W9-CNZ-034

{STRATEGIES FOR SUCCESSFUL WRITING}
A Rhetoric, Research Guide, Reader, and Handbook

James A. Reinking

Robert von der Osten

Sue Ann Cairns
KWANTLEN POLYTECHNIC UNIVERSITY

Robert Fleming
KWANTLEN POLYTECHNIC UNIVERSITY

Pearson Canada
Toronto

We dedicate this book to our students, whose earnest efforts to improve their writing have challenged us to improve our teaching.   *S.A.C. & R.F.*

Library and Archives Canada Cataloguing in Publication

Strategies for successful writing : a rhetoric, research guide, reader, and handbook / James A. Reinking ... [et al.].—4th Canadian ed.

Includes bibliographical references and index.
ISBN 978-0-13-208401-7

1. Report writing—Textbooks. 2. English language—Rhetoric—Textbooks.
3. College readers. 4. English language—Grammar—Textbooks. I. Reinking, James A.

PE1408.S77 2009   808'.0427   C2009-901715-6

ISBN-13: 978-0-13-208401-7
ISBN-10: 0-13-208401-5

Vice-President, Editorial Director:
  Gary Bennett
Editor-in-Chief: Ky Pruesse
Acquisitions Editor: David S. Le Gallais
Marketing Manager: Loula March
Supervising Developmental Editor:
  Suzanne Schaan
Developmental Editor: Rachel Stuckey
Production Editor: Avivah Wargon
Copy Editor: Imogen Brian

MLA Updates: Lisa Berland
Proofreaders: Molly Wolf, Lisa Berland
Production Coordinator: Janis Raisen
Compositor: Integra
Permissions Research: Amanda
  McCormick
Art Director: Julia Hall
Cover Design: Black Eye Design
Interior Design: Julia Hall
Cover Image: Black Eye Design

BRIEF CONTENTS

HANDBOOK

CONTENTS

RESEARCH GUIDE

READER

RHETORICAL TABLE OF CONTENTS

HANDBOOK

Preface

The fourth Canadian edition of *Strategies for Successful Writing: A Rhetoric, Research Guide, Reader, and Handbook* is a versatile, all-in-one textbook that offers ample material for either a full-year or a one-term composition course.

While our text is informed by current rhetorical theory, we have aimed to engage students through a relaxed, conversational style that invites students into the book, lessens their apprehensions about writing, and provides a model for their own prose. This style complements our practical, student-based approach to writing.

The organization of *Strategies for Successful Writing*, Fourth Canadian Edition, reflects a view of writing as a process. This edition emphasizes the interrelationship of critical reading, thinking, and writing. It helps students move along a developmental continuum as they learn, practise, and consolidate their writing skills, while also helping them gain insight into the recursive and fluid nature of the writing process. Students learn how to generate ideas in the early prewriting stages; how to arrange these ideas in the drafting stage, employing rhetorical devices such as analysis, comparison, or argument; and how to make strategic changes in the editing stage. Lively and appealing professional and student model essays help students observe and internalize the strategies of effective writing. Practical classroom-tested material draws students in and gives rise to stimulating class discussions.

CHANGES IN THE FOURTH CANADIAN EDITION

The fourth Canadian edition retains the many strengths of the previous Canadian and U.S. editions while incorporating many improvements that enhance the usefulness of the text for a Canadian audience. We have retained the book's reader-friendly layout and tone but have made a number of changes suggested by users and reviewers. Among these changes the following are noteworthy:

- substantial revision of Chapter 14, on persuasion and argument, with more emphasis on the distinction between opinion and argument, as well as clarification of the concepts of induction and deduction.
- updated discussion on doing library and internet research online.
- more extensive coverage of plagiarism.
- thorough updates of the chapter on MLA documentation, and the text as a whole, to reflect the new seventh edition of the *MLA Handbook for Writers of Research Papers,* published in 2009.

- inclusion of process flowcharts at the end of Chapters 1–3, to reach more visually oriented students.
- replacement of some model essays with more Canadian- and academic-focused essays.
- nine new professional essays and four new student essays.
- added information on sentence elements.

THE RHETORIC

The Rhetoric is a streamlined fourteen chapters, which may be used independently or sequentially. The first six chapters are grouped together under the heading *Writing Strategies: A Writing Process.* These chapters help students learn and practise writing strategies for planning, drafting, revising, and editing. Chapter 1 gives an overview of the principles of effective writing: awareness of purpose; awareness of audience, including conventions in different discourse communities; the qualities of strong writing; and ethical concerns in writing. Chapter 2 offers strategies for active reading, including summaries and critiques. Chapter 3 looks at strategies for prewriting, drafting, and finding a thesis. Chapter 4 focuses on strategies for developing paragraphs, including special paragraphs such as introductions and conclusions. Chapter 5 takes students through the various revision stages, starting with a systematic procedure for revising the whole essay and then moving to pointers for revising its component parts. Sets of checklists pose key questions for students to consider. Chapter 6 helps students think about their editing in more subtle ways, as they consider style, tone, diction, sentence rhythm, variety, and emphasis.

The remaining eight chapters in Part 1 are grouped together under the heading *Writing Strategies: Rhetorical Approaches.* These chapters feature the various strategies, or modes, used to develop papers. Each section includes a mini-reader, which contains a student essay and a selection of professional essays that illustrate the relevant rhetorical mode. The first essay in each strategy section is annotated in the margin in order to highlight aspects of the rhetorical strategy under discussion.

The rhetorical strategies are organized progressively: from closer to home and more personal writing to more analytical and eventually to more research-based, formal writing. These strategies also move from relatively straightforward to complex kinds of writing, culminating with persuasion and argument. Note that Chapter 7 identifies the overlap between narration and description, the two modes of writing that are commonly featured in personal writing. Strategies for using illustration follow, since illustration is commonly used to strengthen both personal and formal writing. The next three rhetorical modes—process analysis, cause and effect, and definition—all represent types of analytical writing. Chapters 12 and 13 introduce the organizational patterns of comparison and classification. Finally, Chapter 14, "Strategies for Convincing Others," shows how argument often subsumes many rhetorical modes such as definition, illustration, and analysis. Because argument is an important focus for many writing instructors, we have included eight model essays in Chapter 14, in addition to the four argument essays in the Reader. These essays pair arguments on bioethics and cultural diversity, and instructors can use them either separately or together.

The "Critical Edge" sections that conclude the chapters on rhetorical modes are intended for above-average students. These sections explain and illustrate how students can advance their writing purpose by synthesizing material from various sources. All the rhetorical modes are presented as natural ways of thinking—as problem-solving strategies—and therefore as effective ways of organizing writing. Complete student essays, along with professional essay models and several writing suggestions, accompany these chapters. Instructors who wish to choose different or supplementary essays may choose from those in the Reader.

THE RESEARCH GUIDE

Chapters 15, 16, and 17 constitute the Research Guide. In Chapter 15, students learn about locating, selecting, and integrating secondary sources, while Chapter 16 focuses on the use of primary sources. Chapter 17 gives extensive information on using MLA and APA documentation, including documentation for online sources. This chapter also advises students on ways to avoid plagiarism.

THE READER

The third section of the text is the Reader, organized according to broad rhetorical categories of personal writing, illustration, analysis, organizational patterns, and argument. Within these broader categories instructors will find examples of other rhetorical strategies, such as narrative or definition. Instructors may also choose to approach the essays thematically (see the Thematic Table of Contents on page ix), for example, examining different points of view on cultural identities, popular culture, or health. A brief biographical note about the author precedes each selection, and stimulating questions designed to enhance student understanding of structure and strategy follow it. In addition, a section entitled "Toward Key Insights" poses one or more broad-based questions prompted by the essay's content. Answering these questions, either in discussion or writing, should help students gain a deeper understanding of important issues. Finally, we include one or more writing assignments related to the essay's topic.

THE HANDBOOK

The fourth and final section of the text is a concise grammar and mechanics handbook, which features tab indexing on each page for easy access to all material and consists of five parts: "Sentence Elements," "Editing to Correct Sentence Errors," "Editing to Correct Faulty Punctuation and Mechanics," "Spelling," and "Glossary of Word Usage." Explanations avoid using unnecessary grammatical terminology and are reinforced by sets of sentence exercises in the first three sections. The section "Sentence Elements" explains how students can use sentence structure to improve their writing skills. We also include connected-discourse exercises—unfolding narratives that engage and retain student interest while they correct errors—in the sections "Sentence Errors" and "Punctuation and Mechanics." The unit "Spelling" presents four useful spelling rules and an extensive list of commonly misspelled words. The "Glossary of Word Usage" offers a similarly comprehensive coverage of troublesome words. Instructors can use the Handbook either as a reference guide or as a basis for class discussion.

INSTRUCTOR'S RESOURCE MANUAL

Strategies for Successful Writing, Fourth Canadian Edition, offers an Instructor's Resource Manual, which includes teaching strategies, additional classroom activities, suggested answers to the text's exercises, and a list of additional readings for instructors. The manual is available to instructors for downloading from a password-protected section of the Pearson Education Canada online catalogue at **www.pearsoned.ca/highered**.

COURSESMART

CourseSmart is a new way for instructors and students to access textbooks online anytime from anywhere. With thousands of titles across hundreds of courses, CourseSmart helps instructors choose the best textbook for their class and give their students a new option of buying the assigned textbook as a lower-cost eTextbook. For more information, visit **www.coursesmart.com**.

ACKNOWLEDGMENTS

We offer many thanks to our reviewers for their insightful comments and helpful suggestions:

Sara Beck, St. Lawrence College

Brent Cotton, Georgian College

Brett Josef Grubisic, University of British Columbia

Chandra Hodgson, Humber College Institute of Technology & Advanced Learning

Aurelea Mahood, Capilano College

Colleen Mahy, George Brown College

Mathew Smith, George Brown College

Like all textbook writers, we are indebted to many people—colleagues, reviewers, and the outstanding team at Pearson Education Canada, whose editorial expertise, genial guidance, and promotional efforts have been vital to this project: Acquisitions Editor Christopher Helsby, who provided helpful direction at the early stages of the project; Developmental Editor Rachel Stuckey and Production Editor Avivah Wargon, who offered helpful suggestions and kept us on task; copy editor Imogen Brian and proofreaders Molly Wolf and Lisa Berland, who did an excellent job of making things consistent throughout the book; and our marketing team, Loula March and Bethany Jolliffe, whose efforts will help our book find its way.

Sue Ann Cairns
Robert Fleming

RHETORIC

CHAPTER 1

Writing:
An Overview

Why write? Hasn't the tempest of technology swept all of us into a brave new electronic world? Aren't email, voice mail, cell phones—all the magical devices of our new electronic estate—fast dooming ordinary writing? Not long ago, some people thought and said so, but events haven't supported those predictions. Although electronic devices have made some writing unnecessary, the written word flourishes both on campus and in the world of work.

Writing offers very real advantages to both writers and readers:

1. It gives writers time to reflect on and research what they want to communicate and then lets them shape and reshape the material to their satisfaction.
2. It makes communication more precise and effective.
3. It provides a permanent record of thoughts, actions, and decisions.
4. It saves the reader time: We absorb information more swiftly when we read it than when we hear it.

Many people will expect you to write for them. Instructors ask you to write reports, summaries, reflective journals, research papers, and essay exams. Job hunting usually requires you to write resumes and cover letters. And once you're hired, writing will probably figure in your duties. You might be asked to discuss the capabilities of new computer equipment, report on a conference you attended, or explain the advantages of new safety procedures to supervisors or staff. Perhaps you'll propose that your organization install a new security system, conduct a market survey, or develop an alternative traffic flow pattern. The ability to write will help you earn better grades, land the job you want, and advance in your career.

Writing also yields personal benefits. Sometimes people find that private writing, as in a journal, can help them sort out their emotions and come to greater clarity about decisions. At university, taking notes in class or writing summaries of lecture material can help you understand, remember, and integrate information. Informal, exploratory writing can help you uncover ideas you didn't know you had. In your personal life, writing can bring social and even financial benefits. You might have to write a tactful letter of apology to mend a broken relationship. Or you might need to defend a reimbursement claim that you filed with your dental insurer or document a request to replace a faulty product. Skill and comfort with writing helps you handle these matters.

Although we may write for ourselves in order to explore ideas, to make knowledge our own, or to communicate privately with our inner selves, we more commonly write in response to situations that involve other people. Situations often determine the purpose and audience of our writing as well as its content, style, and organization. Whether we are writing a text-message, an application letter, or an analytical academic essay, we usually write in a specific cultural context according to certain conventions. We write differently depending on whether we are dashing off emails to friends or writing academic papers. We follow different conventions when writing journal entries, emails, instant messages, policy briefs, memos, letters of reference, reflective critiques, and formal research-based essays. To write effectively in different social, business, or academic contexts, we need to be aware that readers have different expectations and values in different situations.

THE PURPOSES OF WRITING

Whenever you write, a clear purpose should guide your efforts. If you don't know why you're writing, neither will your reader. Fulfilling an assignment doesn't qualify as a real writing purpose, although it may well be what sends you to your desk. Faced with a close deadline for a research paper or report, you may tell yourself, "I'm doing this because I have to." An authentic purpose, however, requires you to answer this question: What do I want this piece of writing to do for both my reader and me? As you might expect, purpose grows out of the writing situation.

Here are four common *general writing purposes,* two or more of which often join forces in a single piece:

To Inform   Presenting information is one of the most common writing purposes. The kayaking enthusiast who writes about how to manoeuvre a kayak plays the role of teacher, as does the researcher who summarizes the results of an investigation for co-workers. In school, you will often be asked to demonstrate your understanding of concepts in exams and papers so that instructors can gauge how well you have mastered the course material.

To Persuade   You probably have strong views on many issues, and these feelings may sometimes impel you to try to sway your reader's views. In a letter to the editor, you might attack a proposal to establish a nearby nuclear power facility. Or, alarmed by a sharp jump in provincial unemployment, you might write to your Member of the Legislative Assembly and argue for a youth employment program.

To Express Yourself   Creative writing includes personal essays, fiction, plays, and poetry, as well as journals and diaries. Self-expression has a place in other kinds of writing too. Almost everything you write offers you a chance to display your mastery of words and to enliven your prose with vivid images and fresh turns of phrase.

To Entertain   Some writing merely entertains; some writing links entertainment with a more serious purpose. A lighthearted approach can help your reader absorb dull or difficult material. Satire lets you expose the shortcomings of individuals, ideas, and institutions by poking fun at them. An intention to entertain can add savour to many kinds of writing.

Besides having one or more *general purposes,* each writing project has its own *specific purpose.* Consider the difference in the papers you could write about herbal medicines. You might explain why readers should take herbal medicines or argue why these medicines should be federally regulated.

Having a specific purpose assists you at every stage of the writing process. It helps you define your audience; select the details, language, and approach that best suit their needs; and avoid going off in directions that won't interest them. The following example from Celia Milne's essay, "Pressures to Conform," has a clear and specific purpose.

> Unhappiness with body image seems to be a national preoccupation. According to statistics compiled by the National Eating Disorder Information Centre in Toronto, 90 percent of Canadian women are dissatisfied with some aspect of their bodies. One of the main battlegrounds in the fight for improvement, of course, is eating. According to *Maclean's* year-end poll published in late December, 43 percent of Canadian women—compared with 33 percent of men—believe they are overweight. The eating disorder centre says that its surveys show that fully 70 percent of Canadian women are preoccupied with their weight, and 40 percent are yo-yo dieting. "For most women, when they get together in a group a common topic is trying to lose weight," says Dr. Christine Davies, a family physician in Saint John, N.B., who is concerned about how that may rub off on their daughters. Margaret Beck, acting director of the eating disorder centre, affirms that danger. "The research," she says, "does seem to suggest that mothers who are food- and weight-preoccupied tend to have daughters who are the same."

The topic sentence that begins Milne's paragraph clearly focuses on her claim that dissatisfaction with "body image" is a widespread concern in Canada. The subsequent four sentences provide statistical evidence from the National Eating Disorder Information Centre in Toronto and a *Maclean's* poll reinforcing her specific argument that the majority of women are unhappy with their weight or appearance. The final three sentences corroborate Milne's argument by introducing statements from medical experts who confirm that weight and body image concerns among Canadian women are prevalent and likely to continue.

Now examine the next paragraph, which does *not* have a firmly fixed specific purpose:

> Community is a sea in which people swim unconsciously, like fish. We fail to recognize our neighbours as fellow humans, and they show the same lack of fellow feeling for us. A complete lack of concern for one another is evident in today's complex society. What is community? Is it a plant? A building? A place? A state of being? Knowing what it is, we can see if such a place exists. To know community, one must realize who he or she is. Identity of a person is the first step in establishing a community.

This student writer can't decide what aspect of community to tackle. The opening sentence attempts a definition, but the next two veer onto the shortcomings of the modern community. Notice how aimlessly the thoughts drift. The vague leadoff sentence asserts "Community is a sea . . . ," but the later question "What is community?" contradicts this opening. Also, if community is a plant, a building, or a place, why must we realize who we are in order to know it? This paragraph reveals a writer groping for a purpose.

The paragraph, however, isn't a wasted effort. These musings offer several possibilities. By developing the first sentence into a full paragraph, the writer could show some interesting similarities between community and a sea, so that instead of taking community for granted, readers could see it in a new light. By pursuing the idea in the second and third sentences, the writer might show the callous nature of modern society and encourage readers to act more humanely. The last two sentences might lead the writer to discover a connection between personal identity and one's place in community. Thus, a specific purpose can sometimes emerge from preliminary expression.

THE AUDIENCE FOR YOUR WRITING

Everything you write is aimed at a particular audience—a person or group you want to reach. The ultimate purpose of all writing is to have an effect on a reader (even if that reader is you), and therefore purpose and audience are closely linked. Whether you are writing to inform *someone* of something, to persuade *someone* to believe or do something, to express feelings or insights to *someone,* or to entertain *someone,* you will write better if you know or can at least imagine a particular someone who is the audience for your writing.

Moreover, in both personal and academic writing, you can't assume that the reader is able to read your mind and understand what you really meant to say. In face-to-face conversations, you can observe your listeners' reactions and instantly respond to signs of confusion, boredom, or anger. You can clarify your meaning by offering examples. Or you can alter your tone, ask a question, or even change the subject. You can even use gestures and facial expressions to emphasize your main points. But when you write, the words on the page are all that carry your meaning. Once written or sent into cyberspace, your written work is on its own, even if the tone is wrong and the message garbled or incomplete. Readers will not charitably fill in gaps in meaning. Of course, when you write to friends or someone else you know well, you can usually anticipate how they might respond to what you say. But when you write for people you know only casually or not at all, such as employers, customers, or the general public, you need to assess your audience before starting to write. The more you understand their assumptions, expectations, needs, and desires, the more strategically you can tailor your writing to them, and the more they will understand.

A good way to assess your readers is to develop an audience profile. This profile emerges gradually as you answer the following questions:

1. What are the educational level, age, and economic status of the audience I want to reach?
2. Why will this audience read my writing? to gain information? learn my views on a controversial issue? enjoy my creative flair? be entertained?
3. What attitudes, needs, and expectations do they have?
4. How are they likely to respond to what I say? Can I expect them to be neutral? opposed? friendly?
5. How much do they know about my topic? (Your answer here will help you gauge whether you're saying too little or too much.)
6. What kind of language will communicate with them most effectively?

Assignment instructions sometimes ask you to envision a reader who is intelligent but not an expert, someone receptive to new ideas but unwilling to put up with boring or confusing material. Another assignment may ask you to write for a certain age group, especially one with particular interests. At other times, you'll be asked to write for a specialized audience—one with some expertise in your topic. These differences affect what you say to each audience and how you say it.

The Effect of Audience on Your Writing

Let's examine how audience can shape a paper. Suppose you are explaining how to take a certain type of X-ray. If your audience is a group of lay readers who have never had an X-ray, you might explain at the outset that taking an X-ray is much like taking an ordinary photograph. Then you might explain the basic process, including the positioning of the patient and the equipment; comment on the safety and reliability of the procedure; and describe how much time it takes. You probably would use few technical terms. However, if you were writing for radiology students, you might instead emphasize exposure factors, film size, and required views. This audience would want technical terms and detailed explanations of the procedure. You would speak to these readers as colleagues who appreciate precise information.

Audience shapes all types of writing in similar fashion, even your personal writing. Assume you've recently become engaged while away at university, and to share your news you write two letters: one to your parents, the other to your best friend back home. You can imagine the differences in details, language, and tone of each letter. Without doubt, different readers call for different approaches.

Discourse Communities

Professionals often write as members of specific communities that have their own conventions, shared assumptions, and specialized language or discourse. For example, environmental biologists with similar interests might exchange information about their research into the effects of environmental policies related to global warming. The members of a community share goals, values, concerns, background information, and expectations, and this shared knowledge in turn affects how they write. Because such writing is closely tied to the interests of the community, professional articles often start with a section linking the content to previous research projects and articles. In addition, custom often dictates what information must be included, what pattern of organization should be used, and what style the paper should follow. For example, in formal academic writing, documentation of sources follows different conventions in the humanities (such as English) than in the social sciences (such as psychology).

In addition, different academic disciplines may emphasize different writing structures and may have different approaches. For example, in a marketing class, you might be asked to do a case study; in a communications class, you might be asked for a technical report and PowerPoint presentation; and in an economics class, you might be asked to identify an economic problem and explore a hypothetical solution to the problem. A chemistry instructor might expect you to write a lab report in such a way that someone with your background could repeat the experiment exactly as you did. In a literature class, an instructor will probably be more interested in your in-depth analysis or interpretation of a story than in your exact recounting of the plotline. So throughout your studies, you will discover that learning to write well means becoming familiar with the values and customs of different discourse communities. To do this, you need to read carefully in a particular field, acquainting yourself with its current issues and concerns and learning how to write about them. Ask yourself these questions as you start reading in any professional area:

1. What are the major concerns and questions in this discourse community?
2. What seems to be common knowledge?
3. To what works do writers regularly refer?
4. How do those in the field go about answering questions?
5. What methods do they follow?
6. Which kinds of knowledge are acceptable? Which are not?
7. What values seem to guide the discourse community?
8. What kinds of information must writers include in papers?
9. How are different writing projects organized?
10. What conventions do writers follow?

Of course, we all belong to many different communities; but the more comfortably you can move from one discourse community to another, the more you will be in a position to exert influence in your world. At university, as you gain familiarity with the language, conventions, and expectations of different academic audiences in psychology, philosophy, or economics, you will find it easier to write papers in these different discourse communities.

EXERCISE *The three excerpts below deal with the same subject—antigens—but each explanation is geared to a different audience. Read the passages carefully; then answer the following questions:*

    a. What audience does each author address? How do you know?

    b. Identify ways in which each author appeals to a specific audience.

1. The human body is quick to recognize foreign chemicals that enter it. "Foes" must be attacked or otherwise got rid of. The most common of these foes are chemical materials from viruses, bacteria, and other microscopic organisms. Such chemicals, when recognized by the body, are called *antigens*. To combat them, the body produces its own chemicals, protein molecules called *antibodies*. Each kind of antigen causes the production of a specific kind of antibody. Antibodies appear in the body fluids such as blood and lymph and in the body's cells.

        L. D. Hamilton, "Antibodies and Antigens," *The New Book of Knowledge*

2. [An] *antigen* [is a] foreign substance that, when introduced into the body, is capable of inducing the formation of antibodies and of reacting specifically in a detectable manner with the induced antibodies. For each antigen there is a specific antibody, the physical and chemical structure of which is produced in response to the physical and chemical structure of the antigen. Antigens comprise virtually all proteins that are foreign to the host, including those contained in bacteria, viruses, protozoa, helminths, foods, snake venoms, egg white, serum components, red blood cells, and other cells and tissues of various species, including man. Polysaccharides and lipids may also act as antigens when coupled to proteins.

        "Antigen," *Encyclopaedia Britannica*

3. The substance which stimulates the body to produce antibodies is designated antigen (antibody stimulator). . . .

    Most complete antigens are protein molecules containing aromatic amino acids, and are large in molecular weight and size. However, it has been demonstrated that other macromolecules, such as pure polysaccharides, polynucleotides, and lipids, may serve as complete antigens.

    However, certain other materials, incapable of stimulating antibody formation by themselves can, in association with a protein or other carrier, stimulate antibody formation and are the antigenic determinants. These determinants are referred to as *incomplete antigens* or *haptens*, and they are able to react with antibodies which were produced by the determinant-protein complex.

    However, before an antigen can stimulate the production of antibodies, it must be soluble in the body fluids, must reach certain tissues in an unaltered form, and must be, in general, foreign to the body tissues. Protein taken by mouth loses its specific foreign-protein characteristics when digested in the alimentary tract. It reaches the tissues of the body as amino acids or other altered digested products of protein. Consequently, it no longer meets the requirements for antigenic behavior.

        Orville Wyss and Curtis Eklund, *Microorganisms and Man*

Level of Diction

How does a writer choose the right level of diction, or word choice, for a particular audience? It depends on the writer's purpose, as well as which discourse community the writer is addressing. Think about a safety engineer who investigates a serious industrial accident on which she must write two reports, one for the safety director of the company, who represents a technical audience, and another for the local newspaper, which represents a general audience. Although the two accounts would deal with the same matter, they would clearly need to use very different language: specialized and formal in the first case, everyday and more relaxed in the second. In both cases, the language would have to reflect the background of the audience. As you write, always choose language suited to your audience and purpose.

Edited standard English follows the familiar grammatical rules maintained in most formal and academic writing. Generally, everything you write for university courses or on the job should be in edited standard English. *Nonstandard English* refers to any version of the language that deviates from these rules. Here is an example from Dionne Brand's short story, "Blossom: Priestess of Oya, Goddess of Winds, Storms and Waterfalls":

> This was Blossom's most successful endeavour since coming to Canada. Every once in a while, under she breath, she curse the day she come to Toronto from Oropuche, Trinidad. But nothing, not even snarky white people could keep Blossom under. When she first come it was to babysit some snot-nosed children on Oriole Parkway. She did meet a man, in a club on Henry Street in Port-of-Spain, who promise she to take care of she, if she ever was in Toronto. When Blossom reach, the man disappear and through the one other person she know in Toronto she get the work on Oriole.

As this example shows, nonstandard English does have a place in writing. Fiction writers use it to narrate the talk of characters who, if real, would speak that way; journalists use it to report eyewitness reactions to accidents and crimes; and people who compile oral histories use it to record the recollections of people they interview.

Edited standard English includes four levels of usage: formal, informal, formal–informal, and technical. Another commonly recognized category is colloquial language and slang.

Formal Level   The formal level, dignified and serious, is suitable for important political, business, and academic occasions. Its vocabulary is marked by many abstract and multisyllabic words but no slang or contractions. Long sentences and deliberately varied sentence patterns help give it a strong, rhythmic flow. The more formal cadence of these sentences comes, in part, from relatively complex parallel or balanced structures. (See Chapter 6 on periodic sentences, which are sentences that delay their main point until the end.) Overall, formal prose impresses the reader as authoritative, stately, and graceful.

The following excerpt from the introduction to the third edition of Susanna Moodie's *Roughing It in the Bush* illustrates the formal level:

> In most instances, emigration is a matter of necessity, not of choice; and this is more especially true of the emigration of persons of respectable connections, or of any station or position in the world. Few educated persons, accustomed to

the refinements and luxuries of European society, ever willingly relinquish those advantages, and place themselves beyond the protective influence of the wise and revered institutions of their native land, without the pressure of some urgent cause. Emigration may, indeed, generally be regarded as an act of severe duty, performed at the expense of personal enjoyment, and accompanied by the sacrifice of those local attachments which stamp the scenes amid which our childhood grew, in imperishable characters upon the heart. Nor is it until adversity has pressed sorely upon the proud and wounded spirit of the well-educated sons and daughters of old but impoverished families, that they gird up the loins of the mind, and arm themselves with fortitude to meet and dare the heart-breaking conflict.

In this address to readers of the third edition of her journals recounting expatriate life in Canada during the nineteenth century, Susanna Moodie formally expresses her sense that "emigration is a matter of necessity, not of choice." This initial parallelism is characteristic of the contrast throughout the passage as Moodie notes the dire circumstances of life in the colony, removed from "the protective influence of the wise and revered institutions" of Europe. All of the sentences use complex causal relationships and modification. The sense that the European emigrant performs a noble task in an ignoble place is reinforced by elevated diction—longer words such as *educated, protective, revered, sacrifice, imperishable, impoverished,* and *fortitude,* along with shorter abstract words like *duty, proud, spirit,* and *mind.* The carefully controlled language and syntax lend an earnest, altruistic tone to this passage directed toward a largely European audience.

Informal Level   Informal writing resembles orderly, intelligent conversation. Earmarked by relatively ordinary words, loose sentences (sentences in which the main clause comes at the beginning), and numerous shorter, less varied sentence structures than formal prose, informal writing may include contractions or even slang, and it is more likely than formal writing to use the pronouns *I, me, my, you,* and *yours.* Casual and familiar rather than dignified and rhythmic, informal writing does not usually call attention to itself. Nevertheless, the language is precise and effective. Here is an example:

> There was a distressing story in the paper a few months ago. I wish I'd clipped it out and saved it. As it is, I can only hope I remember it fairly accurately. There was a group of people who wanted a particular dictionary removed from the shelves of the local library because it contained a lot of obscenity. I think they said there were sixty-five or so dirty words in it. Some poor woman who was acting as a spokesman for the group had a list of offending words, which she started to read aloud at a hearing. She managed to read about twenty of them before she started sobbing uncontrollably and couldn't continue.
>
> Thomas H. Middleton, "The Magic Power of Words"

Unlike the Moodie excerpt, this paragraph has relatively uncomplicated sentences. The passage also includes two contractions (*I'd* and *couldn't*), one casual expression (*a lot of*), and the pronoun *I.* Most of the words are very short, and none would be out of place in an ordinary conversation.

Formal–Informal Level   As life has become less formal, informal diction has become increasingly widespread. Today many articles and books, even ones on relatively serious topics, mix informal and formal elements. Here is an example:

> Faith in sports has been vigorously promoted by industry, the military, government, the media. The value of the arena and the locker room has been imposed on our national life. Coaches and sportswriters are speaking for generals and businessmen, too, when they tell us that a man must be physically and psychologically "tough" to succeed, that he must be clean and punctual and honest, that he must bear pain, bad luck, and defeat without whimpering or making excuses. A man must prove his faith in sports and the American Way by whipping himself into shape, playing by the rules, being part of the team, and putting out all the way. If his faith is strong, he will triumph. It's his own fault if he loses, fails, remains poor.
>
> Robert Lipsyte, *Sports World*

Although a few expressions in this excerpt—*bear, the American Way, triumph*—echo formal diction, most of the words have an informal ring, and two expressions, *whipping himself into shape* and *putting out all the way,* skirt the edges of slang.

Technical Level   A specialist writing for others in the same field or for sophisticated nonspecialists writes on the technical level, a cousin to the formal level. Technical language uses specialized words that may be unfamiliar to a general audience. Its sentences tend to be long and complex; but unlike formal diction, the writing doesn't lean toward periodic sentences, parallelism, and balance. Read this example from the field of entomology, the study of insects:

> The light organs of fireflies are complex structures, and recent studies using the electron microscope show them to be even more complex than once supposed. Each is composed of three layers: an outer "window," simply a transparent portion of the body wall; the light organ proper; and an inner layer of opaque, whitish cells filled with granules of uric acid, the so-called "reflector." The light organ proper contains large, slablike light cells, each of them filled with large granules and much smaller, dark granules, the latter tending to be concentrated around the numerous air tubes and nerves penetrating the light organ. These smaller granules were once assumed by some persons to be luminous bacteria, but we now know that they are mitochondria, the source of ATP [adenosine triphosphate] and therefore of the energy of light production. The much larger granules that fill most of the light cells are still of unknown function; perhaps they serve as the source of luciferin.
>
> Howard Ensign Evans, *Life on a Little-Known Planet*

Note the specialized vocabulary—*granules, uric acid, mitochondria,* and *luciferin*—as well as the length and complexity of the sentences. Five sentences make up the passage, the shortest having twenty-four words. None is periodic, and none has a parallel or balanced structure.

Every field has *jargon,* specialized terms or inside talk that provides a convenient shorthand for communication among its members. For example, for an audience of biologists, you may write that two organisms have a *symbiotic relationship,* meaning "mutually beneficial"; for psychology majors, you might use *catalepsy* instead of "a temporary loss of consciousness and feeling, often accompanied by muscular rigidity." As a general rule, use technical terms only if your audience will know their meanings. If you must use technical words when writing for a general audience, define them the first time they appear.

Colloquial Language and Slang   *Colloquial* originally meant "the language of ordinary conversation between people of a particular region." *Slang*, according to *The Canadian Oxford Dictionary*, is defined as "words, phrases, and uses that are regarded as very informal and are often restricted to special contexts." These two categories blend into each other, and even authorities sometimes disagree on whether to label a term *colloquial* or *slang*. The word *bender*, meaning "a drinking spree," seems firmly in the colloquial camp, and *bummer*, a term recently used by young people to mean "a bad time," is just as clearly slang. *Break a leg* is theatre slang used to wish a performer success. But what about *guy* and *kid*? Once they were slang; but so many people have used them for so long that they have now become colloquial.

Regardless of their labels, colloquial and slang terms are almost never appropriate in formal writing. They sometimes serve a useful purpose in informal writing by creating a special effect or increasing audience appeal. Even so, careful writers use them sparingly. Some readers may not understand some colloquial language, and slang usually becomes dated quickly. The following paragraph uses colloquial and slang expressions successfully:

> When I was just a kid on Eighth Avenue in knee pants . . . [Big Bill] was trying to get himself killed. He was always in some fight with a knife. He was always cutting or trying to cut somebody's throat. He was always getting cut or getting shot. Every Saturday night that he was out there, something happened. If you heard on Sunday morning that somebody had gotten shot or stabbed, you didn't usually ask who did it. You'd ask if Big Bill did it. If he did it, no one paid much attention to it, because he was always doing something like that. They'd say, "Yeah, man. That cat is crazy."
>
> Claude Brown, *Manchild in the Promised Land*

Kid, yeah, and *cat* reflect the speech of Brown's characters and thus add authenticity to his account. Despite the informal diction, Brown uses parallelism in the second, third, and fourth sentences; repetition of *he was always* emphasizes the single-minded self-destructiveness of Big Bill's behaviour.

EXERCISE *Identify the level of diction in each of the following passages. Support your answers with examples from the passages. Point out slang or colloquial expressions.*

1. In some ways I am an exceptionally privileged woman of thirty-seven. I am in the room of a private, legal abortion hospital, where a surgeon, a friend of many years, is waiting for me in the operating room. I am only five weeks pregnant. Last week I walked out of another hospital, unaborted, because I had suddenly changed my mind. I have a husband who cares for me. He yells because my indecisiveness makes him anxious, but basically he has permitted the final choice to rest in my hands: "It would be very tough, especially for you, and it is absolutely insane, but yes, we could have another baby." I have a mother who cares. I have two young sons, whose small faces are the most moving arguments I have against going through with this abortion. I have a doctorate in psychology, which among other advantages, assures me of the

professional courtesy of special passes in hospitals, passes that at this moment enable my husband and my mother to stand in my room at a nonvisiting hour and yell at each other over my head while I sob.

Magda Denes, *In Necessity and Sorrow: Life and Death in an Abortion Hospital*

2. I have just spent two days with Edward T. Hall, an anthropologist, watching thousands of my fellow New Yorkers short-circuiting themselves into hot little twitching death balls with jolts of their own adrenalin. Dr. Hall says it is overcrowding that does it. Overcrowding gets the adrenalin going, and the adrenalin gets them queer, autistic, sadistic, barren, batty, sloppy, hot-in-the-pants, charred-in-the-flankers, leering, puling, numb—the usual in New York, in other words, and God knows where else. Dr. Hall has the theory that overcrowding has already thrown New York into a state of behavioral sink. Behavioral sink is a term from ethology, which is the study of how animals relate to their environment. Among animals, the sink winds up with a "population collapse" or "massive die-off." O rotten Gotham.

Tom Wolfe, *The Pump House Gang*

Whether you choose a relatively formal or casual level of diction depends on your audience, purpose, and situation. Moreover, as you shape your paper, the writing must please you as well as your audience—it must satisfy your sense of what good writing is and what the writing task requires.

THE QUALITIES OF GOOD WRITING

Three qualities—fresh thinking, a sense of style, and effective organization—help ensure that a piece of prose will meet your reader's expectations.

Fresh Thinking   You don't have to astound your readers with something never before discussed in print. Genuinely unique ideas and information are scarce commodities. You can, however, freshen your writing by exploring personal insights and perceptions. Using your own special slant, you might show a connection between seemingly unrelated items. Do not strain too desperately for originality, because far-fetched notions spawn skepticism.

Sense of Style   Whatever context you are writing in, once you have figured out what you want to say, say it as clearly as you can. Sometimes students think that vague, mysterious writing intrigues readers; however, most readers do not want to play guessing games. Write to communicate, not to impress. Good writing is clear, with a style appropriate for the particular situation, audience, and purpose. It may be quite appropriate to write without capital letters or apostrophes in an online chat room, but not in an academic essay. In technical, scientific, or legal documents, readers expect a neutral tone. If you are writing a narrative essay or persuasive argument, well-chosen verbs and nouns, and vivid examples or metaphors can help to draw your reader in. Your style should be suited to the writing situation, whether informal or formal.

Effective Organization   While some personal writing and cyber-writing does not have a linear structure, readers expect academic papers to have a beginning, a middle, and an end—that is, an introduction, a body, and a conclusion. The introduction sparks interest and acquaints the reader with what is to come. The body delivers the main message and exhibits a clear connection between ideas so that the reader can easily follow your thoughts. The conclusion ends the discussion so the reader feels satisfied rather than suddenly cut off. Overall, your paper should follow a pattern that is suited to its content.

WRITING AND ETHICS

Accuracy, fairness, and honesty in your writing help inspire trust in your readers. Like you, readers expect that what they read contains dependable information. If you are writing a report, a brief or abstract, or a review or recommendation, you do not want to skew your conclusions by failing to mention important evidence that contradicts your conclusions. In research writing, you establish credibility when you give credit to authorities and clarify sources of your information. Few readers would bother with a carelessly presented or even deliberately deceptive piece of information.

Think for a minute about how you would react to the following situation. You decide to vacation at a Canadian country resort after reading a brochure that described its white-sand beach, scenic trails, fine dining, and peaceful atmosphere. When you arrive, you find the beach overgrown with weeds, the trails littered, and the view unappealing. The gourmet restaurant is a greasy-spoon cafeteria. Worse, whenever you go outside, swarms of vicious black flies attack you. Wouldn't you feel cheated? In addition, think how you'd feel if you decided to attend a university because of its distinguished faculty members only to discover upon arrival that they rarely teach on campus. The university uses the scholars' reputations to attract students, even though these scholars are usually unavailable. Hasn't the university done something unethical?

Ethical writing, which is accurate, fair, and honest, reflects the integrity of the writer.

The Principles of Ethical Writing

Accuracy   Writing perceived as truthful should *be* truthful. Granted, a writer may use humorous exaggeration to make us laugh, and some sales pitches may stretch the truth a bit in order to entice buyers ("Try Nu-Glo toothpaste and add sparkle to your life"). But most readers recognize and discount such embellishments as harmless. However, deliberate distortions and falsehoods may hurt not only the reader but the writer as well. If you were angered by misrepresentations in the vacation brochure, you would likely warn your friends against the resort; you might even take legal action.

No Deliberate Omissions   To be perceived as truthful, a document should tell the whole truth, omitting nothing the reader needs to know in order to make an informed decision. The text should not be deliberately incomplete so as to mislead. Suppose a university's recruitment brochure stresses that 97 percent of its students get jobs upon graduation, but omits the fact that only 55 percent of these jobs are in the graduates' chosen field of study. Certainly these brochures are deceptive, perhaps attracting students who would otherwise choose schools with better placement records.

Clarity   Writing should be clear to the reader. All of us know the frustration of trying to read an important legal document that is impossible to comprehend. Moreover, a person who writes instructions so unclear that they result in costly or harmful mistakes is partially (and often legally) responsible for the consequences. An annual report that deliberately obscures information about its yearly losses is not fair to potential investors.

Honest Representation   Writing should not present itself as something different from what it is. It would be unethical for a drug company to prepare an advertisement in the form of an unbiased news story.

No Intentional Harm   Writing should not be intended to harm the reader. Certainly it is fair to point out the advantages of a product or service that readers might not need. But think how unethical it would be for a writer to encourage readers to follow a diet that the writer knew was not only ineffective but harmful. Think of the harm a writer might cause by attempting, deliberately, to persuade readers to try crack cocaine.

　　Good writing is also ethical writing. A good test of the ethics of your writing is to determine how you would react after you had read your own work and acted on the basis of the information. Would you feel comfortable with it, or would you feel cheated, manipulated, belittled, or deceived? By practising the principles of ethical writing, you show respect to your readers and to yourself.

Plagiarism

Pivotal to ethics in writing is avoiding plagiarism. When you turn in a piece of writing, you designate it as your own work in your own words. If you have taken material from sources (including the internet) without using the proper documentation discussed in Chapter 17, even if it is in your own words, it is plagiarism, an unacceptable practice for any writer. If you use another writer's language, even in part, without using quotation marks, you are also engaged in plagiarism. Most faculty members check carefully for plagiarism and many automatically give a paper a failing mark for academic dishonesty. Some even give the student an F for the entire course.

　　Why is this an important issue?

1.　Other people have worked hard to develop ideas, do research, and write effectively. They deserve credit for their work when someone else uses it; it is their property. The authors of this text, for example, pay fees to use the essays of others. You would probably not like it if others used material from your papers without giving you credit.

2. Proper documentation strengthens your work since the source, often written by an expert, can add credibility to your claims if properly recognized.

3. If you take some material from a source and use it in your paper without documentation or quotation, you are falsely presenting another writer's work as your own. It is not much different from presenting an entire paper purchased from the internet as your own work.

4. You are in the process of being trained in university to be professionals. Professionals need to be ethical. You wouldn't want someone to take credit for the computer program you wrote, charge you for repairs they didn't make, or write you a ticket for a traffic violation you didn't commit. Journalists have been fired, politicians have lost elections, and companies have been sued because they have been involved in plagiarism.

5. You certainly cannot develop as a writer if your writing isn't mostly your own work.

How can you avoid plagiarism and the failing grade that often comes with it?

1. Be committed to honesty. You should make certain your writing is your own work.

2. If an assignment does not ask you to use sources but you believe information from sources would be useful, talk to your teacher. There may be a reason that you are not asked to use sources. If sources are acceptable, you may be asked to follow a specific procedure for that assignment such as turning in copies of your sources.

3. If sources are required for an assignment or seem reasonable and acceptable, carefully review Chapter 17, including the section on plagiarism. Be meticulous in documenting your sources, even if the material is in your own words, and in quoting and documenting any wording that comes from another writer, even if it is only part of a sentence.

4. Carefully double-check to make certain that all the content in your text is your own and that if you used a source at all, it is documented.

5. Carefully double-check to make certain that all of your text uses your own language and that if you did use another writer's language, you used quotation marks.

6. If you are not sure about whether documentation or quotation marks are necessary, check with your teacher.

You must make a conscious effort to avoid plagiarism. Ignorance and carelessness are rarely accepted as an excuse by professors trying hard to make certain that students are graded fairly and no one gets credit for work that is not their own. If you follow the guidelines in this text and ask your teacher for help when you are confused, you will easily avoid the embarrassment and the often dire consequences of being accused of plagiarism.

A First Look at Your Writing

Know your discourse community.

- What are shared questions?
- What counts as knowledge?
- What conventions do they follow?

Know your purpose.

- Are you going to inform, persuade, express yourself, entertain?
- What specific purpose do you want to accomplish?

Know your audience.

- What do they already know?
- Why will they read my writing?
- How are they likely to respond?
- How can I best reach them?

Apply principles of good writing.

- Write with fresh thinking that offers your own slant.
- Use a clear style in your own voice.
- Use effective organization.

Make certain your writing is ethical!

- Is your writing truthful, unslanted, complete, clear, helpful rather than harmful?
- Is your writing your own? Have you carefully avoided plagiarism?

CHAPTER 2

Strategies for Active Reading

Effective reading is not a passive process, but requires the ongoing interaction of your mind and the printed page. Bringing your knowledge and experience to bear on a piece of writing can help you assess its ideas and conclusions. For example, an understanding of marriage, love, and conflict, as well as experience with divorce, can help readers comprehend an essay that explores divorce. As you read, try to understand each point that's made, consider how the various parts fit together, and anticipate the direction the writing will take. Active reading requires attention. Using specific reading strategies can help you take in more of what you read.

ORIENTING YOUR READING

When reading for pleasure, you can read at any pace you choose, and break off reading when you feel distracted or bored. Reading for academic purposes, however, requires more focused attention. Before starting to read, ask yourself these questions:

- **Why am I reading this material?** Is it for a project you are working on? Is it for a class or an exam? Is it a building block to understanding more material?

- **How well do I need to know the material in the article?** Can you look back to the article as a reference? Is there only one main point you need to know? Are you going to be tested on much of the material in depth?

- **Is some material in the article more important to me than other material?** Sometimes in doing research you may be looking for a specific bit of information that is only one paragraph in a long article. If so, you can skim for the information. In most documents you read, certain sections are more important than others. Often you can read to get the main points of the article and not focus on all the details. Other times, of course, you need to understand all the material in depth.

- **What will I do with the information in the article?** If you are looking for ideas for your own writing, you might read quickly. If you are responsible for writing a critique of the article, you need to read carefully and critically.

- **What kind of reading does the material suggest?** The significance, difficulty, and nature of the writing can all influence how you read. You may read an easy, humorous narrative quickly, but you may need to slow down when you read an argument for or against an important issue, paying careful attention to the main points put forward, perhaps even asking questions about them.

EXERCISE

Reading Activity *Look briefly at "The Appeal of the Androgynous Man" on pages 25–28. Identify three purposes you could have for reading this essay. Identify how these purposes would affect how you would read the essay and what you would look for in the essay.*

A FIRST READING

When going on a trip or an outing, you don't just jump in your car and take off. Usually you take some time to think about where you want to go. Sometimes you even have to check your route. The same is true of effective reading. Because of the challenging nature of most university-level reading assignments, you should plan on more than one reading. The goal of a good first reading is to orient yourself to the material.

Orient Yourself to the Background of the Essay   Before you begin, examine information accompanying the essay for clues about the essay's relevance. Scan the accompanying biographical sketch (if available) to determine the writer's expertise and biases on the topic. Read any notes by the author or editor about the process of researching or writing this essay. For professional essays, look for an abstract that provides a brief summary of the article. At this point, you may want to judge the credibility of the source, a topic discussed in Chapter 15.

Use the Title as a Clue   Most titles identify the topic and often the author viewpoint as well. Thus, "The Sweet Smell of Success Isn't All That Sweet" (page 243) suggests that the author isn't overly impressed with the conventional attitudes toward success.

Skim to Get the Gist of the Article   Sometimes you can just read the introductory and concluding paragraphs and the topic sentences (often the first or last sentences of paragraphs) to get the overall meaning of the article. Other times you will need to read the whole essay quickly. In your first reading, you can skim the more difficult sections without trying to understand them fully. Just try to get an idea of the essay's main thrust, the key ideas that support it, and the ways that they are organized.

Make Connections   When you've finished skimming the essay, think about what you have learned, and then express it in your own words. Until you can state its essence in your own words, you don't really understand what you've read, and you will be unlikely to remember it. Then make connections between the ideas. Go back and underline the thesis statement, or, if there isn't one, try to formulate one in your own words. Identify what you already know about the topic, and examine your personal connection with the topic. You will read more effectively if you can connect what you read to your own knowledge and interests. Finally, jot down questions that the first reading raises in your mind.

EXERCISE
Reading Activities

1. Using the author biography statement at the beginning of the article "The Appeal of the Androgynous Man" (page 25), identify what you can about the author's background, interests, and biases.
2. Before reading, write what you expect to be the essay's main idea, based on the title.
3. After skimming the essay, identify the main points of the essay and the thesis. Jot down at least two questions you have at the end of your first quick reading.

SECOND READINGS

If you find the material difficult, or if thorough comprehension is essential, a second or even third reading may be necessary. On the second reading, you read more slowly than the first reading so that you can carefully absorb the writer's ideas.

Read Carefully and Actively   Read at a pace suitable to the material. Underline significant topic sentences as well as other key sentences and ideas or facts that you find important, but keep in mind that underlining in itself doesn't ensure comprehension. Restating the ideas in your own words is more effective. Depending on your purposes, you may also want to write down the main points in your own words or jot down ideas in the margins. As you proceed, examine the supporting sentences to see how well they back up the main idea. Keep an eye out for how the essay fits together.

Consider Reading as a Kind of Conversation with the Text   Develop the habit of asking questions about facts, reasons, ideas—practically anything in the essay. Jot down your queries and their answers in the margins. (On pages 29–30, you can see how a student interacted with the first page of Amy Gross's essay, "The Appeal of the Androgynous Man.") Good writers anticipate questions and answer them somewhere in the essay. Moreover, because you have posed the questions yourself, you are more likely to see the connections in the text. If the author hasn't answered your questions anywhere in the essay, then you have discovered some weaknesses in the writing and research.

Master Unfamiliar Words   At times, unfamiliar words can hinder your grasp of the material. Whenever you encounter a new word, circle it, use context to help gauge its meaning, check the dictionary for the exact meaning, and then record the meaning in the margins or some other convenient place. If the writing is peppered with words you don't know, you may have to read the whole piece to figure out its general drift, then look up key words, and finally reread the material.

Take Conscious Steps to Understand Difficult Material   When the ideas of a single section prove difficult, write down the points of those sections you do understand. Then experiment by stating in your own words different interpretations of the problem section to see which one best fits the writing as a whole.

Sometimes large sections or entire texts are extremely difficult to understand. Use these strategies to improve your comprehension:

- State the ideas that are easier for you to understand and use them to unlock more difficult (but not unintelligible) meanings in related sections. Save the most difficult sections until last. But don't assume that you have to understand everything completely. Some works take a lifetime to fully understand.
- Discuss the essay with other students who are reading it.
- Read simpler material on the topic to get a basic knowledge of the topic.
- Ask your instructor for help. He or she may help you find background material that will make the selection easier to understand.

Pull the Entire Essay Together   Whenever you finish a major section of a lengthy essay, express your sense of what it means. Say it out loud or write it down. If you have difficulty seeing connections between the ideas, try representing them visually. You might make an outline that states the main points followed by sub-points (see pages 418–420 for ways to outline). For a comparison paper, you might create a table with the main points of the comparison side by side. In addition, you can draw a diagram, list chronological steps, or write out main facts.

You can also use special techniques to strengthen your grasp of material that you may need to remember for a long time. Try restating the main points a couple of days after the second reading to test your retention. Sometimes it is helpful to explain the material to a sympathetic listener; then, if anything has become hazy or slipped your mind, reread the appropriate section(s). But if you must learn the material very thoroughly, make up a test and give it to yourself.

MASTERING READING PROBLEMS

Master the Problems That Interfere with Reading   If your environment is too noisy, if you are too tired, or if you have something on your mind, you can have difficulty reading. Do your reading at the time of day when you are most alert. Be sure you are in a well-lit environment that allows you to concentrate. Try to be rested and comfortable. If you get tired, take a short break or go for a short walk. If something else is bothering you, try to resolve the distraction or put it out of your mind. To avoid boredom, read more actively by connecting the topic to your interests and goals.

If you have extensive problems with your course reading, ask for help. Most universities offer courses in reading and provide tutors and workshops. Higher education usually requires a lot of reading, so take the steps necessary to become the most effective reader possible.

EXERCISE
Reading Activities

1. Reread "The Appeal of the Androgynous Man." Write more questions and notes in the margin as you deepen your understanding of the main points.
2. Create a table with two columns comparing the author's points about the "all-man" and those about the "androgynous man."
3. Find three difficult or unusual words in the essay. Determine their meaning from the context before checking them in a dictionary.
4. Try explaining the main ideas of the article to a friend or roommate.

READING TO CRITIQUE

In university, you usually read not only to understand but also to evaluate what you read. Your instructors want to know what you think about what you've read. Often you are asked whether you agree or disagree with a writer's argument. Sometimes you are asked to write an explicit critique of what you have read.

Your instructors want to see if you can distinguish facts and well-supported arguments from opinions and assumptions. Merely because information and ideas are in print does not mean that they are true or acceptable. For example, an essay might have faulty logic, unreasonable ideas, suspect facts, or unreliable authorities, despite its professional look. Don't hesitate to dispute the writer's information. Ask yourself these questions:

- Does the main point of the essay match your experience or prior learning about this subject?
- Does the evidence support the claim?
- Do the ideas appear reasonable?
- Do other works contradict these claims? Has the author omitted other pieces of evidence that might contradict the main points?
- Do the ideas connect in a logical way?

By knowing the principles of argumentation and various reasoning fallacies, you can critique any piece of writing. These issues are discussed in Chapter 14.

EXERCISE

Reading Activities *Prepare your critique of "The Appeal of the Androgynous Man" by doing the following:*

1. Identify where and how the claims fail to match your experience.
2. Indicate where the evidence does not support the claims.
3. Indicate at least three places where the ideas do not appear reasonable.
4. Identify any evidence that seems to contradict the author's claims.
5. Evaluate whether the ideas connect in a logical way.

READING ASSIGNMENTS CAREFULLY

Many students could get better grades by simply reading their assignments more carefully. In assignments, instructors often indicate possible topics, suggest additional readings, identify the kinds of information that should and **should not** be included, set expectations on style and format, and establish procedures for the assignment such as the due date. You should read the assignment several times. Carefully note any specifications on topic, audience, organizational strategy, or style and format. Be sure to jot down procedures, such as due dates, in an assignment log or your calendar. Do not make assumptions. If you are not clear about a part of the assignment, ask your instructor.

Below is a very specific assignment; read it over carefully to determine what it requires.

OBJECTIVE DESCRIPTION
SHORT ASSIGNMENT (50 POINTS)

Typed final draft following the class format guide is due in class September 12. This assignment page should be turned in with your completed description:

The corner of Perry and King Street, near the Starr building, has been the scene of a terrible accident. The insurance company has asked you to write a brief objective description (approximately two pages double spaced) of the intersection for a report for possible use in court. Your description should not try to take a position about the relative danger of the intersection but rather provide as clear a picture as possible of the situation. The description should include the arrangement of the streets including the number of lanes, the businesses located immediately around the intersection, traffic and pedestrian flow, and the timing of the lights and the effect of that timing on traffic.

Checklist:

The description should:

1. Provide the general location of the intersection.
2. Indicate the streets' traffic function—i.e., major route from 131 into downtown Big Rapids.
3. Describe the actual roads.
4. Identify the businesses and their locations.
5. Describe traffic and pedestrian flow.
6. Detail the timing of the lights.
7. Maintain objective language.
8. Use clear, nontechnical language.

The assignment specifies the topic (a specific intersection), an audience (a court of law and an insurance company), key elements that are required as part of the description, a general style of writing (objective without taking a stance), and procedures including a deadline and format constraints. Clearly a short paper about the accident would not be acceptable since the assigned topic is the actual structure of the intersection. A style of writing that stressed the "horribly short lights that force students to scurry across like mice in front of a cat" would lose points since it takes a position and is not objective. Any description that left out any of the required elements (such as the timing of the lights) would also lose points.

READING AS A WRITER

When you write, you can use reading as a springboard for improving your writing. Reading about the views of others, their experiences, and the information others present often deepens your understanding of yourself, your relationships, and your surroundings. In turn, this broadened perspective can supply you with writing ideas. When you get an idea from your reading, it's helpful to record possibilities by jotting down your thoughts or summarizing what you have read. You can also write down specific ideas, facts, and perhaps even a few particularly interesting quotations that you may want to use later. Be sure to record the source so that you can document it properly in order to avoid plagiarism (see pages 492–494).

When you read several sources that explore the same topic or related topics, you may notice connections among their ideas. Since these connections can be fertile ground for a paper of your own, don't neglect to record them. Once you have jotted down these ideas, circle or label the ideas they connect to. You can also draw lines linking different thoughts to each other and back to the main point. Then express your view of how these ideas fit together as a thesis statement. Interacting with multiple sources and using their ideas to advance the purpose of your writing is a form of synthesis (see pages 423–425). When you synthesize ideas into a new paper, review your information, determine the points you want to make, and experiment until you find the order that works best. As you write, use the material from your sources, but be careful to credit the authors properly in order to avoid plagiarism.

You can also learn new techniques and strategies from other writers. If you find an organizational pattern or a style you like, study the writer's technique. Perhaps you can use it yourself. Similarly, observe when a piece of writing fails and try to determine why.

EXERCISE
Reading Activities

1. Identify at least two strategies used in "The Appeal of the Androgynous Man" that you would find useful.
2. Identify at least two phrases that you found effective.
3. Identify at least two ideas that sparked ideas you could use in your own writing.

Amy Gross

both male and female in one

The Appeal of the Androgynous Man

Amy Gross, a native of Brooklyn, New York, earned a sociology degree at Connecticut College. Upon graduation, she entered the world of fashion publishing and has held writing or editorial positions at various magazines, including Talk, Mademoiselle, Good Housekeeping, Elle, _and_ Mirabella. _She is the editor-in-chief of Oprah Winfrey's_ O _Magazine. In our selection, which first appeared in_ Mademoiselle _in 1976, Gross compares androgynous men favourably to macho "all-men."_

1   James Dean was my first androgynous man.[1] I figured I could talk to him. He was anguished and I was 12, so we had a lot in common. With only a few exceptions, all the men I have liked or loved have been a certain kind of man: a kind who doesn't play football or watch the games on Sunday, who doesn't tell dirty jokes featuring broads or chicks, who is not contemptuous of conversations that are philosophically speculative, introspective, or otherwise foolish according to the other kind of man. He is more self-amused, less inflated, more quirky, vulnerable and responsive than the other sort (the other sort, I'm visualizing as the guys on TV who advertise deodorant in the locker room). He is more like me than the other sort. He is what social scientists and feminists would call androgynous: having the characteristics of both male and female.

2   Now the first thing I want you to know about the androgynous man is that he is neither effeminate nor hermaphroditic. All his primary and secondary sexual characteristics are in order and I would say he's all-man, but that is just what he is not. He is more than all-man. _both male and female sex organs_

Right margin notes:

Does she favour androgynous men? What kind of appeal?

She will give a woman's perspective. She writes for and edits women's magazines.

Seems as if she is going to talk about the advantages of androgynous men as compared to other men. Sees them as better.

Attempt to counter stereotype? Can't androgynous men also be effeminate?

[1]James Dean (1931–1955) was a 1950s film star who gained fame for his portrayals of restless, defiant young men.

Suggests "all-men" men
reject behaviours and
interests they consider
feminine, but isn't she
stereotyping? Are all these
men like this? She seems
to be exaggerating.

3   The merely all-man man, for one thing, never walks to the grocery store unless the little woman is away visiting her mother with the kids, or is in the hospital having a kid, or there is no little woman. All-men men don't know how to shop in a grocery store unless it is to buy a 6-pack and some pretzels. Their ideas of nutrition expand beyond a 6-pack and pretzels only to take in steak, potatoes, scotch or rye whiskey, and maybe a wad of cake or apple pie. All-men men have absolutely no taste in food, art, books, movies, theatre, dance, how to live, what are good questions, what is funny, or anything else I care about. It's not exactly that the all-man's man is an uncouth illiterate. He may be educated, well-mannered, and on a first-name basis with fine wines. One all-man man I knew was a handsome individual who gave the impression of being gentle, affectionate, and sensitive. He sat and ate dinner one night while I was doing something endearingly feminine at the sink. At one point, he mutely held up his glass to indicate in a primitive, even ape-like, way his need for a refill. This was in 1967, before Women's Liberation. Even so, I was disturbed. Not enough to break the glass over his handsome head, not even enough to mutely indicate the whereabouts of the refrigerator, but enough to remember that moment in all its revelatory clarity. No androgynous man would ever brutishly expect to be waited on without even a "please." (With a "please," maybe.)

4   The brute happened to be a doctor—not a hard hat—and, to all appearances, couth. But he had bought the whole superman package, complete with that fragile beast, the male ego. The androgynous man arrives with a male ego too, but his is not as imperialistic. It doesn't invade every area of his life and person. Most activities and thoughts have nothing to do with masculinity or femininity. The androgynous man knows this. The all-man man doesn't. He must keep a constant guard against anything even vaguely feminine (i.e., "sissy") rising up in him. It must be a terrible strain.

5   Male chauvinism is an irritation, but the real problem I have with the all-man man is that it's hard for me to talk to him. He's alien to me, and for this I'm at least half to blame. As his interests have not carried him into the sissy, mine have never taken me very far into the typically masculine terrains of sports, business and finance, politics, cars, boats and machines. But blame or no blame, the reality is that it is almost as difficult for me to connect with him as it would be to link up with an Arab shepherd or Bolivian sandalmaker. There's a similar culture gap.

6   It seems to me that the most masculine men usually end up with the most feminine women. Maybe they like extreme polarity. I like polarity myself, but the poles have to be within earshot. As I've implied, I'm very big on talking. I fall in love for at least three hours with anyone who engages me in a real conversation. I'd rather a man point out a paragraph in a book—wanting to share it with me—than bring me flowers. I'd rather a man ask what I think than tell me I look pretty. (Women who are very pretty and accustomed to hearing that they are pretty may feel differently.) My experience is that all-men men read books I don't want to see paragraphs of, and don't really give a damn what I or any woman would think about most issues so long as she looks pretty. They have a very limited use for women. I suspect they don't really like us. The androgynous man likes women as much or as little as he likes anyone.

7   Another difference between the all-man man and the androgynous man is that the first is not a star in the creativity department. If your image of the creative male accessorizes him with a beret, smock and artist's palette, you will not believe

the all-man man has been seriously short-changed. But if you allow as how creativity is a talent for freedom, associated with imagination, wit, empathy, unpredictability, and receptivity to new impressions and connections, then you will certainly pity the dull, thick-skinned, rigid fellow in whom creativity sets no fires.

8   Nor is the all-man man so hot when it comes to sensitivity. He may be true-blue in the trenches, but if you are troubled, you'd be wasting your time trying to milk comfort from the all-man man.

9   This is not blind prejudice. It is enlightened prejudice. My biases were confirmed recently by a psychologist named Sandra Lipsetz Bem, a professor at Stanford University. She brought to attention the fact that high masculinity in males (and high femininity in females) has been "consistently correlated with lower overall intelligence and lower creativity." Another psychologist, Donald W. MacKinnon, director of the Institute of Personality Assessment and Research at the University of California in Berkeley, found that "creative males give more expression to the feminine side of their nature than do less creative men. . . . [They] score relatively high on femininity, and this despite the fact that, as a group, they do not present an effeminate appearance or give evidence of increased homosexual interests or experiences. Their elevated scores on femininity indicate rather an openness to their feelings and emotions, a sensitive intellect and understanding self-awareness and wide-ranging interests including many which in the American culture are thought of as more feminine. . . . "

10   Dr. Bem ran a series of experiments on college students who had been categorized as masculine, feminine, or androgynous. In three tests of the degree of nurturance—warmth and caring—the masculine men scored painfully low (painfully for anyone stuck with a masculine man, that is). In one of those experiments, all the students were asked to listen to a "troubled talker"—a person who was not neurotic but simply lonely, supposedly new in town and feeling like an outsider. The masculine men were the least supportive, responsive or humane. "They lacked the ability to express warmth, playfulness and concern," Bem concluded. (She's giving them the benefit of the doubt. It's possible the masculine men didn't express those qualities because they didn't possess them.)

11   The androgynous man, on the other hand, having been run through the same carnival of tests, "performs spectacularly. He shuns no behavior just because our culture happens to label it as female and his competence crosses both the instrumental [getting the job done, the problem solved] and the expressive [showing a concern for the welfare of others, the harmony of the group] domains. Thus, he stands firm in his opinion, he cuddles kittens and bounces babies and he has a sympathetic ear for someone in distress."

12   Well, a great mind, a sensitive and warm personality are fine in their place, but you are perhaps skeptical of the gut appeal of the androgynous man. As a friend, maybe, you'd like an androgynous man. For a sexual partner, though, you'd prefer a jock. There's no arguing chemistry, but consider the jock for a moment. He competes on the field, whatever his field is, and bed is just one more field to him: another opportunity to perform, another fray. Sensuality is for him candy to be doled out as lure. It is a ration whose flow is cut off at the exact point when it has served its purpose—namely, to elicit your willingness to work out on the field with him.

13   Highly masculine men need to believe their sexual appetite is far greater than a woman's (than a nice woman's). To them, females must be seduced: Seduction is

a euphemism for a power play, a con job. It pits man against woman (or woman against man). The jock believes he must win you over, incite your body to rebel against your better judgment: in other words—conquer you.

14   The androgynous man is not your opponent but your teammate. He does not seduce: he invites. Sensuality is a pleasure for him. He's not quite so goal-oriented. And to conclude, I think I need only remind you here of his greater imagination, his wit and empathy, his unpredictability, and his receptivity to new impressions and connections.

WRITING ABOUT WHAT YOU READ

Often in university, you are asked to write about what you read. Sometimes this assignment is a major research paper, which is discussed in Chapters 15 and 16. However, sometimes you have to write shorter summaries and critiques. Though similar to the research paper, these shorter assignments focus on testing your ability to understand what you read.

Writing a Summary

A summary states the main points of an essay in your own words. A good summary lets someone who hasn't read the essay understand what it says. A summary can be one or more paragraphs. It should

- provide a context for the essay,
- introduce the author of the essay, and
- state the thesis.

These first three elements often form the introduction of a multiparagraph summary. Then

- state the main points of the essay (sometimes but not always based on the topic sentences), and
- conclude by summarizing the author's final point.

To prepare to write a summary, follow the steps in effective reading. Briefly outline the main points that make the writing easier. But avoid using the author's exact wording unless you use quotation marks. You may want to review the section on plagiarism on pages 492–494 before starting. Also, don't interject your own views. A summary should reflect only the author's ideas.

A Sample Single-Paragraph Summary of
"The Appeal of the Androgynous Man"

What kind of man should appeal to women? According to Amy Gross, the editor-in-chief of *O Magazine*, in "The Appeal of the Androgynous Man," the ideal is the "androgynous man," a man who shares the personality characteristics of both male and female. To make her point, Amy Gross contrasts the all-man man and the androgynous man. She believes that the all-man man does not share in activities like shopping, has no taste in the arts, is imperialistic, resists anything feminine, and is interested only in exclusively male topics. Worse, she points to studies that show that more masculine men are less creative. Further, she argues that the all-man man tends to see women as something to conquer rather than as partners. The androgynous man, by comparison, is very different. He does not resist things that are feminine and so shares in domestic activities, is comfortable with the arts, and can share interests with women. He is shown by studies to be more creative. Further, according to Gross, "The androgynous man is not your opponent but your teammate." As a result, she concludes that the androgynous man has the qualities that women should really look for in a man.

Writing a Critique

Often instructors ask you to give your views on an essay, indicating where you agree and disagree with the author's position. Keep in mind that you can agree with some points and still disagree with others. A critique combines a summary of the article with your thoughtful reaction. Most critiques consist of several paragraphs. A critique usually includes

- a description of the context of the essay
- an introduction of the author
- a statement of the essay's thesis
- the thesis for your critique
- a summary of the essay's main points
- a statement of the points with which you disagree
- a statement with reasons and evidence for your disagreement
- a conclusion

You are well prepared to write a critique if you follow the steps for reading effectively and reading critically.

A Sample Multiparagraph Critique of
"The Appeal of the Androgynous Man"

1   What kind of man should appeal to women? According to Amy Gross, the editor-in-chief of *O Magazine,* in "The Appeal of the Androgynous Man," the ideal is the "androgynous man," a man who shares the personality characteristics typically considered masculine and feminine. But matters are not so simple. Amy Gross falsely divides men into two stereotyped categories. In fact, real men are much more complex.

2   To make her point, Amy Gross contrasts the all-man man and the androgynous man. She states that the all-man man does not share in activities like shopping, has

no taste in the arts, is imperialistic, resists anything feminine, and is interested only in exclusively male topics. In addition, she points to studies that show that more masculine men are less creative. Further, she argues that the all-man man tends to see women as something to conquer rather than as partners. The androgynous man, by comparison, is very different. He does not resist things that are feminine and so shares in domestic activities, is comfortable with the arts, and can share interests with women. He is shown by studies to be more creative. Further, according to Gross, "The androgynous man is not your opponent but your teammate." As a result, she concludes that the androgynous man has the qualities that women should really look for in a man.

3   Gross would be correct if the all-man male were as she described him, because he would truly be undesirable. No woman should want a partner who takes her for granted, doesn't share her interests, or treats her simply as someone to conquer. But is that really what men are like? My brother plays football and loves to watch it on television. He also hunts and fishes. However, that isn't all he does. He plays with kittens, loves to cook, plays the guitar and sings, and secretly likes "chick flicks." As far as I can tell, he treats his girlfriend well. He seems genuinely concerned about her, will spend hours shopping with her, goes to events that interest her, and generally seems sensitive to her needs. Is he an "all-man man" or an "androgynous man"? Equally a man can write poetry, love Jane Austen, cook gourmet meals, and still take women for granted.

4   Gross presents evidence from psychological studies that show that more masculine men are less creative than more feminine men. But she doesn't provide enough evidence for the reader to assess the studies. How did the researchers actually measure masculinity and femininity? How many people were tested? What did they count as creativity? Certainly, the author, who was writing in the mid-70s, would have been influenced by the first wave of feminism, and by the rhetoric of the women's liberation movement. At this time, people were just beginning to question financial and social inequalities between men and women. However, much has changed since then. What was relevant in Gross's time is not necessarily relevant today.

5   Moreover, the fundamental mistake Gross makes is that she believes that women should select men according to types. They shouldn't. Women should date, love, and marry individual men. As a result, a woman should really be concerned about whether the man shares her interests, treats her well, has qualities she can love, and will be faithful. Where the man fits in a chart is far less important than the kind of man he is, regardless of whether he is "androgynous."

Successful Reading

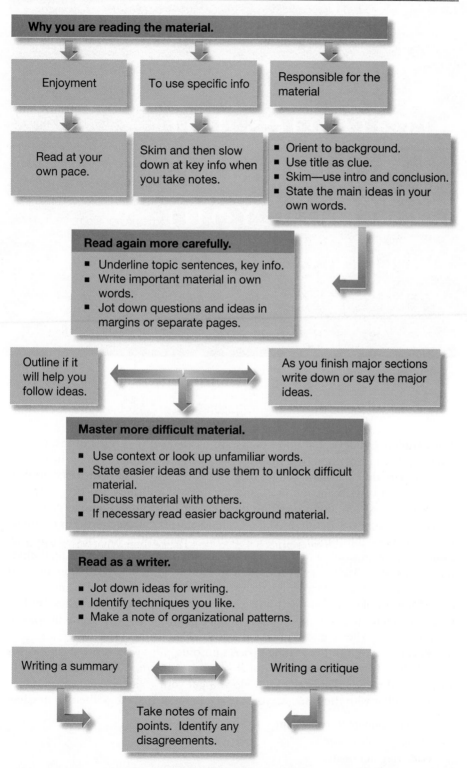

Why you are reading the material.

Enjoyment

To use specific info

Responsible for the material

Read at your own pace.

Skim and then slow down at key info when you take notes.

- Orient to background.
- Use title as clue.
- Skim—use intro and conclusion.
- State the main ideas in your own words.

Read again more carefully.

- Underline topic sentences, key info.
- Write important material in own words.
- Jot down questions and ideas in margins or separate pages.

Outline if it will help you follow ideas.

As you finish major sections write down or say the major ideas.

Master more difficult material.

- Use context or look up unfamiliar words.
- State easier ideas and use them to unlock difficult material.
- Discuss material with others.
- If necessary read easier background material.

Read as a writer.

- Jot down ideas for writing.
- Identify techniques you like.
- Make a note of organizational patterns.

Writing a summary

Writing a critique

Take notes of main points. Identify any disagreements.

CHAPTER 3

Strategies for Planning and Drafting Your Writing

Many students believe that good essays are dashed off in a burst of inspiration. Students themselves often boast that they cranked out their best papers in an hour or so of spare time. Perhaps. But for most of us, writing is less an innate talent than a process that takes time, attention, and the work of informed practice. Although popular writers sometimes describe their favourite formula for success, writing isn't a fixed process with one-size-fits-all rules that work for everyone. For example, some writers establish their purpose and draft a plan at the start of every project, while others begin with a tentative purpose or plan and discover their final direction as they write. Writers can proceed in an orderly, straightforward sequence, but more commonly they leapfrog backward and forward. Partway through a first draft, for example, a writer may think of a new point to present, then pause and jot down the details needed to develop it. Similarly, part of the conclusion may come to mind as the writer is gathering the details for supporting a key idea.

Regardless of how the writing process unfolds, most writers use the six stages listed below. If you have no plan, or if you run into snags with your approach, advancing through each stage will help you get your essay under control. Once you're familiar with these stages, you can combine or rearrange them as needed.

Understanding the assignment

Zeroing in on a topic

Gathering information

Organizing the information
Developing a thesis statement
Writing the first draft

Types of Writers

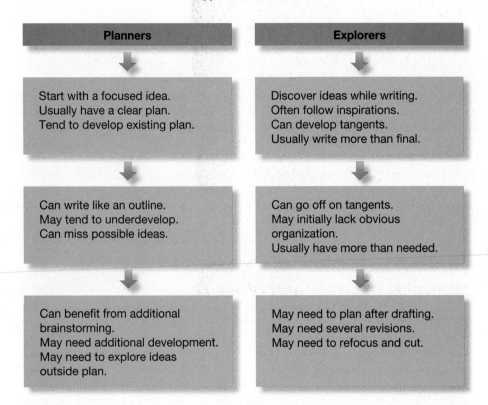

Planners	Explorers
Start with a focused idea. Usually have a clear plan. Tend to develop existing plan.	Discover ideas while writing. Often follow inspirations. Can develop tangents. Usually write more than final.
Can write like an outline. May tend to underdevelop. Can miss possible ideas.	Can go off on tangents. May initially lack obvious organization. Usually have more than needed.
Can benefit from additional brainstorming. May need additional development. May need to explore ideas outside plan.	May need to plan after drafting. May need several revisions. May need to refocus and cut.

UNDERSTANDING THE ASSIGNMENT

Different instructors give different kinds of writing assignments. Some specify the topic; some give you several topics to choose from; and still others offer you a free choice. Likewise, some instructors dictate the length and format of the essay, whereas others don't. Whatever the case, be sure you understand the assignment before you start.

Think of it this way: If your boss asked you to report on ways to improve working conditions at your office, and you turned in a report on improving worker benefits, would you expect the boss's approval? Following directions is crucial. So if you have any questions about the assignment, ask your instructor to clear them up right away. Also make sure that you understand the instructor's expectations and the emphasis for a particular assignment. For example, some assignments require formal academic writing, while others may call for a more informal and personal style. An essay for a sociology class will follow different conventions than an essay for an English class. Don't be timid; it's much better to ask for clarity than to receive a low grade for failing to follow directions.

Once you understand the assignment, consider the project *yours*. Whether you are writing for a local newspaper, for a friend, or for your instructor and classmates, here is your chance to tell others about something important to you. By asking yourself who your audience is, and what the assignment allows you to accomplish, you can find your purpose.

ZEROING IN ON A TOPIC

A subject is a broad discussion area: for example, sports, academic life, or Canadian culture. A topic is one small segment of a subject: for example, if you are interested in public education, you might explore a topic such as testing in the province's public schools, or internet access in the schools, or ways of dealing with school violence. If you choose your own topic, pick one narrow enough that you can develop it properly within the length limitation. Avoid sprawling, slippery topics that result in a string of trite generalities.

In addition, choose a topic you can learn enough about in the time available. Avoid overworked topics, which repeat information that most people are already familiar with. Instead, select a topic that lets you offer a fresh perspective to your reader.

Strategies for Finding a Topic

Students sometimes prefer having a larger, more general area to write about than a more focused topic. However, writing is usually easier—and more interesting for you and your reader—if you take on a topic that is more specific and manageable. Would you be more interested in an essay entitled "Hockey in Canada" or one entitled "Why Hockey Is No Longer Canadian"? Whenever your instructor assigns a general subject area, you need to stake out a limited topic suitable for your paper. If you're lucky, the right one will come to mind immediately. More often, though, you'll need to resort to some special strategy. Here are six strategies that many writers use. Not all of them work for everyone, so experiment to find those that produce a topic for you.

Tapping Your Personal Resources   If your instructor asks for writing that draws from personal experience, you may be able to tap into your memories of family gatherings, school activities, movies, concerts, plays, parties, jobs, books you've read, TV programs, dates, discussions, arguments, and so on. All these experiences can provide suitable topics. Suppose you've been asked to write about some aspect of education. Recalling the difficulties you had last term at registration, you might argue for better registration procedures. Or if you're a hopeless TV addict, why not analyze advertising techniques you have seen on TV for a specific consumer item such as a hybrid car or a new health product?

Anything you've read in magazines or journals, newspapers, novels, short stories, or textbooks can also trigger a topic. Alice Munro's short story "Boys and Girls," in which a girl growing up in rural Canada comes to accept the gender role she is assigned, might suggest a paper on gender socialization, or another on farm work. An article reviewing the career of a well-known politician might stir thoughts of a friend's experience in running for the student council. Possibilities crowd our lives, waiting for us to recognize and seize them. But one word of caution: When using personal experience, ensure that it fits the assignment and the instructor's expectations. Instructors who ask for formal academic papers may not want to see personal material or personal reflections. As always, the key is to determine your audience and the situation or context for your writing.

EXERCISE *Select five of the subjects listed below. Use your personal resources to come up with one topic for each. Then for each topic, list three questions that you might answer in a paper.*

City life	An aspect of nature
A particular field of work	Contemporary forms of dancing
Drugs	Youth gangs
Concern for some aspect of the environment	Fashions in clothing
Saving money	Trendiness
Home ownership	Human rights

Keeping a Journal   Many writers record their experiences in a journal—a private gathering of entries accumulated over a period of time. In addition to helping writers remember and reflect on their experiences, journal keeping provides an abundance of possible writing topics as well as a valuable opportunity for writing practice.

The hallmark of the journal entry is the freedom to explore thoughts, feelings, responses, attitudes, and beliefs. In your own private domain, you can express your views without reservation, without concern for "doing it right." *You* control the content and length of the entry without being held to a specified topic or number of words. Journal writing does not represent a finished product, but rather an exploration. In addition to personal journals, learning journals— where you reflect on what you've learned in your classes—can yield interesting topics for formal research papers.

It can help your writing if you get in the habit of writing regularly in a journal— five times a week if possible. You can write in any format that appeals to you; many people prefer to take notes on computers, while some like to carry a small notebook where they can jot down observations and musings when they have a few spare minutes.

Let's examine a typical journal entry by Sam, a first-year composition student. This journal entry could spawn several essays. Sam might explore the causes of residential deterioration, define sportsmanship, explain how Mrs. Wynick made learning a game, or argue for stricter pollution control laws.

> Last week went back to my hometown for the first time since my family moved away and while there dropped by the street where I spent my first twelve years. Visit left me feeling very depressed. Family home still there, but its paint peeling and front porch sagging. Sign next to the porch said house now occupied by Acme Realtors. While we lived there, front yard lush green and bordered by beds of irises. Now an oil-spattered parking lot. All the other

houses on our side of the street gone, replaced by a row of dumpy buildings housing dry cleaner, bowling alley, hamburger joint, shoe repair shop, laundromat. All of them dingy and rundown looking, even though only a few years old.

Other side of the street in no better shape. Directly across from our house a used-car dealership with rows of junky looking cars. No trace left of the park that used to be there. Had lots of fun playing baseball and learned meaning of sportsmanship. To left of the dealership my old grade school, now boarded and abandoned. Wonder about my Grade 5 teacher Mrs. Wynick. Is she still teaching? Still able to make learning a game, not a chore? Other side of dealership the worst sight of all. Grimy looking plant of some sort pouring foul smelling smoke into the air from a discoloured stack. Smoke made me cough.

Don't think I'll revisit my old street again.

EXERCISE *Write journal entries over the next week or two for some of the following items that interest you. If you have trouble finding a suitable topic for a paper, review the entries for possibilities.*

Pleasant or unpleasant conversations   Cultural or sporting events

Developing relationships   Academic life: myth vs. reality

Single or married life   Public figures—politicians; movie,

Parents   rock, or sports stars

Sorting Out a Subject   All of us sort things. We do it whenever we tackle the laundry, clear away a sinkful of dishes, or tidy up a basement or bedroom. Consider how we might begin organizing a cluttered basement. We might sort the contents according to type: books in one place, clothing in a second, toys in a third. That done, chances are we'd do still more sorting, separating children's books from adults' and stuffed animals from games. As we looked over and handled the different items, long-buried, bittersweet memories might start flooding from our subconscious: memories of an uncle, now dead, who sent this old adventure novel . . . of our parents' pride when they saw their child had learned to ride that now battered bicycle . . . of the dance that marked the debut of the evening gown over there.

Sorting out a subject is similar. First, we break our broad subject into categories and subcategories, and then we allow our minds to roam over the different items to see what topics we can turn up. The chart on page 38 shows what one student found when she explored the general subject of public transportation.

As you'll discover for yourself, some subjects yield more topics than others; some, no topics at all.

EXERCISE *Select two of the following subjects, and then subdivide them into five topics each.*

Advertising	Movies	Transportation
Computers	Occupations	Sports
Fashions	Popular music	Television programs

Asking Questions   Often, asking questions such as those below can lead you to a manageable topic:

How can this subject be described?

How is this subject accomplished or performed?

What is an example of my subject?

Does the subject break into categories?

If so, what comparisons can I make among these categories?

If my subject is divided into parts, how do they work together?

Does my subject have uses? What are they?

What are the causes of my subject?

What is the impact of my subject?

How can my subject be defined?

What case could be made for or against my subject?

Let's convert these general questions into specific questions about a broad general subject: telescopes.

Narration:	What is the story of the telescope?
Description:	How can a telescope be described?
Illustration:	What are some well-known telescopes?
Process:	How does one use a telescope?
Analysis:	What are the parts of the telescope, and how do they work together?
Functional analysis:	How is a telescope useful?
Causal analysis:	Why did the telescope come about?
Analysis of effects:	What effects have telescopes had on human life and knowledge?
Classification:	What are the different kinds of telescopes?
Comparison:	How are they alike? How are they different?
Definition:	What is a telescope?
Argument:	Why should people learn to use telescopes?

Each of these questions offers a starting point for a suitably focused essay. For example, Question 3 might be answered in a paper about the Hubble Space Telescope and the problems experienced with it. Question 10 might launch a paper that compares reflecting and refracting telescopes.

Results of Sorting Out the Subject Public Transportation

Land			Water		Air	
Buses	Taxis	Trains	Seagoing	Lake, River	Airplanes	Helicopters
Local bus services for the handicapped	Rights of passengers	The Orient Express, the Twentieth Century Limited	The Titanic	Barge cruises	Delays from security checks	Air taxis
Bus tours	Preventing crimes against drivers	Subways	Luxury liners		Airline strikes	Cargo
City buses		Via Rail	Theme cruises		Overbooking flights	Search and rescue
Improving bus terminals		Japan's high-speed trains	Modern sea pirates		Making air travel safer	Hospital transfers
Designing buses to accommodate the handicapped		Deterioration of railway track beds	Travelling by freighter		Threats from terrorists	
			The impact of overseas flights on ship travel		Causes and prevention of jet lag	
					Noise pollution around airports	

EXERCISE *Convert two of the general subjects below into more manageable topics. Then, drawing from the list of questions suggested above, ask specific questions about the topics. Finally, come up with two essay topics for each of the two subjects.*

> *Example:* Take a general subject, such as Music, and then narrow it to a more manageable topic, such as "Downloading Music from the Computer." After running through the list of questions above, you might choose two essay topics, such as "How to Download Music from the Internet" and "The Advantages of Downloading Music."

Tourism	Games	Health
Sports	Free trade	Business schools
Languages	Television	

Freewriting   The freewriting strategy snares thoughts as they race through your mind, yielding a set of sentences that you then look over for writing ideas. To begin, turn your pen loose and write for about five minutes on your general subject. Put down everything that comes into your head, without worrying about grammar, spelling, or punctuation. What you produce is for your eyes alone. If the thought flow becomes blocked, write "I'm stuck, I'm stuck . . ." until you break the mental logjam. When your writing time is up, go through your sentences one by one and extract potential topic material. If you draw a blank, write for another five minutes and look again.

The following example shows the product of one freewriting session. Jim's instructor had assigned a two- or three-page paper on a sports-related topic; and since Jim had been a member of his high school tennis team, his thoughts naturally turned toward tennis.

> Sports. If that's my subject, I'd better do something on tennis. I've played enough of it. But what can I say that would be interesting? It's very popular, lots of people watch it on TV. Maybe I could write about the major tennis tournaments. I'm stuck. I'm stuck. Maybe court surfaces. That sounds dull. I'm stuck. Well, what about tennis equipment, clothing, scoring? Maybe my reader is thinking about taking up the game. What do I like about tennis? The strategy, playing the net, when to use a topspin or a backspin stroke, different serves. I'm stuck. I'm stuck. Maybe I could suggest how to play a better game of singles. I used to be number one. I can still remember Coach harping on those three C's, conditioning, concentration, consistency. I'm stuck. I'm stuck. Then there's the matter of special shots like lobs, volleys, and overheads. But that stuff is for the pros.

This example suggests at least three papers. For the beginning player, Jim could focus on equipment and scoring. For the intermediate player, he might write on conditioning, concentration, and consistency; for the advanced player, special shots.

Brainstorming   Brainstorming, a close cousin of freewriting, captures fleeting ideas in words, fragments, and sometimes sentences, rather than in a series of sentences. Brainstorming garners ideas faster than the other strategies do. But unless you move immediately to the next stage of writing, you may lose track of what some of your fragmentary jottings mean.

To compare the results of freewriting and brainstorming a topic, we've converted our freewriting example into this list, which typifies the results of brainstorming:

Popularity of tennis	Equipment
Major tournaments	Clothing
Court surfaces	Scoring
Doubles strategy	Conditioning
Singles strategy	Concentration
Playing the net	Consistency
Topspin	Special shots—lobs, drop volleys,
Backspin	overheads
Different serves	

EXERCISE *Return to one set of five topics you selected for the exercise on page 37. Freewrite or brainstorm for five minutes on each one. Then choose a topic suitable for a two- or three-page essay. State your topic, intended audience, and purpose.*

Narrowing a familiar subject may yield not only a topic but also the main divisions for the paper. Jim's freewriting session uncovered several possible tennis topics as well as a way of approaching each: for example, by focusing on lobs, drop volleys, and overheads when writing about special shots. Ordinarily, though, the main divisions emerge only after you have gathered material to develop your topic.

Identifying Your Audience and Purpose

You can identify your purpose and audience at several different stages in the writing process. Sometimes both are set by the assignment: For example, you might be asked to write to your university or college president to recommend improvements in the school's registration system. At other times, you may have to write a draft before you can determine either. Usually, though, selecting audience and purpose occurs when you determine your topic. Think of the different types of information Jim would gather if he wrote for (1) beginning players, to offer advice on improving their game; (2) tennis buffs, to point out refinements of the game; or (3) a physics professor, to show the physical forces controlling the behaviour of tennis balls in flight.

Case History

Now that you're familiar with some narrowing strategies, let's examine the first segment of a case history showing how one student handled a writing assignment. This segment illustrates the use of a narrowing strategy to find a topic. Later segments focus on the remaining stages of the writing process.

Trudy's class has been talking and reading about memories from childhood, and about how these memories change their meaning over time. Trudy's instructor assigns a three- or four-page paper describing or narrating a childhood experience that led to an insight of some kind. Trudy begins by sorting out possible experiences to write about and comes up with two major categories: memories from elementary school and memories from secondary school. Under the first category, she includes memories of teachers who made an impression on her, a soccer game in which she scored the winning goal, and an autistic boy she knew who had trouble fitting in. In the second category, she includes memories of struggling with French and her experience of losing her boyfriend. Because the secondary school experiences still seem too close to her to write about, she decides to write about one of the memories from elementary school. After weighing the possibilities, she decides that she will be able to write the most interesting narrative about the autistic boy she once knew.

This case history continues on page 43.

GATHERING INFORMATION

Once you have a topic, you need things to say about it. This supporting material can include facts, ideas, examples, observations, sensory impressions, and memories. Without this kind of support, papers lack force, vividness, and interest, and may confuse or mislead readers. The more support you can gather, the easier it will be for you to write a draft. Time spent gathering information is never wasted.

Strategies for Gathering Information

If you are writing on a personal topic for a creative writing class, much of your supporting material may come from your own head. Brainstorming is the best way to retrieve it. However, with academic, professional, and fact-oriented topics, you have to use research for your supporting material. But whatever the topic—personal or academic—using friends, parents, and neighbours as sounding boards and talking to local experts can also produce useful ideas.

Brainstorming   Brainstorming a topic, like brainstorming a subject, yields a set of words, fragments, and occasionally sentences that furnish ideas for the paper. Assume that Jim, the student who explored the subject of tennis, wants to show

how conditioning, concentration, and consistent play can improve one's game. His brainstorming list might look like this:

Keeping ball in play	Courtside distractions
Don't try foolish shots	Temper distractions
Placing ball so opponent runs	Don't continually drive ball with power
Staying in good condition yourself	Two-on-one drill
Running	Lobbing ball over opponent's head
Jogging	Returning a down-the-line
Skipping rope keeps you on your toes	passing shot
Chance for opponent to make mistake	Don't try spectacular overheads
Keeping your mind only on the game	Game of percentages
Personal distractions	Games are lost, not won

You can see how some thoughts have led to others. For example, the first jotting, "keeping ball in play," leads naturally to the next one, "don't try foolish shots." "Placing ball so opponent runs" leads to "staying in good condition yourself," which in turn leads to ways of staying in condition, and so forth.

Clustering and branching are helpful and convenient extensions of brainstorming that allow you to add details to any item in your list. Here's how you might use clustering to approach "courtside distractions." (For branching, see p. 144.)

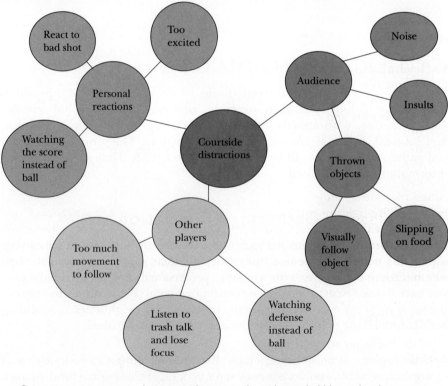

One common strategy is clustering, where you place ideas in bubbles and make as many connections as come to mind.

Don't worry if your brainstorming notes look chaotic and if some seem irrelevant. Sometimes the most unlikely material turns out to be the freshest and most interesting. As you organize and write your paper, you'll probably combine, modify, and omit some of the notes, as well as add others.

EXERCISE *Prepare a brainstorming sheet of supporting details for one of the topics you developed for the exercise on page 40.*

Reading Sometimes we get ideas from our reading, or from what we have heard on the radio and seen on the television news. When you have to grapple with an unfamiliar topic, the library or internet can help you unearth promising leads. Before using library or internet sources, however, you will need to consult Chapter 15 to review research guidelines for using libraries and unearthing promising references to investigate. Depending on the nature of the assignment, you may be asked to compile a list of references, and find books or articles on your topic. If so, look through each source you find and record any information that looks useful, either as direct quotations or as a paraphrase or summary in your own words.

Whenever you use a direct quotation or rephrased material in your paper, you must give proper credit to the source. If you don't, you are guilty of plagiarism (pages 492–494), a serious offence that can result in a failing grade or even expulsion.

Talking with Others You can expand the pool of ideas gained through brainstorming or reading by talking to people around you. Imagine you're writing a paper about a taxpayers' revolt in your province. After checking the leading provincial newspapers at the library, you find that most of the discontent centres on high property taxes. You then decide to supplement what you've read by asking questions about the local tax situation in your town.

Your parents and neighbours tell you that property taxes have jumped 50 percent in the last two years. The local tax assessor tells you that assessed valuations have risen sharply and that the law requires property taxes to keep pace. She also notes that this situation is causing some people on fixed incomes to lose their homes. A city council member explains that part of the added revenue is being used to repair city streets, build a new library wing, and buy more fire-fighting equipment. The rest is going to the schools. School officials tell you they're using their extra funds to offer more vocational courses and to expand the program for special needs students. As you can see, asking questions or even interviewing others can broaden your perspective and provide information that helps you to write a more worthwhile paper.

Case History (continued from page 41)

After choosing to write about a student in elementary school, Trudy brainstorms to generate ideas. The result is a fifteen-item list. After checking her items over, Trudy decides that since the focus of her narrative is on a boy named Steven, she will eliminate items on learning disorders and treatment of autism because they are not directly relevant to her purpose. She also decides not to deal with information on Steven's family, on where Steven is now, or on other bullies today. The remaining items are as follows:

teasing of Steven	why people bully
Steven's appearance	my mother's response
Steven at lunch hour	confronting the bullies
Steven's loneliness	effects of bullying
incident in park	taking time to listen

This case history continues on page 46.

ORGANIZING THE INFORMATION

If you have ever listened to a rambling speaker spill out ideas in no particular order, you know how difficult it is to pay attention to such a speech, let alone make sense of it. So, too, with disorganized writing. A garbled listing of ideas serves no one, but an orderly presentation highlights your ideas and communicates them successfully.

Your topic determines what organizational approach is best. In narrating a personal experience, such as a mishap-riddled vacation, you'd probably trace the events in the order they occurred. In describing a process, say caulking a bathtub, you'd take the reader step by step through the procedure. To describe the parts of a cell, you might work from one end to the other. Or you could first create a general picture of the central features and then fan out in either direction to cover the minor features. Other topics use other patterns, such as illustration, cause and effect, and comparison and contrast (which we discuss in more detail in Chapters 8, 10, and 12, respectively).

For longer pieces of writing, especially research-based writing, formal outlines, described below, are useful road maps. However, for shorter papers, many people use a simple, informal system of *flexible notes*.

The Flexible Notes System

To create a set of flexible notes, write each of your key points at the top of a separate sheet of paper. If your paper requires a thesis statement (see pages 48–49), write it on a separate introduction sheet on its own; but for now, we will just focus on the body of the essay. Next, list under each heading the supporting details that go with that heading. Drop any details that don't fit, and expand any points that need more support. When your sheets are finished, arrange them in the order you expect to follow in your essay. The notes for the body of the tennis paper might look like this:

<u>Conditioning</u>

staying in good condition yourself	two-on-one drill
lobbing ball over opponent's head	running
returning a down-the-line passing shot	jogging
skipping rope keeps you on your toes	

Concentration

keeping your mind only on the game

overcome distractions: personal, courtside, temper

Consistency

keeping ball in play

don't try foolish shots

placing ball so opponent runs

don't continually drive ball with power

don't try spectacular overheads

chance for opponent to make mistake

game of percentages

games are lost, not won

Since conditioning, concentration, and consistency are simultaneous concerns, this listing arranges them according to their probable importance—starting with the least important.

Now you're ready to draft a plan showing how many paragraphs you'll have in each part of the essay and what each paragraph will cover. Sometimes the number of details suggests one paragraph; other times, you need a paragraph block—two or more paragraphs—to cover the topic. Here's a plan for the body of the tennis essay:

Conditioning

staying in good condition yourself

running   off-the-court

jogging   conditioning

skipping rope keeps you on your toes

two-on-one drill

lobbing ball over opponent's head   on-the-court

returning a down-the-line passing shot   conditioning

Concentration

keeping your mind only on the game

overcome distractions: personal, courtside, temper

Consistency

keeping ball in play

don't try foolish shots

placing ball so opponent runs   placing shots

don't continually drive ball with power

don't try spectacular overheads

chance for opponent to make mistake

game of percentages   playing percentage

games are lost, not won

These groupings suggest one introductory paragraph, two paragraphs about conditioning, one about concentration, and two about consistency.

EXERCISE *Organize into flexible notes the supporting details that you prepared for the exercise on page 43. Arrange your note pages in a logical sequence and draft a plan showing the number and content of the paragraphs in each section.*

Case History (continued from page 44)

A careful look at her brainstorming list suggests how Trudy can arrange her items in a logical order. Since she is writing a narrative, she will follow a chronological order, or time sequence. She will begin with a description of Steven in the schoolyard, proceed to the story of the bullies teasing Steven in the park and then to her mother's confrontation with the bullies, and end with the insight about taking time to listen. She draws up the following plan.

Background—Steven at Lunch Time

searching for stick

waving his stick

others whisper and giggle

Steven's Appearance

dirty clothing

gazes into distance

Incident at Park

bullies taunt Steven

I fail to stop them

Going Home for Help

explaining to my mother

heading for the park

Arriving at the Park

Steven is crying

bullies fail to see us

My Mother's Confrontation

Mother yells

bullies leave

We Walk Steven Home

Mother asks Steven where
   home is

Mother seems angry

**Steven Questions Why People
   Are Mean**

Steven's question

no real answer

My Thoughts Today

how Steven made a difference

listening to someone can help

This case history continues on page 51.

Patterns of Development

As you think about ways to organize and develop your ideas, whether for more personal or more academic essays, it may be helpful to think about how you might consciously choose to use different modes of development, such as illustration, analysis, comparison, and argument, that we explore in later chapters.

However, it's important to remember that these modes of developing ideas do not usually occur in isolation. For example, an argument may use some narrative and illustration, and an essay that is primarily a comparison might also analyze the causes or effects of something. A comparative essay is often an argument as well, suggesting that one thing is superior to another.

Since the first writing assignment in Trudy's class asked her to write about a personal experience, Trudy chose to write a narrative about something that affected her emotionally. It's possible that her concern about special needs children could lead her to respond to later writing assignments in more analytical or objective ways. For example, she could decide to write an illustrative essay that shows examples of schoolyard bullying of special needs children. She could also write a research essay comparing different kinds of autism interventions. Or she could write an argument that blended her personal observations with some researched information about how children should be taught empathy for special needs children.

CREATING A FORMAL OUTLINE

Many writers do not write outlines until they have gathered material and even begun writing a draft, since they do not always know what direction they want to take until their ideas have started to unfold. Others prefer more structure early on in the writing process. If it fits your organizational style, especially when you are writing a longer essay, writing a formal outline can show you how to organize your material into paragraphs. In an outline, you organize chunks of information into major units using Roman numerals (I, II, III), letters (A, B, C), and numbers to show the structure you will use in the paper. Introductions and conclusions are not usually included in the outline. There are two kinds of outlines. A topic outline simply states the main topic to be addressed in a section.

    I. Parties
        A. End of the world parties
            1. crowded streets
            2. wild behaviour
        B. Fraternity parties
            1. restricted to university students
            2. guests can be invited

   II. Swimming
        A. Cold water lake
            1. clear water for swimming
            2. a sandy beach

    B. Lake Isabella Dam
      1. large water slide

Topic outlines will quickly let you know if you have enough information for a paragraph. If under one major heading, you only have one letter or under a letter only one number (as in II B), you may need to do more brainstorming.

In a sentence outline, you make full statements or sentences that can often be used in your paper. A sentence outline makes you think about what you really want to say.

    I. Social problems have to be solved for successful reproduction of endangered species in zoos.
      A. Often males and females must be separated until they are ready.
      B. Male–female compatibility can be a social problem.
      C. Captive-born parents may neglect their young.

For a more complete example of a sentence outline, check the example on pages 418–419 in Chapter 15.

To develop your outline, take your brainstorming or notes and mark the major units as I, II, III based on the main ideas they demonstrate. Then start to develop your outline, identifying the major points for each major heading (I, II . . .) and the next major points (A, B, C). You can use your outline as a goad to additional planning as you see the holes. You should rarely have an A without a B or a 1 without a 2.

DEVELOPING A THESIS STATEMENT

A thesis statement—one or two sentences that express the main idea in your essay—can help you stay on track. If you do not have a thesis, or point you are heading toward when you write, your reader will probably feel frustrated. Whether or not it is spelled out explicitly, the thesis statement governs and unifies the entire essay. The thesis statement points you and your reader in a specific direction. In addition, it tells your reader what to expect.

Thesis statements can emerge at several points in the writing process. If an instructor assigns a controversial topic on which you hold strong views, the statement may pop into your head right away. Usually, though, it emerges gradually, after you have gathered and examined supporting information, or during the writing process itself.

Often a preliminary thesis may evolve into something more focused and interesting as you write. In these cases, return to your original thesis and reshape it. A thesis such as "Downloading music from the internet has advantages" could become more refined: "Downloading music from the internet can help musical artists as well as their audience."

As you examine your information, search for the central point and the key points that back it up; then use these to develop your thesis statement. If you convert a topic to a question, the answer to this question may be your thesis statement. For example,

Topic:	The uncertain future of robots in Canadian industry.
Question:	What are some of the drawbacks of using robots in Canadian industry?
Thesis statement:	The expense of producing robots, the lack of qualified personnel to service them, and the moral problems of replacing workers with them all cloud the future of robots in Canadian industry.

The thesis statement stems from the specifics the student unearthed while answering the question.

Requirements of a Good Thesis Statement

Unity   Unless intended for a lengthy paper, a thesis statement *focuses on just one central point or issue.* Suppose you prepare the following thesis statement for a two- or three-page paper:

> New Generation College should re-examine its policies on open admissions, vocational programs, and aid to students.

This sprawling statement would commit you to grapple with three separate issues. At best, you could make only a few general remarks about each one.

To correct matters, consider each issue carefully in light of how much it interests you and how much you know about it. Then make your choice and draft a narrower statement. The following thesis statement would suit a brief paper. It shows clearly that the writer will focus on *just one issue:*

> Because of the rising demand among high school graduates for job-related training, New Generation College should expand its vocational offerings.

Tailored Scope   A good thesis statement also *tailors the scope of the issue to the length of the paper.* No writer could deal adequately with "Many first-year university students face crucial adjustment problems" in two or three pages. The idea is too broad to yield more than a smattering of poorly supported general statements. But paring it down to "Free time is a responsibility that challenges many first-year university students" results in an idea that could probably be developed adequately.

Indication of Writer's Attitude   An essay is not simply a statement of fact or a bland report, but a piece of writing that reflects a particular point of view. The thesis statement implies purpose by suggesting the writer's attitude toward his or her subject. A thesis statement such as "Ethanol is an alternative fuel composed of oxygen, hydrogen, and carbon" simply states a fact, but does not indicate the writer's attitude or position. Consider instead how the following thesis statements suggest the writer's point of view: "Using ethanol as an alternative fuel creates more environmental problems than it solves" or "Despite the costs associated with producing ethanol, it is still an alternative fuel option that the Canadian government should pursue."

Accurate Forecasting   A good thesis statement further provides *an accurate forecast of what's to come.* If you plan to discuss the effects of overeating, don't say "Overeating stems from deep-seated psychological factors and the easy availability of convenience foods." Because this statement incorrectly suggests that the paper will focus on causes, not the effects, it would only mislead and confuse your reader. On the other hand, the statement "Overeating leads to obesity, which can cause or complicate several serious health problems" accurately represents what's to follow.

Preview of Organization   Finally, a good thesis statement is precise, often previewing the organization of the paper, indicating a strategy of development. Assertions built on fuzzy, biased words, such as *fascinating, bad, meaningful,* or *interesting,* or vague statements like "My paper is about . . ." tell neither writer nor reader what's going on. Examine these two examples:

> Montreal is a fascinating city.
> My paper is about health benefits in Canada.

These thesis statements raise too many questions. Why does the writer find Montreal fascinating? Because of its architecture? its night life? its theatres? its restaurants? its museums? its shops? its cultural diversity? And what about health benefits? Will the writer explain how to apply for health benefits, or defend the current system of benefits, trace its history, suggest ways of improving it? Without a clear roadmap sentence suggesting the writer's direction, the readers must labour through the paper, hoping to find their way.

Now look at the rewritten versions of those vague, imprecise thesis statements:

> Montreal's ethno-cultural diversity offers visitors the chance to sample cuisine from every continent.
> Canada's national health care system should be a two-tier system that allows patients the options of receiving medical treatment from private clinics and hospitals at their own expense or from public clinics or hospitals at public expense, because such a system would reduce waiting lists and lower the costs of health care paid by the Canadian government.

These thesis statements tell the reader not only what points the writer will make but also suggest the order and strategy of development they will follow. The Montreal essay will proceed by way of illustration, offering examples of dishes from different parts of the world that a visitor might sample. The health care thesis statement suggests that the writer will argue why a two-tier health care system would be desirable. Note that the second thesis statement could easily be broken into two sentences, with the first sentence stating the writer's position, and the second sentence providing the road map—a preview of the writer's main points.

Placement of Thesis Statement

In most academic essays, the thesis statement comes somewhere in the first paragraph. Many essays take two or three sentences to lead into the thesis, but some, such as an essay for an in-class midterm exam, may need the thesis immediately in the first sentence. Moreover, in persuasive essays, the writer may hold off stating the thesis until close to the end of the first paragraph, especially if it is controversial. Some essays, in particular, narratives and descriptions, or those by professional writers, may have only implied thesis statements. Nonetheless, a core idea underlies and controls all effective writing.

Changing Your Thesis Statement

Unlike diamonds, thesis statements aren't necessarily forever. Before your paper is in final form, you may need to change your thesis statement several times. If you draft the thesis statement during the narrowing stage, you might change it to reflect what you uncovered while gathering information. Or you might amend it after writing the first draft so that it reflects your additions and deletions.

Tentative or final, formulated early or late, the thesis statement serves as a beacon that spotlights your purpose.

Case History   (continued from page 46)

Her essay plan completed, Trudy now drafts a thesis statement—the larger point that her entire essay will make:

> We should listen to other people, even if they seem different from us.

This case history continues on pages 53–55.

EXERCISE

1. Write a thesis statement for the flexible notes that you developed for the exercise on page 46.

2. Using "Requirements of a Good Thesis Statement," explain why each of the following does or does not qualify as an effective thesis statement for a two- or three-page essay.

   a. My paper discusses the problem of employee absenteeism in Canadian industry.

   b. I really like astronomy.

   c. Although I don't know much about running a business, I know that PDT Accounting Inc. is not run well.

   d. Higher education has many problems.

   e. It is not entirely fair for teens that getting a Canadian driver's licence is more difficult than it was a few years ago.

WRITING THE FIRST DRAFT

Of course, sometimes when you sit down to write a first draft or even notes for a draft, the words won't come. All you can do is doodle or stare at the blank page. Perhaps the introduction is the problem. Many writers are terrified by the thought of the opening paragraph. They want to get off to a good start but can't figure out how to begin. If this happens to you, additional brainstorming or freewriting can make you more comfortable and may suggest an opening. Keep in mind that any lead-in you write now can be changed later. If these suggestions don't solve your problem, skip the introduction for now. Once you have drafted the body of the paper, an effective opening should come more easily.

Here are some general suggestions for writing a first draft:

1. Stack your thesis statement, flexible notes, and written plan in front of you. They will help you start thinking.
2. As you are typing, save each version as a different draft so that you can go back later to retrieve material. If you prefer to write by hand, skip every other line (double-space) and leave wide margins so that you'll have room to revise later.
3. Type or write quickly; capture the drift of your thoughts. Concentrate on content and organization. Get your main points and supporting details on paper in the right sequence. Don't spend time correcting grammatical or punctuation errors, improving your language, or making the writing flow smoothly. You might lose your train of thought.
4. Take breaks only at logical dividing points: for example, when you have finished discussing a key point. Before you start to write again, scan what you've written to refresh your memory.

These more specific suggestions can help you deal with writer's block:

1. Enter your thesis statement at the top of your first page to break the ice and build momentum.
2. Type your first paragraph, introducing your essay and stating your thesis. If you get stuck, leave it, and move on to the body of the paper.
3. Follow your plan or outline as you write. Begin with your first main point and work on each section in turn. Remember that you can change the order of main points later if a different arrangement of ideas seems more effective.
4. Look over the supporting details listed under the first heading in your flexible notes. Write a topic sentence stating the central idea of the paragraph before you start entering your supporting facts.
5. Turn the details into sentences. Use one or more sentences to explain each detail. Add other related details, facts, or examples that you could use as concluding statements.
6. When you move from one paragraph to the next, try to provide a transitional word (*However, But, In addition, Moreover,* etc.) or sentence to connect the two.
7. Write your last paragraph, ending your essay in an appropriate fashion. If you get stuck, set your conclusion aside and return to it later.

Of course, writing a draft isn't always so systematic, especially in personal writing. If you are inspired, you may want to abandon your plans and simply use your first draft to explore ideas. You can always revise later, so don't be overly concerned if you get off track. Because writing is an act of discovery, sometimes the best ideas come when you think you are digressing or coming to the end of a preliminary draft.

EXERCISE *Using the plan you prepared for the exercise on page 46, write the first draft of an essay.*

Case History   (continued from page 51)

Trudy now uses her thesis statement and essay plan to write the following draft. Notice that she chooses to write her thesis statement at the end rather than at the beginning of the essay, a common technique in the writing of narratives. Certainly this draft will need revision. We'll return to it in Chapter 5 to discuss the necessary changes.

A Memory

1   When I remember back to elementary school, I remember a boy named Steven Villman. It was said that he had autism, which often involves a withdrawal from reality and difficulty reading others' emotions. It's really hard to understand, and takes lots of patience. I didn't understand Steven. I used to watch him in awe during lunch times as he ran about on his tiptoes with a stick waving about in his hand like a magic wand. His sticks were his trademark. Every lunch hour, rain or shine, he would dart outside and begin his search through the woods behind the school, in search of the best stick. Steven could always be found darting in and out of the trees, gleefully shaking his stick.

2   His high-pitched screeches and nonsense babbling would never fail to catch the attention of children deep in their play. Children always found enough time to stop and stare but never to talk.

3   Steven always seemed to have a dirty film covering his clothing, but he paid no attention to what he wore. He was a large boy with dark, messy hair who always seemed to be looking, not at people, but at something in the distance.

4   Some kids would actually follow him around during lunch time, watching in awe at the odd tasks he'd perform, whispering and giggling about how weird he was.

5   One afternoon I was playing in a park located close to my house. Suddenly loud screeches alerted me as a large boy came running toward the park. Two smaller boys were trailing behind him, creeping up behind him and screeching in his ear to watch Steven's startled reaction for their own amusement.

6   I immediately recognized the terrified boy as Steven Villman. I stood up on top of the slide and stared with wide eyes and mouth open. Murmuring and tightly holding onto his stick, Steven would bolt about like a wild animal full of fear.

7   "Hey, leave him alone, you bullies," I yelled, but the bullies paid no attention. Steven looked up to where I stood, but then quickly turned back to the bullies. I pushed myself down the slide quickly and made my way home to get some help.

8   Inside my home I stood huffing and puffing and babbling out the situation I had witnessed to my mom. I went on to explain how different Steven was from other kids. My mother took a deep breath. We headed back to the park immediately.

9   By the time we arrived at the park, Steven was now blubbering uncontrollably and hollering at the boys. Still fascinated as ever and untouched by Steven's distress, the bullies failed to see my mom and me hustling over to where they stood.

10   "You two should be ashamed of yourselves!" my mother lectured with both hands on her hips. The boys whipped their heads around to be greeted by my furious mother as I watched with a small smirk.

11   The bullies looked at one another and then walked away, without even attempting to explain their behaviour.

12   Steven watched them go with a look of relief. "Where do you live, Steven?" my mom asked.

13   "That way." Steven pointed down the road. He was looking toward the ground as he swayed from side to side, as if he were rocking himself to sleep. He wore no shoes or socks on his feet and was covered from head to toe in dirt. "C'mon, Steven, we'll walk you home," my mother stated dryly, as if she were angry. We walked down the road at a slow pace listening to Steven's bare feet slap the hot concrete with each step he made. "Those bullies tricked me," Steven whined. Steven went on to talk-ing to himself rather than us, and it's a good thing he was, because it was clear that my mom had no answers to why the bullies were so mean.

| 14 | As my mom and I walked back home, we walked in silence. |
| 15 | I still think about Steven Villman. I wonder if he realizes what a difference he can make in the lives of others. When I walked Steven home that day, I learned that we all need to listen to people who are different than we are. |

This essay will be revised in Chapter 5.

PLANNING AND DRAFTING ON COMPUTER

Planning your paper on a computer allows you to take advantage of features that allow you to write, save what you write, insert new material later, delete unwanted material, move sections around, and when you are ready, print copies.

Prewriting

There are many ways to use your computer to generate ideas. When you are simply generating ideas rather than writing a draft, do not be afraid of being messy.

- Generate a list of ideas or key points and then go back and add whatever details or ideas come to mind about those points.
- Pull out the best ideas, and then either on the same page by inserting material, or as part of different files, freewrite about those ideas.
- If you are approaching a topic through the set of questions on page 37, convert them into specific questions related to the broad subject area, and then enter them and your responses to each question on either the same page or create different files for each question, depending how much material you might have.
- Keep a file or two for jotting down ideas for papers, observations about a topic, and even sentences that come to mind.
- Create a table of the main points you want to consider, such as a table for a comparison or argument, and then fill in the table with the details and ideas you will want to include in your paper.
- Use other approaches to get ideas. Some writers get ideas by discussing issues in a chat room, writing emails, or participating in listservs. Remember that if you take ideas from a source, you need to document the information following the method explained in Chapter 17, even if it is something you discovered in a chat room or on a listserv.

Of course, you will want to find your own techniques that work best with your style. Some students get ideas from talking; others prefer computer-based programs that help them organize ideas; still others like to visualize possibilities by drawing on paper.

Planning

If you prefer to write a very rough draft on paper or on the computer, go ahead. If you write your early draft on a computer, it will be easy to revise later by moving material around and using cut and paste features. If you benefit from a more structured approach at the beginning, you can easily create a plan on your computer and experiment with it by deleting, adding, and moving material until you have your points in the order that makes the most sense to you. You can build your draft by inserting material in the appropriate section of your plan. Some people who prefer formal outlines create an outline using the outline view of their program and then fill it in later. If you have created multiple files or sections as you generated ideas and made notes, you can label those sections and from this see how the ideas fit together to form a pattern.

Drafting

Do not let the final look on the screen fool you into being overly meticulous. When you are writing a draft, you know you will revise later, so you can afford to experiment. If you are writing and want to come back to a section later to develop an idea or try a different approach, mark it with an asterisk and then continue to write. You can leave gaps to fill in later. If you have more than one idea for a section, write down the other approaches, either bracketed on the same page or in a separate file. Always save each draft in a separate file, if not in a hard copy. You may want to use parts of an early draft in a later version.

Planning and Drafting Your Paper

Understand the assignment.

- Understand the topic.
- Identify key expectations.
- Make the project yours.

Find your topic.

- Talk with others.
- Keep a journal.
- Sort the subject into categories.
- Brainstorm.

Identify audience, purpose.

Develop details.

Read, talk to others, and brainstorm

Organize the information.

- Create labelled, flexible notes.
- Develop a rough plan—a list of points in order.
- Write a quick draft to find your focus and pattern.

Develop a focused thesis.

- Focus on just one central point or issue.
- Provide an accurate forecast of what is to come.

Draft to capture your thoughts—expect to revise.

CHAPTER 4

Strategies for Developing Paragraphs

Imagine the difficulty of reading a magazine article or book if you were faced with one solid block of text. How could you sort its ideas or know the best places to pause for thought? Paragraphs help guide readers through longer pieces of writing. Some break lengthy discussions of one idea into segments of different emphasis, thus providing rest stops for readers. Others consolidate several briefly developed ideas. Yet others begin or end pieces of writing or link major segments together. Most paragraphs, though, include a number of sentences that develop and clarify one idea. Throughout a piece of writing, paragraphs relate to one another and reflect a controlling purpose. To make paragraphs fit together, you can't just sit down and dash them off. Instead, you first need to reflect on the entire essay and then channel your thoughts toward its different segments. Often you'll have to revise your paragraphs after you've written a draft.

CHARACTERISTICS OF EFFECTIVE PARAGRAPHS

Unity

A paragraph with unity develops one—and only one—key controlling idea. To ensure unity, edit out any stray ideas that don't belong and fight the urge to take interesting but irrelevant side trips; they only create confusion about your destination. The following paragraph *lacks unity:*

> You can start a Registered Retirement Savings Plan (RRSP) as soon as you are 18 years old. You may need to pay off student loans. It is hard to be financially disciplined.

What exactly is this writer trying to say? We can't tell. Each statement expresses a different, undeveloped idea:

1. Starting a Registered Retirement Savings Plan
2. Paying off student loans
3. Financial discipline

In contrast, the following paragraph develops and clarifies only one central idea—the advantages of starting an RRSP early:

> You can start a Registered Retirement Savings Plan (RRSP) as soon as you are 18 years old. Of course, you may need to pay off significant student loans when you are young, but you can start an RRSP before you buy a car or even real estate. Ideally you should maximize your RRSP contributions, even if you have to cut back on some discretionary spending. Making RRSP contributions will save you money since you can reduce your taxable income and defer paying taxes. Retirement may seem a long way off when you are young, but starting an RRSP early will help gain financial discipline while your savings grow.
>
> Paul Johnson, student

Because this paragraph focuses entirely on a discussion of the advantages of starting a Registered Retirement Savings Plan, it has unity. To check your paragraphs for unity, ask yourself what each one aims to do and whether each sentence helps that aim.

EXERCISE *Read the next two paragraphs and answer the questions.*

1   The legend—in Africa—that all elephants over a large geographical area go to a common "graveyard" when they sense death is approaching led many hunters to treat them with special cruelty. Ivory hunters, believing the myth and trying to locate such graveyards, often intentionally wounded an elephant in the

hopes of following the suffering beast as it made its way to the place where it wanted to die. The idea was to wound the elephant seriously enough so that it thought it was going to die but not so seriously that it died in a very short time. All too often, the process resulted in a single elephant being shot or speared many times and relentlessly pursued until it either fell dead or was killed when it finally turned and charged its attackers. In any case, no wounded elephant ever led its pursuers to the mythical graveyard with its hoped-for booty of ivory tusks.

Kris Hurrell, student

2   Mental health practitioners need to be sensitive to the influence of labels and diagnoses. When those in power label the "other" who makes them uncomfortable as deviant in some way, this labelling depersonalizes and objectifies the labelled person. My cousin who was bipolar found it difficult to find and keep a job because of his major mood swings. Educators can be too quick to say that a child who is restless or inattentive has attention deficit disorder, and should take Ritalin. The pharmaceutical industry has a vested interest in getting as many people as possible to take prescription drugs. In the medieval period, women were easily labelled as witches, as madwomen, or as victims of emotional instability.

1. Which of these paragraphs lacks unity? Refer to content in the paragraphs when answering.
2. How would you improve the paragraph that lacks unity?

The Topic Sentence

The topic sentence states the main idea of the paragraph. Think of the topic sentence as a rallying point, with all supporting sentences developing the idea it expresses. A good topic sentence helps you gauge what information belongs in a paragraph, thus ensuring unity. At the same time, it informs your reader about the point you're making.

Placement of the topic sentence varies from paragraph to paragraph, as the following examples show. As you read each, note how supporting information develops the topic sentence, which is italicized.

Topic Sentence Stated First   Many paragraphs open with the topic sentence. The writer reveals the central idea immediately and then builds from a solid base.

Starting about one million years ago, the fossil record shows an accelerating growth of the human brain. It expanded at first at the rate of one cubic inch of additional gray matter every hundred thousand years; then the growth rate doubled; it doubled again; and finally it doubled once more. Five hundred thousand years ago the rate of growth hit its peak. At that time, the brain was expanding at the phenomenal rate of ten cubic inches every hundred thousand years. No other organ in the history of life is known to have grown as fast as this.

Robert Jastrow, *Until the Sun Dies*

Topic Sentence Stated Last   In order to emphasize the support and build gradually to a conclusion, a topic sentence can end the paragraph. Since this position creates suspense for the reader who anticipates the climactic or summarizing point, it can be particularly useful in personal or narrative writing.

An experience of my own comes handily to mind. Some years ago, when the Restaurant de la Pyramide in Vienne was without question one of the best half-dozen restaurants in the world, I visited it for the first time. After I had ordered my meal, the sommelier [wine steward] appeared to set before me a wine list of surpassing amplitude and excellence. But as I cast my eyes down this unbelievable offering of the world's most tantalizing wines, the sommelier bent over me and pointed out a wine of which I had never heard, ticketed at a price one-fifth that of its illustrious neighbors. "Monsieur," said the sommelier, "I would suggest this one. It is a local wine, a very good wine. It is not a great wine, but after all, monsieur, you are likely to pass this way only once. The great wines you will find everywhere; this wine you will find only in Vienne. I would like you to try it, while you have the opportunity." *This, to my mind, was true sophistication—on the part of M. Point for having the wine and on the part of the waiter for offering it.*

Stephen White, "The New Sophistication: Defining the Terms"

Topic Sentence Stated First and Last   Some paragraphs lead with the main idea and then restate it, usually in different words, at the end. This technique allows the writer to repeat an especially important idea.

Everything is changing. . . . This is a prediction I can make with absolute certainty. As human beings, we are constantly in a state of change. Our bodies change every day. Our attitudes are constantly evolving. Something that we swore by five years ago is now almost impossible for us to imagine ourselves believing. The clothes we wore a few years ago now look strange to us in old photographs. The things we take for granted as absolutes, impervious to change, are, in fact, constantly doing just that. Granite boulders become sand in time. Beaches erode and shape new shorelines. Our buildings become outdated and are replaced with modern structures that also will be torn down. Even those things which last thousands of years, such as the Pyramids and the Acropolis, also are changing. This simple insight is very important to grasp if you want to be a no-limit person, and are desirous of raising no-limit children. *Everything you feel, think, see, and touch is constantly changing.*

Wayne Dyer, *What Do You Really Want for Your Children?*

Topic Sentence Stated in the Middle   Occasionally, the topic sentence falls between background information and sentences that develop the central idea. This midpoint positioning of the topic sentence allows the writer to shift the emphasis and at the same time continue to build on the original idea. It can be particularly useful in longer, complex paragraphs.

> Over the centuries, China has often been the subject of Western fantasy. In their own way, a number of scholars, journalists, and other travelers have perpetuated this tradition in recent years, rushing to rediscover the country after its long period of isolation. Some of these visitors, justifiably impressed by the Communists' achievements in eliminating the exploitative aspects of pre-1949 mandarin society, propagated the view that the revolution, after its initial successes, had continued to "serve the people," and that China was "the wave of the future"—a compelling alternative to the disorder and materialism of contemporary Western society. Human rights were not at issue, they argued, because such Western concepts were inapplicable to China. *In the past year, however, the Chinese have begun to speak for themselves, and they are conveying quite a different picture.* In the view of many of its own people, China is a backward and repressive nation. "China is Asia's Gulag Archipelago," an elderly Chinese scholar said to me shortly after I had arrived in China last spring. "I was in Germany right after the Second World War, and I saw the horrors of Buchenwald and other concentration camps. In a way—in its destruction of the human spirit these past two decades—China has been even worse."
>
> David Finkelstein, "When the Snow Thaws"

Topic Sentence Implied   Some paragraphs, particularly in narrative and descriptive writing, have no topic sentence. Rather, all sentences point toward a main idea that readers must infer for themselves.

> [Captain Robert Barclay] once went out at 5 in the morning to do a little grouse shooting. He walked at least 30 miles while he potted away, and then after dinner set out on a walk of 60 miles that he accomplished in 11 hours without a halt. Barclay did not sleep after this but went through the following day as if nothing had happened until the afternoon, when he walked 16 miles to a ball. He danced all night, and then in early morning walked home and spent a day partridge shooting. Finally he did get to bed—but only after a period of two nights and nearly three days had elapsed and he had walked 130 miles.
>
> John Lovesey, "A Myth Is as Good as a Mile"

The details in this paragraph collectively suggest a clear central idea: that Barclay had incredible physical endurance. In most academic writing, however, clearly formulated topic sentences will help focus and unify your paragraphs.

EXERCISE *Identify the topic sentences in each of the following paragraphs and explain how you arrived at your decisions. If the topic sentence is implied, state the central idea in your own words.*

1. The immigrant dream—of financial and social success; of carving out a place within the larger society—is grand in its simplicity. Requiring great courage, it is self-limiting on no level. All one asks is the freedom and fairness—through anti-discrimination legislation, if necessary—to fulfill one's potential. A vital part of that freedom is the

latitude to recognize and welcome inevitable change in society and the migrant. One may treasure a private, personal identity built from family lore and experience, all the while pursuing the public integration vital to wider success. To be put in the position of either obliterating the past or worshipping it is, for the individual, an unnecessary burden that leads to a false and limiting theatre of the self.

Neil Bissoondath, "No Place Like Home"

2. What my mother never told me was how fast time passes in adult life. I remember, when I was little, thinking I would live to be at least as old as my grandmother, who was dynamic even at ninety-two, the age at which she died. Now I see those ninety-two years hurtling by me. And my mother never told me how much fun sex could be, or what a discovery it is. Of course, I'm of an age when mothers really didn't tell you much about anything. My mother never told me the facts of life.

Joyce Susskind, "Surprises in a Woman's Life"

3. It was funny how everyone in the second half of the twentieth century suddenly started buying these large, lumpy, sculptured, multicolored shoes. It was as though people discovered overnight that their footwear didn't have to be black or brown, and didn't need to conform to what was streamlined and quietly tasteful. The traditional shoe was challenged, and it collapsed at the first skirmish. Shoes could trumpet their engineered presence, their tread, their aggressive padding; they could make all manner of wild claims, converting whole populations to athletic splendor and prodigious fitness. Larry's running shoes are red and white, with little yellow insignias located near the toe. Each of the heels has a transparent built-in bubble for additional comfort and buoyancy when running on hard pavement.

Carol Shields, *Larry's Party*

4. That empty building on the left was once a school. Here in Cutback World we have discovered that the educational system operates far more efficiently if schools are not open. You should not conclude from this that we have closed all our schools. That would be foolish. There is a school downtown somewhere. Every city of at least 100 000 people in Cutback World is entitled to have a school. Ours has 15 000 students in it, which enables it to offer a full range of courses. When we pass it, you might notice some students hanging out the open windows. We regard this as a sign that classroom space is being fully utilized.

Charles Gordon "A Guided Tour of the Bottom Line"

EXERCISE

1. **Develop one of the ideas below into a topic sentence. Then write a unified paragraph that is built around it.**

   a. The career (or job or profession) I want is _____.

   b. The one quality most necessary in my chosen field is _____.

   c. The most difficult aspect of my chosen field is _____.

   d. One good example of the Canadian tendency to waste is _____.

   e. The best (or worst) thing about fast-food restaurants is _____.

2. **Write a topic sentence that would control a paragraph on each of the following:**
   a. Preparations for travelling away from home
   b. Advantages of having your own room
   c. Some landmark of the community in which you live
   d. The price of phone cards
   e. Registering for university courses

Adequate Development

Students often ask for guidelines on paragraph length: "Should I aim for fifty to sixty words? seven to ten sentences? about one-quarter of a page?" The questions are natural, but the approach is wrong. Instead of targeting a particular length, ask yourself what the reader needs to know. Then supply enough information to make your point clearly. Skimpy, undeveloped paragraphs frustrate readers by forcing them to fill in the gaps for themselves. On the other hand, a rambling paragraph stuffed with useless padding dilutes the main idea and often loses the audience. The extent of paragraph length and development is influenced by the reader's expectations, as well as the writing genre or publication medium. A newspaper article might feature short paragraphs including only key facts, whereas a scientific journal might have lengthy paragraphs that offer detailed development of facts. Personal narrative writing is more likely to use short paragraphs to control dramatic pacing, while formal academic writing usually contains well-developed paragraphs of several sentences.

The details you supply can include facts, figures, thoughts, observations, steps, lists, examples, and sometimes personal experiences. Individually, these bits of information may mean little, but combined, they clearly illustrate your point. Keep in mind, however, that development isn't an end in itself, but instead advances the purpose of the entire essay.

Here are two versions of a paragraph, the first inadequately developed:

Underdeveloped Paragraph

Many sports have peculiar injuries associated with them. Repetitive use of certain body parts can cause chronic injuries in athletes who play baseball, football, or basketball. All of these common sports injuries are a result of the overuse of specific body parts. However, these injuries can be greatly reduced if athletes train properly, rest fully, and respect their bodies.

Adequately Developed Paragraph

Many sports have peculiar injuries associated with them. Repetitive use of certain body parts can cause chronic injuries in athletes who play baseball, football, or basketball. *Baseball pitchers can throw up to one hundred and fifty pitches per game. This repetitive throwing action can cause pitchers' elbows to swell. Over time, tendonitis often develops. Similarly, football linemen also suffer chronic injuries related to their sport. The constant jarring pressure during physical contact can cause severe back pain. Many linemen struggle with spinal disc injuries throughout their lives. In addition, basketball players often suffer from shin splints because of the repetitive pounding on their legs when running and jumping on a hard surface.* All of these common sports injuries are a result of the overuse of specific body parts. However, these injuries can be greatly reduced if athletes train properly, rest fully, and respect their bodies.

The first paragraph lacks examples of particular sports injuries, whereas the second one provides the needed information.

Readability also helps set paragraph length. Within a paper, paragraphs signal natural dividing places, allowing the reader to pause and absorb the material presented up to that point. Too little paragraphing overwhelms the reader with long blocks of material. Too much creates a choppy Dick-and-Jane effect that may come across as simplistic or even irritating. To counter these problems, writers sometimes use several paragraphs for an idea that needs extended development, or they combine several short paragraphs into one.

EXERCISE

1. **Indicate where the ideas in this long block of material divide logically; explain your choices.**

   During the summer following graduation from high school, I could hardly wait to get to university and be on my own. In my first weeks at university, however, I found that independence can be tough and painful. I had expected the kind of raucous good times and a carefree collegiate life depicted in old beach movies and suggested by the selective memories of sentimental alumni. Instead, all I felt at first was the burden of increasing responsibilities and loneliness. I discovered that being independent of parents who kept at me to do my homework and expected me to accomplish certain household chores did not mean I was free to do as I pleased. On the contrary, living on my own meant that I had to perform for myself all the tasks that the family used to share. Studying became a full-time occupation rather than a nightly duty to be accomplished in an hour or two, and my instructors made it clear that they would have little sympathy for negligence or even for my inability to do an assignment. However, what was more troubling about my early university life than having to do laundry, prepare meals, and complete stacks of homework was the terrifying sense of being entirely alone. Although I was independent, no longer a part of the world that had seemed to confine me, I soon realized that confinement had also meant security. I never liked the feeling that people were watching over me, but I knew that my family and friends were also watching out for me—and that's a good feeling to have. At the university, no one seemed particularly to be watching, though professors constantly evaluated the quality of my work. I felt estranged from people in those first weeks, desperately needing a confidant but fearful that the new and tenuous friendships I had made would be damaged if I were to confess my fears and problems. It was simply too early for me to feel a part of the university. So there I was, independent in the fullest sense, but feeling like a person without a country.

2. **The following short, choppy units are inadequately developed. List some details you could use to expand one of them into a good paragraph.**

Teachers should have strong interpersonal skills. When teachers fail, they usually fail in relationships.

The commercialism of Canadian society affects children from an early age. When they watch television, they are bombarded with commercials that re-inforce the message that happiness comes from buying things.

3. **Scan the papers you have written in other classes for paragraphs that are over- or underdeveloped. Revise any you find.**

Organization

An effective paragraph unfolds in a clear pattern of organization so that the reader can easily follow the flow of ideas. Usually when you write your first draft, your organization reflects the flow of your thoughts. Sometimes this logic of association makes sense, but when you revise, you will often see how you can organize paragraphs more effectively. Writers do not ordinarily stop to decide on a strategy for each paragraph, but when you revise or are stuck, it's useful to understand the available choices. Here are some options:

1. The strategies discussed in Chapters 7–14, including narration, description, illustration, process analysis, cause and effect, definition, comparison, classification, and argument and persuasion
2. Commonly used sequencing patterns, including time sequence and space sequence
3. Order of climax

Four example paragraphs follow. The first, organized by *time sequence*, traces the final years of the Model T Ford, concluding with a topic sentence that sums up its impact.

In 1917, the Model T lost much of its attraction when its exterior appearance was drastically altered. The famous flat-sided brass radiator disappeared and the new style featured (in the words of the catalogue) "the stream-lined hood, large radiator and enclosed fan, crown fenders, black finish and nickel trimmings" ("crown fenders" would be described in England as domed mud-guards). Electric lighting and starting followed in 1919, and the model then continued with little alteration until 1927, when it was finally withdrawn. After a considerable pause, it was replaced by the Model A, a very conventional machine with wire wheels, three-speed gearbox and four-wheel brakes (the "T" had never made this concession to progress and continued to the last with two minute brake drums on the back wheels only). While it was in preparation, others had taken the lead, and the "A" never replaced the immortal "T" in the public fancy. Indeed, the "Tin Lizzy" or "Flivver" had become almost a national characteristic, and at the end of its eighteen years in production, the total number sold was fifteen million.

Cecil Clutton and John Stanford, The Vintage Motor-Car

Common spatial arrangements used to organize paragraphs include top to bottom, left to right, right to left, nearby to far away, far away to nearby, clockwise, and counterclockwise. Consider how the following descriptive paragraph moves from outside to inside.

> Next to the laundry, across the alley, which ran like a sparkling river of broken glass and urine produced by the hordes of feral cats, giant rats and stumbling drunks who waded therein, was the Jewish Tailor. His narrow house, barely a door and a window wide, extended backwards from his work room and housed his wife and daughter, a sewing machine and a steam iron. An air of sadness, like the tape measure he wore around his neck, enveloped the place.

Moses Milstein, "Memories of Montreal—and Richness"

The next paragraph, written by a student, illustrates development by *comparison*. As in many descriptive or narrative paragraphs, the topic sentence is implied.

> I have pictures of the three girls in our peach coloured skirts that Mom had made for us, our moving away skirts. My sisters' skirts had sewn pleats that looked sleek and sophisticated; my skirt had box pleats that were sewn to the waist, and opened up like a Scottish kilt, and that made me feel chunky. We all had decorative dolls, but there was a difference. Their dolls looked glamorous; my doll looked dumpy. My sisters' dolls had skirts made of flexible foam that swirled and swirled. My doll's skirt looked hard, and was shaped like a bell. Their dolls' skirts were turquoise and mauve; my doll's skirt was reddish pink, the colour of not quite cooked meat. It wasn't a real pink, or even red, but something in between.

Order of Climax   Climactic order, often used in personal writing, creates a crescendo pattern starting with the least emphatic detail and progressing to the most emphatic. The topic sentence can begin or end the paragraph, or it can remain implied. This pattern holds the reader's interest by building suspense. Occasionally, writers reverse the order, landing the heaviest punch first; but such paragraphs can trail off, leaving the reader dissatisfied. Here is a paragraph illustrating climactic order:

> The speaking errors I hear affect me to different degrees. I'm so conditioned to hearing "It don't make any difference" and "There's three ways to

solve the problem" that I've almost accepted such usage. However, errors such as "Just between you and I, Arnold loves Edna" and "I'm going back to my room to lay down" still offend my sensibility. When hearing them, I usually just chuckle to myself and walk away. The "Twin I's"— <u>irrevelant</u> and <u>irregardless</u>—are another matter. More than any other errors, they really grate on my ear. Whenever I hear "that may be true, but it's irrevelant" or "Irregardless of how much I study, I still get C's," I have the urge to correct the speaker. It's really surprising that more people don't clean up their language act.

Valerie Sonntag, student

EXERCISE *From a magazine or newspaper article, select four paragraphs that illustrate different patterns of organization. Identify the topic sentence in each case; or if it is implied, state it in your own words. Point out the organization of each paragraph.*

Coherence

Coherent writing flows smoothly and easily from one sentence and paragraph to another, clarifying the relationships among ideas and thus allowing the reader to grasp connections. In contrast, incoherent writing, which fails to make connections clear, can confuse and even irritate readers. Consider how the following paragraph jumps around confusingly.

At certain times counselling can be extremely beneficial. People should be committed to becoming healthy. They should never be forced to go to counselling. Sometimes people do need to be told in a gentle way that maybe they should consider seeking counselling. A person who decides to try counselling should do some research. They have to find a counsellor who is suited to their specific needs. Sometimes it is hard for people to reach out and admit they need help. Mental health is as important as physical health. Finding a counsellor with whom a person feels safe and comfortable is important. Now that you have found a good counsellor, therapy can begin and your mental health is on its way to recovery.

This paragraph has some degree of unity, because most of its sentences relate to the writer's interest in the benefits of counselling. Unfortunately, though, its many gaps in logic create rather than answer questions, and in very bumpy prose. How does the third sentence relate to the fourth? And what do the seventh and eighth sentences have to do with the writer's main purpose: to explain how people can benefit from counselling at certain critical moments?

Now read this rewritten version. Note what has been deleted, and what has been added to improve coherence. Transitions and content additions are italicized:

People who *are in emotional crisis or who have experienced trauma* can benefit from counselling. They should not be forced to go into counselling, *because forced treatment is not likely to be effective. Although* it can be hard at times for people to reach out and admit that they need help, counselling is most effective *when people come to it on their own and feel committed to the process. After* they decide to seek counselling, they should do some research in order to find a counsellor who is suited to their specific needs, and with whom they feel safe.

As this example shows, changing the order of sentences, and inserting connecting words or phrases can make paragraphs smoother and more coherent.

EXERCISE *Rewrite the following student paragraph to improve coherence. You may rearrange sentence order, combine and condense sentences, or add any connecting words that seem appropriate.*

Many elderly people, as well as people who can no longer care for themselves, are placed in long-term care facilities. These surroundings can be unpleasant for many, and can cause residents to become very depressed. Within the last few years, animal therapy has become recognized as a way to improve health. Many care facilities arrange weekly visits from a local handler and their best friend, which is usually a well-trained dog. These visits provide patients with something to look forward to. The presence of a loving animal companion can comfort lonely people. Visiting with animals helps to lower blood pressure. It also can reduce stress. In turn, many patients generally become more responsive to their treatment. Residents seem happier overall and feel better when animals are allowed to visit their facility.

Coherence derives from a sufficient supply of supporting details and from your firm sense of the way your ideas go together.

As you write, and especially when you revise, signal connections to the reader by using *transitions*—devices that link sentences to one another. These common transitions are grouped according to function:

1. Connecting words and phrases
2. Repeated key words
3. Pronouns
4. Parallelism

You can use them to furnish links both within and between paragraphs.

Connecting Words and Phrases   Connectors clarify relationships between sentences. The following list groups them according to function:

Showing similarity: in like manner, likewise, just as, similarly

Showing contrast: at the same time, but, even so, however, in contrast, instead, nevertheless, still, on the contrary, on the other hand, otherwise, yet

Showing results or effects: accordingly, as a result, because, consequently, hence, since, therefore, thus

Adding ideas: also, besides, first (second, third . . .), furthermore, in addition, in the first place, moreover, too

Drawing conclusions: as a result, finally, in brief, in conclusion, in short, therefore

Pointing out examples: for example, for instance, to illustrate

Showing emphasis and clarity: above all, after all, again, as a matter of fact, besides, in fact, in other words, indeed, nonetheless, that is

Indicating time: at times, after, afterward, from then on, immediately, later, meanwhile, next, now, once, previously, subsequently, then, until, while

Conceding a point: granted that, of course, to be sure, admittedly, certainly

Don't overload your paper with connectors; use them only when they improve the flow of your prose.

In the following excerpt, which clarifies the difference between workers and workaholics, the connectors are italicized:

> My efforts to define workaholism and to distinguish workaholics from other hard workers proved difficult. *While* workaholics do work hard, not all hard workers are workaholics. Moonlighters, *for example,* may work 16 hours a day to make ends meet, but most of them will stop working when their financial circumstances permit. Accountants, *too,* seem to work non-stop, but many slow down after the April 30 tax deadline. Workaholics, *on the other hand,* always devote more time and thought to their work than their situation demands. Even in the absence of deadlines to meet, mortgages to pay, promotions to earn, or bosses to please, workaholics still work hard. What sets them apart is their attitude toward work, not the number of hours they work.
>
> Marilyn Machlowitz, "Workaholism: What's Wrong with Being Married to Your Work?"

DISCUSSION QUESTIONS

1. What ideas do each of the italicized words and phrases above connect?
2. What relationship does each show?

Repeated Key Words   Repeating key words, especially those that help convey a paragraph's central idea, can smooth the reader's path. The words may appear in different forms, but their presence keeps the main issues before the reader. In the following paragraph, coherence is achieved through repetition of simple phrases ("it adds," "it is") along with the word "blandness."

> What is the point of the battered fry? *It adds* crunch. *It adds* weight. *It adds* calories. *What it* does not *add* is flavour. *What it* removes *is* potato-ness. *It is* a blandifier.

And *it is* its very *blandness* that makes it popular. *Blandness* is more tenacious than any virus: *It* will always conquer a host population, wherever *it is* introduced.

Russell Smith, "Battered by Blandness"

EXERCISE *Write a paragraph using one of the following sentences as your topic sentence. Insert the missing key word and then repeat it in your paragraph to help link your sentences together.*

1. _____ is my favourite relative.
2. I wish I had (a, an, some, more) _____ .
3. _____ changed my life.
4. _____ is more trouble than it's worth.
5. A visit to _____ always depresses me.

Pronouns   Pronouns stand in for nouns that appear earlier in the sentence or in previous sentences. Mixing pronouns and their nouns throughout the paragraph prevents monotony and promotes clarity. We have italicized pronouns that aid coherence in the following excerpt from an address about Canadian literature by Robertson Davies.

In psychological terms, Canada is very much an introverted country, and *it* lives cheek by jowl with the most extroverted country known to history. Let me explain the terms. In personal psychology, the extrovert is *one* who derives *his* energy from *his* contacts with the external world; for *him*, everything lies outside and *he* moves outward toward *it*, often without much sensitivity to the response of that toward which *he* moves. The introvert, on the other hand, finds *his* energy within *himself*, and *his* concern with the outside world is a matter of what approach the outside world makes to *him*. It is absurd to say that one psychological orientation is superior to the other. Both have *their* values, but difficulties arise when *they* fail to understand one another.

Robertson Davies, "Living in a Country without a Mythology"

Some words such as *this, that, those*, and *these* also may contribute to coherence, or flow, by referring to something that has come just before. Sometimes they function as pronouns; at other times, they function as demonstrative adjectives.

Experience with diversity shows that inequities must be acknowledged and addressed for a diverse people to move forward together. *This* is a slow and sometimes painful process, but it is essential if all Canadians are to enjoy the same sense of belonging and attachment to their country. It also serves to familiarize Canadians with the history they share and the obligations that their history confers. *These* obligations include honouring the proclamations and negotiated arrangements made with First Nations peoples.

Government of Canada, "Canadian Multiculturalism:
An Inclusive Citizenship"

EXERCISE *In a magazine, newspaper, textbook, or some other written source, find two paragraphs that use pronouns or demonstrative adjectives to increase coherence. Copy the paragraphs, underline the pronouns, and explain what each refers to.*

Parallelism   Parallelism uses repetition of grammatical form to express a series of equivalent ideas. Besides giving continuity, the repetition adds rhythm and balance to the writing. Note how the following italicized constructions tie together the unfolding definition of poverty:

> *Poverty is staying up* all night on cold nights to watch the fire, knowing one spark on the newspaper covering the walls means your sleeping children die in flames. In summer *poverty is watching* gnats and flies devour your baby's tears when he cries. The screens are torn and you pay so little rent you know they will never be fixed. *Poverty means* insects in your food, in your nose, in your eyes, and crawling over you when you sleep. *Poverty is hoping* it never rains because diapers won't dry when it rains and soon you are using newspapers. *Poverty is seeing* your children forever with runny noses. Paper handkerchiefs cost money and all your rags you need for other things. Even more costly are antihistamines. *Poverty is cooking* without food and cleaning without soap.
>
> Jo Goodwin Parker, "What Is Poverty?"

PARAGRAPHS WITH SPECIAL FUNCTIONS

Special-function paragraphs include introductions, transitional paragraphs, and conclusions. Although introductions and conclusions may be more than one paragraph, generally one-paragraph introductions and conclusions appear in shorter essays. Transitional paragraphs may function like hinges, helping the writer swing into a different section of the paper—perhaps a different timeframe in a narrative essay, or a different argument in a more formal essay.

Introductions

A good introduction acquaints and coaxes. It announces the essay's topic and may directly state the thesis. In addition, it sets the tone for what will follow—a sombre, lighthearted, or angry introduction for personal writing, or an authoritative, confident, or persuasive introduction for an academic paper. The tone of the introduction should fit the purpose of the paper. Thus, an amusing anecdote would not be an appropriate opening for a paper about torture.

With essays, as with people, first impressions are important. If your opening rouses interest, it will draw the readers into the essay and pave the way for their acceptance of your ideas. If your beginning is mechanical, plodding, and dull, you will likely turn readers away. Consider these weak openings:

In this paper I intend to . . .
Wars have always afflicted humankind.
As you may know, having too little time is a problem for many of us.
In the modern world of today . . .

Are you yawning yet? Ask yourself that same question about every opening you write.

A Directly Stated Thesis   This is a common type of opening, orienting the reader to what will follow. After providing some general background, the writer of our example narrows her scope to a thesis that previews the upcoming sections of her essay.

> An increasing number of midlife women are re-entering the workforce, pursuing degrees, and getting more involved in the public arena. Several labels besides "midlife" have been attached to this type of person: the mature woman, the older woman, and, more recently, the re-entry woman. By definition, she is between thirty-five and fifty-five years old and has been away from the business or academic scene anywhere from fifteen to thirty years. The academic community, the media, marketing people, and employers are giving her close scrutiny, and it is apparent that she is having a greater impact on our society than she realizes.
>
> Jo Ann Harris, student

A Definition   This kind of introduction works particularly well in a paper that acquaints the reader with an unfamiliar topic.

> You are completely alone in a large open space and are struck by a terrifying, unreasoning fear. You sweat, your heart beats, you cannot breathe. You fear you may die of a heart attack, although you do not have heart disease. Suppose you decide you will never get yourself in this helpless situation again. You go home and refuse to leave its secure confines. Your family has to support you. You have agoraphobia—a disabling terror of open spaces.
>
> "Controlling Phobias through Behavior Modification"

A Quotation   A beginning quotation, particularly from an authority in the field for formal papers, can be an effective springboard for the ideas that follow. Make sure any quotation you use relates clearly to your topic.

> "Girl Power!" "Girls Rule!" These slogans now appear weekly as educators, the entertainment industry and the media celebrate spunky young women's rising successes.
>
> Douglas Todd, "In a Girl's World, It Can Be Tough Being a Boy"

An Anecdote or Personal Experience   A well-told personal anecdote or experience can draw readers in. Like other introductions, this kind should bear on what comes afterward. In the following example, an essay that decries the plight of foreign domestic workers in Canada begins with an anecdote about one typical morning for a struggling domestic worker.

> When Joyelle arrives at work, it is 7:45 on Monday morning and the bags of garbage from the weekend are stacked in the hallway of the Pintos' well-appointed condominium. The half-empty wineglasses are strewn around her employers' living room, and the faint odour of stale beer is in the air. Lugging the plastic bags down the hallway to the garbage chute and clearing up the dishes from the previous night's party have become rituals for Joyelle (all names have been changed to protect privacy).
>
> Marina Jiménez, "Domestic Crisis"

An Arresting Statement   Sometimes you can jolt the reader to attention by using surprising or even shocking content, language, or both, particularly if your essay develops an unusual or extreme position. An essay about bulimia uses shock to draw readers in:

> I no longer remember the first time I forced myself to throw up. What I do remember is how inexpert I was and how long it took before I succeeded in actually vomiting instead of just gagging and retching. I began by sticking my finger down my throat and wiggling it around, but this produced few results; it wasn't until articles about bulimia appeared in women's magazines that I finally thought to use the handle of a toothbrush instead of my forefinger. It became easy after that.
>
> Evelyn Lau, "An Insatiable Emptiness"

Intriguing Claim   An essay about anger makes an initial claim that may puzzle and intrigue readers.

> We carry around a lot of free-floating anger. What we do with it is what fascinates me.
>
> Dan Greenburg, "Sound and Fury"

Unusual Slant on a Familiar Theme   It can be difficult to find a fresh approach to the familiar subject of success and failure, but this writer cites paradoxical examples of "failure" to intrigue readers by causing them to examine their assumptions.

> John Milton was a failure. In writing "Paradise Lost," his stated aim was to "justify the ways of God to man." Inevitably, he fell short of accomplishing that and only wrote a monumental poem. Beethoven, whose music was conceived to transcend Fate, was a failure, as was Socrates, whose ambition was to make people happy by making them reasonable and just. The inescapable conclusion seems to be that the surest, noblest way to fail is to set one's own standards titanically high.
>
> Laurence Shames, "The Sweet Smell of Success Isn't All That Sweet"

Interesting Details   These details pique curiosity and draw readers in.

> You were once a single cell. Every one of the 100 trillion cells in your body today is a direct descendent of that zygote, the primordial cell formed by the union of mother's egg and father's sperm. Each one is genetically identical (allowing for copying errors and environmental damage along the way) to that cell. Therefore, if we scraped a cell from, say, the inner lining of your cheek, its DNA would be the same DNA that, years ago in the original zygote, contained the entire plan for creating you and every part of you.
>
> Charles Krauthammer, "Crossing Lines"

A Question or Problem   A provocative question or problem can entice the reader into the essay to find the answer.

> When you leave your apartment or house, do you begin to feel better? If you leave for a week-long trip, do you find your head clears, your migraine disappears, dizziness stops, your aches and pains subside, depression fades away, and your entire attitude is better? If so, chemical pollution of the atmosphere in your home may be making you ill.
>
> Marshall Mandell, "Are You Allergic to Your House?"

In the following introduction, the writer describes an inner conflict she experiences about the fascination with the Barbie doll that she observes in her daughter and other young girls.

> I've always known there was something wrong with Barbie. She looks nice enough. And she has her own Corvette, her own band, and her own dream house. Still, I just didn't want my daughter playing with her. But how can we snub Barbie? Little girls all over Charlottesville, all over Virginia, and, yes, all over the world, seem to be spending hour after hour with her.
>
> Mariflo Stephens, "Barbie Doesn't Live Here Anymore"

Blended Strategies   Many effective introductions contain more than one way to draw the reader in and frame their topic or argument. The following example blends a definition with a quotation and a direct statement of the thesis.

> Loyal: 1. Steadfast in support and devotion to and never betraying the interests of one's homeland, government, or sovereign. 2. Faithful to a person, ideal or custom; constantly supporting or following. (French, from Old French loyal, loial, leial, fait)
>
> —*Reader's Digest Illustrated Encyclopedic Dictionary*

> The Roman senator, Seneca, called it "the holiest virtue in the human head." For most of the 2000 years since, few would have disagreed with his call for loyalty to the gods, to the state, to family and to duty. But loyalty, that once-essential virtue, is fading fast, and our sense of community and identity is disappearing with it.
>
> Bob Harvey, "Loyalty: A Last Virtue; Me-First Attitude Is Stripping Away Our Sense of Community"

Note that the title as well as the introduction announces the direction of the essay.

Transitional Paragraphs

In the midst of a lengthy essay, you may need a short paragraph that announces a shift from one group of ideas to another. Transitional paragraphs summarize previously explained ideas, repeat the thesis, or point to ideas that follow. In our example, Bruno Bettelheim has been discussing a young boy named Joey, who has turned into a kind of human machine. After describing Joey's assorted delusions, Bettelheim signals his shift of emphasis from the delusions to the fears that caused them.

> What deep-seated fears and needs underlay Joey's delusional system? We were long in finding out, for Joey's preventions effectively concealed the secret of his autistic behavior. In the meantime we dealt with his peripheral problems one by one.
>
> Bruno Bettelheim, "Joey: 'A Mechanical Boy'"

The following transitional paragraph looks back as well as ahead:

> Certainly these three factors—exercise, economy, convenience of shortcuts—help explain the popularity of bicycling today. But a fourth attraction sometimes overrides the others: the lure of the open road.
>
> Mike Bernstein, student

Conclusions

A conclusion rounds out a paper and signals that the discussion has been completed. But not all papers require a separate conclusion. For example, narratives and descriptions generally end when the writer finishes the story or completes the details. Although some papers, especially personal narratives, do not always require a separate conclusion, most essays benefit from at least one concluding paragraph that drives the point home. To be effective, a conclusion must mesh logically and stylistically with what comes earlier. A long, complex paper often ends with a summary of the main points, but other options may be used for shorter papers with easy-to-grasp ideas. Most short essays have single-paragraph conclusions, while longer papers may require two or three paragraphs.

Here are some suggestions for writing solid conclusions:

1. Don't introduce new material. Draw together, round out, but don't take off in a new direction.
2. Don't tack on a trite ending in desperation when the hour is late and the paper is due tomorrow—the so-called midnight special. Your reader deserves better than "All in all, skiing is a great sport" or "Thus we can see that motorcycle racing isn't for everyone."
3. Don't apologize. Saying that you could have done a better job makes a reader wonder why you didn't.
4. Don't moralize. A preachy conclusion can undermine the position you have established in the rest of your composition.

The following examples illustrate several common types of conclusions.

Restatement of the Thesis   The following conclusion reasserts the writer's thesis that "the term *youth* has been co-opted by government and corporate interests."

> By replacing the term *adult* with *youth,* governments, corporations, and the media can offer the majority of the electorate and the majority of society (baby boomers, if you will) an easy explanation for why those aged 18–35 are not receiving what they as adults need—namely employment, a living wage, and a minimal level of independence. At the same time, those with a vested interest in the status quo are creating a diversion from a multitude of other issues that will inevitably have to be addressed. All of this with one word.
>
> Andrew Beyak, "The Sweet Bird of Youth Is Showing Signs of Age"

A Summary   A summary draws together and reinforces the main points.

> In conclusion, using nuclear-transfer cloning to allow people to have a child introduces a different way of reproduction for our species. Once we breach this barrier, it leaves us with no place to stop. Given all the problems outlined, the reasons for permitting cloning to produce a person are insufficiently compelling. Even in the few circumstances where the case for human cloning seems justified, there are alternative solutions. We are at an appropriate stopping place on a slippery slope. Not all reasons why a person might wish to copy his or her cells are unethical, but given there are other options open to people wishing to form a family, concerns about individual and social harms from cloning are strong enough that it is not justified to permit it. These issues affecting the creation of the next generation are important for the future of our species; we must deal with them wisely. I hope we can.
>
> Patricia Baird, "Should Human Cloning Be Permitted?"

A Question   A final question often prompts the reader to think further on the topic. If your essay is meant to be persuasive, be sure to phrase a concluding question so that the way a reasonable person would answer emphasizes your point of view. The paragraph below concludes an argument that running should not be elevated to a religion, that its other benefits are sufficient.

> Aren't those gifts enough? Why ask running for benefits that are plainly beyond its capacity to bestow?
>
> James Fixx, "What Running Can't Do for You"

A Quotation   A quotation can capture the essence of your thought and end the essay with authority.

> "We had no idea of the emotional involvement and the commitment of these women," Richard says. "Suddenly a constituency arose. Suddenly there are thousands and thousands of women who don't care about your moral position or mine—they want a baby."
>
> David Zimmerman, "Are Test-Tube Babies
> the Answer for the Childless?"

Ironic Twist or Surprising Observation   These approaches prompt the reader to think further about a paper's topic. The following paragraph highlights the irony of the writer's regret after he has fulfilled a seemingly desirable dream. Although living now in a premium Vancouver locale, the author regrets that his son is missing out on the cultural and economic diversity of his own youth in Montreal.

> When I grew up I bought a house in the gentle forests of the Pacific and my son walks to school among the cherry blossoms. And sometimes I am sad for him.
>
> Moses Milstein, "Memories of Montreal—and Richness"

In the following conclusion, the writer makes a surprising admission that leaves us thinking.

> I'm glad I'm greedy. I would hate to be envious.
>
> Marilyn Baker, "Greed Works"

Clever or Lighthearted Ending   In humorous or otherwise light essays, clever twists of wording can make effective endings. In this example, capitalizing on the essay's topic (clichés), the writer ends by exaggerating the fault being criticized.

> Because using clichés is as easy as falling off a log, it goes without saying that it would be duck soup to continue in this vein till hell freezes over. However, since that would be carrying coals to Newcastle, let's ring down the curtain and bid adieu to the fair topic of the cliché. (No use beating a dead horse.)

Personal Challenge   A challenge often prompts the reader to take some action.

> And therein lies the challenge. You can't merely puff hard for a few days and then revert to the La-Z-Boy recliner, smugly thinking that you're "in shape." You must sweat and strain and puff regularly, week in and week out. They're your muscles, your lungs, your heart. The only caretaker they have is you.
>
> Monica Duvall, student

Recommendation or Hope   Both a recommendation and a hope may restate points already made in the essay or suggest actions to take in order to arrive at a solution. Tomkins's conclusion conveys not only a recommendation, but also a sense of urgency about the consequences of failing to heed his advice.

> It is not more time we need: it is fewer desires. We need to switch off the cellphone and leave the children to play by themselves. We need to buy less, read less and travel less. We need to set boundaries for ourselves, or be doomed to mounting despair.
>
> Richard Tomkins, "Old Father Time Becomes a Terror"

EXERCISE

1. Explain which of the above conclusions appeals to you. Does your response stem from the topic or from the author's handling of it?

2. Collect effective concluding paragraphs from magazine articles, illustrating at least three different techniques. Then write a paragraph explaining why each impresses you.

CHAPTER 5

Strategies for Revising and Editing Your Writing

All of us at one time or another have said something careless to a friend, date, or partner and then spent the rest of the night regretting our words. When we speak, we cannot cut and paste, add and delete. When we write, however, we can use revision skills to work toward getting the wording right, so that it says exactly what we mean. Even professional writers don't express themselves perfectly on the first try, but they can relax, knowing that writing is a process.

Just what is revision? Don't confuse it with proofreading, the final stage of the writing process, where you carefully inspect your word choice, spelling, grammar, and punctuation. The word revision means *re-seeing*. Revision is much more drastic than proofreading, often involving an upheaval of content and organization as you become more certain about what you want to say. The writer E. M. Forster once asked, "How can I know what I think until I see what I say?" Thus, revising helps people sharpen their own ideas.

Most of what you read, including this book, has been considerably altered and improved as the writers progressed through early drafts. This fact shouldn't surprise you. After all, a rough draft is merely a first attempt to jot down some ideas in essay form. No matter how well you gather and organize your material, your ideas evolve only as you write. Sometimes the best ideas come toward the end of your first or second draft, and you might end up sacrificing entire chunks of your first draft. Moreover, often the first draft is incomplete, unclear in places, and possibly disorganized. You might even discover an entirely different approach buried within it. During revision, you keep changing things—your focus, approach to the topic, supporting material, and thesis statement—until the results satisfy you.

Inexperienced writers often mistakenly view initial drafts as nearly finished products rather than as experiments to alter, or even scrap, if need be. As a result, they often approach revision with a defensive attitude. To revise successfully, you need to control your ego and fear and become your own first critical reader. Set aside natural feelings of accomplishment ("After all, I've put a great deal of thought into this") and dread ("Actually, I'm afraid of what I'll find if I look too closely"). Instead, recognize that revision offers an opportunity to communicate more effectively with your audience. Think of your early drafts simply as works in progress.

PREPARING TO REVISE

To distance yourself from your writing and sharpen your critical eye, set your first draft aside for at least half a day, or longer if time permits. When you return to it, gear up for revision by jotting down your intended purpose and audience before you read your paper. These notations will help keep your changes on track. In addition, note any further ideas that have occurred to you.

The right attitude is vital to effective revision. Far too many students hastily skim their essays to reassure themselves that "Everything sounds O.K." Avoid such a quick-fix approach. If your draft appears fine on first reading, read it again with a more critical eye. You can also read your writing aloud so that two senses—hearing and seeing—can be involved during revision. Reading aloud can also help you gain distance on your writing, so that you can respond more as a reader than as a writer who already knows what is on the page. Look at the paper globally, checking for overall focus, before you begin checking sentences and words. Can you sum up your main idea in a sentence (or two), and is that sentence interesting and clear? Try putting yourself in your reader's place. Will your instructions for a new accounting method be clear to someone who has never done it? Will your recommendation of a new policy to address homelessness convince a cash-strapped community council? Remember: If you aren't critical now, anticipating confusion and objections, your reader certainly will be later.

Read your essay at least three times, once for each of these reasons:

To improve the focus and development of the essay as a whole

To strengthen paragraph structure and development

To sharpen sentences and words (explored more in the next chapter)

GLOBAL REVISIONS

If you inspect your draft only sentence by sentence, you can easily overlook how its parts work together. As you begin to revise, step back and view the overall essay rather than its separate parts. Consider big picture elements, such as the essay's focus and direction, audience, organization, and development. Ask questions such as "Does the beginning mesh with the end?" "Does the essay wander?" "Has anything been left out?" In this way, you can gauge how part relates to part and to the whole. Use the acronym *FACT* to guide this stage of your revision.

F Ask yourself first whether the whole essay **FITS** together, presenting a central point for a specific audience. Have you delivered what the thesis statement promises? First drafts often include paragraphs or even large sections that have little to do with the main point. Some drafts even contain ideas for different possible essays, threads that pull in different directions. Furthermore, one section of a draft might be geared to one audience (parents, for example), and another section to an entirely different audience (students, perhaps). As you read each part, verify its connection to your purpose and audience. Don't hesitate to chop out sections that don't fit, redo stray parts so they accord with your central idea, or alter your thesis statement to reflect better your supporting material. Occasionally, you might even expand one small, fertile section of your draft into an entirely new essay.

A Whenever we write first drafts, we may know what we mean, but we often do not think about what the reader needs to know. We tend to make assumptions that the reader somehow knows what we know, and so we unwittingly leave gaps. As we revise, we need to identify and fill in these places we have left out essential information or material. Ask yourself: "Where will the reader need more information or examples to understand my meaning?" Then **ADD** the appropriate sentences, paragraphs, or even pages.

C First drafts often contain material that relates to the thesis but doesn't contribute to the essay. Writing quickly, we tend to repeat ourselves, include uninteresting or uninformative examples, and crank out whole paragraphs when one clear sentence would suffice. As you revise, **CUT** away this clutter with a free hand. Such paring can be painful, especially if you're left with a skimpy text, but your final message will emerge with much greater clarity. As you've probably guessed, revising a draft often requires both adding and cutting.

T Carefully **TEST** the organization of your essay. The text should flow smoothly from point to point with clear transitions between the various ideas. Test the organization by outlining your major and minor points, and then check the results for logic and completeness. Alternatively, read the draft and note the progression of its paragraphs and points. Look for places where you can clarify connections between ideas and thus help your readers understand.

Chapters 7–14 explain nine different writing strategies and conclude with revision questions geared specifically to that strategy. Use these questions, together with the *FACT* of revision, to help you revise more effectively.

Case History   *(continued from page 55)*

Now let's apply the *FACT* approach to Trudy's essay on Steven Villman, which you read on pages 53–55. Like most early drafts, this draft needs work.

FIT. The thesis doesn't fit the rest of the essay very well, since the narrative doesn't really demonstrate the importance of listening. Trudy can rewrite her essay to bring out the importance of listening, or she can rewrite her thesis and conclusion so that they fit her essay better.

ADD. Trudy needs to expand her essay in a couple of places, because the reader cannot understand why the bullies tricked Steven, or whether or not the mother really is angry. Trudy also needs to supply a transition between paragraphs 3 and 4, since the reader may be confused by the jump in time and locale. She also needs to work on the conclusion, which seems rushed.

CUT. Since Trudy's purpose is more to promote compassion than to inform readers about autism, she can condense her introduction, zeroing in more immediately on her story. She can also cut some sentences that tell the reader what she has already demonstrated.

TEST. The first five paragraphs can be rearranged, combined, and condensed, since they seem rather choppy. Describing Steven's appearance before giving the description of his activities at lunchtime would be more logical. The essay does flow well for the most part, although the paragraphs seem to be broken up arbitrarily in a few places, creating choppiness.

This case history continues on pages 85–86.

As you read your own essay, note on a separate sheet of paper problems to solve, ideas to add, and changes to try. If you are composing new material on the computer, you can cut, paste, and delete to help you change and move text. If you are revising a hard copy of the complete essay, make your job easier by using these simple techniques:

1. To mark a deletion, cross it out lightly; you may decide to resurrect the deleted material later.

2. To add a section of text, place a letter *(A, B, C, D)* at the appropriate spot; then create the new material in a new file or at the bottom of your draft file, clearly marked with the letter. Make smaller changes within sections by crossing out on the hard copy what you don't want and writing the replacement above it or nearby. Leave inputting changes and moving blocks of new text into place until you have finished reviewing the entire draft—you may end up changing your mind.

3. To rearrange the organization, draw arrows showing where you want things to go, or cut up your draft and rearrange the sections by taping them on new sheets of paper.

4. When you are satisfied with your changes, enter them in a *new copy* of your draft file. Always keep separate files for draft versions in case you need to go back to them.

Then, when you have a new version of your draft, you might want to team up with one or more classmates and read one another's work critically. The fresh eye you bring to the task can uncover shortcomings that would otherwise go unnoticed. Pages 91–97 discuss peer editing in detail.

REVISING ON THE COMPUTER

Computer programs allow you to write over unwanted sections of your draft, add new information, cut useless material, track changes, and move parts of the text around—all without going to hard copy. Learn all the commands of your particular software and experiment to see exactly what your options are before trying to revise on-screen. The following tips will improve your efficiency:

1. Always keep backup copies of drafts, using the *Save As* function and renaming, possibly dating, each revision. Accidentally erasing a file or losing your work to an electrical power surge is not uncommon. In addition, save copies of your earlier drafts, either as printouts or on disk. Selected parts may prove useful later, and new papers sometimes sprout from old drafts. You can either save each draft under variations of your file name—"Copy A," "Copy B," "Copy C"—or keep deleted sections in specially labelled files.

2. Jot down helpful ideas or comments in your text as you revise. Enclose them with a special symbol, such as < >. Delete them later if they serve no purpose.

3. If you struggle with a section of the text, create two or three versions and then pick your favourite. You might even open a new file, experiment freely, and then use the best version in your draft.

4. Don't allow the program to control how you revise. Easy-to-use, gentle-touch keyboards can lull you into a lapse of judgment and cause you to forget whether your words are worth writing. Pages of worthless material could pile up. Furthermore, don't be tempted to do what the commands make easiest—fiddling and moving. Your job in revising is to develop the essay as a whole, not to tweak sentences or move blocks of text around indiscriminately.

5. If you have to do a major revision, consider doing it on a hard copy. Hard copy revisions allow you to see the "big picture" of your essay and to compare and work with several pages at once.

6. When you finish revising, check the coherence of your draft. The writing must flow smoothly at the points where you have added, deleted, or moved sections of text. In addition, altered sentences must be clearly written and logically constructed. You can best check the essay's flow with a printout.

7. Relying on spell-checking tools to proofread your paper can create major problems. For example, a spell-checker can't judge whether you used the wrong word (*form* instead of *from*) or confused identical sounding but differently spelled words (*their, there, they're*). *You* are still the ultimate proofreader.

8. Some programs, such as Microsoft Word (under *View, Toolbar, Reviewing*), have options to Track Changes, which let you make revisions that then appear in colour with the record of changes noted in the margin. Later you can go back and accept or reject the changes. This feature can be especially useful if you are getting peer feedback or working on a collaborative writing project.

EXERCISE *Use the FACT acronym to revise the draft you prepared for the exercise on page 53.*

Case History   (continued from page 83)

After setting her draft aside for a couple of days, Trudy revises it carefully. Compare the original draft with the revised version below. What changes has Trudy made?

A Memory

1   I remember watching Steven Villman in horrified awe during lunch times at my elementary school. It was said that he had autism, which often involves a withdrawal from reality and difficulty reading others' emotions. Steven always seemed to have a dirty film covering his faded clothing. He was a large boy with dark hair, and always appeared to be gazing at something in the distance.

2   Sticks were his trademark. Every lunch hour Steven would rush outside to begin his search through the woods behind the school, in search of the best stick. Darting around the trees, he would run on his tiptoes, with a stick grasped tightly in his hand, waving it about like a magic wand.

3   His high-pitched screeches and nonsense babbling would never fail to catch the attention of children deep in their play. Sometimes a couple of children would follow him, giggling about how weird he was.

4   One summer afternoon I was playing alone in a park in my neighbourhood. Suddenly, loud screeches alerted me as a large boy came running toward the park like a drunken ballerina. Two smaller boys trailed him with a look of mischief sparkling in their eyes. For their own amusement the boys were sneaking up behind Steven and screeching in his ear, just to watch Steven's terrified reaction. I stared with wide eyes and mouth open. Steven's stick shook uncontrollably as he bolted like a wild animal, trying to escape the bullies. I quickly pushed myself down the slide and made my way home to get some help.

5   Inside my home, I stood huffing and puffing as I informed my mother about what I had witnessed. I went on to explain how Steven was different from other kids. When I finished my story my mother took a deep breath. We headed back to the park immediately.

6   When we arrived at the park Steven was blubbering like a baby and hollering at the boys. Still fascinated as ever and untouched by Steven's distress, the bullies failed to see my mother and me hustling over to where they stood, poking and laughing at Steven. With both hands on her hips my mother lectured, "You two should be ashamed of yourselves." Shocked, the bullies looked at one another and then just walked away, without even attempting to explain their behaviour. Steven watched them with a look of relief as they walked out of sight. "Where do you live, Steven?" Steven pointed. "That way." He looked toward the ground as he swayed from side to side, as if he were rocking himself to sleep. Without shoes or socks on his feet, he was covered from head to toe in dirt.

7   "C'mon Steven, we'll walk you home," my mother said dryly, as if she were angry. Now I know differently.

8   We walked down the road at a slow pace, listening to Steven's bare feet slap against the hot concrete with every step he took.

9   "Those bullies tricked me," Steven whined. "Why would they want my shoes anyway?" He concentrated on his feet as he walked. "Why do kids like them always bug me . . . and what's my mom gonna say?" Steven went on talking to himself rather than to my mother and me, and it's a good thing that he did, because it was obvious my mother had no explanations as to why people could be so mean.

10   After my mother and I brought Steven home, we walked back in silence. It seemed so unfair that Steven had to deal not only with his dis-ability, but also with the stupidity of those who didn't understand. By walk-ing Steven Villman home that day, I learned that we all need to take the time to understand people who are different from we are.

Although this draft is not perfect, Trudy's revisions have considerably improved the paper. As Trudy continues polishing her essay, she can look for ways to cut unnecessary words. By using more accurate words, she can make her essay even stronger. (The final, polished version of the essay appears on pages 89–90). Never stop revising your essay until you are completely satisfied with the result.

This case history continues on pages 88–90.

STRENGTHENING PARAGRAPH STRUCTURE AND DEVELOPMENT

Once you finish considering the essay as a whole, examine your paragraphs one by one, applying the *FACT* approach that you used for the whole paper. Make sure each paragraph *FITS* the paper's major focus and develops a single central idea. If a paragraph needs more support or examples, *ADD* whatever is necessary. If a paragraph contains ineffective or unhelpful material, *CUT* it. *TEST* the flow of ideas from paragraph to paragraph and clarify connections, both between and within paragraphs, as necessary. Ask the basic questions in the checklist that follows about each paragraph, and make any needed revisions.

REVISION CHECKLIST FOR PARAGRAPHS

- Does the paragraph have one, and only one, central idea?
- Does the central idea help to develop the thesis statement?
- Does each statement within the paragraph help to develop the central idea?
- Does the paragraph need additional explanations, examples, or supporting details?
- Would cutting some material make the paragraph stronger?
- Would reorganization make the ideas easier to follow?
- Can the connections between successive sentences be improved?
- Is each paragraph clearly and smoothly related to those that precede and follow it?

Don't expect to escape making any changes; some readjustments will undoubtedly be needed. Certain paragraphs may be stripped down or deleted entirely, others beefed up, and still others reorganized or repositioned. Chapter 4 contains more information on writing effective paragraphs.

EXERCISE *Here are two sample student paragraphs. Evaluate each according to the Revision Checklist for Paragraphs and suggest any necessary changes.*

1. For hours we had been waiting under the overhang of an abandoned hut. None of us had thought to bring ponchos on our short hike through the woods. Soon it would be dark. Earlier in the day it had been a perfectly clear day. We all agreed that we didn't want to stand here all night in the dark, so we decided to make a dash for it.

2. Canadians are beginning to become more and more conscious about the ingredients and production that goes in the food that they are ingesting. There are many reasons that Canadians are choosing to buy organic food whenever

possible. With free-range chicken products, customers know exactly where their food is coming from. Free-range chickens are not raised in factories. They can run around. Vegetables that are grown organically in a garden taste better. People who want to have optimal health should also avoid unnecessary exposure to air-borne chemicals, and should get plenty of exercise.

WRITING THE INTRODUCTION AND CONCLUSION

If you've put off writing your introduction, do it now. (See Chapter 4 for suggestions and examples.) Generally, short papers begin with a single paragraph that includes the previously drafted thesis statement, which sometimes needs to be rephrased so that it meshes smoothly with the rest of the paragraph. The introduction acquaints the reader with your topic; it should clearly signal your intention as well as spark the reader's interest. The conclusion should follow the rest of your essay and should fit your purpose, as well as the type of writing you are doing. If you are writing to inform someone about a business plan, sometimes a summary is the best type of conclusion. For an illustration or persuasive piece of writing, you might want to extend the implications of what you have been writing about, leaving the reader with a question to ponder.

Even when you do not have time to revise extensively, you can almost always improve your writing by going back to the introduction and sharpening your focus. After you have finished a draft or two, you are usually much more clear about what you want to say than when you first sat down to write. Sometimes students actually benefit by starting a whole new draft, using what they thought to be a conclusion as a new starting point.

SELECTING A TITLE

All essays require titles. Unless a good title unexpectedly surfaces while you are writing, wait until you finish the paper before choosing one. Since the reader must see the connection between what the title promises and what the essay delivers, a good title must be both accurate and specific. A specific title suggests the essay's focus rather than just its topic. For example, "A Cruel Joke" is clearer and more precise than "A Memory."

Case History   (continued from page 86)

After carefully proofreading and fine-tuning her essay, Trudy prepares the final version, which follows. Margin notes highlight key changes. Compare the revised and final version for how these changes have improved the essay.

A Cruel Joke

I remember watching Steven Villman in horrified awe during lunch times at my elementary school. Steven always seemed to have a dirty film covering his faded clothing. He was a large boy with dark hair, rough and choppy across his forehead, and always appeared to be gazing at something in the distance. It was said that he had autism, which often involves a withdrawal from reality and difficulty reading others' emotions.

Sticks were Steven's trademark. Every lunch hour he would rush outside to begin his search through the woods behind the school, in search of the best stick. Darting around the trees, he would run on his tiptoes, with a stick grasped tightly in his hand, waving it about like a magic wand. His high-pitched screeches and nonsense babbling would never fail to catch the attention of children deep in their play. Sometimes a couple of children would follow him, giggling, as he performed his usual ritual. Children always found enough time to stop and stare, but never dared to invite him to join them in their play.

I remember one summer afternoon as I played alone in a park in my neighbourhood. Loud screeches alerted me as a large boy, whom I immediately recognized as Steven Villman, came running toward the park like a drunken ballerina. Two smaller boys trailed him with a look of mischief sparkling in their eyes. For their own amusement, the boys were sneaking up behind Steven and screeching in his ear, just to watch Steven's terrified reaction. I stared with wide eyes and mouth open. Steven's stick shook uncontrollably as he bolted like a startled deer, trying to escape the bullies. I quickly pushed myself down the slide and made my way home to get some help.

Inside my home, I stood huffing and puffing as I informed my mother about what I had witnessed. When I finished my story, my mother put down the dishes she was washing and took a deep breath as she dried her hands on a towel. We headed back to the park immediately.

When we arrived at the park Steven was crying and hollering at the boys. Still fascinated as ever and untouched by Steven's distress, the bullies failed to see my mother and me hustling over to where they stood, poking and laughing at Steven. With both hands on her hips my mother scolded, "You two should be ashamed of yourselves." Shocked, the bullies looked at one another and then just walked away, without even attempting to explain their behaviour. Steven watched them with a look of relief as they walked out of sight.

General title made more specific

Second sentence slightly condensed. Third sentence made more vivid, and necessary background information given in the fourth sentence.

Second and third paragraphs combined to improve coherence. Last sentence made more precise.

Transition improved in the first sentence by the cue "I remember one summer afternoon" and the mention of Steven's name right away. "Wild animal" replaced with a more vivid and less derogatory image of "startled deer."

Unnecessary sentence deleted

More explanation of what mother was doing

Tone improved by replacing "blubbering" with less demeaning, more understated "crying," the word "lectured" with more accurate "scolded."

New speaker identified with new paragraph

Better development as possibilities for mother's anger are suggested

Point of essay made clearer. Question is left in reader's mind as well as the writer's.

"Where do you live, Steven?" my mother asked.

"That way." Steven pointed. He looked toward the ground as he swayed from side to side, as if he were rocking himself to sleep. He wore no shoes or socks on his feet and was covered from head to toe in dirt.

"C'mon Steven, we'll walk you home," my mother said dryly. At the time I thought she was angry with Steven for the trouble he brought to our neighbourhood, or maybe at me for interrupting her dishwashing, but now I know she was angry about the cruelty of the bullies.

We walked down the road at a slow pace listening to Steven's bare feet slap against the hot concrete with every step he took.

"Those bullies tricked me," Steven whined. "Why would they want my shoes anyway?" He concentrated on his feet as he walked. "Why do kids like them always bug me? And what's my mom gonna say?" Steven went on talking to himself rather than to my mother and me, and it's a good thing he did, because it was obvious my mother had no explanation for why people could be so mean.

After my mother and I brought Steven home we walked back in silence. Steven's words burned in our minds. Why was it that Steven had to deal not only with his disability, but also with the stupidity of those who didn't understand? By walking Steven Villman home that day, I learned that sometimes the kindest thing is just to take the time to pay attention to others and try to understand.

THE FINAL STAGE: PROOFREADING YOUR DRAFT

Proofreading is the final stage of writing. Check carefully for errors in grammar, punctuation, and spelling. Since we often overlook our own errors simply because we know what we mean, proofreading can be difficult. Some writers find that they catch problems when they read their own writing out loud. Others inch through the draft deliberately, moving a finger along slowly under every word. You can repeat this procedure several times, looking first for errors in grammar, then for sentence errors and problems in punctuation and mechanics, and finally for mistakes in spelling. Be especially alert for problems that have plagued your writing in the past.

Effective proofreading calls for you to assume a detective role and probe for errors that weaken your writing. If you accept the challenge, you will certainly improve the quality of your finished work.

PEER EVALUATION OF DRAFTS

At various points in the writing process, your instructor may ask you and your classmates to read and respond to one another's papers. Peer response often proves useful because even the best writers cannot always predict how their readers will react to their writing. For example, magazine articles designed to reduce the fear of AIDS have in some cases increased anxiety about the disease. Furthermore, writers often have difficulty seeing the problems with their own drafts because so much hard work has gone into them. What seems clear and effective to you can be confusing or boring to your reader. Comments from peers can help you see your writing from a reader's point of view.

Just as the responses of others help you, so too will your responses help them. With another person's essay, you don't have the close, involved relationship that you have with your own. Therefore, you can assess other people's drafts objectively. Moreover, experience with the practice of doing peer reviews will eventually increase your awareness of your own writing strengths and weaknesses. Knowing how to read your own work critically is one of the most important writing skills you can develop.

Responding to Peer Drafts

Responding to someone else's writing is easier than you might imagine. The most helpful way to respond is to let the reader know how you understand what you have read, what draws you in, what loses or confuses you. It's not your job to spell out how to make the draft more effective, how to organize it, what to include, and what language to use. The writer must make these decisions. Your job is not to *solve* problems, but to *identify* them. You can do that best by letting the reader know what goes on in your mind as you are reading.

Some responses are more helpful than others. For example, saying that the draft "looks fine" does not help the writer. Such a response suggests that you have not read carefully and critically. It can take courage as well as attention to give specific, constructive feedback, but it is far more helpful in the long run than polite, generic praise. In addition, critical but vague comments, such as "The introduction is uninteresting," are not helpful either. Point out *why* it is uninteresting. For instance, you might note, "The introduction doesn't interest me because it is very technical, and I get lost. I ask myself why I should read on." Below is another example of an ineffective response and a more effective counterpart.

Ineffective:

The paper was confusing

Effective:

Paragraphs 2, 3, and 4 confused me
when the subject kept jumping around. First you
wrote about your experience on the first
day of university, then you went on to how

much you enjoyed junior high school, and
finally you wrote about what you want to do
for a career. I don't see how these ideas
relate or why they are in the order that they are.

Here are some steps to follow when responding to someone else's draft.

1. Read the essay from beginning to end without interruption.
2. On a separate sheet of paper, indicate what you consider to be the main idea. The writer can then see whether the intended message has come through.
3. Identify the greatest strength and the greatest problem/weakness of the paper. Writers need both positive and negative comments.
4. Reread the paper and write either specific responses to each paragraph or your responses to general questions such as the ones that follow. In either case, don't comment on spelling or grammar unless it really inhibits your reading.

PEER RESPONSE CHECKLIST

- What is the main point of this essay?
- What is the greatest strength? What is the greatest problem?
- What material doesn't seem to fit the main point or the audience?
- What questions has the author not answered?
- Where should more details or examples be added? Why?
- At what point does the paper fail to hold my interest? Why?
- Where is the organization confusing?
- Where is the writing unclear or vague?

As you learn more strategies for successful writing, you will be able to recognize more weaknesses and strengths in peer papers. In addition, the revision questions at the end of Chapters 7–14 can guide more in-depth peer review.

An Example of Peer Response

The following is the first draft of a student essay and a partial peer response to it. The response features three of the nine peer review questions listed above and also comments on one paragraph. Before you read the response, try evaluating this essay yourself, and then compare your reactions to those of the other student.

Captive Breeding in Zoos

1   This paper is about captive breeding. Today, humans hinder nature's

species' right to survive. We are making it hard for over one hundred species of animals to continue to exist. But captive breeding in the world's zoos may be just what the doctor ordered. This rescue attempt is a complex and difficult undertaking. Captive breeding of endangered species is complicated by the special social and physical requirements of individual species.

2   There are many social problems that have to be solved for the successful reproduction of endangered species in zoos. Mating is one of the most important of these problems. One propagation "must" for many felines, pandas, and pygmy hippopotamuses is the complete separation of sexes until they're "ready." Leland Stowe says that cheetahs almost never get together unless they can't see or smell each other ahead of time. When females exhibit a certain behaviour, they bring on the male.

3   Male–female compatibility is a social problem. Great apes seem to be as particular as people in choosing mates. Stowe tells about an orangutan that turned a cold shoulder on the females in the U.S. National Zoo located in Washington, D.C. Then they shipped him to the zoo in Toronto. There, he took up with one of the females. The curator of the zoo, William Zanten, says he's "been siring offspring ever since."

4   Social factors hurt care of infant primates. Sheldon Campbell talks about this in <u>Smithsonian</u> magazine. He writes about the problems of breeding golden marmosets. These are monkeys that live in Brazil. The scientists found that captive-born parents neglected their young. Sometimes they even killed them. The problem was due to the fact that the marmosets had no experience living in a family situation. They didn't know what to do. Emily Hahn writes about gorillas in <u>The New Yorker</u>. She says that those raised by humans make poor mothers. Those raised by dutiful mothers make good parents.

5   The second important stumbling block to successful captive breeding is physical problems. Ignorance of dietary needs can be bad. Stowe talks about the captive breeding of gorillas and says that when this breeding was first getting started, infants exhibited a very high mortality rate. Then the babies were given iron and meat protein, the latter rich in vitamin B-12. They were sprinkled on bananas, and the bananas were fed to the babies. The survival rate markedly improved.

6   Animals can be bred more easily if they are in an environment that duplicates that animal's natural habitat. Hooved and horned animals are an easy job because of the similarity in terrain and climate of their natural habitats to zoo habitats. Polar bears are a lot tougher. Mothers want to be left alone until their

cubs are up and about. Because of this fact, the bears often kill their babies. Stowe says they solved this problem by building replicas of arctic ice caves. The mothers and cubs are left alone until they emerge from the cave. John Perry, Director of the U.S. National Zoo, said this:

> The world is our zoo—a zoo that must be well managed, its resources carefully husbanded, for these are the only resources it can ever have. We have appointed ourselves the keepers of this zoo, but we cannot live outside its gates. We are of it. Our lives are inextricably intertwined with the lives of all that live within. Their fate will be ours.

7   Our endangered species can survive only by nature's implacable test— sustained births by second and third generations. It will take decades to reach such a verdict of success. Thus. we can see that captive breeding is beset by many problems

What is the main point of this essay?

I think this paper is saying that the only chance for endangered species is that they reproduce in zoos but that it is hard to get them to breed in captivity.

What is the greatest strength?

I hadn't thought much about this question, so it was something new for me. I liked the examples about specific animals and the problems that they have in captivity. I especially liked the fact that the writer gave me several problems that occur when animals are bred in captivity. The writer didn't oversimplify.

What is the greatest problem/weakness?

I can't see how the paragraphs connect to the main part of the paper or to each other. They seem disconnected. What does Male-female compatibility is a social problem have to do with the problem of reproduction or with the previous paragraph on mating? Also, there are a number of very unclear statements that leave me with many questions. How are we making it hard for over a hundred species to exist? What do you mean when you say Almost never get together, bring on the male, took up with, and an easy job?

Response to paragraph 4

Do social factors always hurt the care of infant primates? Your statement seems too general. Shouldn't you combine some of your sentences? The first six sentences seem to abruptly jump from one point to the next; the writing is not smooth. How did you get from marmosets to gorillas? The jump confuses me. Also, were the dutiful mothers humans or gorillas?

Acting Upon Your Peers' Responses

Sometimes you need strong nerves to act upon a peer response. You can easily become defensive or discount your reader's comments as foolish. Remember, however, that as a writer you are trying to communicate with your readers, and that means taking reader feedback seriously. Of course, you decide which responses are appropriate, but even an inappropriate criticism sometimes sets off a train of thought that leads to good ideas for revision.

Examine the revised version of the captive breeding essay that follows and note how the writer has taken some of the peer responses into account. Clear transition sentences link paragraphs to the thesis statement and to each other. Vague statements identified in the earlier draft have been clarified. In paragraph 4, the writer connects the discussion of the marmosets to that of the gorillas by changing the order of the sentences and combining them, thereby identifying poor parenting as the key problem with both kinds of primates. Finally, she indicates that either gorillas or humans can be "dutiful mothers."

As you read this version, carefully examine the margin notes, which highlight key features of the revision.

Captive Breeding: Difficult but Necessary

1   Today, as in the past, humans encroach upon the basic right of nature's species to survive. Through ignorance, oversight, and technological developments, we are threatening the survival of over one hundred animal species. Until their environments can be safeguarded against harmful human intrusion, the last chance for the threatened species may be captive breeding in zoos. But this rescue attempt is a complex and difficult undertaking. In particular, each species presents social and physical problems that must be solved if breeding is to succeed.

2   Among the social problems that complicate successful reproduction, mating problems loom especially large. For instance, the male and female of many feline species must be kept completely separated until both animals are ready to mate.

Title: specific and accurate

Introduction: arresting statement

Thesis statement and statement of organization

Topic sentence with link to thesis statement

Specific details: problems with cheetahs

Mention of other species with mating problems

Topic sentence with link to preceding paragraph; linking device

Specific example: problem with particular orangutan

Topic sentence with link to preceding paragraph

Specific details: problems with marmosets

Mention of other species with rearing problems

Linking device

Transition sentence: signals switch to discussing physical problems

Topic sentence with link to transition sentence

Specific details: problems with gorillas

Linking device

Topic sentence

Linking device

Conclusion: quotation plus statement reinforcing idea that captive breeding presents difficulties

Leland Stowe, writing in *National Wildlife* magazine, notes that cheetahs almost never mate unless kept where the one cannot see or smell the other. Once the female shows signs of receptivity, a male is placed in her cage, and mating then occurs. Pandas and pygmy hippopotamuses show the same behaviour.

3   A related social problem with certain species is male–female compatibility. Great apes, for instance, seem to be as particular as human beings in choosing mates. Stowe relates an amusing case of a male orangutan that totally spurned the females in the Washington, D.C., National Zoo. Shipped to a zoo in Toronto, he succumbed to the charms of a new face and has, according to curator William Zanten, "been siring offspring ever since."

4   Social factors can also imperil proper care of infant primates. In a *Smithsonian* magazine article, Sheldon Campbell talks about the problems scientists encountered in trying to breed golden marmosets, a species of Brazilian monkey. Early attempts failed because the captive-born parents neglected and sometimes accidentally killed their babies. Observation showed that the problem occurred because the marmosets had no experience living in a family situation—they simply didn't know how to handle their offspring. Gorillas reared by humans may also make poor mothers, reports Emily Hahn in *The New Yorker*. On the other hand, those reared by dutiful mothers, whether human or gorilla, are usually good parents themselves.

5   Physical problems rival social problems as stumbling blocks to successful captive breeding. Ignorance of a species' dietary needs, for instance, can have disastrous consequences. Early in the captive breeding of gorillas, infants exhibited a very high mortality rate, Stowe notes. Then meat protein and iron, the former rich in vitamin B-12, were sprinkled on bananas and fed to the babies. As a result, the survival rate markedly improved.

6   An environment that duplicates a species' natural habitat favours easy propagation. Hooved and horned animals present few breeding problems because the zoo habitats are similar in terrain and climate to their natural habitats. Polar bears, on the other hand, present difficult problems. Unless the mothers have complete privacy until the cubs can get around, they often kill the babies. To prevent this from happening, Stowe says, zoos now construct replicas of arctic ice caves and leave mothers and cubs completely alone until the new family emerges from the cave.

7   In his book *The World's a Zoo*, John Perry, director of the U.S. National Zoo, has spoken of the need to save our endangered species:

The world is our zoo—a zoo that must be well managed, its resources carefully husbanded, for these are the only resources it can ever have. We have appointed ourselves the keepers of this zoo, but we cannot live outside its gates. We are of it. Our lives are inextricably intertwined with the lives of all that live within. Their fate will be ours.

The difficulty, unfortunately, is as great as the urgency of this problem. Only sustained births by second- and third-generation captive animals can ensure the survival of our endangered species. And it will take decades to achieve the necessary success.

COLLABORATIVE WRITING

In many professions, workers have to cooperate as a group to produce documents. Recognizing this fact, many instructors assign collaborative writing projects. Writing as part of a group offers some advantages but poses some interesting challenges. A group can draw on many different perspectives and areas of expertise, split up the work, and enjoy the feedback of a built-in peer group. On the other hand, the group must also coordinate several efforts, resolve conflicts over the direction of the project, deal with people who may not do their fair share, and integrate different styles of writing.

Moreover, even though you write as part of a group, the final product should read as though it were written by one person. Therefore, take great pains to ensure that the paper doesn't resemble a patchwork quilt. You can help achieve this goal by following the principles of good writing discussed throughout this book. Here are some suggestions for successful collaborative work:

1. Select a leader with strong organizational skills.
2. Make sure each person has every other group member's phone number and email address.
3. Analyze the project and develop a work plan with clearly stated deadlines for each step of the project.
4. Assign tasks on the basis of people's interests and expertise.
5. Schedule regular meetings to gauge each person's progress.
6. Encourage ideas and feedback from all members at each meeting.
7. If each member is working on a different portion of the paper, submit each contribution to other members of the group for peer evaluation.
8. To ensure that the finished product is written in one style and fits together as a whole, assign one person to compile the submissions and write the complete draft.
9. Allow plenty of time to review the complete draft so necessary changes can be made.

Collaborative writing provides an opportunity to learn a great deal from other students. However, problems arise if one or more group members don't do their work or skip meetings entirely. This irresponsibility compromises everyone's grade. The group should insist that all members participate, and the leader should immediately contact anyone who misses a meeting. If a serious problem develops despite these efforts, contact your instructor. But keep in mind that working out the groupwork challenges is part of the assignment, and some instructors expect groups to solve these problems on their own.

Collaboration Using Email, Instant Messaging, or Chat Rooms

Increasing numbers of university students are using electronic communication to collaborate on writing projects. This allows you to exchange material and comments at every stage of the writing process. To illustrate, you can share

1. Brainstorming ideas developed during the search for a writing topic
2. Brainstorming ideas developed during the search for supporting information
3. Tentative thesis statements or any general statement that will shape the document
4. Individual sections of the writing project
5. Copies of the entire original draft

Whenever you use email for collaborative writing, it's a good idea to designate a project leader who will ensure that all members participate and who will receive and distribute all materials. Your instructor may request copies of the email exchanges in order to follow your work.

MAINTAINING AND REVIEWING A PORTFOLIO

A portfolio is an organized collection of your writing, usually kept in a binder or folder. It's a good idea to retain all your work for each assignment, including the instruction sheet, your prewriting notes, and all your drafts, in case the instructor asks to see them. Organize this material either in the order of completion or by type of assignment.

Why keep a portfolio? Not only can a portfolio be a source of ideas for future writing, but it also allows you to review the progress of your current papers. In addition, should any confusion arise about a grade or an assignment, the contents of your portfolio can quickly clarify matters.

Moreover, some instructors may require you to maintain a portfolio. They will probably specify both what is to be included and how it is to be organized. Many instructors believe that portfolios help students track their progress. Furthermore, portfolios give your instructor a complete picture of all your work.

You can review your own portfolio to gain a better understanding of your writing capabilities. Answer these questions as you look over your materials:

1. With what assignments or topics was I most successful? Why?
2. What assignments or topics gave me the most problems? Why?
3. How has my planning changed? How can I make it more effective?

4. What makes my best writing effective? How does this writing differ from my other work?

5. What are the problem areas in my weakest writing? How does this writing differ from my other work?

6. Did I make significant changes in response to my own critical review, a peer evaluation, or my instructor's comments? If not, why not? What kinds of changes did I make? What changes would improve the quality of my work?

7. What organizational patterns have I used? (See Chapters 7–14.) Which ones have been effective? Why? Which ones have given me trouble? Why?

8. What kinds of introductions have I used? What other options do I have for effective introductions?

9. What kinds of conclusions have I used? What other options do I have for effective conclusions?

10. What kinds of grammar or spelling errors get in the way of my effectiveness as a writer? Focus on these errors in future proofreading.

CHAPTER 6

Strategies for Working with Sentences, Diction, Tone, and Style

Learning to write well means learning to revise in order to sharpen the effectiveness of what you want to say. Even after making larger, global revisions related to your thesis, organization, and development, you also need to make smaller, more local changes to sentences and words. By using more varied sentence structures, you will sound like a more mature and sophisticated writer. Getting rid of excess clutter in sentences also gives your writing a pleasing crispness and authority. Finding the right word, instead of the good-enough or almost-right word, is like getting the puck into the net—instead of almost doing it.

To gain control over your writing, you need to be able to recognize what a sentence is. A sentence is a group of words that begins with a capital letter; ends with a period, question mark, or exclamation point; and makes sense by itself. The elements that comprise sentences include subjects, predicates, direct objects, indirect objects, subject complements, object complements, phrases, and clauses.

Sentences take many forms, some straightforward and unadorned, others intricate and ornate, each with its own stylistic strengths. Becoming familiar with these forms and their uses gives you the option to

- emphasize or de-emphasize an idea
- combine ideas into one sentence or keep them separate in more than one sentence

- make sentences sound formal or informal
- emphasize the actor or the action
- achieve rhythm, variety, and contrast

Effective sentences bring exactness and flair to your writing.

SENTENCE STRATEGIES

Effective sentence writing is not an accident; it requires practice and hard work. To create stronger sentences, use these strategies: avoiding wordiness; using clear diction; varying sentence length, complexity, and word order; building a rhythm for your reader; and selecting the right verb voice. Usually it's best to work on these different strategies as you revise, rather than pausing to refine each sentence after you write it.

Avoiding Unnecessary Wordiness

Sometimes in first drafts we write flabby sentences.

It is my considered opinion that you will make an excellent employee.

Joan will give a presentation on our latest sales figures to the CEO.

Mr. Headly, who was my Grade 7 biology teacher, recently was honoured for the research he had done over the years with his classes.

My neighbour's Subaru that was old and rusty still could navigate the winter streets better than most other cars.

Although there may be stylistic reasons for these sentences, such as creating variety or adding a particular emphasis, a writer could sharpen them by reordering the sentence structure and eliminating unnecessary words.

You will make an excellent employee. (The fact that you write it makes it clear that it is your opinion.)

Joan will present our latest sales figures to the CEO. (Many times we use verbs as nouns with a filler verb—"have a meeting," "give a talk," "go running." Change these nouns back to verbs and dragging sentences can be energized.)

Mr. Headly, my Grade 7 biology teacher, recently was honoured for the research he had done over the years with his classes. (The rules of English let you delete some redundant phrases, even repeated subjects, to tighten your language.)

My neighbour's rusty, old Subaru still could navigate the winter streets better than most other cars. (Changing a relative clause to simple adjectives makes this sentence crisper. Often you can change word order to produce more emphatic sentences.)

The actual rules for tightening sentences are discussed in the Handbook. How do most writers do it? Cut out words that seem unnecessary, organize sentences different ways, and let verbs do more of the work.

A type of wordiness referred to as *deadwood* can result from unconscious use of redundancies. Watch for redundant word pairs such as "advance planning," "near proximity," and "twelve midnight," which can be written more simply as "planning," "proximity," and "midnight."

Another type of wordiness, called *gobbledygook,* consists of long, abstract, or technical words that create unnecessarily long and complex sentences. Some people mistakenly believe this fancy talk sounds more dignified. Others who may be trying to impress rather than communicate end up clouding their meanings even from themselves with gobbledygook. Consider how the following examples of gobbledygook can be clarified and simplified.

Original Version	Revised Version
The fish exhibited a 100 percent mortality response.	All the fish died.
We have been made cognizant of the fact that the experiment will be terminated in the near future.	We have learned that the experiment will end soon.

Gobbledygook can result from the practice of transforming verbs into their noun forms. The result is heavy text and dragging sentences. Wherever possible, use a verb in its verb form:

She had a *discussion* about methods for *improvement* of writing.	She *discussed* ways to *improve* writing.

EXERCISE *Rewrite the sentences to avoid unnecessary wordiness.*

1. The principal will give a talk to the parents at the school council meeting about how vitally important it is for their children to get to school on time.
2. I would like to say that no playwright has ever used language as effectively as Shakespeare.
3. Mozart, who was a musical prodigy, is best known for his operas.
4. The jewellery store sold me a watch that was stolen.
5. The meeting that was scheduled for 3 P.M. was cancelled because Mr. Rushton, the consultant who was giving the presentation about the results on our computer security, was arrested for creating computer viruses that were very destructive.

Varying Sentence Complexity and Length

Sentences that are all the same length yield a repetitive, tedious prose.

Janice hated pain. She had her nose pierced. She had her bellybutton pierced. She had her tongue pierced. She wanted to be different. She ended up just like her friends.

This string of simple sentences unnecessarily repeats word phrases and gives the reader a bumpy ride. Combining these sentences results in a smoother and more varied prose style.

> Although Janice hated pain, she had her nose, bellybutton, and tongue pierced in order to be different. She ended up, however, just like her friends.

You can combine and condense sentences by learning to use coordinate and subordinate conjunctions that show the relationship between ideas.

Coordination

Coordinating conjunctions join phrases or clauses of equal weight or importance. They include *and, but, or, nor, for, yet,* and *so.*

> The audience was young, friendly, and responsive, so it cheered for each speaker.

> Either we hang together or we hang separately.

> A tornado ripped through our town, but fortunately it spared our house.

Subordination

Subordinate conjunctions can link a dependent clause to the main clause. Subordinate conjunctions such as *because, since, although, if, unless, while, before, during, after,* and *instead of,* can join clauses and create emphasis. Subordinate conjunctions show the logical relationship of one idea to the other.

> Millicent swam 400 laps today *because* she was feeling unusually strong.

> Arthur collapsed on the sofa *after* the dance was over.

> *After* they had reached the lakeshore, the campers searched for a level spot *because* they wanted to pitch their tent there.

Relative Clauses

Sentences may also be combined and condensed using groups of words called *relative pronoun clauses* (clauses that contain pronouns such as *who, whose, which, that*).

> Students work hard, and they usually succeed.

> Students *who* work hard usually succeed.

> You ordered books on the history of Crete, and they have finally arrived.

> The books on the history of Crete *that* you ordered have finally arrived.

Intentional Fragments

A fragment is a part of a sentence that is capitalized and punctuated as if it were a complete sentence. Although fragments are seldom used in academic writing, they form the backbone of most conversations and thus are popular in fiction. Here's how a typical bit of dialogue might go:

> "Where are you going tonight?" (*sentence*)
>
> "Woodland Mall." (*fragment*)
>
> "What for?" (*fragment*)
>
> "To buy some shoes." (*fragment*)

Moreover, writers of nonfiction use fragments to create special effects. In the following passage, the fragment emphasizes the importance of the question it asks and varies the pace of the writing:

> Before kidney transplants, people had an ethical unease about renal dialysis—the artificial kidney machine. Unquestionably it was a great technical advance making it possible to treat kidney dysfunctions from which thousands die. But the machine was, and is, expensive and involves intensive care of the patient by doctors and nurses. *For whom the machine?* In the United States, the dilemma was evaded but not solved by having lay panels, like juries, making life-or-death choices. In Britain, where the National Health Service entitles everyone, rich or poor, to have access to any necessary treatment, the responsibility rests on the medical staff. It was (and still is) a difficult decision.
>
> Lord Ritchie-Calder, "The Doctor's Dilemma"

Once in a while, a writer uses a whole series of fragments. In the following paragraph, fragments create an impressionistic effect that mirrors the central kaleidoscope image:

> The Jazz Age offers a kaleidoscope of shifting impressions. Of novelties quickly embraced and quickly discarded. Of flappers flaunting bobbed hair and short skirts. Of hip flasks and bootleg whisky, fast cars and coonskin coats, jazz and dancing till dawn. And overall a sense of futility, an uneasy conviction that all the gods were dead.
>
> Elliott L. Smith and Andrew W. Hart,
> *The Short Story: A Contemporary Looking Glass*

A word of caution: Before using any fragment in your own writing, think carefully about your intended effect and explore other ways of achieving it. Unless only a fragment will serve your needs, don't use one; fragments are likely to be viewed as unintentional—and thus errors—in the work of inexperienced writers.

EXERCISE *The following passage includes one or more fragments. Identify each and explain its function.*

> He [Richard Wagner] wrote operas; and no sooner did he have the synopsis of a story, but he would invite—or rather summon—a crowd of his friends to his house and read it aloud to them. Not for criticism. For applause. When the complete poem was written, the friends had to come again, and hear that read aloud. Then he would publish the poem, sometimes years before the music that went with it was

written. He played the piano like a composer, in the worst sense of what that implies, and he would sit down at the piano before parties that included some of the finest pianists of his time, and play for them, by the hour, his own music, needless to say. He had a composer's voice. And he would invite eminent vocalists to his house, and sing them his operas, taking all the parts.

Deems Taylor, "The Monster"

Gaining control over these techniques—coordination; subordination; relative clause use; and selective, intentional fragment use—can help you create rhythm and pacing and flow in your writing style. Note the variety in sentence length in this paragraph.

> To protest that some fairly improbable people, some people who could not possibly respect themselves, seem to sleep easily enough is to miss the point entirely, as surely as those people miss it who think that self-respect has necessarily to do with not having safety pins in one's underwear. There is a common superstition that "self-respect" is a kind of charm against snakes, something that keeps those who have it locked in some unblighted Eden, out of strange beds, ambivalent conversations, and trouble in general. It does not at all. It has nothing to do with the face of things, but concerns instead a separate peace, a private reconciliation.

Joan Didion, "On Self-Respect"

Much of the appealing rhythm of this passage stems from varied sentence length. The first two rather long sentences (forty-nine and thirty-six words) are followed by the very brief "It does not at all," which gains emphasis by its position. The last sentence adds variety by means of its moderate length (nineteen words), quite apart from its interesting observation on the real nature of self-respect.

Varying sentence length can also help you emphasize a key idea. Instead of burying a key point in a long sentence, you can highlight it as a separate, shorter sentence, giving it the recognition it deserves.

Original Version

Employers find mature women to be valuable members of their organizations. They are conscientious, have excellent attendance records, and stay calm when things go awry, but unfortunately, many employers exploit them. Despite their desirable qualities, most remain mired in clerical and retail positions. On the average, they earn two-thirds as much as men.

Revised Version

Employers find mature women to be valuable members of their organizations. They are conscientious, have excellent attendance records, and stay calm when things go awry. *Unfortunately, many employers exploit them.* Despite their desirable qualities, most remain mired in clerical and retail positions. On the average, they earn two-thirds as much as men.

EXERCISE *Combine the sentences in the following passages to reduce length and improve smoothness while keeping the original meaning.*

1. He played the piano. He played the organ. He played the French horn. He did not play the viola.

2. The weather was icy cold and windy. Lee was wearing only a T-shirt and athletic shorts.

3. Life on Venus may be possible. It will not be the kind of life we know on Earth. Life on Mars may be possible. It will not be the kind of life we know on Earth.

4. He felt his classmates were laughing at his error. He ran out of the room. He vowed never to return to that class.

5. Albert lay in bed. He stared at the ceiling. Albert thought about the previous afternoon. He had asked Kathy to go to dinner with him. She is a pretty, blonde-haired woman. She sits at the desk next to his. They work at Hemphill's. She had refused.

6. I went to the store to buy a box of detergent. I saw Bill there, and we talked about last night's game.

7. Tim went to the newsstand. He bought a magazine there. While he was on the way home, he lost it. He had nothing to read.

Varying Word Order

What other tools do you have to create more interesting prose? One powerful technique is to vary word order in a sentence.

Word Order in Independent Clauses

Most independent clauses follow a similar arrangement. First comes the subject, then the verb, and finally any other element needed to convey the main message.

> Barney blushed. (*subject, verb*)
>
> They built the dog a kennel. (*subject, verb, indirect object, direct object*)
>
> Samantha is an architect. (*subject, verb, subject complement*)

This typical order of sentences puts the emphasis on the subject, right where it's usually wanted.

However, the pattern doesn't work in every situation. Occasionally, you want to emphasize another part of the sentence, create a special effect, or give the subject unusual emphasis. In these situations, you may use inverted order and the expletive construction.

Inverted Order   To invert a sentence, move to the front the element you want to emphasize. Sometimes the rest of the sentence follows in regular subject-then-verb order; sometimes the verb precedes the subject.

> Lovable he isn't. (*subject complement, subject, verb*)
>
> This I just don't understand. (*direct object, subject, verb*)
>
> Tall grow the pines in the mountains. (*subject complement, verb, subject*)

Sentences that ask questions typically follow an inverted pattern.

> Is this your coat? (*verb, subject, subject complement*)
>
> Will you let the cat out? (*verb, subject, verb, direct object*)

Keep in mind that most of your sentences should follow normal order: Readers expect it and read it most easily. Furthermore, don't invert a sentence if the result sounds strained and unnatural. A sentence like "Fools were Brett and Amanda for quitting school" only hinders communication.

Expletives   An expletive fills a vacancy in a sentence without contributing to the meaning. English has two common expletives, *there* and *it*. Ordinarily, *there* functions as an adverb, and *it* as a pronoun; and either can appear anywhere in a sentence. As expletives, however, they alter normal sentence order by beginning sentences and anticipating the real subjects or objects.

Expletives are often used unnecessarily, and can be eliminated to reduce wordiness:

> There were twenty persons attending the sales meeting.

This sentence errs on two counts: Its subject needs no extra emphasis, and it is very clumsy. Notice the improvement without the expletive and the unneeded words:

> Twenty persons attended the sales meeting.

Sometimes, when the subject or object needs highlighting, leading off with an expletive calls it more forcefully to the reader's attention by altering normal order.

Normal order:	A fly is in my soup.
	He seeks her happiness.
Expletive construction used to highlight subject:	There is a fly in my soup.
Expletive construction used to highlight object:	It is her happiness he seeks.

Once in a while, you find that something just can't be said unless you use an expletive.

> There is no reason for such foolishness.

EXERCISE *Indicate which expletive constructions below are used for necessary emphasis, and which are unnecessarily wordy.*

1. There is a traitor in our midst.
2. There are some people who need to have it gently pointed out that they should consider counselling.
3. There are many dead fish on the beach.
4. It is usually women who appear in weight loss advertisements.
5. There are a few cheques which I have to deposit.

REVISION CHECKLIST FOR SENTENCES

- What sentences are not clearly expressed or logically constructed?
- What sentences seem awkward, excessively convoluted, or lacking in punch?
- What words require explanation or substitution because the reader may not know them?
- Where does the writing become wordy or use vague terms?
- Are there carelessly omitted or wrongly used words?

Positioning of Movable Modifiers

Movable modifiers can appear on either side of the main statement or within it.

Modifiers after Main Statement   Sentences that follow this arrangement, frequently called *loose* sentences, occur more commonly than either of the others. They mirror conversation, in which a speaker first makes a statement and then adds on further thoughts. Often, the main statement has just one modifier.

> Our company will have to file for bankruptcy *because of this year's huge losses.* (*phrase as modifier*)

Or the main statement can be followed by a series of modifiers.

> He burst suddenly into the party, *loud, angry, obscene.* (*words as modifiers*)

> The family used to gather around the hearth, *doing such chores as polishing shoes, mending ripped clothing, reading, chatting, always warmed by one another's presence as much as by the flames.* (*words and phrases as modifiers*)

> Sally stared in disbelief, and then she smiled, *slowly, tremulously, as if she couldn't believe her good fortune.* (*words and clause as modifiers*)

> There are three essential qualities for buzzard country: *a rich supply of unburied corpses, high mountains, a strong sun.* (*noun-base groups as modifiers*)

> John D. Stewart, "Vulture Country"

A sentence may contain several layers of modifiers. In the following example, we've indented and numbered to show the different layers.

1. The men struggled to the top of the hill,
   2. thirsty,
   2. drenched in sweat,
   2. and cursing in pain
      3. as their knapsack straps cut into their raw, chafed shoulders
         4. with every step.

In this sentence, the terms numbered 2 refer to *men* in the item numbered 1. Item 3 is linked to *cursing* in the preceding item 2, and item 4 is linked to *cut* in item 3.

The modifiers-last arrangement works well for injecting descriptive details into narratives and also for qualifying, explaining, and presenting lists in other kinds of writing.

Modifiers before Main Statement Sentences that delay the main point until the end are called *periodic*. In contrast to loose sentences, periodic sentences lend a formal note to what is said, slowing its pace, adding cadence, and making it more serious.

If you can keep your head when everyone around you is panicking, you can probably survive the situation. (*clauses as modifiers*)

From the outset of his journey to the heart of darkness, Marlow witnesses many incidents that reveal the human capacity for evil. (*phrases as modifiers*)

The danger of sideswiping another vehicle, the knowledge that a hidden bump or hole could throw me from the dune buggy, both of these things added to the thrill of the race. (*noun plus phrase and noun plus clause as modifiers*)

When so many of our students admit to cheating, when so many professors practise grade inflation, and when administrators fail to face up to these problems, our schools are in serious trouble. (*clauses as modifiers*)

1. *When the public protests,*
2. *confronted with some obvious evidence of the damaging results of pesticide applications,* it is fed little tranquilizing pills of half truth. (*clause and phrase as modifiers*)

Rachel Carson, *Silent Spring*

As shown in the preceding example, periodic sentences can also have layers of modifiers.

Positioning the modifiers before the main point throws the emphasis on the end of the sentence, adding force to the main point. The delay also lets the writer create sentences that, like the first example, carry stings, ironic or humorous, in their tails.

Modifiers within Main Statement   Inserting one or more modifiers into a main statement creates a sentence with *interrupted order.* The material may come between the subject and the verb or between the verb and the rest of the predicate.

> The young girl, *wearing a tattered dress and looking anything but well-off herself,* gave the beggar a twenty-dollar bill. (*phrases between subject and verb*)

> Dewey declared, *with a cheery flourish of his ticket,* that the concert was the best he'd ever heard. (*phrase between verb and rest of predicate*)

> The bedsprings, *bent and rusted, festooned with spider webs,* lay on top of the heap. (*words and phrase between subject and verb*)

> The evolutionists, *piercing beneath the show of momentary stability,* discovered, *hidden in rudimentary organs,* the discarded rubbish of the past. (*one phrase between subject and verb, another between verb and rest of predicate*)

By stretching out the main idea, the inserted modifiers in these sentences slow the forward pace, creating a more formal tone.

EXERCISE *Identify each sentence as loose, periodic, or interrupted. Rewrite each as one of the other kinds.*

1. Victoria, rejected by family and friends, uncertain where to turn next, finally decided to start a new life in Halifax.
2. When told that she had to have her spleen removed, the woman gasped.
3. Tom missed the bus because his wife had forgotten to reset the alarm after she got up and he had cut himself several times while shaving.
4. Good health, warm friends, a beautiful summer evening—the best things cannot be purchased.
5. A customer, angry and perspiring, stormed up to the claims desk.
6. Stopping just short of the tunnel entrance, the freight train avoided a collision with the crowded commuter train stalled inside.
7. The new boy, the fire of determination in his eyes, hammered away at the fading champ.
8. The Grade 1 students stood in line, talking and giggling, pushing at one another's ball caps and backpacks and kicking one another's shins, unmindful of the drudgery that awaited them inside.

Using Parallelism

Parallelism presents equivalent ideas in grammatically equivalent form. Dressing them in the same grammatical garb calls attention to their kinship and adds smoothness and polish. The following sentence pairs demonstrate the improvement that parallelism brings:

Nonparallel:	James's outfit was *wrinkled, mismatched,* and *he needed to wash it.* (*words and independent clause*)
Parallel:	James's outfit was *wrinkled, mismatched,* and *dirty.* (*words*)
Nonparallel:	Oscar likes *reading books, attending plays,* and *to search for antiques.* (*different kinds of phrases*)
Parallel:	Oscar likes *reading books, attending plays,* and *searching for antiques.* (*same kind of phrases*)
Nonparallel:	Beth performs her tasks *quickly, willingly,* and *with accuracy.* (*words and phrase*)
Parallel:	Beth performs her tasks *quickly, willingly,* and *accurately.* (*words*)
Nonparallel:	The instructor complimented me *for taking part in class discussions* and *because I had written a superb theme.* (*phrase and clause*)
Parallel:	The instructor complimented me *for taking part in class discussions* and *for writing a superb theme.* (*phrases*)

As the examples show, revising nonparallel sentences smooths out bumpiness, binds the ideas together more closely, and allows for faster comprehension.

Parallelism doesn't always stop with a single sentence. Writers sometimes use it in a series of sentences:

> He had never lost his childlike innocence. He had never lost his sense of wonder. He had never lost his sense of joy in nature's simplest gifts.

For an example of parallelism that extends over much of a paragraph, see page 72 (Chapter 4, "What Is Poverty?").

Repeating a structure through several sentences of a paragraph adds intensity to meaning and rhythm to the prose.

Balance, a special form of parallelism, positions two grammatically equivalent ideas on opposite sides of some pivot point, such as a word or punctuation mark.

> Hope for the best, and prepare for the worst.

> Many are called, but few are chosen.

> When I'm right, nobody ever remembers; when I'm wrong, nobody ever forgets.

> The sheep are in the meadow, and the cows are in the corn.

Like regular parallel sentences, balanced sentences sometimes come in series. Balanced sentences can be especially resonant in speeches.

> We want to live in a country in which French Canadians can choose to live among English Canadians and English Canadians can choose to live among French Canadians without abandoning their cultural heritage.
>
> Pierre Elliot Trudeau, "Statement on Introduction of the Official Languages Bill"

Balance works especially well for pitting contrasting ideas against each other. It sharpens the difference between them while achieving compactness and lending an air of insight to what is said.

EXERCISE *Identify each sentence as nonparallel, parallel, or balanced; then rewrite each nonparallel sentence to make it parallel.*

1. Professor Bartlett enjoys helping students, counselling advisees, and participation in faculty meetings.

2. I can still see Aunt Alva striding into the corral, cornering a cow against a fence-post, try to balance herself on a one-legged milking stool, and butt her head into the cow's belly.

3. The city plans on building a new fishing pier and on dredging the channel of the river.

4. Michèle plans on vacationing in Quebec City, but Robert wants to golf in Charlottetown.

5. Being half drunk and because he was already late for work, Tom called his boss and said he was too ill to come in that day.

6. The novel's chief character peers through a tangle of long hair, slouches along in a shambling gait, and gets into trouble constantly.

7. You can take the boy out of the country, but you can't take the country out of the boy.

8. Joe's problem is not that he earns too little money but spending it foolishly.

9. The room was dark, gloomy, and everything was dusty.

10. The apparition glided through the wall, across the room, and up the fireplace chimney.

Choosing the Right Verb Voice

A sentence's verb voice derives from the relationship between the subject and the action. A sentence in the *active voice* has a subject that does something plus a verb that shows action.

> The boy hit the target.

> The girl painted the garage.

This pattern keeps the key information in the key part of the sentence, making it strong and vigorous and giving the reader a close-up look at the action.

The *passive voice* reverses the subject–action relationship by having the subject receive, rather than perform, the action. It is built around a form of the verb *to be* (*is, are, was, were*). Some sentences identify the actor by using a prepositional phrase; others don't mention the actor at all.

> The target was hit by the boy. (*actor identified*)

> The federal debt is to be targeted for reduction. (*actor unidentified*)

Occasionally passive voice can be useful. For example, it can emphasize the passivity of the subject (e.g. "The man was murdered.") Reporters may use it to conceal the identity of a source. Scientific writing customarily uses the passive voice to explain processes. Consider how the passive voice in the following example of scientific writing provides a desirable objective tone and places the emphasis where it's most important: on the action, not the actor.

> In the production of steel, iron ore is first converted into pig iron by combining it with limestone and coke and then heating the mixture in a blast furnace. Pig iron, however, contains too many impurities to be useful to industry, and as a result must be refined and converted to steel.

On occasion, everyday writing also uses the passive voice.

> The garbage is collected once a week on Mondays.
>
> These caves were formed about ten million years ago.

In the first case, there's no need to tell who collects the garbage; obviously, garbage collectors do. In the second, the writer may not know what caused the formation, and saying "Something formed these caves about 10 million years ago" makes the sentence sound mysterious. In both situations, the action, not the actor, is paramount.

Usually, however, passive voice takes away from the energy of a piece of writing. It dilutes the force of the sentence, puts greater distance between the action and the reader, and almost always adds extra words to the message.

Most writers who overuse the passive voice simply don't realize how it bogs their writing down. Read this paragraph, written mainly in the passive voice:

> Graft becomes possible when gifts are given to police officers or favours are done for them by persons who expect preferential treatment in return. Gifts of many kinds may be received by officers. Often free meals are given to them by the owners of restaurants on their beats. During the Christmas season, they may be given liquor, food, or theatre tickets by merchants. If favoured treatment is not received by the donors, no great harm is done. But if traffic offences, safety code violations, and other infractions are overlooked by the officers, corruption results. When such corruption is exposed by the newspapers, faith is lost in law enforcement agencies.

This impersonal, wordy passage plods across the page. Now note the livelier, more forceful tone of this rewritten version.

> Graft becomes possible when police officers accept gifts or favours from persons who expect preferential treatment in return. Officers may receive gifts of many kinds. Restaurant owners often provide free meals for officers on the beat. During the Christmas season, merchants may give them liquor, food, or theatre tickets. If donors do not receive favoured treatment, no great harm is done. But if officers overlook traffic offences, safety code violations, and other infractions, corruption results. When the newspapers expose such corruption, citizens lose faith in law enforcement agencies.

Unless special circumstances call for the passive voice, use the active voice.

EXERCISE *After determining whether each sentence below is in active or passive voice, rewrite the passive sentences as active ones.*

1. Mary's parents gave her a sports car for her sixteenth birthday.
2. Fires were left burning by negligent campers.
3. The new ice arena will be opened by the city in about two weeks.
4. Harry left the open toolbox out in the rain.
5. Papers were handed back to the students by the instructor.
6. Cyril took a trip to Whitehorse.
7. We have just installed a new computer in our main office.
8. The club president awarded Tompkins the Order of the Golden Mace.
9. The sound of war drums was heard by the missionaries as they floated down the river.
10. Objections were raised by some members of the legislature to the ratification of the proposed amendment.

Beyond the Single Sentence

Like players on a hockey team, your sentences need to work together to be effective. You need to vary sentence length, word order, and rhythms, but in a way that is not obvious or clumsy. This takes work. A good place to start is by studying the essays in the Reader of this textbook to see what kinds of combinations the authors use—a series of questions that are then answered; long sentences with modifiers leading up to and emphasizing a short sentence; a series of fragments followed by a long sentence. In your own writing, keep an eye on what kind of sentences you are creating and how those sentences create a pattern. Once you have finished a draft, read it to hear how its rhythms strike your inner ear, and mark sections that "sound" wrong. Play with your sentences to get the results that you want.

EXERCISE *Revise the following passage to improve its style.*

From 1868 to 1870, Louis Riel was the leader of the Métis. The Métis were the French-speaking majority of the North-West Territories. Riel was a skilful politician. He forced the Canadian government to protect his people's rights. He united his people against exploitative American and Canadian fur trading interests. As a result of his efforts, Canada was compelled to create the province of Manitoba in 1870. Riel fled Manitoba in 1870 to avoid prosecution for hanging a racial bigot, Thomas Scott. He fled to America and became a citizen. In 1885, he came to Northern Saskatchewan to lead another rebellion. He was caught and hanged in the fall of 1885. Many people view him as a symbolic French-Canadian victim of English Canada.

Using Clear Diction

Clear diction stems from choosing words with the right meanings, using abstract and concrete words appropriately, and picking terms that are neither too specific nor too general.

Word Meanings   Make sure the words you use mean what you think they do, so that inaccurate word use does not distort your message. Sound-alike word pairs often trip up unwary writers. Take *accept* and *except* for example. *Accept* means "to approve." *Except,* when used as a verb, means "to exclude or omit." If you want to indicate approval but you say, "The following new courses were *excepted* by the committee," think of the obvious consequences. Likewise, consider the distinction between *continual* (frequently or regularly repeated) and *continuous* (uninterrupted). If you illustrate your popularity by saying "My phone rings *continuously,*" your reader will wonder why you never answer it and how you ever sleep.

Now consider the following sentences:

> Just Mary was chosen to write the report.
>
> Mary was just chosen to write the report.
>
> Mary was chosen to write just the report.

The first sentence says that no one except Mary will write the report; the second says that she was recently picked for the job; and the third says that she will write nothing else. Each of these sentences expresses a different meaning because the placement of modifiers (adjectives, adverbs, and phrases) determines which words they modify.

Concrete and Abstract Words   Sometimes using more concrete words can bring to life a piece of writing that seems vague or dull. A concrete word names or describes something that we can perceive with one or more of our five senses. A thing is concrete if we can weigh it, measure it, hold it in our hands, photograph it, taste it, sniff it, add salt to it, drop it, smash into it, or borrow it from a neighbour. But if a thing is abstract, we can't do any of these things. *Anne of Green Gables* is a concrete term, as are *Swiss cheese, petroleum, maple syrup,* and *Halifax.* On the other hand, *jealousy, power, conservatism, size,* and *sadness* are all abstract terms.

Concrete words evoke precise, vivid mental images and thus help convey a message. In contrast, the images that abstract terms create differ from person to person. Try this test: Ask several of your friends to describe what comes to mind when they think of *joy, hatred, fear,* or some other abstract term. For example, the word *hatred* might call up images of a person with cold, narrow eyes for some, or a grimly set jaw and tightly clenched fists for another. But concrete terms are more uniformly understood and therefore help us specify what we mean.

In the following passage, the concrete diction is italicized:

> To do without self-respect . . . is to be an unwilling *audience of one* to an interminable *documentary* that details one's failings, both real and imagined, with *fresh footage spliced* in for every *screening.* There's *the glass you broke* in anger, there's *the hurt*

on X's face; watch now, *this next scene, the night Y came back from Houston,* see how you muff this one. To live without self-respect is to *lie awake some night,* beyond the reach of *warm milk, phenobarbital,* and *the sleeping hand on the coverlet,* counting up the sins of commission and omission, the trusts betrayed, the promises subtly broken, the gifts irrevocably wasted through sloth or cowardice or carelessness. However long we postpone it, we eventually lie down alone in that notoriously *uncomfortable bed,* the one we make ourselves. Whether or not we sleep in it depends, of course, on whether or not we respect ourselves.

Joan Didion, "On Self-Respect"

Now note how vague and colourless the passage becomes when the concrete diction is removed:

To do without self-respect is to be continuously aware of your failings, both real and imagined. Incidents stay in your mind long after they are over. To live without self-respect means being bothered by intentional or unintentional failings, trusts betrayed, promises subtly broken, and gifts irrevocably wasted through sloth or cowardice or carelessness. However long we postpone it, we eventually must come to terms with who we are. How we respond to this situation depends, of course, on whether or not we respect ourselves.

EXERCISE *Underline the concrete terms in the following passage:*

The fog which rises from the river has no color, no texture, no taste, smell, or sound. It is sheer vision, a vision of purity, a slow, mesmeric, inexorable erasure of the slate. You see fog mushrooming along the river's course. Gently, it obliterates the alders tangled on the banks, wipes out the road. Buildings without foundations, trees without trunks, hang in the air like mirages. Sun may be shining brightly on them, or rain drenching them, or stars twinkling above or among them. Slowly the fog reaches higher and spreads. Ridgepoles, small topmost branches, and your own dooryard vanish. There is nothing left now but shining mist. It is all, and you float on it, utterly alone, as one imagines he might in empty space if flung off by earth; as the mind does, drifting into sleep; as the spirit does, having escaped its mortal frame.

Gladys Hasty Carroll, *Sing Out the Glory*

Specific and General Terms   One concrete term can be more specific or more general than another. As we move from *Lassie* to *collie* to *dog* to *mammal* and finally to *animal,* we become less and less specific, ending with a term that encompasses every animal on earth. With each step we retain only those features that fit the more general term. Thus, when we move from *collie* to *dog,* we leave out everything that makes collies different from terriers, greyhounds, and other breeds. The more specific the term, the less difference among the images it calls to mind. For example, if you say *animal* to a group of friends, one may think of a dog, another of a horse, and a third of a gorilla. *Collie,* on the other hand, triggers images of a large, long-haired, brown and white dog with a pointed muzzle.

Typically, a first draft will contain overly general words that are abstract rather than concrete. Ask yourself how specific you need to be and then revise accordingly. Often, the more specific term is the better choice. For example, you might characterize a wealthy jet-setter by noting that he drives a Ferrari, not just a car. However, if you're writing a narrative about your flight to Quebec City and your experience at the winter carnival, nothing is gained by naming the make of car you rented and used during your stay. Choose details that fit your purpose.

Listening for Tone in Writing

Tone reveals the author's attitude toward the topic and the reader. While it is relatively easy to pick up on a speaker's tone of voice—solemn, confident, ironic, or lightly humorous—tone in writing is conveyed through word choice, style, and sentence rhythm.

Word Meaning   Tone is conveyed partly through the words you choose. Use the exact word that you need for the job. Sometimes you have words in your passive vocabularies—words that you have read or heard before but that you have not yourself used. If you are unsure of the meanings of a word, or if you want more information about a word, consult a good dictionary such as *The Canadian Oxford Dictionary, Funk and Wagnall's Standard College Dictionary,* or an unabridged dictionary such as *Webster's Third New International Dictionary* or the *Oxford English Dictionary,* all of which can be found in most libraries.

Dictionaries can help you learn about current and past meanings of a word. They identify parts of speech, variant spellings of a word, pronunciations, and the history, or etymology, of a word. If you are using a word extensively in your paper, including information about the word's etymology can help your reader understand the word's nuances.

Usage Labels   A dictionary's usage labels also help you determine whether a word suits the circumstances of your writing.

Label	Meaning
Colloquial	Relatively casual usage characteristic of informal conversation
Slang	Informal, newly coined words and expressions or old expressions with new meanings
Obsolete	No longer in use but found in writing from the past
Archaic	Old, usually outmoded, but still finds restricted use; for example, in legal documents
Poetic	Used only in poetry and in prose with a poetic tone
Dialect	Used regularly only in a particular geographical region such as parts of Newfoundland or the Scottish Lowlands

Thesauruses list synonyms for words but omit the other elements in dictionary entries. Figure 6.1 shows a typical entry. Note that the items are grouped according to parts of speech, and some are cross-indexed.

A thesaurus helps you find a word with just the right shade of meaning or a synonym when you want to avoid repetition. However, synonyms are never

247. FORMLESSNESS

1. nouns **formlessness, shapelessness;** amorphousness, amorphism, amorphia; **chaos,** confusion, messiness, orderlessness; disorder 62; entropy; anarchy 740.2; **indeterminateness, indefiniteness,** indecisiveness, vagueness, mistiness, haziness, fuzziness, blurriness, unclearness, obscurity.
2. unlicked cub, diamond in the rough.
3. verbs **deform, distort** 249.5; unform, unshape; disorder, jumble, mess up, muddle, confuse; obfuscate, obscure, fog up, blur.
4. adjs **formless, shapeless,** featureless, characterless, nondescript, inchoate, lumpen, blobby *or* baggy [both informal], inform: amorphous, amorphic, amorph(o)-: **chaotic, orderless,** disorderly 62.13, unordered, unorganized, confused, anarchic 740.6; kaleidoscopic; **indeterminate, indefinite,** undefined, indecisive, vague, misty, hazy, fuzzy, blurred *or* blurry, unclear, obscure.
5. **unformed, unshaped,** unshapen, unfashioned, unlicked; uncut, unhewn.

Figure 6.1 A Typical Thesaurus Entry
From *Roget's International Thesaurus,* 5th edition, Peter Mark Roget. Copyright © 1992 by HarperCollins Publishers, Inc. Reprinted by permission of HarperCollins Publishers, Inc.

exactly equal, nor are they always interchangeable. For example, *old* means "in existence or use for a long time"; *antiquated* conveys the notion that something is old-fashioned or outdated. Therefore, use the thesaurus along with the dictionary. Only then can you tell which synonym fits a specific sentence.

Denotation and Connotation   Word meanings often extend beyond dictionary definitions, or *denotations*. Many words carry emotional associations, or *connotations*. For example, a word such as "medicine" denotes a "substance used in treating illness or disease." This definition is objective and neutral: It does not assign any special value or convey any particular attitude toward the word or what the word stands for. However, the word "medicine" could also carry strong positive or negative connotations, depending on how it is used. To say that going into the wilderness is just the "medicine" one needs sounds positive, but to say that something tastes "like medicine" sounds negative. Context—the parts of a passage that precede and follow a word—also affects connotation. Note, for instance, the different associations of *dog* in these sentences:

> That movie is a real dog.

> I sure am putting on the dog!

> It's a dog-eat-dog world.

> Your dog-in-the-manger attitude makes you very unpopular.

Some words—*death*, for instance—almost always carry strong connotations or emotional associations. *The Canadian Oxford Dictionary* defines it as "the final cessation of vital functions" or "the ending of life," but it means much more. All of us have hopes, fears, and memories relating to death, feelings that colour our responses whenever we hear or read the word. Likewise, we have personal responses to words such as *sexy, cheap, radical, politician,* and *mother* based on our experiences. To an Olympic swimmer who has won a gold medal, *swimming* may stir pleasant memories of the victory and the plaudits that went with it. The victim of a near-drowning, however, might react to the same word with something approaching horror.

Cultural connotations are even more important than personal connotations. Cultural connotations develop the way personal ones do, but on a much larger scale, growing out of the common experiences of many speakers and writers and changing with usage and circumstances. For example, the word "problem" literally means "a difficult matter requiring a solution"—a very neutral denotation. But its cultural connotation is negative in most social situations. Imagine if an instructor called you into his or her office and demanded, "Do you have a problem?" Or if a store clerk approached a hesitant customer and asked, "What is your problem?" In both situations, the listener would probably feel insulted and even angry, due to the negative cultural connotation of the word.

Denotation is sometimes called the language of science and technology, and connotation, the language of art. But we need both to communicate effectively. Denotation allows us to convey precise, essential meanings. Connotation adds richness, warmth, and texture. Without these qualities, our language would be bland and sterile, our stories bleak and mechanical.

An objective tone keeps the writer's personality and opinion out of the message. Here is an example of a relatively neutral piece of prose:

> Myopia is a condition of the eye that makes distant vision blurry. In brief, the myopic individual is nearsighted. When the eye is normal, rays of light pass through it and come to focus on the retina, located at the back of the eye. In the myopic eye, however, the rays of light come together a little in front of the retina. As a result, the distant image is not seen clearly. Myopia may result from the eye itself being too long or the lens of the eye being too flat. In either case, the rays converge in front of the retina, and the nearsighted individual is likely to have difficulty making out distant objects.
>
> Janine Neumann, student

This neutral tone suits a popular explanation of a medical condition. The prose is businesslike and authoritative, the sentence patterns uncomplicated, and the person behind the words adequately concealed.

Other Types of Tone In persuasive writing, your tone will be determined by your purpose, your audience, the context of your writing, and your own attitude. In formal academic writing, your tone might be serious, subtle, and calm. In more personal writing, you might be quietly reflective, matter-of-fact, or lightly humorous. Sometimes a mock pompous or playful tone might be the best choice to win your audience over.

Every essay has combined characteristics that give it a special tone. The following excerpt conveys a sophisticated, rather formal tone.

> Unless you have led an abnormally isolated adulthood, the chances are excellent that you know many people who have at one time or another committed an act, or consorted with someone who was committing an act, for which they might have been sent to prison. We do not consider most of these people, or ourselves, criminals; the act is one thing, the criminality of it quite something else. Homicide, for example, is in our law not a crime; murder only is proscribed. The difference between the two is the intention, or to be more accurate, society's decision about the nature of that intention.

> Bruce Jackson, "Who Goes to Prison: Caste and Careerism in Crime"

The formal tone is suggested partly by words such as *consorted* and *proscribed* that do not form part of most people's word kits. The complexity of the first sentence and the varied patterns of the others add to the air of sophistication. The emphatic *quite,* meaning "entirely," is cultivated usage; and along with *society's decision,* it lends the tone a wry touch.

How is the serious and critical tone of the following passage brought out?

> Cans. Beer cans. Glinting on the verges of a million miles of roadways, lying in scrub, grass, dirt, leaves, sand, mud, but never hidden. Piels, Rheingold, Ballantine, Schaeffer, Schlitz, shining in the sun or picked by moon or the beams of headlights at night; washed by rain or flattened by wheels, but never dulled, never buried, never destroyed. Here is the mark of savages, the testament of wasters, the stain of prosperity.

> Who are these men who defile the grassy borders of our roads and lanes, who pollute our ponds, who spoil the purity of our ocean beaches with the empty vessels of their thirst? Who are the men who make these vessels in millions and then say, "Drink and discard"? What society is this that can afford to cast away a million tons of metal and to make a wild and fruitful land a garbage heap?

> Marya Mannes, "Wasteland"

Rhythm and word choice contribute equally to the tone of this passage. The excerpt opens with imagistic sentence fragments that create a panoramic word picture of littered roadways. Then complete sentences and sombre commentary follow. Words and patterns are repeated, mixing the dignified language of epic and religion with common derogatory terms—*testament, purity, vessels,* and *fruitful* set against *savages, wasters, defile,* and *garbage heap*—to convey the contradictions Mannes deplores. The rhetorical questions, used instead of accusations, add a sense of loftiness to her outrage, helping create a tone both majestic and disdainful.

> *Erethizon dorsatus,* an antisocial character of the Northern U.S. and Canadian forest, commonly called a porcupine, looks like an uncombed head, has a grumpy personality, fights with his tail, hides his head when he's in trouble, attacks backing up, retreats going ahead, and eats toilet seats as if they were Post Toasties. It's a sad commentary on his personality that people are always trying to do him in.

> R. T. Allen, "The Porcupine"

The tone of this passage is affectionately humorous. Allen sets this tone by noting the porcupine's tousled appearance, testy personality, and peculiar habits, such as eating outdoor toilet seats (for their salt content, as Allen later explains). The net effect is to personify porcupines, making them seem like the eccentric reprobate humans whom others regard with amused tolerance.

The next example begins by referring to "genuine love": the patience, sharing, forgiveness, trust, and acceptance necessary to reconcile Native cultures with the contemporary North American culture.

> The only thing that can truly help us is genuine love. You must truly love us, be patient with us and share with us. And we must love you—with a genuine love that forgives and forgets . . . a love that forgives the terrible sufferings your culture brought ours when it swept over us like a wave crashing along a beach . . . with a love that forgets and lifts up its head and sees in your eyes an answering love of trust and acceptance.
>
> Chief Dan George, "I Am a Native of North America"

This writing speaks honestly and passionately about love and reconciliation. Its most obvious rhetorical strategy is the personification of love. Love takes on human form when it "lifts up its head and sees . . . an answering love." This personification reinforces the basic humanity, mutual respect, and love that all people must recognize in each other for reconciliation to take place. The repetition of love throughout the passage reinforces the earnest emotional plea. Eloquence comes through parallelism, repetition, and words like *truly* and *genuine*. Vividness comes through the simile describing the impact of colonization on First Nations cultures as akin to "a wave crashing along a beach."

Like George Orwell, Mark Twain, Joseph Conrad, and other masters of tonal effects, Chief Dan George uses both rhythm and diction to create a tone that infuses and invigorates his message.

EXERCISE *Characterize the tone of each of the following paragraphs. Point out how word choice, sentence structure, rhythm, and other elements contribute to it.*

1. When I awoke, dimly aware of some commotion and outcry in the clearing, the light was slanting down through the pines in such a way that the glade was lit like some vast cathedral. I could see the dust motes of wood pollen in the long shaft of light, and there on the extended branch sat an enormous raven with a red and squirming nestling in its beak.

    The sound that awoke me was the outraged cries of the nestling's parents, who flew helplessly in circles around the clearing. . . . And he, the murderer, the black bird at the heart of life, sat there, glistening in the common light, formidable, unperturbed, untouchable. The sighing died. It was then I saw the judgment. It was the judgment of life against death. I will never see it again so forcefully presented. I will never hear it again in notes so tragically prolonged. For in the midst of protest, they forgot the violence. There, in that clearing, the crystal note of a song sparrow lifted hesitantly in the hush. And, finally, after painful fluttering, another took the song, and then another, the song passing from one bird to another, doubtfully at first, as though some evil thing was being slowly forgotten. Till suddenly they took heart and sang from many throats joyously together as birds are known to sing. They sang under the brooding shadow of the raven. In simple truth they had forgotten the raven, for they were the singers of life, and not of death.

Loren Eiseley, "The Judgment of the Birds"

2. The great economic scandal of our times isn't the dotcom crash or even the criminal culture of the corporate oligarchy. It's an economic system that measures the "goods" without the "bads." For every pound of pesticide, we count the bushels of corn but not the cases of cancer; we see the burgers without the obesity, the cows but not the cowshit.

James MacKinnon and Jeremy Nelson, Adbusters

3.　　Babe Ruth was *** The Sultan of Swat ***
　　Babe Ruth was *** THE BAMBINO ***
　　Babe Ruth was what you came to see!!!!
　　It was like going to a carnival, with Babe as both the star performer and the side-show attraction. Hell, that's what we called him: "You big ape." He was what a home-run hitter was supposed to look like. Wide, flat nose. Big feet. Little ankles. Belly hanging over his belt. All he had to do was walk on to the field and everybody would applaud. The air became charged with electricity. You just felt that something great was going to happen.
　　He'd twirl that big 48-ounce bat around in little circles up at the plate as if he were cranking it up for the Biggest Home Run Ever Hit—you felt that—and when he'd hit one he would hit it like nobody has hit it before or since. A mile high and a mile out. I can see him now, as I did so many times, just look up, drop the bat and start to trot, the little pitter-patter pigeon-toed, high-bellied trot that seemed to say, I've done it before and I'll do it again, but this one was for you.

Leo Durocher, Nice Guys Finish Last

SPECIAL STYLISTIC TECHNIQUES

The style of a piece of writing is its character or personality. Like people, writing can be many things: dull, stuffy, discordant, sedate, lively, flamboyant, eccentric, and so on. Figurative language and irony can contribute to your own distinctive writing style.

Figurative Language

Figurative language uses concrete words in a nonliteral way to create sharply etched sensory images that catch and hold the reader's attention. Besides energizing the writing, figurative language helps to strengthen the reader's grip on its ideas. Five figurative devices are especially important: simile, metaphor, personification, overstatement, and understatement.

Simile and Metaphor　A *simile* directly compares two unlike things by the use of *like* or *as*. "Todd is as restless as an aspen leaf in a breeze." "Her smile flicked on and off like a sunbeam flashing momentarily through a cloud bank." A *metaphor* also compares unlike things, but without using *like* or *as*. Some metaphors include a linking verb (*is, are, were,* and so on); others do not. "The moon was a wind-tossed bark" and "The curtain of darkness fell over the land" are both metaphors. Here is an excerpt that contains similes and metaphors:

> The field is a sea of deep, dark green, a sea made up of millions of small blades of grass blended together as one. Each blade is a dark green spear, broad at the bottom and narrowing to a needle point at the tip. Its full length is arched so that, viewed from one end, it looks like a shallow trough with paper-thin sides. On the inner side of this trough, small ridges and shallow valleys run from base to tip. To a finger rubbed across them, they feel like short, bristly hairs.
>
> Daniel Kinney, student

DISCUSSION QUESTIONS

1. Locate the similes in the above passage and explain how they help the reader.
2. Locate the metaphors and point out how each heightens the sensory impact of the writing.

Keep in mind that similes and metaphors must be used well to be effective. Writers too often snatch hastily at the first similes and metaphors that come to mind and end up strewing their pages with overused and enfeebled specimens. Johnny is "as blind as a bat," Mary runs around "like a chicken with its head cut off"—and the writing slips into "trite" gear. Other comparisons link items that are too dissimilar. For example, "The wind whistled through the trees like a herd of galloping horses" would only puzzle a reader.

Personification   *Personification* is a special sort of metaphor that assigns human qualities or traits to something nonhuman: a plant, an abstraction, a nonliving thing. Here are some examples:

> The vine clung stubbornly to the trunk of the tree.
>
> May fortune smile upon you.
>
> The waves lapped sullenly against the base of the cliff.

Each of these sentences assigns its subject a different emotional quality—stubbornness, friendliness, gloom—in a figurative rather than literal sense: Vines aren't stubborn, fortune doesn't smile, and waves aren't sullen.

Personification sometimes extends beyond a single sentence. To illustrate, in a humorous essay about the replacement of the stubby beer bottle in Canada by the long-neck beer bottle, the following passage personifies the short and stubby beer bottle as a proud, but unpretentious and egalitarian man.

> Mr. Long-neck will flop over like a bowling pin and, unless you've got a head on you like a tenpin bowling ball, Mr. Stubby will still be standing proud, if not tall.
> Stubby was unpretentious. No glamour, all function. Stubby was egalitarian. Millionaire or mooch, you got your brew in a stubby.
>
> Perry T. Jensen, "Lament for the Short and Stubby"

Personification works best when it is used in moderation and doesn't make outrageous comparisons. Dishes don't run away with spoons except in nursery rhymes.

Overstatement   *Overstatement,* sometimes called hyperbole, deliberately and drastically exaggerates in order to make a point. In his humorous essay contrasting the stubby and long-neck beer bottles, Perry Jensen writes:

> Time to take a stand, Canada. Let's demand the return of our national beer bottle, the stubby, and refuse to drink from foreign containers until the brewers come crawling on their hands and knees.
>
> Perry T. Jensen, "Lament for the Short and Stubby"

Overstatement may contribute to a humorous effect. If it is used sparingly in persuasive essays, it can sometimes add force and punch. Writers must be careful, however, not to lose credibility through excessive exaggeration.

Understatement   *Understatement* makes a quiet assertion in a matter-of-fact way, as when a sportscaster calls a team's 23–2 record "pretty fair." By drawing attention to the thing it appears to slight, this soft-spoken approach offers writers an effective strategy. Here is an example:

> To assume that Heidi Mansfield lacks the qualifications for this position is not unwarranted.

Without ever actually calling Mansfield unqualified, the statement suggests that she is. Similarly, when a meat company executive says, "It is not unlikely that beef prices will jump a dollar a kilogram in the next two months," we might as well count on spending another dollar. As these statements show, understatement not infrequently has an ulterior motive.

EXERCISE *Identify the similes, metaphors, personifications, overstatements, or understatements in these sentences.*

1. The old table greedily sucked up the linseed oil.
2. Russia's social and economic system is a giant staircase that leads nowhere.
3. Stanley has the bile of human meanness by the litre in every vein.

4. Their music sounds like the drumming of an infant's fists against the sides of a crib.

5. The foundations of our divorce are as strong as ever.

6. It is not unlike Muriel to be late.

7. You're the world's biggest liar!

8. "Fashion, though folly's child, and guide of fools, Rules e'en the wisest, and in learning rules."

9. Einstein's theories have had some impact on modern science.

10. I'm as tired as a farm horse at sunset.

Irony

Irony occurs when a writer intentionally states one thing but actually means something different or even opposite. The sportswriter who refers to the "ideal conditions" for a tennis tournament when rain has drenched the courts and forced cancellation of matches speaks ironically. In an article about government cutbacks, Charles Gordon uses irony to make a serious point:

> Welcome to Cutback World, ladies and gentlemen. We hope you enjoyed your flight. Sorry you had to walk so far in the rain, but spending reductions have made it possible for us to operate the same number of airplanes with fewer unloading ramps. You will notice complimentary newspapers on some of the seats of this bus. We hope you don't mind sharing them. While we wait to begin our tour, you might like to read some of the stories, just to get an introduction to the place we call home. If you turn to page 1, you'll see the little item about what we are doing for our homeless citizens. We have provided 300 beds for them in this city alone. According to the most recent estimates, this means that at least 10 percent of our homeless citizens will be able to find a bed tonight. So across the country, only 20 000 to 40 000 people are sleeping on the streets.
>
> Charles Gordon, "A Guided Tour of the Bottom Line"

The author never directly states that he disagrees with the government's spending reductions, but he uses details that highlight what he considers the injustice or absurdity of government spending cuts. When he states that "at least 10 percent" of the homeless have beds, he pretends to be congratulatory, but is in fact emphasizing the relatively tiny portion of the homeless population that has shelter.

EFFECTIVE STYLE: SAYING WHAT YOU MEAN

As you become conscious of your writing style, you can work toward more directness and clarity. When you revise, stay alert to diction flaws such as euphemisms, clichés, mixed metaphors, and sexist language, and eliminate any that you find.

Euphemisms

Euphemisms are sometimes used to evade unpleasant realities. Familiar expressions include *pass away* for *die, preowned* for *used,* and *sanitation engineer* for *garbage collector.*

In most cases, the writer simply intends to cushion reality. But euphemisms also have grisly uses. Companies don't fire employees; they *restructure* or *downsize.* Mobsters don't *beat up* merchants who refuse *protection* (itself a euphemism); they *lean on* them. Hitler didn't talk about *exterminating the Jews* but about *the final solution to the Jewish problem.* These euphemisms don't just blur reality; they blot out images of horror. Of merchants with broken limbs and bloodied faces. Of cattle cars crammed with men, women, and children en route to death camps. Of barbed wire and gas ovens and starved corpses in the millions.

Any euphemism, however well intentioned, probably obscures an issue. Although on occasion you may need one in order to protect the sensitive reader, usually you will serve readers best by using direct expressions that present reality, not a tidied-up version.

Clichés and Mixed Metaphors

Clichés   Clichés are expressions that have become flat and stale from overuse. They weaken your prose, because these oft-repeated words or phrases stem from patterned thinking. Dullness follows. It is natural that our early drafts will have the trite expressions that spring readily to mind, but when you revise, take the time to replace clichés such as the following, with fresh, evocative language.

acid test	burn the midnight oil	green with envy
better late than never	cool as a cucumber	rears its ugly head
black sheep	easier said than done	set the world on fire
blind as a bat	goes without saying	sick as a dog

Mixed Metaphors   Clichéd writing often suffers as well from mixed metaphors—inappropriate combinations that startle or unintentionally amuse the reader.

> When he opened that can of worms, he bit off more than he could chew.

Did you visualize someone chewing a mouthful of worms? Beware of mixed metaphors.

Inclusive Language

Inclusive language is language that respects all communities. It does not single out traits such as gender, sexual orientation, abilities, age, or ethnicity when they are not relevant to the context or topic at hand. Non-inclusive language is often inadvertently offensive as it may exclude some people, demean them, or assign them to limiting roles. As language evolves, it is best to use the descriptors that members of a particular community prefer. You can make non-inclusive language more inclusive by avoiding assumptions and making it more neutral.

Non-inclusive:	Please consult the chairman of your department.
Non-inclusive:	Anyone who wants a ticket should bring his money tomorrow.
Non-inclusive:	It's hard to find tradesmen these days.
Non-inclusive:	I'm hoping the mailman will bring me a surprise.
Inclusive:	Please consult the chair of your department.
Inclusive:	All those who want tickets should bring their money tomorrow.
Inclusive:	It's hard to find tradespeople these days.
Inclusive:	I'm hoping the letter carrier will bring me a surprise.

Note how, in each case, the sentence has been rewritten as gender-neutral.

EXERCISE *The following sentences are flawed by euphemisms, clichés, mixed metaphors, and non-inclusive language. When you have identified the faults, revise the sentences.*

1. Last summer, I was engaged in the repair of automobiles.
2. You're looking as bright as a button this morning.
3. There was a large amount of collateral damage in the war.
4. Any student wishing to attend summer school must pay her tuition one week before registration day.
5. My brother is in the process of pursuing a curriculum of industrial chemistry.
6. The ball's in your court, and if you strike out, don't expect me to pick up the pieces.
7. Winning first prize for her essay was a real feather in Peggy's cap.
8. Professional interrogation techniques were used in the war.

CHAPTER 7

Strategies for Personal Writing: Narration and Description

DRAWING FROM EXPERIENCE: NARRATIVE

> Clicking off the evening news and padding toward bed, Heloise suddenly glimpsed, out of the corner of her eye, a shadow stretching across the living room floor from under the drawn curtains.
>
> "Wh—who's there?"
>
> No response.
>
> Edging backward toward the phone, her eyes riveted on the shadow, she stammered, "I—I don't have any money."
>
> Still no answer.
>
> Reaching the phone, she gripped the receiver and started to lift it from its cradle. Just then . . .

Just now you've glimpsed the start of a *narrative*. A narrative relates a series of events. The events may be real—as in histories, biographies, or news stories—or imaginary, as in short stories and novels. The narrative urge stirs in all of us, and like everyone else, you have responded almost from the time you began to talk. As a child, you probably traded many stories with your friends, recounting an exciting visit to a circus or amusement park or an unusually funny experience with your pet. Today you may tell a friend about the odd happening in your biology laboratory or on the job.

Many classroom and on-the-job writing occasions call for narratives. Your English instructor might want you to trace the development of some literary character. Your history instructor might have you recap the events leading to a major war, or your sociology instructor could have you relate your unfolding relations with a stepparent or someone else. At work, a police officer may record the events leading to an arrest, a scientist recount the development of a research project, and a department manager prepare a brief history of an employee's work problems.

PURPOSE

A narrative, like any other kind of writing, makes a point or has a purpose. The point can either be stated or left unstated, but it always shapes the writing. Although some narratives simply tell what happened or establish an interesting or useful fact, most narratives go beyond merely reciting events. Narratives of history and biography delve into the motives underlying the events and lives they portray, while narratives of personal experience offer lessons and insights. In the following conclusion to a narrative about an encounter with a would-be mugger, the writer offers an observation on self-respect.

> I kept my self-respect, even at the cost of dirtying my fists with violence, and I feel that I understand the Irish and the Cypriots, the Israelis and the Palestinians, all those who seem to us to fight senseless wars for senseless reasons, better than before. For what respect does one keep for oneself if one isn't in the last resort ready to fight and say, "You punk!"?
>
> Harry Fairlie, "A Victim Fights Back"

ACTION

Action plays a central role in any narrative. Some writing tells about action that has happened offstage. Because it is fairly general, many gaps remain to stimulate the imaginations of readers:

> A hundred thousand people were killed by the atomic bomb, and these six were among the survivors. They still wonder why they lived when so many others died. Each of them counts many small items of chance or volition—a step taken in time, a decision to go indoors, catching one streetcar instead of the next—that spared him. And now each knows that in the act of survival he lived a dozen lives and saw more death than he ever thought he would see. At the time, none of them knew anything.
>
> John Hersey, *Hiroshima*

This passage suggests a great deal of action—the flash of an exploding bomb, the collapse of buildings, screaming people fleeing. However, because it does not recreate the action moment by moment, it does not pull the reader directly into the scene as the following narration does:

> When I pulled the trigger I did not hear the bang or feel the kick—one never does when a shot goes home—but I heard the devilish roar of glee that went up from the crowd. In that instant, in too short a time, one would have thought, even for the bullet to get there, a mysterious, terrible change had come over the

elephant. He neither stirred nor fell, but every line of his body had altered. He looked suddenly stricken, shrunken, immensely old, as though the frightful impact of the bullet had paralyzed him without knocking him down. At last, after what seemed a long time—it might have been five seconds, I dare say—he sagged flabbily to his knees. His mouth slobbered. An enormous senility seemed to have settled upon him. One could have imagined him thousands of years old. I fired again into the same spot. At the second shot he did not collapse but climbed with desperate slowness to his feet and stood weakly upright, with legs sagging and head drooping. I fired a third time. That was the shot that did it for him. You could see the agony of it jolt his whole body and knock the last remnant of strength from his legs. But in falling he seemed for a moment to rise, for as his hind legs collapsed beneath him he seemed to tower upward like a huge rock toppling, his trunk reaching skywards like a tree. He trumpeted, for the first and only time. And then down he came, his belly towards me, with a crash that seemed to shake the ground even where I lay.

George Orwell, "Shooting an Elephant"

Orwell's account offers a stark, vivid moment-to-moment replay of the shooting that readers can see in their minds' eye. A few words of caution are in order here. Action entails not only exotic events, such as the theft of mass-destruction weapons, then the ransom demand, then the recovery of the weapons and the pursuit of the villains; but a wide variety of more normal events also qualify as action, such as a long, patient wait that comes to nothing, an unexpected kiss after some friendly assistance, a disappointing gift that signals a failed relationship. Furthermore, the narrative action must all relate to the main point—not merely chronicle a series of events.

CONFLICT

The events in our lives and our world are often shaped by conflicts that need to be resolved. In narrative writing, conflict and its resolution, if any, usually motivate and often structure the action. Some conflicts pit one individual against another or against a group, such as a union, company, or religious body. In other cases, the conflict may be between a person and nature. Often the conflict is an inner one that involves clashing impulses inside one person's mind. In the following student paragraph, note how common sense and fear struggle within the writer, who has experienced a sharp, stabbing pain in his side:

Common sense and fear waged war in my mind. The first argued that a pain so intense was nothing to fool with, that it might indicate a serious or even life-threatening condition. Dr. Montz would be able to identify the problem and deal with it before it worsened. But what if it was already serious? What if I needed emergency surgery? I didn't want anyone cutting into me. "Now wait a minute," I said. "It's probably nothing serious. Most aches and pains aren't. I'll see the doctor, maybe get some pills, and the problem will clear up overnight. But what if he finds something major, and I have to spend the night in the hospital getting ready for surgery or recovering from it? I think I'll just ignore the pain."

Luis Rodriguez, student

POINT OF VIEW

Narrative writers may adopt either a first-person or third-person point of view. In first-person narratives, one of the participants tells what happened, whereas a third-person narrator tells the story from an outside perspective. Narratives you write about yourself use the first person, as do autobiographies. Biographies and histories use the third person, and fiction may employ either point of view.

In first-person narration, pronouns such as *I, me, mine, we,* and *ours* identify the storyteller. Often the immediacy of first person enhances reader identification. In contrast, the third-person narrator usually stays behind the scenes, quietly shaping events and selecting details. Although the use of third-person narration creates more distance between reader and characters, this narrator can move more freely in time and space. These two paragraphs show how first person narration may create more of a close-up perspective, while third-person narration takes a longer view.

First-Person Narration

After that I took the beer to the front verandah, and some bread and cheese for our supper to have with it, and I sat out there with Nancy and Jamie Walsh while the sun declined, and it became too dark to sew. It was a lovely and windless evening, and the birds were twittering, and the trees in the orchard near the road were golden in the late sunlight, and the purple milkweed flowers that grew beside the drive smelled very sweetly; and also the last few peonies beside the verandah, and the climbing roses; and the coolness came down out of the air, while Jamie sat and played on his flute, so plaintively it did your heart good. After a while McDermott came skulking around the side of the house like a tamed wolf, and leant against the side of the house, and listened also. And there we were, in a kind of harmony; and the evening was so beautiful, that it made a pain in my heart, as when you cannot tell whether you are happy or sad; and I thought that if I could have a wish, it would be that nothing would ever change, and we could stay that way forever.

Margaret Atwood, *Alias Grace*

As this example shows, first-person narrators refer to other characters in the narrative by using nouns and third-person pronouns.

Third-Person Narration

People driving by don't notice Spit Delaney. His old gas station is nearly hidden now behind the firs he's let grow up along the road, and he doesn't bother to whitewash the scalloped row of half-tires someone planted once instead of fence. And rushing by on the Island highway today, heading north or south, there's little chance that anyone will notice Spit Delaney seated on the big rock at the side of his road-end, scratching at his narrow chest, or hear him muttering to the flat grey highway and to the scrubby firs and to the useless old ears of his neighbour's dog that he'll be damned if he can figure out what it is that is happening to him.

Jack Hodgins, "Separating"

KEY EVENTS

Any narrative includes many separate events, enough to swamp your narrative boat if you try to pack them all in. Suppose you wish to write about your recent attack of appendicitis in order to make a point about heeding early warnings of an oncoming illness. Your list of events might look like this:

Awakened	Greeted fellow	Ate lunch
Showered	employees	Returned to work
Experienced acute	Began morning's	Began afternoon's
but passing pain	work	work
in abdomen	Felt nauseated	Collapsed at work
Dressed	Met with boss	station
Ate breakfast	Took coffee break	Was rushed to
Opened garage door	Visited bathroom	hospital
Started car	Experienced more	Underwent
Drove to work	prolonged pain in	diagnostic tests
Parked in employee	abdomen	Had emergency
lot	Walked to cafeteria	operation
Entered building		

A narrative that included all, or even most, of these events would be bloated and ineffective. Thus you need to be selective, building your narrative around key events that bear directly on your purpose. Include just enough incidental details or events to keep the narrative flowing smoothly, but treat them in sketchy fashion. The pain and nausea certainly qualify as key events. Here's how you might present the first attack of pain:

> My first sign of trouble came shortly after I stepped out of the shower. I had just finished towelling when a sharp pain in my lower right side sent me staggering into the bedroom, where I collapsed onto an easy chair in the corner. Biting my lip to hide my groans, I sat twisting in agony as the pain gradually ebbed, leaving me grey-faced, sweat-drenched, and shaken. What, I asked myself, had been the trouble? Was it ulcers? Was it a gallbladder attack? Did I have stomach cancer?

This passage does not simply summarize or tell that an event happened, but actively shows that an attack has occurred. Its details vividly convey the nature of the attack as well as the reactions of the victim. As in any good narrative, the writer communicates an experience to the reader.

DIALOGUE

Dialogue, or conversation, animates many narratives, enlivening the action and helping draw the reader into the story. Written conversation, however, does not duplicate real talk. When speaking with friends, we repeat ourselves, throw in irrelevant comments, use slang, lose our train of thought, and overuse expressions like *you know, uh,* and *well.* Dialogue that reproduced actual conversation would weaken any narrative.

Good dialogue resembles real conversation without copying it. It is selective, featuring economical sentences while avoiding the over-repetition of phrases such as *she said* and *he replied.* If the conversation unfolds smoothly, the speaker's identity is clear. To heighten the sense of reality, the writer may use an occasional sentence fragment, slang expression, or pause, as in this passage:

> Mom was waiting for me when I entered the house.
>
> "Your friends. They've been talking to you again. Trying to persuade you to change your mind about not going into baseball. Honey, I wish you'd listen to them. You're an awesome ballplayer. Just look at all the trophies and awards you've . . . " She paused. "Joe's mother called me this morning and asked if you were playing in the game on Saturday. Davey, I wish you would. You haven't played for two weeks. Please. I want you to. For me. It would be so good for you to go and—and do what you've always . . . "
>
> "O.K., Mom, I'll play," I said. "But remember, it's just for you."
>
> Diane Pickett, student

Note the mother's use of the slang expression "awesome" and of sentence fragments like "your friends" and "for me," as well as the shift in her train of thought and the repetition of "and." This casual, conversational style lends an air of realism to the mother's words.

Besides making your dialogue sound realistic, be sure that you also punctuate it correctly. Here are some key guidelines: Each shift from one speaker to another requires a new paragraph. When an expression like *he said* interrupts a single quoted sentence, set it off with commas. When such an expression comes between two complete quoted sentences, put a period after the expression and capitalize the first word of the second sentence. Commas and periods that come at the end of direct quotations are placed inside the quotation marks.

WRITING A NARRATIVE

Planning and Drafting the Narrative

Most narratives that you write for a composition class will relate a personal experience and will therefore use the first person, although you might use the third person if you are writing about something that happened to someone else. In either case, your narrative needs to make a point, or go somewhere. In your first draft, you may start describing how you violated a friend's confidence; as you keep writing or revise, a point may emerge—for example, you may uncover an idea about the ethical obligations of friendship. Later, as you revise, you can shape and select parts of the narrative that lead to this point in a more conscious way. To get started, do some guided brainstorming, asking yourself these questions:

> What experience in my life or that of someone I know would be worth narrating?
>
> What point does this experience illustrate? (Try to state the point in one or two sentences.)
>
> What people were involved and what parts did they play?

When you have pinpointed a topic, use further brainstorming to garner supporting material. Here are some helpful questions:

> What background information is needed to understand the events?
>
> What action should I include?
>
> What is the nature of the conflict? Was it resolved? If so, how?
>
> Which events play key roles, which are secondary, and which should go unmentioned?
>
> Would dialogue add to the narrative?

Before you start to write, you might sketch out a plot outline showing three or four significant events in your narrative. For each one, jot down what you saw, heard, or did, and what you thought or felt.

Use the opening of your paper to set the stage for what follows. You might tell when and where the action occurred, provide helpful background information, note the incident that activated the chain of events, or identify the problem from which the action grew. If you state your main point directly, you might choose to do it here, or you might want to save it for the conclusion.

The body of the narrative should carry the action forward toward a turning point. Develop the body around your key events. To help your reader follow the story, use time signals when helpful. Words, phrases, and clauses like *now, next, finally, after an hour,* and *when I returned* help the reader understand the sequence of events. Finally, think about how you can best use conflict and dialogue to heighten narrative interest.

The conclusion should tie up any loose ends, settle any unresolved conflicts, and lend an air of completion to the narrative. Effective strategies to think about include introducing a surprise twist, offering a reflective summary, noting your reaction to the story's events, or discussing the aftermath.

Revising the Narrative

As you revise, follow the guidelines in Chapter 5, and in addition ask yourself these questions:

> Have I made the point, stated or unstated, that I intended?
>
> Does all of the action relate to the main point, or is there irrelevant material I could cut?
>
> Is the conflict handled appropriately?
>
> Have I included all of the key events that relate to my purpose? given each the right emphasis? used time indicators where needed?
>
> Is my point of view appropriate?
>
> Does my dialogue ring true?

EXAMPLE OF A STUDENT ESSAY OF NARRATION

Tom Thomas and the Train Ride Home

By Chelsea Edwardson

He didn't say anything that changed my life. It was a random meeting on a train between two strangers, trading banalities about ourselves. But he was free of judgment, and that freedom gave me the chance to make my own decisions. Tom Thomas was a civil engineer and I was a high school drop out—we were worlds apart.

I didn't notice him at first. I had stubbed a half-smoked Camel on the platform, climbed aboard and found my seat, and he was sitting next to me. I smiled at him. He returned the smile and held out his hand.

"Tom Thomas."

"Chelsea," I replied. "Are you on vacation?"

"No, was just down here on business. But if you thought of vacation, I'm guessing you are?"

I laughed. "I just came down to visit my Auntie Maggie."

"All by yourself?"

"Yeah, sure. Why not?"

He didn't reply. He just quietly smiled in muted recognition that he too, had once been in my shoes.

"She smokes all day and has really bad arthritis, but she's an amazing artist. She has a big heart."

"I bet she does," he replied.

"She agreed to take me in for a while. I just had some thinking to do."

He nodded. I looked down into my bag at the pack of Camels.

"I'll be right back," I told him.

As I headed towards the smoking car, I pulled a stick out of my pack. Everything about it made me feel cool: the lighter's inscribed logo – "Route 66," the burning cigarette, being on my own, and travelling across the states. The Camels tasted bad but even that was kind of cool. I was in my element, surrounded by my kind of people. As I drew the smoke into my lungs, it helped me forget that I was restless, unsettled and questioning. In fact, I was so damn unsettled, I didn't even know what questions I was asking. I had always blown away the problems with smoke. Today it wasn't working. Unsatisfied, I stubbed the half-finished cigarette and headed back to my seat.

I found Tom with his eyes closed, peaceful as ever. I did everything I could not to wake him, but in my attempt to climb over him, my Camels fell out of my bag into his lap. He graciously told me that he was glad someone had woken him because he didn't want to miss the scenery. I still felt embarrassed.

"So, you were telling me about your Aunt Maggie. Did you enjoy your time? Did you find what you wanted?" he asked me.

"I didn't say I was looking." But this sounded too harsh. And untruthful. So I added, "but, I think so." I rocked my head up in down in contemplation. "Maggie is inspiring. She's started going back to school. I mean, that takes courage at her age."

"Well, at any age, really."

"True enough." I hadn't thought of that before. "She really got me thinking. You know much about math?"

"I'm an engineer."

"Well I'm not." I laughed. "I've gotta do it at some point though. No point in waiting till I'm 55."

"Why, is there something wrong with that age?"

"No, no," I laughed. "I didn't mean it in that way."

"I know," he confirmed with a smile. "But you're right. Why wait all that time to do something you're able to do now?"

I liked Tom because he didn't make me feel bad about my choices. And, at the same time, he didn't necessarily agree with them. He gave me space to think for myself.

"And what about the boys?" he said, lifting one of his thin eyebrows.

"What about 'em?"

He laughed. "Well, do you have a steady one?"

"Ah. Joel. Yes." Joel is okay, I thought to myself. My reflection peered back at me as I turned my head towards the window. Joel was always Joel. But, on the other hand, Joel was always going to be Joel—next year, ten years from now. My reflection caught my eye again but this time I noticed Tom in the background, still focused intently on me. I quickly turned my head back away from these thoughts and back towards him. "So yeah, things are good, you know? Whatever happens is going to happen, right?" He knew it wasn't a question and he let my words linger.

We continued talking for the next three days, until we came to his stop. He shared his wisdom, his stories and his blackened peppered halibut with me and I'll never forget for a moment what I gained. He never questioned me, but by learning his values, his integrity and how he lived, he made me question myself.

When it was time for him to get off the train, he looked at me as if he'd been saving it up the whole time and asked, "Chelsea, what are you going to do?"

I thought about it carefully but it was clear.

"I'm going to say goodbye to my Camels." I smiled. Sincerely. We hugged goodbye and I've never looked back except to remind myself of the future.

DISCUSSION QUESTIONS

1. Identify the point of view and tone of the narrative.
2. How does the writer use dialogue to carry the narrative? How does the writer identify the speakers without using too many tag phrases such as "he replied"?
3. This narrative spans about three days. At what points has the writer omitted events? Why?
4. What is the turning point in the narrative? What larger point does the narrative make? Is it stated or implied?

SUGGESTIONS FOR WRITING

1. Write a personal narrative about meeting someone who changed your life in a small way, or who helped you, without preaching, to find insight into yourself.
2. Write a narrative that shows how you were able to come to a decision that affected your direction—perhaps about dropping out of school or going back to school, or taking up or quitting a habit. **Keep in mind all the key narrative elements: purpose, action, conflict, point of view, key events, and dialogue.**
3. A *maxim* is a concise statement of a generally recognized truth. Noting the key elements above, write a personal narrative that illustrates one of the following maxims or another that your instructor approves:
   a. A little learning is a dangerous thing.
   b. The more things change, the more they stay the same.
   c. You'll catch more flies with honey than with vinegar.
   d. Don't judge a book by its cover.

DESCRIPTION: DRAWING FROM OBSERVATION

A narrative often blends in description of details and impressions and events to advance the storyline. Occasionally description stands alone as, for example, in a description of lab report procedures. Usually, however, description is a part of other kinds of writing such as histories, biographies, fiction and poetry, journalism, and advertising. Some descriptions create images and mood, such as when a writer paints a word picture of a boggy, fog-shrouded moor. Description can also stimulate understanding or lead to action. A historian may juxtapose the splendour of French court life with the wretchedness of a Paris slum to help explain the French Revolution. Vivid, telling descriptions of objects, persons, scenes, and events that appeal to the reader's senses can enrich your writing. For example, if you were writing a description of food cooking in a county fair, you might choose details that would appeal not only to the reader's sense of sight, but also to the reader's sense of hearing, taste, and smell, as well as touch. Consider the use of sensory impressions in the following description a student wrote about food at a county fair.

> The sound of hot dogs sizzling on a grease-spattered grill gave way to the whirling buzz of a cotton-candy machine. Fascinated, we watched as the white cardboard cone was slowly transformed into a pink, fluffy cloud. Despite their fibreglass appearance, the sticky puffs dissolved on my tongue into a sugar-like sweetness. Soon our faces and hands were gummed with a sticky mess.

Many occasions call for description. Your chemistry instructor might ask you to characterize the appearance and odour of a series of substances prepared in the laboratory; your art instructor might want you to describe a painting; your hospitality management instructor might have you portray an appealing banquet room. On the job, a realtor might write a glowing advertisement to sell a house; a nurse might describe the postoperative status of a surgical incision; and a journalist might describe the eruption of a volcano. All are attempts to capture the world through description.

SENSORY IMPRESSIONS

Precise sensory impressions begin with close physical or mental observation. If you can re-examine your subject, do it. If not, recall it to mind; then capture its features with appropriate words. Rather than piling on adjectives, look for an accurate verb; in the student narrative you read, the writer said that her "reflection *peered* back at her"—a simple, but evocative verb that suggests looking at something from the corner of one's eye. Sometimes a comparison can enrich your description. Ask yourself what your subject (or part of it) might be likened to. Does it smell like a rotten egg? a ripe cantaloupe? burning rubber? Does it sound like a high sigh? a soft rustle? It may take a few attempts to find the most accurate comparison that is not a cliché, but does not strain for novelty. Most descriptions blend several sense impressions rather than focus on just one. In the following excerpt, Mark Twain, reminiscing about his uncle's farm, includes all five. As you read it, note which impressions are most effective.

> As I have said, I spent some part of every year at the farm until I was twelve or thirteen years old. The life which I led there with my cousins was full of charm, and so is the memory of it yet. I can call back the solemn twilight and mystery of the deep woods, the earthy smells, the faint odors of the wild flowers, the sheen of rain-washed foliage, the rattling clatter of drops when the wind shook the trees, the far-off hammering of woodpeckers and the muffled drumming of wood pheasants in the remoteness of the forest, the snapshot glimpses of disturbed wild creatures scurrying through the grass—I can call it all back and make it as real as it ever was, and as blessed. I can call back the prairie, and its loneliness and peace, and a vast hawk hanging motionless in the sky, with his wings spread wide and the blue of the vault showing through the fringe of their end feathers. I can see the woods in their autumn dress, the oaks purple, the hickories washed with gold, the maples and the sumacs luminous with crimson fires, and I can hear the rustle made by the fallen leaves as we plowed through them. I can see the blue clusters of wild grapes hanging among the foliage of the saplings, and I remember the taste of them and the smell. I know how the wild blackberries looked, and how they tasted, and the same with the pawpaws, the hazelnuts, and the persimmons; and I can feel the thumping rain, upon my head, of hickory nuts and walnuts when we were out in the frosty dawn to scramble for them with the pigs, and the gusts of wind loosed them and sent them down. I know the stain of blackberries, and how pretty it is, and I know the stain of walnut hulls, and how little it minds soap and water, also what grudged experience it had of either of them. I know the taste of maple sap, and when to gather it, and how to arrange the troughs and the delivery tubes, and how to boil down the juice, and how to hook the sugar after it is made, also how much better hooked sugar tastes than any that is honestly come by, let bigots say what they will.
>
> Mark Twain, *Autobiography*

EXERCISE *Spend some time in an environment such as a cafeteria or a city intersection. Concentrate on one sense at a time. Begin by observing what you see; then jot down the precise impressions you receive. Now do the same for impressions of touch, taste, smell, and sound.*

DOMINANT IMPRESSION

Skilful writers select and express sensory perceptions in order to create a *dominant impression*—an overall mood or feeling such as joy, anger, terror, or distaste. This impression may be identified or left for the reader to discover. Whatever the choice, a verbal picture of a storm about to strike, for example, might be crafted to evoke feelings of fear by describing sinister masses of slaty clouds, cannon salvos of thunder, blinding lightning flashes, and viciously swirling wind-caught dust.

The following paragraph establishes a sense of security as the dominant impression:

> A marvelous stillness pervaded the world, and the stars together with the serenity of their rays seemed to shed upon the earth the assurance of everlasting security. The young moon recurved, and shining low in the west, was like a slender shaving thrown up from a bar of gold, and the Arabian Sea, smooth and cool to the eye like a sheet of ice, extended its perfect level to the perfect circle of a dark horizon. The propeller turned without a check, as though its beat had been part of the scheme of a safe universe; and on each side of the *Patna* two folds of water, permanent and sombre on the unwrinkled shimmer, enclosed within their straight and diverging ridges a few white swirls of foam bursting in a low hiss, a few wavelets, a few ripples, a few undulations that, left behind, agitated the surface of the sea for an instant after the passage of the ship, subsided splashing gently, calmed down at last into the circular stillness of water and sky with the black speck of the moving hull remaining everlastingly in its centre.
>
> Joseph Conrad, *Lord Jim*

The first sentence directly identifies the impression, "security," to which the "stillness" and the "serenity" contribute. Other details also do their part: the "smooth" sea, the "perfect circle" of the horizon, the "safe universe," the quick calming of the water, and the "moving hull remaining everlastingly" in the centre of water and sky.

EXERCISE *Go to a favourite gathering place on your campus or in your community and write a paragraph that evokes a particular dominant impression. Omit any details that run counter to your aim.*

VANTAGE POINT

Sometimes you need to write a description from either a fixed or a moving vantage point. A fixed observer remains in one place and reports only what can be perceived from there. Here is how Emily Carr describes a Native carving she encounters in a remote coastal village.

> Her head and trunk were carved out of, or rather into, the bole of a great red cedar. She seemed to be part of the tree itself, as if she had grown there at its heart, and the carver had only chipped away the outer wood so that you could see her. Her arms were spliced and socketed to the trunk, and were flung wide in a circling, compelling movement. Her breasts were two eagleheads, fiercely carved. That much, and the column of her great neck, and her strong chin, I had seen when I slithered to the ground beneath her. Now I saw her face.
>
> The eyes were two rounds of black, set in wider rounds of white, and placed in deep sockets under wide, black eyebrows. Their fixed stare bored into me as if the very life of the old cedar looked out, and it seemed that the voice of the tree itself might have burst from that great round cavity, with projecting lips, that was her mouth. Her ears were round, and stuck out to catch all sounds. The salt air had

not dimmed the heavy red of her trunk and arms and thighs. Her hands were black, with blunt fingertips painted a dazzling white. I stood looking at her for a long, long time.

Emily Carr, "D'Sonoqua"

A moving observer views things from a number of positions, signalling changes in location with phrases such as "moving through the turnstile" and "as I walked around the corner." Below, Michael Ondaatje takes us along with a young boy as he goes out of his home in winter.

One winter night when he was eleven years old, Patrick walked out from the long kitchen. A blue moth had pulsed on the screen, bathed briefly in light, and then disappeared into darkness. He did not think it would go far. He picked up the kerosene lamp and went out. A rare winter moth. It was scuffing along the snow as if injured and he could follow it easily. In the back garden he lost it, the turquoise moth arcing up into the sky beyond the radius of the kerosene light. What was a moth doing at this time of year? He hadn't seen any for months. It may have been bred in the chicken coop. He put the hurricane lamp onto a rock and looked over the fields. Among the trees in the distance he saw what looked like more bugs. Lightning bugs within the trees by the river. But this was winter! He moved forward with the lamp.

The distance was further than he thought. Snow above the ankles of his untied boots. One hand in a pocket, the other holding a lamp. And a moon lost in the thickness of clouds so it did not shine a path for him towards the trees. All that gave direction was a blink of amber. Already he knew it could not be lightning bugs.

Michael Ondaatje, *In the Skin of a Lion*

The phrase "walked out" tells the reader that Patrick is a moving observer. The lamp which Patrick carries reveals a progressively widening picture—first the moth, then the fields and trees, and then what look like lightning bugs. The reader, like Patrick, has no idea what the lightning bugs are until later, when Patrick gets to the bank of the frozen river, and sees skaters on the river holding flaming cattails.

Whatever your vantage point, fixed or moving, report only what would be apparent to someone on the scene. If you describe how a distant mountain looks from the perspective of a balcony, don't suddenly leap to a description of a mountain flower; you couldn't see it from your vantage point.

EXERCISE

1. **Writing as a fixed observer, describe in a paragraph your impressions of a place such as a hotel lobby, campus lounge, or waiting room. Be sure to indicate your vantage point.**

2. **Writing as a moving observer, describe in a paragraph or two your impressions as you shop for groceries, walk from one class to another, or cross a long bridge. Clearly signal your movements to the reader.**

SELECTION OF DETAILS

Effective description depends as much on exclusion as on inclusion. Don't try to pack every possible detail into your paper by providing an inventory of, for example, a room's contents or a natural setting's elements. Instead, select details that bring out the mood or feeling you intend to create. Read the following student description:

> At night, a restful stillness falls over the suburbs. . . . Everyone has vanished inside the carefully maintained homes that line the winding streets. The children have gone to bed, leaving the occasional motionless wagon or tricycle in the driveway. A light gleams in some bedroom windows. TV sets silently flicker a tranquil blue in a few living rooms. The street lamps curve protectively over the empty streets and sidewalks. The stillness is only disturbed by the brief, familiar bark of a neighbour's dog, quickly hushed, intensifying in its wake the silence that holds sway with the dark.
>
> Kim Granger, student

This writer evokes a mood of stillness focusing on quiet images such as "the occasional motionless wagon or tricycle," or the "TV sets [that] silently flicker a tranquil blue."

ARRANGEMENT OF DETAILS

Description, like any other writing, must have a clear pattern of organization to guide the reader and help you fulfill your purpose. Often a spatial arrangement works well. For example, you might move systematically from top to bottom, left to right, front to back, nearby to far away, or the reverse of these patterns. To describe Saturday night at the hockey game, you might start with the crowded parking lot, move into the bustling arena, and finally zoom in on the sights and sounds of the rink. Or if you wanted to highlight the surroundings rather than the central event, the order could be reversed. Going another route, you might start with some striking central feature and then branch out to the things around it. To capture the centre of a mall, you might first describe its ornate fountain illuminated with flashing, multicoloured lights, shift to the reflection of the lights on the skylight above, and end by portraying the surrounding store fronts.

Sometimes a description follows a time sequence. For example, a writer might portray the changes in a woodland setting as winter gives way to spring and as spring, in turn, yields to summer.

ETHICAL ISSUES IN DESCRIPTION AND NARRATION

Think how you'd react to a workplace supervisor who wrote a description or narrative about the development of a new product that exaggerated his role and minimized your crucial contribution to the result. Imagine a police description of an auto accident that misstated the length of a car's skid marks or failed to note the icy patches of road at the scene. It might cost a blameless driver a heavy fine and a steep increase in auto insurance premiums. Imagine your irritation if a going-out-of-business sale described as "fabulous" turned out to offer only 10-percent price reductions. Clearly inaccurate and misleading narratives or descriptions create undesirable consequences. Ask yourself these questions about your narratives and descriptions:

Have I provided a truthful account that participants will recognize and accept? Deliberate falsification of someone's behaviour that tarnishes that person's reputation is libel and could result in legal action.

Would the writing expose any participants to possible danger if it became public? Do I need to change any names in order to protect people from potential harm?

Does the narrative or description encourage unethical behaviour? For example, extolling the delights of using the drug ecstasy for a teenage audience is clearly unethical.

Would readers find my writing credible if they were at the scene?

Have I given readers adequate clues so they will recognize deliberate exaggeration?

You have an ethical obligation to present a reasonably honest, fair, and accurate portrayal of your topic.

WRITING A DESCRIPTION

Planning and Drafting a Description

If you're choosing your own topic, always select one that is familiar. Don't describe a ski run at Jasper National Park or the bridge from Prince Edward Island if you've never seen either one. Instead, opt for a place where you've worked or a locale you've visited. If you keep a journal, thumb through it for possible leads.

For each potential topic that surfaces, ask yourself the following questions. They will direct your attention to matters you'll need to address.

What do I want to accomplish by writing this description? Create one or more impressions? help the reader understand something? persuade the reader to act?

Who is my audience, and why would this topic interest them?

What dominant impression will I develop?

To help gather and organize support for your topic, ask yourself these additional questions:

What details should I include?

What sensory impressions are associated with each detail? (Jot down any words that you feel best convey the impressions.)

How does each detail contribute to the dominant impression?

What sequence should I follow in presenting my impressions? (Map out the sequence, setting up a 1-2-3 listing or possibly a paragraph-by-paragraph plan.)

After brainstorming a list of potential details, you might use branching (see page 42) to help you start accumulating sensory impressions. Here's how Kim Swiger, who wrote the passage below, used this technique:

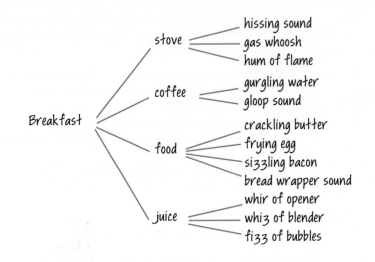

Begin your paper with an introduction that eases the reader into your topic. For example, you might provide a historical overview, ask a provocative question, or snare the reader's attention with an arresting statement.

Develop each major feature in one or more paragraphs. Present each feature in the order you've mapped out. To ensure that the reader follows your thoughts, clearly signal any shifts in vantage point or time. As you write, aim for vivid, original language. It is tempting to use clichés such as describing the "pitter-patter" of raindrops or the "fleecy white" clouds. Consider how the student below finds fresh language, especially strong verbs, to describe the sounds in her kitchen at breakfast time:

> Sure signs of a new day are the sounds in the kitchen as breakfast is prepared. The high sigh of the gas just before it whooshes into flame and settles into a whispering hum blends with the gurgling of the water for the morning coffee. Soon the gloop, gloop, gloop of the coffee sets up a perky beat. Then in mingles the crackle of creamy butter on a hot skillet and the shush of an egg added to the pan. Ribbons of bacon start to sizzle in the spitting grease. The soft rustle of plastic as bread is removed from its wrapper contributes to the medley. The can opener whirs, and the orange juice concentrate drops with a splat into the blender, which whizzes together the orange cylinder and splashed-in water. For minutes after the blender stops, bubbles of various sizes fizz.
>
> Kim Burson Swiger, student

End your paper by pulling your material together in some way. If you've created an impression or mood, you might offer your reaction to it. If you want to ensure that your reader understands the central message, you might spell it out. If you wish to persuade, you might urge some action.

Revising a Description

As you revise, apply the guidelines in Chapter 5 and ask the following questions:

Have I written with a clear sense of purpose and audience in mind?

Have I conveyed sights, sounds, the sense of touch or texture, tastes, or smells?

Have I evoked one dominant impression? Can I strengthen this impression by adding certain selected details? by eliminating details that detract from the impression?

Have I used an appropriate vantage point? If the observer is moving, have I signalled changes in location? Have I included only details that would be visible to the observer?

Have I arranged my details in an order appropriate to the topic?

EXAMPLE OF A STUDENT NARRATIVE THAT INCORPORATES DESCRIPTION

Beth's Finest Hour

Elizabeth Ferguson

1   Eating out is always funny for me; I never feel quite like myself. It might be because I drink so much water (they just keep refilling it) or maybe it is because there is always too much stuff (forks, menus, glasses, etc.) on the table. Often the chairs aren't that comfortable, the atmosphere is too noisy, and the temperature is rarely right. Sometimes it is because of who I'm with. As a result of my relative disorientation and discomfort, I never expect to say or do anything extraordinary while eating out, especially with strangers. I'm usually too preoccupied with clearing my space of all crumbs. I never would have expected that what I call my "finest moment" would occur while eating out.

2   It was the summer of 2002, and I was at my very first rehearsal dinner as my father, brother and I were playing the recessional song at my P.E. teacher's, Mr. Weins's, wedding. The dinner was at a nice restaurant in North Vancouver, and we were all seated at a long white table. I was sitting between Len (my brother) and my dad, but surrounded by strangers. Being a shy 15-year-old, I was feeling particularly self-conscious. I probably went to the bathroom three or four times during the meal just to escape, and also because I was drinking so much water.

3   During one of the moments that I was actually at the table the evening reached its pinnacle. I reached out for my wineglass full of water; however,

I wasn't looking when I reached, and didn't reach far enough. My hand collided with the glass and it started to tip toward the girls across from me. They saw and gasped in horror, the groomsmen saw and their eyes widened, my brother saw and felt sorry for me. I saw my life flash before my eyes . . .

After spilling water all over the Maid of Honour and the other girl, I run out in shame, followed by my father and brother—so ashamed of my unfortunate display that none of us can play at the wedding the next day. In his anger that they didn't have any music for the recessional, Mr. Weins punishes me by making me do squat thrusts and overhand serving drills in P.E. class for the rest of the year.

4   With the image of eternal squat thrusts and utter humiliation before me, the only way to save myself from said fate was quick action. As the falling glass reached a 65-degree angle and the water was about to overflow, I jetted my hand out at lightning speed, grabbed the wineglass by the neck and restored it to its proper position.

5   Silence reigned over the entire table.

6   And then . . . "Whoa! How did you do that? That was crazy! Did you teach her that?" (That last question was addressed to my P.E. teacher)

7   I sat in shock as all the groomsmen looked at me in awe and commented on my savagely fast reflexes. I saw a new future . . . .

LIGHTNING BETH FERGUSON, STAR GOALIE FOR TEAM CANADA, MAKES WICKED SAVES WITH HER SAVAGELY FAST REFLEXES
The next morning, when they interviewed me on Canada AM, *they asked to hear the tale, and then gave me that same strange look of awe after I told it.*

"But how did you do it?"

"I really don't know. It was an out-of-body experience."

Word got around, and before I knew it, my save was a hot topic in every news-paper and a picture of the moment was on every bus stop and billboard. Everyone wanted an interview with that crazy girl who changed an irrevocable fate in one magnificent swoop.

8   Maybe it was only that huge in my mind. My life didn't really change after that moment, but I still remember it vividly with great joy and pride, a moment that could have ruined my appreciation of eating out forever. Now whenever I'm sitting at a cluttered table, and I reach out for my glass of water, I remember the time the Lightning Beth Ferguson took over my body and those good-looking groomsmen looked at me in awe and amazement. Sometimes, I mention it to my brother, and he gives me that same look and says: "That was crazy." I smile, because I'm reliving the moment.

DISCUSSION QUESTIONS

1. Identify descriptions in this essay from fixed and moving vantage points. How is movement indicated?

2. Point out details that appeal to the physical senses and explain how they contribute to the atmosphere in the narrative.

3. How does the essay blend description and narration together? What larger purpose seems to guide the writer in the selection of details?

SUGGESTIONS FOR WRITING *Choose one of the following topics or another that your instructor approves for an essay of description. Create a dominant impression by using carefully chosen, well-organized details observed from an appropriate vantage point. Try to write so that the reader actually experiences your description.*

1. A walk in a forest
2. Your closet
3. An exercise class
4. A classroom when the bell rings
5. A shopping centre
6. A pet store or zoo
7. A busy city intersection
8. The view from your bedroom window
9. Getting caught in a storm
10. Your house after a party

The Critical Edge

Sometimes writers weave together information from different sources. When describing a childhood experience, you might supplement your own recollections by asking relatives and friends to supply details that you've forgotten or clear up points that have become hazy. A police officer investigating an accident questions witnesses and examines physical evidence, and then uses the findings to draft an accurate report.

Integrating material from several sources into a coherent piece of writing is called *synthesis*. When you synthesize, you reflect on ideas you have found in various sources, establish on your own the connections among those ideas, and then determine how the ideas and connections can advance the purpose of your writing. Thus, synthesis features independent thinking in which *you* evaluate, select, and use the material of others—which, of course, must be properly documented—to further your own purpose.

Although synthesis can be challenging and does call for judgment on your part, following an effective procedure can help ensure success. Start by jotting down the main points of information from your sources and identifying where those points agree. A friend's memory of your childhood experience may differ markedly from your own. A police officer may find that two witnesses disagree about how an accident happened. Because different people are likely to see and describe the same event, object, or place differently, you'll need to look for contradictions and weigh each perspective in order to assess credibility. Ask yourself what might have been left out in each account.*

SUGGESTIONS FOR WRITING

1. Read "Memories of Montreal—and Richness," (pages 152–154) "No Place like Home" (pages 363–367), and/or "I'm a Banana and Proud of It" (pages 245–247), and then write a descriptive narrative that relates an experience of a particular community or ethno-cultural group you know well. One of these essays may inspire you to bring in similar kinds of details or explore similar issues. If you would like to incorporate actual material from any of these essays, be sure that you understand the documentation conventions covered in Chapters 15–17.

2. Take notes from several different newspaper accounts of an important or controversial event and write an account of the event that includes your notes.

THE PERSONAL ESSAY: PROFESSIONAL MODELS

NARRATION AND DESCRIPTION READING STRATEGIES

1. Read the essay quickly to get a feel for the story and its main point.
2. Identify the main conflict that moves the story forward. Identify the major characters and what they may represent.
3. Don't get lost in the details. Note (possibly in the margins) the overall impression or mood the description is evoking.
4. Identify a thesis statement (possibly first or last paragraph) and/or a statement of purpose. Read the essay with an anticipation of what the description is intended to accomplish.
5. Read the narrative more slowly with the main point in mind. Keep an eye on how the narrative supports the main point.

---

*Because synthesis involves using several sources, including information from published ones, it is important to read the sections on research in Chapters 15 and 16 and those on handling quotations and avoiding plagiarism in Chapter 17. As always, follow your instructor's guidelines for documenting sources.

READING CRITICALLY

1. Consider whether the narrative would seem different if told from another person's point of view. Consider how a scene or event that is described might look very different from a different vantage point.
2. Examine what principle seems to have guided the selection of details. Has the writer created a certain mood or dominant impression by selecting certain kinds of details?
3. Ask whether the narrative really supports the author's main point. Consider what other possible perspectives or narratives could be included but are not. Would these contradict the writer's claims?

READING AS A WRITER

1. Identify the organizational pattern and decide whether it is the most effective arrangement for this piece of writing.
2. Determine the setting, conflict, characters, and development of the narrative. Note whether the writer gives enough information, or too much in places.
3. Notice any particularly effective movements in the plot. If you find a useful strategy, jot it down.
4. Observe how the writer uses dialogue. Make a note of any especially effective techniques.
5. Examine the essay for particularly effective examples of word choice.

Dan Greenburg

Sound and Fury

Dan Greenburg is a native of Chicago who holds a bachelor of fine arts from the University of Illinois and a master of fine arts from UCLA. A prolific writer, he has authored more than forty books, including such best-sellers as How to Be a Jewish Mother, How to Make Yourself Miserable, *and* How to Avoid Love and Marriage, *plus a series of more than twenty-four children's books,* The Zack Files. *His articles have appeared in a wide and diverse range of popular magazines and been reprinted in many anthologies of humour and satire. He has been a guest on* The Today Show, Larry King Live, Late Night with David Letterman, *and other major TV talk shows.*

1   We carry around a lot of free-floating anger. What we do with it is what fascinates me.

2   My friend Lee Frank is a stand-up comedian who works regularly in New York comedy clubs. Not long ago I accompanied him to one of these places, where he was to be the late-night emcee and where I myself had once done a stand-up act in a gentler era.

3   The crowd that night was a typical weekend bunch—enthusiastic, hostile and drunk. A large contingent of inebriated young men from Long Island had decided that a comedian named Rusty who was currently on stage was the greatest thing since pop-top cans and began chanting his name after almost everything he said: "Rus-TEE! Rus-TEE!"

This familiar expression comes from the title of a famous novel by William Faulkner, and is originally taken from Shakespeare's *Macbeth*: "[Life] is a tale/ Told by an idiot, full of sound and fury,/Signifying nothing." The reader may be intrigued: What does the title signify here?

The brief opening paragraph suggests a larger purpose and point for the story that is about to unfold. Paragraph 2 identifies who, when, where, and why. Paragraphs 2 and 3 set up tension, conflict, even suspense.

Sound impression

Touch impression

Time signal

Dialogue: The off-stage exchange between the writer and his comedian friend helps draw readers into the story.

Conflict arises in key event

Sight impression

His stance as a first-person observer allows the writer close positioning to the drama, as well as the distance to reflect on it from a somewhat detached point of view

Larger point of narrative: The reader draws a larger significance about men's "reservoir of rage" from this incident, thus remind-ing us of his larger point.

4   My friend Lee knew he had a tough act to follow.

5   Indeed, the moment Lee walked on stage, the inebriated young men from Long Island began chanting "Rus-TEE! Rus-TEE!" and didn't give him a chance. Poor Lee, the flop sweat running into his eyes, tried every trick he knew to win them over, and finally gave up.

6   When he left the stage I joined him at the bar in the back of the club to commiserate.

7   "You did the best you could," I told him.

8   "I don't know," he said, "I could have handled it better."

9   "How?"

10   "I don't know," he said.

11   As we spoke, the young men who'd given him such a tough time trickled into the bar area. One of them spotted Lee and observed to a companion that Lee might want to do something about their heckling.

12   Lee thought he heard the companion reply, "I'm down," a casual acknowl-edgment that he was willing to have a fistfight. Lee repeated their remarks to me and indicated that he, too, was "down."

13   Though slight of frame, Lee is a black belt in Tae Kwon Do, has had skir-mishes with three-card monte con men in Times Square, and once even cap-tured a robber-rapist. I am also slight of frame but have had no training in martial arts. I did have one fistfight in my adult life (with a movie producer), but as Lee's best friend, I assumed that I was "down" as well.

14   Considering that there were more than a dozen of them and only two of us, the period of time that might elapse between our being "down" and our being down seemed exceedingly brief.

15   The young man who'd made the remark drifted toward Lee.

16   The eyes of everyone in the bar shifted slightly and locked onto the two men like heat-seeking missiles. Fight-or-flight adrenaline and testosterone spurted into dozens of male cardiovascular systems. Safeties snapped off figurative weapons. Red warning lights lit up dozens of DEFCON systems; warheads were armed and aimed. In a moment this bar area might very well resemble a saloon in a B grade western.

17   "How ya doing?" said Lee, his voice flat as unleavened bread, trying to make up his mind whether to be friendly or hostile.

18   "Okay," said the guy, a pleasant-looking, clean-cut kid in his mid-20s.

19   I was fascinated by what was going on between the two of them, each feeling the other out in a neutral, unemotional, slightly bemused manner. I saw no hos-tility here, no xenophobic loathing, just two young males jockeying for position, going through the motions, doing the dance, willing to engage at the slightest provocation. I had seen my cat do this many times when a stranger strayed onto his turf.

20   And then I had a sudden flash of clarity: These guys could either rip each other's heads off now or they could share a beer, and both options would be equally acceptable to them.

21   I'd felt close to critical mass on many occasions myself. But here, feeling out-side the action, I could see clearly that it had to do with the enormous reservoir

of rage that we men carry around with us, rage that seethes just under the surface and is ready to be tapped in an instant, with or without just provocation.

22   "What're you in town for?" asked Lee casually.

23   The guy was watching Lee carefully, making minuscule adjustments on his sensing and triggering equipment.

24   "It's my birthday," said the guy.

25   Lee mulled over this information for a moment, still considering all his options. Then he made his decision.

26   "Happy birthday," said Lee finally, sticking out his hand.

> Turning point: Lee takes a risk by saying "happy birthday" since the words could be taken as provocative, but instead the potential confrontation is defused in this instant.

27   The guy studied Lee's hand a moment. Then, deciding the gesture was sincere, he took the hand and shook it.

28   "Thanks," he said, and walked back to his buddies.

29   All over the room you could hear safeties snapping on, warheads being unarmed. The incident was over, and in a moment it was as if it had never happened.

30   I felt I had just witnessed in microcosm the mechanism that triggers most acts of aggression, from gang fights to international conflagrations. It was so simple: a minor act of provocation. A decision on how to interpret it. Whether or not to escalate. And, in this particular case, a peaceful outcome. What struck me was how absolutely arbitrarily it had all been decided.

> The writer returns to the larger purpose of the essay—to get us to think about how we have choices in how we deal with conflict. The last sentence leaves readers thinking, perhaps wondering whether they might choose to de-escalate conflict when a potential crisis arises.

DISCUSSION QUESTIONS

1. Discuss the appropriateness of Greenburg's title.

2. Does this essay have a stated or an unstated point? If it is stated, indicate where. If it is unstated, express it in your own words.

3. The expression "our being down" occurs twice in paragraph 14. Explain what it means in each instance.

4. Discuss the effectiveness of the figurative language in paragraph 16.

5. In paragraph 21 Greenburg credits "feeling outside the action" for helping him understand the rage involved in this situation as well as in others. Explain what he means.

6. How often do you think that the "equally acceptable" options mentioned in paragraph 20 occur in confrontations?

TOWARD KEY INSIGHTS

What reasons can you give for the "free-floating anger" that Greenburg mentions at the outset of the essay?

How frequently and in what ways is this anger manifested?

What are some effective strategies for coping with this anger?

SUGGESTION FOR WRITING *Write a narrative about a small incident that turned into a serious confrontation. Possible incidents might include an improper or reckless action of another driver, a minor disagreement with a friend or spouse, or retaliation for an action at a sporting event. The outcome can be peaceful or otherwise. Make sure your essay makes a larger point that could be stated or implied throughout the essay.*

Moses Milstein

Memories of Montreal—and Richness

Moses Milstein was born in 1947 in Austria and grew up in Montreal. He received degrees from McGill University, Université de Montréal, and Guelph University. He now makes his living in British Columbia as a veterinarian and is a regular contributor to the North and West Voice. *In this essay, originally published in* The Globe and Mail, *Milstein recounts memories of growing up in Montreal. He reflects with subtle nostalgia on how his experience of urban, economic, and cultural diversity growing up in Montreal will not be duplicated for his son, who is growing up in a more homogeneous, upper-middle class area of Vancouver. The essay may prompt discussion of generational, class, or ethnic differences, or of gains that may entail losses.*

1   In the April of his youth, my son walks to school in a gentle shower of cherry blossoms. Down the slopes of West Vancouver's Hollyburn Mountain he can see the houses nestled among tall cedars. Bursts of rhododendrons guard the yards and over their tops he can see the sun glinting on the placid waters of Howe Sound. He walks through this serene neighbourhood unmolested, the quiet punctuated by the thwonk of tennis balls coming from cozy courts nearby.

2   And I blame myself.

3   In the April of my childhood in the Montreal of the fifties, the way to school was still studded with chunks of sandy moraine from winter's retreating ice. With the threat of blizzards gone, I could shed my heavy winter boots, and feel the sidewalk strangely close beneath the thin soles of my shoes.

4   The corners of our street, like every street then, were held by the four corner stores. The one we used, the "Jewish" store, could be counted on for an emergency box of matzohs, or kosher Coca Cola during Passover. Although Mr. Auerbach practically lived in his store, he did, in fact, go home at night. His French competitors across the street, though, lived amidst their crowded displays of potato chips, soft drinks and fly-paper rolls—cooking, sleeping, arguing, watching TV, just behind the curtain in the back of the store.

5   You could buy a tiny bag of potato chips for a penny. My mother insisted that it was filled with sweepings.

6   Around the corner was Wing Ling, the Chinese laundry, like all Chinese laundries painted green on the outside. Within, great vats seethed with steam where Mr. Lee and his family washed and ironed our sheets, which he would then hand to me in a package wrapped in brown paper and string.

7   Next to the laundry, across the alley, which ran like a sparkling river of broken glass and urine produced by the hordes of feral cats, giant rats and stumbling drunks who waded therein, was the Jewish Tailor. His narrow house, barely a door and a window wide, extended backwards from his work room and housed his wife and daughter, a sewing machine and a steam iron. An air of sadness, like the tape measure he wore around his neck, enveloped the place.

8   His old, thick-legged wife shared his melancholic mien. Their daughter was my age and wore braces on her legs. I often wondered whether they were her parents or her grandparents, so great was the difference in their ages. According to rumour, they were, like our family, survivors of the "Krieg," the Holocaust. The tailor and his wife had each had families of their own, children and spouses. They perished somehow, I don't remember the details. Every family I knew then had a story of death and they were all mixed up in my mind. In a DP camp after the war, the tailor met and married this woman and she was able to give birth to one more child, with crippled legs, and then no more.

9   I would rush by their sad house, and in one block was on St. Lawrence Street, noisy and bursting with commerce. Two long blocks before I reached my school.

10   My father worked on St. Lawrence Street at the Junior Trend Factory, which he pronounced "Jooniohtren." One April, when school was closed for Passover, I brought him his lunch. The elevator in his building passed floor after floor of angrily buzzing sewing machines. On some floors anonymous contractors were making clothes under other manufacturer's labels; on others I could see fancy offices where men with cigars, manicured fingers and pomaded hair struggled for ascendancy in the *shmatte* business.

11   My father worked among his friends from back home. They would usually greet me with jokes, smiles and much cheek-pinching. But when I saw them at their sewing machines their faces were closed and dark and they worked feverishly at piecework, sewing linings, sleeves, buttonholes under the critical eyes of the foreman. I left quickly.

12   Between these rows of tall, brown brick buildings, I would pass the restaurants that fed the workers. Delicatessens beckoned, their windows steamed from the smoked meat briskets waiting within, festooned with hanging salamis, rows of jars of pickled tomatoes and long banana peppers, green and red. Inside, the esteemed smoked-meat cutter stood resplendent on his pedestal, dispensing thick, greasy, spicy slices of meat onto golden rounds of rye bread. A good cutter was rumoured to be worth his substantial weight in gold and was held in reverential awe by my friends and me. Unhappily, the price of 25 cents, an hour's wages for my father, was beyond our reach.

13   The smells of the delicatessen mixed with the forest of urban smells welling out of each block—fruit stores, bakeries, taverns (for men only), poultry and egg stores, fish stores, bagel bakeries, steak houses, all of which would have me slavering until I reached that pinnacle of sensual delights, the Rachel Market. Here, the smells and sights merged as the French farmers, some able to speak Yiddish, backed their trucks up to the wide sidewalks where they set up their tables and displayed their produce. Beneath the market, down a spiral of stone steps slicked with blood, was a subterranean chamber of death. If you stood halfway down the stairs, you could see the hell waiting for the birds below. An open fire to singe

their pin feathers burned in an alcove. Hooks covered the walls from which the chickens were suspended by their feet while men in bloodied aprons cut their throats, drained their blood and plucked their feathers which floated in the air until they settled among the clots of gray droppings on the floor and walls.

14   Across the street, the large bakery, Richstones, held a secret known only to the few. On Fridays, if you went to the door at the top of the loading bays, you could ask for the seconds, the crumbled cakes, broken doughnuts, smeary cupcakes. Sometimes they would give you some and sometimes they would chase you away angrily. Another example of the incomprehensible capriciousness of adults.

15   As if to remind me of my destination, I would ultimately come to the offices of *Der Kanader Adler*, one of three local Yiddish papers. Occasionally, one of my teachers would publish a poem there, truly the last song of the Last of the Mohicans. The Jewish Peretz School was just around the corner on Duluth Street. We were educated in Yiddish, spoke to each other in English and lived in a French neighbourhood.

16   I can recall every building and business along the two blocks to school. Many of the proprietors knew me and my family. I felt as safe and happy on the streets as in my own home and would often linger until dusk on the return home.

17   When I grew up I bought a house in the gentle forests of the Pacific and my son walks to school among the cherry blossoms. And sometimes I am sad for him.

DISCUSSION QUESTIONS

1. What contrast does the writer introduce in the first three paragraphs? What details are especially effective in highlighting the contrast? Why do you suppose that the second paragraph is only one sentence long?

2. Point out sensory details that reflect sight, sound, taste, smell, touch. Comment on the effect of these sensory impressions.

3. What effect does the description of the Jewish Tailor (paragraphs 7–9), whose place was enveloped by "an air of sadness" have on you while you are reading?

4. An adult writer who is trying to evoke the reality of childhood experiences in the here-and-now often blends the child's perspective with the adult's. How does Moses Milstein reveal a kind of double perspective, as a child and an adult? Consider the fragment that ends paragraph 14, where the writer clearly uses vocabulary he would not have known as a child: "Another example of the capriciousness of adults." What does the writer mean here? Can you find other examples where the adult speaks for the child?

5. In the last paragraph, the father states that he is sad for his son sometimes, even though his son "walks to school among the cherry blossoms." What is the paradox here? Do you think the boy would understand if his father tried to explain to him that he was missing something?

6. Does this essay have a stated or an unstated point? If it is stated, indicate where. If it is unstated, express it in your own words.

TOWARD KEY INSIGHTS

What are the advantages of living in a place of cultural and economic diversity? Are there any disadvantages?

What are the possible losses and/or gains associated with moving away from the place where you grew up?

What does Moses Milstein reveal about the nature of parent–child relationships?

Whose childhood would you prefer—the father's or the son's? Explain.

SUGGESTION FOR WRITING *Create a sense of paradox by recounting a memory of a time or place that at first glance seemed far from perfect, but that has given you riches that you have come to appreciate.*

Lesley Hazleton

Assembly Line Adventure*

Lesley Hazleton (born 1945) is a native of England who earned a B.A. degree from Manchester University and an M.A. degree from the Hebrew University of Jerusalem before emigrating to the United States in 1979. Hazleton is a well-known automotive journalist with wide-ranging interests that include baseball, psychology, and politics. She has authored six nonfiction books, and her numerous shorter pieces have appeared in a variety of major newspapers and popular magazines. Our essay is excerpted from her book Driving to Detroit (1998). In it she describes her brief introduction to auto assembly line work and the lessons she learned from the experience.

1 I'd toured many auto plants before, and physically this was not much different. That is, it was an assault on the senses: an enclosed, windowless world of harsh artificial light and hard concrete floors ringing with the discordant cacophony of industrial production. Metal rang on metal. Stamping presses clanked, power tools whined, pulleys groaned, hoists clanged, welding robots whooshed, sparks crackled, lasers beeped, compressed air hissed, bolts banged into place, trolleys rumbled down the aisles, and all the while, conveyor belts carrying cars in one stage or another of production, from bare metal frames to fully painted bodies, clattered and clanketed beside us and behind us and even over our heads.

2 At five in the afternoon, I started work, joining three other workers stationed around a huge rotating machine. Our job was to feed a robot.

3 Officially, we were preparing dashboard molds for foam injection. In fact, we were simply loading and unloading the machine for the robot, which injected the foam and then wiped its own nozzle as though it were wiping its nose—one of those infuriatingly human gestures that make you think, "Cute," and then hate yourself for having thought it.

*Editors' title.

4   This was one of the simplest tasks on the whole assembly line. Squirt some filler release into a hole. Lift a light plastic mold and place it on a protruding lip of the machine. Bang a board with your knee to drop three locks to hold the mold in place. Check the locks. Push a black button to bring the lip down into the right position for the next guy. Wait for the machine to rotate and present you with a new lip. And that was it. A ten-second job to be repeated ad infinitum.

5   Two hours later, I moved from one of the simplest jobs on the line to one of the most complicated: assembling the whole instrument panel. Steering wheel, indicator and wiper wands, gauges, dashboard line, the lot.

6   Audrey, the woman whose task it was to teach me this job, had a tough challenge ahead of her.

7   I guessed she was in her mid-thirties. Despite a mass of long brown curly hair, she had a boyish way to her, maybe because of the leather builder's apron she was wearing, its pockets so full of connectors and screws and bolts that it took me a while to realize she was six months pregnant.

8   "Is this your first?" I asked.

9   She burst out laughing. "Honey, I'm forty-three years old. And a grand-mother. I married again not long ago, and"—she spread her arms wide and stared at her belly—"just look what happened. This sure is the last thing I ever expected."

10   "How long will you go on working?"

11   She laughed again. "Do you know how much kids cost? I'm staying right here till the day I pop."

12   She hadn't stopped working for a moment as we talked. She couldn't. The line was rolling, and it was either keep up or bring everything to a halt. We were standing *on* the line, a wide conveyor belt rumbling past an array of shelves piled high with parts, and beneath an overhead rack dangling power tools and bins of screws. On the line with us, every six feet or so, was a workstand holding an empty dashboard shell, placed upside down on the stand so that it was easy to work on. Audrey's job was to make it into a complete instrument panel.

13   For the first few moments, standing on the moving belt was almost childishly fun. The world was reversed: you stood still and it went past you. Your mind knew it was you moving, not the world, but your senses told you otherwise. And all the time, the belt vibrated gently underfoot; if it weren't for the noise, it might even have been pleasantly sexy.

14   "Watch your head," Audrey said, and I ducked as a power wrench came dan-gling past my right ear. Followed by another. And yet another. Even though I reminded myself that it was me moving, not them, every time I looked up they seemed to be aiming for my brains with a certain inexorable malevolence.

15   I spent the first half-hour watching Audrey and figuring out how to stay out of the way. So far as I could make out, she had a total of some fifty separate proce-dures to complete in a logic-defying sequence of about three minutes. Each step had to be performed in perfect timing, so that the right parts and tools were at hand exactly when she needed them. And to add to the pressure, this job was what they called a "show-stopper."

16   Farther on down the line, the completed instrument panel would be lowered into the "smile joint"—a large lazy U going from side to side of the car's frame. If

it didn't fit, the line would stop, and the whole plant would start running behind. "You can't go back and do it again," Audrey said. "You got to do it perfect the first time."

17   I knew I'd never be able to do this job. Yet Audrey seemed convinced that I was educable. She talked each movement out loud as she worked, with me following her around like a pet dog. Somehow, she convinced me to do a bit here and a bit there, until within an hour, I had the beginning of it down pat:

18   Walk six stands down the line, past other team members at different stages of the job, and read the manifest hanging on the dashboard shell. Pick up different parts from the shelves alongside the line, depending on whether this is to be a sedan or a wagon, an automatic or a manual shift. Jam a leather sheath over the sharp metal edge to the side of the module. Ease the parts into place. Snap-connect electrical wires: gray to the right, blue to the middle, white to the left.

19   So far so good. I was feeling quite proud of myself. Trouble was, this was only the beginning of the beginning.

20   The rest began to blur: Snap-connect a black fastener, then a yellow one. Don't delay. If you go too slow, the line will take you past the parts you need, and you'll have to start running back and forth for them. Pick up the steering shaft from a shelf and ease its thirty-pound weight down through the center of the module. Arrange the wires to run over the top of the shaft. Slip on and snap a green fastener . . .

21   Or were those last two steps the other way round? "Here," said Audrey, redoing my work.

22   Okay, now pick up two bronze-colored bolts and screws, two black bolts, a circular piece, and two silver bolts from those big bins alongside the line. Insert the silver bolts. Fine. Place the bronze-colored ones in one place, the black ones in another. Great. Pull down a power wrench from the overhead line . . .

23   I grabbed for it and missed. It began to recede from me. I stretched and yanked it down just in time to tighten the bolts. I had no idea of what I was bolting to what, or why. Neither, it turned out, did Audrey.

24   Right, you've got those bolts nice and tight. Now pick different bronze-colored bolts from another bin. No, not alongside the line—right here, hanging overhead. Fine. Insert them and tighten them by hand for now. What about the wrench? Not there yet, that comes soon. First, thread the electrical wires through the back of the module and out through this flap, then loop them over and under the shaft like so, and then . . .

25   Then what? I couldn't remember. And I was only a third of the way through the job.

26   "Don't worry," said Audrey. "It takes most people four days to learn this job. You're doing real good."

27   That was sweet of her, but it didn't feel real good to me. My attention strayed for a moment, I lost a beat, and suddenly the power tools and screw bins were bearing down on me way before I was ready for them. I worked as fast as I could, one eye on my hands, the other on the dangling wrench going past. I swore, lunged for it, and yanked at the cord as though if I pulled hard enough I could pull back the whole line and slow things down to my pace. I remembered Charlie Chaplin's desperation in *Modern Times*, and suddenly there was nothing remotely

funny about it. I dropped a bolt, reached for the wrong wrench, and watched pathetically as Audrey stepped in and put everything to rights. I hadn't felt quite this incompetent since I was a kid trying to thread a sewing machine at school. I never did master that.

28   Every time I thought I had the hang of it all, another two steps somehow reversed themselves in my mind, or one slipped out of existence altogether. My ears were ringing, my mind was reeling, and my hands had never felt clumsier. I began to fumble the screws, inserting them at an angle so that they wouldn't tighten properly and had to be taken out and inserted anew. Audrey was working as hard as I was by now; we stood shoulder to shoulder, me fouling things up, her fixing them.

29   And suddenly it was ten o'clock, and there was a half-hour break for lunch. Ten at night, that is. By now, I was squinting to stop from seeing double. I was convinced that if I could just work through to the end of the shift, I'd get this job down pat. But as the line came to a halt and everything stopped moving, some remote part of my brain managed to signal a weak but just decipherable message that the pressure was getting to me. It was time to call it quits before I damaged a car, or myself, or worse still, somebody else.

30   "Don't you want some lunch before you go?" said Audrey. But I was too exhausted to even look at food. I needed fresh air. And solitude. And silence. I made my excuses, stuffed my yellow Kevlar gloves into my pocket as a memento, got lost twice trying to find the way out, and finally emerged into the parking lot.

31   Never had a parking lot seemed so beautiful: so quiet, so peaceful, so serene. Even the buzzing yellow of the sodium vapor lights seemed soothing. Behind me, the plant hummed gently, its skylights glowing into the night. Mid-shift, I was the only person out here, and I had a flash of guilt mixed with giddy freedom, the kind that comes from playing hooky.

32   I found the truck, climbed in, made to start it up. Then stopped, hand in midair, and sat staring at the instrument panel. Something was wrong. I took a moment to figure it out: I'd spent the past few hours working on upside-down instrument panels, and now I was seeing this one the right way up.

33   I reached out and examined it for its component parts, thinking of the man or the woman who'd put it together, and appreciating the way it had been done. This thing I usually took so for granted that I'd never before paid a moment's attention to it, was now an astounding piece of man-made—woman-made—complexity.

34   I started the truck and drove slowly out of the lot, wondering how long I'd keep this awareness that cars are not merely machines, but things put together by human beings, products of real men and real women doing the kind of work that would drive most people crazy. Not long enough, for sure.

DISCUSSION QUESTIONS

1. Comment on the effectiveness of the essay's title.

2. Which of the five sensory impressions does Hazleton include? Refer to specific paragraphs when answering.

3. What is the dominant impression of this essay?

4. What time signals does Hazleton use? Refer to specific paragraphs when answering.

5. This description takes the form of a narrative with the action moving forward until a turning point is reached. Where does this turning point occur?

6. Identify the conclusion of the essay and what it accomplishes.

7. After reading Hazleton's description, how do you think you would tolerate working on an assembly line as a summer job? Discuss.

TOWARD KEY INSIGHTS

What jobs have you done or heard about that you would consider unbearable? What characteristics make them unbearable? How might these jobs become more tolerable after a while? Use examples.

What jobs have you done or heard about that you would find enjoyable? What characteristics make them enjoyable?

SUGGESTION FOR WRITING *Write an essay describing your introduction to a difficult new job that left you feeling overwhelmed. Use an appropriate number of sensory details that create a dominant impression and lead to a larger point about some insight you gained.*

CHAPTER 8

Strategies for Using Illustration: Making Yourself Clear

"It doesn't pay to fight City Hall. For example, my friend Josie . . . "

"Many intelligent people lack common sense. Take Dr. Brandon . . . "

"Predicting the weather is far from an exact science. Two winters ago, a surprise snowstorm . . . "

Have you ever noticed how often people use *illustrations* (examples) to clarify general statements?

Ordinary conversations teem with "for example . . . " and "for instance . . . ," often in response to a furrowed brow or puzzled look. Diana Krall serves as an excellent example of a singer with broad appeal, and West Edmonton Mall illustrates a multipurpose mall. Teachers, researchers, and writers often present an abstract principle or natural law, then supply concrete illustrations or examples to bring it down to earth. An economics instructor might illustrate compound interest with an example showing how much one hundred dollars earning five percent interest would appreciate in ten years. Examples can also persuade, as when advertisers trot out typical satisfied users of their products to induce us to buy.

Personal writing, business writing, and more formal academic writing are enlivened with the use of illustration. Writing a personal essay about the effects of stress, you might draw examples from personal experience or observation. Writing a more formal research essay about the effects of stress, you will probably include examples from psychological or medical research studies.

A business student writing a paper on effective management may include examples of successful managers and how they operate. A paper defining democracy for a political science course may offer several examples of several democratic governments. In a literature class, a writer illumines the concept of irony with specific examples from stories or poems. At work, writers also use illustration to clarify ideas and support their claims. A teacher asking for more counselling staff might describe particular students who need help but can't get it. An advertising copywriter urging that new copiers be bought might mention different instances of copier breakdown and the resulting delays in customer service. A union steward wanting a better company safety program might call attention to several recent accidents.

Pictures, images, and concrete examples help readers grasp ideas that might otherwise seem too abstract, too general and disembodied.

SELECTING APPROPRIATE EXAMPLES

Make sure that your examples actually support the points that you are trying to make. Sometimes in a first draft, writers get sidetracked with intriguing side issues. For instance, in making the point that the lyrics in a rap group's latest CD were not in good taste, a writer might begin ranting about the thuggish lifestyle of one of the singers. In a revision, however, that writer should substitute more relevant material to support the thesis—excerpts from several song lyrics that illustrate the writer's claim.

Furthermore, ensure that your examples display all the chief features of whatever you're illustrating. Don't offer Avril Lavigne as an example of a singer with broad appeal unless you know she has many different kinds of fans. Alternatively, consider this example of a hacker, a compulsive computer programmer:

> Bob Shaw, a 15-year-old high-school student, is a case in point. Bob was temporarily pulled off the computers at school when he began failing his other courses. But instead of hitting the books, he continues to sulk outside the computer center, peering longingly through the glass door at the consoles within.
>
> Pale and drawn, his brown hair unkempt, Bob speaks only in monosyllables, avoiding eye contact. In answer to questions about friends, hobbies, school, he merely shrugs or mumbles a few words aimed at his sneakered feet. But when the conversation turns to the subject of computers, he brightens—and blurts out a few full sentences about the computer he's building and the projects he plans.
>
> Dina Ingber, "Computer Addicts"

Clearly, Bob Shaw fits Ingber's description of hackers as programmers who have "a drive so consuming it overshadows nearly every other part of their lives and forms the focal point of their existence."

NUMBER OF EXAMPLES

How many examples do you need? One long one, several fairly brief ones, or a large number of very short ones? Look to your topic for the answer. To illustrate the point that a good nurse must be compassionate, conscientious, and competent, your best bet would probably be one example, since one person must possess all these traits.

When dealing with trends, however, you'll need several examples. To show that parents have been raising children more and more permissively in the last few decades, at least three examples are called for: one family from an earlier time around 1970, a second from about 1990, and a third from the present time. Sometimes topics that do not involve trends require more than one example, such as when you demonstrate the sharp differences between Canadian and American attitudes toward handgun registration, health care, or the decriminalization of marijuana.

Finally, some topics require a whole series of examples. If your thesis is that many everyday expressions have their origins in the world of gambling, you'll need many examples to demonstrate your point.

EXERCISE

1. **Choose one of the following topic sentences. Select an appropriate example and write the rest of the paragraph.**

   a. Sometimes a minor incident drastically changes a person's life.

   b. _____'s name exactly suits (her/his) personality.

   c. I still get embarrassed when I remember _____.

   d. Not all education goes on in the classroom.

   e. I learned the value of _____ the hard way.

2. **Explain why you would use one extended illustration, several shorter ones, or a whole series of examples to develop each of the following statements. Suggest appropriate illustrations.**

   a. Many parents I know think for their children.

   b. More and more people are trying to buy local food and products.

   c. The ideal vacation is not what it used to be.

   d. Different university students manage their expenses in different ways.

   e. The quality of youth hostels ranges from excellent to shabby.

ORGANIZING THE EXAMPLES

A single extended example often assumes the narrative form, presenting a series of events in time sequence. To illustrate a trend, sets of examples also rely on chronological ordering, moving either forward or backward in time. This arrangement would work well for a paper on the growing permissiveness in childrearing.

On the other hand, a paper showing that different people exhibit a certain characteristic to different extents would logically be organized by order of climax (from the least to the greatest extent) or perhaps the reverse order. To demonstrate how sales clerks differ in their attitudes toward customers, you might first describe a hostile clerk, then a pleasant one, and finally an outstandingly courteous and helpful one.

Large numbers of examples might first be grouped into categories, and the categories then arranged in a suitable order. For example, if you were writing a paper on types of expressions associated with casino games, you might group together expressions from table games, electronic gaming machines, and random number games. Within each paragraph, you might move from older to newer expressions, or from common expressions to less common ones. Depending upon the specific categories, one arrangement may or may not be preferable to another.

ETHICAL ISSUES

In writing an illustration, we try to show readers something truthful about our understanding of the world. They wouldn't read what we have written if they suspected we were unusually careless in our thinking, or if they thought we were trying to deceive them by skewing our evidence or distorting our examples. For example, parents trying to talk their teenager out of a career in acting would probably cite only examples of failed or struggling performers; but such a distortion isn't fair to the acting profession—or honest to the teenager. Moreover, some distortions can be outright lies. In past debates about welfare, some commentators cited examples of people who were living like millionaires while on welfare. It turned out that the examples were falsified, and no real instances of such massive abuse could be found. To help avoid distortion and deception in examples, ask yourself the following questions:

- Have I given adequate thought to the point I'm making and the examples I'm using?
- Are the examples truthful and representative, or are they slanted and one-sided?
- Could my illustrations have harmful consequences? Do they stereotype an individual or group or harm someone's reputation unjustly?
- Will my examples promote desirable or undesirable behaviour?

WRITING AN ILLUSTRATION

Planning and Drafting the Illustration

If you are writing a paper that draws from personal experience or observation, you could do some freewriting to uncover possibilities for a starting point. Perhaps you will decide to write about something you know well, such as experiences related to school, work, or family life. If you are writing a more formal paper, you can get ideas from reading, as well as from talking to others.

You can begin your illustration paper at either end of the telescope—with the larger point you are trying to make, or with the smaller examples that take you and the reader to a larger point that crystallizes as you write. Ideas for illustrations can be chosen beforehand or can emerge as you write. Even without a clear point-by-point outline or plan, you might begin writing about a vivid personal memory. Then, as you reread your writing, you may see that your central message has to do with learning to accept people rather than trying to change them. Finally, in your revision, you can reshape your paper, editing, deleting, and developing it so that the illustration clearly relates to your larger point.

However, if you prefer to begin with the larger point that you want to make, evaluate your ideas with these questions:

Exactly what point am I trying to make? (Write it down in precise terms.)

Why do I want to make this point? To show how bad something is? To encourage something? To scare people into or away from something?

Who is my prospective audience?

Should I use one extended example, or will I need more? Why?

Once you've picked your topic, ask yourself, "What example(s) will work best with my audience?" Then brainstorm each one for supporting details. Consider using a chart patterned after the one below to help you.

Example 1	**Example 2**	**Example 3**
First supporting detail	First supporting detail	First supporting detail
Second supporting detail	Second supporting detail	Second supporting detail

Review your details carefully and add any new ones you think of; then make a new chart and re-enter the details into it, arranged in the order you intend to present them.

Your introduction should identify your topic and draw your reader into the paper. If you're illustrating a personal belief, you might indicate how you developed it. If you're trying to scare the reader into or away from something, you might open with an arresting statement.

Present your examples in the body of your paper, keeping your purpose firmly in mind as you plan your organization. If you have many brief examples, perhaps group them into related categories for discussion. If you're dealing with a few relatively brief examples—say, to show a trend—you will likely put each in its own paragraph. For a single extended example, use the entire body of the paper, suitably paragraphed. Thus, an extended example of someone who is an ideal teacher might include paragraphs on the person's knowledge and passion for the subject, style of classroom delivery, and relationships with students.

Conclude in whatever way seems most appropriate. You might recommend that the reader do something, or you might issue a personal challenge that grows out of the point you've illustrated.

Revising the Illustration

Think about the following questions and the general revision guidelines from Chapter 5 as you revise your paper:

Exactly what idea am I trying to express? Have I used the best examples to support it?

Do my examples illuminate my idea without introducing irrelevant material?

Are my examples interesting?

Have I used an appropriate number of examples?

Have I organized my paper effectively?

EXAMPLE OF A STUDENT ESSAY OF ILLUSTRATION

If It Is Worth Doing . . .

Janice Carlton

1   Everyone should keep a slogan in his or her back pocket to pull out at difficult times. Mine may seem a bit ridiculous, but I have found it to be a lifesaver: "If it is worth doing, it is worth doing badly." This slogan turns my parent's phrase—If it is worth doing, it is worth doing well—completely upside down. To be clear, I am not suggesting that anyone should deliberately do things badly. No one wants to be operated on by a surgeon whose hand shakes. Hopefully, accountants know their subject and offer sound advice. Still, some activities are so worth doing that the fact that we might do them badly is no reason not to take up the task. Far too often we are tempted to give up art because our paintings are bad, avoid writing because our spelling is poor, or avoid helping a friend build a pole barn because we might make mistakes. My slogan reminds me that my possible failure is no reason to avoid a worthwhile project.

2   Consider singing for a moment. Singing can be tremendous fun. A good song can lift the heart. Singing with others can offer a delightful sense of sharing. My only problem is that I have a terrible voice. It cracks, soars when it should sink, and rises when it should drop. Usually, I hit the right pitch, but

sometimes I have to wiggle into it as though it were a pair of excessively tight jeans. My more musically gifted friends usually cringe when they hear me sing and mutter something under their breath about "the tone-deaf." Should I stop singing just because I do it badly? To me, I sound like a great rock singer, at least when I sing in the shower. Sometimes I sing while I walk from class to class, and I feel, as a result, that I am in an exciting musical. I can even sing with my friends, who only insist that I sing a little more quietly and try, try, try to stay in tune. Probably it would be unfair of me to log in hours at a Karaoke bar, and I usually keep from singing around those who tend to stuff their fingers in their ears. But, with some reasonable precautions, the fact that I sing badly should not prevent me from enjoying the obvious pleasures of singing.

3   Writing poetry is another practice that is worth doing even if we do it badly. What makes poetry worth writing? Writing poetry involves taking time out of the rush of life to reflect on what you're feeling, to perceive more clearly, to hunt for the right word. When it works, you feel like everything in your life has come together.

> As I raced through the forest,
> I stopped to smell a flower,
> A violet, perhaps, a purple pause
> Between home and grandmother's house.
> The flower didn't have any smell,
> But that didn't matter any.
> For a moment, I contemplated
> The breath of a flower,
> And avoided, in the process,
> Meeting any unexpected wolves.

4   The above poem isn't very good, I admit. No one would want to publish it. Most readers may not understand how, feeling like Little Red Riding Hood, I rush from place to place to avoid meeting stray wolves. None of that is the point. When writing the poem, I felt in touch with my life while savoring a creative joy. There is no reason to let anything get in the way of such a delight, not even the poor quality of the resulting poem.

5   Of course, it is easy to sing in the shower and write poetry no one ever sees, even if the results, to put it mildly, stink. What about where others are involved? Imagine my predicament when my big brother called and asked me if I would help him put up a pole barn. "Me," I pleaded, "I'm all thumbs." And I meant it, but somehow he needed my help, so despite my complete

lack of construction experience, I chanted my mantra three times and said "yes." For a day I held up beams, sawed boards (sometimes off the measured line), and hammered in nails (bending more than a few). But I did help my brother. He said that he couldn't have done it without me; and while he probably could have built the barn without me, it would have been harder for him. Besides, working side by side for a day, we got to reconnect in ways that I hadn't thought possible. I also learned some construction skills. Without being willing to help badly, I would have missed a tremendous opportunity.

6　　There are times when doing something badly is significantly better than doing nothing at all. Our local newspaper featured a story about a hiker who was miles from anywhere on the trail when he came across another hiker who was choking on his lunch. What could he do? He couldn't run for help. He was out of his cell phone region. And he didn't know CPR. What he did know was that the man in front of him was starting to turn blue. He pounded the man on the back, but that didn't work. Finally, in desperation he pushed down underneath the man's rib cage. The pressure popped something out of his windpipe and he started breathing again. The point of the article was the importance of learning CPR, the Heimlich Manoeuvre, and other life-saving skills. The hiker, of course, knew none of those skills and could have done tremendous damage, perhaps breaking the victim's ribs. Clearly, it would be worthwhile to be expert at life-saving skills. But what should the hiker have done? If he had just stood there paralyzed by his lack of expertise, the man would have choked to death. Fortunately, he seemed to have believed in my slogan and did what was worth doing, saving a life, even if he did it badly.

7　　There are many pressures in our culture to "leave it to the experts." We can listen to CDs instead of singing ourselves. We can call towing services that are glad to change our flats for us. We can watch soccer instead of play it. With so many skilled people, it would be easy to be embarrassed by our own lack of expertise and abandon everything except what we do well. However, our lives would be significantly poorer with such a surrender. Instead, we would be better off adapting the adage that "if it is worth doing, it is worth doing badly" and step up to the plate at a softball game, grab a sketch pad and draw what we see, write a poem, sing, cook a meal for a friend. In the end, we have nothing to lose but our false pride.

DISCUSSION QUESTIONS

1. How does the writer find an interesting thesis by providing a fresh slant on a familiar expression? How does she then use illustration to support this thesis?

2. With her different illustrations of why doing something badly is preferable to not doing anything, the writer mentions a number of benefits. What positive results come, for instance, from singing, or writing poetry, or helping her brother with construction, even when she is not skilled?

3. Why did the writer include her poem in her essay?

4. What does the paragraph on the use of CPR add to the essay?

5. In the last paragraph, why does the writer use the pronoun "we"? How does the final sentence follow from what has come before, but go beyond a flat re-statement of the thesis to leave the reader with something to consider?

SUGGESTIONS FOR WRITING *Use one of the ideas below or another that your instructor approves for your illustration essay. Select appropriate examples, determine how many you will use, and decide how you will organize them.*

1. Just as the student writer reversed the cliché "If something is worth doing, it is worth doing well," change or reverse a familiar expression such as one of the following:

   ■ The early bird gets the worm.

   ■ If you can't stand the heat, stay out of the kitchen.

   ■ Don't fight City Hall.

2. Use examples to illustrate how

   ■ People have strange remedies for hangovers.

   ■ Canadians can conserve water in small ways that add up over time.

   ■ Some people pride themselves on being busy and stressed.

The Critical Edge

When we write an illustration paper, we don't always draw our examples from personal experience. As we reflect on a topic, we may talk with other people and read various source materials to broaden our understanding. We explore differing perspectives and determine the connections between them en route to arriving at our own views and insights. Take, for instance, the topic of eating disorders. "An Insatiable Emptiness" (pages 499–504), "Distorted Images" (pages 180–183), and "Pressures to Conform" (pages 225–228) offer poignant illustrations of how eating disorders affect people's personal lives. Reading these essays, drawing upon your own observations, and perhaps questioning fellow students could lead you to an important insight: for example, that eating disorders are subtly encouraged by society. You might then synthesize others' illustrations and your own to produce a paper that presents this insight.

Sometimes illustrations don't reflect reality. An author trying to make the point that many students are irresponsible might offer examples of students who skip classes, fail to hand in assignments, and party constantly. These examples, however, overlook the many students who hold part-time jobs while taking a full load of classes, participate in professional organizations, and function successfully as spouses, and even parents, while earning good grades. Because published material can paint an inaccurate picture, develop the habit of judging the examples you read in the light of what your knowledge, further investigation, and other sources reveal. Critical thinking is one of the most important skills a writer can cultivate.*

SUGGESTIONS FOR WRITING

1. Examine the essays on cultural pressures pertaining to body image and weight: "An Insatiable Emptiness" (p. 499), "Pressures to Conform" (p. 225), and "Distorted Images" (p. 180). Then, drawing on examples from the essays and perhaps from your observations of students you know, write a paper illustrating the physical, psychological, and emotional damage that can result from obsession with weight or body image.

2. Read several issues of a Canadian magazine such as *Maclean's, Chatelaine,* or *Canadian Living* and determine what the articles suggest about a particular aspect of Canadian life. Then write an essay that illustrates your conclusions and incorporates relevant material from the articles.

3. Several essays in this book raise questions about how we use our work and leisure time. Drawing from one or more essays, such as "Old Father Time Becomes a Terror," or "Beware the Boredom Boom," as well as your own observations, write an essay that illustrates a specific point about positive or negative uses of time.

ILLUSTRATIVE ESSAYS: PROFESSIONAL MODELS

READING STRATEGIES

1. Read the introductory and concluding paragraphs quickly to determine the thesis for the illustration. Then read the essay quickly to get the main point of the essay. Jot down the key points of the illustration.
2. Based on your purpose for reading and the level of difficulty of the essay, determine if it is necessary to read the essay more carefully.
3. If a more careful reading is warranted, read slowly, noting any key details of the illustration that make a more general point.

*Because this type of paper draws on published information, it is important to read the sections on research in Chapters 15 and 16 and those on handling quotations and avoiding plagiarism in Chapter 17. As always, follow your instructor's guidelines for documenting sources.

READING CRITICALLY

1. Test whether the illustration really demonstrates the main point.
2. Determine whether the illustrations seem representative of the larger point being made. Has the writer chosen typical, realistic examples, or unusual and unlikely examples that are difficult to trust?
3. Test the point by thinking of examples that would argue against the writer's position.

READING AS A WRITER

1. Identify and evaluate the kinds of examples used in the illustration.
2. Notice the strategies used to link the illustrations to a main point.
3. Identify and evaluate how the illustrations were organized (e.g., as short narratives, as descriptions) and jot down any strategies you found useful.

Andrew Struthers

How Spell-Check Is Destroying English: With No Governing Body, Our Language Now Lies Prone to Market Forces

Andrew Struthers is a frequent contributor to "The Mix," the arts and entertainment section in the weekend edition of The Vancouver Sun, *where his article first appeared. His essay uses a wide variety of detailed examples in order to demonstrate how spell-checking tools have influenced our language usage.*

Example shows pressure on Canadian spelling	1 The word "bizarre" is a remnant of the stone age, a verbal coelacanth swimming in the depths of modern English. It comes from Basque, Europe's only aboriginal tongue. The rest were long ago supplanted by Indo-Germanic.

2   "Bizarre" began as "bisare," the Basque word for beard. It was appropriated by the Spanish as "bizarre" (dashing), wended into French as "bizarre" (angry or unstable), and by the time it reached England it meant "just plain weird." So this ancient word's journey tells us how the Spanish saw the Basques, how the French saw the Spanish, and how the English saw the French. <u>As Emerson said,</u> <u>"Language is the archives of history."</u>

Topic sentence

One sentence transition to subject of essay

3   In a bizarre twist, these archives have fallen into the hands of Bill Gates.

Ironic statement of thesis

4   I'm talking about <u>Spell-check, the helpful tool that underlines words it doesn't</u> <u>recognize in red, tacitly pressuring you to change them</u>. A red line is a subtle pressure. But even the strongest swimmer can only buck the tide 'til his arms get tired. Consider the fate of "founder." Time was, when a ship went down we said it "foundered"—from the Latin "fundus" meaning bottom. Today we say it "flounders," because we've confused "founder" with "flounder," the bottom-dwelling fish—probably because it thrashes around then lies down in the mud. The original word and its history are lost, swept into oblivion by the tide of common usage, its only crime having a homonym that was also a synonym.

Example shows how words can be lost

5   <u>Thanks to Spell-check, Canadian spelling now bucks a similar tide.</u> Because of market forces even my Canadian-made (Corel) Spell-check was factory-set on U.S. English, so it encouraged me to love my "neighbor." I changed the setting to Canadian English, but every time I booted up the Yankees were back. I set out to track the problem to its source, but it was easier said than done. I'm no Bill Gates. Last time I tried anything south of the toolbar I accidentally deleted a program file. Next thing I know I'm trying to wangle a Windows 98 product key out of a support technician down in Florida called "Dixie 343629." For problems with Spell-check I was advised to read "Knowledge Base Article Q178238."

Topic sentence

6   Pass.

7   I could turn Spell-check off, but the ugly truth is, I can't live without it. At 3 A.M., fumbling towards deadline, I no longer care whether "theatre" is Canadian or incorrect, I just change the darn word till I get the red out.

Example shows pressure on Canadian spelling

8   Thousands of kids today are doing the same thing without even realizing it. Eventually Bill Gates' spelling will prevail. It's a triumph of the individual over the collective.

9   <u>The situation has a precedent.</u> Spelling was standardized around 1500 by a single individual—William Caxton, the first English printer. He learned his trade in Germany, where "g" and "h" often appear together, which meant he had lots of "gh" blocks lying around his print shop. To cut costs (market forces again) he arbitrarily inserted the "h" in "ghost," which it haunts to this day. And because he worked in London, Southeast dialect was used to determine spelling, supplanting the more widespread East Midlands dialect. So you might say Bill Gates is the William Caxton of our time.

Topic sentence

Example shows historical influence of market forces on spelling

10   Such power should be wielded wisely. Our forebears ascribed a power to spelling that was downright mystical. It's no coincidence we speak of magic "spells." Even the word glamour (originally "to enchant") is an 18th-century pun on "grammar," a tacit reference to occult practices associated with the rules of language.

Topic sentence illustrated with examples

11   Here's a "glamorous" experiment. Write out the alphabet, then underneath write it in reverse:

    A B C D E F G H I J K L M N O . . .
    Z Y X W V U T S R Q P O N M L . . .

12   The letters of certain short words—like the biblical interjection "lo"—land in the same positions in both alphabets, but in the second alphabet the sequence is reversed. The "l" and "o" in the first set of letters line up perfectly over the "o" and "l" of the second set. A handful of two-letter "mirror words" exist, but there are very few with more letters. The odds against a six-letter word working both ways are nearly infinite, so only one has been found: Wizard.

13   This might be sheer coincidence, but remember that the people who decided on the spelling of "wizard" also finalized the order of the alphabet. Perhaps this game offers a glimpse of the deep connection between spelling and history. At the very least, wholesale overhauls of such a delicate and ancient ecosystem should be handled with care.

14   L'Académie française at the Sorbonne in Paris <u>handles French with care.</u> No changes can be made in their lexicon until they've had a few hundred meetings. In Iceland words are government-regulated. In Japan, state control of language is extreme. When the Imperial Army lost WWII, the brass blamed it on spelling.

Repetition of phrase adds coherence

Example of state control of language

There are more than 20 000 characters in Japanese. Only linguists know them all. When generals wrote orders, they used around 5000 characters. But the lead-biters in the trenches could read only 2000. Chaos ensued. When the radioactive dust settled the government reduced the number of characters allowed for mass communication to 1945 (a little reminder of their shame).

15   That degree of government control is unthinkable in English. We immediately flash on Orwell's *1984* and its abbreviated lexicon, Newspeak. Every new edition of the *Newspeak Dictionary* contained fewer words than the one before. The government's evil plan was to control what its citizenry thought by subtracting nouns that described the proscribed.

16   So English has no governing body, and with Spell-check programs vying for eyeballs, our language now lies prone to market forces.

Loops back to thesis

17   Rule #1 of the free market: never offend the marks. To accommodate the strait-laced, Spell-check redlines profanity as a matter of course. Too bad. "Fuck" can teach us things. Fuck, from the Scandinavian "fock," was not written down until the early 16th century, but a 1278 reference to one "John le Fucker" tells us people were saying it at least 300 years prior—proof of the resilience of slang.

Topic sentence

Example of pressures exerted by Spell-check

18   Corel even finds some words guilty by association: "bugger" (how else do I refer to a person who is bugging me?), "cock" (perchance I'm speaking of that herald of the dawn), and the lowly "ass," which is legitimate even in pejorative mode, deriving from the Old English term "oers"—to play the fool.

Topic sentence

19   The market forces that drive Spell-check programs toward smaller, faster, more *ruthless* efficiency also threaten obscure words that describe very specific things. *Lordosis,* that mysterious twisting of the spine. *Deinosis,* the ability to see things at their worst, surely a word Eminem fans might cherish. *Porphyria,* the purple-pissing malady that caused the madness of King George III.

Topic sentence

20   There's a belief that with bigger hard drives this problem will just go away. But I call this "mumpsimus"—a "bigoted adherence to an exposed but customary error."

21   Because simply increasing the size of the program will not help. I own a *Random House Encyclopedic Dictionary* the size of a small couch that has no entry for "mandala," "racist" or "coven," and I'm not convinced lack of space is the reason.

22   An inordinate share of the unwanted words in my Spell-check describe the proscribed—which brings us back to *1984.*

23   The interesting verb "frag"—when soldiers kill an unpopular officer—gets no shrift, even though this four-letter word does more to break down "us and them" stereotypes of war than a stack of Catch-22s. The dark side of the moon is missing from my software ("occultation"), as is the "Antichrist," who's been around since the third century AD. The only way to get the red out is to spell it anti-Christ, which has a whole different meaning.

Examples of words that Spell-check does not recognize

24   "Hocus-pocus" is trapped in a twilight zone—"hocus" is acceptable, "pocus" is not—like siamese twins who won't survive surgery. "Widdershins," a most excellent term for anti-clockwise, left-handed, or God-cursed, is banished.

25   If Orwell was right about words, that it's impossible to think certain things without their help, the New Age will be nipped in the bud. Zen "koans" (what is the sound of one hand clapping?) didn't make the cut. Forget about balancing your kundalini or your ki, because they no longer exist. Nor do the Suds. Mandala has become manana.

26   Perhaps we are facing a word die-off like the one that claimed the megafauna of the paleolithic, a farewell to the "wiccans," the "homos," the "half-assed twats" and "schlongs" of this world, who must now slouch off to the vast tundra of words that never were, like "queendom," and the word for "male muse," whatever that might be.

| Examples of "word die-off" |

27   Or perhaps this arbitrary pruning of Shakespeare's tongue will quicken the sap.

28   Because when all's said and done and run through Spell-check, <u>English has fared better than those state-controlled tongues.</u> Despite centuries of hard work by l'Académie française, fewer people speak French every year. The only people who still speak Icelandic are Bjork and her immediate family. And Japanese is now 30 percent English (their word for velcro is "majiku tapu"—magic tape). In fact, I once tutored a Japanese banker so that he could understand board meetings between Dutch, Thai and Nihon businessmen, all trying to converse in English.

| Topic sentence makes political point |
| Examples support topic sentence |

29   So it looks like English is the lingua franca of the future. But before we celebrate we'd best give a smidgen of thought to what our language will look like once market forces have whittled it so that it fits inside the mall. Here are some words not ostracized by Spell-check: Coca-cola, Pepsi, velcro, Big Mac, Taco Bell.

| Examples reinforce connection between words and market forces |

DISCUSSION QUESTIONS

1. Why do you think that the writer uses such an unusual word as "*coelacanth*" in the first sentence, which readers are unlikely to recognize? What point is the writer illustrating at the outset by tracing the history of the word "bizarre"?

2. How can you tell that this essay is directed to a Canadian audience? Explain what the writer means when he says that "eventually Bill Gates' spelling will prevail" (paragraph 8) or that "our language now lies prone to market forces" (paragraph 16).

3. What examples does the writer use to illustrate his claim (paragraph 10) that spelling has a magical, even mystical power?

4. What is the point of Struthers' references to Orwell's "Newspeak" in the novel *1984* (paragraphs 15, 22, 25)?

5. What examples does the writer use to demonstrate that we may be "facing a word die-off" (paragraph 26)? In your own words, explain why the writer is concerned that there are many words that Spell-check does not recognize.

6. Find examples of irony or humour in this essay (paragraphs 4, 5, 29). What is the effect of using humour?

TOWARD KEY INSIGHTS

What frustrations have you found with computer editing tools such as Spell-check?

What benefits have you found?

What other examples can you think of to illustrate differences between the spelling, pronunciation, or even word meanings from Canada and another English-speaking country?

What other market forces, especially from the United States, are threatening Canadian distinctiveness?

SUGGESTIONS FOR WRITING

1. **Consider some other aspect of technology (email, laptops, BlackBerries, cell phones, etc.) that is supposed to make life easier, and write an essay illustrating the drawbacks of this technology.**

2. **Using a number of examples, write an essay showing how language is enriched or impoverished by the use of slang and/or profanity. If you are interested in the history of words, you may wish to consult the Oxford English Dictionary or a dictionary of etymology.**

Candace Fertile

The Oldest Profession: Shopping

Candace Fertile has a Ph.D. in English Literature from the University of Alberta. She wrote her dissertation on the novels of Lawrence Durrell. She now teaches English at the University of Victoria and Camosun College and reviews books for several Canadian newspapers, mainly to support her addiction to reading. And yes, she loves to shop.

1   My shopping career began in earnest when I was seven. My currency was time and deceit. My boutiques were the garbage cans in the alley behind our apartment house in Edmonton.

2   I could not believe that people threw out such wonderful stuff. What a deal—something for nothing. Perhaps like the first-time gambler who wins and is forever hooked on that adrenaline rush, my love of shopping began with that first magical exposure, on a day when I was wandering home from school, taking my usual route through back alleys. To my extreme delight, I saw peeking out of a galvanized-steel garbage pail what looked like a blue three-ring binder. Acquisition grabbed my seven-year-old soul, and to this day it hasn't let go, fuelled no doubt by relentless advertising and the creation of more and more stuff that announces to the world who we are. Or perhaps who we want to be.

3   In that alley, my paper-loving self honed in on that blue binder like a cat streaking up from the basement at the sound of a can opener, and I started to understand the power of objects. As a second-grader, I was (unjustly, I thought) required to use despised scribblers. The covers were barely more substantial than the rather nasty paper within them. The booklets had three staples in the middle holding the whole ugly mess together. I hated these scribblers, and I hated their name. And I particularly hated the fact that the teacher would stalk around the room, checking to see if we were properly holding our pencils (another affront—I longed to use a pen). Periodically she would sneak up and grab our yellow HBs to make sure that we were not gripping them too tightly. Her actions made me clutch my pencil as if it were keeping my heart pumping. And the choke-hold I had on my pencil meant that I frequently made holes in the flimsy paper of the scribbler. With grim regularity the teacher and I would get into a tug-of-war over my pencil.

4   It was after such a dismal war (I always had to lose) that the bright blue plastic corner of the binder caught my eye. I debated for some time about whether or not I was allowed to look in the can, or if taking something from a garbage can was stealing. I should mention: not only was I polite, but I was also Catholic. I knew God was watching my every move, and should I be so vile as to commit a mortal sin, lightning bolts would descend and incinerate my evil little soul, so that all that would be transported to Hell would be something the size of a barbecue briquette. The possibility of owning a binder seemed worth the risk.

5   I inched closer, then looked up and down the alley to make sure no one was watching me. I carefully removed the lid, which was already precariously perched to one side, and laid it on the ground. A perfect, blue, three-ring binder glowed at me. I was in Heaven. I picked it up and with disbelief discovered an unopened packet of three-hole paper inside. The narrow blue (not even the more babyish wide) lines on the stark white paper with the margins marked with a thin pink line were everything my crummy scribbler wasn't. This paper and binder were for grownups, not little kids.

6   I could hardly wait to write in my new binder. With a pen. I felt instantly grown-up, more important, more substantial, the tug-of-war over my pencil forgotten. I had gained a new status. And this emotional boost into the stratosphere was accomplished by the simplest of means: I had acquired a new object. And it was free. No drug would ever reproduce the rush I felt as my concept of myself and the world tilted.

7   On subsequent shopping expeditions down the back alleys I never found anything as great as the binder and paper, but sometimes I found stuff for my little brother. At two, he would play with just about anything. I enjoyed his delight, and finding free stuff meant saving my allowance. I now suspect my kid-sized version of dumpster-diving sparked my career as a bargain shopper.

8   Once I found a scarf—a sophisticated, almost sheer, leopard-spotted scarf. It spoke of glamour, beauty, and fashion, with just an edge of wildness. It was a scarf worn by elegant and capable women on television. It was perfect for my mother, who set off for work each morning with her matching high heels and handbag.

9   Maybe the scarf wasn't even supposed to have been thrown out, but there it was, dangling from a garbage can a few blocks away from home. (In the space of a few weeks, I had increased my territory substantially.) My mother would love this scarf, I thought, but I had no idea how I would explain the acquisition of such a treasure. I didn't have that kind of money. I had finally revealed the binder to her, as it was too difficult trying to write in it without being found out. Even that was hard, as I'd had to commit what I hoped was a venial sin by lying that a friend's older sister had given me the stuff. I knew that wouldn't work again with a scarf. And I still felt a bit singed around the edges from the lie. For a week I had imagined everyone thought I smelled like a campfire. And while I knew what the wrath of God entailed, I was absolutely sure that the wrath of my mother was worse.

10   I decided to come clean. I took the scarf home, and when my mother got home from work, I presented it to her. She was astonished, and then asked where I got it. I told her. To my bafflement, she burst into gales of laughter, nearly hiccupping herself into a coma while trying to catch her breath.

11   When she regained control, she announced that my garbage-looting days were over. Nice girls didn't do such things. And there could be dangerous things in the garbage. Like what, I wanted to know, but she wouldn't tell me. These events happened decades ago—I'm sure my mother was worried I'd cut myself on a tin can or broken bottle, not get jabbed by some hypodermic needle. Garbage was safer then, but not safe enough for my mother's daughter to play in it.

12   But what sticks indelibly in my mind is that my mother carefully washed and ironed the scarf and wore it faithfully, even proudly, a splash of jungle against her ever-so-fashionable green wool coat with the fur around the sleeves. She would fling one end over her shoulder as she headed out the door in the morning, as if to announce her formidable presence in the universe.

13   Scavenging no longer an option, I had to find another way to satisfy the desire for acquisition now flowing through my veins. Little did I know that I was turning into a good little twentieth-century consumer. According to Lauren Langman, an academic who studies human development:

> In the contemporary world, the signifying and celebrating edifice of consumer culture has become the shopping mall which exists in [a] pseudo-democratic twilight zone between reality and a commercially produced fantasy world of commodified goods, images, and leisure activities that gratify transformed desire and provide packaged self-images to a distinctive form of subjectivity. (40)

14   Langman's thesis certainly helps to explain not only the label-consciousness of shoppers but also the desire of many shoppers to become apparent walking billboards for name-brand products. How much difference, if any, is there between my girlish desire for white go-go boots and the current stampede to wear T-shirts emblazoned with "Roots" or "Nike"?

15   I prefer to think the difference is significant. I could be wrong, in which case, Langman's argument is unassailable. But another academic offers me some hope. In an article in *Vogue* titled "The Professor Wore Prada," Elaine Showalter, professor of English at Princeton and recently president of the Modern Language Association, comments on her love of fashion and shopping. She does so in a humorous way, defending her intellectualism, femininity, and feminism. As she says, "For years I have been trying to make the life of the mind coexist with the day at the mall, and to sneak the *femme* back into feminist" (80). Showalter delineates the various ways female academics (herself included) have dressed in an effort to be taken seriously, and ends her essay by saying, "if you want to deconstruct my feminist criticism, go right ahead. But you'd better not sneer at my angel backpack or step on my blue suede shoes. I've paid my dues dressing 'feminist,' and now I'm going to wear what I like" (92). Showalter's essay is full of the pleasure one can gain from shopping, both the activity of looking and actual purchase. Throughout history and likely before, human beings have been drawn to objects of beauty (although certainly the concepts of beauty change).

16   The acquisition of objects, beautiful or otherwise, is usually an economic transaction. As a child prevented from plundering garbage bins, I needed a new way to get the stuff I wanted. So from time and deceit as currency, I turned to the more usual one: money. Getting that required work. My first job was ironing for my mother. I had seen a T-shirt in Sears, and my mother refused to buy it for me because, as she said, "You don't need it." It's no wonder that nowadays when

I buy yet another object I don't need I think of King Lear's "Oh, reason not the need."[1] The other object that captured my fancy was a particular lava lamp. I loved that lava lamp, but it was out of the realm of financial possibility. And my mother was right about the T-shirt. I didn't need it. I wore a uniform to school, and I had sufficient play clothes. Incessant pestering of my mother resulted in the ironing agreement. I ironed like a demon, encouraging my beleaguered mother to change clothes frequently so I could have something to iron. Eventually I saved enough to buy the T-shirt, and I wore it to shreds. It was the first thing I bought for myself with my own money, and I remember it in every detail. Still. It had short white sleeves, a white back, and a front in four coloured squares of red, yellow, blue, and green. If I had had white go-go boots to match, life would have achieved its pinnacle. (Elaine Showalter, by the way, wore white go-go boots to her Ph.D. defence.)

17   Since those very early days, my shopping has expanded in terms of money, objects, and range. Like many middle-class Canadians, I have more material goods than some small nations, and I am constantly acquiring more. What is interesting is that none of us needs all these things, but lemming-like we hurl ourselves at the nearest mall, which has acquired the status of a cathedral for some. Or else we seek out independent and unique shops in downtowns and other shopping areas. We go to outlets and discount centres. We are the consumer society of which much has been written. Thorstein Veblen's *The Theory of the Leisure Class* (1934), Christopher Lasch's *The Culture of Narcissism* (1979), and Hilary Radner's *Shopping Around: Feminine Culture and the Pursuit of Pleasure* (1995) are just three of the many works written to explore humans' need to shop even when we are way beyond buying what is necessary for our survival. Veblen's term "conspicuous consumption" indicates that the purchase of many unnecessary items is a performance. It's interesting to imagine what the performance means. If we examine advertising, which certainly fuels consumer desire, we see that Langman's view of buying an identity is accurate. To wear a certain brand (a "Roots" or "Nike" T-shirt is infinitely more desirable to certain groups than, say, a "K-Mart" T-shirt) or to drive a certain car or to drink a certain beer is presumably a statement of who we are. Or is it?

18   In his essay "The Individual, Consumption Cultures and the Fate of Community," Rob Shields attends to the performative aspect of purchasing and gives consumers some credit: "Many consumers are now ironic, knowing shoppers, conscious of the inequalities of exchange and the arbitrary nature of exchange value. As social actors, they attempt to consume the symbolic values of objects and the mall environment while avoiding the inequalities of exchange" (100). Shields's essay notes that public spaces have changed and that the mall serves as a gathering place. Thus, the activity of shopping (whether or not a purchase is made) plays a significant social role. Shields argues: "It is necessary to recognize that consumption itself is partly determined by the non-rational, cultural element of society. Shopping is not just a functional activity.

---

[1]When King Lear's daughters Goneril and Regan challenge the necessity of Lear's keeping an army after he has given away his kingdom, Lear protests, saying that for human life to have value, humans need more than the basics of survival (*King Lear* 2.4. 264).

Consumption has become a communal activity, even a form of solidarity" (110). It appears to me that shopping plays a number of roles, and one of these is certainly a communal one, as Shields argues. But it can also be said that in addition to having a connective importance, shopping—and more specifically the purchased goods—can fulfill people's desires both to join a group and to differentiate themselves from one another. For example, clothing choices are laden with meaning, even if the message is inaccurate.

19   Shoppers, as Shields notes, are becoming more sophisticated and particular, if the growth in thrift stores is any indication. A CBC newscast in July 1998 noted that the thrift store business is so popular that charities depending on donations have to be much more competitive. We are still conspicuously consuming, but we want a bargain. Certain sections of the population have always needed to shop for sale goods, but the practice is now losing any stigma it might have had. In fact, getting a bargain, or a "steal," marks one as a consummate shopper. Getting a deal has become a selling point for much commercial activity. I'd like to mention sales, for example. Anyone in western Canada familiar with Woodward's $1.49 Day will remember the thrust and parry of grabbing for the goodies on this once-a-month sale extravaganza. The deals were often extraordinary, and people didn't want to miss this opportunity. Encountering sharp elbows was common. In contrast, the former frenzy of Bay Day has abated now that the sale lasts for ages and has lost any special air. No need to dive in a scrum for the merchandise. No, it's all there in stacks, and then we stand in line to pay. Infrequent sales events such as Boxing Day sales create line-ups hours before the stores open. The sale must appear to be an unusual event or it garners little excitement. I once worked at Harrods, and the annual sale was marked by the sound of crashing crockery as maniacal shoppers stormed the aisles.

20   But what are we doing when we shop, and why do I refer to it as the oldest profession? The answer is simple. Well, sort of. In *Shopping Around: Feminine Culture and the Pursuit of Pleasure,* Hilary Radner argues the following: "Feminine culture emphasizes a process of investment and return, of negotiation, in which the given articulation of pleasure is always measured against its costs, the inevitable price of an invitation that is never extended freely, never absolutely, the terms of which change from day to day, from place to place" (178). While the terms and values change, it is surely the case that a shopper considers the relative costs (whether in time, effort, or money) and the benefits of the object gained. And these judgments will differ from person to person even within the same socio-economic group.

21   Shopping is our contemporary form of hunting and gathering. Men may have hunted, and women may have gathered, but both processes resulted in maintaining life. And if the effort expended exceeded what was gained—the result was death. Such an obvious relationship between acquisition (shopping in a sense) and survival is still evident in the world today. But in rich countries like Canada, hunting and gathering is largely done at the mall, and our survival is not in question. In "Dressed to Kill," Don Gillmor makes fun of men at a clothing sale, and he uses the metaphor of the hunt:

> The big game is on the suit rack, though. Some of the men simply drape a dozen business suits over one arm and then try to find a little room in which to sort and sniff them,

like lions defending their kill. But to bring down a three-button, blue wool crepe 42R Donna Karan (reg. $2295, now $395) in open country requires keen eyesight, stealth, and a burst of cheetah-like speed. . . . [Men] are taking home cashmere and silk and cotton that feels like whipped butter. They have hunted well and they are filled with the self-knowledge that comes with risk and death and loss and dramatic savings. (75)

22   Whether the hunting is done in an exclusive boutique or a thrift store, it's the thrill of the chase that drives shoppers. It could be the lure of low prices, or exclusive merchandise, or the media-created buzz about something completely useless like Cabbage Patch Dolls or Beanie Babies that gets everyone out there, roaming, foraging, stalking, pouncing, occasionally even wrestling another shopper for the item.

23   Then we bag our prize and take it back to our cave, er, home. I bet those cavepeople never stopped and said to each other, "Listen, honey, I think we have too many acorns or dried fish or fur blankets." I think they were out there scooping up whatever they thought might come in handy for survival.

24   And so while many of us shop for a variety of reasons, including pleasure, but rarely need (even grocery stores are full of stuff no one needs to survive; in fact, some of that junk probably shortens lives), perhaps somewhere at the heart of the endeavour is a genetic link to our past, when tracking and locating food was essential for survival. Now different needs drive our shopping expeditions. And survival is perceived in ways beyond the merely physical.

References

Gillmor, Don. "Dressed to Kill: What Really Happens When Men Go Hunting for Deep Discounts." *Saturday Night* 113.5 (June 1998): 75.

Langman, Lauren. "Neon Cages: Shopping for Subjectivity." *Lifestyle Shopping: The Subject of Consumption.* Ed. Rob Shields. London: Routledge, 1992. 40–82.

Radner, Hilary. *Shopping Around: Feminine Culture and the Pursuit of Pleasure.* New York: Routledge, 1995.

Shields, Rob. "The Individual, Consumption Cultures and the Fate of Community." *Lifestyle Shopping: The Subject of Consumption.* Ed. Rob Shields. London: Routledge, 1992. 99–113.

Showalter, Elaine. "The Professor Wore Prada." *Vogue* 187.12 (December 1997): 80, 86, 92.

DISCUSSION QUESTIONS

1. How does the writer use irony in the title and the first paragraph? What does the writer mean when she says that her "currency was time and deceit"?

2. Why does the writer spend so much time describing the "blue binder" she discovers (paragraphs 3–6)? How does the writer suggest the significance of this binder through overstatement or exaggeration, and through metaphorical comparisons?

3. What is the relevance of her religious background (paragraphs 4–5, 9) and the distinction between a "mortal sin" (paragraph 4) and a "venial sin" (paragraph 9)?

4. What is the significance of the scarf (paragraphs 8–12) that the writer presents to her mother? What image of the mother is created in this brief narrative?

Why does the mother's response to the scarf mean that "scavenging is no longer an option" (paragraph 13)? How does the image of scavenging early on connect to the image of bargain hunting (paragraphs 21–22) toward the end of the essay?

5. How does the writer shift from a personal story to a more academic tone in paragraph 13? What different perspectives on shopping are offered by scholars Lauren Langman (paragraph 13) and Elaine Showalter (paragraph 15)? Which perspective does the author Candace Fertile seem to prefer?

6. The writer refers to a theory that "the purchase of many unnecessary items is a performance" (paragraphs 17–18). In your own words, explain what this means.

7. In paragraphs 14, 16, and 19, the writer illustrates general points with concrete examples. Locate places where she uses illustration, and explain the point of these illustrations.

TOWARD KEY INSIGHTS

When she was young, Candace Fertile did ironing jobs for her mother so that she could earn the money to acquire unnecessary but desired possessions: a T-shirt and a lava lamp. When have you been motivated to work in order to buy what might be considered unnecessary but desirable possessions? What different reasons did you have for these purchases? How did you come to view the possessions later?

To what extent do you agree that shopping helps people feel connected to others, as well as "differentiated" from others (paragraph 18)?

In your experience, does "getting a bargain . . . [mark] one as a consummate shopper" (paragraph 19)?

SUGGESTION FOR WRITING *After reading Candace Fertile's essay, reflect on what underlying reasons you might have for going to the mall or for purchasing unnecessary items. Then, using illustrations of your own, write an essay showing that the reasons for shopping often go beyond obvious survival needs.*

Susan McClelland

Distorted Images

Susan McClelland is a frequent contributor to Maclean's *and* THIS Magazine. *Her work includes numerous feature articles on a variety of social issues. In "Distorted Images," Susan McClelland discusses how the West exports body-image anxiety through images of very thin females and steroid-built males.*

1   When Zahra Dhanani was just seven years old, her four-foot frame already packed 100 lb.—so her mother, Shahbanu, put her on her first diet. "My mother, a fat woman, daughter of another fat woman, thought if I was skinny, different from her, I would be happy," says Dhanani. The diet, and many after, did not

have the desired effect. By 13, Dhanani was sporadically swallowing appetite suppressants; at 17, she vomited and used laxatives to try to keep her weight under control. There were times when she wanted to die. "I had so much self-hate," recalls the 26-year-old Toronto immigration lawyer, "I couldn't look in the mirror without feeling revulsion."

2   The hate reflected more than just weight. "It was race," says Dhanani, who had moved with her family to Canada from East Africa when she was 4. "I was straightening my hair—doing anything to look white." Her recovery only began when, at age 19, she started to identify with women in other cultures. "I came to realize that there were people who revered large women of colour," says Dhanani, who now says she loves all of her 200 lb. She blames part of her earlier eating disorders on the images in western media: "When you have no role models to counteract the messages that fat is repulsive, it's hard to realize that you are a lovable human being."

3   Body image may be one of the western world's ugliest exports. Thanks to television, magazines, movies and the Internet, rail-thin girls and steroid-built beef-boys are being shoved in the faces of people all over the world. As a result, experts say, cultures that used to regard bulk as a sign of wealth and success are now succumbing to a narrow western standard of beauty. And that, in turn, is leading to incidences of eating disorders in regions where anorexia and bulimia had never been seen before. But body-image anxiety in ethnic cultures runs much deeper than weight. In South Africa, almost six years after the end of apartheid, black women still use harmful skin-bleaching creams in the belief that whiter is prettier. "We're seeing a homogenization and globalization of beauty ideals," says Niva Piran, a clinical psychologist at the University of Toronto. "It's white. It's thin. And the result is that people come to identify less with their own cultures and more with an image in the media."

4   In most cultures, bigger was considered better until the 19th century. "The larger a man's wife, the more he was seen as a good provider," says Joan Jacobs Brumberg, a professor of American women's history at Cornell University and author of *Fasting Girls: The History of Anorexia Nervosa.* That began to change during the Industrial Revolution, she says, as women in the United States and Great Britain began to see thinness as a way to differentiate themselves from the lower classes. By the 1920s, fat was seen as unhealthy. And in the burgeoning magazine, movie and fashion industries, the women depicted as being successful in love, career and finances were slim and almost always white.

5   Still, eating disorders are not a modern affliction. Records of women starving themselves (anorexia) date back to the medieval period (1200 to 1500). As Brumberg notes in *Fasting Girls,* during this time, a woman who did not eat was admired for having found some other form of sustenance than food, like prayer. Yet, until the last century, the number of women who fasted was low. But, particularly over the past 30 years, the number of anorexics and women who self-induce vomiting (bulimia) or use laxatives has increased dramatically. "It's generally this obsession with the body, constant weight-watching, that introduces a person to these behaviours," says Merryl Bear of the Toronto-based National Eating Disorder Information Centre. It was

commonly believed, however, that sufferers came predominantly from white, middle- and upper-class backgrounds. Experts thought ethnic minorities were immune because of their strong ties to communities that emphasize family and kinship over looks alone.

6   Studies done in the United States with Hispanic, black and Asian college students, however, show that women who are alienated from their minority cultures and integrated into mainstream society are prone to the same pressures of dieting as their white counterparts. In a recent study of South-Asian girls in Peel, Ont., 31 percent responded that they were not comfortable with their body shape and size. Fifty-eight percent compared their appearance with others, including fashion models—and 40 percent wanted to look like them.

7   Some of the most compelling research comes from Harvard Medical School psychiatrist Anne Becker, who was in Fiji in 1995 when the government announced that TV, including western programs, would be introduced. "Fijians revere a body that is sturdy, tall and large—features that show that the body is strong, hardworking and healthy," says Becker. "Thinness and sudden weight loss was seen as some kind of social loss or neglect."

8   In 1998, Becker returned to Fiji and found that this had all changed. Her studies showed that 29 percent of the girls now had symptoms of eating disorders. Many said they vomited to lose weight. But what was most alarming were the girls' responses about the role of television in their lives. "More than 80 percent said that watching TV affected the way they felt about their bodies," Becker says. "They said things such as, 'I watched the women on TV, they have jobs. I want to be like them, so I am working on my weight now.' These teenagers are getting the sense that as Fiji moves into the global economy, they had better find some way to make wages and they are desperate to find role models. The West to them means success, and they are altering their bodies to compete."

9   Cheryl McConney has felt the pressures to alter her body, too. The black 32-year-old native of Richmond Hill, Ont., co-hosts a daytime talk show on cable TV. And although it has not been difficult for her to get where she is in her career, she is concerned about how to navigate her next step. "Looking at Canadian television, I don't see many people who look like me on air," she says. At five-foot-five, and weighing about 145 lb., McConney has never been told she should lose weight. Still, in 1998, she went on a six-month, high-protein, low-carbohydrate diet, hoping to look better in front of the camera. She shed 20 lb. "I felt good. People in the studio thought I looked great, but it wasn't easy to maintain." Within a year, she had gained it all back.

10   For McConney, race has been more of an issue. An industry insider jokingly told her that she would do better if she dyed her hair blond. And just a few months ago, she was discouraged from applying for another on-air host position because of what the casting agents said they were looking for. "They wanted the 'girl next door' and 'peaches-and-cream' pretty, not chocolate and cream," says McConney, adding: "It was pretty clear some women were not invited to participate because of their skin colour." As to the girl-next-door part: "I said it just depends where you live."

11   While McConney says she is determined to make it on air despite the barriers, Linda, who requested *Maclean's* not use her real name, may not be around to

see her success. The 19-year-old—part South African and part East Indian—has anorexia. She says trying to fit into a Canadian suburban community played a big role in her illness. "I was never proud of my different religion, different skin colour," she says. "I would put white baby powder on my cheeks just to make me look white." What alarms her now, Linda says, is that with her skin pale from malnutrition and her weight fluctuating between 75 and 85 lb., other young women often come up to her and say, "You look so good, I wish I looked like you." But she adds: "What they don't know is that my body is decaying. People glamorize eating disorders. But what it is is a lifetime of hospitalization and therapy." As long as the western media promote thinness and whiteness as the pinnacle of beauty, stories like Linda's will remain all too familiar.

DISCUSSION QUESTIONS

1. The essay begins and ends with short narrative illustrations. How do these illustrations relate to the essay's overall purpose and thesis?

2. How does McClelland make the case that the beauty ideal of thinness is linked to the harmful belief that "whiter is prettier" (paragraph 3)?

3. What purpose does it serve for McClelland to discuss the historical perspective that in many cultures bigger used to be "considered better" (paragraph 4)? Why did this positive view of large women change?

4. Why did women from minority cultures in North America, and women from non-Western traditional cultures such as Fiji begin to subscribe to mainstream Western cultural ideals of beauty?

5. What point does the author make in the concluding two paragraphs? How effective is this conclusion?

TOWARD KEY INSIGHTS

How have you or others you know been affected by a one-size-fits-all standard of beauty or sex appeal fostered by the media?

This essay discusses ways that the West is exporting body-image anxiety through images of very thin females and steroid-built males. Are there other ways in which Western values and preoccupations are being exported to non-Western cultures along with economic products? What possible effects do these Western images and ways of thinking have on people in the countries?

How could we address the problems raised by this essay?

SUGGESTIONS FOR WRITING

1. Write a paper illustrating how a certain kind of cultural export to or from Canada may be damaging.

2. Write an essay, using real-life illustrations, showing how Canadian women or men can free themselves from ideals of beauty perpetrated by the media.

CHAPTER 9

Strategies for Analytical Writing: Process Analysis

EXPLAINING HOW

"Hey Bill, I'd like you to take a look at Mr. Gorgerise's car. He's really fuming. Says the engine's burning too much oil, running rough, and getting poor gas consumption. Check it out and see what you can find."

Bill begins by removing the spark plugs, hooking a remote-control starter to the starter in the car, and grounding the ignition to prevent the car's starting accidentally. Next, he fits a compression pressure gauge into the spark plug hole by cylinder number one, starts the engine, and reads and records the pressure; then he does the same for each of the other cylinders. Finally, he compares the readings with one another and the automaker's engine specs. The verdict? An excessively worn engine that needs rebuilding. Bill has carried out a *process,* just one among many that fill his workdays.

As we pursue our affairs, we perform processes almost constantly, ranging from such daily rituals as brewing a pot of coffee to taking a picture, preparing for a date, or replacing a light switch. Often we share our special technique for doing something—for example, making chicken cacciatore—by passing it on to a friend.

Many popular publications feature process analyses that help readers sew zippers in garments, build canoes, live within their means, and improve their wok technique. Process analysis also frequently helps you meet the writing demands of your courses. A political science instructor may ask you to explain how the current premier won the last election. Another instructor may call for directions relating to some process in your field—for example, analyzing a chemical compound, taking fingerprints, or obtaining a blood sample. On the job, a greenhouse crew leader may provide summer employees with directions for planting various kinds of shrubs and flowers. A sanitation department technician may write a brochure telling city residents how to get paper, glass, and metal garbage ready for recycling.

As these examples show, a process can be nontechnical, historical, scientific, natural, or technical.

KINDS OF PROCESS ANALYSIS PAPERS

Process papers fall into two categories: those intended for readers who will perform the process, and those intended to explain the process for nonperformers. Papers in either category can range from highly technical and sophisticated to nonspecialized and simple.

Processes for Readers Who Will Perform Them   The audience for process analysis papers can be either technical and professional personnel who need the information to carry out a work-related task, or individuals who want to perform the process for themselves.

A how-to-do-it paper must include everything the reader needs to know in order to ensure a successful outcome. Its directions take the form of polite commands, often addressing readers directly as "you." This approach helps involve readers in the explanation and emphasizes that the directions must, not merely should, be followed. Here is an illustration:

> To prepare a bacterial smear for staining, first use an inoculating loop to place a drop of distilled water on a clean glass microscope slide. Next, pass the loop and the opening of the tube containing the bacterial culture to be examined through a Bunsen burner flame to sterilize them. From the tube, remove a small bit of culture with the loop, and rub the loop in the drop of water on the slide until the water covers an area four centimetres long and approximately the width of the slide. Next, reflame the opening of the culture tube to prevent contamination of the culture, and then plug it shut. Allow the smear to air dry, and then pass the slide, smear side up, through the flame of the burner until it is warm to the touch. The dried smear should have a cloudy, milky-white appearance.
>
> Darryl Williams, student

Processes for Readers Who Won't Perform Them   These kinds of papers may tell how some process is or was performed or how it occurs or occurred. A paper might, for instance, detail the stages of grief, the procedure involved in an operation, the role of speech in the development of children's thinking, or the sequence involved in shutting down a nuclear reactor. These papers serve many purposes—for example, to satisfy popular curiosity; to point out the importance, difficulty, or danger of a process; or to cast a process in a favourable or unfavourable light. Even though the writers of such papers often explain their topic in considerable detail, they do not intend to provide enough information for readers to carry out the process.

Papers of this sort present the needed information without using polite commands. Sometimes a noun, a pronoun like *I, we, he, she,* or *it,* or a noun–pronoun combination identifies the performer(s). At other times, the performer remains unidentified. Three examples follow.

Pronouns Identify Performer

Thus, when I now approach a stack of three two-inch cinder blocks to attempt a breaking feat, I do not set myself to "try hard," or to summon up all my strength. Instead I relax, sinking my awareness into my belly and legs, feeling my connection with the ground. I breathe deeply, mentally directing the breath through my torso, legs, and arms. I imagine a line of force coming up from the ground through my legs, down one arm, and out through the stone slabs, and down again into the ground, penetrating to the center of the earth. I do not focus any attention on the objects to be broken. Although when I am lifting or holding them in a normal state of consciousness, the blocks seem tremendously dense, heavy, and hard, in the course of my one- or two-minute preparation, their reality seems to change, as indeed the reality of the whole situation changes. . . . When I make my final approach to the bricks, if I regard them at all, they seem light, airy, and friendly; they do not have the insistent inner drive in them that I do.

Don Ethan Miller, "A State of Grace: Understanding the Martial Arts"

Noun–Pronoun Combination Identifies Performers

Termites are even more extraordinary in the way they seem to accumulate intelligence as they gather together. Two or three termites in a chamber will begin to pick up pellets and move them from place to place, but nothing comes of it; nothing is built. As more join in, they seem to reach a critical mass, a quorum, and the thinking begins. They place pellets atop pellets, then throw up columns and beautiful, curving, symmetrical arches, and the crystalline architecture of vaulted chambers is created. It is not known how they communicate with each other, how the chains of termites building one column know when to turn toward the crew on the adjacent column, or how, when the time comes, they manage the flawless joining of the arches. The stimuli that set them off at the outset, building collectively instead of shifting things about, may be pheromones released when they reach committee size. They react as if alarmed. They become agitated, excited, and then they begin working, like artists.

Lewis Thomas, "Societies as Organisms"

Performer Unidentified

The analyzer was adjusted so the scale read zero and was connected to the short sampling tube, which had previously been inserted into the smokestack. The sample was taken by depressing the bulb the requisite number of times, and the results were then read and recorded. The procedure was repeated, this time using the long sampling tube and sampling through the fire door.

Charles Finnie, student

EXERCISE *Examine your favourite newspaper or magazine for examples of process analysis. Bring them to class for group discussion of which kind each represents and the writer's purpose.*

ETHICAL ISSUES

Unclear, misleading, incomplete, or erroneous instructions written for someone to follow can create unwanted consequences. Often frustration and lost time are the only results. Sometimes, though, the fallout is more serious, as in the case of a lab explosion. And in extreme cases, the outcome can be potentially catastrophic, as when an accident occurs in a nuclear power plant. As writers, we have an ethical obligation to write clear and complete instructions. To help you do this, ask yourself the following questions when you're writing a process that the reader will perform.

- Have I used clear and unambiguous language so the reader will not encounter unnecessary frustration and inconvenience?
- Have I clearly indicated all requirements, such as time needed or additional supplies that have to be purchased?
- Have I clearly warned readers about any possible harm they could face?

WRITING A PROCESS ANALYSIS

Planning and Drafting the Process Analysis

As always, when the choice is yours, select a familiar topic. If you're not the outdoor type and prefer to stay at a Holiday Inn rather than the north woods, don't try to explain how to plan a camping trip. Muddled, inaccurate, and inadequate information will result. On the other hand, if you've pitched many a tent, you might want to share your camping knowledge with your readers.

Finding a suitable topic should be easy. But if you do hit a snag, turn to the strategies on pages 34–40. In any event, answer the following questions for each potential choice:

Will the reader find the process important, interesting, or useful?

Should I provide directions for the reader to follow, explain how the process takes place, or explain how others perform it?

Can I explain the process adequately within any assigned length?

Writing Processes for Readers Who Will Perform Them   If you are writing a process for readers to follow, use this second set of questions to help you gather the details you need:

> What separate actions make up the process? (Be especially careful not to omit any action that is obvious to you but wouldn't be to your reader. Such an oversight can ruin your reader's chances of success.)
>
> What is the reason for each action?
>
> What warnings does the reader need in order to perform the process properly and safely?

When you have your answers, record them in a chart similar to this one:

Action	Reason for Action	Warning
First action	First reason	First warning
Second action	Second reason	Second warning

Sometimes a reason is so obvious that no mention is necessary, and many actions don't require warnings. When you've completed the chart, review it carefully and supply any missing information. If necessary, make a revised chart.

Once you've listed the actions, group related ones together to form steps, the major subdivisions of the procedure. The following actions constitute the first step—lighting the gas barbecue—of a paper explaining how to grill hamburgers:

1. Lift lid
2. Spray non-stick spray on the rack
3. Turn on main gas supply
4. Turn on first gas burner
5. Twist automatic starter until burner ignites
6. Turn on second burner
7. Close lid
8. Let barbecue heat for 10 minutes

EXERCISE

1. **Develop a complete list of the actions involved in one of the following processes, then arrange them in an appropriate order.**
   a. Cleaning out a garage
   b. Assembling or repairing some common household device
   c. Giving an effective PowerPoint presentation to a class
   d. Breaking a bad habit

2. **Locate a set of instructions for a new product that requires the purchaser to do something: assemble furniture, activate a phone, make a cappuccino in a cappuccino maker, etc. Evaluate the clarity and helpfulness of these instructions.**

Start your paper by identifying the process and arousing your reader's interest. For example, you might note the importance of the process, its usefulness, or the ease of carrying it out. Include a list of the items needed to do the work, and note any special conditions required for a successful outcome. The paper explaining how to grill hamburgers might begin as follows:

> Grilling hamburgers on an outdoor grill is a simple process that almost any-one can master. Before starting, you will need a clean grill, some hamburger meat, a plate, a spatula, and some water to put out any flames caused by fat drippings. The sizzling, tasty patties you will have when you finish are a treat that almost everyone will enjoy.

DISCUSSION QUESTION *How does the writer try to induce the reader to perform the process?*

Use the body of the paper to describe the process in detail, presenting each step in one or more paragraphs so that each is distinct and easy to understand. If you've ever muttered under your breath as you struggled to assemble something that came with vague or inadequate directions, you know the importance of presenting steps clearly, accurately, and fully. Therefore, think carefully and include everything the reader needs to know. Provide the reason for each action unless the reason is obvious. Flag any difficult or dangerous step with a cautionary warning. If two steps must be performed simultaneously, tell the reader at the start of the first one. In some places, you may want to tell readers what to expect if they have completed the instructions properly. Feedback lets readers know that they are on track or that they need to redo something.

Let's see how the first step of the hamburger-grilling paper might unfold:

> The first step is to light the barbecue. Lift the lid and lightly spray the rack with a nonstick spray for gas barbecues. This will make clean-up easier later on. Next, make sure that the gas supply valve on the tank is open. Then turn the burner closest to the automatic starter to high. Immediately twist the automatic starter until the gas lights. You may have to twist it more than once. Note that, on very windy days, the automatic starter may not work effectively. Once the main burner is lit, turn the other gas burner to high until it lights as well.
>
> Do not squirt on lighter fluid, because a flame could quickly follow the stream back into the can, causing an explosion. Close the lid and let the barbecue heat up. The result will be a hot, even fire, the type that makes grilling a success.

DISCUSSION QUESTIONS

1. At what points has the writer provided reasons for doing things?
2. Where has the writer included a warning?

Some processes can unfold in *only one order.* When you shoot a free throw in basketball, for example, you step up to the line and receive the ball before lining up the shot, and you line up the shot before releasing the ball. Other processes can be carried out in an *order of choice.* When you grill hamburgers, you can prepare the patties either before or after you light the barbecue. If you have an option, use the order that has worked best for you.

End your paper with a few brief remarks that provide some perspective on the process. A summary of the steps often works best for longer, multistep processes. Other popular choices include evaluating the results of the process or discussing its importance. The paper on hamburger grilling notes the results.

> Once the patties are cooked through, remove them from the grill and place them on buns. Now you are ready to enjoy a mouthwatering treat that you will long remember.

Writing Processes for Readers Who Won't Perform Them   Like how-to-do-it processes, process descriptions intended for non-doers require you to determine the steps, or for natural processes, the stages, and their functions before you start to write. In addition, since this type of essay does not enable readers to perform the process, think carefully about why you're presenting the information, and let that purpose guide your writing. For instance, if you're trying to persuade readers that the use of rabbits in cosmetics testing should be discontinued, the choices you make in developing your steps should reflect that purpose.

To arouse your reader's interest, you might begin with a historical overview or a brief summary of the whole process, or you could note its importance, among other possible options. The following introduction to an essay on the aging of stars provides a brief historical perspective:

> Peering through their still-crude telescopes, eighteenth-century astronomers discovered a new kind of object in the night sky that appeared neither as the pinprick of light from a distant star nor as the clearly defined disk of a planet but rather as a mottled, cloudy disk. They christened these objects planetary nebulas, or planetary clouds. . . . Modern astronomers recognize planetary nebulas as the fossil wreckage of dying stars ripped apart by powerful winds.

Because the reader will not perform the process, supply only enough details in the body of the paper to provide an intelligent idea of what the procedure entails. Make sure the reader knows the function of each step or stage and its place in the overall process. Present each in one or more paragraphs with clear transitions between the steps or stages. The following excerpt points out the changes that occur as a young star, a red giant, begins the aging process:

> As the bloated star ages, this extended outer atmosphere cools and contracts, then soaks up more energy from the star and again puffs out: with each successive cycle of expansion and contraction, the atmosphere puffs out a little farther. Like a massive piston, these pulsations drive the red giant's atmosphere into space in a

dense wind that blows with speeds up to 15 miles per second. In as little as 10 000 years, some red giants lose an entire sun's worth of matter this way. Eventually this slow wind strips the star down close to its fusion core.

As with processes aimed at performers, end your paper with a few remarks that offer some perspective. You might, for example, evaluate the results of the process, assess its importance, or point out future consequences. The ending of the essay on star aging illustrates the last option:

> The cloud of unanswered questions surrounding planetaries should not obscure the real insight astronomers have recently gained into the extraordinary death of ordinary stars. In a particularly happy marriage of theory and observation, astronomers have discovered our own sun's fate. With the interacting stellar winds model, they can confidently predict the weather about 5 billion years from now; very hot, with *really* strong gusts from the east.
>
> Adam Frank, "Winds of Change"

Revising the Process Analysis

To revise, follow the guidelines in Chapter 5, and ask yourself these questions:

- Have I written consistently for someone who will perform the process or someone who will merely follow it?
- If my paper is intended for performers, have I included every necessary action? Have I explained any purpose that is unclear? Have I warned about any steps that are dangerous or might be performed improperly?
- Are my steps presented in an appropriate order? Developed in sufficient detail? Have I considered appropriate ethical issues?

EXAMPLE OF A STUDENT ESSAY OF PROCESS ANALYSIS

The ABCs of CPR

Kathy Petroski

1   A heart attack, choking, or an electric shock—any of these can stop a person's breathing. The victim, however, need not always die. Many lives that would otherwise be lost can be saved simply by applying the ABCs of CPR—cardiopulmonary resuscitation. Although presence of mind is essential, CPR requires no special equipment. Here's how it is performed. When you are certain that the victim's breathing and pulse have stopped, start CPR immediately. If breathing and circulation aren't restored within five minutes, irreversible brain damage occurs.

2   <u>A</u> stands for opening the airway. Lay the victim in a supine (face up) position on a firm surface. Then tilt the head as far back as possible by gently lifting the chin with one hand. In an unconscious person, the tongue falls to the back of the throat and blocks the air passages. Hyperextending the head in this fashion pulls the tongue from that position, thus allowing air to pass. At the same time tilt the forehead back with the other hand until the chin points straight upward. The relaxed jaw muscles will then tighten, opening the air passage to the lungs. Remove your hand from the forehead and, using your first two fingers, check the mouth for food, dentures, vomitus, or a foreign object. Remove any obstruction with a sweeping motion. These measures may cause the patient to start breathing spontaneously. If they do not, mouth-to-mouth resuscitation must be started.

3   <u>B</u> stands for breathing. Position one hand on the forehead and pinch the victim's nostrils shut with the index finger and thumb of your other hand. Open your mouth, and place it over the victim's mouth so that a tight seal is formed. Such contact allows air to reach and expand the lungs. If the seal is incomplete, you will hear your own breath escaping. Deliver two quick, full breaths without allowing the victim's lungs to deflate completely between breaths; then remove your mouth and allow him or her to exhale passively. At this point, check the carotid pulse to determine whether the heart is beating. To do so, place the tips of your index and middle fingers laterally into the groove between the trachea (windpipe) and the muscles at the side of the neck. If no pulse is evident, artificial circulation must be started.

4   <u>C</u> means circulation. Locate the lower end of the sternum (breastbone), and move upward approximately the width of two fingers. At this point, firmly apply the heel of one hand, positioning the fingers at right angles to the length of the body and keeping them slanted upward. If the hand is positioned any higher or lower on the sternum, serious internal injuries in the abdomen or chest are possible. Now place the heel of your second hand on top of your first. The fingers may be interlaced or interlocked, but they must not touch the chest, or the force of your compressions may fracture ribs.

5   Keeping your elbows straight and pushing down from the shoulders, apply firm, heavy pressure until the sternum is depressed approximately one and one-half to two inches. Rock forward and backward in a rhythmic fashion, exerting pressure with the weight of your body. This action squeezes the heart against the immobile spine with enough pressure to pump blood from the left ventricle of the heart into general circulation. Compress the chest, and then

immediately release the pressure, fifteen times. Do not, at any point in the cycle, remove your hands from the chest wall. Counting the compressions aloud will help develop a systematic cycle, which is essential for success. When the fifteen have been completed, pinch the nose as described above, seal the victim's mouth with your own, and deliver two quick breaths of air. Then compress the chest an additional fifteen times. Alternate respiration and compression steps, timing yourself so as to deliver approximately eighty compressions per minute.

6   At various intervals, quickly check the effectiveness of your CPR technique. Lift the eyelids and notice if the pupils are constricted—a key sign that the brain is receiving enough oxygen. In addition, if the bluish colour of the victim is decreasing and spontaneous breathing and movement are increasing, the victim has responded favourably.

7   To maximize the chances for survival, do not interrupt this technique for more than five or ten seconds. Continue the ABCs of CPR until competent medical help or life-support equipment arrives.

DISCUSSION QUESTIONS

1. How does the writer use the letters *A, B,* and *C* from the CPR technique in this paper?
2. How does the opening paragraph prepare the reader for what follows?
3. Where does the essay indicate the purposes of actions?
4. What order has the writer used? Explain why this order is a good choice.
5. Is the writer merely explaining how the process is carried out, or does she intend for the reader to follow the directions? Defend your answer.

SUGGESTIONS FOR WRITING *Write a process analysis on one of the topics below or one approved by your instructor. The paper may provide instructions for the reader to follow, tell how a process is performed, or describe how a process develops. Prepare a complete list of steps, arrange them in an appropriate order, and follow them as you write the body of your essay.*

1. A natural process, such as erosion, that you observe or research
2. Breaking a bad habit such as procrastination
3. Getting a tattoo
4. The stages in a student's adjustment to university
5. Buying or selling on eBay

6. Putting CDs on an iPod

7. Planning a personal budget

8. The stages in developing an argument

9. Carrying out a process related to your hobby

10. Throwing a successful small party

The Critical Edge

Is there only one way to study effectively, develop a marketing campaign, or cope with a demanding supervisor? No, of course not. As you've already learned, not all processes unfold in a single, predetermined order. For this reason, there are many different approaches to writing about processes.

Imagine you are writing a process paper about the writing process itself. The steps in the process would be determined by the nature of the writing situation, the purpose and audience for the writing. Informal writing to a friend would require fewer steps than formal, academic writing. For example, when you write an email to a good friend, you probably just start typing without any preliminaries and press "send" as soon as you are finished. However, in formal writing such as job applications or academic research essays, the writing process involves careful planning, drafting, revising, and editing.

Sometimes the same writing occasion may allow for differing procedures. If you're writing a short essay for your English class, you might brainstorm for ideas, develop a detailed outline, rough out a bare-bones draft, and add details as you revise. In talking to other students with the same assignment, you might find that they prefer to write a much longer draft and then whittle it down. Others might do very little brainstorming or outlining but a great deal of revising, often making major changes in several drafts. Even in the complex challenge of writing research essays, variations are possible: One student might prepare the list of works cited before writing the final draft, while another might perform this task last.

But the fact that processes can differ does not mean that all processes are equal—or even correct. Sometimes important and even popular processes have been disputed in print. If you want to assess a process description, you need to do some of your own investigations or research. Informed disagreements exist about the order of processes, such as how language developed, or how children mature emotionally or cognitively. Police officers debate the best way to handle drunks, and management experts argue about how best to motivate employees. When you investigate such controversies, determine which view is supported by the best evidence and seems most reasonable. Then, as a writer, you can present the accounts in an appropriate order, comparing one to the other and perhaps indicating which one you think merits acceptance.*

---

*If you rely on information obtained through interviews, read pages 451–453 in Chapter 16. If you rely on published sources, read the sections on library and internet research in Chapter 15 and those on handling quotations and avoiding plagiarism in Chapter 17. As always, follow your instructor's guidelines for documenting sources.

SUGGESTIONS FOR WRITING

1. Drawing on your own experience and/or interviews with others, write an essay explaining how to make decisions about an area that is important in some way to you right now:

   — a decision about what courses to take
   — a decision about what car to buy
   — a decision about what kind of job or career to pursue
   — a decision about where to travel

2. Write an essay explaining how to manage money, or get out of debt, while one is a student.

PROCESS ANALYSIS ESSAYS: PROFESSIONAL MODELS

READING STRATEGIES

1. Determine the reason you are reading the process essay. If it is to follow instructions, you need to read in one way; if it is to understand a process, you need to read differently.

2. If you are going to follow the instructions, read over the process first to get an understanding of the whole. Look for specific warnings or feedback you should consider. Get an idea of what the end result should look like. Gather any equipment you need. Then follow the process step by step, checking after each step to make certain the results you are obtaining match those described in the process.

3. If you want to understand the process thoroughly, first read it quickly to get an overview. As you read through again more slowly, take notes outlining the major steps of the process.

READING CRITICALLY

1. Check to see if the process could be completed differently or more effectively. Are there any cautions or warnings not included in the essay that should be there?

2. If the writer is explaining a process, is there evidence that his or her account is correct? Verify that there is good reason to believe the given account. If you believe there might be competing accounts of the process, test your suspicion by doing some research.

READING AS A WRITER

1. Observe how the writer uses verbs to indicate actions.

2. Notice how the writer gets from step to step in the process. If there is a strategy you could use, make note of it.

Rod McQueen

Millionaire Questionnaire

Born in Guelph, Ontario, in 1944, Rod McQueen has worked as a reporter, editor, director of public affairs at the Bank of Nova Scotia, and managing business editor at Maclean's. He has won many awards for his writing, including the National Business Book Award for Who Killed Confederation Life? The Inside Story. *He has authored thirteen other books, including* The Last Best Hope—How to Start and Grow Your Own Business *and* The Icarus Factor: The Rise and Fall of Edgar Bronfman, Jr. *He is now a Toronto-based senior writer at* The Financial Post. *Rod McQueen's clear, tightly structured essay "Millionaire Questionnaire" might also have been called "Steps to Starting a Small Business" or "Setting a Goal and Succeeding."*

> Title implies a process: questions and answers on how to become a millionaire

> Several introductory strategies are employed to engage the audience: arresting statement (para. 1), personal challenge (paras. 2 and 3), and rhetorical question (para. 4)

> Thesis: clearly asserts the essay's focus on the top ten steps to success as identified by the presidents of Canada's 50 Best Managed Private Companies (para. 5)

> Each of the ten steps to success is expressed as a direct assertion to the audience, giving the essay a consistent format and focusing the audience on the process (paras. 5–24)

> The use of specific personal examples demonstrates and explains each of the 10 steps to success while engaging the audience with "real" anecdotes that are likely to be relatable to their own experiences.

1   Lottery tickets are a waste of money. Everybody knows the improbable odds—one in 13 million.

2   There's a better way to become a millionaire. You've already got everything you need—right inside.

3   Here's the four-word secret: Start your own business.

4   Have you got what it takes?

5   After five years of interviewing the presidents of Canada's 50 Best Managed Private Companies, I've identified the top 10 steps to success.

6   **1. Find a need and fill it.** Have a plan and follow it. Newfoundland's Lorraine Lush concluded that her neighbours needed work skills. For 14 years she'd been a secretary, so she taught the first 65 students what she knew best: secretarial skills.

7   Today, The Career Academy has 22 programs, 3000 students and 15 campuses.

8   **2. Believe in yourself.** If you don't, who will? When free trade arrived in 1989, observers predicted the demise of Morrison Lamothe Inc., an Ottawa bakery begun in the 1930s. Third-generation president John Morrison didn't heed the so-called experts.

9   The firm focused on private-label frozen dinners. Almost half of the product line is new in the last four years, and the firm is tackling the U.S.

10   **3. Exude optimism.** Nobody wants to deal with a dud. Geoff Chutter runs Whitewater West Industries Ltd., of Richmond, B.C., making waterslides and wave pools.

11   Talking to this man is like taking a tonic. Despite having the best job in the world, Chutter has twice run for Parliament because he believes he can make a public policy difference.

12   **4. Be flexible.** Bend the rules. Take chances. Mining exploration fell two-thirds from 1987 to 1992, and with it went the drilling tool business of Fordia, in St. Laurent, Que.

13   Fordia's Alain Paquet took a chance and chased customers in South America. "Your life is at risk when traveling in those areas," he says after being robbed in Venezuela. "You can get killed for nothing if you're not careful." He and the company both survived. Fordia now sells in 28 countries.

14   **5. Exercise vision.** This is the capacity to see the invisible. In September, 1996, a stranger arrived at Crila Plastic Industries Ltd., in Mississauga, Ont., promoting an unlikely product, a plastic that looked and acted like wood.

15   Intrigued, Crila president Peter Clark flew to Britain, obtained North American rights, and now sells two million board feet of Extrudawood per month in an industry where a million board feet of anything in a year is a good sale.

16   **6. Accept help and advice.** Honour what people have to offer. Edmonton-based Fountain Tire doesn't just wait to hear ideas, it goes looking.

17   Says CEO Brian Hesje: "It's more productive to be humbled by those that succeed rather than have the false sense of security that comes from visiting the less successful."

18   **7. Tap the passion within.** Be resourceful. Trust your instincts. "I believe entrepreneurs are being visited by divine inspiration," says clothing designer Linda Lundström. "I also believe an entrepreneur can visualize something and make it happen."

19   How else to explain the moment when a bird-dropping spattered her car windshield while Lundström drove on an expressway. She combined that unhappy impact with a message she read on a passing truck and concluded that her La Parka line would do well. Her instincts were accurate.

20   **8. Fulfill customers' needs and exceed their expectations.** Glegg Water Conditioning, of Guelph, Ont., shipped a key component to a U.S. client, but customs problems meant a 24-hour delay.

21   A Lear jet was chartered to deliver the item that very day. "We'll do whatever it takes to look after our clients," says president and CEO Robert Glegg.

22   **9. Never give up.** True character means never accepting defeat. Robert Mills and his son, Ray, of Calgary, spent nine months in 1989 making 1000 sales calls. They sold only two of their pumps.

23   In the tenth month, Ray sold 15 pumps to one company. Today, Kudu Industries Inc., employs 100 and has annual sales of $35 million.

24   **10. Dream it and do it.** Olympic cyclist Louis Garneau's racing gear and helmet business, based in St.-Augustin, Quebec, began with one sewing machine in his father's garage. Montreal's Karel Velan filled his order book using a four-page leaflet before he'd manufactured his first valve.

25   Not every start-up succeeds; annual failure rates run to 20 percent.

26   But what that also means is that out of 100 new businesses launched tomorrow, 30 will still be alive in five years.

27   Of those, 20 percent will be scraping by, 60 percent will be doing middling well, but 20 percent will be spectacularly successful.

28   Each of those six firms will have anywhere from 30 to 100 employees plus annual sales as high as $50 million.

29   And each of those individual founders will be millionaires.

30   Six millionaires for every 100 entrants.

31   I like those odds. Don't you?

32   You have the power to make of tomorrow exactly what you want.

> The inspirational tone throughout the essay is reasserted at the end with the personal challenge to become successful by applying the process steps explained in the essay (paras. 31 and 32).

DISCUSSION QUESTIONS

1. Why do you suppose the writer uses examples to illustrate each step? What examples do you find especially vivid?

2. Consider the brevity of the paragraphs in this article, especially the introductory and concluding paragraphs. Why do you think the writer has written such short paragraphs?

3. Find examples of the writer's use of numbers and statistics, quotations, and rhetorical questions. Comment on their effect.

4. Do you trust the writer's advice in this essay? Why or why not?

TOWARD KEY INSIGHTS

What reasons besides financial ones might people have for starting a small business? If you were to "find a need and fill it," what business would you start?

If you were to start a business or become a partner in an existing business immediately after leaving school, would you prefer to start your own small business or join a corporation? Explain.

Some people believe that superstores, large chains, and shopping malls make it difficult for small businesses to compete successfully. What is your view? Where do you prefer to take your business?

SUGGESTION FOR WRITING *Think of an endeavour outside the business realm where it is important to "believe in yourself," and write an essay explaining how to be successful in this activity.*

Mark Kingwell

Ten Steps to Creating a Modern Media Icon

Mark Kingwell is a professor of philosophy at the University of Toronto, where he is a fellow of Trinity College and senior fellow of Massey College. Kingwell, born in 1963 in Toronto, is the author of several books of political and cultural theory and popular philosophy, including Concrete Reveries: Consciousness and the City *(2008),* Nearest Thing to Heaven: The Empire State Building and American Dreams *(2006), and* Catch and Release: Trout Fishing and the Meaning of Life *(2003). His work has appeared in a wide range of publications from leading academic journals to mainstream magazines such as* Harper's, Adbusters, the Walrus, *and the* New York Times Magazine. *Kingwell is also a contributing editor to several North American publications.*

1.   **1.** "Icon" is from the Greek *eikon*, which means "image," which is everything: The name of a camera. The word for all those little point-and-click pictures on your computer screen. Greek and Roman Orthodox religious objects. Little oil paintings of saints with elaborate gold panel coverings. Anybody who represents something to someone somewhere. The image that gives a debased Platonic suggestion of reality without ever being it. So create an image — one the cameras, and therefore we, will love.

2.   **2.** The image must be drastically beautiful or else compellingly ugly. It must, for women, show a smooth face of impenetrable maquillage and impeccably "tasteful" clothing (Chanel, Balenciaga, Rykiel; not Versace, not Moschino, definitely not Gauthier), a flat surface of emotional projection, the real-world equivalent of a keyboard emoticon. Icon smiling at the cheering crowds: :-). Icon frowning bravely at diseased child or crippled former soldier in hospital bed: :-(. Icon winking slyly at the crush of press photographers as she steps into the waiting limousine: ;-). There should be only one name, for preference a chummy or faux-intimate diminutive: Jackie, Di, Barbra. Sunglasses are mandatory whenever the ambient light rises above building-code-normal 250-foot candles. These can be removed or peered over to offer an image of blinking vulnerability.

3.   Or else the image should be, in men, so overwhelmingly tawdry and collapsed, preferably from some high-cheekbone peak of youthful beauty, that it acquires a can't-look-away magnetism, the sick pull of the human car wreck. (The only exceptions: (1) Athletes—Tiger, Michael—whose downy smoothness and transcendental physical abilities offer a male counterpoint that is almost female in appeal; they are the contraltos of the icon chorus. And (2) actors, whose malleable faces are so empty of particular meaning as to be innocent of intelligence.) Folds of leathery skin, evidence of drug use and chain-smoking, the runes of dissipation etched on the pitted skin of hard living—they all have them. Johnny Cash, Mick Jagger, Leonard Cohen, Kurt Cobain, Chet Baker, late Elvis: the musician in ruins, the iconic face as crumbling stone monument.

4.   Basic black attire is effective but must be Armani, never Gap. This suggests wisdom and sexual power, deep and bitter knowledge of the world—but with dough. The face need never change, its very stasis a sign of rich inner troubles. Sunglasses are superfluous. They smack of effort.

5.   **3.** There must be a narrative structure that bathes the icon in the pure light of the fairy tale or morality play. Beautiful princess beset by ugly siblings or nasty stepmother. Lovely rich girl mistakes the charisma of power for true character. Overweening ambition turns simple boy into gun-toting, pill-popping maniac. Feisty rebel takes on the establishment of (circle one) Hollywood/big business/government/rock music/professional sports. Prodigy singled out for great things at an early age by psycho father.

6.   Indispensable words in the story: "trapped," "betray," "tragic," "love," "promise" (as both verb and noun), "happiness" (always without irony), "fame" (always with venom), and "money" (never spoken). The details of the story may change, but the overarching structure cannot: you can improvise and elaborate, but never deviate.

Sometimes a new story (thrill-happy slut consorts with swarthy and disreputable jet-setter) will be temporarily substituted for an old one that no longer applies (virginal bride is unloved by philandering husband). We can't be sure which story will win out until. . . .

7 **4.**   Death. Already, at step four? Yes, absolutely, for iconography is very much a postmortem affair.

8   The death ends the life but does not quite complete it: that is the business of story-tellers and their audience, the cameras and their lights. Death is just the beginning. It should be, if possible, violent, messy and a bit mysterious. Unwise confrontations with fast-moving industrial machines—sports cars, airplanes, cargo trucks, high-speed trains, bullets. Accidents are good, having as they do an aura of adventitious innocence, followed closely in order of preference by murder, assassination, execution and suicide. If suicide it must be either a gun or an overdose of illicit drugs, usually in colorful and nasty combination: alcohol and barbiturates, crack and benzedrine, heroin and anything.

9   In all cases, the death is "shocking" and "tragic," though in neither instance literally.

10 **5.**   Now, an outbreak of hysterical mourning, baseless and all the more intense for being so. (Nobody feels so strongly about someone they actually know.) Extended retrospectives on television. Numerous panel discussions and attempts to "make sense," to "assess the life," to "provide context." Long broadcasts of the funeral or memorial service complete with lingering, loving shots of weeping crowds. Greedy close-ups of the well-known people in attendance, the bizarre fraternity of celebrity which dictates that those famous for being born in a certain family have everything in common with those famous for singing pop tunes or throwing a ball in a designated manner.

11   News agencies and networks must spend a great deal of money sending a lot of people somewhere distant to cover the death. They must then justify that expense with hours and hours of coverage. We must see images of the iconic face, beautiful or ruined, over and over and over. "Ordinary" people must be shown, on the media, insisting that the media have nothing to do with their deep feelings of loss. They must say that they "felt they knew him (her)," that "she (he) was like a member of the family." This keeps them happy and ensures that no larger form of public participation—say, protesting a tax hike or program cut, resisting a corporate takeover—will ever cross their minds as possible, let alone desirable.

12 **6.**   A small backlash must gather strength, a token gesture of cultural protest that, in pointing out the real faults and shortcomings of the dead icon, unwittingly reinforces the growing "larger-than-life" status of the image. This is the culture's way of injecting itself with a homeopathic inoculation, introducing a few strains of mild virus that actually beef up the dominant media antibodies. Those who have the temerity to suggest that the dead icon was not all he (she) is thought to be will be publicly scorned, accused of cynicism, insulted at dinner parties, but secretly welcomed.

13   The final storyline of the icon-life will now begin to set, rejecting the foreign elements as dead-ends or narrative spurs, or else accepting them as evidence that the icon was "after all" human—a suggestion that, in its very making, implies the opposite. The media coverage will fall into line in telling this story because individual producers and anchors will be unable to imagine doing otherwise. Taglines and feature-story titles will help set the narrative epoxy for good, providing catchy mini-stories for us to hang our thoughts on to. Quickie books with the same titles will begin to appear—things like *Icon X: Tragic Ambition* or *Icon Y: Little Girl in Trouble.*

14   The producers and anchors must then claim that they are not creating this tale, simply "giving the people what they want." Most people will accept this because to do otherwise would hurt their brains.

15 **7.** The image will now be so widely reproduced, so ubiquitously mediated on television, at the supermarket, in the bookstore, that it seems a permanent feature of the mediascape, naturalized and indispensable. It will now begin its final divorce from the person depicted. Any actual achievements— touchdowns thrown, elections won, causes championed—fall away like the irrelevancies they are. The face (or rather, The Face) looms outward from glossy paper, T-shirts, fridge magnets, posters, Halloween masks and coffee mugs.

16   Kitschification of the image is to be welcomed, not feared. It proves that the icon is here to stay. The basic unit of fame-measurement is of course, as critic Cullen Murphy once argued, the *warhol*, a period of celebrity equal to fifteen minutes. Kitsch versions of the image auger well: we're talking at least a megawarhol icon or better (that's fifteen million minutes of fame, which is just over 10,400 days, or about 28.5 years—enough to get you to those standard silver-anniversary retrospectives). No kitsch, no staying power: a hundred kilowarhols or less, a minicon.

17 **8.** There follow academic studies, well-meaning but doomed counter-assessments, sightings, and cameo appearances of the icon on a *Star Trek* spinoff series or as an answer on *Jeopardy*. People begin to claim they can commune with the spirit of the dead icon across vast distances of psychic space. Conspiracy theories refuse to be settled by overwhelming evidence of a boringly predictable chain of events involving a drunk driver, too much speed, and unused seatbelts. Or whatever.

18 **9.** Television retrospectives every decade, with a mid-decade special at twenty-five years. The final triumph of the image: entirely cut off now from its original body, it is free-floating and richly polysemous. Always more surface than depth, more depiction than reality, the icon now becomes pure zero-degree image, a depicted lifestyle without a life, a face without a person, a spiritual moment without context or meaning. In other words, the pure pervasive triumph of cultural exposure, a sign lacking both sense and referent. In still other words, the everything (and nothing) we sought all along: communion without community.

19 **10.** Now, for a religious experience, just point. And click.

DISCUSSION QUESTIONS

1. What is Kingwell's definition of the word "icon," and why does he begin with it? What examples does he give of icons from various contexts? Do you understand what he means when he suggests that the icon is "the image that gives a debased Platonic suggestion of reality without ever being it"? What does Plato—a Greek philosopher from the fifth century BCE—have to do with media icons? If necessary, look up Plato's theory of forms to answer this question.

2. Kingwell says that the image (icon) created by the camera is the "flat-screen equivalent of a keyboard emotion"; what does he mean by this comparison? He includes examples of icons along with verbal descriptions such as "Icon frowning bravely at diseased child or crippled former soldier in hospital bed: :-(. Icon winking slyly at the crush of press photographers as she steps into the waiting limousine: ;-)." What is the effect of his inclusion of these "keyboard emotions" (called *emoticons*) that go along with the verbal descriptions in a serious analytical essay? What is the connection between these text messaging icons and the celebrity icons that are the main subject of his essay?

3. Although the public fascination with media icons may seem a harmless form of entertainment, Kingwell makes a serious point about the effect that this obsession with public icons has on "public participation" (paragraph 11). Explain what he means here, and discuss whether or not you agree with this claim.

4. In an essay about a rather abstract phenomenon (the making of a media icon), Kingwell uses a number of metaphors and analogies that appeal to the senses. Consider paragraph 12, for example, where Kingwell suggests that pointing out a media icon's faults is the "culture's way of injecting itself with a homeopathic inoculation, introducing a few strains of mild virus that actually beef up the dominant media antibodies." Explain what Kingwell means by this analogy. Then locate other metaphors or analogies in the same paragraph, and explain their meaning. What is the effect of including these analogies and metaphors?

5. Explain the effect of the one-sentence conclusion. What is the tone here?

TOWARD KEY INSIGHTS

1. The writer suggests a number of possible story lines, or narrative structures, that the media seize upon in their making of icons (for example, "the feisty rebel takes on" a particular kind of establishment such as big business). Kingwell claims, "The details of the story may change, but the overarching structure cannot: you can improvise and elaborate, but never deviate." To what extent do you agree that stories in the media are this formulaic and predictable? Can you think of a particular media story that fits one of the narrative outlines that Kingwell has mentioned? Zeroing in on more examples of a media or movie or even a television series icon, show how the steps or stages in this narrative resemble Kingwell's, but complicate the narrative by adding to or changing the bare bones narrative that Kingwell has offered here.

2. Kingwell claims that "iconography is very much a post mortem affair" (paragraph 4). To what extent do you agree that the media treats the death of celebrities in the way that Kingwell describes?

SUGGESTIONS FOR WRITING

1. Write an essay showing the steps that advertisers follow as they prepare to create consumer demand for a new product, or the steps that the media follow in creating an iconic news story. Use one extended example or several smaller examples to illustrate these steps.

2. Write an essay that explains the steps of text messaging from a cell phone or instant messaging, using shorthand forms of communication such as emoticons, to a member of the older generation who has never done this before.

Steve Whysall

Don't Let Emotion Guide Your Email

Born in Nottingham, England, Steve Whysall has been the garden columnist for the Vancouver Sun *for more than a decade. He is the author of three books:* 100 Best Plants for the Coastal Garden, The Blooming Great Gardening Book, *and* 100 Best Plants for Ontario Gardens. *The first two were No. 1 best-sellers in B.C. In 1999, he was named Communicator of the Year by the B.C. Landscape and Nursery Association. In addition to being a regular lecturer at garden shows and garden clubs, he has also written for magazines and done numerous spots on TV. Before coming to Canada in 1975, he worked for various newspapers in the U.K. including the* London Evening News, *the* Bristol Post, *and the* Nottingham Evening Post.

1   In the movie *Groundhog Day*, Bill Murray kidnaps Pennsylvania's famous weather-forecasting groundhog, Punxsutawney Phil.

2   He plonks the furry, chisel-toothed creature on his lap and lets him steer a truck at high speed. "Don't drive angry, don't drive angry," Murray warns Phil.

3   He might just as well have been laying down rules for email interaction.

4   Email sent in anger is not unlike putting a groundhog behind the wheel of a truck. It might seem like a good idea at the time, but the fact is a wild creature occupies the driver's seat and no matter how good-intentioned, the action is destined to result in a disastrous crash and burn.

5   To avoid misunderstanding and keep the emotional tone on track, some people add to their email animated smiley faces or tiny pictures composed of brackets, commas, dashes and other simple ASCII characters.

6   None of which would change a thing if you "flame" someone by dashing off an angry response in the heat of the moment. The goofy little yellow smileys (winking, cringing, weeping, jumping, clapping and so on) are more likely to add insult to injury than inject clarity and reason.

7   So, what exactly are the rules of email etiquette? Are you obliged to reply to every message? And if so, how quickly are you supposed to respond?

8   Does it matter what you write in the "subject" line? And what about length of the message: Can you give offence by being too blunt, or do you give more offence by waffling or saying too much?

9   For answers, we consulted various sources. The London School of Economics, for instance, has come up with a whole bunch of recommendations.

10   And a survey of 750 European office workers produced a list of the "seven deadly email sins," of which ignoring, long-windedness, blitzing and tactlessness were the top four.

11   Dozens of books have been written on the subject. There's *EMail Etiquette: Do's, Don'ts and Disaster Tales from People Magazine's Internet* by Samantha Miller, *The Wormwood File: Email from Hell* by Jim Forest, and *Office Emails that Really Click* by Maureen Chase.

12   Here's a compilation of the basic rules of email etiquette, most of which you have probably figured out for yourself already.

13   **Ignore or reply.** The London School of Economics says you should always reply, even if a brief acknowledgement is all you can handle. "Ignoring a mail message is discourteous and confusing to the sender," it says. The LSE also thinks replies should be prompt. On the other hand, some say email senders should be patient and not expect an immediate answer. "Just because you don't get an answer from someone in 10 minutes does not mean he or she is ignoring you and is no cause for offence."

14   But it is also worth bearing in mind that the volume of email has increased dramatically, and many people find they don't have time to respond to every message, and you shouldn't respond to junk or spam mail. Bottom line: Always reply (if possible) and don't wait too long to do it.

15   **Think about tone.** *Merriam-Webster* defines tone as "accent or inflection expressive of a mood or emotion." Hitting the right tone is important in email. You should come across as respectful, friendly and approachable, not curt or demanding. Avoid using irony or sarcasm—they are easily misunderstood.

16   **Never write in anger, in the heat of the moment.** Take a walk, think about it, write, then think about it again. Emails lack the facial clues and body language you would normally use in a personal encounter to adjust your response. Angry words almost always come across as more harsh in black and white. "Flaming" is when you deliberately burn someone with an angry message.

17   **Avoid typing in capitals.** It's considered the vulgar equivalent of shouting, and the sender of such emails always comes across as rude and uneducated. Same applies to the excessive use of exclamation marks. Do you really want to be that forceful? Isn't the statement you are making strong enough??????

18   **Be brief but not too brief.** It is possible to be too terse in your email reply. This can come across as rude and tactless. Especially annoying is to have a detailed memo returned with the words: "Me too." That's not good enough. Questions should be answered, partly to pre-empt further questions. It is safe to assume an email is sent because a quick, brief response is called for, but the response should be an appropriate length. The London School of Economics suggests "try to restrict yourself to one or two screenfuls at most."

Another suggestion is to "match your message length to the tenor of the conversation: if you are only making a quick query, then make it short and to the point."

19   **Be clear in your subject line.** The word or words used should be as meaningful as possible, not vague or misleading. The idea is to use the words to focus the topic of the message. The LSE recommends: "Try to restrict yourself to one subject per message, sending multiple messages if you have multiple subjects."

20   **Don't blitz.** This is one of the seven deadly email sins identified in a survey of 750 European office workers. Blitzing (sending the same email more than once) was considered extremely annoying along with "presuming" (assuming the receiver knows who you are and what you are talking about) and "tactlessness" when email is used inappropriately to share or discuss sensitive information. Top of the list, however, was "ignoring" (not replying) and "longwindedness."

21   **Don't pick on emailers who can't spell.** The rules about spelling are much more loosely applied when it comes to email. It is generally regarded as petty, even rude, to point out someone else's spelling mistakes in an email, partly because email is considered conversational.

22   **Keep your signature short.** The signature is the small block of text at the end of your messages that contains your contact information. Keep them short and to the point with only essential information: your mailing address, fax and phone number.

23   **Don't forget your P's an Q's.** It may sound dated, but people still like you to say please and thank you. Interestingly, people who are normally polite in everyday life often forget their manners in their emails.

24   **Don't attach files unless they were asked for.** It can be annoying to have attachments that either cannot be opened or once they are opened were unnecessary. Many people refuse to open unasked-for attachments for fear of releasing a virus.

25   **Do you reply or send a new message?** Some believe when you reply, you must include the original email as reference. Others say you should remove the previous message (since it has already been sent) and reply or send a new email altogether. However, the argument against sending a completely new message is that it creates a "threadless email"—one that the receiver could have difficulty understanding if it were left unread for a time.

DISCUSSION QUESTIONS

1. Why do you suppose the writer uses the example of the movie *Groundhog Day* in the opening paragraphs?

2. What effect results from the writer's use of rhetorical questions in paragraph 7?

3. What appeals to authority does the writer use to reinforce the assertions in this essay? Comment on their effect.

4. Do you agree with the writer's advice in this essay? Why or why not?

TOWARD KEY INSIGHTS

What underlying values relating to the treatment of others inform the advice given in this essay?

When you use email, do you follow the writer's guidelines? Have you ever received or sent email that did not follow these guidelines? How did you feel afterward?

Some people believe that email communication has contributed to a "lowered" standard of written discourse because of the informality of diction and conversational style that is prevalent. What is your view? Explain.

SUGGESTION FOR WRITING *Think of another activity or venue in which appropriate etiquette is often forgotten, and write an essay that explains the guidelines for appropriate interaction there.*

CHAPTER 10

Strategies for Analytical Writing: Cause and Effect

EXPLAINING WHY

Like the two sides of a coin, cause and effect are inseparably linked. Together they make up *causation*. Cause probes the reasons why actions, events, attitudes, and conditions exist. Effect examines their consequences. Causation can help explain historical events, natural happenings, and the actions and attitudes of individuals and groups. It can also help us anticipate the consequences of personal actions, natural phenomena, or government policies.

Everyone uses questions of causation in daily life. For example, Scott wonders why Gina *really* broke off their relationship, and Jennifer speculates on the consequences of changing her major. Many wonder why homeless populations are on the rise in Canadian cities, and millions worry about the effects of deteriorating air and water quality.

At school, your instructors might ask you to write on topics such as the causes of the Quebec separatist movement, the psychological consequences of workplace harassment, the causes or effects of the rise in greenhouse gases in the atmosphere, or the positive effects of urban community gardens. In the workplace, you may need to write a report explaining why a certain product malfunctions, a proposal detailing what might happen if a community redesigns its traffic pattern, or a study explaining how increased energy costs might affect business.

PATTERNS IN CAUSAL ANALYSIS

Several organizational patterns are used in a causal analysis. Sometimes, a single cause produces several effects. For instance, poor language skills prevent students from keeping up with required reading, taking adequate notes, and writing competent papers and essay exams. Below, the outline on the left shows a pattern for a paper that traces a single cause with multiple effects; on the right, we're shown how this pattern could be used for a paper analyzing the effects of having poor language skills in school.

I. Introduction: identifies cause	I. Poor language skills
II. Body	II. Body
A. Effect number 1	A. Can't keep up with required reading
B. Effect number 2	B. Can't take adequate notes
C. Effect number 3	C. Can't write competent papers or exams
III. Conclusion	III. Conclusion

Alternatively, you might discuss the cause after the effects are presented.

On the other hand, several causes may join forces to produce one effect. For example, lumber production in British Columbia has decreased over the last few years because stumpage fees are higher, international demand is lower, and foreign competition is stronger. Note how the outline below on the left shows a pattern for an analysis of how multiple causes may contribute to a single effect; on the right, you'll see how this pattern could be used for an outline on the reasons for a decrease in B.C. lumber production.

I. Introduction: identifies effect	I. Decrease in B.C. lumber production
II. Body	II. Body
A. Cause number 1	A. Higher stumpage fees
B. Cause number 2	B. Lower international demand
C. Cause number 3	C. Stronger foreign competition
III. Conclusion	III. Conclusion

As an alternative, you can also discuss the effects following the presentation of causes.

Often a set of events forms a causal chain, with each event the effect of the preceding one and the cause of the following one. For example, a student sleeps late and so misses breakfast and ends up hungry and distracted, which in turn results in a poor performance on an exam. Interrupting the chain at any point halts the sequence. Such chains can be likened to a row of falling dominoes. The U.S. entry into the Vietnam War illustrates a causal chain: One major cause of the war was a widespread belief in the domino theory, which held that, if one nation in Southeast Asia fell to the communists, all would fall, one after the other. Causal chains can also help explain how devices function and social changes proceed.

In many situations, the sequence of causes and effects is too complex to fit the image of a chain. Suppose you are driving to a movie on a rainy night. You approach an intersection screened by bushes, and, because you have the right-of-way, you start to drive across. Suddenly, a car with unlit headlights looms directly in your path. You hit the brakes but skid on the slippery pavement and crash into the other car, crumpling its left fender and damaging your own bumper. Later, as you think through the episode, you become aware of its complexities.

Obviously, the *immediate cause* of the accident was the other driver's failure to heed the stop sign. But other causes also played roles: the bushes and unlit headlights that kept you from seeing the other car sooner; the starts and stops, speedups and slowdowns that brought the two cars to the intersection at the same time; the wet pavement that made you more likely to skid; and the movie that brought you out in the first place.

You also realize that the effects of the accident go beyond the fender and bumper damage. After the accident, a police officer ticketed the other driver. As a result of the delay, you missed the movie. Further, the accident unnerved you so badly that you couldn't attend classes the next day and therefore missed an important writing assignment. Because of a bad driving record, the other driver lost his licence for sixty days. Clearly, the effects of this accident rival the causes in complexity.

Here's how you might organize a multiple cause–multiple effect essay:

I.	Introduction		I.	The accident
II.	Body		II.	Body
	A.	Cause number 1		A. Driver ran stop sign
	B.	Cause number 2		B. Bushes and unlit headlights impaired vision
	C.	Cause number 3		C. Wet pavement caused skidding
	D.	Effect number 1		D. Missed the movie
	E.	Effect number 2		E. Unnerved so missed classes next day
	F.	Effect number 3		F. Other driver lost licence
III.	Conclusion		III.	Conclusion

In some situations, you might first present the effects, then turn to the causes.

EXERCISE

1. **Read the following paragraph on political change in Ireland, and then arrange the events in a causal chain:**

   At a key moment, labour, business, and government leaders abandoned ideological differences and constructed a shared socio-economic strategy. These factors, in concert with strategic investment in education and a focused effort to attract new foreign direct investment, produced over 500 000 new jobs in the 1990s. Ireland's recent economic success has been achieved, in part, through a social or strategic partnership. Armed with a consensus on the problem, they took a long-term, strategic approach to economic and social change. The steps they took established a positive labour relations climate and stabilized the macro-economic and fiscal situation in Ireland.

   "Strategic Partnership," The Strategic Partnership Study Group,
   Province of Newfoundland and Labrador, June 2002

2. Trace the possible effects of the following occurrences:

    a. You pick out a salad at the cafeteria and sit down to eat. Suddenly, you notice a large green worm on one of the lettuce leaves.

    b. As you leave your science lab, you trip and break your arm.

REASONING ERRORS IN CAUSAL ANALYSIS

Ignoring Multiple Causes

An effect rarely stems from a single cause. The person who believes that permissive parents have caused the present upsurge of sexually transmitted diseases or the one who blames video game violence for the climbing numbers of emotionally disturbed children oversimplifies the situation. Permissiveness and violence perhaps did contribute to these conditions. However, numerous other factors have also undoubtedly played important parts.

Mistaking Chronology for Causation

Don't assume that, just because one event follows another, the first necessarily causes the second. Therese breaks a mirror just before Wade breaks their engagement; then she blames the cracked mirror. Youth crime rates may have declined since the *Youth Criminal Justice Act* was introduced, but does this mean that the introduction of the *Youth Criminal Justice Act* has necessarily caused the decline in youth crime rates? Don't misunderstand: One event *may* cause the next event, but before you go on record with your conclusion, make sure that you're not dealing with mere chronology.

Confusing Causes with Effects

Young children sometimes declare that the moving trees make the wind blow. Similarly, you may assume that Tara's relationship breakdown caused her depression, whereas perhaps, her undiagnosed depression caused her relationship breakdown. Scan your evidence carefully in order to avoid such faulty assertions.

EXERCISE *Which of the following statements point toward papers that focus on causes? Which point toward papers focusing on effects? Explain your answers.*

    1. There are many reasons why more male students than female students drop out of school.

    2. While offshore oil exploration will produce new jobs, it may also damage the marine environment in a number of ways.

    3. Children who live in poverty are twice as likely as other children to have poor health, low scores on school readiness exams, and high remediation needs.

ETHICAL ISSUES

Causation is not immune from abuse, either accidental or deliberate. Imagine the consequences of an article that touts a new medication but fails to mention several serious side effects that could harm many users. Think about the possible strain on your relationship with a friend if she unjustly accuses you of starting a vicious rumour about her. Asking and answering the following questions can help you meet the ethical responsibilities of writing a cause-and-effect paper.

- Have I tried to uncover all of the causes that might result in a particular outcome? A report blaming poor instruction alone for a high failure rate in a town's public schools almost certainly overlooks such factors as over-sized classes, inadequate facilities, and economic deprivation.

- Have I carefully weighed the importance of the causes I've uncovered? If only two or three of the classes in the school system are oversized, then the report should not dwell on the significance of class size.

- Have I tried to uncover and discuss every important effect, even one that might damage a case I'm trying to make? A report emphasizing the beneficial effects of jogging would be negligent if it failed to note the potential for injury.

- What would be the consequences if people acted on my advice?

Careful evaluation of causes and effects shows that you have taken your ethical obligations as a writer seriously.

WRITING A CAUSAL ANALYSIS

Planning and Drafting the Causal Analysis

Because you have probably speculated about the causes and effects of several campus, local, provincial, or national problems, writing this type of paper should pose no great difficulty. For more personal essays, you can draw on your own experience, perhaps exploring a topic such as "Why I Dislike (or Like) Social Networking" or "The Effects of a Learning Disability on My Life." For more formal writing, which may require you to draw on library or other secondary sources, you might explore larger issues such as "What's Behind Teenage Suicides?" or "The Impact of the U.S. Credit Crisis on Canadian Corporations."

The strategies on pages 34–40 can also help you find several topics. Answer these questions about each potential candidate:

What purpose guides this writing?

Who is my audience? Will the topic interest them? Why or why not?

Shall I focus on causes, effects, or both?

Brainstorming your topic for supporting details should be straightforward. If you're dealing with causes, consider these questions about each one:

How significant is this cause?

Could it have brought about the effect by itself?

Does it form part of a chain?

Precisely how does it contribute to the effect?

For papers dealing with effects, ask these questions:

How important is this effect?

What evidence will establish its importance?

Charting your results can help you prepare for writing the paper. You might tabulate causes with an arrangement like this one:

Cause	Contribution to Effect
First cause	Specific contribution
Second cause	Specific contribution

For effects, use this chart:

Effect	Importance
First effect	Why important
Second effect	Why important

Once your items are tabulated, carefully examine them for completeness. Perhaps you've overlooked a cause or effect or have slighted the significance of one you've already mentioned. Think about the order in which you'd like to discuss your items and prepare a revised chart that reflects your decision.

Use the opening of your paper to identify your topic and indicate whether you plan to discuss causes, effects, or both. You can signal your intention in a number of ways. To prepare for a focus on causes, you might use the words *cause, reason,* or *stem from,* or you might ask why something has occurred. To signal a paper on effects, you might use *effect, fallout, consequence,* or *result,* or you might ask what has happened since something took place. Read these examples:

Signals causes: Sudbury's recent decrease in street crime stems from its expanded educational program, growing job opportunities for young people, and falling rate of drug addiction.

Signals effects: The rising cost of gasoline has affected the Canadian tourist industry in a number of ways.

At times, you may choose a dramatic attention-getter. For a paper on the effects of radon, a toxic radioactive gas present in many homes, you might note, "Although almost everyone now knows about the hazards associated with smoking, eating high–trans fat foods, and drinking excessively, few people are aware that just going home could be hazardous to one's health." However, if you use an arresting statement, be sure the content of your paper warrants it.

How you organize the body of the paper depends on your topic. Close scrutiny may reveal that one cause was indispensable; the rest merely played supporting roles. If so, discuss the main cause first. For example, when analyzing your car accident, start with the failure of the other driver to yield the right-of-way; then fan out to any other causes that merit mentioning. Sometimes you'll find that no single cause was at fault but that all of them helped matters along. Combinations of this kind lie at the heart of many social and economic concerns, such as depression and urban crime rates. Weigh each cause carefully and rank the causes in importance. If your topic and purpose would profit from building suspense, work from the least important cause to the most important. For analyzing causal chains, chronological order works most effectively.

If space won't permit you to deal adequately with every cause, pick out the two or three you consider most important and limit your discussion to them. To avoid giving your reader an oversimplified impression, acknowledge that other causes exist. However, ensure that you stay on topic. Even with no length limitation, don't attempt to trace every cause to more remote causes and then to still more remote ones. Instead, determine a sensible cutoff point that fits your purpose.

Treat effects as carefully as you treat causes. Keep in mind that effects often travel in packs, and try to arrange them in some logical order. If they occur together, consider order of climax. If one follows the other in a chainlike sequence, present them in that fashion. If you are close to the maximum length permitted, limit your discussion to the most interesting or significant effects. Whatever order you choose for your paper, don't jump helter-skelter from cause to effect to cause in a way that leaves your reader bewildered.

Moreover, as you write, don't restrict yourself to a bare-bones discussion of causes and effects. For instance, if you're exploring the student parking problem on campus, you might describe the jammed lots or point out that students often miss class because they have to drive around looking for available spots. Similarly, don't simply assert that the administration's insensitivity contributes to the problem. Instead, cite examples of their refusal to answer letters about the situation or to discuss it. To provide statistical evidence of the problem's seriousness, you might note the small number of lots, the limited spaces in each, and the approximate number of student cars on campus.

It's important to remember, however, that you're not just listing causes and effects; you're showing the reader their connection in order to serve a larger purpose. Let's see how one student handled this connection. After you've read "Why Students Drop Out of University," the student essay in this chapter, carefully re-examine paragraph 3. Note how the sentence beginning "In many schools" and the two following it show precisely how poor study habits develop. Note further how the sentence beginning "This laxity produces" and the three following it show precisely how such poor habits result in "a flood of low grades and failure." University students who read this causal analysis are better armed to avoid poor study habits and their consequences.

Causal analyses can end in several ways. A paper discussing the effects of the mountain pine beetle infestation on Canada's forests might specify the far-reaching consequences of failing to deal with the problem or recommend strategies for dealing with it. Frequently, writers use their conclusions to emphasize the larger implications of causes or effects.

Revising the Causal Analysis

Follow the guidelines in Chapter 5 and answer these questions as you revise your causal analysis:

> Have I made the right decision in electing to focus on causes, effects, or both?
>
> Have I determined all important causes and effects? Have I avoided mistakenly labelling something as an effect merely because it follows something else? Have I avoided confusing causes with effects?
>
> Am I dealing with a causal chain? an immediate cause and several supporting causes? or multiple causes and effects?
>
> Have I presented my causes and effects in an appropriate order?
>
> Have I supported my discussion with sufficient details?

EXAMPLE OF A STUDENT ESSAY OF CAUSE AND EFFECT

Why Students Drop Out of University

Diann Fisher

1   Each fall, a new crop of first-year university students, wavering between high hopes for the future and intense anxiety about their new status, scan campus maps searching for their classrooms. They have been told repeatedly that university is the key to a well-paying job, and they certainly don't want to support themselves by flipping hamburgers or working at some other dead-end job. So, notebooks at the ready, they await what university has in store. Unfortunately many of them—indeed, over 30 percent—will not return after the first year. Why do so many students leave? There are several reasons. Some find the academic program too hard, some lack the proper study habits or motivation, others fall victim to the temptations of the environment, and a large group leave for personal reasons.

2   Not surprisingly, the academic shortcomings of university students have strong links to high school. In the past, a high school student who lacked the ability or desire to get postsecondary education or training could still find a job with decent pay, perhaps in the resource sector. Now that possibility scarcely exists, so many poorly prepared students feel compelled to try college or university. Getting accepted by some schools isn't difficult. Once in, though, the student who has taken nothing beyond general mathematics, English, and science faces serious trouble when confronted with advanced algebra, first-year English, and biological or physical science. Most universities do offer remedial

courses and other assistance that may help some weaker students to survive. In spite of everything, however, many others find themselves facing ever-worsening grades and either fail or just give up.

3   Like academic shortcomings, poor study habits have their roots in high school, where even average students can often breeze through with a minimum of effort. In many schools, outside assignments are rare and so easy that they require little time or thought to complete. To accommodate slower students, teachers frequently repeat material so many times that slightly better students can grasp it without opening their books. And when papers are late, teachers often don't mark them down. This laxity produces students who can't or don't want to study, students totally unprepared for the rigorous demands of university. There, courses may require several hours of study each week in order to be passed with even a C. In many programs, outside assignments are commonplace and demanding. Instructors expect students to grasp material after one explanation, and many won't accept late papers at all. Students who don't quickly develop disciplined study habits may face low grades and failure.

4   Poor student motivation aggravates faulty study habits. Students who thought high school was boring find even less allure in the more challenging university offerings. Lacking any commitment to do well, they shrug off assigned papers, skip classes, and avoid doing required reading. Over time, classes gradually shrink as more and more students stay away. With final exams upon them, some return in a last-ditch effort to salvage a passing grade, but by then it is too late. Eventually, repetition of this scenario forces the students out.

5   In addition, the wide range of freedoms offered by the university environment can overwhelm even well-prepared newcomers. While students are in high school, parents are on hand to make them study, push them off to class, and send them to bed at a reasonable hour. Once away from home and parents, however, far too many students become caught up in a constant round of parties, dates, and other distractions that seem more fascinating than school work. Again, if such behaviour persists, poor grades and failure result.

6   Personal reasons also take a heavy toll on students who might otherwise complete their programs successfully. Often, money problems are at fault. For example, a student may lose a scholarship or grant, fail to obtain needed work, or find that the family can no longer afford to help out. Some students succumb to homesickness; some are forced out by an illness, injury, or death in the family; and yet others become ill or injured themselves and leave to recuperate. Finally, a considerable number become disillusioned with their programs or the size, location, or atmosphere of their schools and decide not to return.

7   What happens to the students who drop out? Some re-enroll later, often in less demanding schools that offer a better chance of academic success. Of the remainder, the great majority find jobs. Most, whatever their choice, go on to lead productive, useful lives. In the meantime, campus newcomers need to know about the dangers that tripped up so many of their predecessors and make every effort to avoid them.

DISCUSSION QUESTIONS

1. Identify the thesis statement in this essay. Who is the audience and what is the larger purpose for this essay?
2. Trace the causal chain that makes up paragraph 2.
3. In which paragraphs does the writer discuss causes? effects?

SUGGESTIONS FOR WRITING *Use one of the topics below, or another that your instructor approves, to develop a causal analysis. Determine which causes and/or effects to consider. Scrutinize your analysis for errors in reasoning, settle on an organization, and write the essay.*

1. Effects of the internet or cell phones on family life, social life, or work life
2. Causes and/or effects of a particular kind of stress
3. Causes and/or effects of bullying in public schools or elsewhere
4. Effects of an unwise choice that you have made
5. Reasons for the popularity of a particular trend among teenagers (street racing, iPods, text-messaging, gang culture) or among another group of people
6. Effects of a recent change in policy regarding health care, education, law, or other public policy
7. Effects of media coverage of a recent incident of violence that has occurred in Canada or elsewhere
8. Effects (or mixture of causes and effects) of a particular obsession or minor addiction (worry, gossip, video games, cell phones, etc.)
9. Reasons for (or effects of) your choice to go to university
10. Benefits of participating in a particular healthful practice or sport

The Critical Edge

Although nearly everyone recognizes the role of causation in human affairs, people's opinions differ about the causes and effects of important matters. What factors contribute to childhood obesity in North American culture today? Why are women more likely than men to leave management jobs? How do video games affect children's social or emotional development? What impact does electronic fraud have on society? Obviously such questions lack simple answers; as a result, even when investigators agree on the causes and effects involved, they often debate their relative importance.

Suppose your business instructor has asked you to investigate the departure of women from managerial positions. Library and internet searches reveal several articles on this topic that identify a number of causes. Some women leave because they find it harder to advance than men do, and as a result they seldom attain senior positions. Others leave because they receive lower salaries than their male counterparts. Still others leave because of the stifling effects of corporate rigidity, unrealistic expectations, or the demands of raising a family. Although most articles cite these causes, the relative importance of each cause is debatable. For example, one researcher emphasizes family concerns by discussing them last and at greatest length. Another puts the chief blame on obstacles to upward mobility—the "glass ceiling" that blocks women from upper-level positions along with an "old-boys network" of entrenched executives that parcels out jobs among its members.

Once you've finished your research, your job is to sift through all these causes and synthesize (see pages 423–425) the views of your sources with your own views. Before you start to write, though, take some time to consider carefully each cause and effect you've uncovered. Obviously you should ground your paper on well-supported and widely acknowledged causes and effects, but you might also include more speculative ones as long as you clearly indicate their hypothetical nature. For example, one researcher mentions corporate rigidity as a reason that women leave management jobs, but she also clearly labels this explanation as a theory and backs it with only a single example. As you examine your research, ask yourself these critical questions as well as any others that occur to you: Does any researcher exhibit obvious bias? Do the studies cited include a sufficient number of examples to be meaningful? Do the statistics appear reliable, or are some out of date, irrelevant, or skimpy? Have the researchers avoided reasoning errors? Whenever you find a flaw, note where the problem lies so that you can discuss it in your writing if you choose. Such discussions often clear up common misconceptions.

There are various possibilities for organizing your paper. If your sources substantially agree on the most important cause, you might begin with that cause and then take up the others. A second possibility, the order-of-climax arrangement, reverses the procedure by starting with secondary causes and ending with the most significant one. You can use the same options for organizing effects. When no clear consensus exists about the relative importance of the different causes and effects, organize the material in a way that is easy to understand and interesting to read.*

*Because this type of paper draws on published information, it is important to read the sections on research in Chapters 15 and 16 and those on handling quotations and avoiding plagiarism in Chapter 17 before you start to write. As always, follow your instructor's guidelines for documenting sources.

SUGGESTIONS FOR WRITING

1. Read three articles on the causes of a major social controversy, such as First Nations land claims, drug policies, or food origin labelling requirements, and incorporate those causes and your own views in a paper. Be sure that you have read the chapter on documentation, and cite appropriately where needed.

2. Write an essay that corrects a common misconception about the causes or effects of a matter about which you feel strongly. Possibilities might include the causes of homelessness in your region or the effects of zero tolerance policies in schools.

CAUSE AND EFFECT ESSAYS: PROFESSIONAL MODELS

READING STRATEGIES

1. Identify the central event of the essay around which the causes and effects are organized.
2. Determine whether the writer is identifying a chain of causes that yields a single result or multiple causes for the same event.
3. Read carefully before determining the writer's main point. In more sophisticated academic writing, writers often first present several causes or effects, both worthy and unworthy. Only after ruling some out with key explanations do they reveal which ones they think are most plausible.
4. It can be helpful to make a diagram showing the connection between the causes and the effects.

READING CRITICALLY

1. Evaluate the evidence the writer gives for the relationship between cause and effect. How does he or she prove that the causes link to the effects as described?
2. Determine whether there could be other causes or effects that the writer hasn't mentioned.
3. Writers often confuse "correlation" for causation. Just because something happens before or proximate to another event doesn't mean that it is the cause of the event. Does the writer confuse correlation and causation?

READING AS A WRITER

1. Note how the writer organizes the causes and effects to keep them clear and distinct.
2. Observe what devices the writer uses to demonstrate the connection between the causes and the effects.
3. Examine how the writer pulls his or her ideas together in the conclusion.

Richard Tomkins

Old Father Time Becomes a Terror

Richard Tomkins is consumer industries editor of the Financial Times, *where he has been a member of the editorial staff since 1983. He is currently based at the company's London headquarters, where he leads a team of journalists covering the consumer goods sector and writes about consumer trends. Previously, he was the FT's marketing correspondent; and from 1993 to 1999, he was a correspondent in the newspaper's New York bureau, where he covered the consumer goods sector. Earlier positions in London included writing about the transport sector and corporate news. Tomkins was born in Walsall, England, in 1952. His formal education ended at the age of seventeen. Before becoming a journalist, he was a casual labourer, a factory worker, a truck driver, a restaurant cashier, a civil servant, and an assistant private secretary to a government minister. He left government service in 1978 to hitchhike around the world and, on returning to the U.K. in 1979, joined a local newspaper as a trainee reporter. He joined the FT as a subeditor four years later. In this selection, Tomkins discusses the time squeeze that many people are experiencing and offers a way to combat the problem.*

1   It's barely 6:30 A.M. and already your stress levels are rising. You're late for a breakfast meeting. Your cell-phone is ringing and your pager is beeping. You have 35 messages in your email, 10 calls on your voicemail, and one question on your mind.

> Introduction contrasts the leisurely 1960s (paragraphs 1–5) with the time-stressed present.

2   Why was it never like this for Dick Van Dyke?

3   Somehow, life seemed much simpler in the 1960s. In "The Dick Van Dyke Show," the classic American sitcom of the era, Rob Petrie's job as a television scriptwriter was strictly nine-to-five. It was light when he left for work and light when he got home. There was no teleconferencing during his journey from the Westchester suburbs to the TV studio in Manhattan.

4   At work, deadlines loomed, but there was plenty of time for banter around the office typewriter. There was no Internet, no voicemail, no fax machine, no CNN. The nearest Petrie came to information overload was listening to a stream of wisecracks from his colleague Buddy Sorrell about Mel, the bald producer.

5   Meanwhile, at home, Rob's wife Laura—Mary Tyler Moore—led a life of leisure. After packing little Richie off to school, she had little to do but gossip with Millie, the next-door neighbour, and prepare the evening meal. When Rob came home, the family sat down to dinner: then it was television, and off to bed.

6   Today, this kind of life seems almost unimaginable. The demands on our time seem to grow ever heavier. Technology has made work portable, allowing it to merge with our personal lives. The nine-to-five job is extinct: in the U.S. people now talk about the 24-7 job, meaning one that requires your commitment 24 hours a day, seven days a week.

7   Home life has changed, too. Laura and Millie no longer have time for a gossip: they are vice-presidents at a bank. Richie's after-school hours are spent at karate classes and Chinese lessons. The only person at home any more is Buddy, who went freelance six months ago after being de-layered by Mel.

8   New phrases have entered the language to express the sense that we are losing control of our lives. "Time famine" describes the mismatch between things to do and hours to do them in, and "multi-tasking" the attempt to reconcile the

two. If multi-tasking works, we achieve "time deepening," making better use of the time available: but usually it proves inadequate, resulting in "hurry sickness" and an increasingly desperate search for "life balance" as the sufferer moves closer to break-down.

9   It was not supposed to be this way. Technology, we thought, would make our lives easier. Machines were expected to do our work for us, leaving us with ever-increasing quantities of time to fritter away on idleness and pleasure.

Body: main points presented in paragraphs 10–31

10   But instead of liberating us, technology has enslaved us. Innovations are occurring at a bewildering rate: as many now arrive in a year as once arrived in a millennium. And as each invention arrives, it eats further into our time.

Gives cause and effects of time stress and technology (paragraphs 10–14)

11   The motor car, for example, promised unimaginable levels of personal mobility. But now, traffic in cities moves more slowly than it did in the days of the horse-drawn carriage, and we waste our lives immobilized by congestion.

12   The aircraft promised new horizons, too. The trouble is, it delivered them. Its very existence created a demand for time-consuming journeys that we would never previously have dreamed of undertaking—the transatlantic shopping expedition, for example, or the trip to a convention on the other side of the world.

13   In most cases, technology has not saved time, but enabled us to do more things. In the home, washing machines promised to free women from the drudgery of the laundry. In reality, they encouraged us to change our clothes daily instead of weekly, creating seven times as much washing and ironing. Similarly, the weekly bath has been replaced by the daily shower, multiplying the hours spent on personal grooming.

14   Meanwhile, technology has not only allowed work to spread into our leisure time—the laptop-on-the-beach syndrome—but added the new burden of dealing with faxes, emails and voicemails. It has also provided us with the opportunity to spend hours fixing software glitches on our personal computers or filling our heads with useless information from the Internet.

Gives cause and specific effects of the information explosion

15   Technology apart, the Internet points the way to a second reason why we feel so time-pressed: the information explosion.

16   A couple of centuries ago, nearly all the world's accumulated learning could be contained in the heads of a few philosophers. Today, those heads could not hope to accommodate more than a tiny fraction of the information generated in a single day.

17   News, facts, and opinions pour in from every corner of the world. The television set offers 150 channels. There are millions of Internet sites. Magazines, books and CD-ROMs proliferate.

18   "In the whole world of scholarship, there were only a handful of scientific journals in the 18th century, and the publication of a book was an event," says Edward Wilson, honorary curator in entymology at Harvard University's museum of comparative zoology. "Now, I find myself subscribing to 60 or 70 journals or magazines just to keep me up with what amounts to a minute proportion of the expanding frontiers of scholarship."

Gives cause and effects of rising prosperity

19   There is another reason for our increased stress levels, too: rising prosperity. As ever-larger quantities of goods and services are produced, they have to be consumed. Driven on by advertising, we do our best to oblige: we buy more, travel

more, and play more, but we struggle to keep up. So we suffer from what Wilson calls discontent with super abundance—the confusion of endless choice.

20   Of course, not everyone is overstressed. "It's a convenient shorthand to say we're all time-starved, but we have to remember that it only applies to, say, half the population," says Michael Willmott, director of the Future Foundation, a London research company.

21   "You've got people retiring early, you've got the unemployed, you've got other people maybe only peripherally involved in the economy who don't have this situation at all. If you're unemployed, your problem is that you've got too much time, not too little."

22   Paul Edwards, chairman of the London-based Henley Centre forecasting group, points out that the feeling of pressures can also be exaggerated, or self-imposed. "Everyone talks about it so much that about 50 percent of unemployed or retired people will tell you they never have enough time to get things done," he says. "It's almost got to the point where there's stress envy. If you're not stressed, you're not succeeding. Everyone wants to have a little bit of this stress to show they're an important person."

23   There is another aspect to all of this too. Hour-by-hour logs kept by thousands of volunteers over the decades have shown that, in the U.K., working hours have risen only slightly in the last 10 years, and in the U.S., they have actually fallen—even for those in professional and executive jobs, where the perceptions of stress are highest.

24   In the U.S., John Robinson, professor of sociology at the University of Maryland, and Geoffrey Godbey, professor of leisure studies at Penn State University, both time-use experts, found that, since the mid-1960s, the average American had gained five hours a week in free time—that is, time left after working, sleeping, commuting, caring for children and doing the chores.

25   The gains, however, were unevenly distributed. The people who benefited the most were singles and empty-nesters. Those who gained the least—less than an hour—were working couples with pre-school children, perhaps reflecting the trend for parents to spend more time nurturing their offspring.

26   There is, of course, a gender issue here, too. Advances in household appliances may have encouraged women to take paying jobs: but as we have already noted, technology did not end household chores. As a result, we see appalling inequalities in the distribution of free time between the sexes. According to the Henley Centre, working fathers in the U.K. average 48 hours of free time a week. Working mothers get 14.

27   Inequalities apart, the perception of the time famine is widespread and has provoked a variety of reactions. One is an attempt to gain the largest possible amount of satisfaction from the smallest possible investment of time. People today want fast food, sound bytes and instant gratification. And they become upset when time is wasted.

28   "People talk about quality time. They want perfect moments," says the Henley Centre's Edwards. "If you take your kids to a movie and McDonald's and it's not perfect, you've wasted an afternoon, and it's a sense that you've lost something precious. If you lose some money you can earn some more, but if you waste time you can never get it back."

> Discusses distribution of time stress to balance his arguments (paragraphs 20–26)

> Discusses first general effect of time stress: maximizing pleasure in minimum time

Discusses second general
effect: buying time

29   People are also trying to buy time. Anything that helps streamline our lives is a growth market. One example is what Americans call concierge services—domestic help, child care, gardening and decorating. And on-line retailers are seeing big increases in sales—though not, as yet, profits.

30   A third reaction to time famine has been the growth of the work–life debate. You hear more about people taking early retirement or giving up high-pressure jobs in favour of occupations with shorter working hours. And bodies such as Britain's National Work-Life Forum have sprung up, urging employers to end the long-hours culture among managers—"presenteeism"—and to adopt family-friendly working policies.

Discusses third general
effect: re-evaluating jobs,
long work hours

31   The trouble with all these reactions is that liberating time—whether by making better use of it, buying it from others or reducing the amount spent at work—is futile if the hours gained are immediately diverted to other purposes.

32   As Godbey points out, the stress we feel arises not from a shortage of time, but from the surfeit of things we try to cram into it. "It's the kid in the candy store," he says. "There's just so many good things to do. The array of choices is stunning. Our free time is increasing, but not as fast as our sense of the necessary."

Conclusion: summarizes
sources of time stress and
offers solutions
(paragraphs 33–36)

33   A more successful remedy may lie in understanding the problem rather than evading it.

34   Before the industrial revolution, people lived in small communities with limited communications. Within the confines of their village, they could reasonably expect to know everything that was to be known, see everything that was to be seen, and do everything that was to be done.

35   Today, being curious by nature, we are still trying to do the same. But the global village is a world of limitless possibilities, and we can never achieve our aim.

36   It is not more time we need: it is fewer desires. We need to switch off the cellphone and leave the children to play by themselves. We need to buy less, read less and travel less. We need to set boundaries for ourselves, or be doomed to mounting despair.

DISCUSSION QUESTIONS

1. Identify the thesis statement of this essay and suggest why it is located at this spot.

2. In your own words, explain the paradox around technology that Tomkins explores in paragraphs 9–13. What examples does the writer use to illustrate this paradox?

3. How is "rising prosperity" related to "the confusion of endless choice" mentioned at the end of paragraph 19? Then suggest examples that illustrate this idea.

4. Why do you think Tomkins calls attention to groups that "have too much time, not too little" (paragraph 21)?

5. What is meant by "stress envy" (paragraph 22)? What is the reason for it?

6. What suggestions does the author make to reduce our stress around time (paragraphs 33–35)? How realistic are these suggestions, in your view?

TOWARD KEY INSIGHTS

Regarding the essay's final sentence, what type of boundaries do you think time-stressed individuals should set?

How can people establish these boundaries without sacrificing quality of life?

Do you think that Canadians are generally as time-stressed as Americans? Why or why not?

SUGGESTION FOR WRITING *Write an essay discussing the causes and/or effects of some type of stress other than time stress. Possibilities might include academic or financial stress or the stress associated with personal relationships. Develop your paper with appropriate examples.*

Kristine Nyhout

Send in the Clowns

Kristine Nyhout is a freelance writer living in London, Ontario. She frequently writes on family issues, particularly the joys and challenges of raising a special needs child. "Send in the Clowns" traces the physical and emotional benefits of laughter.

1   You exercise, eat the right foods and take vitamins. If you really want to stay healthy, try laughing more each day. It may sound silly, but health professionals are taking laughter seriously and using it to help people heal. Twenty years ago, the best-seller *Anatomy of an Illness* inspired the first research. When author Norman Cousins was diagnosed with a rare arthritis-like disease, he refused to accept pain as a fact of life. With his physician's approval, he checked in to a hotel and watched funny movies. He timed the effects: a belly laugh kept pain at bay for two hours. Now mainstream scientists are investigating humour's effects on health: it's no joke because jocularity has real psychological and physiological effects—from reducing stress to affecting production of hormones.

2   So the next time you visit a hospital, you may well see a red-nosed therapeutic clown or humour specialist—health professionals trained to get laughs—among white-coated doctors. Comedy carts filled with doses of satirical verse or slapstick films roll down the corridors. Consultants even bring the comedy preventive to workplace wellness seminars—apparently laughter also boosts creativity and productivity. Regina therapist Catherine Ripplinger Fenwick recognized the importance of humour when she battled breast cancer eight years ago. "I didn't laugh enough." She outfitted herself with a laughter first aid kit, took up clowning during her chemotherapy, and noticed the "wows" of life. Now she lectures government employees and others in the benefits of mirth.

3   Bringing humour into hospital helps defuse patient anxiety and change atti-tudes. One of the new healing clowns, registered nurse Dee Preikschas of Kitchener, Ont., tuned in to humour's healing power when her husband became ill. Now she's one of a number of therapeutic clowns in Canada who often work with children. Once Preikschas was dispatched to the bedside of a 10-year-old boy recovering from an appendectomy—he hated his IV and wasn't eating. By giving the kid a "magic" hammer that made a smashing noise at the offending IV, the clown got the boy to laugh—and cooperate. Clowns also bring comfort. Joy Van Herwaarde, who calls herself Joybells when she's clowning, says, "Humour can make someone less aware of the pain and can make them feel less lonely." Indeed, when a 101-year-old woman at Good Samaritan Hospital in Edmonton neared death, she asked for Joybells's brand of comfort. In Hamilton, Ont., nurse Sharon Orovan is using and studying humour to fend off panic attacks.

4   Humour also packs a physical punch. A sort of pharmacist of silliness, humour specialist Barbara Wetmore-Patel of London, Ont., dispenses videos and joke books from her comedy cart. How does it work? The laughing response can lower both heart rate and blood pressure, increase T-cell activity to fend off ill-ness, and may improve digestion. Wetmore-Patel has seen how humour helps seniors in retirement homes and palliative care hospitals feel better physically. Laughing may release endorphins—chemicals in the brain responsible for the feeling of well-being known as runner's high—into the bloodstream, taking the edge off pain.

5   What's more, laughter may actually help keep you from getting sick. When you laugh, an antibody called immunoglobulin A travels from the bloodstream to the salivary glands where it blocks viruses from their usual port of entry, explains Herb Lefcourt, a psychology professor at the University of Waterloo. Lefcourt's research found that people who used humour more in their daily lives had higher levels of immunoglobulin A in their saliva. And when your body is under stress (as in a fight-or-flight confrontation), your immune system is sup-pressed. Lefcourt found humour defuses that state of arousal, allowing the immune system to continue doing its job.

6   Laughter can also lead to deeper breathing and relaxed muscles, according to physiologist David Garlick at the University of New South Wales in Sydney, Australia. Tense muscles can mean increased heart rate and blood pressure. Adrenaline levels and mental stress may also go up, Garlick adds. You may not be able to meditate during a meeting, but as Garlick points out, "Laughter is the usual way of helping to relieve muscle tension."

7   You don't have to be a stand-up comic to reap the health benefits of a chuckle—just look on the light side of life.

DISCUSSION QUESTIONS

1. Study the introductory paragraph and the concluding paragraph. What is the relationship between these two paragraphs? Identify the thesis statement. Where do you find out that the essay will focus on effects?

2. Identify five or six positive effects of laughter that are discussed in paragraphs 2–6.

3. How are paragraphs 4, 5, and 6 related? On what basis did the writer make the decision to separate these paragraphs?

4. What examples, or brief anecdotes, does the writer use to illustrate the benefits of laughter?

5. While this essay focuses on the effects of laughter, it also has a persuasive, or argumentative, slant. What strategies does the writer use to persuade you that laughter is beneficial for health? Why do you suppose the writer does not cite statistics to strengthen her argument?

TOWARD KEY INSIGHTS

To what extent do you agree with Kristine Nyhout that physical health and emotional health may be related?

Can a person decide to seek out opportunities for laughter? Why or why not?

How can humour help with other stressful situations besides physical illness?

Are there ever times when humour could strike the wrong note?

SUGGESTION FOR WRITING *Interview three or four people who are knowledgeable about some aspect of health, and write an essay persuading your reader of the positive effects of a specific healthful practice, such as weight lifting, vegetarianism, or meditation. Explain the benefits with short anecdotes, examples, and quotations from your interviewees.*

Celia Milne

Pressures to Conform

Celia Milne writes for Maclean's *magazine. Her article "Pressures to Conform," which first appeared in* Maclean's, *points out how women have paid dearly for their unhappiness with their body image. Low self-esteem associated with body insecurities has contributed to the prevalence of eating disorders and a boom in plastic surgery. The essay's recommendation of body acceptance should generate lively discussion among students.*

1   "Lose 20 lb. by Christmas!" screams the headline on the cover of a popular women's magazine. Beside it is a picture of a gorgeous, typically stick-thin model. And below her is a photo of . . . guess what? A turkey dinner with all the trimmings. In vivid colour, the cover neatly illustrates the body-image dichotomy: the twin obsessions with thinness and indulgence. Between the extremes of women intentionally so underweight they risk death and others overweight enough to be candidates for cardiovascular disease and adult-onset diabetes, there are millions whose body mass index—relating height and weight—is in the normal range. Yet most of them feel fat.

2   "Oh my God, we are so sick in this society," fumes Dr. Joan Johnston, 48, an Edmonton family physician who suffered from anorexia from her late teens until well into adulthood. As a child, she was surrounded by messages about the importance of thinness. "I don't remember a time when my mother wasn't on a diet," she says. "My cousin and my aunt were always dieting." Johnston traces her eating disorder from the day when she was 19 and her mother patted her on the backside and said: "Better watch out, girl. You're getting a little broad across the beam!"

3   Johnston has recovered from what she now sees as an addiction to dieting. "I am five feet, three inches and I weigh 133 lb., the same as I did before anorexia," she says. "I am extremely comfortable with my body, and it is so liberating to not have to put energy into that. But I'm very atypical." Now, she puts her energy into helping young women who have eating disorders—a societal problem that is not getting any better.

4   Unhappiness with body image seems to be a national preoccupation. According to statistics compiled by the National Eating Disorder Information Centre in Toronto, 90 percent of Canadian women are dissatisfied with some aspect of their bodies. One of the main battlegrounds in the fight for improvement, of course, is eating. According to the Maclean's year-end poll published in late December, 43 percent of Canadian women—compared with 33 percent of men—believe they are overweight. The eating disorder centre says that its surveys show that fully 70 percent of Canadian women are preoccupied with their weight, and 40 percent are yo-yo dieting. "For most women, when they get together in a group a common topic is trying to lose weight," says Dr. Christine Davies, a family physician in Saint John, N.B., who is concerned about how that may rub off on their daughters. Margaret Beck, acting director of the eating disorder centre, affirms that danger. "The research," she says, "does seem to suggest that mothers who are food- and weight-preoccupied tend to have daughters who are the same."

5   Public awareness of eating disorders got a big boost in 1995 when Diana, Princess of Wales, began talking openly about her struggles with bulimia. That bingeing and vomiting condition affects three to five percent of young Canadian women aged 14 to 25. The other main manifestation of food preoccupation is anorexia, affecting one to two percent of that group. And the problems occur among younger girls, too. "There are girls younger than 10, even as young as 6, being admitted to hospital programs," says Beck. "It is still a small number, but it is growing."

6   Another popular route in the quest for a better body is plastic surgery. There are no national statistics on esthetic surgery in Canada, but the trends are visible in figures kept by the American Society of Plastic and Reconstructive Surgeons. From 1994 to 1996, the number of people having tummy tucks rose 103 percent, breast augmentation went up 123 percent, breast lifts increased 60 percent, chemical peels rose 47 percent, retin-A anti-wrinkle treatments grew by 256 percent, buttock lifts rose by 146 percent and thigh lifts went up 93 percent. Dr. Thomas Bell, president of the Canadian Society of Aesthetic Plastic Surgery in Toronto, also notices a trend towards younger patients wanting plastic surgery. "The median age has moved from the mid-50s to the late or mid-40s," he says. "This is part and parcel of body image issues."

7   Perhaps it was media images of ample, perky breasts that persuaded more than 100 000 Canadian women to undergo silicone implant surgery between 1969 and 1992. That type of implant was banned in 1993, and at least 10 000 Canadians blame them for health problems including arthritis, lupus and scarring.

8   Saline implants in a silicone shell are now the norm, and women are still seeking breast enlargement. Vancouver plastic surgeon Kimit Rai says they generally come in two age-groups: the younger women aged 19 or 20 who have never been happy with their breasts, and others who have finished breastfeeding their children and want a pick-me-up. The cost is steep—between $5 000 and $10 000—and there are possible, well-documented risks. Yet for many women, the importance of looking full-figured seems to outweigh the need to feel good. "About five or six percent are unhappy with their implants because they cause discomfort," says Rai, "but because they look good, they don't want them out."

9   In fact, women will go to frightening lengths to achieve their body ideal, according to an extensive reader survey published last year in the U.S. magazine *Psychology Today*. A troubling 24 percent of women said they would give up three years of their life to achieve their weight goals. A few were willing to forgo motherhood because pregnancy would ruin the trim bodies they had worked so hard to achieve. Young women "are being initiated into feelings of body dissatisfaction at a tender age," reported the magazine, "and this early programming may be difficult to undo."

10   The same willingness to pay a high price for an enhanced image is evident in the fact that young women are now the fastest growing group of smokers in Canada. The reason appears to have a lot to do with low self-esteem. Studies indicate that young women who take up smoking consider themselves significantly less attractive than do their peers who never take up the habit.

11   Part of the esteem problem is inevitably related to the impossible ideals with which women are bombarded. "We are constantly shown images of very sick, anorexic women and that's what we are striving for," says Davies. "The average woman is five feet, five inches and 145 lb. The average model is five feet, 11 inches and 110 lb. Ninety-five percent of us don't match up and never will." Ironically, she adds, the average North American's weight has been rising over the past few decades, so most women are moving further away from the physique they seek.

12   Striving for the unattainable creates insecurity among women, says Davies. And that, in turn, leads them to try to please even an unreasonable partner. "A woman is more likely to stay with a man who is abusive if she has low self-esteem," Davies says. "She just doesn't have the confidence to leave." Among teens, low self-esteem can lead to unsafe activities designed to show their worth, such as having sex before they are ready to, which carries with it the risk of HIV and other sexually transmitted diseases.

13   Those tendencies alarm Dr. Sarah Kredentser, who sees a lot of young women in her Winnipeg family practice. "People judge themselves against others and through the eyes of others," she notes with regret. "It is not experience, personality skills and character that counts, but image." According to Kredentser, society's preoccupation with body image has worsened over the past decade.

A 65-year-old woman recently asked about liposuction. "If you haven't solved your body image problems by the time you are 65, then you've got problems," Kredentser says.

14   On the other hand, it can sometimes be a positive step for a woman to have something "done" that has been bothering her for years. "I have seen instances where minor plastic surgery such as nose reshaping has made an enormous difference in self-esteem," Kredentser says. "My concern is that this can become the slippery slope. Then it's, 'Now I'll get my breasts done the way I want them,' and what next?"

15   Women simply have to become comfortable with the fact that their bodies are going to age, she says. "If you don't, you will have a chronic struggle with unhappiness and low self-esteem," says Kredentser. "You can never win this battle." Instead of surgery, women are much better off doing the psychological work necessary to accept the aging process, she says.

16   Acceptance is a vital key to dealing with body insecurities. As an administrative assistant at a student residence at the University of Waterloo, Angela Kelman, 23, has an interesting perspective. At five feet, six inches and weighing between 135 and 140 lb., she says she is not wrapped up in body image issues herself, yet sees those obsessions all around her. First-year students are worried about putting on pounds—"the freshman ten," as they call it. "What I see most is over-exercising," she says. "A couple of my friends do it to maintain a model look." Another trend among female university students is vegetarianism. "They say it is because of allergies, religion or animal rights," says Kelman, "but I think it is to lose weight."

17   Kelman credits her upbringing in Waterloo for her lack of concern about body image. "I come from a very close, large family with five children," she says. "My mother loves to cook, and I cook the way she does. We enjoy very balanced meals, and never a lot of prepackaged foods. I don't worry about it much. I'm lucky."

18   There is no doubt the way a woman views herself can affect those around her, particularly children. A mother-daughter competition to lose weight by dieting and going to the gym is not a healthy New Year's resolution, says Beck. Instead, she suggests such pleasurable activities as walks in the park or games of touch football that do not have to do with food or weight loss.

19   A family life focused on looking good contributed to Joan Frère's obsession with body weight. The 35-year-old Edmonton social worker began to diet about 15 years ago, thinking it would make her a better person. "I thought thinness was equated with intelligence, success, being a good worker, achievement," she says. Over the years, she travelled the long and difficult journey from the depths of anorexia and bulimia, through the ups and downs of healing, and into a healthy way of thinking. Her coping mechanisms include reaching out to friends, taking long walks, focusing on things other than her weight, and listening to her body. "I am five feet, three inches and 128 lb., I will never be five-feet-six and 110 lb.," Frère says. "I eat what I want and I don't beat myself up. I have learned that I have the same feelings as everyone else, and I have acquired the tools to deal with life."

DISCUSSION QUESTIONS

1. In the first paragraph, Celia Milne describes a magazine cover that "illustrates the body-image dichotomy: the twin obsessions with thinness and indulgence." What does she mean? How does her point here relate to her overall argument?

2. What support does the writer give for her claim that "unhappiness with body image seems to be a national preoccupation" (paragraph 4)?

3. While the argument seems largely to emphasize the extreme measures that some women will take to achieve their body ideal (paragraph 9), how does the essay also concede that sometimes changing one's body image through surgery "may be a positive step" (paragraph 14)? What is meant by the term "slippery slope" in this paragraph?

4. Examine paragraph 10. How does it act as a kind of bridging, or transitional, paragraph between what has come before and what comes after? How does the issue of self-esteem (paragraphs 10–16) relate to the essay's larger point about body image?

5. Cite examples of different kinds of rational appeals used in this essay—including expert opinions, primary source information, and statistical findings.

6. What positive recommendations does the writer make about ways to promote body acceptance (paragraphs 16–19)?

TOWARD KEY INSIGHTS

This essay cites a *Maclean's* poll that reports that more women than men believe they are overweight (paragraph 4). How do you account for this difference?

Compare and contrast this essay with Evelyn Lau's descriptive essay entitled "An Insatiable Emptiness" (pages 499–503) or with Susan McClelland's essay "Distorted Images" (pages 180–183). How does Celia Milne approach the subject of eating disorders in a different way than Evelyn Lau or Susan McClelland does? How is the purpose of this essay different from Lau's or McClelland's essay?

Celia Milne recommends acceptance as the best way to deal with body insecurities. How realistic do you think this advice is? In your opinion, what is the best way to promote body acceptance, both within the individual and within the larger society?

SUGGESTIONS FOR WRITING

1. Write an essay that argues that males are increasingly subject to body insecurities too. Bring in as many different kinds of evidence as you can.

2. If your instructor allows you to use secondary research (see Chapter 15), examine the causes and/or effects of a popular surgical treatment such as breast enhancements or botox treatments.

CHAPTER 11

Strategies for Analytical Writing: Definition

ESTABLISHING BOUNDARIES

The holiday movies were coated with schmaltziness.
Once the bandage is off the wound, swab the proud flesh with disinfectant.
That hockey player is a goon.

Do you have questions? You're not alone. Many people would question the sentences above: "What does *schmaltziness* mean?" "How can flesh be *proud*?" "What is a *goon* in hockey?" To avoid puzzling and provoking your own readers, you'll often need to explain the meaning of some term. The term may be unfamiliar (*schmaltziness*), or used in an unfamiliar sense (*proud flesh*), or it may mean different things to different people (*goon*). Whenever you clarify the meaning of some term, you are *defining*.

Humans are instinctively curious. We start asking about meanings as soon as we can talk, and we continue to seek and supply definitions all through life. In school, instructors expect us to explain literary, historical, scientific, technical, and social terms. On the job, a member of a company's human resources department might prepare a brochure that explains the meaning of such terms as *corporate responsibility* and *product stewardship* for new employees. A special education teacher might write a memo explaining *learning delayed* to the rest of the staff.

When you define, you identify the features that distinguish a term, thereby establishing its boundaries and separating it from all others. Knowing these features enables both you and your reader to use the term appropriately.

Sometimes a single word, phrase, or sentence can settle a definition question. To clear up the mystery of "proud flesh," all you'd need to do is insert the parenthetical phrase "(excessively swollen and grainy)" after the word *proud.* But when you're dealing with new terms—such as *cyber war* or *podcasts*—brief definitions won't provide the reader with enough information for proper understanding.

Abstract terms—those standing for things we can't see, touch, or otherwise detect with our five senses—often require extended definitions, too. Terms such as *democracy, hatred,* or *bravery* are too complex to capture in a single sentence, and people have too many differing ideas about what they mean. If you are using concrete terms—those standing for actions and things we can perceive with our five senses—you may also need to provide a longer definition to make sure your audience understands what you are talking about. For example, some people limit the term *drug pusher* to full-time sellers of hard drugs such as cocaine and heroin, while others assume the term applies to full- and part-time sellers of any illegal substance. Thus, writing an argument recommending life sentences for convicted drug pushers would require you to tell just what you mean by the term.

TYPES OF DEFINITIONS

Three types of definitions—synonyms, essential definitions, and extended definitions—serve writers' needs. Although the first two seldom require more than a word or a sentence, an extended definition can run to several pages. Synonyms and essential definitions can be found in dictionaries, and are starting points for extended definitions.

Synonyms

Synonyms are words with very nearly the same meanings. *Lissome* is synonymous with *lithe* or *nimble,* and *condign* is a synonym of *worthy* and *suitable.* Synonyms let writers clarify meanings of unfamiliar words without using cumbersome explanations. To clarify the term *expostulation* in a quoted passage, all you'd have to do is add the word *objection* after it in brackets. However, since synonyms are not identical twins, using them as definitions puts a slightly different shade of meaning on a message. For example, to "protest" and to "object" have similar meanings, but saying that we "object" to the establishment of a toxic waste site in our area sounds much weaker than saying we "protest" against such a site. Still, synonyms may provide convenient shorthand definitions, if used judiciously.

Essential Definitions

An essential definition does three things: (1) names the item being defined, (2) places it in a broad category, and (3) distinguishes it from other items in that category. Here are three examples:

Item Being Defined	Broad Category	Distinguishing Features
A howdah	is a covered seat	for riding on the back of an elephant or camel.
A voiceprint	is a graphical record	of a person's voice characteristics.
To parboil	is to boil meat, vegetables, or fruits	until they are partially cooked.

Suppose your instructor has asked you to write an essential definition of one of the terms listed in an exercise, and you choose *vacuum cleaner*. Coming up with a broad category presents no problem: A vacuum cleaner is a household appliance. The hard part is pinpointing the distinguishing features. The purpose of a vacuum cleaner is to clean floors, carpets, and upholstery. You soon realize, however, that these features alone do not separate vacuum cleaners from other appliances. After all, carpet sweepers also clean floors, and whiskbrooms clean upholstery. What feature then does distinguish vacuum cleaners? After a little thought, you realize that, unlike the other items, a vacuum cleaner works by suction. You then write the following definition:

> A vacuum cleaner is a household appliance that uses suction to clean floors, carpets, and upholstery.

You will need to think carefully to uncover the distinguishing features in any essential definition.

Limitations of Essential Definitions   Essential definitions have certain built-in limitations. Because of their brevity, they often can't do full justice to abstract terms such as *cowardice, love, jealousy, power*. Problems also arise with terms that have several settled meanings. The word *jam* when used as a noun would require at least three essential definitions: (1) a closely packed crowd, (2) a fruit preserve, and (3) a difficult situation. But despite these limitations, an essential definition can be useful by itself or as part of a longer definition.

Pitfalls in Preparing Essential Definitions   When you prepare an essential definition, guard against these flaws:

Circular definition. Don't define a term by repeating it or changing its form slightly. A definition of a psychiatrist as "a physician who practises psychiatry" will only frustrate someone who's never heard of psychiatry. Avoid circularity and choose terms the reader can understand, for example, "A psychiatrist is a physician who diagnoses and treats mental disorders."

Overly broad definition. Shy away from loose definitions that cover too much territory. If you define a skunk as "an animal that has a bushy tail and black fur with white markings," your definition is not precise. Many cats and dogs also fit this description. But if you add "and that ejects a foul-smelling secretion when threatened," you will clear the air—of any misconceptions at least.

Overly narrow definition. Don't hem in your definition too closely, either. The definition of a kitchen blender as "a bladed electrical appliance used to chop foods" is too restricted. Blenders perform other operations, too. To correct the error, add the missing information: "A kitchen blender is a bladed electrical appliance used to chop, mix, whip, liquefy, or otherwise process foods."

Omission of main category. Avoid using "is where" or "is when" instead of naming the main category. Here are examples of this error: "A bistro is where food and wine are served" and "An ordination is when a person is formally recognized as a minister, priest, or rabbi." The reader will not know exactly what sort of thing (a bar? a party?) a *bistro* is and may think that *ordination* means a time. Note the improvement when the broad categories are named: "A bistro is a small restaurant where both food and wine are served" and "An ordination is a ceremony at which a person is formally recognized as a minister, priest, or rabbi."

EXERCISE

1. **Identify the broad category and the distinguishing traits in each of these essential definitions:**

   a. Gangue is useless rock accompanying valuable minerals in a deposit.

   b. A catbird is a small songbird with a slate-coloured body, a black cap, and a catlike cry.

   c. A soldier is a man or woman serving in an army.

2. **Indicate which of the following statements are acceptable essential definitions. Explain what is wrong with those that are not. Correct them.**

   a. A scalpel is a small knife that has a sharp blade used for surgery and anatomical dissections.

   b. A puritan is a person with puritanical beliefs.

   c. A rifle is a firearm that has a grooved barrel and is used for hunting large game.

3. **Write an essential definition for each of the following terms:**

   a. spam   **c.** hit man

   b. summary offence   **d.** consumerism

Extended Definitions

Sometimes it's necessary to go beyond an essential definition and write a paragraph or whole paper explaining a term. Terms with differing meanings also frequently require extended definitions. New technical, social, and economic terms often require extended definitions. For example, a computer scientist might need to define *data integrity* so that computer operators understand the importance of maintaining it. Furthermore, extended definition is crucial to interpretation of the law, when courts must clarify the meaning of terms such as *obscenity*.

Extended definitions are not merely academic exercises. A police officer needs to have a clear understanding of what counts as *reasonable grounds for search and seizure;* an engineer must comprehend the meaning of *stress;* a nuclear medical technologist had better have a solid grasp of *radiation.* And all of us are concerned with the definition of our basic rights as citizens.

Extended definitions commonly draw on other methods of development—narration, description, process analysis, illustration, classification, comparison, and cause and effect. Often, they also define by negation—explaining what a term *does not* mean. The following paragraphs show how one writer handles an extended definition of *sudden infant death syndrome.* The student begins by presenting a case history (illustration), which also incorporates an essential definition and two synonyms.

> Jane and Dick Smith were proud new parents of an eight-pound, ten-ounce baby girl named Jenny. One summer night, Jane put Jenny to bed at 8:00. When she went to check on her at 3:00 A.M., Jane found Jenny dead. The baby had given no cry of pain, shown no sign of trouble. Even the doctor did not know why she had died, for she was healthy and strong. The autopsy report confirmed the doctor's suspicion—the infant was a victim of the "sudden infant death syndrome," also known as SIDS or crib death. SIDS is the sudden and unexplainable death of an apparently healthy, sleeping infant. It is the number-one cause of death in infants after the first week of life and as a result has been the subject of numerous research studies.

DISCUSSION QUESTIONS

1. What synonyms does the writer use?
2. Which sentence presents an essential definition?

In the next paragraph, the writer turns to negation, pointing out some of the things that researchers have ruled out about SIDS.

> Although researchers do not know what SIDS is, they do know what it is not. They know it cannot be predicted; it strikes like a thief in the night. Crib deaths occur in seconds, with no sound of pain, and they always happen when the child is sleeping. Suffocation is not the cause, nor is aspiration or regurgitation. Researchers have found no correlation between the incidence of SIDS and the mother's use of birth control pills or the presence of fluoride in water. Since it is not hereditary or contagious, only a slim chance exists that SIDS will strike twice in the same family.

Finally, the student explores several proposed causes of SIDS as well as how parents may react to the loss of their child.

As might be expected, researchers have offered many theories concerning the cause of crib death. Dr. R. C. Reisinger, a National Cancer Institute scientist, has linked crib deaths to the growth of a common bacterium, *E. coli,* in the intestines of newborn babies. The organisms multiply in the intestines, manufacturing a toxin that is absorbed by the intestinal wall and passes into the bloodstream. Breast milk stops the growth of the organism, whereas cows' milk permits it. Therefore, Dr. Reisinger believes, bottle-fed babies run a higher risk of crib death than other babies. . . .

The loss of a child through crib death is an especially traumatic experience for the family. Parents often develop feelings of guilt and depression, thinking they somehow caused the child's death. To alleviate such feelings, organizations have been established to help parents accept the fact that they did not cause the death.

Trudy Stelter, student

ETHICAL ISSUES

How we define a term can have profound consequences. For centuries, the practice of defining Africans as "subhuman" helped justify slavery. During the 1930s and early 1940s, labelling Jews as "vermin" was used to fuel the attempt to exterminate them in both Nazi Germany and much of the rest of Western Europe. Even in the absence of malice, definitions can have far-reaching effects, both good and bad. Definitions of certain learning disabilities affect whether or not a student in the public school system is eligible for extra assistance. A word such as "terrorism" has critical political, legal, and military implications Answering the following questions will help you think about possible ethical implications of your definitions.

- Have I carefully evaluated all the features of my definition? For example, a definition of "excessive force" by the police would be unfair if it included actions that constitute reasonable means necessary to subdue highly dangerous suspects.

- Have I slanted my definition to reflect a prejudice? Let's say a writer opposed to casino gambling is defining "gambling addicts." The paper should focus on those who spend an excessive amount of time in casinos, bet and often lose large sums of money, and in so doing neglect family, financial, and personal obligations. It would be unfair to include those who visit casinos occasionally and strictly limit their losses.

- Have I avoided unnecessary connotations that might be harmful? A definition of teenagers that overemphasizes their swift changes in mood might be unfair, perhaps even harmful, since it may influence the reactions of readers.

WRITING AN EXTENDED DEFINITION
Planning and Drafting the Extended Definition

As in any type of writing, purpose will guide your choice of topic in writing definitions. Generally you don't want to spend time telling readers something they
already know. For instance, why define *table* when the discussion would likely
bore your reader?

If you are writing an extended definition, choose an abstract term or one that
is concrete but unfamiliar to your reader. An extended definition of an unfamiliar
term that the reader may not understand such as *carbon footprint* might well prove
interesting and informative for a reader. Use one of the strategies on pages 34–40
to unearth promising topics. Then answer these questions about them:

> Which topic holds the most promise? Why?
>
> What purpose will guide my writing?
>> To clarify a technical or specialized concept
>> To show how I am using the term
>> To persuade the reader to adopt my attitude toward it
>> To discuss some neglected facet of the term
>
> For what audience am I writing?

Here's a helpful process to follow as you think your definition through.
Imagine that you are defining an abstract term such as *democracy*. First, select a
clear example that illustrates what you wish to define, and brainstorm to
uncover major identifying characteristics. If you are brainstorming about the
United States as an example for *democracy*, your list might include majority rule,
free elections, a separately elected chief executive, a constitution, and basic
human rights. Next, test these characteristics against other legitimate examples
and retain only the characteristics that apply. Although Canada is clearly a
democracy, it doesn't have a separately elected chief executive. Moreover,
Canada was a democracy for more than a century before getting its own constitution. Finally, the People's Republic of China—which is not a democracy—has
elections. What, then, truly constitutes a democracy? Finally, test your unfolding
definition against a counter-example such as Myanmar (dictatorship) or Saudi
Arabia (kingdom). Your definition should conflict with these examples.

Now evaluate what methods you might use to develop your definition.
Each method has its own set of special strengths, as the following list shows:

Narration.	Tracing the history of a new development or the changing meaning of a term
Description.	Pointing out interesting or important features of a device, event, or individual
Process.	Explaining what a device does or how it is used, how a procedure is carried out, or how a natural event takes place
Illustration.	Tracing changes in meaning and defining abstract terms
Classification.	Pointing out the different categories into which an item or an event can be grouped

Comparison.	Distinguishing between an unfamiliar and a familiar item, or evaluating two ideas or things by putting them side by side
Cause and effect.	Explaining the origins and consequences of events, conditions, problems, and attitudes
Negation.	Placing limitations on conditions and events and correcting popular misconceptions

Examine your topic in light of this list and select the methods of development that seem most promising. Don't hesitate to use a method because the purpose was not mentioned here. If you think that a comparison will help your reader understand some abstract term, use it.

Chart the methods of development you plan to use, and then brainstorm each method in turn to gather the details that will inform the reader. When you've finished, look everything over, rearrange the details as necessary, add any new ones you think of, and prepare a revised chart. The example that follows is for a paper using four methods of development.

Narration	**Classification**	**Process**	**Negation**
First supporting detail	First supporting detail	First supporting detail	First supporting detail
Second supporting detail	Second supporting detail	Second supporting detail	Second supporting detail

Definition papers can begin in various ways. If you're defining a term with no agreed-upon meaning (for example, *conservatism*), you might note some differing views of it and then state your own. If the term reflects some new social, political, economic, or technological development such as a *smart phone,* you might mention the events that brought it into being. A paper defining *chutzpah* might begin by illustrating the brash behaviour of someone with this trait. Occasionally, an introduction includes a short definition, perhaps taken from a dictionary. If you do include a dictionary definition, reference the full name of the dictionary (The *Canadian Oxford Dictionary* says . . .), but usually it is best to come up with your own definition.

In writing the body of the paper, present the methods of development in whatever order seems most appropriate. A paper defining *drag racing* might first describe the hectic scene as the cars line up for a race, then classify the different categories of vehicles, and finally explain the steps in a race. One defining *intellectual* might start by showing the differences between intellectuals and scholars, then name several prominent intellectuals and note how their insights have altered our thinking, and conclude by trying to explain why some people distrust intellectuals.

Definition papers can end in a number of ways. If you're defining some undesirable condition or event you might refer to new research initiatives that may yield solutions. If you're reporting on some new development (such as *nanotechnology*), you might include predictions about its economic or social impact. Choose whichever type of ending best supports your main idea.

Revising the Extended Definition

Use the general guidelines in Chapter 5 and these specific questions as you revise your extended definition:

Are my purpose and audience clear and appropriate?

If I've used an essential definition, does it do what it should, and does it avoid the common pitfalls?

Are the methods of development suitable for the topic?

Is the paper organized effectively?

Are there other factors or examples I need to consider?

Have I considered appropriate ethical issues?

EXAMPLE OF A STUDENT ESSAY OF DEFINITION

Lust and Gluttony

by Bryan Wainwright

1   If I had to choose between lust and gluttony, I would commit myself to a life of lust.

2   Although lust and gluttony may be sinful cousins of sort, the lustful are full of joy, but the gluttonous are simply full. The lustful who fill their emptiness with all life's sensuous pleasures find unsurpassed happiness and delight. The gluttonous, however, who focus on filling their protruding stomachs with all that is fatty and sweet, live with a perpetual sense of anxiety—or guilty over-consumption. The lustful can anticipate the moment of pleasure, and revel in it when it comes. Whether they have been desiring a sexual experience or a high performance car, the lustful can experience true delight and fulfillment. The gluttonous, however, never really enjoy anything. They can't even taste that popcorn they are shovelling into their mouths at the movie. They gobble down their king crab and lobster slathered with buttery cream sauces as quickly as possible, as if they worried someone could take their food away. And before they have wiped the grease from their upper lip, they are already longing for that chocolate amaretto cheesecake with hazelnut crust.

3   One defining characteristic divides the lustful from the gluttonous. Drawing a chubby line in the sand of sins is the fact that the lustful being simply has no boundaries. The lustful may have immense amorous appetite for pleasure, but they are not limited by their physical capacities. They can enhance their pleasure through imagination. They feel delight before, during, and after the lustful

experience. The gluttonous masses, however, are limited by their own earthly selves and their weak fleshy bodies. When the gluttonous finally sit back at the end of the meal, they rub their stomachs sadly, as if they wished they could keep eating forever. As they loosen their belt buckles as far as they possibly can, they may also feel a tinge of shame. The lustful, in contrast, reflect happily on their sexual encounters. Why else would Casanova have written his memoirs, except to re-live his amorous adventures with countless women in the pleasure palace of his imagination?

4   It's true that gluttony and lust are related. Gluttony is the fat, lethargic cousin of legendary lust. The glutton sleeps on the couch in lust's penthouse suite, leaving a lingering stench that all the Glade plug-ins of the world couldn't conquer. Gluttony is merely lust without imagination. Where lust strives to touch the stars and part the seas in hopes of a new high, gluttony waddles to the fridge and drinks milk from the carton to wash down the Twinkies.

5   The glutton is the hot dog cart of the sins: big and slow, full of saturated fat, and grease. Lust is the high octane muscle car that tears through the world at breakneck speeds in search of its next conquest. While lust evolves and discovers new forms of happiness, gluttony is stagnant and watches the world go by, flicking through the channels of life with chocolate-stained fingers and a gut full of trans-fatty acids. Every moment of the lustful life is an affront to the gluttons of the world, suggesting imagination need not be bounded by a kitchen. The desire to stimulate the senses with all the wonderful sensations life has to offer is not a real sin, but could even be considered a virtue that leads to fulfillment. While gluttony is focused on food and drink, lust encompasses much more than sexual pleasure. The lust for love leads to fiery passionate encounters; the lust for power drives people to glory and fame; the lust for blood creates champions and heroes who achieve greatness through sport and combat. To have lust course through one's veins helps one become a titan among mortals.

6   The glutton has great power as well: the power to waste the worlds' supply of food; the power to expand one's girth to the point of eruption; the power to make society pay for the disposal of a monstrously revolting corpse. While the lustful can channel their burning desires in many ways, the gluttonous are limited by their obsession with food and drink. While they may gain a small measure of glory in the so-called sport of food-eating competitions, most people are more disgusted than intrigued by stupendous feats of ingestion. Who would want to gain fame through the rapid consumption of 59 hot dogs, or 72 glazed doughnuts? The gluttonous also tend to die in undignified ways; in one strange CSI ("Crime Scene Investigation") episode focused on extreme eating, a man

who ate too many hot dogs is found in a dumpster after his gut literally exploded. The end of gluttony is not pretty.

7　　　The lustful contribute to society. They are the lovers, fighters, heroes, entrepreneurs, pioneers, and leaders of our world. The lust for knowledge, power and wealth command them to achieve greatness through innovation and revolution. The lustful know the world will not be inherited by the meek but by those who follow their passions.

8　　　The gluttonous leave no legacy. The crooked, pitted headstone of the glutton has no story to tell, but the memorials of the lustful stand tall and proud, pronouncing grand tales and heroic deeds. As the gluttons lie six feet under, filling oversized caskets and extra-large graves, I, the lustful, will be setting out on one more passionate adventure.

DISCUSSION QUESTIONS

1. What methods of development does the writer use to develop an extended definition of lust and gluttony?
2. Find examples where the writer uses metaphors or figurative language to help define his terms.
3. How does the writer use transitions and topic sentences to help create coherence?
4. To what extent does this essay include a persuasive angle? Do you find yourself being persuaded? Why or why not?

SUGGESTIONS FOR WRITING *Write an extended definition using one of the following suggestions or one approved by your instructor. The term you define may be new, misused, or misunderstood, or may have a disputed meaning. Develop the essay by any combination of writing strategies.*

1. Literacy
2. Storm chaser
3. Multiculturalism
4. Stress
5. Emotional intelligence
6. Podcast
7. Biodiversity
8. Carbon footprint

The Critical Edge

Definitions are always social creations. The meaning of a word depends on a shared understanding of how people in communities use the word. Thus writers who use abstract words such as *justice, love,* or *charisma* may need to consult a number of sources to determine how others have used the words. With their findings of this research in mind, the writers can stake out their own meanings of those words.

If you were writing an extended definition of the word *dance* for a humanities class, you would probably discover that people have used the word in different ways. As you read *The Dance as an Artwork,* you might at first like Frank Thiess's definition of dance as the use of the body for expressive gesture; but as you mull over that definition, you realize that it is both too broad and too narrow. While some forms of dance, such as ballet, feature expressive gesture, so does pantomime or even a shaken fist; and neither of these qualifies as dance. A square dance clearly qualifies, but does it represent expressive gesture? Then you turn to *Philosophy in a New Key,* in which Susanne Langer defines dance as "a play of Powers made visible," and stresses that dancers seem to be moved by forces beyond themselves. You recognize that this definition may apply to religious dance forms, that dancers sometimes appear swept away by the music, and that you yourself have experienced a feeling of power when dancing. Nevertheless, upon reflection you decide that people watch dancers for less mystical reasons, and that it's usually the dancer's skill and artistry that attracts viewers. Finally, you discover that Francis Sparshott, in *The Theory of the Arts,* defines dance as a rhythmical, patterned motion that transforms people's sense of their own existence according to the dance they do. As you evaluate Sparshott's contention, you decide that it has considerable merit, although you aren't convinced that every dance transforms our sense of existence. When you think about the kinds of dance you know and the various definitions you have uncovered, you conclude that these writers, like the blind men who felt different parts of an elephant and tried to describe it, are each only partly correct. For your humanities paper, you decide to synthesize (see pages 423–425) the different definitions. You might explain that all dance involves a rhythmical, patterned movement of the body for its own sake. Sometimes such movement can transform our sense of existence, as in trance dances or even waltzes. Other dances, such as story ballets, use rhythmical movements as expressive gestures that tell stories or convey emotions. Still other dances may suggest the manifestation of powers beyond the dances themselves. You proceed to explain each of these features with details drawn both from your sources and from personal experience.

Writing this kind of paper requires you to look critically at the definitions of others. Do they accurately reflect the examples you know about? Do they describe examples that do not fit the definition? Are any parts of the definition questionable? Once you've answered these questions, you can then draw on the appropriate elements of the definitions to formulate your own. You might organize such a paper by developing each definition in a separate section, first presenting it in detail and then pointing out its strengths and weaknesses. In the final section, you could offer your own definition and support it with your reasoning and suitable examples.*

---

*Because you need to draw on published sources, it is important to read the sections on research in Chapters 15 and 16 and those on handling quotations and avoiding plagiarism in Chapter 17 before you start to write. As always, follow your instructor's guidelines for documenting sources.

SUGGESTIONS FOR WRITING

1. Do some reading about an abstract term, such as *pornography, democracy, marriage,* or *terrorism,* in at least three sources. Use the sources to develop your own definition of the term.

2. If you are familiar with a particular type of discourse from an area you know well (sports, computers, music, cooking, etc.), define this language for a reader uninitiated to this specialized language. This essay might blend different strategies of development such as illustration, for you need to provide examples and definitions along the way. Alternatively, you might choose to organize your essay mainly around one extended definition of a significant word or phrase.

DEFINITION ESSAYS: PROFESSIONAL MODELS

READING STRATEGIES

1. Clearly identify the term being defined, and the broad category to which it belongs.
2. As you read, note distinguishing characteristics of the concept.
3. If there is definition by negation, identify what the term is not to be confused with.
4. Observe any analogies, similes, or metaphors that can help readers understand the concept by seeing what it resembles.
5. Consider whether you have unanswered questions or points of confusion.

READING CRITICALLY

1. Ask yourself whether the definition makes sense to you.
2. Test the definition to see if it is too narrow. If a person defines *literature* as works of fiction, the definition could leave out poetry.
3. Test the definition to see if it is too broad. If a person defines *literature* as works of writing, the definition would include phone books—a clearly unintended consequence of the definition.
4. Note whether the definition has a simple explanatory purpose, or a persuasive angle.

READING AS A WRITER

1. Notice how the writer uses the introduction to explain the importance of the concept and the definition.
2. Identify the key strategies the writer uses to construct a definition—stating the broad category and distinguishing characteristics; providing examples; saying what the term is not to be confused with; drawing comparisons.

3. Observe how the writer limits the definition so that it is not too general.

4. Note whether the writer illumines a specialized concept, redefines a term in a new way, clarifies the meaning of the term for a particular context, or calls attention to an overlooked facet of the term.

Laurence Shames

The Sweet Smell of Success Isn't All That Sweet

Laurence Shames (born 1951) is a native of Newark, New Jersey, and a graduate of New York University. After completing his education, he began a career as a nonfiction writer, contributing to such publications as Playboy, McCall's, Esquire, Vanity Fair, *and the* New York Times. *He co-authored Peter Barton's memoir* Not Fade Away *(2003), and has written several works of fiction. His work* The Hunger for More *(1991) focuses on the search for values in a world of greed. This concern for values is also apparent in the following selection, which attacks contemporary attitudes about success.*

1   John Milton was a failure. In writing "Paradise Lost," his stated aim was to "justify the ways of God to men." Inevitably, he fell short of accomplishing that and only wrote a monumental poem. Beethoven, whose music was conceived to transcend Fate, was a failure, as was Socrates, whose ambition was to make people happy by making them reasonable and just. The inescapable conclusion seems to be that the surest, noblest way to fail is to set one's own standards titanically high.

| Introduction: paragraphs 1–4; captures attention by ironically attacking high success standards, defending low standards |

2   The flip-side of that proposition also seems true, and it provides the safe but dreary logic by which most of us live: The surest way to succeed is to keep one's strivings low—or at least to direct them along already charted paths. Don't set yourself the probably thankless task of making the legal system better; just shoot at becoming a partner in the firm. Don't agonize over questions about where your talents and proclivities might most fulfillingly lead you; just do a heads-up job of determining where the educational or business opportunities seem most secure.

3   After all, if "success" itself—rather than the substance of the achievements that make for success—is the criterion by which we measure ourselves and from which we derive our self-esteem, why make things more difficult by reaching for the stars?

4   What is this contemporary version of success really all about?

5   According to certain beer commercials, it consists in moving up to a premium brand that costs a dime or so more per bottle. Credit-card companies would have you believe success inheres in owning their particular piece of plastic.

| Body: paragraphs 5–12 |

6   If these examples sound petty, they are. But take those petty privileges, weave them into a fabric that passes for a value system, and what you've got is a national mood that has vast motivating power that can shape at least the near future of the entire country.

| Development by examples and brief definitions |

| Development by effects |

7   Under the flag of success, modern-style, liberal arts colleges are withering while business schools are burgeoning—and yet even business schools are having an increasingly hard time finding faculty members, because teaching isn't

| Development by comparison, examples, and causes |

considered "successful" enough. Amid a broad consensus that there is a glut of lawyers and an epidemic of strangling litigation, record numbers of young people continue to flock to law school because, for the individual practitioner, a law degree is still considered a safe ticket.

| Development by effect | 8 |

The most sobering thought of all is that today's M.B.A.'s and lawyers are tomorrow's M.B.A.'s and lawyers: Having invested so much time and money in their training, only a tiny percentage of them will ever opt out of their early chosen fields. Decisions made in accordance with today's hothouse notions of ambition are locking people into careers that will define and also limit their activities and yearnings for virtually the rest of their lives.

| Development by effects and argument | 9 |

Many, by external standards, will be "successes." They will own homes, eat in better restaurants, dress well and, in some instances, perform socially useful work. Yet there is a deadening and dangerous flaw in their philosophy: It has little room, little sympathy and less respect for the noble failure, for the person who ventures past the limits, who aims gloriously high and falls unashamedly short.

| Development by effects | 10 |

That sort of ambition doesn't have much place in a world where success is proved by worldly reward rather than by accomplishment itself. That sort of ambition is increasingly thought of as the domain of irredeemable eccentrics, of people who haven't quite caught on—and there is great social pressure not to be one of them.

| Development by effects | 11 |

The result is that fewer people are drawn to the cutting edge of noncommercial scientific research. Fewer are taking on the sublime, unwinnable challenges of the arts. Fewer are asking questions that matter—the ones that can't be answered. Fewer are putting themselves on the line, making as much of their minds and talents as they might.

| Development by effect, cause, and comparison | 12 |

The irony is that today's success-chasers seem obsessed with the idea of *not settling*. They take advanced degrees in business because they won't settle for just a so-so job. They compete for slots at law firms and investment houses because they won't settle for any but the fastest track. They seem to regard it as axiomatic that "success" and "settling" are opposites.

| Conclusion: argues against contemporary notions of success | 13 |

Yet in doggedly pursuing the rather brittle species of success now in fashion, they are restricting themselves to a chokingly narrow swath of turf along the entire range of human possibilities. Does it ever occur to them that, frequently, success is what people settle for when they can't think of something noble enough to be worth failing at?

DISCUSSION QUESTIONS

1. Shames notes in paragraph 3 that "'success' itself—rather than the substance of the achievements that make for success" seems to be the touchstone by which we measure our worth. What do you think he means? Why is the distinction positioned at this point?

2. Why do you think Shames ends his essay with a rhetorical question, that is, one for which no answer is expected?

3. To what extent do you agree with Shames's idea of success? Discuss.

TOWARD KEY INSIGHTS

What evidence do you find that not all people are consumed by the desire for money?

What qualities do you consider crucial to living a "good" life and to happiness?

SUGGESTION FOR WRITING *Write a definition essay explaining how the popular view of responsibility, greed, marriage, single life, friendship, or some other concept needs redefining. Use whatever writing strategies advance your purpose.*

Wayson Choy

I'm a Banana and Proud of It

Wayson Choy is a Canadian author, born in Vancouver in 1939. He is the author of the award-winning novel The Jade Peony *(1995) as well as* All That Matters *(2004), which was nominated for the Giller Prize. As the son of Chinese immigrants, Choy often writes on issues of multiculturalism, assimilation and cultural hybridity and published his memoir* Paper Shadows: A Chinatown Childhood *in 1999. Choy has taught at Humber College in Toronto for over 30 years and is currently on the faculty of the Humber School of Writers.*

1   Because both my parents came from China, I look Chinese. But I cannot read or write Chinese and barely speak it. I love my North American citizenship. I don't mind being called a "banana," yellow on the outside and white inside. I'm proud I'm a banana.

2   After all, in Canada and the United States, native Indians are "apples" (red outside, white inside); blacks are "Oreo cookies" (black and white); and Chinese are "bananas." These metaphors assume, both rightly and wrongly, that the culture here has been primarily anglo-white. Cultural history made me a banana.

3   History: My father and mother arrived separately to the B.C. coast in the early part of the century. They came as unwanted "aliens." Better to be an alien here than to be dead of starvation in China. But after the Chinese Exclusion laws were passed in North America (late 1800s, early 1900s), no Chinese immigrants were granted citizenship in either Canada or the United States.

4   Like those Old China village men from *Toi San* who, in the 1850s, laid down cliff-edge train tracks through the Rockies and the Sierras, or like those first women who came as mail-order wives or concubines and who as bond-slaves were turned into cheaper labourers or even prostitutes—like many of those men and women, my father and mother survived ugly, unjust times. In 1917, two hours after he got off the boat from Hong Kong, my father was called "chink" and told to go back to China. "Chink" is a hateful racist term, stereotyping the shape of Asian eyes: "a chink in the armour," an undesirable slit. For the Elders, the past was humiliating. Eventually, the Second World War changed hostile attitudes toward the Chinese.

5   During the war, Chinese men volunteered and lost their lives as members of the American and Canadian military. When hostilities ended, many more were proudly in uniform waiting to go overseas. Record Chinatown dollars were raised to buy War Bonds. After 1945, challenged by such money and ultimate sacrifices, the Exclusion laws in both Canada and the United States were revoked. Chinatown residents claimed their citizenship and sent for their families.

6   By 1949, after the Communists took over China, those of us who arrived here as young children, or were born here, stayed. No longer "aliens," we became legal citizens of North America. Many of us also became "bananas."

7   Historically, "banana" is not a racist term. Although it clumsily stereotypes many of the children and grandchildren of the Old Chinatowns, the term actually follows the old Chinese tendency to assign endearing nicknames to replace formal names, semicomic names to keep one humble. Thus, "banana" describes the generations who assimilated so well into North American life.

8   In fact, our families encouraged members of my generation in the 1950s and sixties to "get ahead," to get an English education, to get a job with good pay and prestige. "Don't work like me," Chinatown parents said. "Work in an office!" The *lao wah-kiu* (the Chinatown old-timers) also warned, "Never forget—you still be Chinese!"

9   None of us ever forgot. The mirror never lied.

10   Many Chinatown teen-agers felt we didn't quite belong in any one world. We looked Chinese, but thought and behaved North American. Impatient Chinatown parents wanted the best of both worlds for us, but they bluntly labelled their children and grandchildren "*juk-sing*" or even "*mo no.*" Not that we were totally "shallow bamboo butt-ends" or entirely "no brain," but we had less and less understanding of Old China traditions, and less and less interest in their village histories. Father used to say we lacked Taoist ritual, Taoist manners. We were, he said, "*mo li.*"

11   This was true. Chinatown's younger brains, like everyone else's of whatever race, were being colonized by "white bread" U.S. family television programs. We began to feel Chinese home life was inferior. We co-operated with English-language magazines that showed us how to act and what to buy. Seductive Hollywood movies made some of us secretly weep that we did not have movie-star faces. American music made Chinese music sound like noise.

12   By the 1970s and eighties, many of us had consciously or unconsciously distanced ourselves from our Chinatown histories. We became bananas.

13   Finally, for me, in my 40s or 50s, with the death first of my mother, then my father, I realized I did not belong anywhere unless I could understand the past. I needed to find the foundation of my Chinese-ness. I needed roots.

14   I spent my college holidays researching the past. I read Chinatown oral histories, located documents, searched out early articles. Those early citizens came back to life for me. Their long toil and blood sacrifices, the proud record of their patient, legal challenges, gave us all our present rights as citizens. Canadian and American Chinatowns set aside their family tongue differences and encouraged each other to fight injustice. There were no borders. "After all," they affirmed, "*Daaih ga tohng yahn* . . . We are all Chinese!"

15   In my book, *The Jade Peony*, I tried to recreate this past, to explore the beginnings of the conflicts trapped within myself, the struggle between being Chinese and being North American. I discovered a truth: these "between world" struggles are universal.

16   In every human being, there is "the Other"—something that makes each of us feel how different we are to everyone else, even to family members. Yet, ironically, we are all the same, wanting the same security and happiness. I know this now.

17   I think the early Chinese pioneers actually started "going bananas" from the moment they first settled upon the West Coast. They had no choice. They adapted. They initiated assimilation. If they had not, they and their family would have starved to death. I might even suggest that all surviving Chinatown citizens eventually became bananas. Only some, of course, were more ripe than others.

18   That's why I'm proudly a banana: I accept the paradox of being both Chinese and not Chinese.

19   Now at last, whenever I look in the mirror or hear ghost voices shouting, "You still Chinese!" I smile.

20   I know another truth: In immigrant North America, we are all Chinese.

DISCUSSION QUESTIONS

1. Identify the essential definition that Choy gives at the beginning of the essay. To what extent is the rest of the essay an elaboration of this definition?

2. How does Choy use comparison or contrast in the essay? What purpose does the comparison or contrast serve?

3. How does the writer's view of Chinese culture and his Chinese heritage seem to change over time? Why does he decide that he needs "roots" (paragraph 13)?

4. Why does Choy say that he is "proud" to be a banana (paragraph 1, 18)? Why is his pride in this identity a "paradox" (paragraph 18)?

5. What does Choy mean with his closing statement that "In immigrant North America, we are all Chinese" (paragraph 20)? Could you substitute another group name for Chinese? Why or why not?

TOWARD KEY INSIGHTS

Comment on the significance of nicknames in your experience. Do you have a personal nickname now, or did you have one when you were younger? Do you belong to a group that has a nickname? If so, how do you feel about these nicknames?

Wayson Choy writes that in every person, "there is 'the Other'—something that makes each of us feel how different we are to everyone else, even to family members." How do you understand this claim? Does it seem true in your experience? If so, explain.

SUGGESTIONS FOR WRITING

1. Just as Wayson Choy mounts a defence of a term (banana) that some might consider racist, write an essay explaining why a term that some consider offensive could be understood in a positive way—or, conversely, a descriptive term that some consider acceptable could be considered offensive.

2. Read the two essays in the argument chapter related to Canada's multicultural policies, "No Place Like Home" by Neil Bissoondath and "Immigrants, Multiculturalism and Canadian Citizenship" by Will Kymlica. Drawing from these essays, and your own experience, write an extended definition of a term such as *assimilation* or *cultural integration*.

Robert M. MacGregor

I Am Canadian: National Identity in Beer Commercials

Robert M. MacGregor is professor of marketing at Bishop's University in Quebec. His research interests include cultural analysis of national, racial, and ethnic identities through many forms of communications conduits. A major focus of his research is the use of racial and ethnic stereotypes in advertising.

1   Occasionally a television commercial causes social, political, and business ramifications way beyond anyone's initial expectations. In March 2000, a sixty-second television beer commercial became an overnight phenomenon. For approximately three months thereafter, the advertisement became a national and international focus of debates on Canadian nationalism and identity. Some issues concerning national identity will be discussed.

Molson Canadian "The Rant"

2   Sometimes a single television commercial can have such an impact that it takes on a life of its own. A few examples of such advertisements include:

1. Coca-Cola's 1971 song "I'd Like to Buy the World a Coke" that became "I'd Like to Teach the World to Sing," a one-million-units-sales best seller.
2. Life brand cereal—Quaker Oats Company showing Mikey enjoying Life brand. "Hey Mikey" entered the lexicon.
3. The greatest commercial ever made—Apple Macintosh's "1984," showing Big Brother (IBM) in an Orwellian nightmare—caused the Macintosh revolution.
4. Clara Peller barked, "Where's the Beef?!" for Wendy's, and a popular culture phenomenon was born. American presidential candidate Walter Mondale used the phrase in his campaign (Ward Fawcett).

     Molson's beer commercial, in a Canadian context, now stands as an example of a single advertisement that now joins the pantheon of selected "best" television presentations.

3   Montreal-based Molson Company, founded in 1786, is Canada's preeminent brewer and one hundred percent Canadian owned, with sales in excess of $2 billion. One of its top-selling brands is called CANADIAN. Between 1994 and 1998, Molson had used the tag line, "I am CANADIAN." This line was replaced by "Here's where we get CANADIAN," widely criticized as flat-mouthed. Responsibility for reviving the Canadian brand went to Brett Marchand, an Alberta-born marketing executive who had been lured away from Campbell Soup in Philadelphia. Grassroots interviews clearly indicated a growing sense of national pride among the key niche, nineteen- to twenty-five-year-olds. The Toronto agency Bensimon Byrne D'Arcy recommended that Molson revive the "I am CANADIAN" slogan. The "Joe Rant" emerged as a passionate declaration of national pride, a definitive piece of popular culture. As they say, the rest is history.

I AM CANADIAN

Hey.
I'm not a lumberjack, or a fur trader.
I don't live in an igloo, eat blubber, or own a dogsled.
I don't know Jimmy, Sally, or Suzy from Canada.
Although I'm certain they're very nice.

I have a prime minister, not a president.
I speak English and French, Not American,
and I pronounce it 'ABOUT', NOT 'A BOOT.'

I can proudly sew my country's flag on my backpack.
I believe in peace keeping, NOT policing,
DIVERSITY, NOT assimilation
and that the beaver is a proud and noble animal.

A TOQUE IS A HAT,
A CHESTERFIELD IS A COUCH,
AND IT IS PRONOUNCED 'ZED,' NOT 'ZEE', 'ZED.'

CANADA IS THE SECOND LARGEST LANDMASS,
THE FIRST NATION OF HOCKEY
AND THE BEST PART OF NORTH AMERICA.
MY NAME IS JOE
AND I AM CANADIAN
    Thank you.

The copy and visual elements of the advertisement addressed some of the commonly held stereotypes that others perhaps hold of Canadians. Whether it is language pronunciation differences, occupational, eating, and living factors, sports interests, or social and political policies, each of these is fleetingly presented. Two major symbolic icons are also invoked in the ad: the beaver and Canada's national flag, the maple leaf. The ad had been seen in movie theaters since March 17, 2000, and made its national television debut on March 26 during the Academy Awards broadcast.

4   A possible impetus to the immediate success of "The Rant" may have been Robin Williams's same-night, same-show rendition of the *South Park* film's song "Blame Canada." This song was nominated for an Oscar.

5   This song satirized Canada as a tool for satirizing Americans. In the song "Blame Canada," all four mums—Sheila, Sharon, Liane, and Ms. McCormick—sing the wows of parenthood. The last ten lines of the song are:

> Sheila: With all their hockey hubba baloo
> Liane: And that bitch Anne Murray too
> Everyone: Blame Canada
> Shame on Canada
> The smut we must stop
> The trash we must smash
> Laughter and fun
> Must be all undone
> We must blame them and cause a fuss
> Before someone thinks of blaming uuuuuus.

Trey Parker and Matt Stone did not create the flip-top headed characters in *South Park* to offend Canadians; they did so to take a jab at Americans' stereotyping of Canadians. They chose to "Blame Canada" before somebody thinks to blame us—Americans—for the sole reason American mentality is that way. Michael Moore wrote *Canadian Bacon* in 1995, a movie about invading Canada that focused on America's need to have an enemy. The song, the movie, and the Oscar presentation appeared to add to the poignancy of "The Rant" commercial and helped to reinforce some prevailing attitudes of Canadians about Americans.

6   Within days of the initial airing of "The Rant," dozens of Web sites sprung [*sic*] up, numerous parodies of groups and individuals appeared, and Jeff Douglas took on major celebrity status. The many parodies that appeared include: I am a columnist, I am an Albertan, I am a Newfie, I am Chinese, I am Pakistani, I am Indian, I am Italian, I am Irish, I am Jamaican, I am Filipino, I am Torontonian, I am Manitoban, I am British Columbian, I am Not Canadian (parody on Québecers), and I am American. All of the parodies followed the same genre, and the American one read as follows:

I AM AMERICAN

I'm not particularly intelligent, open-minded, or generally well liked.
I don't live in a clean place.
I don't eat nutritiously very often.
And I abandon my car on the side of the interstate until the tires are stolen.

I don't know Shakespeare, Da Vinci or Gutenberg.
Although I'm certain they weren't American.

I drink watery beer.
I don't use utensils when eating.
I believe in guns for settling disputes, not discussions.

And I pronounce it AIN'T, not AREN'T.
I don't say "you're welcome" in response to "thank you," I say "Uh Huh."
I can proudly sew my country's flag on my backpack . . . until I go anywhere.

Burger King IS fine dining and Miss America is a virgin.
Ketchup IS a vegetable and WWF wrestling is real.

The UNITED STATES is the ONLY country in the world.

The FIRST nation of ignorance,
And the BEST part of South America!

My name is Johnny Bob Jimmy Joe Ray, I'm married to my sister, AND
I AM AMERICAN!

7   Joe, the actor, performed at National League Hockey games, appeared on most major television and radio talk shows, did business conferences, and eventually went off to Hollywood. The television commercial won a Bronze Lion at the 2000 Cannes International Advertising Awards, where thirty-two other commercials were on the short list in the alcoholic beverage category. In Canada, it was voted "Best of Show," winning the gold medal for television single over thirty seconds (*Marketing*).

8   In November 2001, "The Rant" won top honours at the advertising industry's CASSIE awards, picking up the covered Grand Prix. The CASSIES are awarded based on how successfully the ad moves the client's business. In a release, the award's group said that the Molson Canadian campaign produced "amazing" results for the brand. From March 2000 to March 2001, the Canadian brand grew by 2.5 percent in market share, while archrival Labatt's Blue declined by 2.9 percent (Heinrich).

9   From a commercial and creative viewpoint, "The Rant" was an extremely successful advertisement. What was unseen initially were the eventual discussions that took place at the political and institutional levels. Ontario Minister of Consumer Affairs Bob Runciman quickly denounced the ad. He was quoted as saying:

> I felt it was saying things that didn't have to be said in terms of saying things of feeling good about our country. You can send out very strong messages about being Canadian—I'm certainly as pro-Canadian as anyone—but I don't think you have to kick anyone else in the shins to do that. I think that this is essentially an anti-American rant which taps into a national lack of self confidence when it comes to dealing with the United States. (Molson Canadian Commercial)

Several well-known Canadian historians, including Michael Bliss of Toronto and Desmond Morton of McGill, voiced their concerns about the negativity of "The Rant." Bliss believed that the advertisement was pathetic, depressing, and an embarrassment to Canada; it was nationalism without content. Morton said that "the mobilization of a sense of Canadianism to peddle beer is a frontal attack on the values Canadians share" (Walker).

10   Other well-known Canadians took an opposing view and voiced their support of the creative rendition. Bob Rae, former premier of Ontario, said:

> This speaks to every stupid question that Americans always ask Canadians. There is a very strong element of nationalism in Canada that never goes away. The closer we get economically, the more we like thumbing our noses, and that's a lot of fun. (Kettle)

Rudyard Griffiths, director of the Dominion Institute in Toronto, saw "The Rant" as an example of tearing a page out of the book of American cultural imperialism—a change in the habits of cultural expression in Canada (a "ra ra-ism"). He believed:

> It's very retro and it's interesting that it's connected with a younger group. Canadian sovereignty has been more of an issue for those who came of age during the late 1960s and early 1970s. That was a time when Canada had a new flag, a hip and

glamourous [*sic*] prime minister in Pierre Trudeau, and a world fair. As tensions over the Vietnam war tore at the social fabric of the United States, Canada emerged as a humane alternative society. There was a conscious rebranding of Canada as independent nation ready to take its place on the world stage (Walker).

Throughout the public debates, two viewpoints were coalescing. The advertisement was seen as an expression of Canadian pride, and critics saw "The Rant" as a declaration of anti-American sentiment. Glen Hunt, who wrote the ad, saw the commercial as pro-Canadian and not anti-American. Brett Marchand, Molson vice president, believed what the ad said ". . . is what more Canadians wish people would do—scream that they are proud to be Canadian" ("Beer ad").

11   Marchand also stated that the ad elements—beer, hockey, and the environment, for example—represented "Canada's patriotic DNA." He believed that the young respondents interviewed for their views on Canada were likened to a "dormant volcano." "We definitely didn't expect it to have the impact it's had, beyond its value as a beer ad," Marchand continued. "You couldn't image [*sic*] the phenomenon it is in Canada. It's been on the front page of newspapers. There are radio talk shows across the country dedicated to the ad. I've been doing interviews almost from first thing in the morning until the end of the day every day. It really has struck a chord with a huge group of consumers" (Bach).

12   One federal politician who saw the social and political implications of the mass appeal of the ad to many Canadians was the Honourable Sheila Copps, Minister of Canadian Heritage. At the International Press Institute World Congress held in Boston on May 1, 2000, she used "The Rant" beer advertisement to present and discuss the importance of national cultural identity to Canadians. After the video of the ad was shown, she presented the following points to the audience:

> Yes, the ad pokes fun at the U.S., and yes, there is a bit of chest thumping—but it also pokes fun at Canadian efforts at self-validation by posing in contrast to Americans. The ad has spun off a huge raft of subsidiary jokes in which Canadians laugh at our teams, our cities and ourselves. The popularity of the ad raises a serious point, though. Some American business people firmly believe that culture is a good allocated solely by the private sector and free markets. When you are the world's cultural juggernaut, at best, this means serious challenges for other nations.
>
> For Canadians, culture is not just like any other good like pork rinds or brass tack. Culture is not just entertainment. It is the expression of the soul and the identity of the country. (*Speaking notes*)

Ms. Copps continued in the speech to discuss cultural pluralism, cultural diversity, and the disappearance of languages and dialects, encouraging free expression and cultural security. Near the conclusion of her speech, she stated,

> I'll undoubtedly catch flak from some commentors back in Canada for bringing "Joe Canadian" to Boston, but I say what better place for a strong call for cultural identity by Joe Sixpack than here where Americans first stated their call for cultural recognition and fair representation. (Speaking notes)

The Minister of Canadian Heritage did not have long to wait. The next day, May 2, Mr. John Solomon (Regina-Lumsden-Lake Centre, NDP) rose in the House of Commons in Ottawa and proudly proclaimed "I am Canadian":

> Mr. Speaker, I am not a Republican or a Democrat. I do not spend millions to run for office or hire American consultants or go negative. I do not know Stockwell or Tom

or Joe but I am sure they are very nice. I have a health card, not an insurance card. I listen to Cross Country Checkup, not Howard Stern or Rush Limbaugh, I speak for people, not multinational corporations. I believe in inexpensive generic drugs, environmental protection and fair trade deals. I believe that Canada can have an independent foreign policy. Canadian taxpayers are citizens too who value our social programs. And it is pronounced medicare, not Bill 11, okay? Canada is the home of public health care, curling, Codco and the NDP.

My name is John and I am Canadian.

Much of Mr. Solomon's "rant" compares various factors that clearly distinguish America from Canada, and clearly suggests his own political party's electoral platform (Solomon).

13   Three days later on May 5, Richard Marceau (Charlesbourg, BQ), member of the nationalist/separatist party, openly mocked Ms. Copp's Boston visit. His declaration clearly illustrated some of the tensions that prevail between the English and French populations in Canada. His statements were as follows:

> Mr. Richard Marceau (Charlesbourg, BQ): Mr. Speaker, on May 1, the Minister of Canadian Heritage went to the ridiculous lengths of promoting "Canadian" culture in Boston with a beer ad. How clever.
>
> How can Quebecers define themselves within this selection of Canadiana when the beer in question is not even sold in Quebec? Molson long ago grasped the specific nature of Quebec and serves us Laurentide.
>
> We in Quebec have a real department of culture, not one for heritage. What we fear is not comparison with the Americans but assimilation with the Canadians.
>
> In Quebec, when we say we are bilingual, that does not mean we just know a few pick-up lines. Our objective is to make Quebec known throughout the world, not to go to other countries and put our foot in our mouth every chance we get.
>
> Above all, when we in Quebec want some pro-Quebec advertising, we do not hire an American. (Marceau)

14   It is not the intent of this article to discuss the individual elements of the ad or to discuss the tensions between English and French politicians. These will be analyzed in other articles as will the American dimension—for example, stereotyping of Canadians and whether the ad was anti-American. Some considerations concerning national identity will conclude this article.

National Identity

15   "Who are we?" is a universal and perennial question. It is a particular question of concern to Canadians, most of whom believe that they are distinctive, and that to have a clear identity is to be different from Americans (Hedley). The advertisement highlights some of the perceived value differences: the protection of the state—peace, order, good government, and inclusive social policies.

16   Douglas Kellner believed that today identity is more mobile, multiple, personal, self-reflexive, and subject to change and innovation. Yet in postmodern society, identity remained social- and other-related. Historically, in Canada the dominant ideology of "being a Canadian" was in the process of being defined as speaking English within a British-type institutional system. This British model, a latent unitarian model of identity, was reasonably successful in Canada but was never unchallenged. To varying degrees, tension has existed within the existing cultural diversity of the nation, and especially within the mainly French population of Québec. The symbolic order and cultural capital factors changed dramatically in the 1960s. One of the ways that changes were made to help assuage

growing tensions and anxiety between the two founding nations was to change the symbolic character of the Canadian national identity. The Official Languages Act of 1969 made Canada a bilingual country, a Canadian Flag was adopted in 1965, Trans-Canada Airline became Air Canada, the Dominion Bureau of Statistics became Statistics Canada, "O Canada" was proclaimed as the national anthem in 1980, stamps were changed (with the elimination of the Queen's portrait), money was redesigned with more Canadian symbols, and the constitution was patriated. The point to emphasize here is to concur with Kellner's point that modern national identity more and more has a degree of flexibility to evolve. The state in Canada intervened substantially to reorient the symbolic national identity order. Some groups, not the Québec nationalists, perceived the changes to be an enrichment of society's symbolic system, and, as a result, their own symbolic identity. Some of these changes are reflected in "The Rant" beer advertisement (Breton).

17   Consumers, beer drinkers, and advertisement viewers are socially and culturally situated individuals seeking to make sense of their lives, identities, and relationships. Ads such as "The Rant" provided symbolic resources to be used for those purposes (O'Donohue). McCracken suggested that in looking at ads, consumers seek "concepts of what it is to be a man or a woman, concepts of what it is to be middle-aged . . . (or) a member of a community or a country" (122). Molson's sixty-second television commercial for its brand of beer, CANADIAN, appeared to motivate many people to be proud to stand up and shout, "I am CANADIAN!"

Works Cited

Bach, Deborah. "Better Ad Hyping Canada Strikes Chord Across Borders." *Baltimore Sun* 25 Apr. 2000. Available at http://www.amarillonet.com.

"Beer Ad Gets 19 000 Fans Excited." 15 Apr. 2000. Available at http://www.canoe.ca/2000_NHL_Playoffs_OrrTor.

Breton, Raymond. "The Production and Allocation of Symbolic Resources: An Analysis of the Linguistic and Ethnocultural Fields in Canada." *Canadian Review of Sociology and Anthropology* 21.2 (1984): 123–44.

CASSIES, short for Canadian Advertising Success Stories, created in 1993. For more information see: http://www.cassies.ca.

Copps, Sheila. *Speaking Notes for the Honourable Sheila Copps, Minister of Canadian Heritage.* International Press Institute World Congress, Boston, 1 May 2000.

Hedley, Alan. "Review Essay, Identity: Sense of Self and Nation. *Canadian Review of Sociology and Anthropology* 31.2 (1994): 200–14.

Kellner, Douglas. "Popular Culture and the Construction of Postmodern Identity." *Modernity and Identity.* Ed. Scott Lash and Jonathan Friedman. Oxford, UK: Basil Blackwell Ltd., 41–77.

Kettle, Martin. "Mocked Canada Finds Hope and Glory in a Beer Ad." *Guardian.* 25 May 2000. Available at http://www.guardian.co.uk/Archive/Article.

Marceau, Richard (Charlesbourg, BQ). *House of Commons Debates.* Volume 136, Number 091, 2nd Session, 36th Parliament, Friday, May 5, 2000, 6443.

Marketing. Awards Issue 26 Mar. 2001, 7, 20.

McCracken, Grant. "Advertising: Meaning or Information?" Ed. Melanie Wallendorf and Paul Anderson. Provo, UT. *Advances in Consumer Research* 14 (1987): 1–2.

"Molson Canadian Commercial." 10 May 2000. Available at http://www.snopes.ca/ia...boxer/petition/joerant.htm.

O'Donohue, Stephanie. "Nationality and Negotiation of Advertising Meanings." Ed. Eric J. Arnould and Linda M. Scott, Montreal. *Advances in Consumer Research* 26: 684–89.

Solomon, John (Regina-Lumsden-Lake Centre, NDP). "I AM CANADIAN" *House of Commons Debate.* Volume 136, Number 088, 2nd Session, 36th Parliament, Tuesday, May 2, 2000, 6282.

South Park. Prod. Scott Rudin, Tracy Parker, and Matt Stone. Paramount Pictures and Warner Brothers, in association with Comedy Central, 1999.

Walker, Ruth. *Christian Science Monitor* 4 May 2000 <http://www.csmonitor.com>.

Ward Fawcett, Adrienne. "The 50 Best." *Advertising Age.* Special Awards Issue spring 1995: 36–39.

DISCUSSION QUESTIONS

1. Why does the writer refer to four other television commercials that are not the focus of his analysis at the outset of the essay?

2. How does the author link the commercial to a larger discussion on national identity?

3. Do you think "The Rant" is an assertion of anti-American sentiment? Explain why or why not.

4. How is this essay an extended definition? What other strategies of development does it employ?

TOWARD KEY INSIGHTS

How do you respond to the claim that "in looking at ads, consumers seek 'concepts of what it is to be . . . a member of a community or country'"? Discuss.

Some people argue that Canadian culture is overwhelmed by American culture. To what extent do you agree? Explain.

SUGGESTION FOR WRITING *Write an essay explaining how you define yourself as Canadian. Use whatever criteria, examples, and writing strategies advance your purpose.*

CHAPTER 12

Strategies for Finding Patterns: Comparison

SHOWING RELATIONSHIPS

Which candidate for mayor should get my vote, Ken Conwell or Jerry Mander?

What is it about online shopping that you prefer?

Doesn't this tune remind you of a Nelly Furtado song?

Is high school in Australia harder or easier than high school in Canada?

Everyone makes *comparisons*, not just once in a while, but day after day. When we compare, we examine two or more items for likenesses, differences, or both. Comparison has a purpose. Sometimes when the similarities between two things are obvious, we may choose to emphasize how two things which appear at first glance to be similar are actually quite different. On the other hand, when the differences are obvious, we may choose to demonstrate how two things which impress us with their differences actually share underlying similarities.

Comparison often serves an evaluative purpose, showing why one person, thing, or plan of action is superior to another. It may help us clarify our preferences and decide on matters small and large. At a restaurant, we may compare the appeal and value of ordering a pasta dinner with the appeal and value of ordering a sub sandwich. Putting items side by side can help us weigh the relative merits of each item and choose between alternatives.

Comparison also influences our more important decisions. We weigh majoring in chemistry against majoring in physics, buying against renting, working for Apple against working for IBM. An instructor may ask us to write a paper comparing the features of two behavioural organization models. An employer may have us weigh two proposals for decreasing employee absenteeism and write a report recommending one of them.

Comparison also acquaints us with the unfamiliar. To help Canadian readers understand the English sport of rugby, a sportswriter might compare its field, team, rules, and scoring system with those of football. To teach students about France's government, a political science textbook might compare the makeup and election of its legislature to that of the Canadian Parliament, and the method of selecting its president and premier to the Canadian method of selecting leaders.

Both academic assignments and jobs call for comparative analysis. A music instructor may ask you to compare baroque and classical music and their contributions to later musical developments. A psychology instructor may want you to compare two different types of psychosis treatment and assess the legal and medical ramifications of each. A biology instructor might have you consider how the features of two different kinds of body cells enable them to perform their functions. A criminology instructor might ask you how a restorative justice model compares with a model of adversarial justice in a specific context. In the workplace, comparisons are also common because they help people make decisions. An office manager may compare several telephone systems to determine which one would be most useful for the company; a nurse may assess the condition of a patient before and after a new medicine is given; an insurance agent may point out the features of two insurance policies to highlight the advantages of one.

SELECTING ITEMS FOR COMPARISON

Any items you compare must share some common ground. For example, you could compare two golfers on driving ability, putting ability, and sand play, or two cars on appearance, gas consumption, and warranty; but you can't meaningfully compare a golfer with a car, any more than you could compare guacamole with Guadalajara or chicken with charcoal. There's simply no basis for comparison.

Any valid comparison, on the other hand, presents many possibilities. Suppose you head the music department of a large store and have two excellent salespeople working for you. The manager of the store asks you to prepare a one- or two-page report that compares their qualifications for managing the music department in a new branch store. Assessing their abilities becomes the guiding purpose that motivates and controls the writing. Rather than comparing irrelevant points such as eye colour, hairstyle, and religion, which have no bearing on job performance, you will focus on what managerial traits the job requires and the extent to which each candidate possesses them. Your thinking might result in a list like this.

Points of Similarity or Difference	Lee	Mike
1. Ability to deal with customers, sales skills	Excellent	Excellent
2. Effort: regular attendance, hard work on the job	Excellent	Excellent
3. Leadership qualities	Excellent	Good
4. Knowledge of ordering and accounting procedures	Good	Fair
5. Musical knowledge	Excellent	Good

This list tells you which points to emphasize and suggests Lee as the candidate to recommend. You might briefly mention similarities (points 1 and 2) in an introductory paragraph, but the report would focus on differences (points 3, 4, and 5), since you're distinguishing the relative merits of two employees.

EXERCISE *Compare two popular restaurants in order to recommend one of them. List the points of similarity and difference that you might discuss. Differences should predominate because you will base your decision on them.*

DEVELOPING A COMPARISON

Successful comparisons depend on ample, well-chosen details that show just how the items under consideration are alike and different. Such support helps the reader grasp your meaning. Read the following student comparative paragraphs and note how the concrete details convey the striking differences between south and north 14th Street:

> On 14th Street running south from P Street are opulent luxury stores such as Birks and Holt Renfrew, and small but expensive clothing stores with richly dressed mannequins in the windows. Modern skyscraping office buildings hold banks and travel bureaus on the ground floors and insurance companies and corporation headquarters in the upper storeys. Dotting the concretescape are high-priced movie theatres, gourmet restaurants, multilevel parking garages, bookstores, boutiques, and fancy gift shops, all catering to the wealthy population of the city. This section of 14th Street is relatively clean: The city maintenance crews must clean up after only a nine-to-five populace and the Saturday crowds of shoppers. The pervading mood of the area is one of bustling wealth during the day and, in the night, calm.
>
> Crossing P Street toward the north, one notes a gradual but disturbing change in the scenery of 14th Street. A panhandler sits nodding on the sidewalk in front of a rundown hotel, too tired, or too drugged, to bother asking for money. A liquidation store promises bargains, but the window display shows an

unattractive tangle of chains, watches, knives, and dusty tools. Outside a tavern with opaque windows, a homeless person is curled up, sleeping beneath a tattered blanket. On the opposite side of the street, a restaurant advertising curry competes for customers with the house of noodles and pizza-to-go restaurant. Sometimes, even when the air is chill, one sees young women in short skirts, low-cut tops, and high boots standing near the curb, or leaning into the windows of cars momentarily stopped, talking to the drivers.

Vivid details depict with stark clarity the economic differences between the north and south ends of the street. These differences contribute to the writer's implied thesis: *The stark contrast between wealth and poverty on opposite ends of the same street is disturbing.*

ORGANIZING A COMPARISON

Comparison papers can be organized in two basic patterns: *block pattern*, also called comparison of wholes; and *alternating pattern*, also called comparison by points or by parts. Typically a comparison paper uses some combination of these two patterns.

The Block Pattern   The block pattern first presents all of the points of comparison for one item and then all of the points of comparison for the other. Here is the comparison of the two salespeople, Lee and Mike, outlined according to the block pattern:

I.   Introduction: mentions similarities in sales skills and effort but recommends Lee for promotion
II.   Specific points about Mike
   A. Leadership qualities
   B. Knowledge of ordering and accounting procedures
   C. Musical knowledge
III.   Specific points about Lee
   A. Leadership qualities
   B. Knowledge of ordering and accounting procedures
   C. Musical knowledge
IV.   Conclusion: reasserts that Lee should be promoted

For a shorter paper or one that includes only a few points of comparison, the block pattern can work well, since the reader can remember all the points from the first block while reading the second. Be careful, however, that you do not dwell too long on one half of the comparison without mentioning the other, or your essay might seem to break in two. Often the reader may find it easier to follow a modified block pattern, in which you refer to the first item of comparison throughout the second block.

The Alternating Pattern   The alternating pattern presents a point about one item, then follows immediately with a corresponding point about the other. Organized in this way, the Lee-and-Mike paper would look like this:

I.   Introduction: mentions similarities in sales skills and effort but recommends Lee for promotion
II. Leadership qualities
    A. Mike's qualities
    B. Lee's qualities
III. Knowledge of ordering and accounting procedures
    A. Mike's knowledge
    B. Lee's knowledge
IV. Musical knowledge
    A. Mike's knowledge
    B. Lee's knowledge
V.   Conclusion: reasserts that Lee should be promoted

If there are many points of comparison, the alternating method, which deals with each point in turn, can help your reader grasp similarities and differences. Be aware, however, that moving back and forth between two different poems or two different historical periods may become rather dizzying. To ground your reader, you may need to blend the two approaches. For example, when comparing protagonists from two works of fiction, you might give an overview of the two works' similarities in the block approach, and then use the alternating approach to focus on salient points of difference.

Once you select your pattern, arrange your points of comparison in an appropriate order. Take up closely related points one after the other. Depending on your purpose, you might work from similarities to differences or the reverse. Often, a good writing strategy is to move from the least significant to the most significant point so that you conclude with a punch.

EXERCISE *Using the points of comparison you selected for the exercise on page 258, prepare two different outlines for a paper, one organized according to the block pattern, and one according to the alternating pattern.*

USING ANALOGY

An *analogy,* a special type of comparison, calls attention to one or more similarities underlying two different kinds of items that seem to have nothing in common. While some analogies stand alone, most clarify abstract or unfamiliar concepts in other kinds of writing. They are commonly used in political and business contexts. In the 1995 Québec referendum on sovereignty, newspaper writers drew analogies comparing separation to divorce or major surgery. In marketing, someone trying to sell a personal digital assistant might compare it to an efficient office secretary.

Drawing parallels through an analogy between seemingly unrelated things can help people get a picture in their mind's eye. Analogies that point out how cells may be like factories, or DNA molecules like ladders, may help people who are not scientists to get a mental picture that clarifies scientific concepts. Consider, for example, how the following passage provides insight by comparing something that is less understood (the atmosphere of the Earth) to something that is more familiar (a window).

> The atmosphere of Earth acts like any window in serving two very important functions. It lets light in, and it permits us to look out. It also serves as a shield to keep out dangerous or uncomfortable things. A normal glazed window lets us keep our houses warm by keeping out cold air, and it prevents rain, dirt, and unwelcome insects and animals from coming in. . . . Earth's atmospheric window also helps to keep our planet at a comfortable temperature by holding back radiated heat and protecting us from dangerous levels of ultraviolet light.
>
> Lester del Ray, *The Mysterious Sky*

Conversely, an analogy sometimes highlights the unfamiliar in order to help illuminate the familiar. The following paragraph discusses the qualities and obligations of an unfamiliar person, the mountain guide, to shed light on a familiar practice—teaching:

> The mountain guide, like the true teacher, has a quiet authority. He or she engenders trust and confidence so that one is willing to join the endeavor. The guide accepts his leadership role, yet recognizes that success (measured by the heights that are scaled) depends upon the close co-operation and active participation of each member of the group. He has crossed the terrain before and is familiar with the landmarks, but each trip is new and generates its own anxiety and excitement. Essential skills must be mastered; if they are lacking, disaster looms. The situation demands keen focus and rapt attention: slackness, misjudgment, or laziness can abort the venture.
>
> Nancy K. Hill, "Scaling the Heights: The Teacher as Mountaineer"

When you develop an analogy, keep these points in mind:

1. Your readers must be well acquainted with the familiar item. If they aren't, the point is lost.
2. The items must indeed have significant similarities. You could develop a meaningful analogy between a kidney and a filter or between cancer and anarchy but not between a fiddle and a flapjack or a laser and Limburger cheese.
3. The analogy must truly illuminate. Overly obvious analogies, such as one comparing a battle to an argument, offer few or no revealing insights.
4. Overextended analogies can tax the reader's endurance. A multipage analogy between a heart and a pump would likely overwhelm the reader with all its talk of valves, hoses, pressures, and pumping.

ETHICAL ISSUES

Although an old adage declares that "comparisons are odious," most people embrace comparisons except when they are unfair. Unfortunately, unfair comparisons are often drawn. For example, advertisers commonly magnify trivial drawbacks in competitive products while exaggerating the benefits of their own merchandise. Politicians run attack ads that distort their opponents' views and demean the opponents' characters. And when scientific theories clash, supporters of one view have been known to alter their findings in order to undermine the other position. Your readers expect all comparisons to meet certain ethical standards. Ask and answer these questions to help ensure that the comparisons you write are solid.

- Have I avoided skewing one or both of my items in order to ensure a particular outcome?
- Are the items I'm comparing properly matched? It would be unethical to compare a student essay to a professional one in order to demonstrate the inadequacy of the former.
- If I'm using an analogy, is it appropriate and ethically fair? Comparing immigration officials to Nazi storm troopers would trivialize the suffering and deaths of millions of Nazi victims and taint immigration officials with a terrible label.

WRITING A COMPARISON

Planning and Drafting the Comparison

Don't write merely to fulfill an assignment; if you do, your paper will likely ramble aimlessly and fail to deliver a specific message. Instead, build your paper around a clear sense of purpose. Do you want to show the superiority of one product or method over another? Do you want to show how sitcoms today differ from those twenty years ago? Purpose governs the details you choose and the organization you follow. Whether you select your own topic or write on an assigned one, answer these questions:

What purpose will my comparison serve?

Who will be my audience and why will they want to read the essay?

What points of similarity or difference will I discuss?

To develop the comparison, draw up a chart similar to this one.

Item A	**Item B**
First point of comparison	First point of comparison
Second point of comparison	Second point of comparison

Next, brainstorm each point in turn, recording appropriate supporting details. When you finish, stand back and ask these questions:

Do all the details relate to my purpose?

Do any new details come to mind?

In what order should I organize the details?

When you decide upon an order, copy the points of comparison and the details, arranged in the order you will follow, into a chart like the one below.

Item A	Item B
First point of comparison	First point of comparison
First detail	First detail
Second detail	Second detail
Second point of comparison	Second point of comparison

Use the introduction to identify your topic and arouse the reader's interest. If you intend to establish the superiority of one item over the other, you might call attention to your position. If you're comparing something unfamiliar with something familiar, you might explain the importance of understanding the unfamiliar item.

Organize the body of your paper according to whichever pattern—block or alternating or a combined approach—that suits its length and the number of points you're planning to take up. If you explain something familiar by comparing it with something unfamiliar, start with the familiar item. If you try to show the superiority of one item over another, proceed from the less to the more desirable one.

Write whatever kind of conclusion will round off your discussion effectively. Unless you've written a lengthy paper, don't summarize the likenesses and differences you've presented. If you've done a proper writing job, your reader already has them clearly in mind. Many comparison papers end with a recommendation or a prediction. A paper comparing a familiar sport, such as ice hockey, with a less familiar one, such as roller hockey, might predict the increasing popularity of the latter. A paper comparing face-to-face poker with online poker might end with a recommendation to try the less familiar form of the game.

Revising the Comparison

Revise your paper in light of the general guidelines in Chapter 5 and the questions that follow:

> Have I accomplished my purpose, whether to examine the advantages and disadvantages of two alternatives or to acquaint the reader with something unfamiliar?
>
> For something unfamiliar, have I shown clearly just how it is like and unlike the familiar item?
>
> Have I consistently written with my audience in mind?
>
> Have I considered all points of similarity and difference that relate to my purpose?
>
> Have I included appropriate supporting details?
>
> Are my comparisons arranged effectively?

EXAMPLE OF A STUDENT ESSAY USING COMPARISON

Real vs. Fake Conversation

William Nichols

1   Have you ever been engaged in a conversation where you have no interest in the subject or who you are talking to? Of course. Now ask yourself what it feels like to be in a conversation that has your full attention. You are sure to notice many differences. For simplicity, I will call these two types of conversations real and fake, the fake conversation being the one which you wish you were never part of. These fake conversations are not limited to talks with teachers, parents, law enforcement officials, but could in fact include even the closest people in your life, since it is the level of interest in the topic that determines engagement. While real and fake conversations are very different, they can be assessed by examining the degree of conversational engagement or disengagement, as the case may be.

2   In a real conversation, the listener is genuinely interested in what the speaker has to say. This is not the case in a fake conversation, where the listener is not really listening, but usually either trying to get away or thinking only about what he or she wants to say. If we examine the body language, eye contact, emotion, and overall interest displayed by the participants in both real and fake conversations, we will see that the differences are reflected in the type and level of engagement.

3   For a conversation to be real, all parties involved should show interest in what the others are saying and be aware of the messages that they are conveying through body language, eye contact, and emotion. The use of body language and eye contact is integral to making good conversation. Body language is often quite subtle, as even the slightest movement such as leaning toward someone or away from someone can be quite revealing. One obvious form of body language is the use of hands. Our hands help us stay focused while conveying our message to the listener. For example, consider how you might use your hands when you are on the phone talking to someone. When you are describing something, you might not even notice how much you are using gestures. If you are trying to describe a building or a shape, you may trace this shape with your hands, even though you are talking on the phone

and no one can see you. It seems ridiculous in hindsight, yet most of us use our hands in such circumstances because we are fully engaged in conversation and genuinely interested in communicating our thoughts to others. Now imagine how you use your hands while talking person-to-person. Using your hands while talking person-to-person shows that you are thinking about what you are saying and that you are trying to get your message across by whatever means possible.

4   Another form of effective body language to use in conversation is eye contact. In a real conversation all persons involved make eye contact quite frequently, but in a fake conversation, people often look off into the distance, or down at a newspaper. Eye contact tells people we are listening intently or that we are speaking directly to them. Both eye contact and the use of hands can directly show emotion.

5   Showing emotion when speaking demonstrates that we care about what we are saying or about what is being said and that we are in fact engaged in a real conversation. The emotion found in a fake conversation is very different from that of a real one. In a real conversation, the participants look animated and attentive; they may smile, laugh, frown, or widen their eyes as they speak and listen. In a fake conversation, sometimes one person is serious about what is being discussed and the other is bored. While in a fake conversation, we may find ourselves becoming distracted by the smallest of things, such as the pattern on the other person's shirt. Obviously, when distracted, we fail to maintain eye contact and are not engaged in animated body language. Our disinterest is readily apparent to all . . . unless we are able to maintain the appearance of interest by staying in the conversation and sending enough body language cues to deceive our conversation partners. By pretending or faking interest, we make the other person feel as if we are genuinely participating. In fake conversations, we may be engaged in a game with ourselves in order to keep us from admitting to the other person that we are in fact totally bored and distracted.

6   When people are engaged in a fake conversation, they lack interest in those with whom they are conversing or the subject of the conversation. Fake conversations, which may occur with a teacher, parent, neighbour, or co-worker, are revealed not only by how we act but also by what we say. Clichéd statements about the nice weather suggest that the person would probably prefer not to be talking at all. Fake conversation is often bland and lacks any real substance. Usually people stay in such conversations out of guilt and fear of offending. We

don't want to admit to the other person—or sometimes even to ourselves—that we are completely bored by the conversation we are in.

7   Although all conversations use similar tools of communication, the body language, eye contact, and degree of emotional engagement are different in real and fake conversations. In a real conversation, participants engage physically in many ways, and there is frequent, focused eye contact, but in a fake conversation, participants are disengaged and eye contact is uncommon. While we all can probably admit to being in a fake conversation, how many of us can really admit to knowing someone was trying to maintain a fake conversation with us? By remaining attentive to the real and fake conversational dynamics described above, next time you'll know.

DISCUSSION QUESTIONS

1. Comment on the significance of the rhetorical questions in the introductory and concluding paragraphs.
2. Point out effective supporting details in the essay. What do they accomplish?
3. What pattern of organization does the writer use? Examine how the whole essay and individual paragraphs are organized.
4. What concrete details does the writer use to distinguish real conversations from fake ones?

SUGGESTIONS FOR WRITING

1. **Write a comparison essay on one of the topics below or another that your instructor approves. Determine the points you will discuss and how you will develop and arrange them. Emphasize similarities, differences, or both.**
   a. An arts education versus a trades education
   b. The physical or mental demands of two jobs
   c. Two advertisements for similar products
   d. An online course and a face-to face course
   e. A day-to-day relationship and a virtual one
   f. Two different forms of exercise
   g. Two cultures' approaches toward dating
2. **Develop an analogy based on one of the following sets of items or another set that your instructor approves. Proceed as you would for any other comparison.**
   a. Ending a relationship and leaving a job
   b. Drug addiction and shopping addiction

   c. Troubleshooting a computer and writing an essay

   d. Learning to drive and learning a new language

   e. Taking an exam and going to the dentist

   f. A parent and a farmer

   g. A workaholic and an alcoholic

The Critical Edge

Although you may rely on your own knowledge or findings to develop many comparisons, in some cases you may synthesize (see pages 423–425) material from other sources.

   Let's say that your business management instructor has asked you to prepare a report on the management styles of two high-profile chief executive officers (CEOs) at successful companies that manufacture the same kinds of products. You realize that you need to do some reading in business periodicals such as *Canadian Business, The Economist,* and *Fortune* in order to complete this assignment. Your sources reveal that the first CEO favours a highly centralized managerial structure with strict limits on what can be done by all employees except top executives. The company has pursued foreign markets by establishing factories overseas and has aggressively attempted to merge with or acquire its domestic competitors. The second CEO has established a decentralized managerial structure that allows managers at various levels of the company to make key decisions. The company has also established a strong foreign presence, but it has done so primarily by entering into joint ventures with foreign firms. Most of its domestic expansion has resulted from the construction of new plants rather than from mergers or takeovers. Both CEOs have borrowed heavily to finance their companies' expansion. These three differences and one similarity are your points of comparison, which you can organize using either the block or alternating pattern. You might conclude by indicating which of the two management styles is more effective.

   After you've read the views expressed by your sources, examine them critically. Does any of the information about the two CEOs seem slanted so that it appears to misrepresent their management styles? For example, do any of the writers seem to exaggerate the positive or negative features of centralized or decentralized management? Do appropriate examples support the writers' contentions? Does any relevant information appear to be missing? Does any source contain material that isn't related to your purpose? Judging the works of others in this fashion helps you write a better report.*

---

*Because you rely on published sources for your information, it is important to read the sections on research in Chapters 15 and 16 and those on handling quotations and avoiding plagiarism in Chapter 17 before you start to write. As always, follow your instructor's guidelines for documenting sources.

SUGGESTIONS FOR WRITING

1. Read at least two essays in this book on a similar issue (for example, the articles on cloning or on multiculturalism in Chapter 14), and then compare the views of these two writers. In your comparison, make an argument for which essay or article is more persuasive.

2. After reading several reviews of the same movie, compare and contrast these reviews in order to demonstrate how film critics bring different values to their viewing.

COMPARISON ESSAYS: PROFESSIONAL MODELS

READING STRATEGIES

1. Identify your purpose for reading the comparison and the author's purpose for the comparison. Does the author compare in order to acquaint the reader with something new, or to suggest the relative merits of one thing over another?

2. Identify the items that are being compared, and identify the basis for the comparison.

3. Identify the pattern of organization (alternating point by point, block, or a blended approach) that is used in the comparison.

4. Read carefully to establish the points of similarities and differences. When the information might be necessary for future purposes, it can be helpful to create a table that matches similarities and differences.

READING CRITICALLY

1. Explore whether there are any biases underlying the comparison. Does the writer seem to give fair treatment to all items being compared? Test whether the basis for comparison is logically consistent.

2. Determine if the writer emphasizes similarities, differences, or both. Does the author go beyond ticking off similarities and differences and make a larger point in the essay? Does the writer have something fresh to say and avoid dwelling on the obvious?

3. Identify whether there are other similarities or differences or more illustrative details that could have been brought in.

READING AS A WRITER

1. Examine how the author organized the essay. Was the organization effective in guiding the reader through the essay? Note what organizational pattern was most effective.

2. Notice transitional words and phrases such as *in contrast, on the other hand, while, whereas* that indicate contrast, or words such as *just as, like, similarly,*

both that help the writer draw distinctions and parallels. Note also the sentences that the writer uses for transitions.

3. Observe how much detail was used to substantiate the comparison.

Douglas Todd

In a Girl's World, It Can Be Tough Being a Boy

Title sets up differences, suggests direction

Douglas Todd writes a regular column on religion and ethics for the Vancouver Sun. *He has gathered more than 50 journalism awards, including the 2005 National Newspaper award for a piece about his father's battle with schizophrenia. He is the author of* Brave Souls: Writers and Artists Wrestle with God, Love, Death and the Things That Matter. *In the following essay, Todd argues that boys are now on the losing end of the gender battle, particularly in education.*

1   "Girl Power!" "Girls Rule!" These slogans now appear weekly as educators, the entertainment industry, and the media celebrate spunky young women's rising successes.

Introduction: paragraphs 1–4; background and social context; significance of following contrasts

2   Girls now do better in school than boys. Many employers are patting themselves on the back for hiring more females than males. Vancouver's Sarah McLachlan, who organized a big money-making all-women concert festival called Lilith Fair, is becoming an international icon for "Girl Power."

3   Unfortunately, the cheering for girls' triumphs is drowning out the quiet worries of a bunch of others—boys. Just as girls were stereotyped as sweet low-achievers in the '50s, now boys seem to be suffering from being pigeon-holed as unruly good-for-littles.

4   The notion of gender inequity has been turned on its head. While some commentators declare it's now a good time to be a girl, they're not dropping the other shoe: it's a troublesome, even crummy, time to be a boy.

5   A recent *Globe and Mail* column is typical of the current blindness. Education writer Jennifer Lewington analysed an Ontario study that found Grade 3 girls were doing better than boys at writing, as well as being more confident than boys about writing. Grade 3 girls were also doing better than boys at math, but weren't quite as confident as boys about numbers.

Body: paragraphs 5–17; alternating pattern throughout

Differences in elementary school

6   What angle did the *Globe* column pursue? It explored ways to improve girls' confidence in math—even though they were already doing better than boys in the subject. It didn't focus on the more pressing problem: helping Grade 3 boys catch up in both math and writing.

7   Lewington's column is just one small example of an education bias that drives at least one Vancouver school teacher to distraction. The teacher says many of her colleagues, like much of the public, generally view girls as delightful, boys as trouble.

8   The teacher was at a recent conference where a female education specialist told the audience the only things boys are better at than girls is sports. As a mother of boys and a teacher, she could barely contain herself. (As a father of boys, I can also tell you this is increasingly becoming a topic among pro-feminist mothers and fathers of boys, at least those not afraid to discuss such spicy issues.)

9   It's a mug's game to try to figure out whether boys or girls are more hard-done-by today. Both are undoubtedly having a tough time, particularly because of meaner economics, higher divorce rates, and greater role confusion. But girls, at least, are winning the fight for attention.

Compares boys and girls   10   We see a flood of lifestyle articles about girls who lose confidence when they become adolescents.
in adolescence

11   But we see little about a similarly devastating emotional slide for boys. We hear a lot about how parents and teachers with low expectations for girls will fulfill their own prophecies; we don't hear how the same attitude can doom boys to mediocrity or worse.

12   One of the few people to raise the alarm for boys is B.C. Teachers Federation professional development specialist Patrick Clarke. He believes the public hasn't noticed what's befallen boys because the switch has happened so fast—within the past 10 years.

Research and statistics   13   Clarke's research has found almost 80 percent of B.C. honour-roll students
reinforce claims   now are girls. B.C.'s education ministry also says about 60 percent of current graduates with honours are girls (with the highest marks going to Asian girls, who, prevailing wisdom falsely argues, should be twin victims, of both their ethnicity and gender), which reverses test results of the early '80s.

Contrasts level of   14   What's more, girls dominate school clubs and student councils. "To put it
participation in extra-   bluntly, the girls are running the place," says Clarke, who, rightly or wrongly,
curricular activities   carefully avoids blaming teachers or feminism for boys' crisis.

15   Confirming the trend, British and Australian studies show at least one out of three boys succumbing to mass images that say the only way to glory lies in professional sports, or Beavis and Butthead–style laziness and mischief.

Broadens scope   16   In Britain, while girls 15 to 17 are becoming more optimistic, boys are becom-
of discussion   ing more pessimistic and introverted, suffering from low self-esteem and lack of ambition, which lead to poor study habits. A large minority of Britain's young men may be forming a new rogue underclass, writes Edward Balls in *Danger: Men Not at Work.*

17   As a father of girls, Clarke says part of him recognizes that every boy who drops off the career path opens up another place for his daughters in an increasingly competitive marketplace. But his sense of social justice tells him he can't give in to such self-interest.

Conclusion: paragraphs   18   And while many others declare it's about time girls ruled the world, or at least
18–20; recommends   the Western world (where girls' advances are far more pronounced), they might
change in educational   not enjoy telling that directly to a struggling 12-year-old boy. After all, he had
policy   absolutely nothing to do with centuries-old customs that confined women to narrow roles.

19   While it's undeniable the top echelon of the business world is still dominated by men in suits, that doesn't mean much for boys (and the vast majority of men) who are just trying to get by, who weren't raised among the wealth and privilege that often opens the doors to such million-dollar positions. Young women are now doing fine in most professions.

20   Although it might seem shocking to some people stuck in outdated gender trenches, it could be time for affirmative-action education programs for boys similar to those that encouraged girls in the maths and sciences.

DISCUSSION QUESTIONS

1. Identify the thesis statement. Why do you think it is located where it is?

2. Consider colloquialisms such as the word "crummy," as Todd declares "it's a troublesome, even crummy, time to be a boy" (paragraph 4). What other examples of colloquialisms or slang can you find? Given that this article was originally written for a newspaper, comment on how Todd can use such an informal, casual writing style without losing authority.

3. How does the writer support his claim that girls are now "winning the fight for attention" (paragraph 9)?

4. How is the writer careful to qualify his argument by acknowledging the problems that females have faced? What does he mean when he refers to "outdated gender trenches" (paragraph 20)?

TOWARD KEY INSIGHTS

To what extent do you think that the problems for boys that Todd alludes to may be an inevitable result of feminist gains? What disturbing implications about gender equity are raised by this article?

Do you agree that for many boys today, "the only way to glory lies in professional sports, or Beavis-and-Butthead–style laziness and mischief" (paragraph 15)? Why or why not?

In your view, what different issues do males and females face in adolescence?

What do you think of Todd's suggestion that it could be time "for affirmative-action education programs for boys" (paragraph 20)?

SUGGESTION FOR WRITING *Drawing from your own experience, compare and contrast the treatment of males and females in a particular context, such as a specific sport, a place of employment, the news media, or Hollywood.*

Mariflo Stephens

Barbie Doesn't Live Here Anymore

Mariflo Stephens lives in Charlottesville, Virginia, where she writes essays and fiction. Her work appears in a number of major periodicals such as the Washington Post *and the* Virginia Quarterly Review. *This essay, from her memoir in progress,* Last One Home: Life After Oprah, *compares the place of the common Barbie doll in her and her daughter's lives to demonstrate the differences between two generations of women.*

1   I've always known there was something wrong with Barbie. She looks nice enough. And she has her own Corvette, her own band, and her own dream house. Still, I just didn't want my daughter playing with her. But how can we snub Barbie? Little girls all over Charlottesville, all over Virginia, and, yes, all over the world, seem to be spending hour after hour with her.

2   I considered relying on my own experience. When, in 1962, I was presented with my first Barbie doll, I did what all the other little girls did with their Barbies: I took her clothes off. Wow! I could hardly wait to have a pair of my very own.

3   Then I put her clothes back on. It was hard. There was a snap the size of a pinhead and Barbie hardly cooperated. I pulled the tight dress up her legs, over her hips; and it stopped right there. Had a liquid Barbie been poured into this to harden? She was stiff as stone but still smelled like new rubber. I had to put her head between my teeth to get her dress past that chest. I was exhausted. But was it ever fun, I told myself.

4   Now where were those high heels and that pair of long white gloves? I found one glove. Later my friend Jane came over to play. She took the dress off, too. We waited for something to happen. Then we went out to climb some trees. Four hours later, we told our mothers we'd had a great time playing Barbie. (This was lobbying. Jane's mother looked quizzical and noted the leaves in our hair.)

5   I was twelve in 1962, so I didn't have too many good years left for Barbie. Soon I would be Barbie. I was blond, wasn't I? And I would be an American teenager with no time left for playing. My time would be devoted to the serious business of dressing and dating and talking on the telephone.

6   In the months to come, I made the best of it. I spent my entire piggybank savings on Barbie clothes—sequined evening gowns, fake-fur wraps, and high heels. The outfits had themes like Barbie Goes to the Prom and Barbie Steps Out printed in a fast-moving script with exclamation marks at the end. There wasn't much to do, however, but dress and undress Barbie, and I found I had to spend most of my time looking for a lost pink high heel the size of my little fingernail.

7   Buying the clothes was the exciting part. Since I liked horses, I picked out Barbie's rodeo skirt set with white high-heeled boots and fringe. These weren't Barbie's clothes, they were mine. If I could've worn Barbie's lavender loungewear with its pink feather boa to my seventh-grade classroom, I would have. If, that is, I could find it. Much was located under the sofa cushions, but far too late, I'm afraid.

8   Barbie retired early. I waited for my body to fill out, Barbie-style. My legs didn't grow to those proportions and neither did anything else. I got the idea that every time a teenage boy looked at me he saw only what was missing—what Barbie had that I didn't.

9   Even the blond hair didn't live up to expectations. Mine was fuzzy and its shape varied from day to day. Barbie's seemed to stay in a permanent coiffure. Evening gowns weren't even in style.

10   And not very many blondes can manage a nose that turns up that way.

11   Worst of all, Barbie doesn't do anything but lose her clothes. I had wasted a lot of money, not to mention rich fantasy time, on a false goddess.

12   When my daughter, Jane, was born, I told myself there would be no false goddesses. I didn't name her after a goddess, I named her after the girl I'd climbed trees with.

13   When relatives started to inquire about birthday gifts, I didn't say "No Barbies, please," though I wanted to. I said instead that books were very nice gifts. I mentioned there wasn't much to do with a Barbie doll except comb her hair and I was sure we'd lose those little combs.

14   Jane turned seven. She had five Barbie dolls. I didn't see her playing with them much, although every few days I would find a pink high heel somewhere. I would spot the dolls around the house—their legs splayed crazily and scarves tied around their bodies for clothes.

15   One day Jane said: "Barbies don't do anything. They don't even bend their legs when you sit them down. Their legs stick straight out." I knew she was on to something. Then we cleaned up her room. I found most of the clothes and even some of the high heels. I was pretty proud of myself. But behind me I heard Jane saying: "Let's get rid of the Barbies."

16   "Huh?"

17   "They're dumb and prissy. They clutter up everything. Let's sell them."

18   "What do you mean by 'dumb and prissy'?"

19   "They look like this," she said and raised to tiptoe and smiled maniacally. "They've got globs of blue makeup over their eyes and they can't do anything. You can't even bend their legs to sit them on a model horse."

20   I seized the moment. "What else is wrong with the Barbies?"

21   "They don't have toes. Their shoes fall off. They're always on tiptoe."

22   "That would be tiring," I said, sympathetically.

23   "They never get tired. They don't do anything."

24   "What else is wrong?"

25   "They don't wear socks or pants. Just dresses or fish-net stockings or they go barefoot. All the commercials compliment their hair, but once their hair is tangled, it never goes back."

26   "Anything else wrong?" I asked—and here she won my heart if ever there was a contest for it.

27   "They're all the same age. There are no Barbie babies and no old people."

28   "Sounds like Barbie lives in a dull world," I said.

29   "No, not dull. Dumb and prissy. Let's sell them."

30   "How much should we charge for each one?"

31   "A penny," she said disgustedly, then immediately saw her error. "No, no. A dollar."

32   "Oh," I said, seeing my own error. Just because I considered Barbie small change didn't mean everyone else did. Six Barbies went out the back door to a secondhand shop and, in a matter of minutes, six dollars came in the front door.

33   Maybe Barbie's business suit with its one-inch briefcase inspired Jane's market wisdom.

34   After all, the new Barbies are still in stores, housed in pink boxes with bold script that seems to shout: Barbie Goes to the Office! My old dolls, with their narrow eyes and puckered lips, are upstairs like other mad women of the attic, whispering: "Who stole my feather boa?"

DISCUSSION QUESTIONS

1. This essay compares the different reactions of mother and daughter to Barbie dolls. What are the differences in their responses? What is the real point of this comparison?

2. How does this writer organize her comparison? What is the effect of this strategy?

3. Crucial to this essay is the dialogue between mother and daughter. What does the dialogue accomplish in the essay?

4. Reread the last paragraph. What point is the author trying to make in the conclusion? Is the conclusion effective?

5. How is the image of the feather boa used in the essay? What is the meaning of the feather boa for the author? What clues in the text demonstrate this meaning?

TOWARD KEY INSIGHTS

What role do Barbies have in the developing attitudes of girls, and is that role positive or negative?

How do you imagine that contemporary toys such as Hannah Montana toys, Transformer action figures, etc., influence young girls' and boys' self-image?

SUGGESTIONS FOR WRITING

1. Compare how a toy such as G.I. Joe or a particular video game has changed over a specific period of time.

2. Select a male or female whom you know well and write an essay comparing how you and the other person, as adolescents, handled such matters as peer pressure, self-image, dating, and relationships with family members. Develop the essay with relevant supporting material.

Trevor Herriot

Generation unto Regeneration

Trevor Herriot is an accomplished prairie naturalist, illustrator, and writer. His award-winning book, River in a Dry Land, *is a personal reflection on life and landscape in the Qu'Appelle Valley, where he grew up. As is evident in the essay here, Trevor Herriot's respect and enthusiasm for people and the natural environment is a prominent feature of his writing.*

1   Yesterday, 90-kilometre-per-hour winds blew glacial loess onto my desk through a crack in the window, but this afternoon the rain has finally come. For the first time this spring, the kale and lettuce in my front-yard patch will be plunging root hairs into moisture that has come from the skies instead of the city's water system.

2   The need for rain has lately become something urban and rural people in Saskatchewan can agree upon, though we have more in common than we generally admit. To be a thoroughgoing urbanite in even the largest cities of this, the most rural of provinces, one has to go out of one's way to cultivate the illusion.

3   I live in central Regina, where I can walk downtown in 20 minutes or turn the other way and walk to fields on the western outskirts in 15 minutes. (I clocked myself the other day: 12 minutes from my front porch to the first meadowlark song.) Most of us living here grew up on farms, in villages, or on reserves, yet we talk about one another—urban and rural—as though we still had walls to keep the pagans at bay.

4   Our disprivileging of rural people is at least that old: Pagan, from the Latin *paganus*, means "of the country." It entered our lexicon when Christianity, a persecuted cult on the fringes of the Roman polis, snuck past the walls of civilization to become the Church of Emperors. When the marginal make it to the centre, their first act is to declare a new margin.

5   In this city, our "pagan" roots surface now and then, no matter how long we've lived away from the farm. You meet people here who garden by the moon and the fuzz on caterpillars. Office and government employees commonly give up vacation days each spring and fall to help with seeding and harvest on a relative's farm.

6   And when conversation shifts from the weather to the latest blow to rural community, stories and opinions come easily. Some are damning, others compassionate; most are discouraging, some manage to console.

7   "We might be the last generation of people who will remember days spent killing and plucking geese to make a feather tick." This from a friend, Joanne, who moved to Regina decades ago from the village of Limerick in south-central Saskatchewan.

8   I was suggesting that, as the rural economy slips, community-building skills and traditional lifeways become all the more vital. I asked how Limerick was getting by. In reply she told me about the system they use to keep community events going—fairs, weddings, funerals, feasts and dinners of all kinds.

9   The village's families, about 150 people, are divided into four work groups, and they do all the catering and organizing on a rotation, apportioning the labour among three of the groups. The fourth group gets a break and then at the next event it cycles to the "A" position responsible for the main load of work—cooking the food.

10   I had to ask the urban question: What if someone doesn't want to help? There isn't really any choice, she said. If you want to be well regarded and included in the community, you participate. The system finds a way for everyone to help; even young men are in there pinching perogies and basting turkeys.

11   Older citizens, like Joanne's father, 81 and long retired from active farming, have their role too in maintaining the well-being of Limerick. People are holding onto their cash more than ever in rural areas, but a fundraiser who has local knowledge and the respect of his neighbours can charm, beg, guilt and cajole enough money out of savings accounts and mattresses to bring almost any community dream into the light of day. Con, as Joanne's father is known throughout the district, has been Limerick's chief arm-twister until poor health recently forced him to quit.

12   A modest man, he won't stand up in front of a small gathering of family and neighbours to receive community service awards (Joanne suspects he has them mail the certificate), but as a fundraiser he'll wade in where others fear to tread, pin the most parsimonious of old bachelors against the wall and talk them into donating to the rink-building fund. "What do I want a rink for?" they'd say. "I ain't got kids or even a niece or a nephew to use it." Con's reply: "That doesn't matter. You live here, don't you?"

13   A simple notion that, but it works because Con and everyone else in Limerick knows that to live in a place is to be responsible for its welfare. Forgetting that truth, I will admit, is easier here in the city, where we protect the Prairie polis with walls made of all we choose to forget: that the country surrounds the city and not the reverse, that a civilization's social and spiritual renewal almost always comes from the margins, and that we ourselves are marginal and therefore more pagan than Roman. Perhaps worst of all, we forget that to keep a culture vital, its seed stock of lifeways must be resown in situ in the new soil of each generation.

14   Thomas Cahill has argued, convincingly I think, that after Rome fell, Western civilization was saved by a few Roman-educated monks living among Celtic pagans just beyond the reach of the empire. When our current dispensation finally goes the way of all empires, the seeds that will keep our cultural practices, subsistence skills, and communal values alive will come from places far from the centre where pagans and Romans have been quietly mixing and planting their lifeways, sowing the old amongst the new.

15   A new day now and my garden is consoled by the rain, as I am by the thought of people living in places as far-flung as Limerick who still know how to get things done.

16   And one of them, bless his soul, is named Constantine, after the Roman emperor who let the Christians into the city in the first place.

DISCUSSION QUESTIONS

1. Why does the writer emphasize his position as an urban person in a primarily rural setting (see paragraphs 1–3, 5, and 10)? How might his perspective be different if he had never moved to a city, or if he had never lived in the country? What similarities and differences between rural and city people are suggested? Can you locate other, less obvious examples of comparison in these paragraphs?

2. What is the significance of the writer's references to "pagans" and to ancient Roman civilization (paragraphs 3–5, 13, 16)? Explain what the author means when he says, "When the marginal make it to the centre, their first act is to declare a new margin" (paragraph 4).

3. Why does the writer zero in on one community member, the older citizen named Con (paragraphs 11–13, 16)?

4. Identify the thesis statement, and speculate about why you think it comes so late in the essay (paragraph 13).

5. Explain how the title could be read in more than one way. Find examples of references, whether stated or implied, to the idea of "generation" or "generations" in the essay. Where does the writer use images or metaphors from farm life?

TOWARD KEY INSIGHTS

If you have experienced life on a farm, on a reserve, or in a small village, how much of this essay can you identify with? If you have lived only in cities, what is your response to this portrait of rural life?

What is your view of the argument that as rural and village life falters, "community-building skills" become increasingly important?

What experiences have you had of community-building events or customs, and how are they similar to or different from the ones described in the essay?

SUGGESTIONS FOR WRITING

1. Reflect on two different cultures or ways of life (urban/rural; working class/ middle class; Eastern/Western, etc.) you have experienced. Write an essay that compares and contrasts the different perspectives on community, or nature, or a particular custom associated with each culture.

2. Compare this essay with "Memories of Montreal" (pages 152–154) in order to show how different writers convey regret for lost values of community and tradition.

CHAPTER 13

Strategies for Finding Patterns: Classification

GROUPING INTO CATEGORIES

Help Wanted, Situations Wanted, Real Estate, Personal. Do these terms look familiar? They do if you've ever scanned the classified ads of the newspaper. Ads are grouped into categories, and each category is then subdivided. The people who assemble this layout are *classifying*. Figure 13.1 (see page 279) shows the main divisions of a typical classified ad section and a further breakdown of one of them.

As this figure indicates, grouping allows the people who handle ads to divide entries according to a logical scheme and helps readers find what they are looking for. Imagine the difficulty of checking the real estate ads if all the entries were run in the chronological order in which they were received.

Our minds naturally sort information into categories. Within a few weeks after their birth, infants can tell the faces of family members from those of outsiders. Toddlers learn to distinguish between cats, dogs, and rabbits. In both cases the classification rests solely on physical differences. As we mature we start classifying in more abstract ways, and by adulthood we are constantly sorting things into categories.

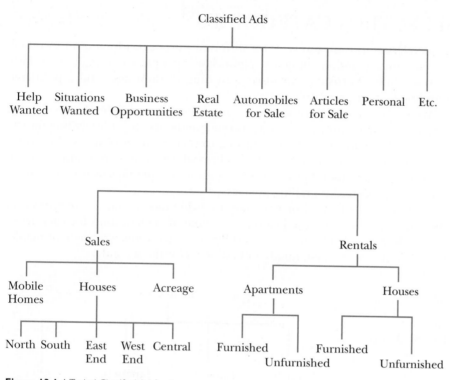

Figure 13.1 A Typical Classified Ad Section

Classification helps writers and readers come to grips with large or complex topics. It breaks a broad topic into categories according to some specific principle, presents the distinctive features of each category, and shows how the features vary among categories. Segmenting the topic simplifies the discussion by presenting the information in small, neatly sorted piles rather than in one jumbled and confusing heap.

Furthermore, classification helps people make choices. Identifying which groups of consumers—students, accountants, or teachers—are most likely to buy a new product allows the manufacturer to advertise in appropriate media. Knowing the engine size, manoeuvrability, seating capacity, and gas consumption of typical subcompact, compact, and intermediate-size cars helps customers decide which one to buy.

Because classification plays such an important part in our lives, it is a useful writing tool in many situations. Your accounting instructor may ask you to categorize accounting procedures for retail businesses. In a computer class, you may classify computer languages and then specify appropriate applications for each grouping. The communications director of an investment firm might write a customer letter categorizing investments according to their degree of risk.

SELECTING CATEGORIES

People classify in different ways for different purposes, which tend to reflect their interests. A clothing designer might classify people according to their fashion sense, an advertising executive according to their age, and a politician according to their party affiliations.

When you write a classification paper, choose a principle of classification that suits not only your purpose but also your audience. If you're writing for students, don't classify instructors according to their manner of dress, their body build, or their car preferences. These breakdowns aren't relevant. Instead, organize by a more useful principle of classification—perhaps by teaching styles, concern for students, or grading policies.

Sometimes it's helpful or necessary to divide one or more categories into subcategories. If you do, use just one principle of classification for each level. Both levels in Figure 13.2 meet this test because each reflects a single principle: place of origin for the first, number of cylinders for the second.

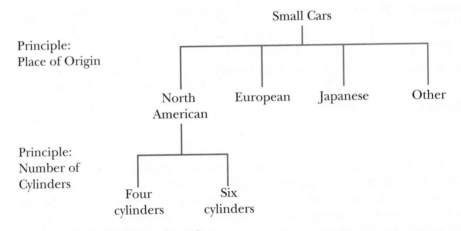

Figure 13.2 Proper Classification of Small Cars

Now examine Figure 13.3. This classification is *improper* because it groups cars in two ways—by place of origin and by kind—making it possible for one car to end up in two different categories. For example, the German Porsche is both a European car and a sports car. When categories overlap in this way, confusion reigns and nothing is clarified.

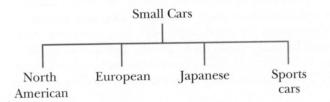

Figure 13.3 Improper Classification of Small Cars

EXERCISE

1. **How would each of the following people be most likely to classify the families living in a Canadian town?**

   a. The member of Parliament who represents the city

   b. A social worker

   c. The director of the local credit bureau

2. **The following lists contain overlapping categories. Identify the inconsistent item in each list and explain why it is faulty.**

Nurses	Pictures	Voters in Saskatoon
Surgical nurses	Oil paintings	Liberals
Psychiatric nurses	Magazine illustrations	Conservatives
Emergency room nurses	Lithographs	Saskatchewan Party
Terminal care nurses	Watercolours	New Democrats
Night nurses	Etchings	Nonvoters

NUMBER OF CATEGORIES

Some classification papers discuss every category included within the topic. Others discuss only selected categories. Circumstances and purpose dictate the scope of the discussion. Suppose you work for a city finance department and you have been asked to write a report that classifies the city's major nonservice industries and also assesses their strengths and weaknesses. Your investigation shows that food processing, furniture making, and the production of auto parts account for over 95 percent of all nonservice jobs. Two minor industries, printing and toy making, provide the rest of the jobs. Given these circumstances, you'd probably focus on the first three industries, mentioning the others only in passing. However, if printing and toy making were significant industries, they too would require detailed discussion.

DEVELOPING CATEGORIES

Develop every category using specific, informative details that provide a clear picture. The following excerpt from a student paper classifying public restrooms for women discusses two of the writer's three categories:

> Luxurious washrooms are found in upscale department stores, chic boutiques, and the better restaurants. This aristocrat of public facilities usually disdains the term *washroom*, masquerading instead under the alias of *ladies' room*. Upon entering its plush environs, the user is captivated by its elegance. Thick carpet reaches up to cushion tired feet, wood panelled or brocade velvet walls shut the outside world away, and softly glowing wall sconces soothe the eyes. Inviting armchairs and gold-and-velvet tables add to the restful, welcoming

atmosphere, and the latest issues of upscale magazines such as *Elle* and *Flare* entice customers to sit and read. Mirrors in carved frames, designer basins with gleaming gold faucets, and creamy scented soap suggest a spa-like luxury. Soft music, piped in through invisible speakers, may take patrons back in time, as if no one is waiting for them outside the door.

The adequate washroom offers utility without the swankiness of its lavish cousin. Typically located in a large shopping mall or mass-market department store, it is a stark world of hard, unadorned surfaces—tile floors, tile walls, and harshly glaring fluorescent lights recessed in the ceiling. For those who wish to rest, there is a garishly coloured Naugahyde couch and next to it a battered metal or wood table holding a few tattered copies of *Homemakers, People, Canadian Living*, and similar publications. The mirrors have steel frames; the sinks, set in a formica counter, have plain chrome faucets; and the soap dispenser emits a thin stream of unscented liquid. There is no soothing music—just the relentless whining of someone's tired child.

The concrete details in these paragraphs effectively characterize each category and clearly distinguish between them. Imagine how vague and indistinct the categories would be without these details.

ETHICAL ISSUES

Classification can seem quite innocent, yet can cause great harm. In India, millions of people were once classified as "untouchables" and so were denied the rights of other citizens. In Canada during World War II, innocent people of Japanese descent were classified as a threat and were stripped of property and moved away from their homes. In many high schools, students are often lumped into categories with labels such as "preps," "geeks" or "nerds," "jocks," or "druggies." Clearly you have to evaluate the appropriateness and consequences of your classification scheme. To avoid problems, ask and answer these questions:

- Is my classification called for by the situation? It may be appropriate to classify students in a school environment according to their reading skills, but classifying factory workers in this fashion may be inappropriate and unfair to the people involved.
- Have I avoided the use of damaging classifications? People naturally resent stereotyping.
- Have I applied my classification without resorting to overgeneralization? In a paper classifying student drinkers, it would be a mistake, and even harmful, to imply that all university students drink excessively.
- Could my classification promote harmful behaviour? When classifying the behaviour patterns of young urban dwellers, it would be unethical to present favourably the lifestyle of a group that uses hard drugs and engages in criminal activities.

We are ethically responsible for the classification systems that we use in our writing. Always examine the ones you use for suitability, fairness, and potential harm.

WRITING A CLASSIFICATION

Planning and Drafting the Classification

Many topics that interest you are potential candidates for classification. If you're selecting your own topic, you might explain the different kinds of rock music, take a humorous look at different types of teachers, or, in a more serious vein, identify different types of discrimination. As always, use one or more of the narrowing strategies on pages 34–40 to help stimulate your thinking. As possibilities come to mind, examine each one in light of these questions:

What purpose will this classification serve?

Who is my audience and what will interest them?

What are the categories of this topic?

What features distinguish my categories from one another?

Next, determine whether you'll discuss every category or only selected ones, and then set up a classification chart similar to the one following.

Category 1	**Category 2**	**Category 3**
First distinguishing feature	First distinguishing feature	First distinguishing feature
Second distinguishing feature	Second distinguishing feature	Second distinguishing feature

Such a chart helps you see the relationships among categories and provides a starting point for developing your specific details. Proceed by jotting down the details that come to mind for each distinguishing feature of every category. Then prepare a second chart with the distinguishing features and details arranged in the order in which you want to present them.

Begin your paper by identifying your topic and capturing your reader's attention in some way. A paper classifying types of problems associated with substance abuse on campus might start with a short narrative about a university student who managed to overcome a debilitating drug or alcohol dependency. In more personal writing, you could cite a personal experience that relates to your topic. As always, circumstances dictate your choice.

In the body, discuss your categories in whatever order best suits your purpose. Order of climax—least important, more important, most important—often works well. Or perhaps your topic suggests arranging the categories by behaviour, income, education, or physical characteristics. Whatever your arrangement, signal it clearly to your reader. Don't merely start the discussions of your categories by saying *first . . .*, *second . . .*, *another . . .*, *next . . .*, or *last*. These words offer no rationale for your order.

In addition, make sure the arrangement of material within the categories follows a consistent pattern. Recall the two categories of washrooms discussed on pages 281–282. In each case, after noting where the washroom can be found, the writer discusses its floor, walls, and lighting, moves to the furniture, and ends by discussing the sinks, soap, and sound.

The strategies for ending a classification paper are as varied as those for starting it. A paper on problems linked to substance abuse on campus might conclude by exploring the wider cultural implications of this substance abuse, or by suggesting ways that universities could address these problems more productively. In other cases, you might weigh your evidence that one item is more useful than another for a particular purpose.

Revising the Classification

Revise your paper by following the guidelines in Chapter 5 as well as by asking yourself these questions:

Does my classification have a clear sense of purpose and audience?

Does my principle of classification accord with my purpose?

Do any of my categories overlap?

Have I chosen an appropriate number of categories?

Are these categories developed with sufficient details?

Are the categories and details arranged in an effective order?

EXAMPLE OF A STUDENT ESSAY USING CLASSIFICATION

Get Used to It

Luke Kingma

1   In the world of education, there are those that are meant to teach, and there are those that should stay away. The poor teachers mix with the good and form the education system that we are acquainted with today. Unfortunately, those individuals who have yet to find the right job for their talents can add to the frustrations of student life. I suppose it could be argued that students must learn to deal with all personality types and levels of competence when interacting with others throughout life. Indeed, students owe a debt of gratitude to all those teachers who can take even the most ill-shaped mind and mould it into an objective-thinking unit; however, struggling students should be aware that teachers often fall into the following categories before they sign up for a class.

The Genius

2   Viewed by average students as second only to Einstein, this mastermind is primarily a knowledge-focused individual who ignores all other aspects of life. A teacher like this is hired for credentials, not for an amazing teaching record. This teacher's intellect is on display each class in a plethora of mind-boggling detail. Imagine someone who can explain the Standard Model of Quantum Mechanics on the blackboard in ten seconds or less. This person may be smart, but intelligence alone does not make a teacher.

3   Although naturally intelligent, this teacher does not comprehend how some students do not understand the lecture. A question directed at a genius teacher from a perplexed student will result in a confused and slightly frustrated look, followed by an explanation exactly like the one given before. This teacher puts forth no effort to make certain a student understands the material before progressing. Students who understand what is being taught are able to move on; those who do not are left grasping at straws. Lecturing is the teacher's job; students must teach themselves if they are to keep up.

The Hider

4   Hiders are excessive introverts. Why these people chose teaching as a career is beyond most students. They shy away from the limelight and avoid communication as best they can. Chameleon-like, they blend in with the chalkboard, quietly scribbling notes for the class to copy down. They avoid eye contact when students attempt to ask questions. The floor, the lecture notes, or the wall behind the students often make for a better target. An excellent tactic they use for avoiding questions is directing the struggling student back to the textbook. Unfortunately, the textbook is usually the source of the student's confusion. There is only one thing worse than a two-hour class with a hider—a three-hour one. Through these gruelling hours, students can only strive to stay awake and not miss anything for the big exam. Morning and evening classes worsen the dryness of the session. The drone of the fan, tapping on the chalkboard, and lack of enthusiasm entice students into a long nap.

The Crammer

5   These tough guys assume that students are only taking one class each semester: theirs. They often begin the semester by telling the class in an almost evangelistic way, "This will be the one most important and interesting class in all of your schooling . . . and perhaps provide your greatest lesson in life." A summary of grades for a past class is also given, and the particular focus is on those who failed or barely passed. The audience is not given any encouragement that

they will achieve their usual grade average in this class. Students are left to try their best to keep up in the class, with no time for questions—they can review at home. The pile of homework given every night assumes that every other class is unimportant, so grades in the other classes may suffer. To top it off, this teacher often wears a slight, arrogant smirk while watching students frantically jot down notes and scramble to raise a seemingly "un-raisable" grade. Nothing is ever good enough for crammers.

The Know-It-All

6   Often spotted in universities, these instructors know everything there is to know about everything—except the subject they supposedly majored in. More often than not, these teachers establish their authority on the first day about how many and which kinds of high-profile institutions they have taught at. Of course, these biographies never include reasons why they moved from one university to another; we are left to assume that they came to their current position of their own accord.

7   Somehow, these often loud attention-seekers get away with teaching nothing of the subject, and they justify leaving half-way through a class to let students "discuss their studies and work on projects." Often, if a student manages to gather up enough nerve to ask a Know-It-All a question about the course, the Know-It-All shoots back: "It's in the textbook. READ IT!" After struggling through the course, those students who survived move on without a secure foundation, often wondering what they actually learned and floundering in subsequent classes.

The Class Master

8   This may be the first undesirable teacher a grade-school student will encounter, and perhaps is the most damaging to a young mind. These teachers love to point out the obvious faults of their students—small or large—both in school-work and in personality. The tough survive; the weak get pounded. Every word that comes out of Class Master's mouth is undeniable, undisputable truth—at least in this teacher's own mind. These educators are on a mission: to make clones of themselves. Really, it's a "god complex," as many students have put it. These teachers want to save the world from drowning in its own stupidity. They seem to stick with the job simply because of the power it holds: a reign of terror over quivering students. When Class Masters step outside their classroom, they're just regular "schmos" walking down the street. Of these five undesirable types, the Class Master is the one students could do without the most.

9   Students encounter these types of undesirable teachers all too often, so students and administrators should be on the alert. Sadly, it is probably a fact of life

that these types will forever be in our education system, so we might as well get used to it and learn from our experiences. In fact, no matter where we end up in life, we will have to deal with people such as these, so we might as well learn how to deal with them while we are growing up.

DISCUSSION QUESTIONS

1. What is the writer's purpose in developing this classification? Where does he state it?
2. In what order has the author arranged his categories? Refer to the essay when answering.
3. Demonstrate that the writer has avoided overlapping categories.
4. How might he have refined further the categories of undesirable teachers?

SUGGESTIONS FOR WRITING *Write a classification paper on one of the topics below or one approved by your instructor. Determine your purpose and audience, select appropriate categories, decide how many you'll discuss, develop them with specific details, and arrange them in an effective order.*

1. University pressures
2. Pet owners (or types of pets)
3. Computer games
4. Alternative medicines
5. Websites
6. Alternative energy sources
7. Extreme sports
8. Music for driving
9. Attitudes toward death
10. Lies
11. Canadian TV shows
12. Ways to break off a relationship
13. Bores

The Critical Edge

Classification provides an effective tool for organizing material into categories. Sometimes you will be able to draw on your own knowledge or experience to determine or develop categories, but often you will supplement what you bring to a writing assignment with research.

Suppose that for an introductory business course, you're asked to prepare a paper that explores major types of investments. After consulting a number of books and magazines, you conclude that stocks, bonds, and real estate represent the three main categories of investments and that each category can be divided into several subcategories. Bonds, for example, can be grouped according to issuer: corporate, municipal, provincial, and federal.

At this point, you recognize that the strategy of classification would work well for this assignment. Reading further, you learn about the financial risks, rewards, and tax consequences associated with ownership. For example, Canada Savings

Bonds offer the greatest safety, while corporate bonds, as well as stocks and real estate, entail varying degrees of risk depending on the financial condition of the issuer and the state of the economy. Similarly, the income from the different categories and subcategories of investments is subject to different kinds and levels of taxation.

After assimilating the information you've gathered, you could synthesize (see pages 423–425) the views expressed in your sources as well as your own ideas about investments. You might organize your categories and subcategories according to probable degree of risk, starting with the least risky investment and ending with the most risky. For your conclusion you might offer purchase recommendations for different groups of investors such as young workers, wealthy older investors, and retirees.

When preparing to use the material of others in your writing, be sure to examine its merits. Do some sources seem more convincing than others? Why? Do any recommendations stem from self-interest? Are any sources overloaded with material irrelevant to your purpose? Which sources offer the most detail? Asking and answering questions such as these will help you write a more informed paper.*

SUGGESTIONS FOR WRITING

1. Examine professional essays on gender issues or cultural diversity in this text-book, and then write a paper that classifies their content.
2. Reflect on the professional essays that you've studied and then write a paper that presents an appropriate classification system for them, perhaps based on the writers' levels of diction, tone, or reliance on authorities.

CLASSIFICATION ESSAYS: PROFESSIONAL MODELS

READING STRATEGIES

1. Identify your purpose for reading the essay and the writer's purpose for the classification.
2. Identify the principle of classification that is being used, and the distinguishing features of each category. It can be useful to make a table that identifies each major classification and identifies the distinctive features of each category.

---

*Because you'll rely on published sources, it is important to read the sections on handling quotations and avoiding plagiarism in Chapter 17 before you start to write. As always, follow your instructor's guidelines for documenting sources.

READING CRITICALLY

1. Determine the purpose for the classification.
2. Try to come up with an alternative classification system.
3. Check whether the categories of the classification are clear and distinct, or whether they overlap.
4. Note whether the principle of classification is logically consistent. Note whether it is a complete system, or whether some categories are omitted.

READING AS A WRITER

1. Note whether the essay arranges categories in a logical sequence such as largest to smallest, or least desirable to most desirable.
2. Observe whether the writer gives each category about the same amount of space, and gives similar kinds of information for each category.

Marion Winik

What Are Friends For?

Marion Winik (born 1958) is a graduate of Brown University and of Brooklyn College, where she earned a master of fine arts degree in creative writing. Since graduation, she has pursued a career in education, writing, and marketing. Her writings include poems, short stories, essays, and books, and the shorter pieces have appeared in a variety of major newspapers and popular magazines. Her 1998 book Lunch-Box Chronicles: Notes from the Parenting Underground *discusses her experiences of raising her sons after her husband's death. In this selection, Winik takes a humorous look at the different categories of friends and the benefits derived from each one.*

1   I was thinking about how everybody can't be everything to each other, but some people can be something to each other, thank God, from the ones whose shoulder you cry on to the ones whose half-slips you borrow to the nameless ones you chat with in the grocery line.

> Introduction describes the value of friends.

2   Buddies, for example, are the workhorses of the friendship world, the people out there on the front lines, defending you from loneliness and boredom. They call you up, they listen to your complaints, they celebrate your successes and curse your misfortunes, and you do the same for them in return. They hold out through innumerable crises before concluding that the person you're dating is no good, and even then understand if you ignore their good counsel. They accompany you to a movie with subtitles or to see the diving pig at Aquarena Springs. They feed your cat when you are out of town and pick you up from the airport when you get back. They come over to help you decide what to wear on a date. Even if it is with that creep.

> Body begins. (Paragraphs 2–14)

> First category: buddies

3   What about family members? Most of them are people you just got stuck with, and though you love them, you may not have very much in common. But there is that rare exception, the Relative Friend. It is your cousin, your brother, maybe

> Second category: relatives

even your aunt. The two of you share the same views of the other family members. Meg never should have divorced Martin. He was the best thing that ever happened to her. You can confirm each other's memories of things that happened a long time ago. Don't you remember when Uncle Hank and Daddy had that awful fight in the middle of Thanksgiving dinner? Grandma always hated Grandpa's stamp collection; she probably left the window open during the hurricane on purpose.

4   While so many family relationships are tinged with guilt and obligation, a relationship with a Relative Friend is relatively worry-free. You don't even have to hide your vices from this delightful person. When you slip out Aunt Joan's back door for a cigarette, she is already there.

Third category: co-workers 5   Then there is that special guy at work. Like all the other people at the job site, at first he's just part of the scenery. But gradually he starts to stand out from the crowd. Your friendship is cemented by jokes about co-workers and thoughtful favors around the office. Did you see Ryan's hair? Want half my bagel? Soon you know the names of his turtles, what he did last Friday night, exactly which model CD player he wants for his birthday. His handwriting is as familiar to you as your own.

6   Though you invite each other to parties, you somehow don't quite fit into each other's outside lives. For this reason, the friendship may not survive a job change. Company gossip, once an infallible source of entertainment, soon awkwardly accentuates the distance between you. But wait. Like School Friends, Work Friends share certain memories which acquire a nostalgic glow after about a decade.

Fourth category: faraway friends 7   A Faraway Friend is someone you grew up with or went to school with or lived in the same town as until one of you moved away. Without a Faraway Friend, you would never get any mail addressed in handwriting. A Faraway Friend calls late at night, invites you to her wedding, always says she is coming to visit but rarely shows up. An actual visit from a Faraway Friend is a cause for celebration and binges of all kinds. Cigarettes, Chips Ahoy, bottles of tequila.

8   Faraway Friends go through phases of intense communication, then may be out of touch for many months. Either way, the connection is always there. A conversation with your Faraway Friend always helps to put your life in perspective: when you feel you've hit a dead end, come to a confusing fork in the road, or gotten lost in some crackerbox subdivision of your life, the advice of the Faraway Friend—who has the big picture, who is so well acquainted with the route that brought you to this place—is indispensable.

9   Another useful function of the Faraway Friend is to help you remember things from a long time ago, like the name of your seventh grade history teacher, what was in that really good stir-fry, or exactly what happened that night on the boat with the guys from Florida.

Fifth category: former friends 10   Ah, the Former Friend. A sad thing. At best a wistful memory, at worst a dangerous enemy who is in possession of many of your deepest secrets. But what was it that drove you apart? A misunderstanding, a betrayed confidence, an unrepaid loan, an ill-conceived flirtation. A poor choice of spouse can do in a friendship just like that. Going into business together can be a serious mistake. Time, money, distance, cult religions: all noted friendship killers . . . .

Sixth category: love-to-hate friends 11   And lest we forget, there are the Friends You Love to Hate. They call at inopportune times. They say stupid things. They butt in, they boss you around, they embarrass you in public. They invite themselves over. They take advantage.

You've done the best you can, but they need professional help. On top of all this, they love you to death and are convinced they're your best friend on the planet.

12   So why do you continue to be involved with these people? Why do you tolerate them? On the contrary, the real question is, What would you do without them? Without Friends You Love to Hate, there would be nothing to talk about with your other friends. Their problems and their irritating stunts provide a reliable source of conversation for everyone they know. What's more, Friends You Love to Hate make you feel good about yourself, since you are in so much better shape than they are. No matter what these people do, you will never get rid of them. As much as they need you, you need them too.

13   At the other end of the spectrum are Hero Friends. These people are better than the rest of us, that's all there is to it. Their career is something you wanted to be when you grew up—painter, forest ranger, tireless doer of good. They have beautiful homes filled with special handmade things presented to them by villagers in the remote areas they have visited in their extensive travels. Yet they are modest. They never gossip. They are always helping others, especially those who have suffered a death in the family or an illness. You would think people like this would just make you sick, but somehow they don't.

> Seventh category: hero friends

14   A New Friend is a tonic unlike any other. Say you meet her at a party. In your bowling league. At a Japanese conversation class, perhaps. Wherever, whenever, there's that spark of recognition. The first time you talk, you can't believe how much you have in common. Suddenly, your life story is interesting again, your insights fresh, your opinion valued. Your various shortcomings are as yet completely invisible.

> Eighth category: new friends

15   It's almost like falling in love.

> Conclusion uses a memorable observation that meshes stylistically with rest of essay.

DISCUSSION QUESTIONS

1. Comment on the effectiveness of Winik's title.
2. Characterize the level of diction that Winik uses in her essay
3. What elements of Winik's essay interest you the most? What elements interest you the least?

TOWARD KEY INSIGHTS

What traits characterize the various types of friends that you have?

In what ways are these friendships mutually beneficial?

SUGGESTION FOR WRITING *Write an essay classifying the various types of dates, employers, sales techniques, or vacations that you consider undesirable. Choose an appropriate number of categories and support them with appropriate specific details.*

Kerry Banks

As a Dad, Will I Do Right by My Daughter?

Kerry Banks is a freelance journalist. He has written 15 books and has won many writing awards for his feature magazine work. He has written articles for numerous publications, including Equinox, Harrowsmith, Maclean's, Canadian Geographic, Canadian Business and Chatelaine. For ten years, he wrote a weekly sports column for the Vancouver news-and-entertainment weekly, The Georgia Straight. Banks's essay, "As a Dad, Will I Do Right by My Daughter?" reflects on the contemporary pitfalls of being a first-time father of a daughter. Having read a book about the different kinds of fathers who affect their daughters' self-image in different, sometimes troubling ways, Banks questions women he knows about their experiences of fathers.

1   My daughter's first word was "Da-Da." At least, that's how I remember it. Her mother, Anne, insists it was actually "dog." Whatever the true order, it was a thrill to hear her identify me by name. I think the bond between us grew a little closer at that moment. I know the weight of responsibility suddenly gained several pounds.

2   Riley is our first child and she is full of surprises. As she nears one year of age, we are amazed to discover how much she enjoys books, how quickly she can ransack a room and how deeply she is attached to the TV remote control. The first surprise, though, was her sex.

3   Both Anne and I come from families dominated by male progeny, and the odds seemed to suggest a son. When he turned out to be a she, it immediately struck me how little I knew about girls. With a son, I would be on familiar turf; I would instinctively know where he was heading and how he would feel when he got there. With a daughter, I would only be guessing. Each stage of her development would be a mystery to me.

4   Being a first-time parent is never easy, but I think it is especially tough for fathers these days. Our role is in flux. The "good provider" and "stern father" figures are as out of style as the hula-hoop. Modern dads are expected to be more actively involved in child rearing. We are supposed to change more diapers, spend more time at home, be more sensitive, and avoid gender stereotyping of our children at all costs.

5   Unfortunately, we have no role models on whom to base our behaviour. It is hard to feel confident when you are making things up as you go along. Pressured by society to be different from our fathers and struggling to achieve domestic equilibrium with our wives, we cannot help but feel anxious. So, as I confronted the reality of having a daughter, I could only wonder: what sort of father was I going to be?

6   As I was mulling over this conundrum, a book entitled *Women and Their Fathers: The Sexual and Romantic Impact of the First Man in Your Life* came across my desk. Contrary to popular wisdom, the author, New York journalist Victoria Secunda, contends it is the father, not the mother, who has the more profound impact in shaping a daughter's self-image. According to Secunda, the way dad

and daughter get along largely determines how the daughter will see herself as an adult, and what she will expect from men.

7　　Secunda classifies fathers into categories—"templates for their daughters' future attachments," she calls them. Fathers are doting, distant, demanding, absent or seductive. She classifies daughters too. A particular type of father does not necessarily produce a single type of daughter, but the way the relationship plays out produces daughters who are favoured, good, competitive, fearful or maverick. As I read the sobering litany of the ways in which each father type can damage his daughter's psyche, little Riley began to assume the fragility of a package of gelignite. Did so much of what she would become depend on me?

8　　I began questioning women I knew about the impact of their fathers on their lives. Few of their relationships fit Secunda's categories precisely, but some patterns were evident. It was, for example, not difficult to find examples of the **distant father**—most of the women I spoke with had fathers who were remote in some way. But it was harder to correlate cause and effect. According to Secunda, distant fathers can produce a myriad of emotional consequences. Their daughters may or may not become sexually promiscuous, suffer from anorexia nervosa, be unable to achieve orgasm or marry men who don't notice them.

9　　Sometimes, women raised by distant fathers deliberately seek out men who are diametrically different. Terrie Orr is a case in point. Orr, a soft-spoken but strong-willed 39-year-old Vancouver homemaker, says she has always been drawn to men with dynamic outgoing characters—men quite unlike her father, who is a quiet, unemotional reserved man. Orr refers to her dad as an "armchair father." His main interest, she recalls, was his job on the Canadian Pacific Railway. He occupied most of his leisure time with solitary pursuits, such as watching TV, doing carpentry and gardening. Orr says it was her effervescent mother who kept the family's five kids in line. "It was strange. Even though Dad was around a lot, you never had the feeling that he was really there."

10　　Orr's most vivid memory of her father was one rare occasion when he stepped out of character. On Mother's Day, when Orr was 10, her father suggested that his wife sleep in as a treat while he took the kids out for a stroll in the woods near their home in Winnipeg. "We walked for two or three hours. I remember sunshine and open fields and laughing and skipping along. It was one of the only times he initiated something with the family."

11　　Orr still finds her father an enigma, although she knows that her own reserved personality somewhat resembles his. Ironically, her relationship with her sales manager husband, Laurie Stein, is in some respects a mirror image of her own parents' merger of opposites. But, in this case, it is her husband who is the socializer.

12　　Orr says that one of the things that attracted her to Laurie was his natural affinity for children: "He likes to play and fool around with our two boys and be naughty."

13　　Orr's distant father does not sound much like me, but I do tend to be the introspective type. In fact, my wife does not hesitate to describe me as "moody." And truth be told, I exhibit other "distant father" danger signs—obsession with my work and a reluctance to discuss my feelings on personal subjects openly. Uptight, macho, WASP, self-obsessed: as I read Secunda's book, these psychological buzzwords began doing a noisy dance in my male psyche.

14   Maybe it's just self-justification, but I think some of the distance that exists between fathers and daughters is a product of our sexual blueprints. Men tend to deal with their emotions differently from women. It does not mean we do not have any. The challenge I will face with Riley is to make sure our differences never destroy the bonds between us.

15   At the other end of the emotional spectrum is the **doting father**—the daddy who makes everything all right. Annemarie Beard, 35, a stylish, sassy production manager with a Vancouver advertising firm, says she was "always the light in my father's eye." In sharp contrast to her two brothers, she was "spoiled and treated like a princess." Beard says her father, a chemical engineer, was always physically affectionate and ready to play. Only when she reached puberty did "the bubble burst," as her father began to pull away.

16   This is evidently a common reaction among fathers, according to Vancouver family therapist Mary Trokenberg. "As daddy's little girl grows into womanhood and becomes more sexually aware, many men don't know how to handle it. When men feel fragile and in doubt, they withdraw, and as a result, children feel abandoned."

17   Today, Annemarie Beard says the bond with her father has been restored. Yet, she admits that her early idealization of him had its consequences. "It took me a long time to grow up. I had to discover that not all men are like my father."

18   Author Secunda says many women with doting fathers are drawn to men who resemble their fathers—men who will protect them and keep them in the pampered style to which they are accustomed. Often, they tend to be older men. This is certainly true of Beard. "I had my first date at 15," she says. "He was 35." Today, she continues to feel most comfortable with older men. She likes their secure nature and the attentive manner in which they treat her. "Older men seem delighted just to have a younger woman around."

19   Doting and distant are polar opposites. Logically, therefore, I can't possibly be the doting type. So, why is it that Anne and I are already divided over the issue of protectiveness, which is one of the characteristics Secunda attributes to doting dads? I think Anne is too carefree with Riley; she feels I worry too much. And yet, how can I not worry? Our once benign household has suddenly become a nest of dangers—electrical outlets, open staircases, hot liquids, bottled poisons. So, if I am doting now, it is only for Riley's own good. This stage will surely pass. Once she is old enough to take care of herself, I will let her climb trees and play tackle football. Maybe.

20   Another of Secunda's archetypes, the **demanding father,** casts a dual-edged shadow over his daughter's life. Secunda says the best sort of demanding fathers are those who are stern but fair—they inspire confidence and ambition in their daughters. But when the sternness is not balanced by tenderness and support, daughters may be left with painful legacies.

21   Bonita Thompson, a vivacious, high-energy, 45-year-old Vancouver lawyer, traces much of what she has accomplished in life to her demanding father's

influence. A chartered accountant, he was wrapped up in his career and spent little time with her three sisters and one brother. But Thompson forged a bond with him through sports. "From age 6 to 16, I was dad's caddie on the golf course. He taught me a sense of gentlemanly conduct, sportsmanship, ethics and setting high standards for yourself."

22 But some of his standards were impossibly high. "I'd bring home my report card with an average of 94 percent, and he'd say, 'Why isn't it 100 percent?' He was joking, but there was a barb underneath it."

23 As far back as she can recall, Thompson always had a strong desire to achieve. Yet, even as her law career flourished, she sensed there was something lacking. "After each of my achievements, I'd feel empty." Eventually, Thompson realized that "all I had done in life was a continuing effort to elicit my father's praise."

24 Thompson's failed first marriage was to a man very similar to her father. Her current husband is the antithesis. "He's a free spirit, a warm, outgoing humorous person. And he's a bit of a rascal and a rule breaker. He's the nurturer in our family. He stayed home and raised our child."

25 The problem of fathers who are grudging with praise often surfaced in my conversations with women. I may be in dangerous waters here too. Neither of my parents expressed support easily, and it's going to be hard for me to break the mould.

26 The discussions with my female friends did little to relieve my angst. I kept seeing bits of my character reflected in the darker side of their fathers' images. As for Secunda's book, I was left wondering whether a healthy relationship between a father and a daughter is possible at all.

27 Mary Trokenberg, the therapist, helped me put it in perspective: "Some of the ways in which daughters develop has to do with their fathers, but not all. The danger with these sorts of self-help books is that people will think one-dimensionally. When you divide people into categories, you lose the nuances and fail to see other possibilities."

28 This makes sense to me. While I will undoubtedly have a major influence on Riley, I suspect her view of men will also be shaped by what she sees in the relationship between my wife and me, and in her mother's attitudes toward men generally.

29 As for being distant, doting or demanding, I will try to keep my conflicting impulses in balance. Like any new parent, I have hopes. I want Riley to be an independent thinker, confident and creative. I want her to be a woman who is involved in the world, a woman who likes men and who can tell a joke. Most of all, I want her to be happy.

30 I don't know yet how I will deal with the familiar crises of fatherhood, such as when Riley begins dating boys with green hair and nose rings. But there is time to learn, and I will need to trust my instincts. For now, I am content simply to share the extraordinary discoveries of Riley's young life—and her awe at seeing the night stars for the first time, the giddy tingle of walking barefoot on a freshly mown lawn, the magical spell of a street musician's guitar. For now, just being Da-Da is enough.

DISCUSSION QUESTIONS

1. Why does the writer think that being a father today is more difficult for him personally than it might be for other people? (See paragraphs 2–3.) Why is being a father generally more difficult today than it might have been for fathers in the past? (See paragraphs 4–5.) How does this discussion of difficulties with the paternal role make the reader receptive to what follows?

2. Discuss what you think Kerry Banks means when he says, "As I read the sobering litany of the ways in which each father type can damage his daughter's psyche, little Riley began to assume the fragility of a package of gelignite" (paragraph 7).

3. Why does Kerry Banks follow his description of the "distant father" with the description of the "doting father" (paragraph 15)? Explain the three main categories of fathers that the writer deals with in your own words. Why do you suppose that Banks does not discuss two other categories of fathers—the absent or seductive father—(paragraph 7) in detail? What is the principle for classification of fathers in the essay?

4. Why does Kerry Banks talk to women he knows about their relationships with their fathers (paragraph 8)? What does he find out from these women? How do these interviews influence the writer's attitude toward fathering?

5. Study the conclusion of this essay. How does Kerry Banks expand the scope of his essay outward, enlarging the context and significance of what he has been discussing? How does he also come full circle?

TOWARD KEY INSIGHTS

From your own experience, do you also conclude that the roles of fathers are "in flux" (paragraph 4)? Why or why not?

Kerry Banks writes that "men tend to deal with their emotions differently from women" (paragraph 14). How does he qualify this claim? To what extent do you agree with this generalization? Is it possible to make meaningful generalizations about such gender differences? Why or why not?

Kerry Banks quotes a therapist as saying, "When you divide people into categories, you lose the nuances and fail to see other possibilities" (paragraph 27). Do you also see problems with classifying people? Why or why not? What are the reasons that we put people into categories?

SUGGESTION FOR WRITING *Write an essay that classifies a certain group of people into categories according to a clear principle—kinds of university students, instructors, coaches, concert-goers, clothes shoppers. In your essay, acknowledge any potential problems with classifying in this way.*

Bernice McCarthy

A Tale of Four Learners

Bernice McCarthy, Ph.D., earned her doctorate in education and learning theory from Northwestern University. She founded About Learning, Inc., a consulting firm on educational theory and research. She has published a number of articles and presented workshops at major institutions. In this essay, she classifies learners based on the 4MAT System® she created.

1   A young man at a midwestern middle school said of his social studies teacher, "She doesn't label us, and she helps us do all kinds of things." That student expressed very simply my evolving understanding of style since I created the 4MAT System in 1979. The way one perceives reality and reacts to it forms a pattern over time. This pattern comes to dominate the way one integrates ideas, skills, and information about people and the way one adapts knowledge and forms meaning.

2   But to learn successfully, a student also needs expertise in other learning styles; together these styles form a natural cycle of learning. That middle school teacher apparently honored the unique style that each student brought to her classroom, while helping each one do some stretching and master all the ways of learning.

3   Following are true stories about four types of learners. They illustrate how students with different learning styles experience school and why we must create opportunities for diverse learning experiences for every child.

4   Linda was in 6th grade when she hit the wall in math. She had loved school up until then. Her teachers and classmates agreed that her poetry was quite good, and her poems often appeared in local publications. But math was a problem. She couldn't connect it to anything—she simply could not see the patterns. Her teachers were not pleased with her and she longed to please them.

5   Linda went on to college, and when she was a junior, a new professor arrived on campus. The day before Linda's statistics class began, she met him in the hallway. He said, "Oh, you're Linda; I've been reading your poetry. You are going to do very well in statistics."

6   She looked at him in amazement. "How can you say that? I have such difficulty in all my math classes."

7   He smiled and answered, "I can tell from your poetry that you understand symmetry. Statistics is about symmetry. As a matter of fact, statistics is the poetry of math." Linda went on to earn an A in that class. Her professor had connected statistics to her life and showed her the patterns (McCarthy 1996).

8   Linda is a Type 1 learner—the highly imaginative student who favors feeling and reflecting. These learners

9   ■ are at home with their feelings, people-oriented, outstanding observers of people, great listeners and nurturers, and committed to making the world a better place.

10   ■ prefer to learn by talking about experiences; listening and watching quietly, then responding to others and discussing ideas; asking questions; brainstorming; and examining relationships. They work well in groups or teams but also enjoy reading quietly.

11   ■ experience difficulty with long verbal explanations, with giving oral presentations, and with memorizing large chunks of abstract information. They dislike confusion or conflict, environments where mistakes are openly criticized, or where they cannot discuss their perceptions.

12   ■ have a cognitive style that puts perception before judgment, subjective knowledge before objective facts, and reflection before action. They prefer to make decisions based on feeling, are visual/auditory/kinesthetic, and experiential before conceptual.

13   As a Type 1 learner, Linda needed to connect math to her real life, to know why it was useful as a way of thinking and a way of formulating problems and solutions. She also needed her teachers to believe in her and to spend time with and nurture her.

14   Marcus was in 1st grade, and he loved school. Everything he longed for was present there—the teacher's loving interest, the thrill of deciphering the symbols that meant things, the things he could touch and feel, the addition problems that the teacher wrote on the chalkboard. He could always see the answers. His excitement was like that of the basketball player who knows that if he can just get his hands on the ball, he can sink it. Each question became an exciting foray into even more questions. And as his reading improved rapidly, he could not get enough of books. He welcomed the words and ideas of each new writer. He felt confident; he knew he belonged (McCarthy 1996).

15   Marcus is a Type 2 learner—the analytic student who favors reflecting and thinking. These learners

16   ■ have a knowledge-oriented style; are outstanding at conceptualizing material; analyze and classify their experiences and organize ideas; are highly organized and at home with details and data; are good at step-by-step tasks; are fascinated with structure; believe in their ability to understand; and are committed to making the world more lucid.

17   ■ prefer to learn through lectures and objective explanations, by working independently and systematically, and by reading and exchanging ideas.

18   ■ experience difficulty in noisy, high-activity environments, ambiguous situations, and working in groups. They also have trouble with open-ended assignments, as well as with presentations, role-playing, and nonsequential instructions. They have difficulty talking about feelings as well.

19   ■ have a cognitive style that is objective thinking, reflection before action, impersonal, auditory/visual/kinesthetic, conceptual over experiential. They tend to make judgments first, then support them with their perceptions.

20   As a Type 2 learner, Marcus found school an absolute joy. Testing, so frightening to Linda, was a tonic for him, a chance to prove he could do it. Because he was naturally verbal and school is mostly a verbal challenge, he was—and continues to be—successful.

21   When Jimmy was in 2nd grade he did not like to read, and that made school difficult. He did enjoy having others read to him, and his younger brother, a

1st grader, read him stories every night. Jimmy did excel in math and art. He loved to work alone on projects and never wanted help. When he was asked to illustrate a story or build something to depict a math concept, he approached the task excitedly. He was happiest when he could solve a problem by creating a three-dimensional solution.

22 Unfortunately, Jimmy had a rigid teacher whose timing was always different from his own. Jimmy either finished too fast or took too long when he got really interested in a project. Once his teacher said in exasperation, "I didn't say you had to do your best work, Jimmy, just get it done!" When Jimmy's family bought a new VCR, they read the directions aloud to figure out how it worked. Jimmy stepped up and simply made it work. His reading problem continued into 3rd grade when he caught up with the others, but he never let it get him down—he was simply too busy doing other kinds of things (McCarthy 1996).

23 Jimmy is a Type 3 learner—the common-sense learner who favors thinking and doing. These learners

24 ■ are great problem solvers and are drawn to how things work. They are at home with tasks and deadlines, are productive and committed to making the world work better, and they believe in their ability to get the job done. They are also active and need opportunities to move around.

25 ■ prefer to learn through active problem solving; step-by-step procedures; touching, manipulating, and constructing; demonstrations; experimentation and tinkering; and competition.

26 ■ experience difficulty when reading is the primary means of learning and whenever they cannot physically test what they are told. They have trouble with verbal complexity, paradoxes or unclear choices, subtle relationships, and open-ended academic tasks. They also have difficulty expressing feelings.

27 ■ have a cognitive style that features objective thinking and facts over ideas, action before reflection, and judgment before perception. Their style is impersonal and kinesthetic/auditory/visual.

28 As a Type 3 learner, Jimmy needed to work things out in his own way, to create unique solutions to problems, and, most of all, to show what he learned by doing something concrete with it. His verbal skills did not kick in until well into the 3rd grade. Although this is not unusual with highly spatial learners, teachers treated it as an aberration. School was simply too regimented and too verbal for Jimmy. What saved him was his focus on his own learning.

29 When Leah was a high school freshman, she liked her new friends and some of her teachers. But she had a fierce need to learn, and school was not nearly exciting enough for her. She found so much of it deadening—memorizing endless facts that were totally irrelevant to her life. Leah had a wonderful spontaneity, and when it took hold of her, she focused so intensely that time became meaningless. Her teachers came to regard this spontaneity as a liability that was taking her away from the things she needed to know.

30 At first Leah persevered. Instead of preparing a juvenile justice report based on her social studies text, she asked to be allowed to go to juvenile court and see for herself, and then present her findings in a skit. Her teachers seldom agreed to her proposals, and after a while Leah stopped trying. She had natural leadership

talent, which she expressed through her extra-curricular activities—the one part of school she came to love. She graduated, but has believed ever since then that real learning does not happen in school (McCarthy 1996).

31   Leah is a Type 4 learner—the dynamic learner who favors creating and acting. These learners

32   ■ are proud of their subjectivity, at home with ambiguity and change, and great risk takers and entrepreneurs. They act to extend and enrich their experiences and to challenge the boundaries of their worlds for the sake of growth and renewal, and they believe in their ability to influence what happens. They initiate learning by looking for unique aspects of the information to learn and they sustain learning through trial and error.

33   ■ prefer to learn by self-discovery, talking, convincing others, looking for creative solutions to problems, and engaging in free flights of ideas. They also like to work independently and tackle open-ended academic tasks with lots of options, paradox, or subtle relationships. Their interpersonal skills are good.

34   ■ experience difficulty with rigid routines when they are not allowed to question. They also have trouble with visual complexity, methodical tasks, time management, and absolutes.

35   ■ have a cognitive style that is perception first with slight attention to judgment, subjective, relational, action-oriented, kinesthetic/auditory/visual, and experiential over conceptual.

36   Leah found learning for school's sake incomprehensible. As in Jimmy's case, doing was crucial to her approach. She preferred interviewing over reading, going to court to see for herself, exploring instead of hearing how others see things.

37   In any classroom, Linda, Marcus, Jimmy, Leah, and their many shades and varieties sit before the teacher—challenging and waiting to be challenged. The frustrating question is: why are some learners honored in our schools and others ignored, discouraged, or even frowned upon? Why did Marcus fare so well, while Linda, Jimmy, and Leah struggled to be accepted?

38   In my definition of learning, the learner makes meaning by moving through a natural cycle—a movement from feeling to reflecting to thinking and, finally, to acting. This cycle results from the interplay of two separate dimensions—perceiving and processing (Kolb 1984).

39   In perceiving, we take in what happens to us by (1) feeling, as we grasp our experience, and then by (2) thinking, as we begin to separate ourselves from the experience and name and classify it. The resulting concepts become our way of interpreting our world (Kegan 1982).

40   We also process experiences in two ways: by (1) reflecting on them, and then by (2) acting on those reflections. We also try things; we tinker.

41   The places in this cycle that we find most comfortable—where we function with natural ease and grace—are our learning preferences or styles, the "spins" we put on learning.

42   Unfortunately, schools tend to honor only one aspect of perceiving—thinking. This is very tough on kids whose approach to learning is predominately feeling. Linda and Leah, like many other Type 1 and 4 learners—both male and female—are

naturals on the feeling end of experience. Jimmy and Marcus, the Type 2 and 3 learners, favor the thinking end.

43   As with feeling and thinking, reflecting and acting need to be in balance. But our schools favor reflecting. Marcus excelled at that, while both Jimmy and Leah needed to act. The lack of hands-on learning created difficulties for both of them.

44   Even as I define styles in my work, I caution that we must be wary of labels. Over time, and with experience, practice, and encouragement, students become comfortable with learning styles that aren't naturally their own. Successful learners, in fact, develop multiple styles.

45   The 4MAT framework is designed to help students gain expertise in every learning style. We design lesson units as cycles built around core concepts, each of which incorporates experiencing (Type 1), conceptualizing (Type 2), applying (Type 3), and creating (Type 4). The styles answer the questions:

46   ■ Why do I need to know this? (the personal meaning of Type 1).

47   ■ What exactly is this content or skill? (the conceptual understanding of Type 2).

48   ■ How will I use this in my life (the real-life skills of Type 3).

49   ■ If I do use this, what possibilities will it create? (the unique adaptations of Type 4).

50   Had the teachers of Linda, Marcus, Jimmy, and Leah used the entire cycle of learning styles, including those areas in which each student needed to stretch, all four students would have acquired expertise in all facets of the cycle. They would have made personal connections to the learning, examined expert knowledge, used what they were learning to solve problems, and come up with new ways to apply the learning—both personally and in the world at large. (As it happened, the students learned to do these things on their own.)

51   In addressing the various learning styles, the 4MAT System also incorporates elements of brain research—in particular, the different ways that the right and left hemispheres of the cerebral cortex process information (Benson 1985, McCarthy 1981 and 1987, Sylwester 1995, Wittrock 1985). I call these contrasting mental operations the Left and Right Modes.

52   The Left Mode is analytical and knows those things we can describe with precision. It examines cause and effect, breaks things down into parts and categorizes them, seeks and uses language and symbols, abstracts experience for comprehension, generates theory, and creates models. It is sequential and works in time.

53   The Right Mode knows more than it can tell, filling in gaps and imagining. It is intuitive. It senses feelings; forms images and mental combinations; and seeks and uses patterns, relationships, and connections. It manipulates form, distance, and space.

54   Excellence and higher-order thinking demand that we honor both sides of the brain, teaching interactively with hands-on, real-life, messy problem solving. Learners speak in words, signs, symbols, movement, and through music. The more voices students master, the more new learning they will do. Unfortunately, however, teachers persist in lecturing and using logical, sequential problem solving most of the time.

55   In assessing student performance, traditional methods work fairly well for Type 2 learners, who like to prove themselves, and Type 3 learners, who do well on tests in general. Traditional testing doesn't work as well for Types 1 and 4, however. Type 1 learners have difficulty in formal testing situations, especially when tests are timed and call for precise answers. Type 4 learners have trouble doing things by the book and with absolutes and rigid routines when they are not allowed to ask questions.

56   Further, students change roles as they move through the learning cycle. Tests that require students to recall facts obviously do not reflect the subtlety of these changes.

57   We need assessment tools that help us understand the whole person. We must assess the students' ability to picture the concept, to experiment with the idea, to combine skills in order to solve complex problems, to edit and refine their work, and to adapt and integrate learning. We need to know how students are connecting information to their own experiences, how they are blending expert knowledge with their own, and how creative they are. We also need some way of measuring how students reflect on material, conceptualize, and represent what they have learned through various kinds of performances.

58   Successful learning is a continuous, cyclical, lifelong process of differentiating and integrating these personal modes of adaptation. Teachers do not need to label learners according to their style; they need to help them work for balance and wholeness. Leah needs to learn the ways of Marcus; Jimmy needs Linda's ways. And all learners need encouragement to grow.

59   Learning is both reflective and active, verbal and nonverbal, concrete and abstract, head and heart. The teacher must use many instructional methods that are personally meaningful to each student. The more students can travel the cycle, the better they can move to higher-order thinking.

60   As a final note, what became of the students I described earlier? Linda directs the management division of a major human resources consulting firm. Marcus, a former professor of statistics at a prestigious university, is now president of a research firm. Jimmy will be a senior in high school this fall. He scored 100 percent on the Illinois State Math Achievement Test and achieved cum laude in the International Latin Exam. He also had his art portfolio favorably reviewed by the Art Institute of Chicago. And Leah? Leah is a pseudonym for the author of this article.

References

Benson, D. F. "Language in the Left Hemisphere." *The Dual Brain: Hemispheric Specialization in Humans.* Ed. D. F. Benson and E. Zaidel. New York: Guilford, 1985.

Kegan, R. *The Evolving Self: Problems and Process in Human Development.* Cambridge, MA: Harvard UP, 1982.

Kolb, D. A. *Experiential Learning: Experience as the Source of Learning and Development.* Englewood Cliffs, NJ: Prentice-Hall, 1984.

McCarthy, B. *The 4MAT System: Teaching to Learning Styles with Right/Left Mode Techniques.* Barrington, IL: Excel, Inc., 1981, 1987.

McCarthy, B. *About Learning.* Barrington, IL: Excel, Inc., 1996.

Sylvester, R. A *Celebration of Neurons: An Educator's Guide to the Human Brain.* Alexandria, VA: ASCD, 1995.

Wittrock, M. C. "Education and Recent Neuropsychological and Cognitive Research." *The Dual Brain: Hemispheric Specialization in Humans.* Ed. D. F. Benson and E. Zaidel. New York: Guilford, 1985.

DISCUSSION QUESTIONS

1. The author starts with an example of praise for a teacher who did not "label" her students but then goes on to classify learning styles. Is this a contradiction?

2. With each type of learning style, the author follows the same pattern. What is the pattern that she uses and is it effective?

3. In paragraphs 4, 22, and 30, the author identifies the problems three out of the four sample students had in school. Why does she do this? Is it effective?

4. After discussing the four learning styles, the author discusses in paragraphs 38–50 what she identifies as the learning cycle. What is the connection between this learning cycle, and how is this important in relation to the classification system?

5. It could be easy to imagine someone who had qualities of more than one learning style. Is this a problem for the writer's classification of learning styles?

6. In the conclusion, the author informs us of the successes of her four example students. How is this conclusion important to the essay?

TOWARD KEY INSIGHTS

Try to match yourself to the four learning styles. Does one learning style seem most like you? What does this say about the classification system?

What learning styles do you observe in your classes? To what extent do instructors and professors appeal to these learning styles?

SUGGESTION FOR WRITING *Write an essay classifying teaching styles, including the different kinds of activities involved in the classroom and the different kinds of assessment.*

CHAPTER 14

Strategies for Convincing Others: Argument and Persuasion

"What did you think of that movie?"

"It was fun."

"Did you really think so? I thought it dragged on too long. I had a hard time believing in the story too."

"I don't know how you can say that!"

"Well, that's my opinion!"

Although the word *opinion* sometimes refers to an informed judgment, as when an opinion is issued by a judge on a weighty matter, what we call opinions are often simply take-it-or-leave-it expressions of personal taste that cannot really be debated or defended ("Well, that's what I think, so how can you challenge that?"). An academic argument is different from a mere statement of opinion. An opinion that is really a preference or an untested belief may, however, be a starting point for developing a more formal argument, which works to persuade its audience of a central claim, or debatable proposition, through the strategic use of logic, relevant evidence, and consideration of other points of view.

Imagine that you have been asked to write an argumentative or persuasive paper. You decide that you will start with your opinion that development of

Alberta tar sands should be stopped at once. However, after you start digging into your subject, you discover that the issue is more complicated than you realized. As you examine different sides of the issue, including opposing arguments, your opinion may become a more reasoned and nuanced proposition—the central claim of your argument that names the issue and indicates which position the writer will take:

> Multinational oil companies that are profiting from oil reserves in Alberta should pay much higher taxes.

As you investigate more deeply, it is possible that your original idea will shift its focus considerably:

> The Canadian government should start investing more heavily in alternatives to fossil fuels in order to meet Kyoto Protocol commitments.

Some people think that an argument, like a quarrel, implies angry disagreement between two people who will never see eye to eye, but who seek to vanquish each other by drowning out the other's voice. However, a well-presented academic argument is not a heated shouting match. Yes, it involves taking a stand, but it also involves taking other points of view into account. Even when writers of academic argument have strong passions, they demonstrate respect for their audience, and for the complexities of the issue. Successful arguers do not oversimplify or distort evidence in order to score points or advance a claim. They convey a sense of being reasonable and fair people by presenting honest, logically sound arguments that display knowledge of the subject, and understanding of their audience. They certainly do not, like some television talk show hosts, work to inflame the passions of their audience through sensationalizing the topic and polarizing people. They avoid inflammatory statements, particularly those which attack the character of the opposition.

It is impossible to write any essay, including an argumentative essay, without clarifying for yourself why you are writing. An argumentative essay is not to be confused with a factual report, although arguers use facts and evidence to support their central claim. What do you want your audience to think or believe or do? Academic arguments may attempt to convince others to accept a proposal, to support a cause, or to take action. At the very least, a formal argument is a sincere attempt to persuade the audience that a particular point of view or judgment is worthy of consideration.

Many people think of arguments as having just the two clear-cut opposing sides of classical debates, which aim to confirm or refute a particular position, attitude, or hypothesis. While it's true that arguments have at least two sides, many arguments have multiple sides. Some arguments take the form of exploratory dialogues, in which people test different perspectives or possibilities. Exploratory arguments allow you to air doubts about your own position, explain why certain reasons and evidence have weight with you, and address alternative positions and arguments that attract you. They can also help you to find a position before you craft a more committed and focused argument. Using exploratory arguments can help clarify your assumptions and values as you consider other points of view and acquire new information. Engaging in exploratory argument as a kind of social conversation can be an enjoyable and enlivening experience.

Some arguments, especially the informal arguments that are a part of daily life, are attempts to establish a common ground or seek consensus, such as when a family discusses where to go on a holiday, or company managers debate the best ways to boost productivity. Sometimes people use arguments to persuade neutral or undecided others to a point of view or a new course of action, as when a salesperson tries to convince someone to try a new product or a social or political activist tries to influence people to sign a petition.

In the many communities to which you belong, there are no doubt some things you would like to be different. For example, you might like to see more healthy food choices in your university cafeteria, or more bicycle paths in your local community. You might want to influence young people on campus to get out and vote. In your family, you might wish to persuade other family members to have a more structured arrangement for doing household chores. The ability to argue well can help you effect positive change by influencing other people in school, work, and civic communities.

At university, you are often asked to demonstrate through argument what you have learned. A business instructor may ask you to defend a particular management style. A political science instructor may want you to support or oppose limiting the number of terms that members of Parliament can serve. A special education instructor may have you write a case for increased funding for exceptional students. If you identify a problem, such as an inefficient schedule, and propose a workable solution, you are using a common form of argument. In the workplace, a computer programmer may argue that the company should change its account-keeping program, an automotive service manager call for new diagnostic equipment, or a union president make a case that a company's employees merit raises. In many arenas, argument is used to justify or defend a previously established decision or course of action, such as when a department manager sends her boss a memo justifying some new procedure that she implemented.

When preparing to write an argument, you need to be aware that certain kinds of topics just aren't arguable. There's no point, for instance, in trying to tackle questions of personal preference or taste (Is red prettier than blue?). Such contests quickly turn into "it is," "it isn't" exchanges that establish nothing except the silliness of the contenders. Questions of simple fact (Was Pierre Trudeau prime minister in 1972?) don't qualify either, because only one side has the facts as ammunition. We turn to argument only when there is room for debate.

APPEALS IN ARGUMENT AND PERSUASION

Argument is a form of persuasion. The word *argument*, however, connotes an emphasis on logic and reason, while the word *persuasion* has a broader meaning, suggesting an emphasis on swaying the reader's attitudes by appealing to values and emotions. Arguments about practical issues such as the necessity for civic improvements may emphasize reasons, evidence, and rational appeals. Other writing that seeks to persuade people to, say, take in foster children may emphasize emotional appeals. Effective arguments are grounded in logical, structured evidence—rational appeals known as *logos*. However, since people are not just thinking machines, most effective arguments also include appeals to people's emotions; emotional appeals in argument are classically referred to as *pathos*. Ethical appeals known as *ethos* are based on the ethical implications of the case being argued—often an appeal to the reader's sense of fairness and the common good. Ethical appeals are also based on the character of the speaker/writer that is conveyed through language and tone of the argument. Since readers often form conclusions based on their judgments of the writer's trustworthiness, effective arguers convey attitudes of authority, accuracy, and integrity.

Using Qualifiers to Strengthen Your Credibility

One way to convey your trustworthiness as a writer is to ensure that the claims you make are suitably limited and accurate rather than over-generalized; most people know how resistant they feel when a family member accuses them of *never* cleaning up or *always* making a mess. Be careful not to make overly general, sweeping claims. For example, a student writing about drug use at raves originally claimed, "Raves offer the opportunity for young people to find the respect and acceptance that is lacking in our culture." Yet after reflection, the student carefully revised her sweeping claim that respect is lacking in our culture: "Raves offer the opportunity for young people to find the respect and acceptance that *often appear* to be lacking in teen culture." Rather than making blanket claims that the reader may take exception to, academic arguers often qualify their claims with words such as "perhaps" or phrases such as "often appears." When you are making large claims that could be disputed, consider using qualifiers such as "it seems that," "often," "may," or "it appears" to limit your claim and make it more persuasive. For example, if you are arguing about the importance of manners for young people, you do not want to charge all young Canadians with rudeness. Instead, you could qualify your claim by saying something such as "Many young people aren't aware of the social rules that make social interactions smooth and enjoyable."

Using Primary and Secondary Research in Argument

While it is possible to use your own experience, observations, and skills in logic to build a strong argument in a personal writing assignment, for formal academic writing, you will probably be expected to use research to support your claims. Let's say that you're taking an education course and are asked to write a paper arguing for or against the effectiveness of computers as an educational tool in elementary schools. Obviously, this assignment would require you to synthesize (see pages 423–425) the results of your outside reading as well as your own conclusions drawn from your observations of computer use in the classrooms.

It would, in short, require both secondary (that is, library) research and direct observation (see Chapter 16), which is itself a form of primary research. Remember that before you use library and internet sources, you will need to read the sections on taking notes, handling quotations, and avoiding plagiarism in Chapter 17. As always, follow your instructor's guidelines for documenting sources.

RATIONAL APPEALS

Among family, friends, and your community, and certainly in professional circles, you are usually expected to reach your conclusions on the basis of sound reasons and appropriate evidence. Reasons are the key points you use to defend your conclusions. For instance, if you support safe injection sites for intravenous drug users, one reason might be the reduction in AIDS-related deaths that could result. You could cite figures that project the number of deaths likely to be prevented by safe injection sites. If you oppose the program, one reason might be the drug dependency that will continue. To support this concern, you could quote a respected authority who verifies that dependency will become entrenched. Often the reasons you cite will draw on causal logic, with the word *because* showing the link between reasons and the conclusion you draw. Consider how a student writer uses the word *because* to link two reasons with the claim which follows.

> The drug ecstasy is especially dangerous when it is used at raves, because participants dance continuously and don't drink enough fluids.

Even if you do not entirely convince your audience, they should at least be able to see your position as a plausible one. If you or your readers have rigid, unmovable assumptions, there can be no real argument, because you are not really listening to one another. Argument presupposes that both you and your readers are reasonable people who have a vested interest in reaching some kind of common ground. You and your audience need to have some shared principles about what counts as evidence.

The different kinds of rational evidence used in argument include established truths, personal experience, primary source information, statistical findings, and the opinions of authorities.

Established Truths

These are facts that no one can seriously dispute. Here are some examples:

Historical fact:	The Canadian Charter of Rights and Freedoms prohibits racial discrimination.
Scientific fact:	The layer of ozone in the earth's upper atmosphere protects us from the sun's harmful ultraviolet radiation.
Geographical fact:	Alberta has the largest oil reserves in Canada.

Established truths aren't arguable themselves but do provide strong backup for argumentative propositions. For example, citing the abundant oil supply in the western regions could support an argument that Canada should promote the increased use of Canadian oil to supply its energy needs.

Some established truths, the result of careful observations and thinking over many years, basically amount to enlightened common sense. The notion that everyone possesses a unique combination of interests, abilities, and personality characteristics illustrates this kind of truth. Few people would seriously question it.

Opinions of Authorities

An authority is a recognized expert in some field. Authoritative opinions—the only kind to use—help win readers to your side. Quotations from metropolitan police chiefs and criminologists could support your position on ways to control urban crime. Citing the research of scientists who have investigated the effects of air pollution could help you argue for stricter smog-control laws. Whatever your argument, use credible, recognized authorities from the field, and, when possible, mention their credentials to your reader. This information makes their statements more persuasive. For example, "Ann Marie Forsythe, a certified public accountant and vice-president of North American operations for Touche Ross Accounting, believes that the finance minister's tax cut proposal will actually result in a tax increase for most Canadians." Of course, citing the opinions of experts will sway readers only if the audience accepts the expert as authoritative. Although advertisers successfully present hockey players as authorities on shaving cream and credit cards, most people would not accept their views on the safety of nuclear energy.

The following paragraph from an article arguing that youth crime is becoming more violent illustrates the use of authority:

> According to Roy O'Shaughnessy, clinical director of British Columbia's Youth Court Services, Youth Forensic Psychiatric Services, the perception that a segment of young people is becoming more brutally violent is well-founded. "The type of crime we're seeing now is different from what we saw 10 years ago," says O'Shaughnessy, whose unit does psychiatric assessments of delinquents between the ages of 12 and 17. "We're seeing more use of weapons, more gang-related activity, more violent behaviour."
>
> Brian Bergman, "When Children Are Vicious"

Beware of biased opinions. The agribusiness executive who favours farm price supports or the labour leader who opposes any restrictions on picketing may be writing merely to guard old privileges or garner new ones. Unless the opinion can stand close scrutiny, it will weaken rather than strengthen your case. Be especially careful with internet sources. If you are using a general search engine such as Google, the first results of your key word search may be those sites that have paid for priority placement on the list. If you are writing a formal academic argument, you might want to search scholarly databases such as Academic Search Premier, Canadian NewsDisc, or Canadian Periodical Index for articles that have been juried by specialists in the field. Follow your instructor's guidelines for citations and documentation.

Primary Source Information

You need to support some types of arguments with primary source information—documents or other materials produced by individuals directly involved with the issue or conclusions you reached by carrying out an investigation yourself. For example, to argue whether or not Newfoundland should have joined Confederation, you would want to examine the autobiographies of those involved in making the decision and perhaps even the historical documents that prompted it. To take a position on the violence in gangster rap, you would want to analyze the actual lyrics in a number of songs. To make a claim about media coverage of a terrorist act, you would want to read the newspaper and magazine accounts of correspondents who were on the scene. To convince readers to adopt your solution for the homeless problem, you might want to visit a homeless shelter or interview (in a safe place) some homeless people. This type of information can help you reach sound conclusions and build strong support for your position. Most university and college libraries contain a significant amount of primary source materials that you can draw on for an argument. Document the sources you use according to your instructor's guidelines.

Statistical Findings

Statistics—data showing how much, how many, or how often—can also buttress your argument. Most statistics come from books, magazines, newspapers, handbooks, encyclopedias, and reports, but you can use data from your own investigations as well. The Statistics Canada website is a good source of authoritative statistics on many different topics.

Because statistics are often misused, many people distrust them, so any you offer must be credible and reliable. First, make sure your sample isn't too small. Don't use a one-day traffic count to argue for a traffic light at a certain intersection. City Hall might counter by contending that the results are atypical. To make your case, you'd need to count traffic for perhaps two or three weeks. You must have a large enough representative sampling to support the kinds of conclusions you draw. In addition, do not push statistical claims too far. You may know that two-thirds of Tarrytown's factories are polluting the lake, but don't argue that the same figures probably apply to a different town. There's simply no carryover. Also, keep alert for biased or poorly researched statistics; they can cause as serious a credibility gap as biased opinions. Generally, recent data are better than old data, but either must come from a reliable source. For example, older information from *The Globe and Mail* would probably be more accurate than current data from tabloid newspapers. Note how the following writer uses statistics to support the argument about the influence of the news media:

> And, the news media plays an important role in feeding the public view that we're in the middle of a crime wave. In 1995, the Fraser Institute studied media coverage of violent crime. In 1989, the murder rate in Canada was 2.4 per 100 000 people, and the two national networks (CBC and CTV) spent 10 percent of their airtime covering murder stories. By 1995, the murder rate had dropped to

2.04 per 100 000 people. However, national television news coverage of murder had more than doubled on both networks to fill 25 percent of airtime.

Susan McClelland, "Distorted Picture"

Statistics from newspaper or journal articles, graphs, tables, and charts can help strengthen your case, but be sure to select data responsibly from credible sources, and to document them correctly.

Personal Experience

You yourself may be a credible authority on some issues. Personal experience can sometimes deliver an argumentative message more forcefully than any other kind of evidence. Suppose that two years ago a speeder ran into your car and almost killed you. Today you're arguing for stiffer laws against speeding. Chances are you'll rely mainly on expert opinions and on statistics showing the number of people killed and injured each year in speeding accidents. However, describing the crash, the slow, pain-filled weeks in the hospital, and the months spent hobbling around on crutches may well provide the persuasive nudge that wins your reader over.

Often reports of others' experiences and observations, gathered from books, magazines, or interviews, can support your position. If you argue against chemical waste dumps, the personal stories of people who lived near them and suffered the consequences—filthy ooze in the basement, children with birth defects, family members who developed a rare form of cancer—can help sway your reader.

Despite its usefulness, personal experience generally reinforces but does not replace other kinds of evidence. Some readers will discount personal experience as biased. Moreover, unless personal experience has other more objective support, readers may reject it as atypical or trivial.

EVALUATION OF EVIDENCE

Once you have gathered the appropriate evidence, you need to use certain standards to evaluate that evidence before you use it. That a piece of information is in some way connected to your topic does not make it good evidence or qualify it for inclusion in your paper. Readers won't be convinced that trains are dangerous merely because you were in a train wreck. You should not reach a conclusion based on such flimsy evidence either. In order to reach a reasonable conclusion and defend a position with suitable evidence, you should apply the following principles.

Evaluation Criteria	Explanations
How credible are the sources of the information? How reliable is the evidence?	Not all sources are equally reliable. For example, Statistics Canada data about population change is more credible than a local newspaper's estimate, and both are likely more valid than your own estimate.

How much confirming evidence is there?	With evidence, more is better. One scientific study on the efficacy of high-protein diets would be good, but several would be better. One authority who claims that global warming is a reality becomes more credible when confirmed by several other authorities.
How much contradictory evidence is there?	If several scientific studies or authorities point to the efficacy of high-protein diets while several other studies find such diets harmful, clearly you would need to weigh the evidence carefully. To present the evidence honestly, you would have to include evidence from both sides in your paper.
How well established is the evidence?	Extremely well-established evidence, such as the evidence for atoms, becomes the basis for textbooks and is assumed in most other research. This evidence is usually unquestionable (although occasionally it can be overturned). Such evidence makes a solid foundation for arguments.
How well does the evidence actually fit or support the claim?	False connections between ideas weaken arguments. For example, the fact that most Canadians are immigrants or descendents of immigrants has no bearing on whether the country is admitting too many or too few immigrants. To make a case for or against some policy on immigration, the evidence would have to focus on good or bad results, not numbers.
What does the evidence actually allow you to conclude?	Conclusions should flow from the evidence without exaggeration. For example, studies showing that TV violence causes children to play more aggressively do not warrant the conclusion that it causes children to kill others.

Sometimes unwarranted conclusions result because a writer fails to take competing claims and evidence into consideration. You need to weigh the credibility, quantity, reliability, and applicability of all the available evidence to reach and defend a conclusion.

REASONING STRATEGIES

An argument, then, consists of a conclusion or claim that you want to support, your reasons for arriving at that conclusion, and the evidence that supports your reasons. But how are reasons and evidence fitted together? Arguments with different purposes and audiences are constructed differently. Many arguments depend on inductive reasoning—that is, they move from specific pieces of evidence to a general conclusion. Other arguments emphasize deductive logic—that is, they may follow from a general principle that most people accept as true to a specific argument. Arguments may also employ all the strategies of development such as illustration, definition, comparison, or causal analysis covered earlier in this book. It will often be necessary for arguers to use examples, to explain how a particular process works, to define unfamiliar or abstract terms, to compare two models, or to use a special kind of comparison called an analogy, which compares two seemingly unlike things which yet have one or more features in common. It could be argued, in fact, that arguments underlie almost any kind of writing we do.

Induction

An argument that uses inductive reasoning proceeds from specific evidence, whether observations, statistical data, testimony of experts, or scientific studies, to a general claim or conclusion. We use inductive reasoning in our daily lives when we form expectations based on patterns of repeated observations or experiences that lead us to expect similar results. For example, we expect that we will feel more energy after exercise when we have experienced this result many times. When we conclude that a movie is worth watching because our friends liked it, when we decide a university program is effective because most of the graduates get jobs, or even when we support a scientific hypothesis based on formal experimentation, we are drawing inductive generalizations from an accumulation of bits of evidence. After observing many specific instances of lung cancer seen in smokers, and noting that there were significantly fewer cases of lung cancer in non-smokers, scientists reasoned inductively that smoking was a contributing cause of lung cancer. We might think of inductive argument as building from the bottom up, from bits of evidence to a broad conclusion that is probable, given the evidence. Inductive conclusions are based on probability, not absolute certainty. To be absolutely certain of our conclusions, we'd have to check each possible case or piece of evidence, and that's not usually feasible. If you ask ten out of fifteen thousand students whether they like the meal plan, you cannot draw a conclusion about the tastes of the entire student body, but the greater the number of observations and the larger the sample, the stronger your conclusion will be. Of course, we need to be thoughtful about our conclusions, and carefully consider the trustworthiness of the evidence we use to make our case.

You have several options for organizing an inductive argument. Many essays state the central claim, or proposition, directly at the beginning, sometimes even in the title. Sometimes it is strategic to withhold the thesis until later in the essay, after you have first given the background necessary for the reader to understand the issue. The strategy of withholding the thesis can be especially effective if the argument is a solution to a problem that readers need to be convinced exists before they will be receptive to hearing your recommendations. Stating the thesis later in the essay may be an effective strategy if the audience is likely to be resistant or skeptical. Once you have established rapport with the reader and answered possible objections that he or she might have, you can ease your reader into agreement more readily. Sometimes students think that their argument papers are being marked on whether or not the professor agrees with their point of view, but in fact your academic argument will be assessed on how successfully you win the reader over, in part by anticipating and countering possible objections, and making concessions where necessary. For example, when you offer your recommendations to change a current practice, you might need to admit that the new approach will be expensive in the short run. However, you may also be able to add that not accepting your proposals will cost more in the long run, or that the costs of not following these recommendations will be social, emotional, or environmental.

The body of the paper provides the supporting evidence for your claims. When you make a claim, you cannot simply expect that readers will take your word for it. To prove your point, you may need to draw on many kinds of evidence, including examples, references to authorities, illustrations, facts and statistics, even charts and graphs in some kinds of papers. Some successful arguers call on narratives at times to help them reinforce a point and draw the audience closer. It is in the body of your paper that you will address possible objections to your argument as well.

In the conclusion, you reaffirm your position or suggest the consequences of that position. You can also raise a general question, evaluate how your evidence answers that question, and then draw your conclusion from that answer.

The following short example illustrates inductive argument:

> Bologna is perhaps the most popular of all luncheon meats. Each day, thousands of individuals consume bologna sandwiches at noontime without ever considering the health consequences. Perhaps they should.
>
> The sodium content of bologna is excessively high. On the average, three ounces contain over 850 milligrams, three times as much as a person needs in a single day. In addition, bologna's characteristic flavour and reddish colour are caused by sodium nitrite, which is used to prevent the growth of botulism-causing organisms. Unfortunately, sodium nitrite combines with amines, natural compounds already in most foods, to form nitrosamines, which have been proved to cause cancer in laboratory animals. Finally, from a nutrition standpoint, bologna is not a good food choice. The fat content is around 28 percent, the water content ranges upward from 50 percent, and the meat includes very little protein.
>
> Health-conscious people, then, will choose better fare for lunch.
>
> Alison Russell, student

When writing an inductive argument, in addition to presenting the available evidence, there are two other important things you should do. First, demonstrate the credibility of your evidence. Why should the reader find the evidence credible? In the above example, the argument would have been much stronger if the writer had established the source of the evidence.

> On the average, as indicated on any store package, three ounces contain over 850 milligrams of sodium, three times as much as a person needs in a single day, according to Health Canada.

If possible, try to show how the evidence fits the conclusion you want to reach.

> Excess sodium and fat, low protein content, and the presence of a possible carcinogen are all considered by nutritionists to be unhealthy. Health-conscious people, then, will choose better fare for lunch.

Deduction

Unlike inductive reasoning, which builds its case from the bottom up, from the specific to the general, deductive reasoning follows a top-down strategy, arguing from the general rule or observation to the specific instance. Instead of formulating a general conclusion after considering pieces of evidence, deductive arguments begin with an observation that most people accept as true and then show how certain conclusions follow from that observation. For example, to convince a friend to study harder, you begin with the assumption that a profitable career requires a good education; proceed to argue that for a good education students must study diligently; and conclude that, as a result, your friend should spend more time with the books. Of course, if your friend does not agree with what seems to you a self-evident truth (a profitable career requires a good education), then your friend will not accept the conclusion that follows from that premise either. It is important that the premises from which you argue are indeed ones which your audience will accept. When politicians draw from agreed-upon premises that we all want to act in ways beneficial to future generations and then point out how the policies they favour will ensure that outcome, they are using deductive reasoning; most people will accept general premises based on principles of obvious ethical fairness—for example, the idea that community or long-term values are more important than short-term self-interest. However, arguments are weakened when people argue from premises they wrongly assume to be self-evident and commonly shared; for example, a person who argues from the premise that "everyone agrees" that all couples who have children should get married assumes an agreement that is not justified, and will likely not convince an alert audience.

Syllogism   Sometimes a deductive argument is built around a three-part formula called a syllogism, a set of three statements that follow a fixed pattern to ensure sound reasoning. The first statement, called the major premise, names a category of things and says that all or none of them share a certain characteristic. The minor premise notes that a thing or group of things belongs to that category. The conclusion then states that the thing or group logically must share the characteristics of the category. Here are two examples:

Major premise:	All persons are mortal.
Minor premise:	Sue Davis is a person.
Conclusion:	Therefore, Sue Davis is mortal.
Major premise:	No dogs have feathers.
Minor premise:	Spot is a dog.
Conclusion:	Therefore, Spot does not have feathers.

Note that in each case, both major and minor premises are indisputably true, and so the conclusion follows logically. A syllogism in which one premise or both is false will not be logical. For example, if the major premise of your syllogism is that all Canadians support keeping troops in Afghanistan, your unsound premise invalidates your conclusion.

Syllogisms frequently appear in stripped-down form, with one of the premises or the conclusion implied, but unstated. The following example omits the major premise: "Because Wilma is a civil engineer, she has a strong background in mathematics." Obviously the missing major premise is: "All civil engineers have strong backgrounds in mathematics."

Consider how the following syllogism works and then finds its way into a short piece of writing:

Major premise:	All stereotypes are dangerous.
Minor premise:	Female sex objects shown in the media are stereotypes.
Conclusion:	Therefore female sex object stereotypes are dangerous.

The ideal of physical beauty portrayed by female stereotypes in the media is unattainable and unrealistic. Most women do not have this idealized body shape: full breasts, tiny waist, and narrow hips that air-brushed models appear to have. To attain these features, most women would have to resort to surgical alterations or starvation diets. Even so, all women must ultimately fail this beauty test in time, for the sex object is, above all else, young. Mere mortals cannot compare with these perpetually young, airbrushed, and anorexic visions of beauty. Like other stereotypes, the unrealistic images of female beauty reflected in the media are damaging to women and to the larger society.

To accept the deductive argument above, you would have to accept both the major premise above (the commonsense notion that stereotypes are dangerous) and the minor premise (female sex objects in the media are stereotypes).

When arguing from deduction, you need to make clear how your conclusions follow from the agreed-upon premises. One student who wrote a persuasive paper cautioning people about the risks of cosmetic surgery organized her paper partly around the following syllogism:

All surgery carries risks.

Cosmetic procedures done under the knife are surgeries.

Therefore cosmetic surgeries carry risks.

The student then proceeded to give examples of risks from respected medical authorities. These examples led to inductive conclusions such as "There are psychological risks after cosmetic surgery" and "There is a risk that some men and women can become addicted to plastic surgery." This essay, like many, blended inductive with deductive reasoning.

As with induction, you have several options when organizing a deductive argument. You might begin with the position you intend to prove, with a question that will be answered by the argument, or with a synopsis of the argument. The body of the paper works out the implications of your assumption. In the conclusion, you could directly state (or restate, in different words) your position, suggest the consequences of adopting or not adopting that position, or pose a question that is easily answered after reading the argument.

Reductio ad Absurdum   A common and powerful form of deduction called *reductio ad absurdum* ("to reduce to absurdity") is used to attack an opponent's position by showing that its consequences are absurd if carried to their logical end. For example, to counter the position that the government should impose no restrictions on parents' rights to discipline their children, you might point out that, carried to its logical extreme, such a policy would allow individuals to beat their children. This absurd result makes it clear that certain restrictions should apply. The question then becomes where we should draw the line.

Avoiding the Misuse of Syllogisms   Two cautions about the use of syllogisms are in order. *First,* make sure any syllogism you use follows the proper order. The writer of the following passage has ignored this caution:

> Furthermore, Robinson has stated openly that he supports a ban on all clearcut logging practices. For many years now, the Green Party has taken the same environmentalist stand. Robinson's position places him firmly in the Green Party camp. I strongly urge anyone supporting this man's candidacy to reconsider. . . .

Restated in syllogistic form, the writer's argument goes like this:

> Green Party members support a ban on all clearcut logging practices.
>
> Robinson supports a ban on all clearcut logging practices.
>
> Therefore, Robinson is a supporter of the Green Party.

The last two statements reverse the proper order, and as a result the syllogism proves nothing about Robinson's politics: He may or may not be "in the Green Party camp."

Second, make sure the major premise of your syllogism is in fact true. Note this example:

> All Conservatives are opposed to environmental protection.
>
> Mary is a Conservative.
>
> Therefore, Mary is opposed to environmental protection.

But *is* every Conservative an anti-environmentalist? In some communities, political conservatives have led fights against air and water pollution, and most conservatives agree that at least some controls are worthwhile. Mary's sympathies, then, may well lie with those who want to heal, rather than hurt, the environment.

EXERCISE *Which of these syllogisms is satisfactory, which have false major premises, and which is faulty because the last two statements reverse the proper order?*

1. All singers are happy people.

   Mary Harper is a singer.

   Therefore, Mary Harper is a happy person.

2. All cowards fear danger.

   "Chicken" Cacciatore is a coward.

   Therefore, "Chicken" Cacciatore fears danger.

3. All cats like meat.

   Towser likes meat.

   Therefore, Towser is a cat.

4. No salesperson would ever misrepresent a product to a customer.

   Sabrina is a salesperson.

   Therefore, Sabrina would never misrepresent a product to a customer.

Analogy in Argument

An analogy compares two unlike situations or things. Arguers often use analogies to contend that, because two items share one or more likenesses, they are also alike in other ways. Familiar analogies assume that humans respond to chemicals as rats do and that success in school predicts success on the job. You have used analogy if you ever pressed your parents for more adult privileges, such as a later curfew, by arguing that you were like an adult in many ways.

However, because its conclusions about one idea rest upon observations about a different idea, analogy is the weakest form of rational appeal. Analogies never prove anything, but they often help explain and show probability and therefore can be quite persuasive.

For an analogy to be useful, it must feature significant similarities that bear directly on the issue. In addition, it must account for any significant differences between the two items. It is often helpful to test an analogy by listing the similarities and differences. Here's an effective analogy, used to back an argument that a liberal education is the best kind to help us cope successfully with life:

> Suppose it were perfectly certain that the life and fortune of every one of us would, one day or other, depend upon his winning or losing a game of chess. Don't you think that we should all consider it to be a primary duty to learn at least the names and the moves of the pieces; to have a notion of a gambit, and a keen eye for all the means of giving and getting out of check? Do you not think that we should look with a disapprobation amounting to scorn, upon the father who allowed his son, or the state which allowed its members, to grow up without knowing a pawn from a knight?
>
> Yet it is a very plain and elementary truth, that the life, the fortune, and the happiness of every one of us, and, more or less, of those who are connected with

us, do depend upon our knowing something of the rules of a game infinitely more difficult and complicated than chess. It is a game which has been played for untold ages, every man and woman of us being one of the two players in a game of his or her own. The chessboard is the world, the pieces are the phenomena of the universe, the rules of the game are what we call the laws of Nature. The player on the other side is hidden from us. We know that his play is always fair, just, and patient. But also we know, to our cost, that he never overlooks a mistake, or makes the smallest allowance for ignorance. To the man who plays well, the highest stakes are paid, with that sort of overflowing generosity with which the strong shows delight in strength. And one who plays ill is checkmated—without haste, but without remorse. . . .

Well, what I mean by Education is learning the rules of this mighty game. In other words, education is the instruction of the intellect in the law of Nature, under which name I include not merely things and their forces, but men and their ways; and the fashioning of the affections and of the will into an earnest and loving desire to move in harmony with those laws. For me, education means neither more nor less than this. Anything which professes to call itself education must be tried by this standard, and if it fails to stand the test, I will not call it education, whatever may be the force of authority, or of numbers, upon the other side.

Thomas Henry Huxley, "A Liberal Education and Where to Find It"

To develop an argument by analogy, brainstorm the two items being compared for significant similarities and prepare a chart that matches them up. The greater the number and closeness of these similarities, the better the argument by analogy.

EMOTIONAL APPEAL

Although effective argument relies mainly on reason, an emotional appeal can lend powerful reinforcement. Indeed, emotion can win the hearts and the help of people who would otherwise passively accept a logical argument but take no action. Each Christmas, newspapers raise money for local charities by running stark case histories of destitute families. Organizations raise funds to fight famine by displaying brochures that feature skeletal, swollen-bellied children. Still other groups use emotion-charged stories and pictures to solicit support for environmental protection, to combat various diseases, and so on. Less benignly, advertisers use emotion to play upon our hopes, fears, and vanities in order to sell mouthwash, cars, clothes, and other products. Politicians paint themselves as fiscally responsible, trustworthy toilers for the public good while lambasting their opponents as being callous and unconcerned with social justice. In evaluating or writing an argument, ask yourself whether the facts warrant the emotion. Is the condition of the destitute family truly cause for pity? Is any politician unwaveringly good, any other irredeemably bad?

The following passage from a student argument favouring assisted suicide for the terminally ill represents an appropriate use of emotion:

When I visited Grandpa for the last time, he seemed imprinted on the hospital bed, a motionless, skeleton-like figure tethered by an array of tubes to the droning, beeping machine at his bedside. The eyes that had once sparkled with delight as he bounced grandchildren on his knee now stared blankly at the ceiling, seemingly ready to burst from their sockets. His mouth, frozen in an open grimace, emitted raspy, irregular noises as he fought to breathe. Spittle leaked from one corner of his mouth and dribbled onto the sheet. A ripe stench from the diaper around his middle hung about the bedside, masking the medicinal sickroom smells. As I stood by the bedside, my mind flashed back to the irrepressible man I once knew, and tears flooded my eyes. Bending forward, I planted a soft kiss on his forehead, whispered "I love you, Gramps," and walked slowly away.

Dylan Brandt Chafin, student

To develop an effective emotional appeal, identify the stories, scenes, or events of the topic that arouse the strongest emotional response within you. Do some thinking about the types of words that best convey the emotion you feel. Then write the section so that it builds to the kind of emotional conclusion that will help your argument.

ETHICAL APPEAL

Before logic can do its work, the audience must be willing to consider the argument. If a writer's tone offends the audience, perhaps by sounding arrogant or mean-spirited, the reasoning will fail to penetrate. But if the writer comes across as pleasant, fair-minded, and decent, gaining reader support is much easier. The writer who conveys a sense of integrity uses an ethical appeal.

If you write with a genuine concern for your topic, a commitment to the truth, and a sincere respect for others, you will probably come across reasonably well. When you finish writing, check whether occasional snide comments or bitter remarks slipped unnoticed onto the page. In the following excerpt from Martin Luther King's famous "I Have a Dream" speech, King does not give way to angry venting, but makes a strong ethical appeal to people's sense of justice:

Now is the time to make real the promises of democracy; now is the time to rise from the dark and desolate valley of segregation to the sunlit path of racial justice; now is the time to lift our nation from the quicksands of racial injustice to the solid rock of brotherhood; now is the time to make justice a reality for all of God's children.

Martin Luther King, Jr., "I Have a Dream"

FERRETING OUT FALLACIES

Fallacies are lapses in logic that weaken your argument. The fallacies described below are among the most common. Correct any you find in your own arguments, and call attention to those used by the opposition.

Hasty Generalization

Hasty generalization results when someone bases a conclusion on too little evidence. The student who tries to see an instructor during one of her office hours, finds her out, and goes away muttering, "She's never there when she should be" is guilty of hasty generalization. Perhaps the instructor was delayed by another student, or had gone home ill. However, the student who fails to find the instructor during office hours several times is more justified in drawing such a generalization.

Non Sequitur

From the Latin meaning "It does not follow," this fallacy draws unwarranted conclusions from seemingly ample evidence. Consider this example: "Bill's been out almost every night for the last two weeks. Who is she?" These evening excursions, on their own, point to no particular conclusion. Bill may be studying in the library, participating in campus organizations, taking night classes, or walking. Of course, he could be with a new girlfriend, but that conclusion requires other evidence.

Stereotyping

A person who commits this fallacy attaches one or more supposed characteristics to a group or one of its members. Typical stereotypes include "Latins make better lovers," "Blondes have more fun," and "Teenagers are lousy drivers." Stereotyping racial, religious, ethnic, or national groups can destroy an argument. The images are often malicious and are always offensive to fair-minded readers.

Card Stacking

In card stacking, the writer presents only part of the available evidence on a topic, deliberately omitting essential information that would alter the picture considerably. For instance: "University students have a very easy life; they attend classes for only twelve to sixteen hours a week." This statement ignores the many hours that students must spend studying, doing homework and/or research, writing papers, and earning enough money to pay tuition.

Either/Or Fallacy

The either/or fallacy asserts that only two choices exist when in fact several options are possible. A salesperson who wants you to buy snow tires may claim, "Either buy these tires or plan on getting stuck a lot this winter." But are you really that boxed in? You might drive only on main roads that are plowed immediately after every snowstorm. You could use public transportation when it snows. You could buy radial tires for year-round use, or you could buy tires from another dealer. If very little snow falls, you might not need special tires at all.

However, not all either/or statements are fallacies. The instructor who checks a student's record and then issues a warning, "Make at least a C on your final, or you'll fail the course," is not guilty of a reasoning error. No other alternatives exist. Most situations, however, offer more than two choices.

Begging the Question

A person who begs the question asserts the truth of some unproven statement. Here is an example: "Vitamin A is harmful to your health, and all bottles should carry a warning label. If enough of us write to the Minister of Health, we can get the labelling we need." But how do we know vitamin A does harm users? No evidence is offered. People lacking principles often use this fallacy to hit opponents below the belt: "We shouldn't allow an environmental terrorist like Paul Watson to run for political office." Despite a lack of suitable evidence, voters are sometimes swayed by such faulty logic and vote for the other candidate.

Circular Argument

Circular argument, a first cousin to begging the question, supports a position merely by restating it. "Pauline is a good manager because she runs the company effectively" says, in effect, that "something is because something is." Repetition replaces evidence.

Arguing off the Point

The writer who commits this fallacy, which is sometimes called "ignoring the question" or "a red herring," sidetracks an issue by introducing irrelevant information. To illustrate, "Vancouver has a more moderate climate than Toronto. Besides, too many Torontonians are moving to Vancouver. They are creating congestion and driving up the price of real estate. Many Vancouverites are angry that the cost of buying a home is so high." The writer sets out to convince that Vancouver offers a more enjoyable climate than Toronto but then abruptly shifts to increasing congestion and rising house prices in Vancouver—a trend that has no bearing on the argument.

The Argument *ad Hominem*

The Latin term "to the man" designates an argument that attacks an individual rather than that individual's opinions or qualifications. Note this example: "Sam Bernhard doesn't deserve promotion to personnel manager. His divorce was a disgrace, and he's always writing critical letters to the editor. The company should find someone more suitable." This attack completely skirts the real issue—whether Sam's job performance entitles him to the promotion. Unless his personal conduct has caused his work to suffer, it should not enter into the decision.

Appeal to the Crowd

An appeal of this sort arouses an emotional response by playing on the irrational fears and prejudices of the audience. Terms like *terrorists, fascists, bleeding hearts, right-wingers, welfare chisellers,* and *law and order* are tossed about freely to sway the audience for or against something. Consider the following excerpt from a famous speech:

> The streets of our country are in turmoil. The universities are filled with students rebelling and rioting. Communists are seeking to destroy our country. Russia is threatening us with her might, and the public is in danger. Yes, danger from within and without. We need law and order. Yes, without law and order our nation cannot survive. Elect us, and we shall by law and order be respected among the nations of the world. Without law and order our republic shall fall.

Tapping the emotions of the crowd can sway large groups and win acceptance for positions that rational thinking would reject. Think what Adolf Hitler, the author of the foregoing excerpt, brought about in Germany.

Guilt by Association

This fallacy points out some similarity or connection between one person or group and another. It tags the first with the sins, real or imagined, of the second. The following excerpt from a letter protesting a speaker at a lecture series illustrates this technique:

> The next slated speaker, Dr. Sylvester Crampton, was for years a member of the Economic Information Committee. This foundation has very strong ties with other ultraright-wing groups, some of which have been labelled fascistic. When he speaks next Thursday, whose brand of patriotism will he be selling?

Post Hoc, ergo Propter Hoc

The Latin meaning, "after this, therefore because of this," refers to the fallacy of assuming that because one event follows another, the first caused the second. Such weak thinking underlies many popular superstitions ("If a black cat crosses your path, you'll have bad luck") and many connections that cannot be substantiated ("Since video games have become so popular, childhood obesity rates have risen. Therefore, video games cause childhood obesity."). Sometimes one event does cause another: A sudden thunderclap might startle a person into dropping a dish. At other times, coincidence is the only connection. Careful research and thinking will help determine whether A caused B, or whether these two events just happened to occur at about the same time.

Faulty Analogy

This is the error of assuming that two circumstances or things are similar in all important respects, when in fact they are not. Here's an example: Sean McIntyre, midget hockey coach, tells his players, "Scotty Bowman has won the Stanley Cup seven times by insisting on excellent defensive positional play and requiring excellent physical conditioning. We're going to win the midget championship by following the same methods." McIntyre assumes that because he and Bowman are coaches, he can duplicate Bowman's achievements by using Bowman's methods. Several important differences, however, mark the two situations:

1. Bowman has had very talented players, obtained through the player draft or trades; McIntyre can choose only from the children in his community.
2. Bowman's players have been paid professionals who very likely were motivated, at least in part, by the financial rewards that come from winning the Stanley Cup; McIntyre's players are amateurs.
3. "Excellent defensive positional play" is probably easier for professional players than for midget players to attain.
4. Very few of Bowman's players could resist his insistence on "excellent physical conditioning" because they were under contract. Could McIntyre expect his players, essentially volunteers, to accept the same physical demands that Bowman has expected?

EXERCISE *Identify and explain the fallacies in the following examples. Remember that understanding the faulty reasoning is more important than merely naming the fallacy.*

1. After slicing a Golden Glow orange, Nancy discovers that it is rotten. "I'll never buy another Golden Glow product," she declares emphatically.
2. A campaigning politician states that, unless the federal government appropriates funds to help people living in poverty, they will all starve.
3. A husband and wife see an X-rated movie called *Swinging Wives*. A week later the husband discovers that his wife, while supposedly attending an evening class, has been unfaithful to him. He blames the movie for her infidelity.
4. "Look at those two motorcycle riders trying to pick a fight. All those cycle bums are troublemakers."
5. "Bill really loves to eat. Some day he'll have a serious weight problem."
6. "Because no-fault divorce is responsible for today's skyrocketing divorce rate, it should be abolished."
7. "This is the best-looking picture in the exhibit; it's so much more attractive than the others."
8. "I am against the proposed ban on smoking in public places. As long as I don't inhale and I limit my habit to ten cigarettes a day, my health won't suffer."

ETHICAL ISSUES

When writing an argument, we may wish to raise awareness, change attitudes, or spark some action. These objectives create an ethical responsibility for both the quality and the possible consequences of our arguments. Suppose a doctor writing a nationally syndicated advice column recommends an over-the-counter product that may cause a serious reaction in users who also take a certain prescription drug. Clearly this writer has acted irresponsibly and risks legal action if some readers suffer harm. Asking and answering the following questions can help you avoid any breach of ethics.

■ *Have I carefully considered the issue I'm arguing and the stance I'm taking?* Since you're trying to get others to adopt your views, you'll need to make sure they are very credible or make clear that your position is tentative or dependent on certain conditions.

■ *Am I fair to other positions on the issue?* Careless or deliberate distortion of opposing views is ethically dishonest and could raise doubts about your credibility.

■ *Are my reasons and evidence legitimate?* It is unethical to present flawed reasons as if they were credible or falsify evidence.

■ *Do I use fallacies or other types of faulty thinking to manipulate the reader unfairly?*

■ *What consequences could follow if readers adopt my position?* Say a writer strongly opposes genetically modified foods and advocates disruption of installations that help develop them. If some who are convinced by the argument then proceed to act on the writer's advice, innocent people could be injured.

WRITING AN ARGUMENT
Planning and Drafting the Argument

When you write an argument, you don't simply sit down and dash off your views as though they came prefabricated. Instead, look at argument as an opportunity to think things through, to gradually and often tentatively come to some conclusions, and then begin to draft your position in stages with the support you have discovered. If you are using outside sources to find support for your argument, you need to use your active reading and critical thinking skills as you sift and evaluate potential supporting materials. You need to weigh the merits of different writers' opinions, look for evidence of bias, weigh the type and amount of support backing each assertion, and select the key points to include in your paper. Try to keep an open mind as you are formulating your thesis.

Some instructors assign argument topics, and some leave the choice of topic to you. If you are choosing, many options are available. Interesting issues—some local, some of broader importance—crowd our newspapers, TV airways, and the internet, vying for attention. Because several of them have probably piqued your interest, there's a good chance you won't have to rely on the strategies on pages 34–40 to help you choose your topic.

Some students approach an argument with such strong attitudes that they ignore evidence that contradicts their thinking. Don't make this mistake. Instead, maintain an open mind as you research your issue, and then, after careful thought, choose the position you'll take. Often, several possible positions exist; and sometimes you end up changing your position after you have researched the topic.

Exploring Your Topic

You never really start an argument with a blank page. There is almost always an ongoing conversation about issues, so when you know that an argumentative paper will be assigned, it helps to be alert to controversies as you surf the net, read the news, and go about your daily life. Once you decide on a general subject, it helps to be informed by researching the topic. If your paper is based on sources, you may want to look at Chapters 15 and 17 for ideas and information about proper documentation. You may want to talk to others to get their views on the matter. Or you might make your own formal or informal observations; if so, you may be helped by the additional research strategies in Chapter 16.

As you investigate possible positions, ask and answer the following questions about each:

What are the reasons for the various positions?

What values are at stake, and what conclusions do they imply?

What common ground or shared principles exist among various positions?

What kinds of evidence support the position?

How substantial is the evidence?

If the evidence includes statistics and authoritative opinions, are they reliable? Or are they flawed for some reason?

What are the objections to each position, and how can they be countered?

If the issue involves taking some action, what might be its consequences?

To help with this stage of the process, prepare a chart that summarizes your findings for each position; then examine it carefully to identify the best position to argue for. The example below illustrates a three-position issue:

Position 1	Position 2	Position 3
Evidence and evaluation	Evidence and evaluation	Evidence and evaluation
Objections and how countered	Objections and how countered	Objections and how countered
Consequences	Consequences	Consequences

One effective technique for developing an argument is to first write a dialogue between two or three people that explores the various sides of an issue without trying to arrive at any conclusion. Writing such a dialogue can help start your mental energy flowing, reveal the issue from many sides, and give you ideas about developing effective material for your paper.

Arguments for Different Purposes

Arguments take many different forms, depending on the purpose, audience, and genre for the argument. When you write any kind of argument, you may find yourself drawing on all the different writing strategies you have previously learned. As you contemplate your position and evidence, consider the purpose of your argument and how the purpose will affect the strategies you choose to employ. An argument that takes the form of a critique may include a comparative analysis that demonstrates the relative merits of one item over another. An argument that takes the form of a complaint letter may use causal analysis to outline a problem and then propose a solution. An argument in a business context may also establish that something is a problem, and then recommend a new policy. An argument that takes the form of a formal academic research paper is likely to use definition and illustration as it makes its case with the help of information from primary and secondary sources.

Some arguments try to establish that something is a fact—nursing is hard work, residences are poor study places, bologna is an unhealthy food. This type of paper usually relies on assorted evidence, perhaps some combination of statistics, authoritative opinion, and personal experience. For example, to prove that nursing is demanding, you might narrate and describe some of the strenuous activities in a typical nursing day, cite hospital nursing supervisors who verify the rigours of the job, and perhaps give statistics on nurses who quit the profession because of stress.

Argument as Problem and Solution

If you want to propose a change to an existing structure or policy, you must first prove that a problem exists before your audience will be receptive to hearing about a solution. As you investigate the extent of the problem, you may decide that it does not really need solving, or even that the real problem is different than you originally thought. As you attempt to convince your audience to accept your solution, you are likely to blend different writing strategies into your argument. You may use description and illustration to identify the problem, and cause/effect analysis as you examine causes, including hidden causes, and possible effects. Sometimes you can come up with effective solutions by addressing the causes, or you can explore new ways to improve the situation. In some cases, you may have to explain the process of implementing your solution and/or defend (argue) its feasibility by showing that it will not have unacceptable consequences.

Arguments that propose a new action or policy may identify a need or a problem, and they generally recommend the implementation of a practical project, program, or action that will meet existing needs. For example, if there is no place on campus where students can gather to meet each other informally or study, a writer might propose the construction of a study lounge for students. Arguments that defend or oppose a broader social, political, or cultural policy— for example, whether Olympic athletes should have random drug-testing, or whether Canadian ports should have stricter security measures—must demonstrate the need for a new policy, how the need can best be addressed, and the benefits that will result. Arguments that propose a new policy or recommend a new action often use verbs such as *should*, *need*, or *ought*.

Argument as Evaluation and Critique

Reviews and critiques are arguments that evaluate something against specific criteria. Some reviews provide a short summary of content as background information, but the overall thesis should reflect your judgment, and the rest of the review develops reasons for this judgment. If you are asked to critique a movie, you need to commit yourself to a point of view on the quality of that movie rather than simply summarizing what happened. For example, your thesis for a movie review might be something like "The latest Harry Potter movie does not live up to the hype it has generated." If you are looking at criteria such as the quality of acting, special effects, music, and pacing, use specific examples and details for each criterion you are evaluating. Remember to establish criteria for your evaluation that are in accord with what the movie, or restaurant, or writer is trying to do; you can't fault the movie for not being a book, a café for not being a five-star restaurant, or an essay for not having music. Moreover, if you are evaluating a text, you need to establish that you have not come to it with preformed judgments, but have tried to understand and appreciate it on its own terms.

If you are evaluating a text or comparing two texts, your evaluation does not have to be absolutely negative or positive, but you do have to decide whether to emphasize strengths or weaknesses. Typically the evaluation of a text, movie, or essay is mixed, something like "Although this movie features amazing chemistry between the two stars, other weaknesses seriously compromise its quality." If you want to emphasize weaknesses, subordinate the strengths and put the weaknesses afterward, since whatever you end with makes the greatest impression on the reader. If you want to emphasize positives, end on a positive note. By the way, evaluations of texts and works of art usually employ the present tense throughout, except in the beginning when you are describing your experiences of entering a movie theatre, or picking up a book. If you are asked to write a comparative evaluation, in which you assert the greater value of someone or something as compared to a similar person, thing, or work of art, you can refer to Chapter 12 on structuring comparisons.

Considering Your Audience in Argument

With an argument, as with any essay, purpose and audience are closely linked. You should always imagine that your audience is a group of readers who are neutral or opposed to your position, because there's no point in preaching to the converted. Take a little time to analyze these readers so that you can tailor your arguments appropriately. Pose these questions as you proceed:

What are the readers' interests, expectations, and needs concerning this issue?

What evidence is most likely to convince them?

What objections and consequences would probably weigh most heavily with them?

How can I win people over and deal with objections?

Building Bridges with a Rogerian Argument

As you reflect on the issues that concern you, consider who the people are who have the power to change things, why they might resist change, and how you could overcome their resistance. If your audience is likely to be resistant or even hostile, you may want to use a *Rogerian argument.* Named for psychologist Carl Rogers, this type of argument emphasizes the speaker or writer's ability to look at things from the other's point of view. You can show that you understand and respect the position of the other by summarizing and acknowledging opposing points of view in a fair and accurate way. If you seek to establish some common ground before getting into your argument, you can often reduce the antagonism that people with opposing views might feel toward your position. For example, if you are arguing about emotionally charged issues that affect people directly such as assisted suicide or introducing user fees to Canada's health-care system, you can acknowledge in your introduction that these challenging issues have troubling ethical implications that people are right to worry about. After you build a bridge of shared values and respect with your audience, you can then present a position that addresses opposing concerns without compromising your views.

You can also reduce audience resistance if you acknowledge possible objections early on, responding to them if you can, or making concessions where necessary. For example, if you are arguing that the province needs to allocate more money for autistic children's therapy, you can acknowledge that these therapies are costly, but then emphasize that the long-term benefits include a more equitable society.

If your argument is highly controversial or your audience highly resistant, delay stating your thesis until you have built a case by establishing common ground, anticipating possible objections, providing necessary background, and using other strategies such as humour or an apt illustrative narrative to draw your audience to your side.

In addition, you can adapt the language of your argument to the audience's concerns and interests. To convince an audience of farmers that organic farming is viable, you might stress the added income they would gain from selective consumers willing to pay more for organic food; while for an audience of nutritionists, you might note the health benefits that would result. Even though you are unlikely to convince everyone, it is best to adopt the attitude that most readers can be convinced if your approach is appealing and your evidence is sound.

Drafting the Argument

When you have a good grasp of your position, reasons, evidence, and approach, you're ready to draft your paper. A typical introduction arouses the reader's interest and sometimes presents the proposition—a special thesis statement that names the issue and indicates which position the writer will take. It can declare that something is a fact, support a policy, call for a certain action, or assert that something has greater value than something else. Here are examples:

1. Carron College does not provide adequate recreational facilities for its students. *(Declares something is fact.)*
2. Our company's policy of randomly testing employees for drug use has proved effective and should be continued. *(Supports policy.)*

3. Because the present building is overcrowded and unsafe, the people of Midville should vote funds for a new middle school. *(Calls for action.)*

4. The Toyota Prius is more fuel-efficient and versatile than the Honda Civic hybrid. *(Asserts value.)*

Any of the techniques on pages 72–76 can launch your paper. For example, in arguing for stepped-up AIDS education, you might jolt your reader by describing a dying victim. If your issue involves unfamiliar terms, you might define them up front; and if the essay is long, you could preview its main points.

After the introduction comes the evidence, arranged in whatever order you think works best. If one of your points is likely to arouse resistance, hold it back and make points your reader can more easily accept first. Where strong resistance is not a factor, you could begin or end with your most compelling piece of evidence.

The strategies discussed in earlier chapters can help you develop an argument. Some papers incorporate one strategy, while others rely on several. Let's see how you might combine several in an argument against legalized casino gambling. You might open with a brief *description* of the frantic way a gambling addict keeps pulling the lever of a slot machine, his eyes riveted on the spinning dials, his palms sweating, as flashing lights and wailing sirens announce winners at other machines. Next, you could offer a brief *definition* of gambling fever so that the writer and reader are on common ground; and then, to show the dimensions of the problem, *classify* the groups of people who are especially addicted. Finally, after detailing the negative *effects* of the addiction, you might end by *comparing* gambling addiction with drug addiction, noting that both provide a "high" and both kinds of addicts know their habits hurt them.

Whatever strategies you use, make sure that substantiating evidence is embedded within each one. Strategies by themselves don't convince. For example, in discussing the negative effects of gambling, you might cite statistics that show the extent and nature of the problem. An expert opinion might validate your classification of addicts. Or you might use observation data to verify gambling's addictive effects.

Besides presenting evidence, use this part of your paper to refute—that is, to point out weaknesses or errors in—the opposing position. You might try the following:

- *Point out any evidence that undermines that position.* If one viewpoint holds that drug testing violates cherished privacy rights, you might note that employers already monitor phone calls, check employees' desks, and violate privacy in other ways.

- *Identify faulty assumptions and indicate how they are faulty: They don't lead to the implied conclusion, they lack the effectiveness of an alternative, or they are false or unsupported.* If you oppose drug testing, you could point out problems in the assumption that such tests are necessary to protect the public. Closer supervision of work performance might be a better protection; after all, fatigue, stress, negligence, and alcohol abuse can all result in serious problems, and they are not detected by drug tests.

- *Identify problems in the logic of the argument.* Are there missing premises, faulty connections between reasons, or conclusions that don't follow from the premises? The argument against drug testing usually proceeds by asserting that privacy is a fundamental right, that drug testing violates privacy, and that therefore drug testing should not be allowed. There is a missing premise, however: that because privacy is a fundamental right it should never be violated. This premise is, in fact, at the heart of the dispute and therefore cannot be accepted as a reason to disallow drug testing.

You can place refutations throughout the body of the paper or group them together just ahead of the conclusion. Whatever you decide, don't adopt a gloating or sarcastic tone that will alienate fair-minded readers. Resist the urge to engage in straw man tactics—calling attention to imaginary or trivial weaknesses of the opposing side so that you can demolish them. Shrewd readers easily spot such ploys. Finally, don't be afraid to concede secondary or insignificant points to the opposition. Arguments always have two or more sides; you can't have all the ammunition on your side. (If you discover that you must concede major points, however, consider switching sides.) Here is a sample refutation from a student paper:

> Not everyone agrees with workplace drug testing for employees in public transportation companies, electric utilities, nuclear power plants, and other industries involving public safety. Critics assert that such tests invade privacy and therefore violate one of our cherished freedoms. While the examination of one's urine does entail inspection of something private, such a test is a reasonable exception because it helps ensure public safety and calm public fears. Individuals have a right to be protected from the harm that could be caused by an employee who abuses drugs. An airline pilot's right to privacy should not supersede the security of hundreds of people who could be injured or killed in a drug-induced accident. Thus the individual's privacy should be tempered by concern for the community—a concern that benefits all of us.
>
> Annie Louise Griffith, student

Conclude in a manner that sways the reader to your side. Depending on the argument, you might restate your position, summarize your main points, predict the consequences if your position does or doesn't prevail, or make an emotional appeal for support or action.

Revising the Argument

Review the guidelines in Chapter 5 and ask yourself these questions as you revise your argument paper:

Appropriate topic and thesis Is my topic a clearly debatable one? Have I narrowed my topic to a clearly defined thesis that runs throughout the essay? Is my proposition clearly evident and of the appropriate type—that is, one of fact, policy, action, or value?

Focus Do I have a clear purpose I want to achieve through my argument, and do I maintain this sense of purpose and direction throughout? Is my thesis clear and strategically positioned? Are my main points clearly related to my thesis?

Awareness of audience Is the paper aimed at the audience I want to reach? Have I tailored my argument to appeal to that audience? Have I kept a respectful tone throughout, even when dealing with possible objections to my argument?

Thoroughness Have I examined all of the main positions? Have I assessed the evidence supporting each one? Have I considered the objections to each position and either countered these objections or made concessions where necessary?

Rational appeal Do I have enough solid evidence to support my claims? Is my evidence sound, adequate, and appropriate to the argument? Are my authorities qualified? Have I established their expertise? Are they biased? Will my audience accept them as authorities? Do my statistics adequately support my position? Have I pushed my statistical claims too far?

Emotional appeal If I've included an emotional appeal—perhaps by including a short narrative or story that fits with my larger purpose—does it centre on those emotions most likely to sway the reader? Have I addressed possible reader resistance by adequately refuting opposing arguments? Have I avoided sentimentality and self-pity?

Ethical appeal Have I made a conscious effort to present myself as a fair and reasonable person? Have I weighed the possible consequences if my paper were to persuade someone to take action?

Logic Have I established logical links between my claims and my evidence? Have I avoided overly broad claims and sweeping generalizations, especially ones that contain words such as "all" and "never"? If the proposition takes the form of a syllogism, is it sound? If faulty, have I started with a faulty premise, or reversed the last two statements of the syllogism? If I've used analogy, are my points of comparison pertinent to the issue? Have I noted any significant differences between the items being compared? Is my argument free of fallacies?

Organization Does my argument follow an effective organizational plan, such as the order of climax? Have I developed my position with one or more writing strategies? Are transitions smooth, from one point to the next? Do I end with an effective conclusion, rather than going on too long or stopping short?

EXAMPLE OF A STUDENT ESSAY OF ARGUMENT

Teaching Boys to Be Nonviolent and Still Be Boys

Kelly Dussin

1   This week I attended a memorial service for a colleague's daughter-in-law. She was only 39 years old and the mother of two young children, and was the alleged victim of a domestic dispute. Just about every day, the news is filled with stories of violence such as murders, stabbings, domestic abuse, robberies, abductions, sports violence, and school shootings like the one by a 14-year-old in Taber, Alberta, in 1999. The news reports note the youth of those engaged in violence, but do not dwell on the fact that most of these crimes of violence are

committed by males. Anti-violence educator Jackson Katz states in his video *Tough Guise* that "in the United States, 85 percent of all murders are committed by men and over 90 percent of all assault, domestic abuse, date abuse, rape, [and] child sexual abuse are committed by men." He also notes that "81 percent of boys who are abused will grow up to abuse and 76 percent of all homicides are males killing males." Of course, while many crimes of violence are committed by males, most males do not grow up to be abusers or criminals. Still, as a teacher assistant who works with adolescents, many of them male, and as mother of two boys, I am concerned about what kinds of cultural messages boys are receiving about what it means to be a man.

2   Many people might argue that boys have always engaged in acts of violence and that fighting at school or at home was just part of what being a boy was all about. Some might say that we can't always expect boys will always want to sit quietly and talk things out, and that most young males are active, sometimes more active than teachers would like. Some schools are so alarmed about bullying that they may have a policy of zero tolerance for the roughhousing that boys are prone to. As a teaching assistant, parent and citizen, I find it difficult to know how to promote peaceful alternatives to violence while still respecting boys' needs to be active and physical. How can we teach boys to be nonviolent in a culture of masculinity that glorifies violence, while still allowing boys to be boys?

3   In North America, the culture of masculinity promotes ideals of toughness, independence, and cool. Myriam Miedzian, author of *Boys Will Be Boys,* describes the values of "the masculine mystique as toughness, dominance, repression of empathy, [and] extreme competitiveness" (Introduction). She believes these values are reflected in "criminal activity and are evidenced in the messages and policies of political leaders" (Introduction). William Pollack, Ph.D., author of *Real Boys*, believes we need to rescue our sons from the "myths of boyhood." Pollack suggests that we expect boys to grow up too fast, "with too little preparation for what lies in store, too little emotional support, not enough opportunity to express feelings and often with no option of going back or changing course" (xxiv). This emphasis on independence in turn leads to boys "feeling ashamed of their vulnerability, masking their emotions and ultimately their true selves" (xxiv). Experts such as Miedzian, Pollack, and Katz all agree that our culture teaches boys to follow an unwritten code of boyhood that encourages toughness.

4   This unwritten code of what it means to be a man contributes to male violence. When Jackson Katz interviewed teen boys for his video *Tough Guise* to find out what their definition of being a man was, teens used words such as the following: "physical, strong, intimidating, powerful, tough, independent, control."

Katz theorizes that "masculinity is a guise, a front put up to gain respect by being violent." When Katz asked these same teens what happens when males do not fit the above definition, they used labels such as "wuss, wimp, sissy, fag."

5   When I asked my 19-year-old son, who viewed Katz's video with me, what he thought about Katz's claims, he agreed that boys are taught to be tough. My son went on to say that he always felt that he had to be tough at school or he would have been labelled a "wimp or a wuss." I asked him what "tough" meant, and he said, "I played rugby and hockey and I never backed down from a fight even if I knew it was wrong." I was saddened to realize that my son knowingly admits he can distinguish right from wrong, but the fear of not meeting the expectations of what a man is could make him choose wrong over right. The scary thing is that he still feels the same way as he did in high school.

6   Even young boys' toys have evolved to reflect our cultural fascination with male toughness. Katz shows in *Tough Guise* how toys such as GI Joe action figures (not dolls) have become more mean and menacing over the years, and their body shape has changed drastically since their introduction in 1964. GI Joe (in relation to human biceps) had a "biceps measurement of 12.2″" in 1964 and in 1998, his biceps measured 26.8″. In comparison, baseball player Mark McGuire's biceps measurement was 20″ at the height of his career." GI Joe also does something Barbie never did: he goes to war, a violent game that boys can learn from movies, television, video games and the daily news.

7   The link between masculinity and violence is perpetrated by the media—especially movies and video games. Many of the movies today are full of violence; man against man; man against woman. Slasher films are particularly disturbing in which sexualized violence is "deliberately designed to arouse" (*Tough Guise*). Some might argue that movies have always been violent, but the images have become much more disturbing over the years. Katz points out the difference between 1950's tough guy Humphrey Bogart, 1980's Sylvester Stallone in *Rambo*, and 1990's Arnold Schwarzenegger in *The Terminator*. Bogart has a little pistol while Schwarzenegger and Stallone both have huge guns. But it is not just the size of the guns that have changed. Schwarzenegger and Stallone also have very large, well-muscled bodies designed to intimidate. Boys can't help internalizing messages about the power of violence from movies such as *Terminator* or *Die Hard*. Recreation for boys is often linked with violence. Many of the video games that boys play, sometimes for hours a day, are full of graphic violence. "Young Canadians in a Wired World" reported that almost half of Canadian males aged 9–17 play video games every day, and about 60 percent prefer what are euphemistically

called "action games." According to the Media Awareness Network, in September 2002, the extremely "violent <u>Grand Theft Auto 3</u> was the second most popular game in the world."

8 Violence in sports, with few exceptions (e.g., golf, bowling, swimming) seems to be increasing. Fights in hockey, football, basketball not only take place during the play, but at times even involve the fans. Players are expected to participate in fights and some are hired for that very reason. Violence in sports has always been considered to be outside of the law, and even though some violent incidents have been dealt with in the courts, the convictions have had little effect in decreasing the violence. But it is not only violence in sports that affects our boys: it is the expectation that they will play tough under any circumstances, even when injured, and that winning is worth any cost. Miedzian gives the example of Bobby Knight, a university basketball coach who would "put a box of sanitary napkins in the locker of one of his players so that he would get the point that Knight considered him less than masculine" (198). This same coach also commented on television that "if a woman can't do anything about rape, she may as well lie back and enjoy it" (199). These are very powerful messages being sent to our boys.

9 Music with violent lyrics sends antisocial messages to boys. The Media Awareness Network reports that "'rage' music, filled with profanity and hate" has moved from the margins to the mainstream. In recent years, the music of singers such as "Eminem, Dr. Dre and Limp Bizkit—all known for their bleak anthems of violence and hatred, often aimed at women, gays and lesbians" has become hugely popular. Heavy Metal, Rap and Gangsta Rap music often contain lyrics that talk of violence, drugs, and suicide. Lyrics such as Motley Crue's "Get my ways at will / Go for the throat, / Going in for the kill" (Miedzian, 249) describe a fantasy about assaulting a woman. Often these kinds of music are delivered by artists in a mean and menacing manner. In *Boys Will Be Boys*, Miedzian talks about the "violence that often occurs at or after concerts" (250). Rapes, stabbings or murders are not uncommon occurrences at these concerts.

10 So what can we do to teach our boys to be nonviolent and still be boys? How can we help boys learn more positive images of masculinity?

11 I interviewed Jesse Padget, a pastor, and youth care worker, Paul McClelland, who has developed Hot Rod High, an innovative new program to teach youths about hot rods and life skills. While the program is for both males and females, the majority of the students are male. When I asked Jesse why he thought so many of our boys are struggling in school and life in general, he

replied that "we are teaching boys to be good, not to be boys." He went on to say, "Over my years of ministering, I have learned that the males in my congregation were bored out of their trees during my sermons. But when the guys were doing something, like working on a car, they would talk. Guys need to be hands-on, and boys need to be taught where they fit in society. They are often disoriented and rebellious when they start school." Paul McClelland set up Hot Rod High not only for young people to build hot rods, but also to develop skills in communication, teamwork, goal-setting and safe street smarts that boys can use throughout their lives. I can vouch for the power of this program, as my youngest son has been a student. For the last three years, things at school and in his life were in turmoil. Attending this program has given him a new sense of belonging and a new direction.

12   We need to appreciate that boys develop differently from girls, and that many boys do need outlets for their physical energy. However, we can attempt to counter the destructive messages about violence boys often receive from popular culture while still allowing them to be boys. We can encourage positive male role models and mentoring, we can teach empathy and nurturing skills, and we can enroll our boys in programs such as Hot Rod High that encourage positive, hands-on learning. Most importantly, we can, once we are aware of the factors that contribute to male violence, do what we can to eliminate the onslaught of violent messages from the media and other areas in our homes. While we cannot eliminate violence, or the cultural messages that approve it, we can teach boys critical thinking skills that will allow them to choose healthy models of what it means to be a man.

Works Cited

Dussin, Aaron. Personal interview. 24 Mar. 2005.

Hot Rod High. DVD. GS Productions, 2005.

Katz, Jackson. *Tough Guise.* Video. Media Education Foundation, 1999.

McClelland, Paul. Personal interview. 30 Mar. 2005.

Media Awareness Network. "The Business of Media Violence." 18 Aug. 2005. <http://www.media-awareness.ca/english/issues/violence/business_media_violence.cfm 2005>.

Media Awareness Network. "Young Canadians in a Wired World." 2001. 15 Aug. 2005. <http://www.cfc-efc.ca/docs/mnet/00002_en.htm>.

Miedzian, Myriam. *Boys Will Be Boys.* New York: Doubleday, 1991.

Padgett, Jesse. Personal interview. 30 Mar. 2005.

Pollack, William. *Real Boys: Rescuing Our Sons from the Myths of Boyhood.* New York: Henry Holt and Company, LLC, 1998.

DISCUSSION QUESTIONS

1. Identify the author's central purpose. What is her thesis, or proposition? Is it one of fact, policy, action, or value?

2. Why does the writer include a discussion of how action figures have changed over the years? How does this observation relate to her argument?

3. What type of supporting evidence does the writer use in her argument? Identify examples.

4. What is the effect of the rhetorical question that is used throughout the essay?

5. What type of conclusion does the writer use?

SUGGESTIONS FOR WRITING *Write an argument on a topic you feel strongly about. Study all sides of the issue so you can argue effectively and appeal to a particular audience. Be sure to narrow and focus your argument. Support your proposition with logical evidence. Here are some possibilities to consider:*

1. Compulsory writing courses
2. Cyberbullying in youth culture
3. Nuclear or wind power
4. Corporate involvement in education
5. A controversial First Nations issue
6. Online privacy issues
7. Raising the minimum wage
8. Export of Canadian water
9. Carbon taxes
10. Canadian food safety

The Critical Edge

By its very nature, a successful argument requires critical thinking. This chapter has given you the tools you need to test the logic and evaluate the evidence of argumentative positions. After all, rarely are writers assigned to generate an idea on their own and then argue for it. Instead, because most important issues have already been debated in print, they enter a discussion that's already underway. Sometimes it's on a topic of national interest, such as the desirability of politically correct speech and writing or the need to limit the number of terms elected officials can serve. At other times, the topic may be more localized: Should your province outlaw teacher strikes, your company install new equipment to control air pollution, or your university or college reduce its sports programs? On any of these issues, form your view as you read and assess the arguments of other writers.

A good way to take stock of conflicting opinions is to make a chart that summarizes key reasons and evidence on each side of the argument. Here is a segment of a chart that presents opposing viewpoints on whether industrial air pollution is related to the threat of global warming:

Pro-threat side	No-threat side

Industrial emissions of carbon dioxide, methane, and chlorofluorocarbons let sun's rays in but keep heat from escaping.
 	
          Andrew C. Revkin, student
	Natural sources account for almost 50 percent of all carbon dioxide production.
	
	          Dixy Lee Ray

Atmospheric levels of carbon dioxide are now 25 percent higher than in 1860. Computer models indicate continuing rise will cause temperature increase of 3–9°F.
 	
          Revkin
	The computer models are inaccurate, don't agree with each other, and fail to account for the warming effects of the oceans.
	
	          H. E. Landsberg

Even though you investigate the reasons and evidence of others, deciding what position to take and how to support it—that is, establishing your place in the debate—is the real work of synthesis. (See pages 423–425.) Therefore, after evaluating your sources, outline the main points you want to make. You can then incorporate material that supports your argument. Let's say that you're considering the issue of global warming. After examining the differing viewpoints, you might conclude that, although those who believe that global warming is occurring sometimes overstate their case, those who disagree tend to dismiss important scientific evidence. Moreover, when comparing the credentials of the pro-threat group against the no-threat group, you discover that many of the researchers in the no-threat group are indirectly members of lobby groups and are not themselves scientists. Since you have decided that global warming is a serious threat, you decide to argue for immediate environmental action. You might begin your paper by pointing out the dire environmental consequences of global warming if it is proved beyond the shadow of a doubt, then offer evidence supporting this possibility, acknowledge and answer key opposing viewpoints, and finally offer your recommendations for averting a crisis.*

SUGGESTION FOR ORAL ARGUMENTATION

Oral argumentation through formal debate is an enjoyable and effective exercise that promotes research and argumentation skills, a commitment to honesty and truth, and an attitude of respect for others and their ideas. In preparing for a formal debate, the debaters must first conduct primary and/or secondary research on the proposition they will be addressing so that they may defend either a pro or a con position. Because the debaters are not aware of the position they will

---

*Note that papers requiring research must be documented correctly. Before starting to write this type of paper, read the sections on handling quotations and avoiding plagiarism in Chapter 17. As always, follow your instructor's guidelines for documenting sources.

take on the proposition while conducting their research, their priority is to establish clear facts and specific arguments that could be offered as proofs for either side of the proposition. Once debaters are aware of the side of the proposition they will argue, they can draw from their research to develop a clear and concise argument for or against the proposition. Since the debaters have conducted their research prior to taking a pro or con position, they should be able to advance either argument with a thorough understanding of opposing views. This knowledge encourages an atmosphere of respect and tolerance.

After the debaters have completed their research on a proposition, they divide into teams representing pro and con positions. Each team then prepares opening statements outlining its arguments and compiles a set of proofs or examples that defends its positions. The actual debate can be structured in the following way:

STRUCTURING A DEBATE (ABOUT 60 MINUTES)

- Moderator asserts resolution and invites speakers from each team to direct opening statements to audience
- Each side gives opening statements outlining argument (3–5 minutes each)
- Speakers from each team give proofs
- Short break allows students to prepare statements and questions for cross-examination
- Cross-examination: Each side presents responses and rebuttals in turn (may also include questions from audience)
- Moderator asks audience to render written decision assessing debate teams according to criteria:
  - clarity of expression
  - thoroughness of research
  - effective use of rational, emotional, and/or ethical appeals
  - effectiveness of oral delivery
- Moderator announces results at end of debate

PROPOSITIONS FOR DEBATE

Propositions for debate can be found after the readings classified as "argument." Alternatively, try one of the following propositions.

- Canada's policy on refugees should be stricter (or more liberal).
- Decriminalization of marijuana is (or is not) justifiable.
- Victims of crimes should (not) be compensated by the perpetrator.
- The internet should be subject to stricter (looser) controls.
- Animal testing should (not) be banned.
- Grading for university English classes should (not) be abolished.
- Seal hunting in Canada should be illegal (legal).
- Government invasion of personal privacy in cyberspace is (un)justifiable.
- Exclusive corporate advertising on university campuses is (un)ethical.
- High schools should (not) put stronger emphasis on trades and apprenticeships.
- Cigarette taxes should (not) be raised.

SUGGESTIONS FOR RESEARCH-BASED ARGUMENTS

1. Use primary and secondary sources to investigate the placement of special needs students with mental and emotional disabilities in mainstream rather than special classes in your community. To gather primary information, you might interview people who work in the school system, or visit classrooms with and without students who have disabilities. To gather secondary research, you might consult educational journals or websites. After researching this issue, write a paper addressed to the school board or other stakeholder arguing for a change in the present policy.

2. Read several sources that explore problems related to a broad topic such as mortgage rules, or policies on drugs, health care, or the environment, and then write an argument that incorporates the views expressed in the sources and that suggests the extent of the problem. Be sure to narrow your subject and define your thesis.

3. Using outside sources, investigate a current social problem in your community, such as an increase in homelessness, drug abuse, or reckless street racing. Then write a paper addressed to a community council recommending a new course of action or policy.

4. Identify something you consider to be a problematic law or policy. Perhaps you see this law or policy as unjust, unfairly applied, outdated, or too expensive to enforce. Examine several sources that discuss this law, and then write a paper that identifies the problem and proposes a reasonable solution.

5. Analyze the rhetorical strategies in a recent influential speech by a major politician. If you prefer, you might choose to analyze an article from a website, such as the Canadian Centre for Policy Alternatives (www.policyalternatives.ca), The Fraser Institute (http://www.fraserinstitute.org/), or the Canadian Federation of Students (http://www.cfs-fcee.ca/html/english/home/index.php). Draw on your knowledge of argument and other writing strategies in order to show why you think the article or speech is or is not persuasive. Remember that your purpose is not simply to say whether or not you agree with the speaker or writer, but to evaluate the quality of the logic and other persuasive techniques in this speech or article.

6. If your instructor gives you free choice of topics, you could consult a Canadian website, such as one of the following, that features articles on controversial issues for ideas to get you started:

   www.policyalternatives.ca (Canadian Centre for Policy Alternatives)

   www.Canadians.org (Council of Canadians—a citizens' watchdog group devoted to social and environmental concerns)

   www.rabble.ca (progressive alternative to mainstream media)

   Alternatively, you could look for topical ideas in opinion pieces, columns, or commentary available on Canadian newspaper websites. Examples:

   www.canada.com (contains daily newspapers from Canadian cities; the section called "Forums" features colloquial debate from ordinary Canadians that might trigger an idea for you if you're stuck)

   www.globeandmail.com/columnists

ARGUMENT AND PERSUASION ESSAYS: PROFESSIONAL MODELS

READING STRATEGIES

1. Identify the background of the author if possible. Does the author bring any expertise or experience that helps make the argument credible?
2. Read the introduction and conclusion to gain a sense of the thesis and main points of the argument.
3. Read the argument quickly to gain an overall sense of the major points of the essay.
4. Look for the organizational pattern of the essay, and keep an eye out for transition sentences. Be aware of weak organizational patterns. Sometimes an inexperienced author argues by first presenting the viewpoints of several other authors, then pointing out limitations of those views, then presenting his or her own position and offering support, and finally admitting possible limitations and problems with this position (possibly answering these objections). This pattern makes it difficult to understand the writer's position.
5. Read carefully to identify the major claims of the argument, the reasons for the author's position, and any evidence presented for any of the claims. It can be very helpful to outline the argument, making a special note of the major reasons and evidence for the claim. Note the author's approach. Is the argument mostly deductive or inductive? Does the author try to show the negative consequences of opposing views? Does the author base the argument on authority?

READING CRITICALLY

1. Check whether the author demonstrates any overt bias.
2. Determine whether the reasons given really support the author's thesis.
3. Test whether the evidence is adequate. Does the evidence support the claims? Is the source of the evidence trustworthy and unbiased? Is the evidence extensive or scanty? Could contrary evidence be offered?
4. Check the essay for logical fallacies.
5. Try to offer objections to the author's claims. Write objections in the margins or on a separate piece of paper.
6. Formulate alternative conclusions to those proposed by the author.
7. Formulate reasons and concerns that the author may have neglected.
8. Read essays that present other viewpoints and compare.

READING AS A WRITER

1. Note the organizational pattern of the argument. Identify how you might use the pattern in one of your argument papers.
2. Examine how the writer connects the reasons with the major thesis.

3. Identify how the evidence is presented and connected as support.
4. Notice effective word choice that helps cement the emotional argument.
5. Evaluate how the author establishes tone and ethos.
6. Examine how the author answers possible objections.

Patricia Baird

Should Human Cloning Be Permitted?

Dr. Patricia Baird was trained as a pediatrician and then specialized in medical genetics. She has been Head of the Department of Medical Genetics at the University of British Columbia for over a decade and has been a member of numerous national and international bodies, among them the National Advisory Board on Science and Technology, chaired by the prime minister; the Medical Research Council of Canada (and its Standing Committee on Ethics in Experimentation); and International Ethics Committees. She headed the Canadian Royal Commission on New Reproductive Technologies and has served as an advisor to the World Health Organization in recent years. Since the mid-1980s she has been associated with the Canadian Institute for Advanced Research, where she currently chairs the Advisory Committee for the Population Health and Human Development Programs. She has received three honorary degrees and the Order of British Columbia. She is also an Officer of the Order of Canada, a Fellow of the Royal Society of Canada, and a "University Distinguished Professor" at the University of British Columbia. The following article, from Annals 33(4), June 2000, can be found on the Web.*

Introduction and Background

1   In 2001, a California state legislature committee invited individuals to present their recommendations on what position should be taken on human cloning, and outline their reasons. This article is an abridged version of an invited presentation in January 2000 to that committee.

A Qualitatively Different Type of Reproduction

> Introduction includes background, extended definition, and comparison.

2   Producing humans by somatic-cell nuclear-transfer cloning differs from sexual reproduction—it separates reproduction from recombination. Normally, in an outbred species such as humans, we cannot predict what the overall characteristics of an embryo will be. In sexual reproduction, it is unpredictable which combination of the parents' thousands of genes will occur. To date, in creating the next generation, we have had to give ourselves over to chance. But if nuclear transfer is used, the nucleus can be taken from an adult whose characteristics are known—and the process reproduces the biology of the former individual. It becomes possible to select by known characteristics which humans will be copied. The new technology allows the asexual replication of a human being, the ability to predetermine the full complement of a child's nuclear genes, and the easier alteration of the genes of prospective individuals. Cloning is a change in the integrity of our species, and we must think about the long-term consequences.

> Indication of writer's attitude: forecasting statement

Public Reaction to Human Cloning

3 <u>Cloning used to produce a human is rejected by the overwhelming majority of people.</u> Polls on new scientific developments have limitations, but *The Economist* reported that over 90 percent of Americans were opposed to human cloning.[1] Other polls have shown similar results.[2,3] Polls, however, are affected by how the questions are asked, so an in-depth approach is needed. Many experts believe that lay people cannot understand complicated scientific topics, but there are data showing that they can assimilate and make judgments about complex issues. The Wellcome Trust did a qualitative focus-group study and reported that opposition to human cloning was "nearly universal" among participants.[4] Most were against the idea of using cloning for reproductive purposes, stemming from concerns for the children and society, as much as from fears about interfering with nature. When over 90 percent of citizens in a democracy oppose human cloning, it is difficult for a government to justify a policy that permits it. There are a few people, however, who would pursue cloning because they see potential advantages for themselves.

> Topic sentence

> Rational appeal: statistics, citation of study

Foreseeable Requests for Cloning

4 <u>There are foreseeable situations where individuals may want to pursue cloning,</u> for example, for couples where both are infertile and have neither eggs nor sperm, or where the male produces no sperm. <u>Given that there are new treatment techniques using cells from testicular biopsy, such problems are rare.</u> A second example is where a lesbian couple might wish to use one partner's body cell and the enucleated egg of the other to produce a child together. <u>In these scenarios, there are other options available to form a family—such as sperm donation, egg and embryo donation, or adoption.</u> Other situations where cloning may be pursued is when a couple's child is dying or is killed, and they want to replace him or her by using one of his or her cells in nuclear-transfer cloning; or when a clone could provide a genetically compatible organ for transplantation. There will be instances where people wish to pursue cloning for particular reasons. [5,6,7]

> Topic sentence

> Refutation

> Development by example

> Refutation

5 <u>The arguments about physical and psychological harm to clones have also been well delineated.</u>[8,9] For example, with regard to possible physical harms, congenital malformations, handicap, early death, increased risk of cancer, premature aging, and death have all been raised. Possible psychological harms to cloned individuals (replicands) have also been outlined, including diminished individuality, a sense of foreclosed future, or a disturbed sense of identity. An important part of human identity is the sense of arising from a maternal and a paternal line while at the same time being a unique individual. Many children who are adopted, or conceived from donor insemination, show a deep need to learn about their biological origins. Making children by cloning means that they do not have this dual genetic origin; they are not connected to others in the same biological way as the rest of humanity. The first person born this way would have to cope with being the first not to come from the union of egg and sperm. Social, family, and kinship relationships that support human flourishing have evolved over millennia—but there is no way to place replicands. Is the DNA source the twin? The mother? The father?

> Topic sentence combines two claims

> Support for first claim

> Support for second claim

Widening the Frame

6   Most debate on human cloning focuses on a weighing of harms and benefits to individuals. This is a dangerously incomplete framing. Looking at the issue as a matter of reproductive technology choice, although it focuses on individual autonomy, reproductive freedom, and protection of children, means that other issues are omitted.[10] We need to shift from the framing as individual choice to a framing that reveals how permitting cloning affects future generations and society. I am reminded of one of the consultations of the Royal Commission on New Reproductive Technologies with an Aboriginal group in Canada. They told the commission about their seventh-generation rule. They said that when they had to make a big decision in their community, they always considered what the consequences were likely to be in the seventh generation. This is a useful perspective to have, because viewing cloning as a personal matter inappropriately minimizes potentially serious social consequences. Individual choices in reproduction are not isolated acts—they affect the child, other people, and future generations. The wider consequences must be considered because we all have a stake in the type of community that we live in. We do not want it to be one where the use of cloning commodifies children, commercializes family formation, or increases social injustice. Cloning raises issues about the future of our species. We have not yet found the wisdom to deal with hunger, poverty, and environmental degradation—we are unlikely to have the wisdom to direct our own evolution.

7   Nuclear-transfer cloning allows third parties to choose the genotypes of people who will be cloned. Before, when two people mated, no one could control which genes the child received out of a myriad of possibilities. This lottery of reproduction has been a protection against people being predetermined, chosen, or designed by others—including parents.

8   Cloning directs the production of human beings in an unprecedented way. When a child of a particular genetic constitution is "made," it is easier to look on him or her as a product, rather than a gift of providence. If we can, and some people do, make children "to order," it is likely to change the way we view children.

9   An impetus to developing nuclear-transfer cloning for producing animals has been that it could then be combined with genetic enhancement—genes could be added to give the animals desired traits. Genes are inserted into cells in culture, then the cells screened to pick the ones that have incorporated the desired genes. These altered cells are used as the donors of nuclei for cloned animals. It is then possible to create transgenic cloned animals with commercially desirable genetic traits (for example, heavier meat yield or production of insulin in the milk).[11]

10   Reproduction by nuclear-transfer cloning makes it possible to think about genetically enhancing humans. A person's cells could be cultured, genes inserted, and those cells taking up the desired genes used to produce a cloned "improved" individual. We could insert genes for viral-disease resistance, or to protect against baldness or degenerative diseases, or insert genes related to height or intelligence. If nuclear-transfer cloning is permitted, what will stop genetic enhancement being used eventually? There would be strong individual motivation to have a taller or disease-resistant child. We would then be taking human evolution into our own hands. Are we wise enough to manage it or the social consequences? Most people will want their child to be brighter, taller,

Marginal annotations:

- Ethical and emotional appeal
- Established truth
- Established truth
- Development through comparison
- Topic sentence
- Development through effects
- Definition of key term: scientific fact
- Refutation of argument for genetic enhancement

disease-resistant—so this technology could make people more standard, based on individual choices and market forces. If it works, it is likely to become used more often than just occasionally.

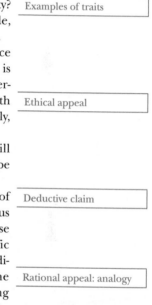

Qualification of claim

11   Who would have access to cloning or genetic improvements? Everyone? It is likely that those with financial resources would have access, but not other people, because cloning or enhancement would have to be provided as a socially underwritten "good" if it were to be available to everyone. And it is unlikely that most countries would provide publicly supported cloning, given that there are few social benefits and many potential harms.

12   If cloning or enhancement technology were provided as a public good to ensure equality of access, the government would have to decide in what circumstances people may clone themselves, and what traits were desirable. Docility? Height? Ability to provide a tissue transplant? Unless the market is to decide, criteria as to who may clone themselves, and a regulatory body will be needed.

Examples of traits

13   If cloning is used, will we undermine the unconditional parental acceptance of offspring that is central to nurturing human beings? Parental acceptance is likely to become conditional when we are able to program for certain characteristics. If cloning technology or genetic enhancement is permitted, people with disabilities, or members of racial or ethnic minorities, will be affected differently, and in a way unlikely to lead to greater equality and respect.

Ethical appeal

14   There are forces favouring the use of cloning—particular individuals will pursue it, and it will benefit financially those who provide it, so it is likely to be marketed to the public.

15   Many issues arising from cloning cannot be resolved in the framework of individual autonomy and reproductive choice. The focus on autonomy leads us to overlook the collective and transgenerational consequences of leaving the use of reproductive technologies to individual choices.[12] The use of scientific technology focused on individual wishes may result in social harms because individual interests differ from the public good at times. It is analogous to the tragedy of the commons,[13] which is exemplified by ranchers sharing grazing land, or fishers sharing a fishing ground. There is an incentive for individuals to overgraze or overfish because the benefits of doing so accrue to the individual, whereas the costs and harms occur to the community. The aggregate effect of individually beneficial choices may harm the long-term common good, and the cumulative impact of individual choices can result in an unethical system. Public policy-making differs from individual-based decision-making—because the moral unit of a physician is the patient, while the moral unit of public policy is all citizens.[14] If there is a conflict between the total social good and the good of an individual, public policy must uphold the public interest.

Deductive claim

Rational appeal: analogy

16   All members of the public have a stake in whether cloning is permitted, because if cloned people exist, the changes affect everyone. Even though a majority do not want to allow it, if it is permitted, we would all live in a world where people are cloned. Even though initially, individuals on whom cloning technology had a direct impact would be a minority, their collective experiences would influence social values. In public policy-making, it is inappropriate to subordinate every consideration to the question of whether it helps a couple to have a family. Society has a legitimate role in deciding whether cloning will be used. The far-reaching

nature of this choice means more voices must be involved in making decisions. The decisions should not be taken preemptively by a clinical facility or a group of scientists who ignore the wishes of the rest of the community. We need the perspectives not just of those who are knowledgeable in biology or science; we also need the perspectives of sociologists, humanists, and citizens from a variety of life experiences. On something that affects our species' future, it would be valuable to have the perspectives of people from many countries.

Conclusions Regarding Policy

17 There is no compelling case to make people by asexual means; human reproductive cloning is without potential benefits to almost all citizens, and other options are available in most situations. Many institutions have come to this conclusion; the prospects of making human beings by cloning have elicited concern in many countries, and there have been calls for a worldwide ban on cloning used to produce humans by many political and religious leaders, and by organizations such as the World Health Organization, the World Medical Organization, the American Medical Association, and UNESCO. Nineteen countries in the Council of Europe have signed an agreement that bans human cloning. Medicine, science, and technology are worldwide endeavours, so this is an issue facing humans as a species. For this reason, WHO is making an international effort to co-operate on guidelines for cloning in humans.

18   History shows that where there is a demand for a new service and the ability of a few to pay for it, unless there is legislation, there will be professionals willing to provide it. There is licensing of fertility clinics in several European countries, but in some other countries, reproductive technologies are highly commercialized and little regulated. If human cloning were permitted in the United States, it would likely proceed in the billion-dollar private reproductive-medicine sector. In this market-driven context, its use is unlikely to be controlled. It is now possible to peruse catalogues if you wish to buy eggs or surrogate pregnancies, so it seems likely that if human cloning is permitted in the United States, it is only a matter of time before pressure from individuals with specific interests would open up the field. Legislation is needed to ban the implantation into a woman of an egg cell that has had its nucleus transferred from a body cell. When such legislation is written, its wording should not inadvertently ban non-reproductive cloning research, or animal cloning research that may be of benefit, and that many people see as acceptable.

19   How we use cloning is not an individual or medical matter. It is a matter of social policy that cannot be viewed in a narrow framework of reproductive technology and individual choice. How we choose to use this technological capacity will shape society for our children, their children, and after. How it is used is likely to entrench existing inequalities, and create new ones.

Ethical appeal

Conclusion

Thesis statement

20   In conclusion, using nuclear-transfer cloning to allow people to have a child introduces a different way of reproduction for our species. Once we breach this barrier, it leaves us with no place to stop. Given all the problems outlined, the reasons for permitting cloning to produce a person are insufficiently compelling. Even in the few circumstances where the case for human cloning seems justified, there are alternative solutions. We are at an appropriate stopping place on a

slippery slope. Not all reasons why a person might wish to copy his or her cells are unethical, but given there are other options open to people wishing to form a family, concerns about individual and social harms from cloning are strong enough that it is not justified to permit it. These issues affecting the creation of the next generation are important for the future of our species; we must deal with them wisely. I hope we can.

Ethical appeal

References*

1. Whatever next? *The Economist* 1997 March 1;79-81.

2. Time/CNN poll. 1997 March.

3. International Food Information Council. *Wirthlin group quorum survey*, 1997 March 21-24.

4. *Public perspectives on human cloning, medicine in society program.* The Wellcome Trust, 1999 June (**http://www.wellcome.ac.uk/en/1/awtpubrepcln.html).**

5. McGee G. The human cloning debate. Berkeley: Berkeley Hills Books, 1998.

6. Hummer J, Almeder R. Human cloning. Biomedical Ethics Reviews. Totowa: 1998.

7. Andrews L. *The clone age: 20 years at the forefront of reproductive technology.* New York: Henry Holt, 1999.

8. Wilson JQ, Kass L. The ethics of human cloning. Washington: American Enterprise Press, 1999:10(2).

9. Cloning human beings. Report of the national bioethics advisory commission. *Hastings Center Report* 1997:27(5).

10. Baylis F. Human cloning: three mistakes and a solution. Unpublished manuscript.

11. Pennis E. After Dolly, a pharming frenzy. *Science* 1998:279;646-8.

12. Baird PA. Individual interests, societal interests, and reproductive technologies. *Perspectives Biology Medicine* 1997;40(3):440-51.

13. Hardin G. The tragedy of the commons. *Science* 1968;162:1243-8.

14. Lamm RD. Redrawing the ethics map. *Hastings Center Report* 1999;29(2):28-9.

DISCUSSION QUESTIONS

1. What use does the writer make of polls on people's attitudes toward cloning? What possible objection to the use of polls does the writer anticipate and counter?

2. According to Baird, what are three reasons that people might wish to pursue cloning? How does she support her claim that cloned individuals may feel "a disturbed sense of identity" (paragraph 5)?

3. What does Baird imply by her call to "shift the framing" of the debate about human cloning? In her ethical appeal, what undesirable consequences does she imagine could result from cloning (paragraph 6)?

4. Locate the questions that Baird asks the reader (paragraphs 10, 11, 12, 13). Why do you suppose that most of the questions are positioned later in the paper? What effect does Baird create through the asking of these questions?

*Please note that these References follow the CBE (Council of Biology Editors) style in effect at the time of publication, not the MLA style usually recommended for essays in English classes. This style is now known as CSE (Council of Science Editors) style and has undergone some changes.

5. Explain the point of the analogy which Baird uses in paragraph 15. Does this analogy help persuade you to Baird's point of view? Why or why not?

6. What concerns does Baird express about letting market forces decide whether or not cloning should be permitted (paragraphs 10–14)?

7. As in many arguments, the thesis statement comes in the last paragraph. Why do you suppose it comes toward the end?

8. What kinds of sources does Baird cite? To what extent does the use of sources bolster her argument?

9. Baird's views on cloning differ from those of Chris MacDonald in the following pages. Read MacDonald's argument and summarize the main points of difference.

TOWARD KEY INSIGHTS

How do you respond to Baird's emphasis on the psychological harm to individuals that might result from cloning?

Do you believe that cloning would be more psychologically harmful than other forms of reproductive technology that are currently permitted? Why or why not?

SUGGESTION FOR ORAL ARGUMENT *After researching both sides of the argument on the internet or elsewhere, come to class prepared to argue either side of the following proposition:*

As a society, we should support stem cell research.

SUGGESTION FOR WRITING *Write an essay that emphasizes either the potential benefits or the potential drawbacks in one type of reproductive or medical technology such as embryo research, genetic testing, pre-natal diagnostic screening, in-vitro fertilization, or surrogacy. Convey a sense of balance by considering opposing arguments as well.*

A useful starting point might be any of the sources cited in the article by Patricia Baird; or an electronic weekly digest of news stories related to assisted reproduction, www.progress.org.uk; or a related link that contains an annotated bibliography.

Chris MacDonald

Yes, Human Cloning Should Be Permitted

Dr. Chris MacDonald is a Canadian philosopher whose research interests include business ethics, health care ethics, professional ethics, and ethical theory. Some of his most recent publications have been related to ethical issues in the biotechnology industry. As you read the article "Yes, Human Cloning Should Be Permitted,"* note how he responds to specific points in Patricia Baird's argument calling for a ban on human cloning.

*©The Royal College of Physicians and Surgeons of Canada.

1   Patricia Baird's discussion of human cloning (*Annals RCPSC*, June 2000) challenges the prospect of nuclear-transfer cloning for the purposes of human reproduction. Baird reviews a long list of familiar worries about human cloning, but the most striking feature of her discussion is its frankness in placing the onus of justification on the shoulders of those who would permit human cloning. The reasons for permitting cloning, she argues, are "insufficiently compelling," so cloning should be prohibited. The implication is that any new technology should be forbidden unless and until enough justification can be found for allowing its use.

2   Baird is to be commended for her frankness. But the onus is misplaced, or at least too severe. One need not be a single-minded defender of liberty to think that, contrary to Baird's implication, we need good reasons to limit the actions of others, particularly when those actions do no clear and specific harm. The fact that a portion of society—even a majority—finds an activity distasteful is insufficient grounds for passing a law forbidding it. For example, it is presumably true that at one point, roughly 90 percent of the public (the same proportion that Baird says is against human cloning) was opposed to homosexuality. Does (or did) this justify action on the part of government to ban homosexual lifestyles? Surely not.

3   There may be a flaw in my analogy. Human cloning, according to critics, has harmful effects (or at least risks). Indeed, Baird suggests that the arguments regarding potential physical and psychological harm to clones have been "well delineated." In fact, a convincing case has yet to be made for the claim that the physical and psychological risks to clones are more severe than, or different in kind from, those faced by children produced in more traditional ways. Identical twins live with the psychological "burden" of not being genetically unique. Children born to women over 35 are at an increased risk of genetic illness. Children resulting from in-vitro fertilization or other reproductive technologies live with the knowledge that their origins were unusual. They may even live with the knowledge that their genetic profile has been manipulated (for example, through pre-implantation selection of embryos). Human cloning for reproductive purposes is another novel—and as yet untested—medical technology. As such, it should be approached with caution. Thorough animal trials should be completed before attempts on humans are contemplated. But this is true of any new medical technology.

4   Baird worries about the shift that human cloning might provoke in the way that we view children. This in turn would change the type of community that we are. The central worry is that human cloning "commodifies" children (i.e., that cloning may make us think of children as a commodity or product to be bought and sold). Why would cloning have this effect? Is it simply because it is likely to be expensive, so that it costs money to have children? Surely this is insufficient to worry us. Raising children already costs money—the statistics show us how many hundreds of thousands of dollars it costs to raise a child through to adulthood. Yet no one has suggested that we see our children as products, or love them any less. (In the mid-1940s—before publicly funded health care—my grandparents sold their car to pay the hospital bill related to my father's birth, so "purchasing" the birth of a child is nothing new!)

5   Baird argues that an "important part of human identity is the sense of arising from a maternal and a paternal line while at the same time being a unique individual." Yet without supporting evidence, this sounds like pop psychology. And we can reply in kind: most people I know do not identify with both their maternal and paternal lineages. One of my friends, who was raised by a single mother, identifies with her maternal eastern European heritage, and not with the French paternal heritage implied by her surname. Another friend identifies with his father's black heritage, rather than with his maternal Chinese lineage, despite his Asian physical features. Such patterns are not unusual. Dual heritage may be normal, but it hardly seems central to our conception of ourselves as humans. And identical twins seem none the worse for the knowledge that they are not genetically unique individuals. Claims about challenges to what makes us "human" may be powerful rhetorical devices, but they must be substantiated if they are to be convincing.

6   Baird is correct to exhort us to look beyond harms to identifiable individuals to the social implications that human cloning might have. As a comparison, think of fetal sex selection. Most of us think that sex selection is a bad thing—not because of any purported harm to the child, but because we worry about the social implications of valuing children of one sex over those of another. So Baird rightly reminds us that focusing on potential harms to individuals constitutes a "dangerously incomplete framing" of the problem. Furthermore, cloning (and genetic technology in general) is sufficiently new—and its implications sufficiently poorly understood—to warrant a healthy respect, and even the allowance of a margin of safety. But this does not suggest the need for the ban that Baird (with others) proposes. What these worries suggest is a need for caution, for discussion, and for regulation. For instance, laws limiting the number of clones that might be created from one individual, restricting the combination of cloning with genetic modification, and defining lines of parental obligation, would alleviate many of the concerns associated with human cloning. (Françoise Baylis argues that cloning is so likely to be used in combination with gene transfer that we should think of cloning as an enhancement technology rather than as a reproductive technology, in her article "Human cloning: three mistakes and a solution," which has been accepted for publication in the *Journal of Medicine and Philosophy*.)

7   What I have said here should not be taken as an absolute defence of human cloning in all circumstances. (Indeed, there may be only a few circumstances in which cloning is appropriate.) Nor have I suggested that public monies should be spent on cloning research. All I have suggested is that a ban on research leading toward human cloning is unwarranted by the arguments raised thus far. Caution and discretion are warranted; a ban is not.

8   Finally, I worry that Baird's point of view exemplifies the way in which human reproductive cloning is being singled out, among cloning-related techniques, as a bogeyman. Almost in chorus, scientists are pleading with regulators not to place restrictions on cloning experimentation per se. At the same time, most scientists seem to be more than willing to swear off reproductive cloning, and indeed to wring their hands over the moral implications of its use. Yet this has the air of a too-hasty concession. The scientific community seems to be too willing to condemn one unpopular application of cloning technology, on the basis of too little convincing argumentation, to appease those who oppose

cloning technology in general. But human cloning for reproductive purposes has legitimate, morally acceptable applications—for example, for infertile couples, and for gay couples. And none of the criticisms have been convincingly made. We should not let reproductive human cloning be abandoned as the moral sacrificial lamb of the cloning debate.

DISCUSSION QUESTIONS

1. Chris MacDonald's essay is a rebuttal to the arguments offered by Patricia Baird in her essay "Should Human Cloning Be Permitted?" What major premise of Baird's argument does MacDonald think is "misplaced, or at least too severe" (paragraph 2). Explain MacDonald's objection and the major argumentative premise of his essay.

2. While taking issue with many of Baird's claims, MacDonald acknowledges the strengths of her argument as well. Find an example showing how MacDonald praises an aspect of Baird's argument and then adapts it to serve his own argument.

3. Identify the main claims of Baird's argument to which MacDonald responds. Are his responses compelling? Does he succeed in raising doubt about Baird's conclusion?

4. Unlike Baird, MacDonald (except through one parenthetical reference to an unpublished article by Françoise Baylis) does not refer to the scholarship of others to reinforce his position. Is his argument weakened by this lack of secondary scholarly support? Explain why or why not.

5. While Baird's essay is written almost entirely in the third-person voice, MacDonald's is written almost entirely in the first-person voice. How does this first-person point of view enhance or diminish MacDonald's persuasive appeal? Explain, using examples from the essay.

6. What rational, emotional, and ethical appeals does MacDonald use in the two concluding paragraphs of this essay?

TOWARD KEY INSIGHTS

How do you respond to MacDonald's assertion that there is no clear evidence that our humanity is predicated on being able to recognize and identify with both our parental lineages?

SUGGESTION FOR ORAL ARGUMENT *After researching both sides of the argument on the internet or elsewhere, come to class prepared to argue either side of the following proposition:*

Human cloning for reproductive purposes could be appropriate in some circumstances.

SUGGESTIONS FOR WRITING *After considering the issue of animal cloning, develop an argument that makes a strong ethical appeal for or against animal cloning. Use specifics in your argument.*

Charles Krauthammer

Crossing Lines

Dr. Charles Krauthammer majored in political science and economics at McGill University, studied at Oxford University, and received his medical degree from Harvard. He practised medicine and became chief resident in psychiatry at Massachusetts General Hospital. In 1978, he served as the director of psychiatric research for the Carter Administration. Since then he has written articles and commentary for The New Republic *and* The Washington Post, *with his syndicated columns appearing in more than 100 newspapers. He won the 1987 Pulitzer Prize for distinguished commentary and has been named by* the Financial Times *as the most influential commentator in the U.S. In this essay he argues against cloning research.*

Problem

1   You were once a single cell. Every one of the 100 trillion cells in your body today is a direct descendent of that zygote, the primordial cell formed by the union of mother's egg and father's sperm. Each one is genetically identical (allowing for copying errors and environmental damage along the way) to that cell. Therefore, if we scraped a cell from, say, the inner lining of your cheek, its DNA would be the same DNA that, years ago in the original zygote, contained the entire plan for creating you and every part of you.

2   Here is the mystery: Why can the zygote, as it multiplies, produce every different kind of cell in the body—kidney, liver, brain, skin—while the skin cell is destined, however many times it multiplies, to remain skin forever? As the embryo matures, cells become specialized and lose their flexibility and plasticity. Once an adult cell has specialized—differentiated, in scientific lingo—it is stuck forever in that specialty. Skin is skin; kidney is kidney.

3   Understanding that mystery holds the keys to the kingdom. The Holy Grail of modern biology is regenerative medicine. If we can figure out how to make a specialized adult cell dedifferentiate—unspecialize, i.e., revert way back to the embryonic stage, perhaps even to the original zygotic stage—and then grow it like an embryo under controlled circumstances, we could reproduce for you every kind of tissue or organ you might need. We could create a storehouse of repair parts for your body. And, if we let that dedifferentiated cell develop completely in a woman's uterus, we will have created a copy of you, your clone.

4   That is the promise and the menace of cloning. It has already been done in sheep, mice, goats, pigs, cows, and now cats and rabbits (though cloning rabbits seems an exercise in biological redundancy). There is no reason in principle why it cannot be done in humans. The question is: Should it be done?

5   Notice that the cloning question is really two questions: (1) May we grow that dedifferentiated cell all the way into a cloned baby, a copy of you? That is called reproductive cloning. And (2) may we grow that dedifferentiated cell just into the embryonic stage and then mine it for parts, such as stem cells? That is called research cloning.

6   Reproductive cloning is universally abhorred. In July 2001, the House of Representatives, a fairly good representative of the American people, took up

the issue, and not a single member defended reproductive cloning. Research cloning, however, is the hard one. Some members were prepared to permit the cloning of the human embryo in order to study and use its component parts, with the proviso that the embryo be destroyed before it grows into a fetus or child. They were a minority, however. Their amendment banning baby-making but permitting research cloning was defeated by 76 votes. On July 31, 2001, a bill outlawing all cloning passed the House decisively.

7   Within weeks, perhaps days, the Senate will vote on essentially the same alternatives. On this vote will hinge the course of the genetic revolution at whose threshold we now stand.

The Promise

8 This is how research cloning works. You take a donor egg from a woman, remove its nucleus, and inject the nucleus of, say, a skin cell from another person. It has been shown in animals that by the right manipulation you can trick the egg and the injected nucleus into dedifferentiating—that means giving up all the specialization of the skin cell and returning to its original state as a primordial cell that could become anything in the body.

9   In other words, this cell becomes totipotent. It becomes the equivalent of the fertilized egg in normal procreation, except that instead of having chromosomes from two people, it has chromosomes from one. This cell then behaves precisely like an embryo. It divides. It develops. At four to seven days, it forms a "blastocyst" consisting of about 100 to 200 cells.

10   The main objective of cloning researchers would be to disassemble this blastocyst: pull the stem cells out, grow them in the laboratory, and then try to tease them into becoming specific kinds of cells, say, kidney or heart or brain and so on.

11   There would be two purposes for doing this: study or cure. You could take a cell from a person with a baffling disease, like Lou Gehrig's, clone it into a blastocyst, pull the stem cells out, and then study them in order to try to understand the biology of the illness. Or you could begin with a cell from a person with Parkinson's or a spinal cord injury, clone it, and tease out the stem cells to develop tissue that you would reinject into the original donor to, in theory, cure the Parkinson's or spinal cord injury. The advantage of using a cloned cell rather than an ordinary stem cell is that, presumably, there would be no tissue rejection. It's your own DNA. The body would recognize it. You'd have a perfect match.

12   The conquest of rejection is one of the principal rationales for research cloning. But there is reason to doubt this claim on scientific grounds. There is some empirical evidence in mice that cloned tissue may be rejected anyway (possibly because a clone contains a small amount of foreign—mitochondrial—DNA derived from the egg into which it was originally injected). Moreover, enormous advances are being made elsewhere in combating tissue rejection. The science of immune rejection is much more mature than the science of cloning. By the time we figure out how to do safe and reliable research cloning, the rejection problem may well be solved. And finally, there are less problematic alternatives—such as adult stem cells—that offer a promising alternative to cloning because they present no problem of tissue rejection and raise none of cloning's moral conundrums.

13   These scientific considerations raise serious questions about the efficacy of, and thus the need for, research cloning. But there is a stronger case to be made. Even if the scientific objections are swept aside, even if research cloning is as doable and promising as its advocates contend, there are other reasons to pause.

14   The most obvious is this: Research cloning is an open door to reproductive cloning. Banning the production of cloned babies while permitting the production of cloned embryos makes no sense. If you have factories all around the country producing embryos for research and commerce, it is inevitable that someone will implant one in a woman (or perhaps in some artificial medium in the farther future) and produce a human clone. What then? A law banning reproductive cloning but permitting research cloning would then make it a crime not to destroy that fetus—an obvious moral absurdity.

15   This is an irrefutable point and the reason that many in Congress will vote for the total ban on cloning. Philosophically, however, it is a showstopper. It lets us off too early and too easy. It keeps us from facing the deeper question: Is there anything about research cloning that in and of itself makes it morally problematic?

Objection I: Intrinsic Worth

16 For some people, life begins at conception. And not just life—if life is understood to mean a biologically functioning organism, even a single cell is obviously alive—but personhood. If the first zygotic cell is owed all the legal and moral respect due a person, then there is nothing to talk about. Ensoulment starts with Day One and Cell One, and the idea of taking that cell or its successor cells apart to serve someone else's needs is abhorrent.

17   This is an argument of great moral force but little intellectual interest. Not because it may not be right. But because it is unprovable. It rests on metaphysics. Either you believe it or you don't. The discussion ends there.

18   I happen not to share this view. I do not believe personhood begins at conception. I do not believe a single cell has the moral or legal standing of a child. This is not to say that I do not stand in awe of the developing embryo, a creation of majestic beauty and mystery. But I stand in equal awe of the Grand Canyon, the spider's web, and quantum mechanics. Awe commands wonder, humility, appreciation. It does not command inviolability. I am quite prepared to shatter an atom, take down a spider's web, or dam a canyon for electricity. (Though we'd have to be very short on electricity before I'd dam the Grand.)

19   I do not believe the embryo is entitled to inviolability. But is it entitled to nothing? There is a great distance between inviolability, on the one hand, and mere "thingness," on the other. Many advocates of research cloning see nothing but thingness. That view justifies the most ruthless exploitation of the embryo. That view is dangerous.

20   Why? Three possible reasons. First, the Brave New World Factor: Research cloning gives man too much power for evil. Second, the Slippery Slope: The habit of embryonic violation is in and of itself dangerous. Violate the blastocyst today and every day, and the practice will inure you to violating the fetus or even the infant tomorrow. Third, Manufacture: The very act of creating embryos for the sole purpose of exploiting and then destroying them will ultimately predispose us to a ruthless utilitarianism about human life itself.

Objection II: The Brave New World Factor

21 The physicists at Los Alamos did not hesitate to penetrate, manipulate, and split uranium atoms on the grounds that uranium atoms possess intrinsic worth that entitled them to inviolability. Yet after the war, many fought to curtail atomic power. They feared the consequences of delivering such unfathomable power— and potential evil—into the hands of fallible human beings. Analogously, one could believe that the cloned blastocyst has little more intrinsic worth than the uranium atom and still be deeply troubled by the manipulation of the blastocyst because of the fearsome power it confers upon humankind.

22 The issue is leverage. Our knowledge of how to manipulate human genetics (or atomic nuclei) is still primitive. We could never construct ex nihilo[1] a human embryo. It is an unfolding organism of unimaginable complexity that took nature three billion years to produce. It might take us less time to build it from scratch, but not much less. By that time, we as a species might have acquired enough wisdom to use it wisely. Instead, the human race in its infancy has stumbled upon a genie infinitely too complicated to create or even fully understand, but understandable enough to command and perhaps even control. And given our demonstrated unwisdom with our other great discovery— atomic power: As we speak, the very worst of humanity is on the threshold of acquiring the most powerful weapons in history—this is a fear and a consideration to be taken very seriously.

23 For example. Female human eggs seriously limit the mass production of cloned embryos. Extracting eggs from women is difficult, expensive, and potentially dangerous. The search is on, therefore, for a good alternative. Scientists have begun injecting human nuclei into the egg cells of animals. In 1996, Massachusetts scientists injected a human nucleus with a cow egg. Chinese scientists have fused a human fibroblast with a rabbit egg and have grown the resulting embryo to the blastocyst stage. We have no idea what grotesque results might come from such interspecies clonal experiments.

24 In October 2000, the first primate containing genes from another species was born (a monkey with a jellyfish gene). In 1995, researchers in Texas produced headless mice. In 1997, researchers in Britain produced headless tadpoles. In theory, headlessness might be useful for organ transplantation. One can envision, in a world in which embryos are routinely manufactured, the production of headless clones—subhuman creatures with usable human organs but no head, no brain, no consciousness to identify them with the human family.

25 The heart of the problem is this: Nature, through endless evolution, has produced cells with totipotent power. We are about to harness that power for crude human purposes. That should give us pause. Just around the corner lies the logical by-product of such power: human-animal hybrids, partly developed human bodies for use as parts, and other horrors imagined—Huxley's Deltas and Epsilons—and as yet unimagined. This is the Brave New World Factor. Its grounds for objecting to this research are not about the beginnings of life, but about the ends; not the origin of these cells, but their destiny; not where we took these magnificent cells from, but where they are taking us.

---

[1] ex nihilo means "from nothing."

Objection III: The Slippery Slope

26   The other prudential argument is that once you start tearing apart blastocysts, you get used to tearing apart blastocysts. And whereas now you'd only be doing that at the seven-day stage, when most people would look at this tiny clump of cells on the head of a pin and say it is not inviolable, it is inevitable that some scientist will soon say: Give me just a few more weeks to work with it and I could do wonders.

27   That will require quite a technological leap because the blastocyst will not develop as a human organism unless implanted in the uterus. That means that to go beyond that seven-day stage you'd have to implant this human embryo either in an animal uterus or in some fully artificial womb.

28   Both possibilities may be remote, but they are real. And then we'll have a scientist saying: Give me just a few more months with this embryo, and I'll have actual kidney cells, brain cells, pancreatic cells that I can transplant back into the donor of the clone and cure him. Scientists at Advanced Cell Technology in Massachusetts have already gone past that stage in animals. They have taken cloned cow embryos past the blastocyst stage, taken tissue from the more developed cow fetus, and reimplanted it back into the donor animal.

29   The scientists' plea to do the same in humans will be hard to ignore. Why grow the clone just to the blastocyst stage, destroy it, pull out the inner cell mass, grow stem cells out of that, propagate them in the laboratory, and then try chemically or otherwise to tweak them into becoming kidney cells or brain cells or islet cells? This is Rube Goldberg. Why not just allow that beautiful embryonic machine, created by nature and far more sophisticated than our crude techniques, to develop unmolested? Why not let the blastocyst grow into a fetus that possesses the kinds of differentiated tissue that we could then use for curing the donor?

30   Scientifically, this would make sense. Morally, we will have crossed the line between tearing apart a mere clump of cells and tearing apart a recognizable human fetus. And at that point, it would be an even smaller step to begin carving up seven- and eight-month-old fetuses with more perfectly formed organs to alleviate even more pain and suffering among the living. We will, slowly and by increments, have gone from stem cells to embryo farms to factories with fetuses in various stages of development and humanness, hanging (metaphorically) on meat hooks waiting to be cut open to be used by the already born.

31   We would all be revolted if a living infant or developed fetus were carved up for parts. Should we build a fence around that possibility by prohibiting any research on even the very earliest embryonic clump of cells? Is the only way to avoid the slide never to mount the slippery slope at all? On this question, I am personally agnostic. If I were utterly convinced that we would never cross the seven-day line, then I would have no objection on these grounds to such research on the inner cell mass of a blastocyst. The question is: Can we be sure? This is not a question of principle; it is a question of prudence. It is almost a question of psychological probability. No one yet knows the answer.

Objection IV: Manufacture

32   Note that while, up to now, I have been considering arguments against research cloning, they are all equally applicable to embryonic research done on a

normal—i.e., noncloned—embryo. If the question is tearing up the blastocyst, there is no intrinsic moral difference between a two-parented embryo derived from a sperm and an egg and a single-parented embryo derived from a cloned cell. Thus the various arguments against this research—the intrinsic worth of the embryo, the prudential consideration that we might create monsters, or the prudential consideration that we might become monsters in exploiting post-embryonic forms of human life (fetuses or even children)—are identical to the arguments for and against stem-cell research.

33   These arguments are serious—serious enough to banish the insouciance of the scientists who consider anyone questioning their work to be a Luddite—yet, in my view, insufficient to justify a legal ban on stem-cell research (as with stem cells from discarded embryos in fertility clinics). I happen not to believe that either personhood or ensoulment occurs at conception. I think we need to be apprehensive about what evil might arise from the power of stem-cell research, but that apprehension alone, while justifying vigilance and regulation, does not justify a ban on the practice. And I believe that given the good that might flow from stem-cell research, we should first test the power of law and custom to enforce the seven-day blastocyst line for embryonic exploitation before assuming that such a line could never hold.

34   This is why I support stem-cell research (using leftover embryos from fertility clinics) and might support research cloning were it not for one other aspect that is unique to it. In research cloning, the embryo is created with the explicit intention of its eventual destruction. That is a given because not to destroy the embryo would be to produce a cloned child. If you are not permitted to grow the embryo into a child, you are obliged at some point to destroy it.

35   Deliberately creating embryos for eventual and certain destruction means the launching of an entire industry of embryo manufacture. It means the routinization, the commercialization, the commodification of the human embryo. The bill that would legalize research cloning essentially sanctions, licenses, and protects the establishment of a most ghoulish enterprise: the creation of nascent human life for the sole purpose of its exploitation and destruction.

36   How is this morally different from simply using discarded embryos from in vitro fertilization (IVF) clinics? Some have suggested that it is not, that to oppose research cloning is to oppose IVF and any stem-cell research that comes out of IVF. The claim is made that because in IVF there is a high probability of destruction of the embryo, it is morally equivalent to research cloning. But this is plainly not so. In research cloning, there is not a high probability of destruction; there is 100 percent probability. Because every cloned embryo must be destroyed, it is nothing more than a means to someone else's end.

37   In IVF, the probability of destruction may be high, but it need not necessarily be. You could have a clinic that produces only a small number of embryos, and we know of many cases of multiple births resulting from multiple embryo implantation. In principle, one could have IVF using only a single embryo and thus involving no deliberate embryo destruction at all. In principle, that is impossible in research cloning.

38   Furthermore, a cloned embryo is created to be destroyed and used by others. An IVF embryo is created to develop into a child. One cannot disregard

intent in determining morality. Embryos are created in IVF to serve reproduction. Embryos are created in research cloning to serve, well, research. If certain IVF embryos were designated as "helper embryos" that would simply aid an anointed embryo in turning into a child, then we would have an analogy to cloning. But, in fact, we don't know which embryo is anointed in IVF. They are all created to have a chance of survival. And they are all equally considered an end.

39   Critics counter that this ends-and-means argument is really obfuscation, that both procedures make an instrument of the embryo. In cloning, the creation and destruction of the embryo is a means to understanding or curing disease. In IVF, the creation of the embryo is a means of satisfying a couple's need for a child. They are both just means to ends.

40   But it makes no sense to call an embryo a means to the creation of a child. The creation of a child is the destiny of an embryo. To speak of an embryo as a means to creating a child empties the word "means" of content. The embryo in IVF is a stage in the development of a child; it is no more a means than a teenager is a means to the adult he or she later becomes. In contrast, an embryo in research cloning is pure means. Laboratory pure.

41   And that is where we must draw the line. During the great debate on stem-cell research, a rather broad consensus was reached (among those not committed to "intrinsic worth" rendering all embryos inviolable) that stem-cell research could be morally justified because the embryos destroyed for their possibly curative stem cells were derived from fertility clinics and thus were going to be discarded anyway. It was understood that human embryos should not be created solely for the purpose of being dismembered and then destroyed for the benefit of others. Indeed, when Senator Bill Frist made his impassioned presentation on the floor of the Senate supporting stem-cell research, he included among his conditions a total ban on creating human embryos just to be stem-cell farms.

42   Where cloning for research takes us decisively beyond stem-cell research is in sanctioning the manufacture of the human embryo. You can try to regulate embryonic research to prohibit the creation of Brave New World monsters; you can build fences on the slippery slope, regulating how many days you may grow an embryo for research; but once you countenance the very creation of human embryos for no other purpose than for their parts, you have crossed a moral frontier.

43   Research cloning is the ultimate in conferring thingness upon the human embryo. It is the ultimate in desensitization. And as such, it threatens whatever other fences and safeguards we might erect around embryonic research. The problem, one could almost say, is not what cloning does to the embryo, but what it does to us. Except that, once cloning has changed us, it will inevitably enable further assaults on human dignity. Creating a human embryo just so it can be used and then destroyed undermines the very foundation of the moral prudence that informs the entire enterprise of genetic research: the idea that, while a human embryo may not be a person, it is not nothing. Because if it is nothing, then everything is permitted. And if everything is permitted, then there are no fences, no safeguards, no bottom.

DISCUSSION QUESTIONS

1. What are the main points of Krauthammer's argument against cloning research?
2. Krauthammer directly identifies the reasons individuals might want cloning research. What is the effect of this discussion on Krauthammer's argument?
3. Krauthammer rejects the argument based on intrinsic worth. Why does he reject this argument? What effect does this have on his overall argument?
4. What is the overall tone of Krauthammer's argument? What impact does that have on the relative effectiveness of the essay?
5. Krauthammer raises a number of horrifying possibilities in his essay, including humans without heads, living infants being carved up into parts, and human genes being mixed with animal genes. Does such speculation help or hurt his arguments?
6. Krauthammer directly refers to "the slippery slope" (see paragraph 20). What does he mean here? Are his slippery slope arguments legitimate? Do they help or hurt his overall argument?

TOWARD KEY INSIGHTS

Krauthammer states that humans lack the wisdom to handle the complex power of nature. Should scientific and technological development that holds powerful implications beyond our wisdom be restricted?

SUGGESTION FOR ORAL ARGUMENT *After researching both sides of the argument on the internet or elsewhere, come to class prepared to argue either side of the following proposition:*

The potential benefits from genetic enhancement of human beings outweigh the potential detriments.

SUGGESTION FOR WRITING *Write a paper responding in more depth to one of the arguments Krauthammer raises.*

Peter McKnight

The Specious Arguments against Human Cloning

Peter McKnight is an award-winning columnist and editor at The Vancouver Sun *who serves as a legal analyst for Global National, and teaches in the School of Criminology at Simon Fraser University. A former lawyer and parole officer, McKnight writes on a variety of subjects, including law and justice issues, science, social science, philosophy, religion and ethics. His work has appeared in several North American newspapers and in 2007, McKnight became the first and only Canadian named a Templeton-Cambridge Fellow in Science and Religion at the University of Cambridge.*

1   When Dolly the sheep was cloned in 1997, many people worried that cloning of humans was just around the corner. But they were reassured that the substantial differences between sheep and humans meant that it would be a long time before human reproductive cloning was possible.

2   In the rapidly progressing world of science, however, 10 years can be a long time. Indeed, just 10 years after Dolly, the Oregon National Primate Research Center announced that it had cloned 20 monkey embryos.

3   This doesn't mean that human reproductive cloning is around the corner, but that scientists are now able to clone primates has once again stoked fears that human cloning will soon be a reality.

4   In fact, the United Nations University-Institute for Advanced Studies (UNU-IAS), fearing that reproductive cloning might now be inevitable, recently issued a report in which it lamented that "regulators missed an opportunity to develop clear and unequivocal measures banning cloning intended for the purposes of bringing about the birth of human life."

5   Yet many organizations have done exactly that—the World Health Organization, the United Nations Educational Scientific and Cultural Organization (UNESCO) and more than 50 countries have outlawed the practice, and none explicitly permit it.

6   The problem therefore seems to revolve not around a lack of legislation, but around disagreements as to the morality of human reproductive cloning. Certainly, most bioethicists oppose the practice, but a significant minority remain unconvinced because the arguments against cloning depend more on intuition than reason, when they're not downright fallacious.

7   The UNU-IAS report reviews the main arguments, though it carefully avoids relying on any as conclusive. Nevertheless, there is one argument that governments can rely on without reservation. Given the significant health and safety concerns associated with cloning, it would be unethical and unacceptable to create children who might suffer immeasurably.

8   However, given the rapid progress of science, this argument might ultimately lose its force as improvements in technique might eliminate health and safety concerns. The real challenge, then, is to find arguments that apply always and everywhere, and this is not easy.

9   One of the most popular arguments is also one of the most fallacious. Cloning, we are told, compromises people's individuality. Most countries, including Canada, that have banned reproductive cloning have relied heavily on this argument, which is astonishing since it is an example of crude genetic determinism.

10   In effect, the argument says that our individuality is the result of our genes—indeed, that we are nothing more than our genes. This notion of reducing people to their bodies—thereby making us machines—is not only morally problematic but is simply false.

11   After all, we know that our individuality is the result of the complex interplay of genetics, the environment, and perhaps most importantly, of our freely made choices. No one would ever suggest that identical twins lack individuality, for example, despite the fact that they are (natural) clones of each other.

12   A third branch of arguments relies on the Kantian categorical imperative, and suggests that allowing people to clone themselves would amount to treating clones as means rather than ends. According to these arguments, the close is created merely to satisfy some purpose, such as to replace a dead child.

13   This could happen of course, but it would not be peculiar to cloning. There are, unfortunately, people who have their own interests in mind when they have children through in vitro fertilization or indeed, by natural means. And there is no reason to assume that those who use cloning will be more likely to do so for selfish reasons.

14   Of all the justifications for banning reproductive cloning, though, by far the most popular one suggests that cloning represents an affront to human dignity. Governments and international organizations rely heavily on this position, which isn't surprising since it's impossible to counter because it's not an argument.

15   Instead, the appeal to human dignity relies on "the yuck factor," the immediate visceral reaction of revulsion some people have at the thought of human cloning. Normally, people's visceral reactions would not form the basis of a philosophical position, but the yuck factor has received plenty of play in relation to cloning thanks to Leon Kass, former chairman of the U.S. President's Council on Bioethics.

16   In *The Wisdom of Repugnance*, an essay now incorporated into his book *Life, Liberty and the Defense of Dignity*, Kass admits that "revulsion is not an argument," but, "In crucial cases, however, repugnance is the emotional expression of deep wisdom beyond reason's power fully to articulate it."

17   Now two problems immediately arise here. First, Kass never tells us what constitutes a crucial case, and second, he is trying to convince us that the inability to make an argument is somehow better than argument itself!

18   Nevertheless, this notion of repugnance is worth considering. As Yale University psychologist Paul Bloom argues, disgust plays an important evolutionary role in that it helps us to avoid ingesting substances that might make us sick. In effect, our feelings of disgust toward certain things, such as disease and decay, increase our chances of survival, which seems to support Kass's position.

19   Yet as other psychologists have shown, socialization plays a large role in repugnance. Relying on this research, University of Chicago philosophy and law professor Martha Nussbaum argues that through socialization—though associating certain groups with things that disgust us—cultures have managed to engender feelings of revulsion towards Jews, women, homosexuals, and people of lower castes in caste-based societies.

20   Similarly, though less problematically, Nussbaum notes that people have also reacted with disgust towards certain great literature, including James Joyce's *Ulysses*, and to many advances in reproductive therapies, including in vitro fertilization (Kass also opposed IVF.)

21   This should lead us to question the wisdom of repugnance, and to avoid making policy solely on the basis of people's feelings of disgust. More specifically, it should lead us to re-examine appeals to human dignity as a basis for banning human reproductive cloning.

22   Indeed, Tim Caulfield, Canada research chair in health law and policy, and research director of the Health Law Institute at the University of Alberta, argues that "using human dignity as a blanket argument against all forms of human cloning makes it much more difficult to reflect rationally on the true risks and benefits of the technology."

23   Even worse, Caulfield notes that by employing human dignity in this way, we risk downgrading its importance, as it comes to stand for nothing more than "a symbol of amorphous cultural anxiety."

24   Despite this, it's not altogether surprising that policy-makers have relied on appeals to human dignity as justification for banning reproductive cloning. After all, the panic produced by the rapid advance of science has convinced legislators that they must act immediately to outlaw reproductive cloning, even if the arguments are wanting.

25   But policy by panic is never a good idea. And we don't need to panic. Our ability to produce human clones is likely still years away, and we should spend those years discovering what human dignity really means, rather than reflexively and unreflectively appealing to it whenever something makes us uncomfortable.

DISCUSSION QUESTIONS

1. What is the thesis that the author is trying to support? Why does he place it where he does?

2. What are the four commonly offered arguments against human cloning identified by the author?

3. The author takes care to respond to each of the four arguments offered against human cloning. What argumentative strategies does he employ in response?

4. In response to claims that human cloning is an affront to human dignity, the author asks us to reflect upon what human dignity means. By what strategies does the author persuade the audience to consider carefully the meaning of an emotionally charged phrase such as *human dignity*?

5. Throughout the essay, McKnight never offers his opinion on the appropriateness (or not) of human cloning. What might be the reason for this strategy? What effect does this have?

TOWARD KEY INSIGHTS

Often scientific progress is met with fear. Should scientific progress be unregulated, or should society create legal and moral limits on scientific research?

What should be the basis of such limits?

SUGGESTION FOR ORAL ARGUMENT *After researching both sides of the argument on the internet or elsewhere, come to class prepared to argue either side of the following proposition:*

As a society, we should support research into therapeutic cloning.

SUGGESTION FOR WRITING *Read all four articles on human cloning in this section and write a critique (see page 328) on the strengths and weaknesses of each. Proceed from what you consider to be the least effective to the most effective essay.*

Neil Bissoondath

No Place Like Home

Neil Bissoondath has written several critically acclaimed books of fiction and nonfiction that explore themes of migration, alienation, and identity. His works of fiction include A Casual Brutality, The Worlds Within Her, *and* The Unyielding Clamour of the Night. *Neil Bissoondath's provocative discussion of identity politics and multiculturalism,* The Cult of Multi-Culturalism in Canada *(1994), provides a broader and more in-depth discussion of the ideas and concerns raised in his essay "No Place Like Home,"* which is reproduced below.*

1   Three or four years into the new millennium, Toronto, Canada's largest city, will mark an unusual milestone. In a city of three million, the words "minorities" and "majority" will be turned on their heads and the former will become the latter.

2   Reputed to be the most ethnically diverse city in the world, Toronto has been utterly remade by immigration, just as Canada has been remade by a quarter-century of multiculturalism.

3   It is a policy which has been quietly disastrous for the country and for immigrants themselves.

4   The stated purpose of Canada's *Multiculturalism Act* (1971) is to recognize "the existence of communities whose members share a common origin and their historic contribution to Canadian society." It promises to "enhance their development" and to "promote the understanding and creativity that arise from the interaction between individuals and communities of different origins." The bicultural (English and French) nature of the country is to be wilfully refashioned into a multicultural "mosaic."

5   The architects of the policy—the Government of then–Prime Minister Pierre Elliot Trudeau—were blind to the fact that their exercise in social engineering was based on two essentially false premises. First, it assumed that "culture" in the large sense could be transplanted. Second, that those who voluntarily sought a new life in a new country would *wish* to transport their cultures of origin.

6   But "culture" is a most complex creature; in its essence, it represents the very breath of a people. For the purposes of multiculturalism, the concept has been reduced to the simplest theatre. Canadians, neatly divided into "ethnic" and otherwise, encounter each other's mosaic tiles mainly at festivals. There's traditional music, traditional dancing, traditional food at distinctly untraditional prices, all of which is diverting as far as it goes—but such encounters remain at the level of a folkloric Disneyland.

**New Internationalist*, September 1998, Issue 305, p. 20+.

7   We take a great deal of self-satisfaction from such festivals; they are seen as proof of our open-mindedness, of our welcoming of difference. Yet how easily we forget that none of our ethnic cultures seems to have produced poetry or literature or philosophy worthy of our consideration. How seductive it is, how reassuring, that Greeks are always Zorbas, Ukrainians always Cossacks: we come away with stereotypes reinforced.

8   Not only are differences highlighted, but individuals are defined by those differences. There are those who find pleasure in playing to the theme, those whose ethnicity ripens with the years. Yet to play the ethnic, deracinated and costumed, is to play the stereotype. It is to abdicate one's full humanity in favour of one of its exotic features. To accept the role of ethnic is also to accept a gentle marginalization. It is to accept that one will never be just a part of the landscape but always a little apart from it, not quite belonging.

9   In exoticizing and trivializing cultures, often thousands of years old, by sanctifying the mentality of the mosaic-tile, we have succeeded in creating mental ghettos for the various communities. One's sense of belonging to the larger Canadian landscape is tempered by loyalty to a different cultural or racial heritage.

10   When, for instance, war broke out between Croatia and Serbia, a member of the Ontario legislature, who was of Croatian descent, felt justified in declaring: "I don't think I'd be able to live next door to a Serb." That he was speaking of a fellow Canadian was irrelevant. *Over there* mattered more than *over here*—and the cultural group dictated the loyalty. Ironic for a country that boasted about its leading role in the fight against apartheid.

11   Often between groups one looks in vain for the quality that Canadians seem to value above all—tolerance. We pride ourselves on being a tolerant country, unlike the United States, which seems to demand of its immigrants a kind of submission to American mythology. But not only have we surrendered a great deal of ourselves in pursuit of the ideal—Christmas pageants have been replaced by "Winterfests"; the anti-racist Writers Union of Canada sanctioned a 1994 conference which excluded whites—but tolerance itself may be an overrated quality, a flawed ideal.

12   The late novelist Robertson Davies pointed out that *tolerance* is but a weak sister to *acceptance*. To tolerate someone is to put up with them; it is to adopt a pose of indifference. Acceptance is far more difficult, for it implies engagement, understanding, an appreciation of the human similarities beneath the obvious differences. Tolerance then is superficial—and perhaps the highest goal one can expect of Canadian multiculturalism.

13   Another insidious effect of this approach is a kind of provisional citizenship. When 100-metre sprinter Ben Johnson won a gold medal at the Seoul Olympics, he was hailed in the media as the great Canadian star. Days later, when the medal was rescinded because of a positive drug test, Johnson became the Jamaican immigrant—Canadian when convenient, a foreigner when not. Tolerated, never truly accepted, his exoticism always part of his finery, he quickly went from being one of *us* to being one of *them*.

14   This makes for an uneasy social fabric. In replacing the old Canada, based on British and French tradition, with a mosaic (individual tiles separated by

cement), we have shaken our sense of identity. In a country over 130 years old, we are still uncertain who we are.

15   A major 1993 study found that 72 per cent of the population wants, as one newspaper put it, "the mosaic to melt." Canadians were found to be "increasingly intolerant" of demands for special treatment made by ethnic groups—a Chinese group who wanted a publicly funded separate school where their children would be taught in Chinese by Chinese teachers; a Muslim group who claimed the right to opt out of the Canadian judicial system in favour of Islamic law. Canadians wanted immigrants to adopt Canada's values and way of life.

16   Many immigrants agree. They recognize that multiculturalism has not served their interests. It has exoticized, and so marginalized, them, making the realization of their dreams that much harder. The former rector of the Université du Québec à Montréal, Claude Corbo, himself the grandson of Italian immigrants, has pointed out that multiculturalism has kept many immigrants "from integrating naturally into the fabric of Canadian and Quebec society. . . . We tell people to preserve their original patrimony, to conserve their values, even if these values are incompatible with those of our society."

17   Which leads to the other false premise on which multiculturalism is based. It assumes that people who choose to emigrate not only can but also *wish to* remain what they once were.

18   The act of emigration leaves no-one unscathed. From the moment you board a plane bound for a new land with a one-way ticket, a psychological metamorphosis begins—and the change occurs more quickly, more deeply and more imperceptibly than one imagines.

19   I arrived alone in Toronto from Trinidad in 1973, an 18-year-old with dreams but no experience of the world. A year later, I returned to Trinidad to visit my parents. Within days I realized the extent of the change that had come not only to me, but to all I had left behind. Even after so short a time, old friends had become new strangers, and old places remained only old places. Already Trinidad—its ways, its views, its very essences—was receding, becoming merely a memory of place and childhood experience. *Feeling* had already been wholly transferred to the new land, to this other country which had quickly become my home. Certainly, for others the process is slower and often less evident—but it is inexorable. The human personality is not immutable.

20   Multiculturalism, which asked that I bring to Canada the life I had in Trinidad, was a shock to me. I was seeking a new start in a land that afforded me that possibility. I was *not* seeking to live in Toronto as if I were still in Trinidad—for what would have been the point of emigration? I am far from alone in this. As the political scientist Professor Rias Khan of the University of Winnipeg put it: "People, regardless of their origin, do not emigrate to preserve their culture and nurture their ethnic distinctiveness. . . . Immigrants come here to become Canadians; to be productive and contributing members of their chosen society. . . . Whether or not I preserve my cultural background is my personal choice; whether or not an ethnic group preserves its cultural background is the group's choice. The state has no business in either."

21   The immigrant dream—of financial and social success; of carving out a place within the larger society—is grand in its simplicity. Requiring great courage, it is

self-limiting on no level. All one asks is the freedom and fairness—through anti-discrimination legislation, if necessary—to fulfill one's potential. A vital part of that freedom is the latitude to recognize and welcome inevitable change in society and the migrant. One may treasure a private, personal identity built from family lore and experience, all the while pursuing the public integration vital to wider success. To be put in the position of either obliterating the past or worshipping it is, for the individual, an unnecessary burden that leads to a false and limiting theatre of the self.

22   Not long ago, my daughter's teacher wanted to know what kind of family the children in her first-grade class came from. For most of the children, born in Quebec City into francophone families that have been here for over 200 years, the answer was straightforward.

23   Then it was my daughter's turn. Her father, she explained, was born in Trinidad into an East Indian family; having lived in Canada for a long, long time, he was Canadian. Her mother was born in Quebec City, a francophone. She herself was born in Montreal.

24   "Ahh!" the teacher exclaimed brightly, "So you're from a West Indian family!"

25   My daughter returned home deeply puzzled. At six years of age she had been, with the best of intentions, handed an identity crisis.

26   In some ways she was lucky. We were able to sort out her confusions. In other parts of the country—in Toronto or Vancouver—where ethnic identity has become a kind of fetish, my daughter would have had to deal with a far more complex proposal. To be true to her inherited ethnicities, she would be: Franco-Québécoise-First Nations-Indian-Trinidadian-West Indian-Canadian. Indeed, for her to describe herself as simply "Canadian" with no qualifying hyphen would be almost antagonistic.

27   The weight of this hyphen was signalled as far back as 20 years ago by the feminist writer Laura Sabia when she said: "I was born and bred in this amazing land. I've always considered myself a Canadian, nothing more, nothing less, even though my parents were immigrants from Italy. How come we have all acquired a hyphen? We have allowed ourselves to become divided along the line of ethnic origins, under the pretext of the 'Great Mosaic.' A dastardly deed has been perpetuated upon Canadians by politicians whose motto is 'divide and rule'. . . I am a Canadian first and foremost. Don't hyphenate me."

28   Or, one might add, future generations.

29   Canadian multiculturalism has emphasized difference. In so doing, it has retarded the integration of immigrants into the Canadian mainstream while damaging Canada's national sense of self. Canada has an enviable record in dealing with racism; our society, while hardly perfect (we too have our racists of all colours), remains largely free of racial conflict. And yet we do ourselves a disservice in pursuing the divisive potential in multiculturalism. With an ongoing battle against separatism in Quebec, with east-west tensions, we are already a country uncomfortably riven. Our "mosaic" does not help us.

30   In recognition of its growing unpopularity, official multiculturalism has had its status downgraded from a ministry, to a directorate, to a department. Canada, for the foreseeable future, will continue to be a nation open to immigrants—and one committed to combating racism, sexism and the various other forms of discrimination we share with other societies. Beyond this, because of the damage

already inflicted by multiculturalism, we need to focus on programs that seek out and emphasize the experiences, values and dreams we all share as Canadians, whatever our colour, language, religion, ethnicity or historical grievance. And pursue *acceptance* of others—not mere *tolerance* of them.

31 Whatever policy follows multiculturalism, it should support a new vision of Canadianness. A Canada where no one is alienated with hyphenation. A nation of cultural hybrids, where every individual is unique and every individual is a Canadian, undiluted and undivided. A nation where the following conversation, so familiar—and so enervating—to many of us will no longer take place:

32 "What nationality are you?"

33 "Canadian."

34 "No, I mean, what nationality are you *really*?"

35 The ultimate goal must be a cohesive, effective society enlivened by cultural variety; able to define its place in the world. Only in this way might that member of the Ontario legislature and his neighbour no longer see each other as Serb and Croat but as Canadians with a great deal more in common than their politically sanctioned blindness allows them to perceive.

36 In the end, immigration is a personal adventure. The process of integration that follows it is a personal struggle within a social context that may make the task either more or less difficult. Multiculturalism in Canada has the latter effect but it may matter very little, because integration—the remaking of the self within a new society with one's personal heritage as invaluable texture—is finally achieved in the depths of one's soul. Many Canadians, like me, have simply ignored multiculturalism, by living our lives as fully engaged with our new society as possible, secure in the knowledge of the rich family past that has brought us here.

37 I will never forget the bright summer evening many years ago when, fresh off the plane from a trip to Europe, I stood on my apartment balcony gazing out at the Toronto skyline, at the crystal light emanating off Lake Ontario and beyond. I took a deep breath of the cooling evening air and knew, deep within my bones, that it was good to be home.

DISCUSSION QUESTIONS

1. In your own words, explain the rationale for Canada's *Multiculturalism Act* (paragraph 4). Why does the writer say the policy is an "exercise in social engineering" (paragraph 5)?

2. What does the writer see as the "two false premises" (paragraph 5) or flawed assumptions embedded in the policy of multiculturalism? Identify places where he uses rational, emotional, and ethical appeals throughout the essay to convince readers that these premises are mistaken.

3. What is the distinction that the writer makes between "tolerance" and "acceptance" (paragraph 12)? How does the example of Ben Johnson (paragraph 13) support his claim that tolerance does not necessarily translate into acceptance?

4. How does the writer gain credibility and authority from the inclusion of his personal background (paragraphs 19–20)? How might his point of view be affected by his country of origin, his marriage, and his social class? How might you have read this essay differently if the writer did not have the experience of being an immigrant?

5. What is the point of Bissoondath's anecdote about his daughter's school experience (paragraphs 22–25)? What does Bissoondath mean when he refers to "the weight of this hyphen" (paragraph 27)?

6. What positive alternatives to multiculturalism does Bissoondath envision (paragraphs 30–36)?

TOWARD KEY INSIGHTS

Do you agree that ethnic festivals are a kind of "folkloric Disneyland" (paragraph 6), or do you think they have value that Bissoondath does not discuss?

How do you respond to the idea of melting the cultural mosaic?

What, in your view, has Bissoondath left out of his argument that might have made it more persuasive?

SUGGESTION FOR ORAL ARGUMENT *After researching both sides of the argument on the internet or elsewhere, come to class prepared to argue either side of the following proposition:*

To promote social justice, the Canadian government should implement an affirmative action program for ethnic minorities.

SUGGESTIONS FOR WRITING *After reading the* Canadian Multiculturalism Act *at www.solon.org/Statutes/Canada/English/C/CMA.html or the 2004 Speaking Points on "Serving Canada's Multicultural Population: Practical Approaches for Public Servants" by Judith Larocque, Deputy Minister, Canadian Heritage, write an essay weighing the claims of both Bissoondath and the statement put out by the Canadian government. Demonstrate that you understand the arguments for and against the policy of multiculturalism, but take a position, and emphasize either the advantages or disadvantages. You may choose to elaborate on, or to refute, arguments made in either piece of writing.*

Will Kymlicka

Immigrants, Multiculturalism and Canadian Citizenship

Will Kymlicka received his B.A. in philosophy and politics from Queen's University in 1984, and his D.Phil. in philosophy from Oxford University in 1987. He is the author of six books: Liberalism, Community, and Culture (1989), Contemporary Political Philosophy (1990 and 2002), Multicultural Citizenship (1995), which was awarded the Macpherson Prize by the Canadian Political Science Association and the Bunche Award by the American Political

Science Association, Finding Our Way: Rethinking Ethnocultural Relations in Canada *(1998),* Politics in the Vernacular: Nationalism, Multiculturalism and Citizenship *(2001),* *and* Multicultural Odysseys: Navigating the New International Politics of Diversity *(2007).* *His works have been translated into 30 languages. He served a three-year term as President of the American Society for Political and Legal Philosophy (2004–6).*

1   In 1971, Canada embarked on a unique experiment by declaring a policy of official "multi-culturalism." According to Pierre Trudeau, who introduced the policy in the House of Commons, the policy had the following four aims: to support the cultural development of ethnocultural groups; to help members of ethnocultural groups to overcome barriers to full participation in Canadian society; to promote creative encounters and interchange among all ethnocultural groups; and to assist new Canadians in acquiring at least one of Canada's official languages.

2   Although the policy of multiculturalism was first adopted by the federal government, it was explicitly designed as a model for other levels of government, and indeed it has been copied widely. "Multiculturalism programs" can now be found, not just in the multiculturalism office of the federal government, but also at the provincial or municipal levels of government, and indeed within a wide range of public and private institutions, such as schools or businesses.

3   These policies are now under attack, perhaps more so today than at any time since 1971. The debate has heated up lately, in part because of two recent critiques of the multiculturalism policy: Neil Bissoondath's *Selling Illusions: The Cult of Multiculturalism in Canada* (Penguin 1994), and Richard Gwyn's *Nationalism Without Walls: The Unbearable Lightness of Being Canadian* (McClelland and Stewart 1995). Both make very similar claims about the results of the policy. In particular, both argue that multiculturalism has promoted a form of ethnic separatism amongst immigrants.

4   Thus Bissoondath says that multiculturalism has led to "undeniable ghettoization" (111). Rather than promoting integration, multiculturalism is encouraging the idea that immigrants should form "self-contained" ghettos "alienated from the mainstream." This ghettoization is "not an extreme of multiculturalism but its ideal: a way of life transported whole, a little outpost of exoticism preserved and protected" (110). He approvingly quotes Arthur Schlesinger's claim that multiculturalism rests upon a "cult of ethnicity" which "exaggerates differences, intensifies resentments and antagonisms, drives even deeper the awful wedges between races and nationalities. The endgame is self-pity and self-ghettoization" (98), or what Schlesinger calls "cultural and linguistic apartheid." According to Bissoondath, multiculturalism policy does not encourage immigrants to think of themselves as Canadians, and indeed even the children of immigrants "continue to see Canada with the eyes of foreigners. Multiculturalism, with its emphasis on the importance of holding on to the former or ancestral homeland, with its insistence that There is more important than Here, encourages such attitudes" (133).

5   Gwyn makes the same claim in similar language. He argues that "official multiculturalism encourages apartheid, or to be a bit less harsh, ghettoism" (274). The more multiculturalism policy has been in place, "the higher the cultural walls have gone up inside Canada" (8). Multiculturalism encourages ethnic

leaders to keep their members "apart from the mainstream," practising "what can best be described as mono-culturalism." In this way, "Our state encourages these gatekeepers to maintain what amounts, at worst, to an apartheid form of citizenship" (234).

6   If these claims were true, it would be a serious indictment of the policy. Unfortunately, neither Bissoondath nor Gwyn provide any empirical evidence for their claims. In order to assess their claims; therefore, I have tried to collect together some statistics which might bear on the question of whether multiculturalism has promoted ethnic separatism, and discouraged or impeded integration. I will start with evidence from within Canada, comparing ethnocultural groups before and after the adoption of the multiculturalism policy in 1971. I will then consider comparative evidence, to see how Canada compares with other countries, particularly those countries which rejected the principle of official multiculturalism.

The Domestic Evidence

7   How has the adoption of multiculturalism in 1971 affected the integration of immigrant groups in Canada? To answer this question requires some account of what "integration" involves. It is one of the puzzling features of the Gwyn/Bissoondath critique that they do not define exactly what they mean by integration. However, we can piece together some of the things which they see as crucial ingredients of integration: adopting a Canadian identity rather than clinging exclusively to one's ancestral identity; participating in broader Canadian institutions rather than participating solely in ethnic-specific institutions; learning an official language rather than relying solely on one's mother-tongue; having inter-ethnic friendships or even mixed-marriages rather than socializing entirely within one's ethnic group. These sorts of criteria do not form a comprehensive theory of "integration," but they seem to be at the heart of Gwyn and Bissoondath's concerns about multiculturalism, so they are a good starting-point.

8   *Citizenship:* I will start with the most basic form of integration—the decision of immigrants to become Canadian citizens. If the Gwyn/Bissoondath thesis were true, one would expect naturalization rates to have declined since the adoption of multiculturalism in 1971. In fact, however, naturalization rates have increased since 1971. This is particularly relevant since the economic incentives to naturalize have lessened over the last 25 years. Taking out Canadian citizenship is not needed to gain access to the labour market in Canada or to have access to social benefits. There are virtually no differences between citizens and permanent residents in their civil rights or social benefits—the right to vote is the only major legal benefit gained by naturalization. The primary reason for immigrants to take out citizenship, therefore, is that they identify with Canada: they want to formalize their membership in Canadian society and participate in the political life of the country.

9   Moreover, if we examine which groups are most likely to naturalize, we find that it is the "multicultural groups"—that is, immigrants from non-traditional sources for whom the multiculturalism policy is most relevant—which have the highest rate of naturalization. By contrast, immigrants from the United States and United Kingdom—neither of whom are seen in popular discourse as an "ethnic" or "multicultural" group—have the lowest rate of naturalization.

In other words, those groups which fall most clearly under the multiculturalism policy have shown the greatest desire to become Canadian, while those groups which fall outside the multiculturalism rubric have shown the least desire to become Canadian.

10   *Political Participation:* If the Gwyn/Bissoondath thesis were true, one would expect the political participation of ethnic groups to have declined since the adoption of multiculturalism in 1971. After all, political participation is a symbolic affirmation of citizenship and reflects an interest in the political life of the larger society. In fact, however, there is no evidence for a decline in participation. To take one relevant indicator, in the period prior to the adoption of multiculturalism between Confederation and the 1960s, non-British, non-French groups became increasingly underrepresented in Parliament, but since then the trend has been reversed, so that today they have almost as many MPs as one would expect given their share of the population.

11   Moreover, it is important to note the way ethnocultural groups participate in Canadian politics. They do not form separate ethnic-based parties, either on a group-by-group basis or even on a coalition basis. Instead, they participate overwhelmingly within pan-Canadian parties. Indeed, the two parties in Canada which are closest to being ethnic parties were created by and for those of English or French ancestry—namely, the Parti/Bloc Québécois, whose support is overwhelmingly found amongst Quebecers with French ancestry; and the Reform party, whose support is concentrated amongst WASPs. And perhaps the purest case of an ethnic party in Canada—the COR Party—was exclusively a WASP-based party. By contrast, immigrants have shown no inclination to support ethnic-based political parties and instead vote for the traditional national parties.

12   This is just one indicator of a more general point—namely, that immigrants are overwhelmingly supportive of, and committed to protecting, the basic political structure in Canada. We know that, were it not for the "ethnic vote," the 1995 referendum on secession in Quebec would have succeeded. In that referendum, ethnics overwhelmingly expressed their commitment to Canada. More generally, all the indicators suggest that immigrants quickly absorb and accept Canada's basic liberal-democratic values and constitutional principles, even if they came from countries which are illiberal or non-democratic. As Freda Hawkins puts it, "the truth is that there have been no riots, no breakaway political parties, no charismatic immigrant leaders, no real militancy in international causes, no internal political terrorism . . . , immigrants recognize a good, stable political system when they see one."

13   In short, if we look at indicators of legal and political integration, we see that since the adoption of multiculturalism in 1971 immigrants are more likely to become Canadians, and more likely to participate politically. And when they do participate, they do so through pan-ethnic political parties which uphold Canada's basic liberal democratic principles.

14   This sort of political integration is the main aim of a democratic state. But I suspect that individual Canadians are often more concerned with the social integration of immigrants than their political integration. Immigrants who participate in politics may be good democratic citizens, but if they can't speak English or French or are socially isolated in self-contained ethnic groups, then many

Canadians will perceive a failure of integration. So let us shift to two indicators of societal integration: namely, official language acquisition and intermarriage rates.

15   *Official Language Competence:* If the Gwyn/Bissoondath thesis were true, one would expect the desire of ethnocultural minorities to acquire official language competence to have declined since the adoption of multiculturalism in 1971. If immigrant groups are being "ghettoized" and "alienated from the mainstream," and are attempting to preserve their original way of life intact from their homeland, then presumably they have less reason to learn an official language. In fact, however, demand for ESL and FSL classes has never been higher, and indeed exceeds supply in many cities. Recent census statistics show that 98.6% of Canadians say that they can speak one of the official languages. This is a staggering statistic when one considers how many immigrants are elderly and/or illiterate in their mother-tongue, and who therefore find it extremely difficult to learn a new language. It is especially impressive given that the number of immigrants who arrive with knowledge of an official language has declined since 1971. If we set aside the elderly—who form the majority of Canadians who cannot speak an official language—the idea that there is a general decrease in immigrants' desire to learn an official language is absurd. Immigrants want to learn an official language, and do so. Insofar as their official language skills are lacking, the explanation is the lack of accessible and appropriate ESL classes, not the lack of desire.

16   *Inter-marriage Rates:* One final indicator worth looking at is inter-marriage rates. If the Gwyn/Bissoondath thesis were true, one would expect intermarriage rates to have declined since the adoption of multiculturalism in 1971, since the policy is said to have driven "even deeper the awful wedges between races and nationalities," and encouraged groups to retreat into their "monocultural" ghettoes, and hide behind "cultural walls." In fact, however, intermarriage rates have consistently increased since 1971. We see an overall decline in endogamy, both for immigrants and their native-born children. Moreover, we see a dramatic increase in social acceptance of mixed marriages. For example, whereas 52% of Canadians disapproved of black-white marriages in 1968, 81% approved of them in 1995.

17   In short, whether we look at naturalization, political participation, official language competence, or intermarriage rates, we see the same story. There is no evidence to support the claim that multiculturalism has decreased the rate of integration of immigrants or increased the separatism or mutual hostility of ethnic groups.

18   If we examined other indicators, we would get the same story. As Orest Kruhlak puts it, "In sum, irrespective of which variables one examines, including [citizenship acquisition, ESL, mother-tongue retention, ethnic association participation, intermarriage] or political participation, the scope of economic involvement, or participation in mainstream social or service organizations, none suggest a sense of promoting ethnic separateness."

The Comparative Evidence

19 I can make the same point another way. If the Bissoondath/Gwyn thesis were correct, we would expect Canada to perform worse on these indicators of integration than other countries which have not adopted an official multi-culturalism policy.

Both Gwyn and Bissoondath contrast the Canadian approach with the American approach, which exclusively emphasizes common identities and common values and refuses to provide public recognition or affirmation of ethnocultural differences. If Canada fared worse than the U.S. in terms of integrating immigrants, this would provide some indirect support for the Bissoondath/Gwyn theory.

20   In fact, however, Canada fares better than the United States on virtually any dimension of integration. Canada has higher naturalization rates than the United States—indeed, much higher, almost double. We also have higher rates of political participation, higher rates of official language acquisition, and lower rates of residential segregation. Canada also has higher rates of inter-ethnic friendships, and much greater approval for inter-marriage. Whereas 72% of Canadians approved of inter-racial marriages in 1988, only 40% of Americans approved of them, and 25% felt they should be illegal!

21   In short, on every indicator of integration, Canada, with its multiculturalism policy, fares better than the United States, with its repudiation of multiculturalism. We would find the same story if we compared Canada with other immigration countries which have rejected multiculturalism in favour of an exclusive emphasis on common identities—e.g., France.

22   Canada does better than these other countries, not only in our actual rates of integration, but also in our day-to-day sense of ethnic relations. In a 1997 survey, for example, people in twenty countries were asked whether they agreed that "different ethnic groups get along well here". The percentage of people who agreed was far higher in Canada (75%) than in the United States (58%) or France (51%).

23   This should not surprise us, since Canada does better than virtually any other country in the world in the integration of immigrants. The only comparable country is Australia, which is interesting, since it too has an official multiculturalism policy. Indeed, its multiculturalism policy was largely inspired by Canada's policy, although of course it has been adapted to Australia's circumstances. The two countries which are head and shoulders above the rest of the world in the successful integration of immigrants are the two countries with official multiculturalism policies. They are much more successful than any country which has rejected multiculturalism.

24   In short, there is not a shred of evidence to support the claim that multiculturalism is promoting ethnic separateness or impeding immigrant integration. Whether we examine the trends within Canada since 1971, or compare Canada with other countries, the conclusion is the same—the multiculturalism program is working. It is achieving what it set out to do: it is helping to ensure that those people who wish to express their ethnic identity are respected and accommodated, while simultaneously increasing the ability of immigrants to integrate into the larger society. Along with our fellow multiculturalists in Australia, Canada does a better job of respecting ethnic diversity while promoting societal integration than any other country.

Explaining the Debate

25 This raises a genuine puzzle. Why do so many intelligent and otherwise well-informed commentators agree that multiculturalism policy is impeding

integration? Part of the explanation is that many people have simply not examined the policy to see what it actually involves. For example, Gwyn and Bissoondath claim that *multiculturalism* tells new Canadians that they should practice "monoculturalism," preserving their inherited way of life intact, while not interacting with or learning from the members of other groups, or the larger society. According to Gwyn and Bissoondath, this sort of self-ghettoization is not so much an unintended consequence of the policy, but rather one of its explicit aims. Yet neither author quotes a single document published by the multiculturalism unit of the federal government to support this claim—none of their annual reports, demographic analysis, public education brochures, or program funding guidelines.

26   In reality, most of the focus of multiculturalism policy (and most of its funding) has been directed to promoting civic participation in the larger society and to increasing mutual understanding and cooperation between the members of different ethnic groups. More generally, the multiculturalism policy has never stated or implied that people are under any duty or obligation to retain their ethnic identity/practices "freeze-dried," or indeed to retain them at all. On the contrary, the principle that individuals should be free to choose whether to maintain their ethnic identity has been one of the cornerstones of the policy since 1971, and continues to guide existing multiculturalism programs. Multiculturalism is intended to make it possible for people to retain and express their identity with pride if they so choose, by reducing the legal, institutional, economic or societal obstacles to this expression. It does not penalize or disapprove of people who choose not to identify with their ethnic group, or describe them as poor citizens or as lesser Canadians.

27   One could multiply examples of these sorts of misinterpretations of the basic guidelines and purposes of the policy. But I think these are just symptoms of a deeper problem. The real problem, I think, is that critics of multiculturalism view the policy in isolation, as if it was the only government policy affecting the integration of immigrants. But multiculturalism is not the only, or even the primary, policy affecting the integration of immigrants. Instead, it is a modest part of a larger package of policies, which includes citizenship, education and employment policies. It is these other policies which are the major engines of integration. They all encourage, pressure, even legally force immigrants to take steps towards integrating into Canadian society.

28   For example, it is a legal requirement for gaining citizenship that the immigrant know an official language (unless they are elderly), as well as some basic information about Canadian history and institutions. Similarly, it is a legal requirement under provincial education acts that the children of immigrants learn an official language and learn a common core curriculum. Moreover, immigrants must know an official language to gain access to government-funded job training programs. Immigrants must know an official language in order to receive professional accreditation or to have their foreign training recognized. The most highly skilled pharmacist won't be granted a professional license to practice pharmacy in Canada if she can only speak Portuguese. And of course knowledge of an official language is a precondition for working in the bureaucracy or for gaining government contract work.

29   These citizenship, education and employment policies have always been the major pillars of government-sponsored integration in Canada, and they remain fully in place today. Moreover, if we examine the amount of money spent on these policies, it eclipses the money spent on multiculturalism. The government spends billions of dollars a year on language training and job training for immigrants, and on education for their children, compared to under $20 million a year for multiculturalism programs.

30   So Canada spends billions of dollars encouraging and pressuring immigrants to integrate into common educational, economic and political institutions operating in either French or English. This is the context within which multiculturalism operates, and multiculturalism can only be understood in this wider context. With such a tiny budget, multiculturalism could not possibly hope to compete with this government-sponsored integration, and does not try to do so. On the contrary, from the very beginning, multiculturalism has explicitly gone hand-in-hand with government measures to promote societal integration.

31   For example, one of the guiding principles of multiculturalism has been to promote official bilingualism in Canada. This is reflected in the very terminology which Trudeau employed when introducing the policy—namely, "multi-culturalism within a bilingual framework." It has been explicit from the beginning that multiculturalism works alongside the linguistic and institutional integration of immigrants.

32   Some critics see the phrase "multiculturalism within a bilingual framework" as incoherent or meaningless. But I think it has a very simple and compelling meaning. The idea is this: If Canada is going to pressure immigrants to integrate into common institutions operating in English or French, then we need to ensure that the terms of integration are fair. To my mind, this has two basic elements:

33   (a) we need to recognize that integration does not occur overnight, but rather is a difficult and long-term process which operates intergenerationally. Hence special accommodations are often required for immigrants on a transitional basis. For example, certain services should be available in the immigrants' mother tongue, and support should be provided for those groups and organizations within immigrant communities which assist in the settlement/integration process;

34   (b) we need to ensure that the common institutions into which immigrants are pressured to integrate provide the same degree of respect, recognition and accommodation of the identities and practices of ethnocultural minorities as they traditionally have been of WASP and French-Canadian identities. Otherwise, the promotion of English and French as official languages is tantamount to privileging the lifestyles of the descendants of the English or French settlers.

This requires a systematic exploration of our social institutions to see whether their rules, structures and symbols disadvantage immigrants. For example, we need to examine dress-codes, public holidays, or even height and weight restrictions to see whether they are biased against certain immigrant groups. We need to examine the portrayal of minorities in school curricula or the media to see if they are stereotypical or fail to recognize the contributions of ethnocultural groups to Canadian history or world culture. And so on.

35   These measures are needed to ensure that Canada is offering immigrants fair terms of integration. The idea of multiculturalism within a bilingual framework is, I think, precisely an attempt to define such fair terms of integration. And in my view, the vast majority of what is done under the heading of multiculturalism policy, not only at the federal level, but also at provincial and municipal levels, and indeed within school boards and private companies, can be defended as promoting fair terms of integration. Others may disagree with the fairness of some of these policies. The requirements of fairness are not always obvious, particularly in the context of people who have chosen to enter a country. How to define fair terms of integration is a debate that we can and should have. The claim that multiculturalism is anti-integrationist, however, is a red herring.

DISCUSSION QUESTIONS

1. What claims does the writer identify as ones made by Bissoondath and Gwyn that "would be a serious indictment of the policy" if they were accurate?

2. What evidence does the writer offer countering the claims made by Bissoondath and Gwyn?

3. Identify some of the argumentative technique used by the writer to persuade the audience of the inaccuracy of the claims made by Bissoondath and Gwyn.

4. The author chooses to end and not begin his essay with a section entitled "Explaining the Debate." What possible reasons might he have had for the positioning of this section here? Would the essay be more or less effective if organized differently? Explain.

5. In your own words, explain what you think the writer means by "fair terms of integration," and how he thinks that the multiculturalism policy promotes "fair terms of integration."

TOWARD KEY INSIGHTS

Do you agree that Canada more successfully integrates immigrants into society than do most other countries? Explain.

Explain the author's assertion that "the requirements of fairness are not always obvious . . . in the context of people who have chosen to enter the country." Do you agree or not?

In your view, what has Kymlicka left out of his argument that might have made it more persuasive?

SUGGESTION FOR ORAL ARGUMENT *Review the* Multiculturalism Act of Canada *and research statistics on the cultural diversity of Canada's population over the past 40 or so years. Also consider evidence on the level of acceptance and tolerance of cultural diversity in Canada. Come to class prepared to argue either side of the following proposition:*

The *Multiculturalism Act of Canada* has been successful in contributing to the development of Canada as a country that encourages and welcomes cultural diversity.

SUGGESTIONS FOR WRITING *Write a persuasive essay directed to people in a particular community about one of the following topics:.*

The value, for the individual or for the larger Canadian society, of people retaining their ethnic heritage.

The need for more inclusiveness and acceptance of cultural differences.

The need for more governmental support of English language training and/or other services for immigrants.

Marina Jiménez

Domestic Crisis

Marina Jiménez, a 40-year-old Edmonton-born journalist, has worked at CBC TV, the Vancouver Sun, *the* National Post, *the* Edmonton Journal *and the* Globe and Mail *for 16 years. She has covered stories in Latin America, the Middle East, Asia, and North America. She has won numerous awards, including a 2003 National Newspaper Award for her coverage of the immigration and refugee beat at* The Globe and Mail, *and two 2001 National Magazine Gold Awards for a story in* Saturday Night *magazine on the Chinese boat people who washed up on the shores of British Columbia in 1999, and then headed for New York City's Chinatown. She lives in Toronto and works for* The Globe and Mail *newspaper.*

1   When Joyelle arrives at work, it is 7:45 on Monday morning and the bags of garbage from the weekend are stacked in the hallway of the Pintos' well-appointed condominium. The half-empty wineglasses are strewn around her employers' living room, and the faint odour of stale beer is in the air. Lugging the plastic bags down the hallway to the garbage chute and clearing up the dishes from the previous night's party have become rituals for Joyelle (all names have been changed to protect privacy).

2   In the bathroom, the mirror squeaks as she wipes it down with Windex. She grimaces at herself in the glass before passing a sponge over the white-tiled walls. Joyelle hates cleaning almost as much as she hates the pungent smells of Tilex, Javex and the other produces stacked inside the bathroom cupboard.

In the bedroom, dirty tissues litter the floor. And then there's the bedding. She has to wash and iron several sets of sheets and pillowcases. "*Mwen anwajé Bon Dyé ou Kay endé mwen* [I'm angry. God help me]," Joyelle murmurs under her breath in the Creole patois of her homeland, St. Lucia.

3   Dusting and vacuuming are not the life Joyelle had hoped for when she became the Pintos' nanny more than three years ago. Back then, she spent her days taking Maria, the family's only child, to the park, pushing her on the swing and going to the library to read Maria's favourite Robert Munsch books out loud. But now that Maria goes to kindergarten all day, Joyelle's job as a caregiver has been transformed into that of a cleaning lady. She is being paid $300 a week, while the average salary for live-out nannies in Toronto starts at about $400.

4   Joyelle doesn't know how much longer she can put up with this job and its many indignities. She eats the family's leftovers for lunch, knowing her employers would balk if she helped herself to their freshly made food or the fruit and vegetables they say are for the child. She accepts the cast-off clothing they eagerly give her, knowing she will throw out or donate most of it.

5   I am interested in Joyelle's plight because I have a nanny, and her story makes me reflect on what kind of employer I am: do I take care to buy my nanny her favourite foods? Do I treat her with respect?

6   While nannies were once thought of as servants of the upper classes, today many middle-class parents hire them because of the high cost of putting multiple children in day care. Moreover, many day cares close at 6 p.m., leaving people who must work late struggling to pick up their kids on time.

7   Joyelle knows there are better employers out there, yet she feels trapped: If she quits and leaves on bad terms, she is confronted by the real possibility the family will reveal her secret. Because although Joyelle's life has all the trappings of normalcy—she has a bank account, a library card, a bus pass and a position at the local church—she shouldn't even be in Canada. If the government discovered she was working, it could deport her back to St. Lucia.

8   Joyelle is one of many nannies who toil in Canada's underground army of illegal workers. St. Lucians do not need visas to enter the country, and they know that within days they can land jobs in this vast hidden economy. Some Canadian families even prefer illegal nannies because they do not have to remit taxes, CPP or employment insurance to the government on their nanny's behalf.

9   "This is not what I signed up for," says Joyelle. "If I'd wanted to be a cleaner, I'd be a cleaner and earn a lot more money and come and go as I please." The petite 29-year-old is fashionably dressed in black wedge-heel shoes and chunky silver jewelry; her long braids are gathered in a loose ponytail, and accountant's glasses perch on her nose. "When you get really fed up with your job, it turns you into a monster and you start cursing inside," she says.

10   Illegal workers like Joyelle wait tables in Halifax, wash dishes in Montreal and pick fruit in British Columbia's Lower Mainland. It's easy to judge these black-market workers and their employers harshly, but anyone who has ever paid cash for a backyard deck or an evening of babysitting has helped to keep this market afloat.

11   Of course, not all illegal labourers are in the same boat. Take construction workers, for example. Unions and organizations such as the Greater Toronto Home Builders' Association are lobbying on behalf of this almost exclusively male workforce. Last September, former citizenship and immigration minister Judy Sgro was reviewing a proposal to regularize the status of more than 10 000 undocumented workers—including house framers, painters and builders—as long as they had found work and had not relied on social assistance. Joe Volpe, Sgro's successor, is expected to be in favour of legalizing these undocumented workers as well.

12   But no union is lobbying for nannies—legal and otherwise—who care for thousands of Canadian children while their mothers and fathers go to work. Nannies' jobs are not as high-profile as construction workers'—nor are they as clearly tied to big business and economic growth. Instead they are a largely

invisible and overlooked workforce, performing women's work and answering to mainly female employers.

13   As one of these employers myself, I have to ask, Is building houses really more important than caring for the nation's children?

14   When Joyelle was a girl, she helped out on her mother's banana plantation. They didn't have a lot of money, so her mother relied on an extended network of friends and relatives to help raise her large family. There was no such thing as a nanny, though Joyelle's mother had seven children.

15   After she finished high school, Joyelle decided to come to Canada for an extended visit—a rite of passage for many young people from Trinidad, St. Lucia, St. Vincent and other Caribbean islands. Back then, Joyelle had never heard of Canada's Live-In Care-giver Program—one of the few legal entry routes for foreign nannies. The program requires applicants to have the equivalent of a high-school education and six months of training or 12 months of experience as care-givers, and it allows them to apply for permanent residence in Canada after two years of employment. Unlike the Philippines, where nanny training schools often help students navigate the Live-In Caregiver Program, the Caribbean islands are not well set up to exploit this legal mode of entry into Canada. (From 2001 to 2004, 15 893 Filipinos received work permits through the program, compared with 38 Caribbeans.)

16   Instead, Joyelle simply flew into Toronto as a visitor and got lucky. Within weeks, she was hired as a live-in care-giver by a couple with a three-month-old daughter. The family didn't mind that she had no legal right to work—something Joyelle never tried to hide. Best of all, unlike the Pintos, Joyelle's first employers were genuinely nice people who valued her and her work, even if they didn't have deep pockets.

17   "The truth is, we couldn't afford to pay a Canadian live-out nanny," recalls her former employer. "They had degrees in early childhood education and wanted as much as $32 000 a year. I'm not saying they don't deserve it, but we just couldn't do it on our salaries. We were really lucky to find Joyelle." They paid her $275 a week plus board and a room with an ensuite bathroom—an arrangement that worked for everyone.

18   "I really felt like a member of their family," says Joyelle. "The more the parents treat you like you are their people, the more you feel comfortable, and the more love you'll have in your heart. You will pass that love on to their kids."

19   She would fuss over her young charge, singing her Creole church songs such as *Bon Dyé pardonné mwen* [God forgive me]." The baby girl loved her and even called her mama, but Joyelle never noticed any jealousy from the child's mother, Terri—only a sense of wistfulness as she rushed out the door to commute from Pickering, Ont., to her sales job in Toronto. She would kiss her daughter goodbye every day and say, "I love you both." After Joyelle's first week on the job, Terri gave her a journal, and after her first year, a gold cross, in recognition of Joyelle's devout Roman Catholicism.

20   Brian, the father, spent hours studying the Citizenship and Immigration Canada website to see if he could help his young employee resolve her immigration problems. "I really wanted to sponsor her, but she would have had to leave the country and wait six months, and there was no guarantee it would work out," he says. "In the end, we decided it was too complicated."

21   After two years with the family, Joyelle also began to question whether being a nanny was really her long-term goal. She decided to enroll in an evening business program at a downtown college so that, if she were ever deported, she would at least return to St. Lucia with a new skill. But going to school meant she had to find an employer closer to the city's centre. "I cried for nights on end. I told myself I wouldn't get as close to the next child," Joyelle says.

22   The family was heartsick at her decision to leave but understood that she felt isolated living in the suburbs without a car to drive and unable to go home for a vacation because of her illegal status. Brian faxed in her registration for school and drove her downtown on the first day of classes. "I never would have found my way around campus without him," Joyelle says.

23   If the fit is right, the relationship between a nanny and her employer is like no other. I know because I have come to consider the nanny we employ as part of our family. I am heartbroken wondering how I will cope when she goes on maternity leave to have a baby of her own. What other person has seen me in my pyjamas, my hair askew, with dark bags under my eyes? Who else has observed me lose my car keys every morning, and then when I finally do leave for work, watch me drive my car over my rock garden, becoming impaled on a large stone? Still, she has the tact and sensitivity not to laugh—at least not in my face—at my foibles. And, of course, she loves my child as her own.

24   It is with this mutual understanding—a shared recognition of the peculiar intimacy of the nanny-employer relationship—that Joyelle and I connect. When I visit her apartment, she tells me what she liked best about her old employers— their respect—and what she likes least about her current bosses—their stinginess.

25   The three St. Lucian roommates she shares her $1400-a-month townhouse with all work as nannies. Only one has an official work authorization. Though they try not to dwell on it, these young women are consumed by one thing: how to regularize their status.

26   "The fear of being found out as an illegal is something you carry with you wherever you go, even if you try not to think about it," says Joyelle, flopping down on the couch. "When you hear on the news about someone being deported, your heart beats faster and you begin to think of all the different things you should be doing to better yourself in case it happens to you."

27   "People come here and they know it's risky, but they also know there's a demand for them," adds one of her roommates. "And back home, it's hard to get a job. The key is to get a good family."

28   Suddenly, Joyelle turns to me, knowing that I have a 2-year-old boy at home, and says, "What do you think? I could go back home for six months, then you could bring me in under the Live-In Caregiver Program. Will you do it? Will you sponsor me?"

29   Briefly, I consider the possibility of sponsoring and hiring Joyelle, who seems an ideal replacement for our soon-to-depart nanny. But I know I can't wait six months for her. Who will care for my boy in the meantime?

30   It is Sunday, the following week. The rain pounds down outside, while inside a modest church in the north end of Toronto, a few dozen Caribbean congregants interrupt the pastor with hallelujahs. They affirm their belief in Christ before breaking into joyful hymns. Joyelle worships at this Pentecostal church because she finds Catholic mass—as celebrated in Canada—too austere. On this particular day, she fingers her Bible and prays for courage.

31   The next day, Joyelle finally feels ready. She approaches her employer, Mrs. Pinto, in the dining room and looks her straight in the eye. "I am unhappy cleaning all the time, and there is no enjoyment now that your daughter is in school. I don't want to be a cleaner," she blurts out.

32   "I would like to keep you, but if you are unhappy, you can go," Mrs. Pinto replies. Relief washes over Joyelle. Implicit in Mrs. Pinto's release is the indication that there will be no serious consequences for Joyelle. Still, the Pintos are stingy until the end: They let Joyelle go almost right away, after more than three years of employment, and they don't offer her an extra cent.

33   Again out of work, Joyelle finally seeks the advice of a Toronto immigration lawyer who has seen hundreds of cases like hers. He outlines three choices: Joyelle can file an application to be granted permanent-resident status on a humanitarian basis, but he doesn't like her odds. She can return to St. Lucia and apply to the Live-In Caregiver Program (though he worries she may be penalized for working here without legal status). Or Joyelle can bide her time and see if the immigration minister really will introduce a program to regularize the status of all illegal labourers—and not just construction workers.

34   In the end, Joyelle decides to stay in the shadows and wait for a time when the contribution she and other illegal nannies are making to our economy—and our society—is recognized and valued. "All I am doing is trying to better myself," she says. "I think I would make an ideal new Canadian."

35   I think so, too.

DISCUSSION QUESTIONS

1. How does the writer draw the reader in?
2. What is the effect of the writer's first person point of view and use of personal experience?
3. How does the writer show sympathetic understanding of those who hire illegal nannies?
4. Why does the writer compare construction workers to nannies (paragraphs 12–13)?
5. How does the writer use emotional and ethical appeals?
6. What is the thesis, and why is it located so late in the argument? What hope does the writer express toward the end of the essay?

TOWARD KEY INSIGHTS

To what extent does the Canadian economy depend in part on the labour of undocumented workers such as nannies like Joyelle? What ethical problems are raised by the use of undocumented workers?

The writer refers to the "peculiar intimacy of the nanny–employer relationship." Have you ever been an employee or an employer in a relationship such as this— perhaps housecleaning or tutoring—that produced an unusual kind of intimacy? What were the power dynamics like? What were the pluses and minuses of this kind of connection?

SUGGESTION FOR ORAL ARGUMENT *After researching both sides of the argument, come to class prepared to argue either side of the following proposition:*

The Canadian government should fund a free daycare program for children aged five and younger.

SUGGESTIONS FOR WRITING

1. After investigating the problem parents have of finding high-quality, affordable daycare for their children, write an essay arguing for one or more solutions to this problem. You may decide to address parents or a governmental agency.

2. Research the problems associated with a different kind of undocumented labour, such as immigrant agricultural work in Canada, and write an argument proposing a different policy.

Julie Traves

The Church of Please and Thank You

Julie Traves has spent several years in the publishing industry in roles ranging from promoting writers to promoting her own writing. She is currently based in Toronto, where she is part of The Globe and Mail's *editorial team and contributes pieces on arts, society and ideas to newspapers and magazines including* The Globe, *the* Toronto Star, *the* National Post, Maisonneuve, The Walrus, Canadian Business, *and* THIS.

1   Michelle Szabo smiles encouragingly as a young businessman talks about his hobbies in broken English. She is a Canadian teacher at Aeon's language school in Kawagoe, Japan. He is a prospective student she's charged to recruit as part of her job. The two meet in a drab five-storey office building outside the train station. The room is so small it fits only a table and two chairs. But making the sell to would-be learners has little to do with décor. What counts is Szabo's final handshake.

2   More than contact with an attractive young woman, her personal touch symbolizes a grasp on a better life. In the competitive marketplace of Japan, English test scores make or break job applications. Getting ahead means getting into classes with teachers like Szabo. "I would ask so many people, 'Do you expect to use English in your life?' And most people would say 'No, no, no, I just need this test score,'" says Szabo. "I think it's sort of a given for all families—it's like food, shelter, English." Some sarariiman (salarymen) were so excited they trembled when they took her hand.

3   In addition to the 380 million people worldwide who use English as their first language, it's estimated there are 350 million to 500 million speakers of English as a foreign language (EFL)—and the number is growing. For people from affluent and developing nations alike, it is clear that the secret passwords to safety,

wealth and freedom can be whispered only in English. Even 66 percent of French citizens, linguistic protectionists *par excellence*, agreed they needed to speak English in a 2001 Eurobarometer poll. While thinkers such as John Ralston Saul proclaim the death of globalization, locals from countries around the world are clamouring for English training.

4   Enter thousands of Westerners who spread the English gospel overseas each year. Like the Christian missionaries who came before them, many are young, have a blind faith in the beliefs they've grown up with and are eager to make their mark on the world. Unlike the 19- to 26-year-olds who proselytize for the Latter-day Saints, however, these new missionaries are also out for adventure, good times—and hard cash. Part of a $7.8-billion industry, instructors can earn $400 a month plus room and board in China and up to $4000 a month in Japan. That's a lot more than a McJob back home.

5   But students expect more than lessons in syntax and style. EFL teachers are also hired to share Western customs and values. "'Let's have lunch sometime' doesn't mean stop by my office tomorrow and we'll go out and have lunch. It means something more general, like 'It's been nice talking to you and maybe at some point I'd like to continue the conversation,'" says Diane Pecorari, a senior lecturer at the University of Stockholm. "When you're teaching formulae like 'Please,' 'Thank you,' 'Can I split the cheque?' you also have to teach the context in which they come up. That means teaching culture."

6   But what is the effect of that culture on students' dialects, customs—their very identity? Ian Martin, an English professor at York University's Glendon College in Toronto, points to a troubling precedent for the current explosion of EFL. "One of the big moments in the spread of English took place in India in 1835. [British politician] Thomas Babington Macaulay proposed that English be used to create a class of Indian middlemen who would be sympathetic to British interests, without the necessity of large numbers of British citizens coming out and running the show." Instead of invading India at great economic and human cost, English allowed the British to transform the country from within. With English on the tip of their tongues, Indians could much more easily swear allegiance to England.

7   Today's linguistic imperialism has a similar goal. Where once English facilitated the staffing of colonial offices, now it helps fill the cubicles of multinational corporations. Teaching locals Western speech and when it's appropriate to use it no longer transforms them into perfect Englishmen: it makes them into perfect businessmen and women. The politics of English haven't changed—the language simply serves a new corporate master.

8   To be sure, even those who are fascinated by the countries where they teach sometimes can't help transforming "the natives" as part of their work abroad. Canadian Michael Schellenberg, who taught in Japan more than a decade ago, loved learning about Japanese customs but also sheepishly admits he urged students to express themselves—quite against the Japanese grain. "One of the sayings in Japan is that the nail that sticks up will get pounded down. They wanted people to conform," he says. "I remember classes where I'd be like, 'Just be yourself!' As someone in my early 20s, I had a pretty good sense of how I thought the world should be. I felt pretty confident being forthright about that."

9   Teaching materials subtly suggest the superiority of Western values. Produced primarily in the US and UK, textbooks propagate the advantages of materialism, individualism and sexual liberation. For example, Ian Martin recalls an Indian friend's reaction to one textbook that showed Jack and Jane meeting in lesson one and dancing alone together by lesson three. "Where are the parents?" his friend wondered.

10   Some newer textbooks are more culturally sensitive. But in many of the books currently in circulation, says Martin, "there's nothing about environmentalism, nothing about spirituality, nothing about, say, respecting non-native [English] speakers. And there's very little realism in any of the language learning material that I've seen. It's this mythic world of dream fulfillment through consumerism and Westernization." The Aeon language franchise in Japan uses Cameron Diaz and Celine Dion as its poster girls.

11   Of course, not all teachers aggressively peddle a mythic world—some have their soapbox thrust upon them. In her book *The Hemingway Book Club of Kosovo*, California writer Paula Huntley chronicles her experience teaching English to the survivors of the area's brutal ethnic clashes. Huntley doesn't believe her language and culture are better than any other. She wants to learn from the Kosovars as much as they want to learn from her. It's her students who are convinced that the American way is the way forward, that English is the true language of progress.

12   Before leaving for Kosovo, Huntley crams for four weeks to complete an English as a second language instructors' certificate. But this is not what impresses the owner of the Cambridge School in Kosovo, a man named Ahmet whose house and library of 5000 books were destroyed by the Serbs. Barely looking at her CV, he tells her she's hired. "'You are an American,'" he says. "'So you can teach our students more than English. You can teach them how to live together, with others, in peace. You can teach them how to work, how to build a democracy, how to keep trying no matter what the odds.'"

13   Then there is the conflicted experience of Kathy Lee. She teaches at Guangdong Industry Technical College in China. In a suburb called Nanhai, the school is putting up satellite facilities eight times larger than the main campus. Teaching labs have banks of computers and a plasma screen TV. But like so much of the country, there is such impatience to forge ahead that Lee conducts her three classes a week amid construction because the school is expanding so fast.

14   Her pupils are equally anxious to take part in the country's massive business boom. Though most of them have been studying English since primary school, their fluency is strained. They tell her: "The world is growing and many people speak English. If I want to do business with them, I must speak English well too!" What students want is a foreign teacher to help them get up to speed. That's why the college has hired the 23-year-old Canadian at 4000 RMB a month, two to three times the average salary for Chinese teachers.

15   The payoff is more than just monetary for Lee. Born in China but raised in Canada, she accepted the job so she could live in Hong Kong, within a short train ride from her sick grandmother. But now, her feelings have deepened. "When the schools were asking me why I wanted to teach in China, I BS'd and

said it's because I wanted to learn about my 'other' culture," she says. "But the more I said it, the more I believed it. Now, I feel that I need to be here and learn what it means to be a Chinese person."

16   Yet the way of life Lee is trying to understand is challenged by her methodology in the classroom. By the end of term, her students will be well practised in communication modes that are entirely un-Chinese. Lee worries about this— and the general English fever sweeping the country that even includes television programs that aim to teach English.

17   "I know that if everyone spoke English in the world there would still be cultural differences, but the differences between cultures will become less and less," she says. "Why is China pushing English so hard? [My students] get the sense that their own language is not good enough. To prosper, they need English. What was wrong with the way it was before? Why do you have to be Western to be competitive in business?"

18   If it is tough for teachers to come to terms with these questions, it is even more complex for students. While some are in what Martin calls a "process of self-assimilation," others are much more ambivalent about the course they are on. These students may be struggling with the political implications of learning English in places where the language is associated with American or British hegemony. Or they may simply recognize that as English proliferates, the survival of their own customs and dialects is under threat.

19   Take 27-year-old Sanghun Cho of South Korea. He is a graduate student in Toronto and has a Canadian girlfriend. But when he thinks of English, he also thinks of the US. "It's a kind of dilemma for Koreans," he says. "I don't like America in Korea because they want to control the Korean government; but to survive in this kind of competitive environment I have to speak English and I have to know what English culture is."

20   Another South Korean student puts it even more bluntly. Part of a multinational research project Martin has been conducting over the past five years to examine why students study English as a foreign language, the student was asked to draw a picture of his future with English and describe the picture. He sketched Uncle Sam extending a fishing line from the US across the Pacific Ocean, a hook dangling above the student's open mouth. His description: "English is the bait that Americans are using to catch Koreans in their net."

21   Marta Andersson is a part of the last generation of Poles forced to learn Russian in school. When she was able to study English after the fall of communism, she was thrilled. On the one hand, it paid off: she got a good job in Poland, is now studying abroad and speaks English at home with her husband. On another level, though, Andersson is aware that using English is eroding part of what her people fought for. "I have just started to lose the sense of my native language and just wait when it will become moribund," she says, "Yet I cannot imagine my future without the presence of English."

22   Swede Hélène Elg is also concerned about the fate of her language as English words invade it the way they do in "Chinglish" and "Franglais." "I think it's important to separate the languages in order to 'protect' our own," she says. "I realize that languages evolve, allowing new words to come into use, but we should be aware of that development and be cautious about it. The reason I feel

this is because languages are so much more than just words. Words have cultural connotations. As with languages, cultures evolve, but that development should not be about adopting another culture."

23   Can students fight back? it's arguable that withdrawing from English would exact too high a cost for those who want to be a part of a global economy. Instead, what's changing is how people from around the world use English. Rather than simply conforming to an English steeped in Western values, many students are co-opting the language for themselves.

24   On an internet discussion board for EFL teachers, one teacher writes: "I feel the need of reminding our students and young colleagues that the purpose of learning English is not for us to 'speak and act' like an English person . . . but to 'speak English' as an educated Indonesian." Similarly, one Cuban who participated in Martin's project drew a picture of a rocket being launched into the sky with the description: "English is the rocket which will allow Cuba to tell its own stories to the world."

25   A new "global" English is emerging that is a bridge language between cultures, not simply a language that supplants other cultures. As Salman Rushdie is quoted as saying in the best-selling history *The Story of English*, "English, no longer an English language, now grows from many roots; and those whom it once colonized are carving out large territories within the language for themselves. The Empire is striking back."

26   Along with students, many teachers are joining the fight to create a more egalitarian English. They do not want to be cultural colonialists. As David Hill, a teacher in Istanbul, writes in *The Guardian Weekly*: "English is global for highly dubious reasons: colonial, military and economic hegemony, first of the British, now of the US. . . . If we are not to be imperialists then we must help our students to express themselves, not our agenda."

27   To do that, new programs are emerging, like the Certificate in the Discipline of Teaching English as an International Language, which Martin coordinates at Glendon College. It pays close attention to issues of cultural sensitivity and autonomy when training teachers. As Martin says, "We're trying to come to grips with the effect of globalization on language teaching. Do we want a globalization that is going to be assimilationist to Western models of communication only? Or do we want to help people gain a voice in English?"

28   Michelle Szabo is one teacher who has tried to give her students a voice. After her stint in Japan, she took a job at Chonbuk National University in South Korea from 2003 to 2004. On one November morning, she recalls encouraging discussion about the power of English. Her hope was to give pause to students who'd never considered the impact of studying English on their lives—as well as a place for those who had thought about it—a rare place to vent.

29   And there was plenty of venting as students heatedly debated face-to-face from desks arranged in a conversation-friendly horseshoe configuration. "One side was feeling very pressured and resentful," says Szabo, "and one side was saying, 'No, [English is] opening doors for us.'" Szabo tried to "equalize" the class by sitting among the students. She also said little. She wanted a forum that conveyed the message, "I'm not here to change you, to acculturize you, to force my beliefs on you," she says.

30   But even Szabo's new self-consciousness about what it is she is selling to her students along with English grammar has limits. English has irrevocably changed and acculturated the world already. Even if locals don't want to participate in the global capitalist machine, they need English to truly challenge it. As one of Szabo's students couldn't help but point out during the debate, "Isn't it ironic we're discussing the effect of English—in English?"

DISCUSSION QUESTIONS

1. Explain the significance of the title.

2. What do you think is the thesis of the essay? If it is explicit, where is it located? Why does it come here rather than earlier?

3. How does the writer build a bridge with her audience by showing that she understands the ambiguities and complexities of her issue? How does she avoid blaming English teachers and thus alienating potential readers (paragraphs 8, 10, and 11)?

4. Cite examples where the author uses rational appeals such as statistics or expert opinion, and where she uses emotional and ethical appeals in her argument.

5. This essay incorporates writing strategies such as illustration, and cause/effect analysis. What is the point of illustrations such as those used in paragraphs 1–2, 8, 9, 11, 12–16, 18, 19, 20, and 21? What is the point of the cause/effect analysis used in paragraphs 4, 6, 8, 13, 14–16, and 19?

6. In some ways, this essay is structured as a problem/solution argument. What is the problem, and why does the author spend so much time establishing that there is a problem? What possible solutions are suggested for students of English and for teachers of English?

7. How effective is the concluding paragraph? What irony does it point out?

TOWARD KEY INSIGHTS

This essay argues that Westerners who teach English overseas cannot help but teach Western values along with teaching the language. How does learning a new language necessitate learning different ways of seeing, or different values? How can learning a new way of seeing bring losses as well as gains?

This essay criticizes the subtle bias of teaching materials that promote Western values (paragraph 9). Have you noticed any kind of bias in textbooks or teaching materials that you have been exposed to? Explain.

Think of jobs that you have done, or different kinds of work that you have considered going into. What unintended social consequences, negative or positive, might follow from doing this kind of work?

SUGGESTION FOR ORAL ARGUMENT *After researching both sides of the argument, come to class prepared to argue either side of the following proposition:*

In Canada, linguistic diversity must be maintained in order to ensure that cultural diversity is maintained.

SUGGESTIONS FOR WRITING

1. If you have taught or studied English as a second language, respond to Julie Traves's argument that teaching English is a form of "linguistic imperialism."

2. Write an argument that some other kind of activity usually viewed as positive—for example, travelling to a Third World country, or adopting a baby from a foreign country—may have negative effects on people's values or sense of identity.

3. Following the structure of this argument, establish that something usually perceived as benign is actually a problem; then recommend some possible solutions.

RESEARCH GUIDE

Much of your academic and workplace writing requires some type of research—obtaining information from one or more sources to help achieve your writing purpose. The nature of your writing task and the demands of the situation determine the format you use and the way you document your sources.

This section explores the research tools and procedures you can use to develop papers and reports. Writers commonly draw from secondary sources such as books, magazines, newspapers, and other printed sources, as well as electronic sources, in order to prepare research papers. Other situations call for primary research—the type that you plan and carry out yourself. The three chapters in this section will help you to meet these writing demands.

Chapter 15 explains how to choose a suitable library research topic and then carry out the necessary steps to write research papers in both MLA and APA style. The chapter includes a continuing case history that leads to a finished paper, complete with margin notes that provide guidance as you prepare your own paper.

Chapter 16 explains and illustrates the most common types of primary research strategies—interviews, questionnaires, and direct observations. In each case, student models, annotated with margin notes, embody the key features of that strategy.

Chapter 17 shows how to prepare correct references for your paper's "Works Cited" page or bibliography. It also shows the correct formats for references within the body of the paper, explains how to handle quotations, and offers guidelines for avoiding plagiarism.

Together, the material in these three chapters should provide all the information you need to complete your research assignments.

CHAPTER 15

Strategies for Researching: Using Secondary Research

Scene: A dark, sinister-looking laboratory. In the centre of the stage stands a large laboratory bench crowded with an array of mysterious chemistry apparatus. Tall, cadaverous, and foreboding, Dr. Frankenslime leers as he pours the contents of a tube through a funnel and into a bubbling flask. A short, hunched-over figure looks on with interest. Suddenly the doctor spreads his arms wide and flashes a sardonic smile.

Frankenslime: Igor! At last! At last I've got it! With this fluid, I can control . . .

Research, yes. But not all researchers are mad scientists, or even scientists—or mad, for that matter. You might not be any of these things, but no doubt you have been asked to prepare *research papers* for writing classes in the past. This type of assignment typically asks you to gather information from a variety of sources and then focus, organize, and present it in a formal paper that documents your sources. When you finish the paper, you have a solid grasp of your topic and pride in your accomplishment. Moreover, the research process familiarizes you with the correct handling of documentation. Finally, the experience helps you learn how to meet the research demands of future courses and jobs.

For many students, the thought of writing a research paper triggers feelings of anxiety and fears of drudgery. Some feel overwhelmed by the amount of material in a college or university library and the need to make a lengthy search for useful information. Others doubt that they could have anything to say about a topic that hasn't already been said: What's the point of simply rehashing what experts have already said much better? Still others are daunted by how much there might actually be to say about their topic.

But writing a research paper really isn't so formidable. Once you acquaint yourself with library and electronic resources that contain information related to your area of interest, you can learn to limit the scope of your topic so that it doesn't balloon out of control. As you read what others have written about your topic or research question, you will develop new ideas and begin to formulate your own conclusions. You may even notice that you have begun to enjoy the process of becoming a relative expert on your topic!

Research writing is common to both coursework and on-the-job writing. A history professor might ask you to write about the economic effects of World War II on the Canadian homefront. A business instructor might ask you to trace the history of a company, evaluate an internet advertising campaign, or review corporate management strategies. A building trades instructor might call for a short report comparing the effectiveness of several new insulating materials. At work, a marketing analyst might report on the development costs, sales potential, and competition for a product the company is developing. An engineer might write a journal article that summarizes recent developments in plastic fabrication. A physical therapist might prepare a seminar paper that evaluates different exercise programs to follow arthroscopic surgery.

Whatever the writing project, let your purpose guide your research and determine the information you use. Rather than trying to include everything you have read or learned in your final paper, sift through your information to select that which is relevant to your thesis and your conclusions.

LEARNING ABOUT YOUR LIBRARY

Before starting a library research paper, take time to familiarize yourself with your library. Many libraries offer guided tours, and almost all of them display floor plans that show where and how the resources are organized; your school may even offer or require a library orientation seminar. If your library doesn't offer learning sessions, you can explore it on your own, or ask a librarian for help. As you do, note the following features:

> *Library Catalogue:* All libraries have an internal index of their books and often most of their other holdings as well. These indexes are usually computerized and can be accessed through the internet. Pages 399–400 explain how to use library catalogues.

> *Databases:* Databases provide searchable listings of articles in magazines and newspapers and often even provide the full text of the article. Most libraries purchase subscriptions to commercial databases specializing in particular subject areas. Pages 401–404 explain how to use databases effectively.

> *Internet Search Terminals:* Most libraries have computers reserved for internet access. Internet access to library catalogues and databases is often available as well,

allowing users to search and order materials from home, prior to picking them up at the library. Pages 405–407 discuss effective use of the internet.

Stacks: These are the bookshelves that hold books and bound periodicals (magazines and newspapers). Stacks are either open or closed. Open stacks allow you to go directly to the books you want, take them off the shelf, and check them out. Closed stacks do not allow you direct access to shelved material. Instead, a staff member brings you what you want.

Periodical Area: Here you find current and recent issues of magazines, journals, and newspapers. If your topic calls for articles that have appeared within the last few months, you're likely to find them in this area.

Microfilm and Microfiche Files: Microfilm is a filmstrip bearing a series of photographically reduced printed pages. Microfiche is a small card with a set of photographically reduced pages mounted on it. While many larger publications have been archived online, most of a library's magazine and newspaper collection is often only available on film. Ask a librarian how to work the viewing machines.

Reserve Area: This area contains books that instructors have had removed from general circulation so students can use them for particular courses. Ordinarily, you can keep these books for only a few hours or overnight.

Reference Area: This area houses the library's collection of specialized encyclopedias and indexes, almanacs, handbooks, dictionaries, and other reference tools that you may want to use as you delve into your topic. You'll also find one or more reference guides—for example, Eugene P. Sheehy's *Guide to Reference Books* (1996)—that can direct you to useful reference tools. To ensure that these books are always available, most libraries require that they be read within the building. A librarian is usually on duty in the reference area to answer questions.

CHOOSING A TOPIC

Instructors take different approaches in assigning library research papers. Some instructors want explanatory papers which aim to inform readers about a topic with which they are unfamiliar; others want research papers which take a definite position on a controversial issue. Many research papers are, in essence, arguments or persuasive papers that aim to influence readers to adopt a certain perspective. Even an essay that is primarily informative may have a persuasive angle; for example, an essay that describes the advantages of wind power as an energy source may aim to clear up certain popular misconceptions. In order to influence readers to accept a controversial idea—for example, the argument that sex trade workers should be protected by the government—a writer will need to draw on research. Some instructors specify not only the type of research paper but also the topic. Others restrict students to a general subject area, ask them to pick topics from lists, or give them free choice. If you have little say in the selection, take a positive view: At least you won't have to wrestle with finding a topic.

Whatever the circumstances, it's a good idea to follow a paced schedule that establishes completion dates for the various stages of your paper. A timetable encourages planning, clarifies both your progress and the work remaining, and provides an overview of the entire project. You can use the following sample schedule as a guide.

Sample schedule for a library research paper

Activity	Target Date	Completion Date
Topic Selection	_____	_____
Working Bibliography	_____	_____
Research Question and Tentative Thesis	_____	_____
Note Taking	_____	_____
Working Outline	_____	_____
First Draft	_____	_____
Second Draft	_____	_____
Revised Drafts	_____	_____
Date Due:		_____

Topics to Avoid

If you have free rein to pick your topic, how should you proceed? To begin, rule out certain types of topics.

- Those based entirely on personal experience, personal taste or opinion, such as "The Thrills I Have Enjoyed Snowboarding" or "Newfoundland Has More Scenic Beauty than Ontario." Essays such as these don't go anywhere, and the topics can't be supported by library research.

- Those fully explained in a single source. An explanation of a process, such as cardiopulmonary resuscitation, or the description of a place, such as the Alberta Badlands, does not require co-ordination of materials from various sources. Although you may find several articles on such topics, they will basically repeat the same information.

- Those that are overly broad. Don't try to tackle such elephant-sized topics as "The Technology of War" or "Recent Medical Advances." Instead, slim them down to something like "The Legal Status of Chemical Warfare" or "Eye Surgery with Laser Beams: Risks and Benefits."

- Those that have been worked over and over, such as the decriminalization of marijuana, and those on which people tend to have entrenched, unmovable positions: for example, abortion or euthanasia. Why re-hash an argument that is probably familiar to you and to your reader already?

EXERCISE *Using the advice on topics to avoid, explain why each of the following would or would not be suitable for a library research topic:*

1. genetic engineering
2. social networking on the internet
3. climate change
4. steroid use among young athletes

5. buying locally grown food

6. a Third World disaster as described on the evening news

7. reforming the financing of municipal election campaigns

Drawing on Your Interests

Let your interests guide your choice. A long-standing interest in hockey might suggest a paper on the pros and cons of expanding the number of teams in the National Hockey League. An instructor's lecture might spark your interest in a historical event or person, an economic crisis, a scientific development, a socio-logical trend, a medical milestone, a political scandal, or the influences on an author. An argument with a friend might spur you to investigate carbon taxes. A television documentary might arouse your curiosity about the impact of residen-tial schools on First Nations communities. A lecture in your Criminology class might inspire you to research restorative justice programs in Canada.

Be practical in selecting a topic, and choose something that will interest you or serve your needs. You could, for example, get a head start on a particular aspect of your major field by researching it now. Think about your audience, the availability of information, and the instructor's guidelines for your paper.

When you are developing the focus of your paper, it's often helpful to brain-storm your topic, skim internet articles, and sketch ideas using the branching or clustering techniques. For example, if you're exploring the topic of child abuse, preparing a clustering diagram like the one in Figure 15.1 can help you decide how to narrow your topic, as well as providing a rough map of areas to research.

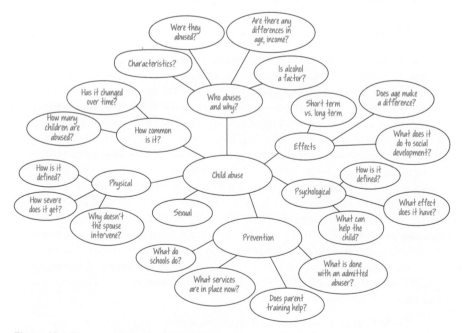

Figure 15.1 Clustering Diagram on Child Abuse

The more you brainstorm, the richer your map will be. Brainstorming often yields a set of questions, perhaps based on the writing strategies discussed earlier, that can guide your research. Often it is helpful to write down your main research question, followed by a series of related questions that elaborate on it. For example, a student wishing to explore the topic of psychological abuse might use a clustering diagram to develop the following set of questions:

What can be done to help victims of psychological abuse?

What is psychological abuse?

What long-term and short-term effects does it have on a child?

How can a child living at home be helped?

Are there services to help limit the abuse?

Is family therapy an option?

What is family therapy, and what does it do?

What psychological help is available for an adult who experienced childhood abuse?

What therapies work best?

What do they do?

How effective are they?

These questions make research easier. After all, the purpose of research is to answer questions. Later, as you examine source material, you will seek specific answers to specific questions, instead of randomly generating information.

However, more often than not, ideas don't fall neatly into place as you probe for a topic and a focus. Don't be discouraged by false starts and blind alleys. Sometimes it is necessary to try out more than one idea before alighting on one that really works.

Case History

Keith Jacque was a first-year composition student studying criminal justice when he wrote the library research paper at the end of this chapter. The assignment was to write about a recent technological development or an innovative solution to a social problem. Intrigued by the possible solutions to the problem of prison overcrowding, Keith decided to explore several options: building more prisons, developing early release programs for the least dangerous criminals, setting up house-arrest programs verified by electronic monitoring systems, better utilizing halfway houses, converting empty military bases into prisons, and re-evaluating legal codes to determine which offences should require incarceration. After a little thought, Keith realized that in order to develop his paper properly he would need to concentrate on only one option. Because he had recently watched a televised report on electronic monitoring and had found it interesting, he decided to investigate this topic.

To establish a focus for his paper, Keith drafted a series of questions suggested by the writing strategies discussed in Chapters 7–14. Here are the questions he developed:

Could I *narrate* a brief history of electronic monitoring?

Could I *describe* how a monitoring system works?

Could I *classify* monitoring systems?

Could I *compare* monitoring systems to anything?

Could I explain the *process* involved in monitoring?

What *causes* led to the development of monitoring?

What kind of *effects* is monitoring likely to have?

What systems best *illustrate* the essence of monitoring?

Is there a widely accepted *definition* of electronic monitoring?

Could I *argue* for or against the expanded use of monitoring?

For background reading, Keith consulted two general information sources: the Corrections Canada website and the online *Encyclopaedia Britannica*. After preparing a list of possible entries ("electronic monitoring," "electronic surveillance," "electronic incarceration," "home incarceration," and "house arrest"), he began searching for those entries and found some general information. However, none of it helped him to focus a thesis, a specific point of view, for his paper.

At this point, drawing on what he had learned from his criminal justice instructor and the television report, Keith brainstormed in order to determine a possible focus for his paper. He came up with the following list:

1. Brief history of electronic monitoring
2. Technical problems in developing systems
3. Types of monitoring systems
4. Benefits of monitoring
5. Problems associated with monitoring

Upon reflection, Keith eliminated the second item because it would require reading highly technical material, which he might not understand. The other items were interesting to him, and he believed that they would also interest his audience—fellow students in his university class.

Next, Keith used branching to expand his list and guide his research, concentrating on what he knew at this stage.

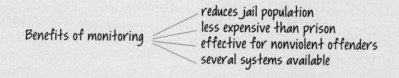

Benefits of monitoring
- reduces jail population
- less expensive than prison
- effective for nonviolent offenders
- several systems available

Problems associated with monitoring
- signal interference problems
- legal concerns

This case history continues on page 408.

ASSEMBLING A WORKING BIBLIOGRAPHY

Once you have a topic, you're ready to see whether the library has the resources you need to complete the project. This step includes checking additional reference tools and compiling a working bibliography—a list of promising sources of information. This section discusses some common reference tools and how to use them.

Encyclopedias

What They Are   Although encyclopedias are usually not accepted as sources for university-level research papers because their information is so broad, they may be useful starting points to get an overview of your topic. General encyclopedias, such as *The Canadian Encyclopedia* and the *Encyclopaedia Britannica*, offer articles on a wide range of subjects. Specialized encyclopedias such as the *Encyclopedia of Education* or *Encyclopedia of World Art* cover one particular field. Today most encyclopedias, both general and specialized, are available online or on CD. They are easy to search and often allow you to search for a key phrase such as "Canadian wine regions." The results will guide you not only to articles devoted to your topic, but also to others that refer to your topic, even if only briefly. If you use an electronic encyclopedia, write down, in addition to the other source information, the publication medium, the name of the vendor (Microsoft, for example), and the name and date of the electronic publication. Study and learn how to use the search options for each electronic encyclopedia to improve your searches.

How to Use Them   For a nonspecialized topic, such as the impact of commercial television during the 1950s, you could begin by checking articles on *television* in one or more general encyclopedias. For a specialized aspect of television, such as the development of the picture tube, consult specialized encyclopedias, such as *Harper's Encyclopedia of Science* and the *McGraw-Hill Encyclopedia of Science and Technology*, along with the general encyclopedias.

Some instructors allow you to use encyclopedias as a source; others prohibit their use; and still others allow material from specialized, but not general, encyclopedias. As an open forum that allows users to write and edit entries, the online encyclopedia Wikipedia has become a convenient "go-to" place for information in our society, especially for extremely recent material on popular culture or technology. However, because the information is largely unregulated and constantly changing, and because it does not always come from reliable sources, Wikipedia has uneven quality control. Thus many instructors will not allow Wikipedia as an academic source for a formal paper; others will allow it only for minor, non-controversial points that are not likely to be disputed. Because it is constantly mutating, if you are allowed to use Wikipedia as one of your sources, it is especially critical to include the date that you accessed the information. As always, follow your instructor's requirements.

Library Catalogue

What It Is Library catalogues list all the books in the library, along with other holdings, such as journals, newspapers, government documents, CD-ROMs, videos, and electronic recordings. They may also provide additional information, such as whether a book has been checked out and, if so, the return date. Some catalogues include links to the catalogues of other libraries.

Online library catalogues may require a student number or library card number. Libraries also have computers available specifically for searching the catalogue. To use the catalogue search function properly, read the instructions at the terminal or ask a librarian. Remember, if you misspell a word, the catalogue will not find any matches.

Search systems usually allow you to restrict your searches by material type and location. These systems also let you conduct searches by author, title, subject, or key term (those appearing in book titles and descriptions). Typically, you begin a search by selecting a category—such as Author, Title, Subject, or Key Words—and then entering your specific search request. The search results in a list of works with the call number, date of publication or production, location, and availability of each work. Selecting an entry from the list will reveal a brief description of the contents and a list of categories that could be used in additional searches. The search system may also provide links to additional searches for works by the same author and for works on similar topics.

Often, a key term search can be the most useful way to approach a topic. In this type of search, the computer checks the titles and descriptions of books for the key terms you enter and lists any that it finds. Different key terms produce varying strings of articles, so it is a good idea to try different words or phrases for the same topic. For example, if you're searching for material on "hybrid cars," you might also try "green cars," "alternative fuels," and so on. Because these searches are very rapid, you can experiment with different combinations of terms to focus your search. For instance, if you're asked to write a paper on some aspect of Japanese culture, you might investigate such combinations as "Japanese business," "Japan AND education," and "Japanese feminists." Because key term searches allow you to use Boolean logic terms like *and, or, near, but,* and *not,* they are especially useful for narrowing a broad focus.

Obtaining the Books Successful subject and key term searches often turn up more book titles than a single screen can accommodate. With especially long lists, you may need to narrow your focus and start a new search. For example, "Japan AND education" might be narrowed to "Japan AND primary arts education."

Subject searches are more focused than key word searches. But when searching with subjects, rather than key words, you may be surprised that the subject you entered yielded nothing.

Consider for a moment the vast number of possible wordings that exist for each subject. For example, the subject *multiculturalism* could be worded as *cultural pluralism* or *cultural integration* or *diversity*. No library system could sort all their books under all the possible headings. So the subject you enter must exactly match the subject headings that the library system uses. To find the right headings, locate the *Library of Congress Subject Headings*, a large book usually located near the search terminals, and look up your subject. (If it uses the Dewey decimal system, then consult the *Sears List of Subject Headings*.) For example, if you're researching *multiculturalism* (a Canadian term), you will not find books catalogued under that heading. Instead, as the *Subject Headings* guide shows, books on multiculturalism are catalogued under "Pluralism" (social studies). So you would use that subject for the search, instead of *multiculturalism*.

When you have found a promising title, click on the appropriate command to call up the relevant information. Most systems indicate whether the book is in the library or checked out and allow you to reserve a book by entering the request into the computer.

If you cannot print a list of results, record the following information:

Author(s)

Title

Editor(s) and translator(s), as well as author(s) of any supplementary material

Total number of volumes (if more than one) and the number of the specific volume that you want to use

City of publication

Name of publisher

Date of publication

Call number (for future reference)

Next, go to the stacks to scan the books themselves. If the stacks are closed, give the librarian a list of your call numbers and ask to see the books. If you can visit the stacks, locate the general areas where your books are shelved. Once you find your book, spend a few extra minutes browsing in the general area around it. Since all books on a topic are shelved together, you may discover other useful sources.

Skim each book's table of contents and any introductory material, such as a preface or introduction, to determine its scope and approach. Also check the index and note the pages with discussions that relate to your topic. Finally, thumb through any portions that look promising. If the book isn't relevant, place it in the reshelving area and discard the reference information.

Note that if a book is missing from the shelf and the computer indicates that nobody has checked it out, then it's probably on reserve or in the reshelving area. Check at the circulation desk. If the book is on reserve, go to that section and examine it there. For a book in reshelving, you may need to return the next day to see if it shows up. You can also check the catalogue to see if another library location has a copy of the book.

EXERCISE

1. **Select five of the following topics. Go to the online catalogue and find one book about each. List each book's call number, author, title, publisher, and date of publication. Because subject headings may vary, use more than one subject search. For example, if you find nothing under "mountaineering," check "mountain climbing" or "backpacking."**

   a. Adolescent emotional development   **h.** Mountaineering

   b. Albania   **i.** Tattoos

   c. Canadian youth violence   **j.** CUSO opportunities

   d. Terry Fox   **k.** Professional hockey wages

   e. Multiple intelligences   **l.** Fly fishing

   f. Music piracy on the internet   **m.** Telecommunications

   g. Online gaming   **n.** Zen Buddhism

2. **Provide your instructor with a list of the books you found that appear useful for developing your paper's topic. For each book, furnish the information specified in Exercise 1 above, along with a brief note indicating why you think the book will be useful.**

Periodical and Database Indexes

What They Are   Periodical indexes catalogue articles in magazines and newspapers. Older indexes may be on microfilm, microfiche, or CD, or even in book form. However, the most current databases are computerized and available to libraries only through subscription. This means that, although they are available on the internet, you cannot access them from home unless you log in to the library system first.

Updated frequently, sometimes every week, periodical indexes provide access to information that hasn't yet found its way into books and perhaps never will. Their listings allow you to examine new topics, follow developments in older ones, and explore your topic in greater depth than you could by using books alone.

Most library database terminals are intended for student operation, but some are restricted to library personnel. For specialized database services, you may have to pay a service fee, but it's likely to be small.

The *Readers' Guide to Periodical Literature*, available since 1900 in printed form (see page 402), is now available online in many subscription services and on CD-ROMs. The *Guide* indexes the material in over 200 widely circulated magazines— articles by subject and author, and other categories by title and author. The *Guide* is especially useful for finding material on historical events and on social, political, and economic developments. The *Guide* also includes scientific, technical, and even literary articles intended for a general audience rather than specialists, but such articles do not include all the available research.

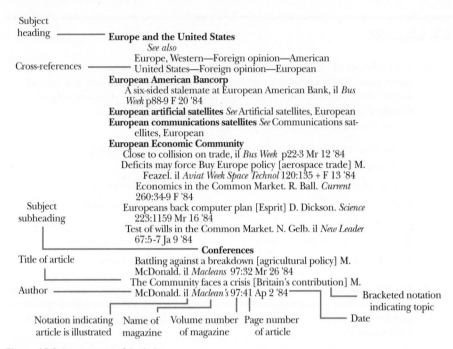

Figure 15.2 Arrangement of the Index

From *Readers' Guide to Periodical Literature*, May, 1984. Copyright ©1984 by the H. W. Wilson Company. Reproduced by permission.

The *Magazine Index,* available on microfilm or online, indexes some 400 popular publications by author, title, and subject. Updated monthly, it covers a five-year period and includes references to articles no more than two weeks old. The microfilm viewers resemble small television sets and allow you to read articles and obtain printed copies. Your librarian can demonstrate how these machines work.

Two helpful periodical indexes that refer exclusively to Canadian sources are the *Canadian News Disc* and the *Canadian Business and Current Affairs Index.* The *Canadian News Disc* compiles articles from eleven major Canadian daily newspapers, including *The Globe and Mail, The Toronto Star,* and *The Vancouver Sun.* The *Canadian Business and Current Affairs Index* covers most major Canadian magazines and periodicals. Both of these indexes, and others like them, are accessible online at most libraries.

General-Purpose and Professional Database Indexes

Periodical databases are efficient because they allow you to search quickly in a wide range of journals, magazines, and newspapers. Some databases, such as *ERIC* (Educational Resources Information Center) or *Medline* (National Library of Medicine), provide access to articles appearing in professional journals. These articles, however, are usually aimed at a specialized audience and may be difficult to comprehend. Perhaps the best place to start a search is with a general periodical database, such as *First Search* or *InfoTrac*. These databases provide access to listings of articles, arranged and subdivided by subject, that have appeared in over a thousand magazines and newspapers, including the entries in various other indexes. Articles are sometimes accompanied by abstracts—brief summaries of the articles' main points—and in some cases, the full articles can be accessed. *A word of caution: Don't mistake an abstract for the full article; an abstract is a 200- to 300-word summary of a journal article and should not be used as a source. Always locate and read the full article before taking notes.*

Subject Search   Because most periodical indexes are organized by subject headings, it's a good idea to try a variety of subject terms, since each yields different articles. If what you enter matches a subject heading, the computer directs you to a list of articles.

Along the way, one of the screens may list subdivisions of the request being searched, as in the following example:

Acquaintance rape, subdivisions of

—analysis

—cases

—investigation

—laws, regulations, etc.

—media coverage

—moral and ethical aspects

—personal narratives

—prevention

—psychological aspects

—research

—social aspects

—statistics

—studying and teaching

—usage

Such a listing can uncover facets of your topic that you hadn't considered and that might enrich your final paper. For example, the subdivision "personal narratives" might contain an experience that would provide a powerful opening for the paper. Similarly, articles catalogued under "statistics" could provide information on the scope of the acquaintance rape problem. Often these subdivisions or alternate subject headings are active links; so you can click on them to be directed to more specific information.

Key Word Search   If your entries don't match a subject heading, the computer may automatically switch to a key word search and display a list of articles anyway. If your subject yields only a few articles, you can initiate a key word search that may uncover more. Just follow the instructions for beginning the search and then enter your key words. For example, if your topic is "teenage suicide," you could enter two key words with AND—"teenagers AND suicide." The computer will check titles and abstracts for the key terms and provide a list of the corresponding articles. This search may not be as specific as a subject search, but it will bring up at least a few relevant titles. Once you have found a relevant article, search the entry for a subject link to click on. This will bring up more closely related articles.

Advanced Search   The final result of any search is a listing of articles which includes the article title, publication title, author name, and information such as whether a physical copy is available in your library, or whether an abstract or the full text is available online.

Besides the previously mentioned specialized indexes, many others, such as the *Education Index, Humanities Index,* and *Social Sciences Index,* are available online and can help supplement your search of general indexes.

With periodical indexes and databases, as with the library catalogue, don't give up if a subject heading yields few or no entries. Instead, explore related headings. For example, if your topic is teenage marriages, look also under "adolescence," "divorce," and "teen pregnancies." Browse through the system and try a variety of options. Use this search as an opportunity to gain different perspectives on your research project.

Obtaining the Articles   Many indexes will allow you to print a list of selected entries; you may also be able to email copies of the article or listing to yourself. Otherwise, record the following information.

> Author(s), if identified
>
> Title of article
>
> Name of periodical
>
> Volume or issue number (for professional and scholarly journals only)
>
> Date of periodical
>
> For newspapers, the edition name (city, metro) if more than one published, and section letter
>
> The page range of the entire article

Obtain hard copies of any articles you might use for your paper (either by photocopying the article or printing it out), and check the topic sentences of paragraphs for essential points. Also, scan any accompanying abstracts or summaries. If an article appears useful, check its bibliography, which might include additional useful sources. Keep the records for articles that seem promising and useful, and discard the others.

Check the remaining references against the library's periodical catalogue to see which periodicals are available and where they are located. Libraries frequently keep current issues in a periodical room or some other special section. Back issues of magazines are often kept on microfilm or bound into hardcover volumes and shelved. Most newspapers are on microfilm or in online databases.

EXERCISE *Select five of the following topics and find one magazine or journal article about each. Use at least three different periodical indexes or databases to locate the articles. List the author, if given; the title of the article; the name of the magazine; its date; the page range; and the name of the index/database used.*

1. Northwest Passage
2. Identity theft
3. Black holes
4. Campaign funds
5. Collective bargaining
6. Fibre optics
7. Fundamentalism
8. Plea bargains
9. Investment trusts
10. Leveraged buyouts

11. Louis St. Laurent
12. Tim Horton
13. Oral history
14. Roots Canada Co.
15. Racial profiling
16. Unemployment
17. Vegetarianism
18. Sidney Crosby
19. Greenpeace
20. York University

The Internet

Using the Internet   Many students use the internet—a worldwide network that links the computer systems of educational institutions, government agencies, businesses, professional organizations, and individuals—as a research tool. The internet allows you to check the holdings of university and municipal libraries; obtain information from online books, magazines, and newspapers; access research and government documents; gather viewpoints and information from numerous organizations and individuals; and communicate with people around the world or at the next computer station. This abundance of information and perspectives can greatly enhance your research, although you need to be careful to evaluate the credibility and relevance of the sources you find. The irony of internet searches is that because the internet offers a stupendous amount of information, finding just the material you want can be quite difficult. To solve this problem, several indexes, or *search engines,* the best known of which is Google, have been developed to connect any search term or terms with potentially millions of sites that include the key words. While each search engine works in a slightly different manner, they all provide similar sorts of information and reduce to a much more manageable size the job of finding what you want on the internet. For example, Google provides several targeted search engines such as Google Scholar, which searches online academic journals, and Google Book Search, which searches scanned copies of books.

You also need to understand that everything on the internet is copyright and must be cited just as print sources are: see the detailed discussion of plagiarism in Chapter 17, pages 492–494.

Remember that in addition to using the internet, most research assignments require you to consult traditional print sources as well.

Evaluating Internet Material   Because anyone can post anything on the internet, it is crucial that you check the accuracy and validity of any information you obtain from it. A source that sounds like a research centre—for example, the Institute for Social Justice—could be a political or even a cult organization giving out one-sided or false information for its own purposes. While articles in professional journals (both paper and online) are reviewed by experts to ensure that the information is reliable, no such safeguard exists for general information on the internet, even for targeted search engines. Carelessly researched or ethically questionable material is commonplace. Here are some guidelines for checking the validity of an internet source:

1. Is the source a reputable professional organization (for example, the Canadian Medical Association, McGill University, or *Maclean's* magazine)? Keep in mind that anyone can make up a professional-sounding name, so be alert. If in doubt, do a search on that organization's name to see what other websites have to say about it.
2. Is there an identified author whose credentials can be checked? If there is no email contact listed or if you can't find another way to verify the contents of the website, don't use it. You can also do a search using the author's name to see what other websites have to say about him or her.
3. Is the information presented in an appropriately scholarly manner?
4. Has the information undergone a critical peer review process?
5. Is the tone of the site professional?
6. Is the information consistent with the other material you have found?
7. Does the site explain how the data were obtained?
8. Does the site appear to misuse any data? For instance, is the sample too small? Are the claims pushed too far? Are the statistics biased? Does it use data from nonexistent studies or falsely quote other researchers?

Inclusion of the author's name usually increases the credibility of the information source or report. However, it's a good idea to complete a search of the author, organization, and publication names to identify expertise, credibility, and potential bias. Many websites are created by individuals or organizations trying to sell products or ideas and may not make that intention immediately obvious.

Sometimes, of course, you may want to check out webpages that present the views of individuals or organizations with strong but slanted positions to gain a better understanding of their perspective. But don't consider such pages to be reliable sources. When using the internet, "Reader beware" is a prudent attitude.

Email   You can use email as a research tool to contact knowledgeable people about your research topic and sometimes get swift answers to your questions. If you have already read background information and done fairly extensive research, you might use email for specific answers to questions that you still have.

Most search engines have clearly identified directories that allow you to look up an email address if you know a person's name. Sometimes you can find the name of an expert through the webpages of major universities. If you do get a response to your query, evaluate it carefully, as you would any material you are thinking about using in your paper.

Newsgroups   A newsgroup is composed of people who discuss a common interest by posting messages to a common address. Newsgroup discussions can be informal and often are not monitored; as a result, they leave something to be desired as a source for research. Still, your university system will likely give you access to newsgroups, so ask your computer centre for an instruction sheet. A word of caution: Many newsgroups are intolerant of uninformed people intruding upon their conversation. Common *netiquette* calls for you to read what has already been written, learn the rules of the list, and think before you write.

Listservs   A listserv contains many email addresses that make up a mailing list of people interested in a particular topic. Once you sign up to a listserv, everything posted to that listserv is sent to your email address. As with newsgroups, netiquette calls for you to acquire an understanding of your subject and follow the discussions on the listserv for some time before you post a question or a response.

FAQs   Whenever you find a promising website, newsgroup, or listserv, you will often see a link for FAQs (frequently asked questions). It's a good idea to read the FAQs first, since they may well answer your questions.

EXERCISE

1. **Using an appropriate search engine, find information on each of the following topics:**
   a. the United Nations
   b. current crime statistics
   c. workplace bullying
   d. current government immigration policy

2. **Enter the name of a major university into a search engine. You should find that university's homepage. Try to access the university's library to find what books are available on a topic of your choice. You might try Simon Fraser University, Queen's University, or the University of New Brunswick.**

PRIMARY RESEARCH FINDINGS

Besides relying on library materials, you may wish to use information obtained by conducting primary research. Chapter 16 provides detailed instructions for interviewing specialists, sending out questionnaires, and making direct observations. Before doing any type of primary research, always get your instructor's permission.

Adjusting Your Topic

After finishing your search for sources, you may need to adjust the scope and emphasis of your topic. If you start with "Early Nuclear-Powered Submarines" but fail to turn up enough sources, you might expand your emphasis to "Early

Nuclear-Powered Warships." On the other hand, if you're working with "Early Nuclear-Powered Warships" and find yourself floundering in an ocean of sources, you might zero in on one type of vessel. Gathering evidence helps develop your judgment about how many sources you need to do the job.

Case History   (continued from page 397)

Once Keith Jacque had selected a focus for his paper on electronic monitoring, he began compiling his working bibliography. First, he turned to the library's computer catalogue and began his search for books and government documents by entering the subject "house arrest." But he found nothing. Next he tried "electronic monitoring of prisoners." This entry yielded a cross-reference directing him to the entries "punishment—North America" and "criminal statistics—analysis." These two entries yielded a list of seven books and eleven government documents. Further examination revealed that three of the books and four of the documents appeared promising.

Keith's search for periodical articles took him to his university's *Infotrac* database. Through trial and error, he found three useful subject headings: "home detention," "electronic monitoring of prisoners," and "criminal statistics—analysis." A search of these subjects turned up twenty-four journal articles, all of which were available in the library. Eight looked as if they would be useful. Three newspaper articles seemed suitable, and a search of *NewsBank* revealed another promising newspaper article.

Keith also searched the Web. He used Google and entered complete phrases in quotation marks, such as "electronic incarceration," "home detention," "electronic monitoring," and "incarceration, electronic." Many of the websites he found were not relevant to his topic, but he persisted and finally found three that seemed promising. One, from an organization concerned with public policy, discussed the indirect costs of incarceration. The other two, from Corrections Canada and from the Probation Division of Georgia's Department of Corrections, discussed alternatives to jail sentences.

Keith realized that many of his sources were either very general or exclusively U.S.–based, and he wanted to know more about how electronic monitoring has been perceived in Canada. He sought and obtained his instructor's permission to conduct primary research on electronic monitoring in Canada. His instructor suggested he interview a criminology professor who could tell him about a 1989 pilot project on monitoring in British Columbia, the first of its kind in Canada. Keith was able to obtain a telephone interview, which he carefully recorded with permission. The interview provided information not only on the B.C. pilot study results, but also on advantages and disadvantages of monitoring.

Satisfied that ample information was available, Keith carefully evaluated the content of the articles and of pertinent sections of the books and government documents he had located. His instructor had suggested that one good way to approach a topic is to pose a question about it and then draft a *tentative* answer. Here's how Keith proceeded:

Q. What benefits does electronic monitoring offer jurisdictions that adopt it?

A. Electronic monitoring is less expensive than incarceration, presents no serious problems, and offers a choice among several systems.

This answer provided a *tentative thesis,* an informed opinion that guided Keith's later note taking, giving him a sense of direction and indicating what information would probably prove useful and what was likely to be useless. Tentative theses can be altered or changed if necessary. If later reading indicated that electronic monitoring can sometimes be more expensive than incarceration, Keith could alter his thesis accordingly.

This case history continues on page 417.

Evaluating Your Sources

Evaluate your sources by considering these factors.

The Expertise of the Author   Judge an author's expertise by examining his or her professional status. Let's say you're searching for information on a new cancer treatment drug. An article by the director of a national cancer research centre would be a better source than one by a staff writer for a popular magazine. Similarly, a historian's account of a national figure will probably have more balance and depth than a novelist's popularized account of that person's life. Gauging a writer's credentials is not difficult. Articles in periodicals often note authors' job titles along with their names. Some even supply thumbnail biographies. For a book, check its title page, preface, or introduction, and—if it's been left on—the dust jacket. Finally, notice whether the writer has other publications on this general subject. If your sources include two or more items by one person, or if that person's name keeps cropping up as you take notes, you're probably dealing with an expert.

The Credibility of the Publication   A book's credibility hinges on its approach and its reception by reviewers. Cast a cautious eye on books that take a popular rather than a scholarly approach. For research papers, scholarly treatments are more reliable. In addition, examine what reviewers said when a book first appeared. There are two publications that excerpt selected reviews of new books and provide references to others. The *Book Review Digest* (1905 to present) deals mainly with nontechnical works, while the *Technical Book Review Index* (1935 to present) covers technical and scientific books. Turn first to the volume for the year the book came out. If you don't find any reviews, scan the next year's index. Often books published in the fall are not reviewed until the following year.

Like books, periodical articles can take either a scholarly or a popular tack. Editors of specialized journals and of some wide-circulation magazines—for example, *Equinox* and *The Atlantic Monthly*—publish only in-depth, accurate articles. Most newsstand publications, however, popularize news to some extent, and some deliberately strive for sensationalism. Popularizing may result in overly broad claims unsupported by sufficient evidence or detail. There are times, however, especially when writing about a current topic, when you may want to use material from more popular sources, but, as always, be sure you understand your instructor's expectations and the nature of the assignment.

TAKING NOTES

Notes are the raw materials for your finished product, so develop them accurately. To take notes, read your references carefully and record significant information. You might review or even expand your original research questions so that you can read with a better sense of purpose. You may record notes on note cards or on computer. If you don't have a laptop, you may find it works best to take notes on cards, and then afterward type up the notes and bibliographical references at a computer. You can type notes into one central file and distribute them later to separate files by topic or distribute them as you go along. Remember to save your work after every entry.

If you are using cards, note each important point on a large index card to avoid confusion with the smaller bibliography cards. Record only one note per card, even when you take several notes from a single page of a book, because you may use the notes at different points in your paper. If you can't fit a note on a single card, continue the note on a second card and paperclip or staple the two together. Cards allow you to test different arrangements of notes and use the best one to write the paper.

If you are taking notes on your computer, create a new file called "Notes" in your new essay's main folder. Keep it distinct from your bibliography file. Record each piece of information in its own paragraph or point-form paragraph, skipping a line in between. Separating paragraphs allows you to move information around later to find the best arrangement.

Before you take a note, indicate its source at the bottom of the card or at the beginning (or end) of each paragraph or chunk of information. You will then have all the details necessary for documenting the information if you use it in your paper. Usually, the author's last name and the page number suffice, since the bibliography card or file contains all other details. To distinguish between two authors with the same last name or between two works by the same author, add initials or partial titles. *Don't forget to include the page number or numbers for each note.* Otherwise, you'll have to waste time looking them up when you cite your sources in the paper.

Summarize briefly the contents of the note at the top of the card. If using a computer, you may want to highlight key phrases. Later, when you construct an outline, these notations will help you sort your points into categories and subcategories.

As you proceed, take great care to distinguish between your notes and your thoughts about them. One good way to do this is to establish some system, such as colour-coding if you are recording notes on a card, or using the Highlight feature to help organize notes on your computer. To avoid inadvertently using the exact words of others without giving proper credit, always put quotation marks around directly quoted material. As an added safeguard, you might also use different spacing for quotations. To identify the sources of your notes, you could number them to match the number of the source or end each note with the author's name. Finally, if you are recording your notes on a computer, be sure to keep printouts of your notes and bibliography to guard against accidental erasure or a power surge.

Thinking Critically as You Take Notes

As you take notes, reflect on your topic and try to come up with new ideas, see connections to other notes, and anticipate future research. Think of yourself as having a conversation with your sources, and record your responses on the backs of your note cards or in a separate "New ideas" file. Ask yourself these questions: Does this information agree with what I have learned so far? Does it suggest any new avenues to explore? Does it leave me with questions about what's been said? Although it may take a few minutes to record your responses to a note, this type of analysis helps you write a paper that reflects *your* judgments, decisions, and evaluations, not one that merely patches notes together.

Types of Notes

A note can be a summary, paraphrase, or quotation. Whenever you use any kind of note in your paper, give proper credit to your source. Failure to do so results in plagiarism—a serious offence even when committed unintentionally. Pages 492–494 discuss plagiarism, and pages 476–483 explain proper documentation of sources.

Summary   A summary condenses original material, presenting its core ideas *in your own words*. In order to write an effective summary, you must have a good grasp of the information, and this comprehension ensures that you are ready to use the material in your paper. You may include brief quotations if you enclose them in quotation marks. A properly written summary presents the main points in their original order without distorting their emphasis or meaning, and it omits supporting details and repetition. Summaries, then, gather and focus the main points.

Begin the summarizing process by asking yourself, "What points does the author make that have an important bearing on my topic and purpose?" To answer, note especially the topic sentences in the original document, which often provide essential information. Copy the points in order; then condense and rewrite them in your own words. Figure 15.3 summarizes the Bertrand Russell passage that follows. We have italicized key points in the original.

Under the influence of the romantic movement, a process began about a hundred and fifty years ago, which has continued ever since—a process of revaluing the traditional virtues, placing some higher on the scale than before, and others

Necessity for law

About a century and a half ago, there began a still-existing preference for impulsive actions over deliberate ones. Those responsible for this development believed that people are naturally good but institutions have perverted them. Actually, unfettered human nature breeds violence and brutality, and law is our only protection against anarchy. The law assumes the responsibility for revenge and settles disputes equitably. It frees people from the fear of being victimized by criminals and provides a means of catching them. Without it, civilization could not endure.

Russell (63—65)

Figure 15.3 Summary

lower. The tendency has been to exalt impulse at the expense of deliberation. The virtues that spring from the heart have come to be thought superior to those that are based upon reflection: a generous man is preferred to a man who is punctual in paying his debts. *Per contra,* deliberate sins are thought worse than impulsive sins: a hypocrite is more harshly condemned than a murderer. The upshot is that we tend to estimate virtues, not by their capacity for providing human happiness, but by their power of inspiring a personal liking for the possessors, and we are not apt to include among the qualities for which we like people, a habit of reflecting before making an important decision.

The men who started this movement were, in the main, gentle sentimentalists who imagined that, when the fetters of custom and law were removed, the heart would be free to display its natural goodness. Human nature, they thought, is good, but institutions have corrupted it; remove the institutions and we shall all become angels. Unfortunately, the matter is not so simple as they thought. Men who follow their impulses establish governments based on pogroms, clamour for war with foreign countries, and murder pacifists and Negroes. Human nature unrestrained by law is violent and cruel. In the London Zoo, the male baboons fought over the females until all the females were torn to pieces; human beings, left to the ungoverned impulse, would be no better. In ages that have had recent experience of anarchy, this has been obvious. All the great writers of the Middle Ages were passionate in their admiration of the law; it was the Thirty Years' War that led Grotius to become the first advocate of international law. Law, respected and enforced, is in the long run the only alternative to violent and predatory anarchy; and it is just as necessary to realize this now as it was in the time of Dante and Grotius.

What is the essence of law? On the one hand, it takes away from private citizens the right of revenge, which it confers upon the government. If a man steals your money, you must not steal it back, or thrash him, or shoot him; you must establish the facts before a neutral tribunal, which inflicts upon him such punishment as has seemed just to the disinterested legislators. On the other hand, when two men have a dispute, the law provides a machinery for settling it, again on principles laid down in advance by neutrals. The advantages of law are many. It diminishes the amount of private violence, and settles disagreements in a manner more nearly just than that which would result if the disputants fought it out by private war. <u>It makes it possible for men to work without being perpetually on the watch against bandits. When a crime has been committed it provides a skilled machine for discovering the criminal.</u>

<u>Without law, the existence of civilized communities is impossible.</u> In international law, there is as yet no effective law, for lack of an international police force capable of overpowering national armies, and it is daily becoming more evident that this defect must be remedied if civilization is to survive. Within single nations there is a dangerous tendency to think that moral indignation excuses the extra-legal punishment of criminals. In Germany an era of private murder (on the loftiest grounds) preceded and followed the victory of the Nazis. In fact, nine-tenths of what appeared as just indignation was sheer lust for cruelty; and this is equally true in other countries where mobs rob the law of its functions. In any civilized community, toleration of mob rule is the first step towards barbarism.

Bertrand Russell, "Respect for Law," San Francisco Review, Winter 1958, 63–65.

EXERCISE

1. **Select two passages that your instructor approves from an essay in the Reader, and prepare summary note cards or computer notes for them.**
2. **Submit summaries of three pieces of information that you plan to use in writing your paper, along with complete versions of the original.**

Paraphrase   To paraphrase is to restate material *in your own words* without attempting to condense it. Unlike a summary, a paraphrase allows you to present an essentially complete version of the original material. Be careful not to copy the original source nearly verbatim, changing only a word here and there. To do so is to plagiarize. To avoid this offence, follow a read, think, and write-without-looking-at-the-original strategy when you take notes so that you concentrate on recording the information in your own words. Then verify the accuracy of your notes by checking them against the original source. Here is a sample passage; Figure 15.4 is its paraphrase.

Over time, more and more of life has become subject to the controls of knowledge. However, this is never a one-way process. Scientific investigation is continually increasing our knowledge. But if we are to make good use of this knowledge, we must not only rid our minds of old, superseded beliefs and fragments of magic, but also recognize new superstitions for what they are. Both are generated by our wishes, our fears, and our feelings of helplessness in difficult situations.

Margaret Mead, "New Superstitions for Old,"
A Way of Seeing, New York: McCall, 1970, 266.

Combatting Superstitions

As time has passed, knowledge has asserted its sway over larger and larger segments of human life. But the process cuts two ways. Science is forever adding to the storehouse of human knowledge. Before we can take proper advantage of its gifts, however, we must purge our minds of old and outmoded convictions, while recognizing the true nature of modern superstitions. Both stem from our desires, our apprehensions, and our sense of impotence under difficult circumstances.

Mead (266)

Figure 15.4 Paraphrase

EXERCISE *Paraphrase a short passage from one of your textbooks. Submit a complete version of the passage with the assignment.*

Quotation A quotation is an exact copy of a phrase, line, or passage of original material. Since your paper should demonstrate that you've mastered your sources, don't rely on quotations too much, and be careful not to string quotations together. The language and style of the quoted material will be different from your language and style, so you want to be sure that the quotation is smoothly integrated with your own language. Avoid overly long quotations where possible, and do not expect quotations to make your points for you. As a general rule, use quotations only when

- you really need support from an authority
- you need to back up your interpretation of a passage
- you need to show exactly what someone else has said in order to clarify how your perspective is different
- the original displays special elegance or force

Paraphrasing a passage as well-written as the one below would rob it of much of its force.

> Man is himself, like the universe he inhabits, like the demoniacal stirring of the ooze from which he sprang, a tale of desolation. He walks in his mind from birth to death the long resounding shores of endless disillusionment. Finally, the commitment to life departs or turns to bitterness. But out of such desolation emerges the awful freedom to choose beyond the narrowly circumscribed circle that delimits the rational being.
>
> Loren Eiseley, *The Unexpected Universe*,
> New York: Harcourt Brace Jovanovich, 1969, 88.

Whether your instructor has asked for a full-blown research paper or an essay that incorporates a modest amount of research, you will want to ensure that the quotations you bring in are relevant, and you also want to explain carefully how the quoted material relates to your larger point. When you introduce a quotation, do **not** simply say "My argument is supported by the following quotation," but alert the reader to what he or she should be looking for in the quotation.

■ Alert the reader to the context of your quotation rather than dropping it in out of the blue. You might mention the occupation or credentials of the person or authority you are citing, as well as its significance for the point you are making. For example, if you were attempting to draw from a point that Neil Bissoondath makes in his essay "No Place Like Home" (Chapter 14), you might lead into the quotation as follows:

> In his reflection on cultural identity, writer Neil Bissoondath argues that we need something much stronger than mere tolerance in Canadian society. While tolerance is passive, "acceptance is far more difficult, for it implies engagement" (quoted above on page 364).

■ Give your reader some idea of the issue or theme you are addressing **before** you give a long quotation. That way, the reader can be looking for the issue or theme as she or he reads the evidence. Consider the following:

> Success is not simply a matter of achievement in the material world. According to Laurence Shames, many people are limiting their ambitions to the striving for external, measurable rewards rather than "putting themselves on the line, making as much of their minds and talents as they might" (quoted above on page 244).

Do not expect quotations to speak for themselves. In addition to leading into a quotation with your own words, follow a quotation with your own commentary, integrating it into your larger argument. Allow yourself to elaborate on the quotation rather than leaving it to dangle in mid-air. When you begin to do this, you may find that you think of more examples of your own to reinforce your argument. You may also notice subtle ways in which your ideas are different from those you are quoting. As you begin to explore more in this way, your essay will develop more richness and texture.

Technical Guidelines for Quotations

You may need to add an explanation or substitute a proper name for a personal pronoun when you are quoting. If you need to insert a word for clarity, enclose it in *brackets*.

> The American Declaration of Independence asserts that "the history of the present King of Great Britain [George III] is a history of repeated injuries and usurpations. . . . "

Reproduce any grammatical or spelling errors in a source exactly as they appear in the original. To let your reader know that the original author, not you, made the mistake, insert the Latin word *sic* (meaning "thus") within brackets immediately after the error.

> As Wabash notes, "The threat to our enviroment [*sic*] comes from many directions."

If you're excluding an unneeded part of a quotation, show the omission with an ellipsis—three spaced periods (. . .). Indicate omissions *within sentences* in the following way:

> Writing in *Step by Step*, 1936–1939, Winston Churchill observed, "To France and Belgium the avalanche of fire and steel which fell upon them twenty years ago . . . [was] an overpowering memory and obsession."

When an omission comes *at the end of a sentence* and what is actually quoted can also stand as a complete sentence, use an un-spaced period followed by an ellipsis.

> In his 1967 Canada Centennial Speech, Chief Dan George spoke about the sorrow of his people in the loss of Canada's natural abundance: "I have known you in your streams and rivers where your fish flashed and danced in the sun. . . . "

Also include an ellipsis when you drop *a whole sentence* within a quoted passage.

> According to newspaper columnist Grace Dunn, "Williamson's campaign will undoubtedly focus primarily on the legalized gambling issue because he hopes to capitalize on the strong opposition to it in his district. . . . Nonetheless, commentators all agree he faces an uphill fight in his attempt to unseat the incumbent."

Don't distort the meaning of the original when you delete. Tampering like the following violates ethical standards:

Original passage: This film is poorly directed, and the acting uninspired; only the cameo appearance by Laurence Olivier makes it truly worth seeing.

Distorted version: This film is . . . truly worth seeing.

You can summarize or paraphrase original material but retain a few words or phrases to add vividness or keep a precise shade of meaning. Simply use quotation marks but no ellipsis.

> Government spokesperson Paula Plimpton notes that, because of the "passionate advocacy" of its supporters, the push to roll back property taxes has been gaining momentum across the country.

When you copy a quotation down in your notes, place quotation marks at the beginning and the end so you won't mistake it for a paraphrase or a summary later. If the quoted material starts on one page of the book and ends on the next, use a slash mark (/) to show exactly where the page shift comes. Then if you use only part of the quotation in your paper, you'll know whether to use one page number or two.

Case History (continued from page 409)

Working bibliography in hand, Keith Jacque prepared his Notes file. Most of his notes were summaries of the source material, but in a few cases he chose quotations because of the importance of the source or the significance of the material. For example, one quotation cited a former Canadian Attorney General who pointed out the disproportionate number of crimes committed by habitual violent offenders. Another quotation cited a key reason for the growing use of electronic monitoring: the high cost of prisons. Still another detailed various difficulties encountered in transmitting signals.

As Keith took notes, a plan for his paper began to emerge. The introduction would explain the reasons behind the growing use of electronic monitoring. The body would present a brief history of monitoring and then detail the different kinds of systems available, examine the problems, and point out their effectiveness.

This case history continues on page 419.

ORGANIZING AND OUTLINING

Once you begin to envision a possible shape for your paper, you may begin to plan the arrangement of your ideas. Some people work with a system of flexible notes discussed earlier to help them visualize a logical order for their chunks of material. Especially for longer papers, some find a formal outline to be a useful tool. The outline is a blueprint that shows the divisions and subdivisions of your paper, the order of your ideas, and the relationships between ideas and supporting details.

A formal outline follows a pattern such as the one shown below:

I.
   A.
   B.
      1.
      2.
         a.
         b.
II.

You can see the significance of an item by its numeral, letter, or number designation and by its distance from the left-hand margin; the farther it's indented, the less important it is. All items with the same designation have roughly the same importance.

Developing Your Outline

Developing an outline involves arranging material from various sources in an appropriate manner. Sorting and re-sorting your notes is a good way to proceed. First, determine the main divisions of your paper, and then sort the notes by division.

Next, review each grouping carefully to determine further subdivisions and sort it into smaller groupings. Finally, use the groupings to prepare your outline.

Many programs, such as Word, provide options that facilitate outlining. With some programs you can compare two arrangements side by side; others enable you to call up your stored and organized notes on one side of the screen and create your outline on the other side.

Don't let software limitations cramp your exploration of possibilities. If your program lets you compare two outlines but you'd like to compare more, make a second and if necessary a third printout; then examine them side by side. Similarly, if an outline includes more items than a single screen can accommodate, continue on a second screen and use printouts to check the complete product.

There are two types of formal outlines: *topic* and *sentence*. A topic outline presents all entries as words, short phrases, or short clauses. A sentence outline presents them as complete sentences. To emphasize the relationships among elements, items of equal importance have parallel phrasing. Although neither form is better than the other, a sentence outline includes more details and also your perspective on each idea. Many students first develop a topic outline, then do additional research, and finally polish and expand this version into a sentence outline. While it's easy to be sloppy in a topic outline, forming a sentence outline requires you to reach the kinds of conclusions that will become the backbone of your paper. The following segments of a topic and a sentence outline for a paper on prescription pill abuse illustrate the difference between the two:

Topic Outline

II. Prescription drug abuse problem

    A. Reasons for the problem

        1. Over-promotion

        2. Over-prescription

        3. Easy availability from friends, internet

        4. Multiple prescriptions from doctor-shopping

        5. Lack of awareness about dangers

    B. Ways to address the problem

        1. Education

        2. More monitoring of prescriptions

Sentence Outline

II. Prescription pills such as anti-anxiety drugs, stimulants, and painkillers are being abused in Canada.

    A. Several factors account for the abuse of prescription drugs.

        1. Drug companies over-promote their product.

        2. Doctors may unnecessarily prescribe anti-anxiety pills, stimulants, and painkillers.

        3. People find these pills easily available from friends or the internet.

        4. Some shop for doctors so they can get multiple prescriptions.

        5. Many perceive prescription drugs as safer than street drugs.

B. The problem of prescription drug abuse can be addressed in two ways.

   1. People can become more educated about the potential dangers of prescription drugs.

   2. There can be more monitoring of prescriptions.

Note that the items in the sentence outline are followed by periods, but that those in the topic outline are not.

Keying Your Notes to Your Outline

When your outline is finished, key your notes to it by writing or entering the letter and number combination—such as IIA or IIIB2—at the top of each card or at the beginning of each computer note. Now arrange the notes in the order shown in the outline. (On the computer, you can often use automatic alphabetization.) Finally, starting with the first note, number them all consecutively. That way, if they later get out of order, you can easily reorganize them. You might have a few stragglers left over when you complete this keying. Some of these may be worked into your paper as you write or revise it.

Case History (continued from page 417)

Sorting and re-sorting was challenging and at times frustrating for Keith. Since some of his material could be arranged in different ways, he found himself experimenting, evaluating, and rearranging as he tried various options. After much thought and some trial and error, the following *initial draft* of his outline emerged:

  I.   Reasons why monitoring used

     A. Serious crime problem and number of people in prisons

     B. High cost of prisons

  II.   Brief history of electronic monitoring

 III.   Types of monitoring systems

     A. Programmed-contact systems

     B. Continuous-contact systems

     C. Hybrid systems

  IV.   Problems with these systems

     A. Practical problems

        1. Offenders' problems

        2. Transmission difficulties

     B. Legal problems

        1. Do the systems violate constitutional rights?

        2. "Net-widening" effect

V.   Effectiveness of electronic monitoring
    A. Effectiveness with low-risk offenders
    B. Cost effectiveness
VI. Expanded use of monitoring likely

This version is marked by nonparallel structure and inadequate attention to some points. But despite these weaknesses, it provided an adequate blueprint for the first draft of Keith's paper.

This case history concludes on page 428.

Using Images, Illustrations, and Graphs

If your instructor permits them, visuals can help clarify ideas and concepts, and software programs make it easy to import photographs, illustrations, and graphs into an essay or report. The best way to explain the bones in the skull is to use a labelled drawing. Complicated numbers can be presented best through the appropriate use of graphs or charts.

Pictures   The use of a scanner or digital camera makes it easy to import pictures, which can spice up the text. If you use pictures, make certain they are clear and simple. Readers shouldn't have to spend time trying to decipher the picture.

Tables   Including tables with columns and rows is an excellent way of comparing information such as the features of different computers, the quantity of sales, or even the quality of different employees. Make certain your table is clearly labelled. See Table 15.1 for an example.

Table 15.1 Use Different Classroom Media for Different Purposes

Features	Blackboard	Overhead	PowerPoint
Class Time Used	Extensive; text written out in class	Minimal; prepared before class	Minimal; prepared before class
Equipment Available	Usually in every classroom	In most classrooms or easily obtained	Limited number of computers and screens
Information Presented	Text and handdrawn images or low-resolution graphs	Text and images or graphs; variable resolutions	All text and visuals with good resolution
Flexibility in Classroom Environment	Plans can be easily changed; readily accepts new direction and student input	Limited flexibility: order can be varied between overheads; can write on blank overheads	Limited; hard to change order of presentation or enter new input

Pie Charts   Pie charts are an excellent way to present percentages or quantities of a whole. Figure 15.5 is a sample pie chart.

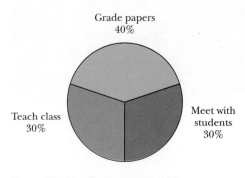

Figure 15.5 How Teachers Use Their Time

Bar Graphs   Bar graphs can help you present and compare data that do not show a continuous trend, as Figure 15.6 illustrates.

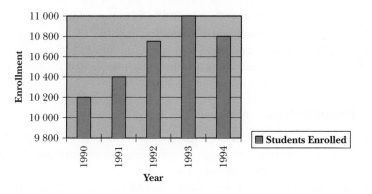

Figure 15.6 Student Enrollment Grows

Line Graphs   Line graphs are an excellent way to present data that are continuous over time and show trends effectively. See Figure 15.7 for an example.

Headers, Numbered Lists, and Bullets

Information in longer pieces of writing is sometimes easier to absorb when it is broken down through headings, subheadings, and lists.

- **Bold headings and subheadings can guide the reader to different sections of the text.** When the sections of a longer report, or even a shorter business memo, can be broken into distinct sections, it can be helpful to label those sections with bold words or phrases that will direct the reader's attention. This text uses headings and subheadings.

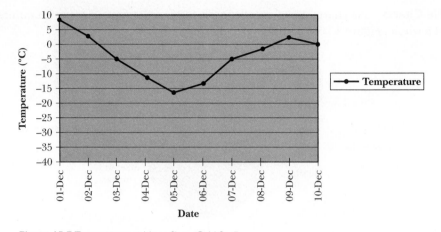

Figure 15.7 Temperatures at Noon Show Cold Spell

- **Lists can be a useful way to present organized information.** Steps in a process, several recommendations, or the identification of important qualities can all be well represented by an indented list. The discussion questions in this text are all presented as numbered lists.
- **Bullets are used when listed information shouldn't be numbered because there is no implied sequence.** The recommendations for using visuals in this section are presented as a bulleted list. Lists and bullets should use parallelism, the same grammatical form, discussed on pages 110–111.

General Principles for Using Visuals

- **Use visuals only when they help.** Visuals should be used only when they are the best way of presenting or illustrating the information. Clichéd clip art only detracts from important messages.
- **Visuals should fit the text.** Visuals shouldn't be just thrown in. Instead, they should have a connection to nearby text so that the meanings are related.
- **Visuals need to be explained.** Visuals don't always stand on their own. You need to explain to readers why they should look at the visual and direct their attention to what they should notice. With graphs and tables, it is helpful to explain first what to look for in the visual and then, after the visual, identify the major conclusion the readers should reach from the visual.
- **Visuals often need a title.** To direct the reader's attention, label all visuals. The title should tell the story of the visual.
- **Place visuals so they do not distract the reader.** You want your page to be attractive but not distracting. Position visuals so the page looks good, but the flow of the text is not seriously interrupted.
- **Visuals should be honest.** It is important to represent the data fairly and not distort the image or graph to slant the information.

ETHICAL ISSUES

When you present information you've gathered from a variety of sources, you want to proceed in an ethically responsible way. Asking and answering the following questions can help you to do just that.

Have I carefully researched my topic, making sure that my conclusions are well founded? Imagine the consequences if slipshod testing by an auto company led to the erroneous conclusion that the steering mechanism on one of its models had met current safety standards.

Have I adequately acknowledged any evidence that runs counter to the conclusions I draw? A paper that stresses the advantages of private schools but deliberately avoids mentioning their disadvantages could be a form of deception.

Have I properly documented my sources? Using someone else's words or ideas without giving proper credit is a form of academic dishonesty.

Have I honestly represented the authority of my sources? If you read an article touting almond extract as a cure for cancer that was written by a practising foot doctor, it would be dishonest to suggest that the article was written by a "prominent research scientist." Refer to someone as an expert only when that person's credentials warrant the label.

Could my information have an undesirable effect on the readers? If so, how can I address their concerns? A report describing a new antibiotic-resistant strain of tuberculosis might alarm some readers, and therefore the writer should provide appropriate reassurances of the limited risk to most people.

WRITING YOUR RESEARCH PAPER

A research paper is not simply a series of quotations, paraphrases, and summaries strung together. Certainly, you use the material of others, but *you* select and organize it according to *your purpose. You* develop insights, and *you* draw conclusions about what you've read. You can best express your conclusions by setting your notes aside, stepping back to gain some perspective, and then expressing your sense of what you've learned. Like all forms of writing, research papers are written for a clearly defined purpose and aimed at a particular audience.

Writing the First Draft

As with other essays you have written, you will need to clarify a thesis for your research paper. You've already drafted a tentative thesis (see pages 46–49), and now you need to refine or revise it to accommodate any changes in your perspective on the topic. Position the thesis in the introductory part of your paper unless you're analyzing a problem or recommending a solution; then you might hold back the thesis until later in the essay. If you do hold it back, state the problem clearly at the outset. Because of the paper's length, it's a good idea to reveal your organizational plan in your introductory section.

Students follow different approaches when writing a draft. Some follow the outline section by section, entering their notes and any thoughts that previously occurred to them, then go through everything again and add material. Others finish off one section before moving on to the next. Some develop ideas by focusing on their notes and then developing thoughts that elaborate on them; others develop their ideas first and then plug in their notes afterward. Follow the procedure that works best for you.

If you discover that it might be better to introduce an item earlier than you intended, go ahead. Just be sure to check your organization later. As you write, think of selecting appropriate material from your notes to support your conclusions, not just throwing your quotations and summaries together willy-nilly. Blend the material from your notes with your own assessments and commentary, but be sure to distinguish between your ideas and other people's ideas throughout.

Don't worry if the style bumps along or connections aren't always clear at first. When you revise, you can improve coherence by connecting major sections with transitional paragraphs to bridge the material already discussed and prepare the reader for what will follow. You can also plug in transitional or topic sentences at the beginning of paragraphs that need more focus. Of course, you will need to know how to document your sources properly, handle quotations, and avoid plagiarism. Chapter 17 presents guidelines on these important subjects.

When you finish writing, let this version sit for a day or two. Then revise it, just as you would with a shorter essay. Keep track of all your sources so that preparing the bibliography goes smoothly.

Revising and Formatting

Students often hesitate to revise research papers because their length makes the task seem daunting, but the cut and paste functions on programs such as Word allow you to isolate sections and experiment with them; move large sections of the text around; or, if you used separate files for different sections, change transitions to reflect different orders. When you make such changes, check to see that you maintain the flow of the paper. An adjustment in one section must mesh logically and stylistically with what precedes and follows. Reviewing a print-out offers the best opportunity to check your paper's continuity. As you revise, always keep copies of earlier versions. Some part that seemed ineffective may fill a gap or take on a new look in view of your changes.

Finally, be sure to take advantage of the formatting capabilities of your software. Most programs will position page numbers, set margins properly, and add your name at the top of each page. Some programs will also indent bibliographic entries properly. Don't, however, neglect your instructor's specifications with regard to spacing, print style, and the like.

Follow the revision guidelines in Chapter 5. In addition, verify that you have

- included all key information
- clearly organized your material
- not overloaded your paper with quotations

- worked in your own observations
- put in-text documentation and source information in proper form

Two systems for formatting and documenting library research papers are in common use: the Modern Language Association (MLA) system, favoured by English and humanities instructors, and the American Psychological Association (APA) system, used by most social science and psychology instructors.

MLA System for Preparing Papers

- Number each page in the upper right-hand corner, 1 centimetre (approximately 1/2 inch) from the top. Precede each number with your last name.
- Starting 2.5 centimetres (1 inch) from the top of the first page, type your full name, the instructor's name, the course designation, and the date, all flush with the left-hand margin.
- Double-space below the date, and centre the title; then double-space before starting the first paragraph.
- Leave 2.5-centimetre (1-inch) margins on all four sides except at the top of the first page. Set the indents for the first line of each paragraph to 1.25 centimetres (1/2 inch).
- The MLA system does not require a title page. If your instructor wants one, however, centre the following on the page: (1) the title of the paper about 5 centimetres (2 inches) below the top of the sheet, (2) your name in the middle of the sheet, and (3) the instructor's name, course designation, and date about 5 centimetres (2 inches) from the bottom. Do not use all uppercase letters. Repeat the title on the first text page, centred about 5 centimetres (2 inches) from the top.
- Begin the works cited on a new page that follows the text of the paper, and give it the heading *Works Cited*. Centre the heading on the page.
- List each bibliographic entry alphabetically according to the author's last name, or, if no author is given, by the first significant word in the title. For a work with more than one author, alphabetize by the name that comes first. If there's more than one entry for an author, use three unspaced hyphens in place of the author's name, followed by a period and a double space, in the second and subsequent entries.
- Begin the first line of each entry at the left-hand margin and indent any subsequent lines 1 centimetre (1/2 inch).

Note: Although the MLA system of documentation calls for a "Works Cited" page at the end of your essay—not a list of footnotes—there may be occasions where you want to include supplementary information that would interrupt the flow of thought if you placed it in the paper. When this happens, use an explanatory note using the footnote function. A typical explanatory note might clarify or elaborate upon a point, discuss some side issue, or define a term used in a specialized way.

APA System for Preparing Papers

- The APA system requires a title page. Centre the following on the page: (1) the title of the paper about 10 centimetres (4 inches) from the top and (2) your name, two lines below the title. About three-quarters of the way from the top, provide the course designation, the name of your instructor, and the date, double-spaced and flush with the right-hand margin. At 5 centimetres (2 inches) from the top of the page, type a running head flush with the left-hand margin. Use the paper's title, abbreviated if necessary to no more than 50 characters, including spaces. Type the running head in capital letters; enter everything else in capital and lowercase letters.

- Repeat the title of the paper on the first text page, centred about 3.75 centimetres (11/2 inches) from the top and typed in capital and lowercase letters.

- Number every page of the text in the upper right-hand corner, starting with the title page. Position the first two or three words of the title five spaces to the left of the page number.

- Leave 2.5-centimetre (1-inch) margins at the bottom and at both sides of each page. Indent the first line of each paragraph 1 centimetre (1/2 inch).

- Begin the bibliography on a new page that follows the text of the paper, and give it the heading *References*. Centre this heading on the page. Follow the alphabetizing and positioning guidelines for the MLA system, except that, if the listing includes more than one entry for an author, repeat the author's name. If the listing includes multiple entries by the same author published in the same year, place letters in sequence after the date (e.g., 2008a, 2008b, 2008c).

- Begin the first line of each entry at the left-hand margin and indent any subsequent lines 1 centimetre (1/2 inch) using a hanging indent. Double space all entries.

Writing Your Research Paper Checklist

Search Checklist

- Brainstorm to focus your topic.
- Get an overview by searching general references such as encyclopedias.
- Search your library for books.
  - Use either key term or subject searches using a computer catalogue.
  - Copy or print out the call number that locates the book.
  - Scan the books in your located section for unexpected finds.
- Search your periodical indexes and databases.
  - Select an index or database that fits your topic.
  - InfoTrac and Wilson Select are often useful starting indexes.
  - Use either key term or subject searches.
  - Use the headings you find to narrow or guide your search.

Print or copy the title of the articles, the author, the magazine, the volume number, the page number, the medium of publication of your source, and the date.

Find the hard copy, microfiche, or microfilm version of your article.

■ Search the internet.

Use an appropriate search engine such as Google or Yahoo.

Try several combinations of terms or modify them to narrow a search.

Assess the credibility of all internet material based on the source for the site, author, quality of the webpages, consistency with other credible information.

Be sure to copy or print the URL, author (if any), and title (if any).

Taking Notes Checklist

■ Evaluate your source by author's qualification, publication's credibility, and obvious bias.

■ Take notes using cards or computer file.

Record the date of access.

Keep track of source and page number for each note.

Record the medium of publication for each source.

You may want to cross-reference notes with bibliography cards.

Give a title to each note card that identifies the notes topic.

■ Respond as you take notes with your own thoughts and observations.

■ Consciously summarize, paraphrase, or quote in your notes.

If you paraphrase, remember to use your own words.

If you quote, be sure to set off your quotations so you don't forget.

■ Always consciously work to avoid plagiarism.

Always carefully record your sources for notes.

Do not simply change a few words in a paraphrase.

Do not forget to identify quotations when you quote.

Ask your teacher or a tutor if you are not sure of the rules.

Drafting Your Paper Checklist

■ Take steps to integrate your information.

Read over your notes.

Possibly write a brief draft without looking at your notes.

■ Write an outline.

Determine the main divisions of your paper.

Read note cards for subdivisions.

Detail either a sentence or topic outline.

■ Key your note cards to your outlines.

■ Determine if you need to perform additional research.

■ Draft your paper in sections.

Work to keep the paper in your own voice.

Don't get stuck on the introduction. Just write.

Use your notes to support your claims but don't just cut and paste.

Be sure to document as you write.

Avoid plagiarism.

Create deliberate transitions between sections.

Go back and rework the introduction and conclusion.

Carefully document using the instructions provided in the next chapter.

Revising Your Draft Checklist

- Do not be afraid to make extensive changes.
- Read and change the paper with an eye to your original purpose.
- Get feedback from other readers.
- Check for material that doesn't fit and needs to be cut.
- Check for holes that may require additional research and do it if needed.
- Check your notes to see that you didn't leave out something important.
- Check to see that the paper is easy to follow.
- Smooth your transitions and add transition paragraphs where needed.
- Make certain the draft is in a consistent voice.

Case History   (continued from page 420)

Using his outline and thesis statement as a guide, Keith prepared a first draft of his paper, following the MLA format required by his instructor. It didn't happen easily. In order to ensure an effective presentation, he checked his notes carefully to determine which material would provide the strongest support for his conclusions. He was careful to use his own words except when he was quoting. To achieve smoothness, he tried to connect his major sections with transitions, aware that he could polish these connections when he revised the paper.

When he had completed the first draft, Keith set it aside for two days in order to distance himself from his writing. Then he returned to it and revised it carefully. Reading the paper from the perspective of a slightly skeptical critic, he looked for unsupported claims, questions that readers might have, sections that might be confusing or poorly organized, and weak transitions. Like most writers, Keith found sections that could be improved. Next, he revised his initial topic outline and followed it when drafting the sentence outline that appears on pages 429–430. Keith then prepared the final draft of the paper itself, which is on pages 431–442. Direct your attention to its noteworthy features, which include italicized notations indicating where Keith used the writing strategies discussed earlier in the text (Chapters 7–14).

MLA STUDENT RESEARCH PAPER

Sentence Outline

Thesis statement: House arrest offers a choice of several monitoring systems, presents no insurmountable problems, proves effective in controlling low-risk offenders, and costs less than incarceration.

I. The use of house arrest stems from serious crime problems in both Canada and the United States.

    A. Extensive use of prisons in Canada and the U.S. has led to economic and social problems.

    B. Violent crimes committed by chronic offenders have led to tougher crime-control legislation.

    C. This legislation has increased the country's prison population and the cost of incarceration.

    D. As a result, many jurisdictions have adopted house-arrest programs for low-risk offenders.

II. Electronic monitoring has a short history.

    A. The idea first appeared in the comic *Spiderman*.

    B. A New Mexico judge asked computer companies to develop an electronic bracelet.

    C. Monitoring was first used in 1984 to control offenders, and the concept quickly spread across the United States.

III. Electronic monitoring devices fall into three categories.

    A. A programmed-contact system calls the offender's home during curfew periods and reports absences.

        1. A computer may simply record the offender's voice.

        2. A computer may compare the voice heard over the phone to a recording of the offender's voice.

        3. The offender may wear an encoded bracelet and insert it into a special telephone transmitter.

        4. A camera may transmit photos of the offender over telephone lines.

> Sentence outline: Note use of complete sentences throughout, the periods following section and subsection markers, and the indentation arrangement.

B.   A continuous-signal system requires the offender to wear a transmitter that sends uninterrupted electronic signals.

C.   A hybrid system combines programmed-contact and continuous-signal techniques.

1.   The programmed-contact component usually includes voice- and photo-transmission units.

2.   Jurisdictions can tailor systems to their needs.

IV.   Electronic systems have created practical and legal problems.

A.   Practical problems include both difficulties experienced by offenders and transmission difficulties.

1.   Encoded bracelets can cause offenders discomfort and embarrassment.

2.   Telephone lines and objects in the offender's home can interfere with signal pickup.

B.   Legal problems include possible infringement of rights and the net-widening effect.

1.   Charging surveillance fees and limiting surveillance to the least dangerous persons may infringe on offenders' equal-protection rights.

2.   Monitoring may violate the right to privacy of others in offenders' homes.

3.   Net-widening can result in an excessive number of individuals under house arrest.

V.   Electronic monitoring has proved effective with low-risk offenders.

A.   Offenders successfully completed monitoring programs in B.C.

B.   Monitoring costs less than incarceration.

VI.   The advantages of house arrest over prison sentences should increase the use of this humane alternative in Canada.

2.5 cm

1 cm

Jacque 1

Keith Jacque

Professor Reinking

English 250

May 8, 1999

double-space throughout

House Arrest: An Attractive Alternative to Incarceration

In Canada, as in the United States, crime is a serious economic and social problem that has led to expanded prison use in both countries. The cost of running the justice system alone in Canada is about $7.3 billion, while the criminal justice system in the United States costs about $26.7 billion to run (Johnson). It is expensive to put people in prisons: It costs about $200 000 to build a Canadian prison cell, and $70 000 annually to keep an offender in prison. Canada also has many of the same problems with overcrowding in prisons as does the United States. Prison cells, like hospital beds, seem to get filled as fast as they are provided. Prisons have also been criticized for failing to rehabilitate; they have even been called "universities of crime," according to Criminology Professor Hollis Johnson. He adds that there is fairly good evidence "that sending people to prison amplifies their deviance" as offenders are socialized into the prison subculture. Yet Canada, which is second only to the United States worldwide in its use of prisons, continues to expand its prison use.

2.5 cm

Although violent crimes have hardened society's attitudes toward criminals and brought about demands for "get tough" policies in dealing with all kinds of offences, most violent crimes are committed by "a tiny fraction of the population" who are often chronic offenders (Barr). In the United States, tough federal legislation such as the Crime Control Act of 1984 and the Anti-Drug Abuse Act of 1986 has led to mandatory incarceration for certain habitual offenders and for persons convicted of specified drug offences, respectively (United States, *Prison Projections* 12).

The introduction of mandatory sentencing guidelines, now common in the United States on both state and federal levels, provides consistent punishment for similar crimes. It has led, however, to an

2.5 cm

Paper is double-spaced throughout.

Title reflects main thrust of paper.

Opening paragraph cites negative effects of extensive prison use.

Causal chain

Effect of nonviolent and violent crimes

Causal chain

Jacque 2

Causal chain

explosion in the number of prison inmates, which by mid-1996 totalled over 1.1 million, according to the U.S. Justice Department's Bureau of Justice Statistics ("BJS Reports" 1). Between 1980 and 1995, the U.S. prison population increased by 242 percent ("Inmate Populations" 10). Many of these inmates are guilty of nonviolent offences. In 1997, three-quarters of all prisoners fell into the non-violent category (Richey 3).

Statistics, forecasts of prisoner increases, costs provide interest, depth

In the United States the prison population is expected to keep growing. The National Council on Crime and Delinquency has esti-mated that the total number of prisoners might reach 1.4 million by the year 2000, a jump of 24 percent over the 1995 level ("Inmate Populations" 10). The Bureau of Prisons has projected construction costs of some four billion dollars for new federal prisons sched-uled to open in the 1996–2006 decade and between ten billion and fourteen billion dollars for the new state prisons required to house the anticipated increase in prisoners ("Inmate Populations" 10).

Author's name introduces short run-in quote within quotation marks; page number follows name.

Even these figures don't tell the whole story. Director of the Federal Bureau of Prisons J. Michael Quinlan comments that, over the lifetime of a prison, "construction costs are only 5–7 percent of the total expense. This means that from 15 to 20 times the construction costs will have to be budgeted over the life of each prison now being built" (114). Underestimating operating costs can result in unused facilities

Effect of underestimating costs

as in Florida where, in 1992, two newly constructed 900-person prisons and a 336-person death-row facility remained empty because the state lacked the money to operate them (Katel 63).

Overcrowding and the high costs of prisons have seriously undermined state spending on public services and created a number of hidden expenses. In Michigan, for example, corrections spending increased over 300 percent between 1979 and 1989, as

Comparison of spending figures

compared to a 98 percent increase in social services spending and a 40 percent increase in education spending (Baird 122). And these figures do not include hidden costs such as welfare pay-ments to the families of imprisoned offenders and the loss of tax revenues from prisoners removed from the job market (Lynch).

Jacque 3

Faced with the social and educational consequences of current policy, many state legislators have recommended using prison space only for violent offenders and developing, for nonviolent ones, low-cost alternatives that provide adequate public protection. At times, results have been mixed. In the early 1980s, for example, the state of Georgia attempted to relieve severe prison overcrowding by greatly expanding the use of closely supervised probation. While significant cost savings were realized, tremendous work overloads on the probation staff resulted (Probation Division).

Another alternative to prison sentences besides probation is a form of house arrest that "confines an offender to a specific site . . . during specific hours" and supervises the offender by means of an electronic monitoring system, sometimes referred to as EMS (BC *EMS Discussion Paper* 2–3). While this technology has been used in the United States since approximately 1984, it was introduced to Canada by some provinces in the late 1980s. Perhaps it is time for us to consider whether electronic monitoring should be promoted more widely in Canada, perhaps even on the federal level. It offers a choice of several monitoring systems, presents no insurmountable problems, is effective in controlling low-risk offenders, and costs less than incarceration.

Electronic monitoring[1] has curious roots—the comic *Spiderman.* The idea first occurred in 1979 to New Mexico Judge Jack Love, who observed that Kingpin, Spiderman's nemesis, used an electronic bracelet to control his crime-fighter enemy. Love asked computer companies to develop a similar device (Scaglione, "Jails" 32; Sullivan 51). The first house-arrest program using electronic monitoring was implemented in 1984, and five years later programs had been established in over a hundred jurisdictions across more than thirty states (Peck 26; Scaglione, "Under Arrest" 26). By 1993, the number of offenders being electronically monitored throughout the United States totalled 65 650 (Carey and McLean 1).

---

[1]This alternative is sometimes called electronic tethering, electronic surveillance, electronic house arrest, or electronic incarceration.

Definition of term	
Omission within sentence, ellipsis	
Rationale for essay's focus	
Thesis statement reflects paper's content, previews organization.	
Narrative relates brief history of monitoring.	
Double citations show two sources with essentially identical information; shortened titles distinguish between separate articles by same author.	
Explanatory note	

Jacque 4

Classification of monitoring systems

The U.S. Department of Justice classifies electronic monitoring systems according to their signalling characteristics (United States, *Electronic Monitoring* 1). Types include programmed contact, continuous signal, and hybrid systems—a combination of the first two.

Definition of system

With a programmed-contact system, a computer calls an offender's residence on a random basis during established curfew periods and reports any unauthorized absence to correctional authorities. Various levels of sophistication are possible depending upon how much certainty is desired. In the simplest system, the computer merely records the offender's voice. Correctional authorities then review the taped responses the next day to determine any curfew violations. A variant approach uses a prerecording of the offender's voice, which the computer compares to the voice heard during random calls. If the two do not match, the computer can immediately notify authorities of a violation. Voice systems are comparatively inexpensive as no special equipment needs to be installed in the offender's home or worn by the individual (Hofer and Meierhoefer 36–37).

Comparison of systems

A more sophisticated means of checking on offenders makes use of an encoded bracelet worn by the offender. Again, a computer calls randomly during curfew. Instead of answering in the usual manner, however, the offender responds by inserting the bracelet into a special transmitter attached to the telephone. The bracelets can be made in such a way that unauthorized attempts to remove them will damage their transmitting ability (Hofer and Meierhoefer 36–37).

Process explained

Visual verification probably offers the best assurance against curfew violation. A special camera that can transmit photographs over telephone lines is installed in the offender's home. During calls, the computer can request the monitored individual to provide a variety of poses to the camera. These photographs can then be stored in the computer for later review or compared immediately to a reference key for the individual (Hofer and Meierhoefer 37).

Comparison of systems; *definition* of system

Continuous-signal systems, unlike programmed-contact systems, require the offender to wear a transmitter that sends a continuous sequence of electronic signals, often several times a minute, to

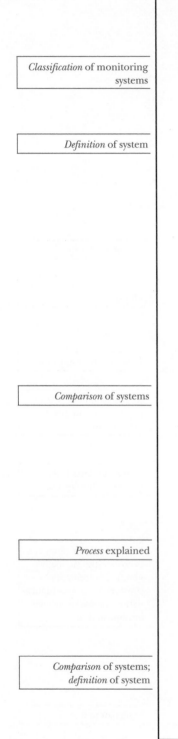

Jacque 5

his or her home telephone. If a break in transmission occurs during a detention period, the monitoring computer notifies authorities. The transmitters are relatively small and generally worn on a tamper-resistant strap around the ankle. Attempts to remove the strap could cause the unit to stop sending signals or could be detected during periodic inspections. These systems provide a greater degree of supervision than programmed-contact systems, which check on offenders only intermittently (Hofer and Meierhoefer 38–39).

Comparison of systems

Hybrid systems combine programmed-contact and continuous-signal techniques in order to realize the advantages of each (United States, *Electronic Monitoring* 1). Typically, the programmed-contact component includes both voice and video units. This component can function as a backup for continuous-signal monitoring or as a supplement to it. In the first case, the computer is programmed to call for voice-video identification whenever the offender's transmitter fails to send a continuous signal. In the second case, the computer randomly calls for voice-video verification as well as receives transmitter signals (Scaglione, "Jails" 36).

Jurisdictions can develop hybrid systems tailored to their individual needs. For example, a house-arrest program for drunk drivers could employ a continuous-signal transmitter supplemented by random telephone verification. Home monitoring equipment could even include a Breathalyzer to determine and transmit to the computer the offender's blood-alcohol level during telephone verification calls (Scaglione, "Jails" 36). A variation of this type of system is used in Annapolis, Maryland, where video cameras have been installed in the homes of some convicted drunk drivers. The offenders are called periodically and required to give themselves a blood-alcohol test in front of the camera (Peck 28).

Not surprisingly, electronic monitoring has resulted in some practical problems and legal concerns. Most problems arise with those who wear encoded verification bracelets or transmitters. These offenders complain that the devices cause physical discomfort or embarrassment. Correction officials can adjust the fit

Jacque 6

of the device or suggest that offenders wear a cut-off tube sock, tennis-type wrist band, or other type of padding under the strap. Wearers, however, must find their own ways of coping with embarrassment. In studying the electronic monitoring of federal parolees, Beck, Klein-Saffran, and Wooten found that offenders could be quite innovative in explaining why they were wearing units. When questioned by strangers, "the majority told the truth, while other parolees stated that [the unit] was a heart monitor, pager, battery charger for a video camera, or a fish caller" (29).

Transmitting difficulties have created other practical problems. In some areas, existing telephone lines may be inadequate or incompatible with the transmitting characteristics of certain monitoring systems. In other cases, the offender's home may cause difficulties. Ford and Schmidt, who conducted research for the U.S. National Institute of Justice, point out that

> The typical room has dead space in which the receiver cannot pick up the transmitter's signal. In particular, metal tends to limit the range of the transmitter; kitchens are therefore an especially difficult environment. Transmission breaks have also been attributed to metal furniture, faulty wiring, other electronic devices, bathroom fixtures, waterbeds, and even certain sleeping positions. Mobile homes constitute a problem for offenders trying to do yard chores: the range outside the building is as little as ten feet, as compared to as much as 200 feet from a mainframe building. (3)

Other researchers have noted similar interference problems. In one situation, authorities suspected noncompliance when they discovered breaks in an offender's continuous signal transmissions. These breaks always occurred during the same time period and only on Sundays. Investigation revealed that a large rock and metal coffee table was blocking the signal from the transmitter on the offender's ankle while he was watching football on television (Beck, Klein-Saffran, and Wooten 27).

Cites article with three authors; page number follows quotation

Brackets enclose explanatory words inserted into quotation.

Examples of problems

Extended quotation indented 2.5 centimetres (1 inch) without quotation marks, double-spaced

Period precedes citation.

Jacque 7

Most practical problems associated with electronic monitoring pose no serious challenge. Troublesome bracelets and transmitters can be adjusted or padded. Offenders often develop ingenious explanations for the units they wear. Difficulties in signal transmission can often be overcome by having trained technicians install equipment or by having offenders slightly modify their routine. Legal problems, on the other hand, pose a greater challenge.

Electronic surveillance programs necessarily involve some type of entry into offenders' homes. Therefore, they need careful examination to ensure that they don't violate the equal protection and right to privacy provisions of the U.S. Constitution. The American Civil Liberties Union is concerned that two common practices—charging a fee to cover surveillance costs and restricting surveillance to classes of offenders least likely to violate house arrest—may infringe on the equal protection clause of the U.S. Constitution. The first practice, the ACLU notes, can discriminate against young and indigent offenders by imprisoning them because they cannot pay their fees. The second, by singling out persons guilty only of property crimes and without serious criminal records or histories of drug abuse, may target disproportionately high numbers of white-collar offenders (Petersilia 3).

Because electronic monitoring programs are always voluntary, participants essentially waive their right to privacy. By agreeing to a program in lieu of prison, they have indicated their willingness to undergo surveillance. Still, as the Bureau of Justice Assistance notes, court rulings may uphold a convicted person's right to privacy if electronic surveillance "cannot be justified in terms of an articulated security interest, ability to deter future criminal conduct or ability to reduce the risk of flight" (United States, *Electronic Monitoring* 5). Furthermore, electronic monitoring can invade the privacy of others in the offender's home. Family members who have not committed an offence and have not waived their right to privacy can accidentally be photographed or recorded. To prevent such intrusions, Kentucky, Nevada, and West Virginia have banned the use of equipment that

> Transition paragraph summarizes solutions to practical problems, looks ahead to legal problems.

> Quotation indicates precise conditions that justify monitoring.

Jacque 8

might accidentally record extraneous sights and sounds. And because North Carolina prohibits photographing juveniles, visual verification cannot be used in that state (Scaglione, "Jails" 34).

Definition of term

Besides protecting an offender's constitutional rights, correction officials must try to avoid a "net-widening" effect when electronic monitoring is used. This effect occurs when a judge approves surveillance for offenders who would formerly have received probation but denies it to anyone who would formerly have gone to prison. The result is a "widening of the net of social control" to encompass more individuals. When such abuses take place, the system does not provide an option for those who would otherwise have gone to prison, and it serves as a new form of punishment for those who would otherwise have been placed on probation. Prison overcrowding is not reduced, and the costs of punishment actually rise because of the excess number of individuals under surveillance (Morris and Tonry 225). The net-widening effect has been avoided in some jurisdictions by establishing strict rules for the selection of participants. New Jersey, for instance, restricts alternative punishment programs to offenders who have already been sentenced to prison (Hofer and Meierhoefer 22).

Argument in favour of monitoring

A pilot project on electronic monitoring introduced in British Columbia in 1987 has provided convincing evidence that electronic monitoring works well in supervising low-risk prisoners. Candidates for this study were carefully screened, and those with a history of violence or those facing a charge of a violent nature were ineligible (BC *EMS Pilot Project Evaluation* 11). The 92 offenders assessed suitable and taken through the entire project all completed their sentences successfully (BC *Pilot Project* 16). In its report afterward, the chair of the Canadian Bar Association (C.B.A.) John Conroy recommended going "on record supporting, in principle, the use of electronic monitoring as an alternative to imprisonment where imprisonment is not considered necessary in the public interest" (20). Conroy also called for legislative changes to the "bail and probation provisions in the *Criminal Code of*

Jacque 9

Canada" to encourage the use of electronic monitoring, though only as an alternative to imprisonment so that judges are not tempted to widen the net (21).

The British Columbia program was also a success on the level of public acceptance. In a personal interview, criminologist Hollis Johnson said that groups such as Mothers Against Drunk Drivers (M.A.D.D.) who were at first opposed to the program later became its greatest proponents. "Once they got involved in the development of the program, they began to see that these people would be placed under greater control than their counterparts who would be sent to prisons on weekends." While the public may see electronic monitoring as overly lenient at first, in fact it can provide an effective, round-the-clock supervision of offenders who would otherwise be contributing to the problem of prison overcrowding.

Although electronic monitoring can reduce prison overcrowding, it is not, of course, a cure-all for the problems associated with our criminal justice system. It is also true that we need to guard against the potential for widening the net "so that increasing numbers of people are placed under . . . surveillance" (Johnson). It is important that we do not violate our Charter of Rights and Freedoms in the implementation of this technology. Still, electronic monitoring may help with economic and human waste of our punitive prison system. While the start-up costs associated with electronic monitoring may seem high, these decrease later once the system is in longer use. With prison sentencing, as Hollis Johnson pointed out, there are hidden costs as well as the obvious ones. Prisoners don't earn a wage, don't contribute to their families or society, and leave prison with a stigma that makes it difficult for them to get hired later. Electronic monitoring offers advantages over prison sentences for nonviolent offenders. Several systems are available; no insurmountable problems are evident; low-risk offenders are effectively controlled; and the costs are less than for incarceration. As we begin the twenty-first century in Canada, we can look to electronic monitoring as a humane, practical alternative to prison sentencing.

Qualification of thesis where necessary

Argument in favour of monitoring

Interview supplements library research.

Independent conclusion acknowledges and answers possible objections.

Independent conclusion draws together and reinforces main points of paper; predicts future of house-arrest programs in Canada.

Works Cited

Entry for collection containing several authors' contributions compiled by three editors	Baird, Christopher. "Building More Prisons Will Not Solve Prison Overcrowding." *America's Prisons: Opposing Viewpoints.* Ed. David Bender, Bruno Leone, and Stacey Tipp. San Diego: Greenhaven, 1991. 118–24. Print.
Entry for newspaper article	Barr, William. "Corraling the Hard-Core Criminal." *Detroit News and Free Press* 18 Oct. 1992, state ed.: B3. Print.
Entry for occupational journal article, with three authors	Beck, James L., Jody Klein-Saffran, and Harold B. Wooten. "Home Confinement and the Use of Electronic Monitoring with Federal Parolees." *Federal Probation* Dec. 1990: 22–31. Print.
Entry for occupational journal article, no author given	"BJS Reports: Nation's Jail and Prison Incarceration Rate Almost Doubled During Last Decade." *Corrections Digest* 24 Jan. 1997: 1–2. Print.
Entry for government discussion paper, no author given	British Columbia. Ministry of Attorney General. Corrections Branch. *Electronic Monitoring System for Offender Supervision.* Discussion Paper. 2nd edition. British Columbia: GPO, 1987. Print.
Entry for government document with more than one author	---. Ministry of Solicitor General. Corrections Branch. *Electronic Monitoring for Offender Supervision: Pilot Project Evaluation* by Linda Neville, et al. British Columbia: GPO, 1989. Print.
Entry for newspaper item with two authors	Carey, Anne R., and Elys A. McLean. "Electronic Prison Bars." *USA Today* 30 Sept. 1993: A1. Print.
Entry for legal report with one author	Conroy, John. *Electronic Monitoring: Report of the Special Committee on Imprisonment and Release.* Canadian Bar Association. Ottawa: GPO, 1988. Print.

Jacque 11

Ford, Daniel, and Annesley K. Schmidt. *Electronically Monitored Home Confinement.* United States. National Institute of Justice, Department of Justice. Washington: GPO, 1989. Print.

Georgia. Probation Division of the Georgia Department of Corrections. *Alternatives to Incarceration* 1 July 1997. Web. 3 Feb. 1998.

Hofer, Paul J., and Barbara S. Meierhoefer. *Home Confinement: An Evolving Sanction in the Federal Criminal Justice System.* Washington: Federal Judicial Center, 1987. Print.

"Inmate Populations, Costs and Projection Models." *Corrections Compendium* Jan. 1997: 10-11. Print.

Johnson, Hollis. Personal interview. 16 Feb. 1999.

Katel, Peter. "New Walls, No Inmates." *Newsweek* 18 May 1992: 63. Print.

Lynch, Allen. *Cost Effectiveness of Incarceration.* Leroy Collins Institute for Public Policy, 1994. Web. 1 July 1997.

Morris, Norval, and Michael Tonry. *Between Prison and Probation: Intermediate Punishments in a Rational Sentencing System.* New York: Oxford UP, 1990. Print.

Peck, Keenan. "High-Tech House Arrest." *Progressive* July 1988: 26–28. Print.

Petersilia, Joan. *House Arrest.* United States. National Institute of Justice, Department of Justice. Washington: GPO, 1988. Print.

Entry for government document, two authors given

Entry for internet report, no author given

Entry for book with two authors

Entry for personal interview

Entry for popular magazine article with one author

Entry for internet report, one author given

Entry for government document, one author given

Jacque 12

Quinlan, J. Michael. "Building More Prisons Will Solve Prison Overcrowding." *America's Prisons: Opposing Viewpoints.* Ed. David Bender, Bruno Leone, and Stacey Tipp. San Diego: Greenhaven, 1991. 112–16. Print.

Richey, Warren. "Bulging Cells Renew Debate over Prisons As Tools to Fight Crime." *Christian Science Monitor* 22 Jan. 1997: 3. Print.

Scaglione, Fred. "Jails without Walls." *American City & County* Jan. 1989: 32–40. Print.

---. "You're Under Arrest—At Home." *USA Today* Nov. 1988: 26–28.3. Print.[1]

Sullivan, Robert E. "Reach Out and Guard Someone: Using Phones and Bracelets to Reduce Prison Overcrowding." *Rolling Stone* 29 Nov. 1990: 51. Print.

United States. Department of Justice. Bureau of Justice Assistance, Office of Justice Programs. *Electronic Monitoring in Intensive Probation and Parole Programs.* Washington: GPO, 1989. Print.

---. Senate. Subcommittee on Federal Spending, Budget, and Accounting, Committee on Governmental Affairs. *Prison Projections: Can the United States Keep Pace?* 100th Cong., 1st. sess. Washington: GPO, 1987. Print.

Entry for occupational journal article with one author

Second entry for author; three unspaced hyphens substitute for author's name

Second entry for government document, no author given

[1]The magazine *USA Today*, not the newspaper of that name.

SAMPLE APA STUDENT
RESEARCH PAPER

Instant Communication Does Not Ensure Good Communication

Bruce Gilchrist

The technological revolution has ushered many new communications technologies and devices into the modern office over the past 25 years. "Every day brings yet another new communication device, software program or piece of computer hardware that workers have to know, need to use, or must have to do their job" (Weil & Rosen, 1999, p. 56). The popularity of these devices at the office and declining costs eventually led to their acceptance for personal use outside the office. After all, who wouldn't want to take advantage of the benefits they offer? The fax machine reduces dependence on the postal system for moving paper documents. Voice mail, pagers, and cell phones make it possible to communicate with others even when they are away from their home or office telephones. Newer technologies such as email and electronic text messaging allow individuals to remain connected with business associates, family, and friends on an almost perpetual basis.

Each new electronic communications gadget is hyped by its creator as yet another labour and time-saving device. Marketing efforts and corporate management describe these devices almost as if they possess magical powers. Simply by using these devices one is suddenly able to do more with less—less time, less manual labour, lower costs, and so on. But are the users of these communications technologies really reaping the benefits that they were promised? Or have the negative aspects of these technologies been masked by clever marketing campaigns and corporate policies? Whether used professionally, personally, or both, many end users of these technologies are unaware of the negative effects to which they are subjecting themselves. Excessive or uncontrolled use of fax machines, voice mail, pagers, cellular phones, email, and text messaging can lead to increased stress levels and decreased productivity.

Speaking in general terms, the first problem presented by instant communication technologies is that they contribute to a

Instant Communication 2

specialized form of stress known as technostress. The term was first defined in 1983 by clinical psychologist Craig Brod as "'a modern disease of adaptation caused by an inability to cope with the new computer technologies in a healthy manner'" (Genco, 2000, p. 1). Brod's original definition was primarily addressing the personal computer revolution and has since been modified to be more inclusive of newer forms of technology. In 1997, clinical psychologists Michelle Weil and Larry Rosen enhanced the definition of technostress to include "'any negative impact on attitudes, thoughts, behaviors, or body psychology caused directly or indirectly by technology'" (Genco, p. 1). Weil further explains technostress as "'our reaction to technology and how we are changing due to its influence'" (Genco, p. 1). Using these expanded definitions it is not difficult to conclude that instant communication technologies can indeed be a source of technostress.

The simplest form of technostress produced by instant communication technologies is the stream of constant interruptions they ultimately produce. As an information technology support specialist, I often find myself working on complex technical problems that require my full attention and mental concentration. Interruptions from pagers, cell phones, and text messaging are distracting as they force me to break away from the task at hand to deal with the incoming communication. Not only do these distractions lengthen the time necessary to complete a task but they can also introduce errors as my attention is not fully focused on a single task.

Adding to this stress is the prevailing attitude that because these technologies provide for instant communication, one should receive an instant response to any messages they send. For me, having to interrupt the task at hand and respond to these incoming messages is indeed disruptive and can lower my productivity when the volume of messages becomes excessive. Personal interviews revealed that my views are shared by others as well. One interviewee stated his biggest complaint is that the constant stream of interruptions brought on by pagers, cell phones, and

Instant Communication 3

email make it difficult for him to prioritize or sometimes even complete tasks (L. Murphy, personal communication, March 25, 2005). He further added that not only does everyone think their message is a top priority, they are also unaware of how many other messages the recipient already has waiting for a response. Another respondent criticizes overzealous management for adding to the problem. In a crisis situation management frequently requests status updates via some form of instant communication. What they fail to realize is that every message they send requires the recipient to divert their focus away from the crisis situation and only lengthens the time it takes to resolve the problem (J. Tice, personal communication, March 25, 2005).

Newly published research supports these individuals' claims that the constant interruptions resulting from instant communications technologies are not only disruptive but detrimental to productivity. In one study, more than 1000 individuals were subjected to persistent interruptions either through email or text messaging. Monitoring and testing of the subjects allowed researchers to determine that such interruptions produce a temporary but measurable drop in intelligence (Burnett & Ortiz, 2005). *The Houston Chronicle* summarized the study by reporting, "Constant E-mailing and text messaging reduces mental ability by 10 IQ points, a more severe effect than smoking cannabis, by distracting the brain from other tasks" (Moore, 2005, p. B3). By comparison, a sleepless night will produce the same effect while smoking marijuana only causes a 4 point reduction (Moore).

Even more troubling is that the disruptions produced by instant communications technologies extend outside the professional and laboratory environments as well. Because pagers, cell phones, and text messaging are portable devices and most employees have Internet access to their corporate email from home, their reach is extended far outside the office. These devices have invaded the home and are eating away at our personal time. Research indicates somewhere between one-half and three-quarters of office professionals use business-related communications technologies

Instant Communication 4

outside the office for up to 1 to 2 hours per day (Weil & Rosen, 2004). A recent article in *Today's Parent* discusses how time spent working outside of office hours is taken away from other activities such as time parents should be spending with their families (Lopez-Pacheco, 2003).

Psychologists concur that all this electronic communication is contributing to a wide array of undesirable psychological changes and increasing personal stress levels. People are becoming more isolated as they choose to use electronic means of communicating over traditional interpersonal methods (Rizzo, 2000). It is becoming increasingly more difficult for one to define their personal space boundaries and separate their personal and professional lives (Rizzo). According to Terrie Hienrich Rizzo, "This boundary break-down leads to a feeling of never being able to get away and contributes to an inability to relax" (p. 1). That anyone may be watching TV or reading a good book when a pager or cell phone beckons with a work-related problem clearly demonstrates this lack of separation and its consequences.

I do not argue that instant communications technologies can offer benefits to the busy professional. However, the growing body of research supports my belief that these devices can elevate stress levels and reduce productivity when used inappropriately. I know from personal experience that I was a victim of the negative effects that these technologies can manifest. The experts call it technostress, multitasking mania, or information overload but for me the end result was career burnout regardless of what term is used to define how or why it happened. In fact, I am probably one of the statistics cited in an *Information Week* report stating that information technology professionals are burning out in ever increasing numbers (Lally, 1997).

The reality is that these electronic communications technologies are not only a current problem we must deal with but if left unchecked the problem will only grow worse in the future. The number one recommendation of experts to reduce the stress manifested by instant communication devices and technologies is to

Instant Communication 5

limit their use. While this seems like an obvious solution, few people fail to put it into practice. Implementing some basic defense strategies to manage the interruptions of instant messages can go a long way towards reducing the stress they can produce (Rizzo, 1999). One is to disable notification of new voice mail and E-mail so that users can check it on their own schedule rather than when it demands their attention (Rizzo, 1999). Another is for users to take regular time out periods where they inform others that they will not be reachable via a pager or cell phone (Rizzo, 1999). This will ensure that today's professionals have some time available to redefine personal space boundaries, spend with their family, or just read a good book (Rizzo, 1999)

References

Burnett, J. H., & Ortiz, V. (2005, April 23). Does more IM = a lower IQ? *Milwaukee Journal Sentinel*, A3.

Genco, P. (2000, September and October). Technostress in our schools and lives. *Book Report*, 42–43. Retrieved from WilsonSelectPlus database.

Lally, R., & Weill, M. (1997, October 6). Managing techno-stress. *Getting Results—for the Hands-on Manager 6,* 5–6. Retrieved from http://www.amanet.org/index.htm

Lopez-Pacheco, A. (2003, February). Baby, baby, don't get hooked on me. *Today's Parent*, 110–112.

Moore, K. J. (2005, April 23). Constant e-mail harms intellect. *The Houston Chronicle*, B3. Retrieved from http://www.chron.com/

Rizzo, T. H. (1999, November and December). Taming techno-stress. *IDEA Health & Fitness*. Retrieved from InfoTrac Onefile database.

Weil, M., & Rosen, L. (1999). Don't let technology enslave you. *Workforce, 78(2)*, 56–60.

Weil, M., & Rosen, L. (2004). *TechnoStress*. Retrieved February 11, 2005, from http://www.technostress.com.

CHAPTER 16

Strategies for Researching: Using Primary Sources

The library and internet aren't the only sources of information for research writing. Investigators also gather information through *primary research,* which includes such activities as consulting public records in local, provincial, and federal archives; performing experiments; conducting interviews; sending out questionnaires; and making direct observations of various kinds.

This chapter focuses on the latter three types, which are the most common primary research strategies.

THE VALUE OF PRIMARY RESEARCH

What makes primary research so valuable? First, it allows individuals and organizations to collect recent information that precisely suits their needs. A company that has developed a new product can't turn to published data to estimate its sales prospects; such information simply doesn't exist. But polling test users with a well-crafted questionnaire could suggest some answers and also some tips for improving the product. Similarly, someone wanting to gauge the success of an ongoing clothing drive by a local charitable organization might interview its director.

Even when published material exists, it may not contain desired information. Although numerous articles discuss student attitudes about required courses, you probably wouldn't find a report that explores student reaction to a new general-education requirement at your university. However, you could assemble this information by distributing a questionnaire. The findings might even contradict and, therefore, cause you to question the conclusions of others.

Primary research can also yield unexpected and significant material. Suppose you're investigating adult illiteracy and you interview a professor with a specialty in this area of study. She explains the reasons why people who can't read often resist help and supplies several relevant examples. Such information might not appear anywhere in print. Certainly the resulting report would carry more weight and elicit more interest than one without such insights.

Primary research can be used to supplement secondary research from external sources. The student who wrote the research paper on electronic monitoring (see pages 431–442) incorporated the results of a personal interview with a criminology professor knowledgeable about a pilot program in British Columbia. This interview provided information on the scope, operation, success rate, and cost advantage of the program. Often, however, writers detail the findings of primary research in separate reports. This would be the case if, for example, your employer asked you to interview users of a new online collaboration tool at work in order to determine their degree of satisfaction with it.

GENERAL PRINCIPLES FOR PRIMARY RESEARCH

Like all research, primary research requires well-formulated questions. Such questions must be specifically focused, contain clearly defined terms, and be answerable by the actual research. A vague, general question such as "What attitudes do Canadians have about their government?" lacks the necessary precision and can't be resolved. What kinds of attitudes? What level or branch of government? Which Canadians? How would you gather their opinions? A more realistic question might be "According to Concordia University students, how adequate is the new federal government proposal for student loan funding in this country?" You could easily develop and distribute to students a questionnaire addressing the different provisions of the proposal. But keep in mind that you can't resolve ethical or philosophical questions through primary research. While you could use a questionnaire to determine public attitudes about the police using sobriety spot checks, such information won't decide the ethical issue of whether the police should use such spot checks.

For valid results, conduct your primary research in a neutral, impartial manner. Always aim to determine facts rather than to justify some belief you hold. This means, first of all, that you must develop questions that have no built-in bias. If you poll students and ask them to tell you "how teachers in English courses mark their papers unreasonably hard," those responding might falsify their answers to give you what you want. Instead, use neutral phrasing such as "To what extent do you believe the grades on your English essays are a fair assessment of quality? Explain."

Second, don't rely on atypical sources and situations for your data. If you investigate the adequacy of parking space on campus, don't deliberately observe the parking lots on a day when some special event has flooded the campus with visitors. Thoughtful readers will see what you have done and reject your findings.

Just as you avoid bias when gathering information, so also should you report your results fairly. For example, don't use inaccurate interpretations of your findings to make them agree with the conclusions you're after. If you believe peer editing produces questionable results, don't claim that the students in a class you observed spent their time sneering at one another's work when in fact they were offering constructive criticism. Similarly, don't report conclusions that are unsupported by your actual research. If you observe several incidents of violence in early morning television cartoons, you can't assume a causal relationship between the violence in the cartoons and children's bullying behaviour later. You simply don't have the evidence needed to show a link between cartoon violence and bullying.

Finally, don't conveniently ignore results that you don't like. If your survey of teachers' marking practices shows that most of your respondents believe instructors mark fairly, don't hide the fact because it doesn't match what you expected to discover. Instead, report your findings accurately and rethink your original position. The following section further explores ethical matters.

ETHICAL ISSUES

Today, most people chuckle at an advertising ploy for a product recommended by "nine out of ten doctors." We recognize that the doctors were handpicked and don't represent an objective sample of adequate size. As a result, little harm occurs. With primary research, however, distorted investigating and reporting are sometimes hard to detect and can have significant consequences.

Let's say the officials of Hafford, Saskatchewan, alarmed at a sharp rise in car accidents caused by distracted drivers, schedule a meeting attempting to ban cell phone use by those driving within city limits. It would be unethical for a reporter opposed to the ban to write a supposedly objective feature article on the issue but include interviews only with people who share his views. Now suppose a presumably neutral group in the city of Winnipeg, Manitoba, distributes a questionnaire to residents to gauge their reaction to a proposed gambling casino. It would be unethical to include a biased question such as "Should the city deprive its residents of the revenue that a casino can provide?" Finally, imagine that a city manager, concerned by reports of motorists running a red light at a major intersection, asks the Department of Transportation to investigate. A department employee conducts a twenty-minute observation and then writes a report indicating that surveillance cameras are not needed there. Clearly, the employee has acted unethically in drawing a conclusion after such a limited observation. To help ensure that your primary research reports are ethically responsible, ask and answer the following questions:

Have I attempted to avoid bias in gathering and evaluating information?

Are my data based on an adequate sample size? If not, have the limitations of the sample been indicated clearly?

Is my information presented objectively and completely without any intentional effort to omit findings that run counter to my position?

Whether I'm preparing an interview, questionnaire, or direct observation report, are the people involved aware that they are part of a study and do they know how the information will be used? Are they protected from any harm that might result from their inclusion?

Do I have permission to name in my report people interviewed or observed?

In an interview report, would the interviewee recognize and accept statements attributed to him or her?

Have I noted any apparent bias in the interviewee?

In a questionnaire, have I avoided any biased questions?

INTERVIEWS

During an interview, questions are asked and answered. Some interviews amount to little more than brief, informal chats. Others, like those discussed here, may feature extended conversations, involve a series of questions, and require careful preparation. Interviewing an informed person provides you with firsthand answers to your queries, lets you ask follow-up questions, and gives you access to the most up-to-date thinking.

If you major in a business program, an instructor may require you to question a personnel manager about the company's employee relations program. If your field is social work, you might have to interview a case worker as part of your study of some kind of family problem. On the job, you might have to talk with prospective employees and then assess their suitability for a position in the company. Police officers routinely interview witnesses to accidents and crimes, and journalists do the same in pursuit of stories.

Choosing the Interviewee

Professional and technical personnel are a rich source of interview candidates. The faculty of any university can provide insights into a wide range of subjects. Doctors, pharmacists, and other health professionals can draw on their expertise to help you, as can lawyers, engineers, researchers, corporation managers, and government employees.

Whom you interview depends, of course, on what you wish to know. For information on the safe disposal of high-level nuclear waste, you might consult a physics professor. If you want an expert view on the causes of homelessness, contact an authority such as a sociologist, who could provide objective information. If, however, you want to gain a sense of what it's like to be homeless, you might interview the manager of a shelter or (in a safe place) one or more homeless people.

Preparing for the Interview

If you don't relish the thought of phoning to request an interview, keep in mind that most interviewees are eager to discuss their areas of expertise and are often flattered by the opportunity. The worst that can happen is that you get turned down; and in that event, you can always find someone else in the same field.

Before you phone, review your own upcoming commitments and try to determine which ones you could reschedule if necessary. You may need to make an adjustment to accommodate the schedule of a busy person. When you call, indicate who you are, why you are calling, what you wish to interview about, and how much time you'd like.

If the person agrees to meet with you, then ask when would be convenient. Carefully record the time, day, and place of the interview; and if for any reason you need to cancel, be sure to call well in advance.

Before the interview, do as much background reading as possible. This reading will help you develop a list of key questions and avoid those with obvious and readily available answers. Write out your questions to help ensure that the interview will proceed smoothly.

Open-ended questions that permit elaboration are more effective than closed questions that ask for simple "yes" or "no" answers. To illustrate:

Poor: Is it difficult to work with adults with low literacy skills? (The obvious answer is simply "yes" or "no," but the answer may stop there).

Better: What have you found most challenging about working with adults who have low literacy skills?

On the other hand, don't ask overly broad questions that can't be answered in a relatively brief interview.

Poor: What's wrong with primary-school education?

Better: Why do you think so many children have trouble paying attention in class?

Avoid questions that are biased and may insult the interviewee.

Poor: Why do you bother to work with adults with low literacy skillsi?

Better: Why did you decide to work with adults with low literacy skills?

Likewise, avoid questions that restrict the interviewee's options for answering.

Poor: What do you think accounts for the poor academic performance of some Canadian secondary-school students—too much screen time, with TV and video games, or overly large classes?

Better: People often blame the poor academic performance of some Canadian high school students on factors such as too much screen time or overly large classes. What importance do you attach to these factors? What other factors do you think might contribute to the problem?

The number of questions you prepare depends on the length of the interview. It's a good idea to draft more questions than you think you'll have time to ask, and then arrange them in order of importance. If the interviewee keeps to the schedule, you'll obtain your desired information. If the interviewee grants you extra time, you will be ready to get more information.

Conducting the Interview

Naturally you'll want to arrive on time and to bring a notepad and a pen. If you want to record the interview, be sure to ask permission first. Because most people warm up slowly, you might start with one or two brief, general, non-threatening questions that provide you with useful background. Possibilities include "When did you start working in this area?" or "What changes have you seen in this field since you started in it?"

Proceed by asking your most important questions first. If you believe that a question hasn't been answered or that an answer is incomplete, don't hesitate to ask follow-up questions.

As the interview unfolds, take notes but don't attempt to copy everything that's said. Instead, jot down key phrases and ideas that will serve as memory prompts. If you want to capture an essential explanation or some other important material in the interviewee's own words, ask the person to speak slowly while you copy them down. When the interview is over, thank the person for talking to you. You may also offer to supply a copy of the finished report. With the answers to your questions fresh in your mind, expand on your notes by filling in details, supplying necessary connections between points that were made, and noting your reactions.

Writing about the Interview

The project you're working on determines how to handle your interview information. If you're preparing a research paper, identify and blend the relevant interview material into your other research and document it properly (see pages 469–483 for MLA and APA style).

Often, however, you are asked to prepare a separate report of the interview. Then, as with any other report, you need to organize and present the material in an effective order, not merely in the order it occurred. Your topic, purpose, and audience determine the arrangement you select. In any event, remember to establish the context for the report, identify the interviewee and his or her position, and present the information accurately.

EXAMPLE OF A STUDENT INTERVIEW REPORT

Budget Cuts Affect Police:

An Interview Report with Officer Robert Timmons

Holly Swain

Confronted with a billion-dollar budget deficit, the provincial government has been forced to make sharp budget cuts. One of these cuts is the allocation to the police. This decision has threatened the loss of some police jobs and aroused considerable controversy. How, many ask, will the police, who were

> Paragraph 1: establishes context for interview

already on a tight budget, be able to provide the public with adequate protection when they have even less money and fewer personnel?

When Officer Robert Timmons first heard that the premier might call for police cutbacks, he didn't believe they would become a reality. Timmons thought the premier was just making "political noise." Actually, the chief of police did at first propose cutting 350 jobs, Timmons' among them, to help meet a $19 million cutback. This proposal was rejected in favour of one that combined demotions, pay cuts, and the elimination of special programs. In addition, the amounts allotted for other purposes were also cut.

All of these actions, Timmons says, have had an unfortunate effect on the operations of the police. As an example, he mentions a sergeant who was demoted to "accident reconstructionist," a job requiring him to review severe accidents and reconstruct what happened for the court. This demotion, Timmons says, has taken an excellent police officer out of the field, where he's most needed, and put him behind a desk.

Timmons notes several bad effects of cuts in the allocation for gasoline. Because of these cuts, police officers are expected to drive just one hundred and fifty kilometres a night. Timmons thinks this limitation has a "direct effect on the public." A motorist stranded on a highway might not be spotted and aided by an officer who is unable to make another run through that territory. Late-night accidents might go undiscovered, with serious or fatal consequences for those involved. Many more speeders and drunk drivers will escape being caught.

As of now, Timmons says, there are only 3000 provincial police, about 400 fewer than needed. Each year, 100 to 200 officers retire. These vacancies need to be filled; however, according to Timmons, the police academy has been closed for over a year. The personnel shortages that already exist and the cutbacks resulting from the budget troubles are making it harder and harder for the police to do an adequate job of protecting the public.

Officer Timmons understands that the government needs to control its spending. However, he believes that the present budget cutbacks for a department that is already understaffed are very unwise. "I feel the premier should have given the matter more thought," he says.

Sentence 1, paragraph 2: identifies interviewee and his position

Remainder of report: presents information provided by interviewee

QUESTIONNAIRES

A questionnaire consists of a series of statements or questions to which recipients are asked to respond. Questionnaires help individuals and organizations determine what select groups of people think about particular products, services, issues, and personal matters. You have probably completed a variety of questionnaires yourself, including teacher evaluations and market surveys.

Questionnaires are used extensively both on campus and in the workplace. A social science instructor might ask you to prepare a survey that explores community reaction to a recently implemented penalty for graffiti artists. A business instructor might want you to survey a test-market group to determine its response to some new product. In fact, some marketing classes focus on survey techniques. But even if marketing isn't your specialty, learning how to construct questionnaires can serve you well in your career. If you work in the hotel, restaurant, or other service field, you could use a questionnaire to gauge customer satisfaction. The same holds true if you manage or own a small repair service. As a landscape specialist, you might survey the people in your community to learn what planting and maintenance services they desire.

Developing the Questionnaire

When you develop a questionnaire, you need to target precisely what you want to know and what group you intend to survey. You could survey restaurant customers to determine their attitudes about the service and the quality of the food or to assess the types of food they prefer. Zero in on only one area of interest, and then explore it with appropriate questions.

Begin the questionnaire with a clear explanation of what you intend to accomplish, and supply brief but clear instructions on how to respond to each part. Keep the questionnaire short, preferably no longer than a page or two. The longer the survey is, the less likely people are to answer all the questions.

As you draw up your questions, take care to avoid these common errors:

1. Don't ask two questions in the same sentence. Their answers may be different.

   Unacceptable: Do you find that your new Toyota Corolla is more reliable and fuel-efficient than the Nissan you had before?

To correct this fault, use separate sentences.

   Better: Do you find that your new Toyota Corolla is more reliable than the Nissan you had before?

   Better: Do you find that your Toyota Corolla is more fuel-efficient than the Nissan you had before?

2. Don't include vague or ambiguous questions. Since people won't understand your intent, their answers may not reflect their beliefs.

   Unacceptable: Is carbon trading a good idea?

   Better: Will a federally monitored carbon trading protocol help Canada reduce emissions significantly in the next five years?

3. Avoid biased questions. They might antagonize those who don't share your views and cause them not to complete the questionnaire.

> *Unacceptable:*   Should taxpayers continue to waste money on renovating the Lion's Gate Bridge?
>
> *Better:*   Should taxpayers spend an additional $10 000 000 to complete the Lion's Gate Bridge renovation?

Most questionnaire items fall into the categories that follow. The information you want determines which you choose. Often you need to include several or all of the categories in your questionnaire.

Two-Choice Items   Some items have two possible responses: yes/no, true/false, male/female.

> *Example:*   Do you plan to repaint your house during the summer months?
>
> ☐   yes
>
> ☐   no

Multiple-Choice Items   Often there are several possible responses to a questionnaire item. When you prepare this type of item, make sure that you include all significant choices and that the choices share some common ground. Don't ask if someone's primary vehicle is subcompact, compact, full-size, automatic, or manual, because size and type of transmission are unrelated. To determine whether the vehicle is automatic or manual, use a separate item.

> *Example:*   Check the income group that describes your combined family income.
>
> ☐   less than $10 000 a year
>
> ☐ $10 000–$20 000 a year
>
> ☐ $20 000–$30 000 a year
>
> ☐ $30 000–$40 000 a year
>
> ☐ $40 000–$50 000 a year
>
> ☐   over $50 000 a year

Checklists   Checklists allow respondents to mark more than one option. They can help you determine the range of factors that led to a decision.

> *Example:*   Please check any of the following factors that help explain why you decided not to re-enroll your child in Rose des Vents Private School:
>
> ☐   can no longer afford tuition
>
> ☐   moved
>
> ☐   dissatisfaction with child's progress
>
> ☐   disagree with school's educational approach
>
> ☐   conflict with teacher
>
> ☐   conflict with other staff
>
> ☐   child unhappy with school
>
> ☐   child had conflict with other children

Ranking Lists Sometimes you may need to ask people to rank their preferences. This information allows them to select the most suitable option from among several possibilities.

> *Example:* Designating your first choice as "1," please rank your preferences in music from 1 through 5.
>
> ☐ classical
>
> ☐ country
>
> ☐ jazz
>
> ☐ rock
>
> ☐ rap

Using the responses to this item, the manager of a local radio station could broadcast the type of music that listeners clearly prefer.

Scale Items When you are trying to determine the extent to which members of a group support or oppose some issue, using a scale can be helpful. Be sure to have people respond to a statement, *not* a question.

> *Example:* Please circle the response that best reflects your feelings about the statement below.
>
> SA = strongly agree, A = agree, N = no opinion,
>
> D = disagree, SD = strongly disagree
>
> Women should be allowed to fly combat aircraft in time of war.
>
> SA A N D SD

Open-Ended Items When you want to gather ideas from other people, you might turn to open-ended items—those that don't limit the reader's response. If you do, keep such items narrow enough to be manageable. You should know, however, that readers are less likely to complete open-ended items and that they are difficult to sort and tally.

> *Example:* Please list the three improvements that you would most like to see in Point Grey's high school curriculum.
>
> _____
>
> _____
>
> _____
>
> _____
>
> _____
>
> _____

EXAMPLE OF A STUDENT QUESTIONNAIRE

Survey on Public Smoking

Kelly Reetz

Please take a few minutes to fill out this questionnaire. My purpose is to determine the smoking habits and attitudes toward public smoking of Bartram College male smokers.

Two-choice item

1. Do you smoke cigarettes? (check one)

    ____   yes

    ____   no

Multiple-choice item

2. If you smoke, indicate how many cigarettes each day. (check one)

    ____   less than half a pack

    ____   between a half and a whole pack

    ____   between one and two packs

    ____   more than two packs

Multiple-choice item

3. If you smoke outside, what are you likely to do upon going outside a building to have a smoke? (check one)

    ____   smoke freely

    ____   look around to see whether there are others nearby who might be bothered by your smoke

    ____   ask others if they would be bothered by your smoke

    ____   not smoke

Checklist

4. Check the statements you believe are true.

    ____   My health is at risk only if I am a smoker.

    ____   Secondhand smoke contains the same ingredients as directly inhaled smoke.

    ____   Secondhand smoke poses no health risk to nonsmokers.

    ____   Secondhand smoke poses a health risk to nonsmokers.

    ____   Secondhand smoke poses less of a health risk than directly inhaled smoke.

Scale items

5. Please rate each of the statements below, using the following scale:

    SA = strongly agree, A = agree, N = no opinion, D = disagree, SD = strongly disagree

    ____   There should be no restrictions on smoking outdoors.

    ____   Smoking should be banned outdoors unless the smoker is at least 5 metres away from a building entrance or exit.

_____ Smoking in people's cars should be banned when there are children under 16 in the car.

_____ Smoking should be banned on outdoor patios.

_____ All public outdoor smoking should be banned.

6. Please add one or two comments you might have regarding public smoking. | Open-ended item |

_____

_____

Testing and Administering the Questionnaire

When you have finished making up the questionnaire, ask several people to respond to the items to test their effectiveness. Are any items vague, ambiguous, biased, or otherwise faulty? If so, rewrite and retest them.

To ensure that you obtain an accurate assessment, make certain that you select an appropriate cross-section of recipients. For example, assume that you and many of your friends dislike early morning classes. You decide to draw up a questionnaire to sample the attitudes of other students. You suspect that many students share your dislike, and you plan to submit your findings to the university president for possible action. To obtain meaningful results, you would have to sample a sizeable group of students. Furthermore, this group would need to include representative numbers of first-year and upper-year students, since these classes may not share a uniform view. Failure to sample properly can call your results into question and cause the administration to disregard them. Proper sampling, on the other hand, pinpoints where dissatisfaction is greatest and suggests a possible response. Thus, if first-year students register the most objections, the administration might decide to reduce the number of first-year classes meeting at 8 A.M.

Totalling the Responses

When the recipients have finished marking the questionnaire, you need to total the responses. Even without computer scoring, this job is easier than you might think. Simply prepare a table that lists the questionnaire items and the possible responses to each; then go through the questionnaire and add up the number of times each response is marked.

When you finish, turn your numbers into percentages, which provide an easier-to-understand comparison of the responses. Simply divide the number of times each possible response is checked by the total number of questionnaires, and then multiply the result by 100.

Writing the Questionnaire Report

When you write your report, don't merely fill it with numbers and responses to the questionnaire items. Instead, look for patterns in the responses and try to draw conclusions from them. Follow the order of the questionnaire items in presenting your findings.

Typically, a report consists of two or three sections. The first, "Purpose and Scope," explains why the survey was performed, how many questionnaires were distributed and returned, and how the recipients were contacted. The second section, "Results," reports the conclusions that you have drawn. Finally, if appropriate, a "Recommendations" section offers responses that seem warranted based on the survey findings.

EXAMPLE OF A STUDENT QUESTIONNAIRE REPORT

**Findings from a Smoking Questionnaire
Distributed to Bartram College Students**

Kelly Reetz

Purpose and Scope of Survey

> Provides background
> details on project, profile
> of respondents

This survey was carried out to determine the smoking habits and attitudes toward public smoking of Bartram College's male students. The assignment was one of my requirements for completing Public Health 201. Each of the 240 male students in Crandall Hall received a copy of the questionnaire in his mailbox, and 72 completed questionnaires were returned. This latter number represents 10 percent of the college's male student population and therefore can be considered a representative sample. Of those responding, 37 students (or 51 percent) were cigarette smokers, and the remaining 49 percent were nonsmokers. Of the smokers, all but 11 percent smoked more than a pack of cigarettes a day.

Results of Survey

> Discusses responses to
> questionnaire item 3

Smokers seemed fairly considerate of nonsmokers in public places. Only 16 percent said they would smoke freely. In fact, 51 percent said they wouldn't smoke at all. The remaining 33 percent indicated they would either look around to see whether they were bothering others or ask others whether they objected to cigarette smoke.

> Discusses responses to
> questionnaire item 4

Surprisingly, all respondents seemed aware that secondhand smoke poses a health risk. Seventy-six percent believe that such smoke contains the same ingredients as directly inhaled smoke, and an amazing 100 percent believe that anyone exposed to secondhand smoke may be at risk.

> Discusses responses to
> questionnaire item 5

Opinions were strongly divided on the matter of banning all public smoking, with 79 percent strongly opposed and 20 percent strongly in favour.

As might be expected, all of the smokers fell into the first group, but just over 50 percent of the nonsmokers did too. A sharp division was equally apparent between supporters and opponents of the ban on smoking in cars with children in them, with 81 percent for or strongly for a ban and 19 percent against or strongly against the idea. There was a similar division in supporters and opponents of the smoking ban on outdoor patios; 80 percent supported the ban, while 20 percent voted against or strongly against the ban.

Responses to items 3–5 reveal an awareness among smokers and nonsmokers alike of the dangers posed by secondhand cigarette smoke. Both the light and heavy smokers showed concern for the well-being of nonsmokers, and a willingness to accept restrictions, though not an outright ban, on public smoking. For their part, about half the nonsmokers showed a tolerant attitude by supporting smoking restrictions but rejecting an outright ban on all public smoking.

> Discusses patterns in responses to items 3–5

No smokers, but 71 percent of the nonsmokers, responded to the request to provide one or two additional comments. All of these comments dealt with how the respondents would act if bothered by someone else's smoke, even on a patio or near a building entrance or exit. Half said they would move to another place, one said he would ask the smoker to stop, and the other one said he would remain silent rather than risk an argument.

> Discusses responses to item 6

Recommendations

As noted previously, this survey included only male students. To determine how its results compare with those for females, the same questionnaire should be administered to a similar group of female students. Perhaps a larger sample of respondents might allow us to better evaluate the proposal for a complete smoking ban on campus.

DIRECT OBSERVATIONS

Often direct observation is the most effective means of answering research questions. If you want to know the extent and nature of violence in children's TV cartoons, watching a number of shows tells you. Similarly, a researcher who seeks information about living conditions in a poor area of some city can obtain it by visiting that locale. Such observations furnish firsthand answers to our questions.

At school and on the job, you may need to report your own observations. If you're majoring in business, an instructor might require a report on the work habits of employees at a small local company. If your field is biology, you might need to assess and report on the environmental health of a marsh, estuary, or other ecological area. On the job, a factory superintendent might observe and then discuss in writing the particulars of some problem-plagued operation. Police officers routinely investigate and report on accidents, and waste-management specialists inspect and report on potential disposal sites.

The following suggestions can help you make your observations, record them, and then write your report.

Preparing to Make the Observations

First, determine the purpose of your observations and keep the purpose firmly in mind as you proceed. Otherwise, you'll overlook important details and record less-than-helpful information. Obviously, observing a classroom to assess the interaction of students requires a different set of notes than if you were observing the teacher's instructional style or the students' note-taking habits.

Next, establish the site or sites that can best supply you with the information you need. If you're trying to determine how students interact in the classroom, then the time of day, kind of class, and types of students all make a difference. You might have to visit more than one class in order to observe the different types of behaviour.

If your observations take place on private property or involve an organized group such as a legislative body, you need to obtain permission and make an appointment. Also, you might want to supplement your observations with an interview. Ordinarily, the interview takes place after you have made your observations so that you can ask about what you've seen. If technical information is needed in advance, the interview should precede the observations. However, you should have done research first so that you do not waste the expert's time and goodwill by asking about information that is reasonably available.

Because you'll probably be making a great many individual observations, try to develop a chart and a code for recording them. Suppose you're comparing the extent to which students interact with one another and with the instructor in first-year and third-year writing courses. After much thought, you might develop a chart like the one following:

Class Designation: English 1100				
Minutes into observation when interaction occurred	Classroom location of interacting students	Number and sex of students	Subject of interaction	Length of interaction

In developing your code, you would undoubtedly use M = male and F = female to distinguish the sexes. To show the location of the interacting students, FC = front of class, MC = middle of class, and BC = back of class would probably work quite well. Coding the kinds of interactions presents a more difficult task. Here, after considering several possibilities, you might decide upon these symbols: CR = class related, SR = school related, SP = sports, D = dating, O = other matters. To save writing time, you'd probably want to use "min." for "minutes" and "sec." for "seconds" when recording the lengths of the interactions.

Making the Observations

If your visit involves a scheduled appointment, be sure to arrive on time and be ready to take notes. Select a location where you can observe without interfering. If you are observing people or animals, remember that they need to adjust to you before they behave naturally.

Before you begin taking notes, record any pertinent general information. If you're observing a class, you might note the time it is meeting, its size, the name of the instructor, and whether he or she is present when you arrive. If you're observing an apartment, record the location and condition of the building, the time of the visit, and the general nature of the environment. Note also whether the landlord as well as the tenant knew you were coming, as foreknowledge may affect conditions. Landlords or tenants noted for maintaining unsanitary living conditions may conduct an exceptional cleaning of an apartment when they know an observer is arriving soon.

Don't feel as though you must take extensive notes. However, do record enough details to ensure that you won't forget any important events, activities, or features. If you have a chart and coding system, rely on it as much as possible when recording information. Refer to the chart on page 462 for how the coded notes for part of a classroom visit might look.

If you haven't developed a chart, take enough notes so that you can produce a thorough report. Try to follow some note-taking pattern. When observing the condition of an apartment, you could proceed from room to room, jotting down observations such as "Front hallway, entranceway: paint peeling in large strips from wall, paint chips on floor. Hallway dark, bulb burned out. Linoleum curling up along sides. Cockroaches running along lower moulding." Remain as objective as possible as you take notes. Record what you see, hear, and smell, and avoid judgmental language. If you must record a subjective impression, identify it as such.

Class Designation: English 1100				
Minutes into observation when interaction occurred	Classroom location of interacting students	Number and sex of students	Subject of interaction	Length of interaction
0 3 Instructor arrived 5 20	FC MC FC, MC, BC FC, MC	M-M F-F M-M-M-F-F M-F-M	SP D CR CR	1 min. 30 sec. 3 min. 45 sec. 1 min.

Ask questions if necessary, but rely primarily on what you observe, not what you're told. If the landlord of a rundown apartment you're visiting tells you that he's repainting the building but you see no signs that this is happening, ignore what he says or report it along with an appropriate cautionary comment.

When you finish, thank the person(s) who made your observations possible or helped you in other ways.

When you leave the observation site, expand your notes by adding more details. Supply any needed connections and record your overall impressions. For example, suppose you are expanding your notes on student interactions in an English class. You might note that the greatest number of interactions occurred before and immediately after the instructor arrived, that all student–student interactions involved individuals seated together, that student–instructor inter-actions included students in all parts of the room, and that all the latter inter-actions were about subject-related matters. This information might stimulate interesting speculation concerning the student–student and student–teacher relationships in the class, causing you to conclude that the students were hesitant about having exchanges with the instructor. As you proceed, record only what you actually observed, not what you wanted or expected to observe.

If upon reviewing your notes you find that you require more information, you may need to arrange a second or even a third visit to the observation site.

Writing the Report

Once your notes are in final form, you can start writing your report. On the job, your employer may specify a certain form to follow. As a general rule, all such reports reflect their purposes, focus on relevant information, and remain objective.

Usually you begin by explaining the reason for the investigation, noting any preliminary arrangements that were made, and if appropriate, providing an overview of the observation site. Depending upon the nature of the report, the primary means of organization may be as follows:

Narration. A report on the changing conduct of a child over a three-hour period in a daycare centre would probably be organized chronologically.

Description. A report assessing the storm damage in a large urban area could present its details in spatial order.

Classification. A visit to a toxic-waste dump suspected of violating government regula-tions might produce a report classifying the types of wastes improperly stored there.

Point-by-point comparison. If you're comparing two possible sites for a baseball stadium, shopping mall, or other structure, a point-by-point comparison probably best suits your purpose.

Cause and effect. This pattern works well for reporting events whose effects are of spe-cial concern, such as the testing of a new siren intended to scare birds from an air-port runway.

Process. This arrangement is indicated when readers want to know step-by-step how a process is carried out: for example, a new test for determining the mineral con-tent of water.

Conclude the report by discussing the significance of the findings and making any other comments that seem justified.

EXAMPLE OF A STUDENT OBSERVATION REPORT

Observations of a Rundown Apartment Building

Caleb Thomas

To fulfill part of the requirements for Social Service 321, I observed the housing conditions in a poor residential area in our city. The building I selected is located at the corner of Division Avenue and Hall Street, an area where most of the residents hold minimum-wage jobs or receive some form of public assistance.

> Gives reason for visit, location of site

I met the building supervisor, who had agreed to this visit, at 9:30 A.M. on Friday, August 15, 2008. The brick sides of the three-storey apartment building appeared to be in good repair, but one second-storey window was broken out and boarded up. Most windows had standard window shades, but a few were blocked with sheets or black plastic bags. Two had no coverings of any kind. Overall, the building's appearance was similar to that of several nearby apartment buildings.

> Notes preliminary arrangements, provides overview of site location

Heavy traffic clogged Division Avenue at the time of my visit. Next to the apartment building stood three single-storey wooden buildings housing an adult video store, a bar, and a novelty shop, all with boarded windows and peeling paint. Across the street, a single-storey Salvation Army Store occupied the entire block. In front of it, three women in short skirts walked slowly back and forth, eyeing the cars that passed. Two men sat on crates, their backs to the building, drinking something out of paper bags.

> Continues overview of site location

The supervisor opened the unlocked metal door of the apartment building, and we went in. The hallway was lighted by a single dim bulb located on the wall toward the rear. Other bulbs along the wall and in two light fixtures hanging from the ceiling appeared burned out. Scraps of newspaper and chips of paint that had peeled from the ceiling and walls littered the floor. A strong urine-like smell pervaded the air.

> Describes building's hallway

Stating that he couldn't show me an occupied apartment because he "respected the privacy of the tenants," the supervisor took me to an unoccupied apartment on the first floor. He had trouble unlocking the wooden door; the key appeared to stick in the lock. The inside of the door had two bolt locks, one just above the door handle and the other one near the floor. The door opened into a short hall with rooms off either side. Here, as in the building entrance, paint chips from the peeling walls and ceiling littered the floor. A battered socket on

> Describes apartment hallway

the wall held a single bulb, but when I flicked its switch, the bulb did not light. On the hall floor, linoleum curled at the edges. When I bent down to examine it more closely, several cockroaches scurried under the curl.

Describes apartment living room

The first door on the right-hand side of the hall led into a 3-by-4–metre room that the supervisor identified as the living room. Here the walls had been recently painted—by a former tenant, the supervisor said—and a strong paint smell was still apparent. However, nothing else had been done to the rest of the room. The radiator was unshielded, several nail heads protruded from the stained and uncovered wooden floor, and the sagging ceiling had several long cracks. Plaster chips dotted the floor.

Describes apartment kitchen

A small kitchen was situated behind the living room. Again, linoleum floor covering curled from the baseboard, and cockroaches scurried for cover. The kitchen was furnished with a battered-looking gas stove, but there was no refrigerator (the supervisor said one was on order). The surface of the sink was chipped and had many brownish stains. When I turned on the faucet, a rusty brown stream of water spurted out. I asked for a sample to be tested for lead content, but the supervisor refused.

Describes apartment bathroom

The bathroom, located at the end of the hall, had no radiator. Its floor tiles, broken in a number of places, exposed a long section of rotted wood. The toilet, with seat missing, would not flush when I tried it but simply made a hissing noise. A brown stain spread over the bottom of the bathtub and a large portion of its sides. The wall tiles around the tub bulged outward and appeared ready to collapse into the tub. The supervisor offered the observation that there had been "some trouble with the plumbing."

Describes apartment bedrooms

Two small bedrooms opened off the left side of the hall. Like the living room both had unprotected radiators, uncovered wooden floors, and cracked ceilings. Walls were papered rather than painted, but long strips of the wallpaper were missing. In one bedroom a piece of plasterboard hung on the wall as if covering a hole. The windows in both bedrooms were covered with sheets tacked to the wall.

When I had finished looking at the bedrooms, the supervisor quickly escorted me from the apartment and the building, declaring that he was too busy to show me any other vacant apartments. He also said he had no time to answer any questions.

Discusses significance of findings

Clearly the building I visited fails to meet the city housing code: The living conditions are not what most people would consider acceptable. A careful investigation, including a test of the water and of the paint for lead content, seems called for to determine whether this apartment constitutes a health risk.

CHAPTER 17

Strategies for Documentation

In order to acknowledge and handle sources, you must know how to (1) prepare proper bibliographical references, (2) document sources within your text, (3) handle quotations, and (4) avoid plagiarism.

The kind of information included in bibliographical references depends on the type of source and the documentation system. Two systems are in common use: the Modern Language Association (MLA) system and the American Psychological Association (APA) system.

Both the MLA and APA systems use a hanging indent for entries in the reference list. Start the first line of each entry flush to the left margin and indent all subsequent lines five spaces.

For more information, consult the *MLA Handbook for Writers of Research Papers,* 7th ed., 2009, and the *Publication Manual of the American Psychological Association,* 5th ed., 2001, as well as the *APA Style Guide to Electronic References,* published in 2007.

For a good general guide:

http://owl.english.purdue.edu/owl/resource/557/01/

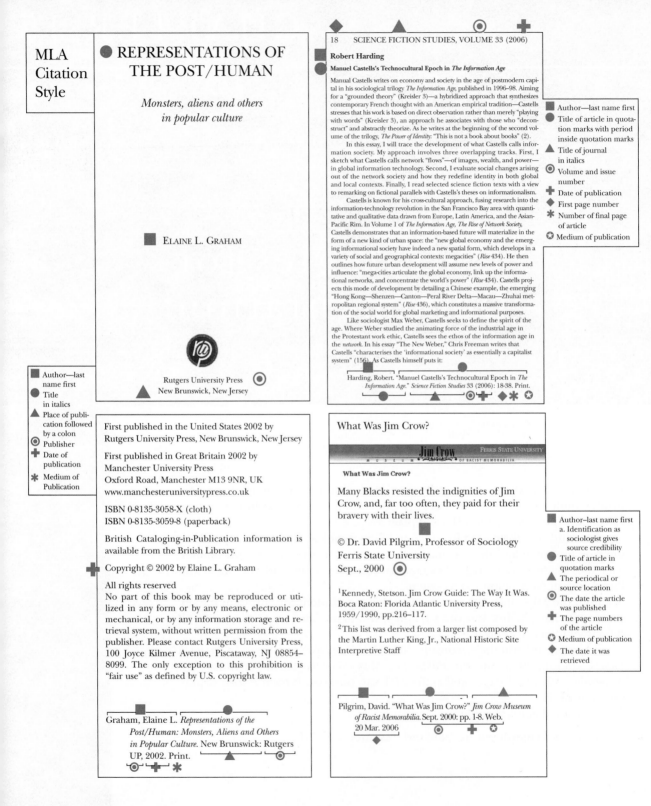

MLA Citation Style

● **REPRESENTATIONS OF THE POST/HUMAN**

Monsters, aliens and others in popular culture

■ ELAINE L. GRAHAM

Rutgers University Press ◉
▲ New Brunswick, New Jersey

■ Author—last name first
● Title in italics
▲ Place of publication followed by a colon
◉ Publisher
✚ Date of publication
✱ Medium of Publication

First published in the United States 2002 by Rutgers University Press, New Brunswick, New Jersey

First published in Great Britain 2002 by Manchester University Press
Oxford Road, Manchester M13 9NR, UK
www.manchesteruniversitypress.co.uk

ISBN 0-8135-3058-X (cloth)
ISBN 0-8135-3059-8 (paperback)

British Cataloging-in-Publication information is available from the British Library.

✚ Copyright © 2002 by Elaine L. Graham

All rights reserved
No part of this book may be reproduced or utilized in any form or by any means, electronic or mechanical, or by any information storage and retrieval system, without written permission from the publisher. Please contact Rutgers University Press, 100 Joyce Kilmer Avenue, Piscataway, NJ 08854–8099. The only exception to this prohibition is "fair use" as defined by U.S. copyright law.

■ ● Graham, Elaine L. *Representations of the Post/Human: Monsters, Aliens and Others in Popular Culture.* ▲ New Brunswick: Rutgers ◉ UP, ✚ 2002. ✱ Print.

◆ ▲ ◉ ✚
18   SCIENCE FICTION STUDIES, VOLUME 33 (2006)

■ **Robert Harding**

Manuel Castells's Technocultural Epoch in *The Information Age*

Manual Castells writes on economy and society in the age of postmodern capital in his sociological trilogy *The Information Age*, published in 1996–98. Aiming for a "grounded theory" (Kreisler 3)—a hybridized approach that synthesizes contemporary French thought with an American empirical tradition—Castells stresses that his work is based on direct observation rather than merely "playing with words" (Kreisler 3), an approach he associates with those who "deconstruct" and abstractly theorize. As he writes at the beginning of the second volume of the trilogy, *The Power of Identity*: "This is not a book about books" (2).

In this essay, I will trace the development of what Castells calls information society. My approach involves three overlapping tracks. First, I sketch what Castells calls network "flows"—of images, wealth, and power—in global information technology. Second, I evaluate social changes arising out of the network society and how they redefine identity in both global and local contexts. Finally, I read selected science fiction texts with a view to remarking on fictional parallels with Castells's theses on informationalism.

Castells is known for his cross-cultural approach, fusing research into the information-technology revolution in the San Francisco Bay area with quantitative and qualitative data drawn from Europe, Latin America, and the Asian-Pacific Rim. In Volume 1 of *The Information Age, The Rise of Network Society*, Castells demonstrates that an information-based future will materialize in the form of a new kind of urban space: the "new global economy and the emerging informational society have indeed a new spatial form, which develops in a variety of social and geographical contexts: megacities" (*Rise* 434). He then outlines how future urban development will assume new levels of power and influence: "mega-cities articulate the global economy, link up the informational networks, and concentrate the world's power" (*Rise* 434). Castells projects this mode of development by detailing a Chinese example, the emerging "Hong Kong—Shenzhen—Canton—Peral River Delta—Macau—Zhuhai metropolitan regional system" (*Rise* 436), which constitutes a massive transformation of the social world for global marketing and informational purposes.

Like sociologist Max Weber, Castells seeks to define the spirit of the age. Where Weber studied the animating force of the industrial age in the Protestant work ethic, Castells sees the ethos of the information age in the *network*. In his essay "The New Weber," Chris Freeman writes that Castells "characterises the 'informational society' as essentially a capitalist system" (156). As Castells himself puts it:

■ Harding, Robert. "Manuel Castells's Technocultural Epoch in *The Information Age*." ▲ *Science Fiction Studies* ◉ 33 ✚ (2006): ● 18-38. ◆ ✱ ✪ Print.

What Was Jim Crow?

Jim Crow FERRIS STATE UNIVERSITY
MUSEUM OF RACIST MEMORABILIA

What Was Jim Crow?

Many Blacks resisted the indignities of Jim Crow, and, far too often, they paid for their bravery with their lives.

■

© Dr. David Pilgrim, Professor of Sociology
Ferris State University
Sept., 2000 ◉

[1] Kennedy, Stetson. Jim Crow Guide: The Way It Was. Boca Raton: Florida Atlantic University Press, 1959/1990, pp.216–117.

[2] This list was derived from a larger list composed by the Martin Luther King, Jr., National Historic Site Interpretive Staff

■ Pilgrim, David. "What Was Jim Crow?" *Jim Crow Museum of Racist Memorabilia*. ● ▲ Sept. 2000: pp. 1-8. ◉ ✚ Web. ✪ 20 Mar. 2006 ◆

Right-side legend (top):

■ Author—last name first
● Title of article in quotation marks with period inside quotation marks
▲ Title of journal in italics
◉ Volume and issue number
✚ Date of publication
● First page number
✱ Number of final page of article
✪ Medium of publication

Right-side legend (bottom):

■ Author–last name first
  a. Identification as sociologist gives source credibility
● Title of article in quotation marks
▲ The periodical or source location
◉ The date the article was published
✚ The page numbers of the article
✪ Medium of publication
◆ The date it was retrieved

For more detailed help with electronic sources:

http://www.thewritesource.com/mla.htm

For answers to frequently asked questions about the MLA guide consult the MLA website:

http://www.mla.org/handbook_faq

In addition, see the detailed chart on the opposite page for examples of how to cite books and journals in MLA style.

MLA

PREPARING MLA BIBLIOGRAPHIC REFERENCES

Books

The basic bibliographic reference for a book includes the name of the author, the title of the book, the place of publication, the name of the publisher, the date of publication, and the medium of publication (*Print*). Other information is added as necessary.

■ A Book with One Author

Ondaatje, Michael. *The English Patient.* Toronto: Vintage Books, 1993. Print.

■ A Book with Two Authors

Finnbogason, Jack, and Al Valleau. *Canadian Writer's Pocket Guide.* 2nd ed. Toronto:
    Nelson, 2002. Print.

■ A Book with More Than Three Authors

Alder, Roger William, et al. *Mechanisms in Organic Chemistry.* New York: Wiley,
    1971. Print.

The MLA system permits the use of "et al." for four or more authors or editors (listing all authors is also permitted).

■ A Book with a Title That Includes Another Title

The MLA offers two options: You may omit italicizing the embedded title, or you may set it off with quotation marks.

Tanner, John. *Anxiety in Eden: A Kierkegaardian Reading of* Paradise Lost. Oxford:
    Oxford UP, 1992. Print.

Tanner, John. *Anxiety in Eden: A Kierkegaardian Reading of "Paradise Lost."* Oxford:
    Oxford UP, 1992. Print.

■ **A Book with Corporate or Association Authorship**

United Nations, Public Administration Division. *Local Government Training.* New York: UN, 1968. Print.

■ **An Edition Other Than the First**

Reinking, James, et al. *Strategies for Successful Writing: A Rhetoric, Research Guide, Reader, and Handbook.* 4th Canadian ed. Toronto: Pearson, 2010. Print.

■ **A Book in Two or More Volumes**

Bartram, Henry C. *The Cavalcade of America.* 2 vols. New York: Knopf, 1959. Print.

■ **A Reprint of an Older Work**

Matthiessen, F. O. *American Renaissance: Art and Expression in the Age of Emerson and Whitman.* 1941. New York: Oxford UP, 1970. Print.

■ **A Book with an Editor Rather Than an Author**

Toye, William, ed. *The Oxford Companion to Canadian Literature.* 2nd ed. Toronto: Oxford UP, 1998. Print.

■ **A Book with Both an Author and an Editor**

Conrad, Joseph. *Heart of Darkness.* Ed. Robert Hampson. London: Penguin, 1995. Print.

■ **A Translation**

Beauvoir, Simone de. *All Said and Done.* Trans. Patrick O'Brian. New York: Putnam, 1974. Print.

■ **An Essay or Chapter in a Collection of Works by One Author**

Woolf, Virginia. "The Lives of the Obscure." *The Common Reader,* First Series. New York: Harcourt, 1925. 111–18. Print.

■ **An Essay or Chapter in an Anthology**

Blaise, Clark. "A Class of New Canadians." *Pens of Many Colours: A Canadian Reader.* Ed. Eva C. Karpinski and Ian Lea. Toronto: Harcourt Brace Jovanovich, 1993. 218–26. Print.

Periodicals

Periodicals include newspapers, popular magazines, and specialized occupational and scholarly journals. The basic information for a periodical article includes the name of the article's author, the name of the periodical, the title of the article, the date of publication, the page range of the entire article, and, for scholarly journals, the volume number and issue number (if there is one) of the periodical for scholarly journals, and the medium of publication. The MLA system capitalizes periodical titles, but omits an introductory *The* from these titles.

MLA

■ An Article in a Scholarly Journal

Pfennig, David. "Kinship and Cannibalism." *Bioscience* 47. 10 (1997): 667–75. Print.

■ An Article in a Scholarly Journal That Uses Only issue Numbers

Zine, Jasmin. "Honour and Identity: An Ethnographic Account of Muslim Girls in a
    Canadian Islamic School." *Topia* 19 (2008): 35-62. Print.

■ An Unsigned Article in a Scholarly Journal

"Baby, It's Cold Inside." *Science* 276 (1997): 537–38. Print.

■ A Signed Article in an Occupational or a Popular Magazine

Gopnik, Adam. "The Good Soldier." *New Yorker* 24 Nov. 1997: 106–14. Print.

■ An Unsigned Article in an Occupational or a Popular Magazine

"Robot Productivity." *Production Engineering* May 1982: 52–55. Print.

■ A Signed Article in a Daily Newspaper

Aird, Elizabeth. "Take Men as Sexual Victims, Please." *Vancouver Sun*
    14 Feb. 1998: A5. Print.

■ An Unsigned Article in a Daily Newspaper

"The Arithmetic of Terrorism." *Washington Post* 14 Nov. 1997:A26. Print.

Encyclopedia Articles

When documenting familiar works, such as *The Canadian Encyclopedia,* the basic information for the MLA system includes the name of the article's author if known, the title of the article, the name of the encyclopedia, the edition number (if provided), and the date of the edition.

Marsh, James. "Photography." *World Book Encyclopedia.* 1991 ed. Print.

Henderson, William. "Aboriginal Self-Government." *The Canadian Encyclopedia.*
    2000 ed. Print.

The MLA system requires additional information for encyclopedia citations when less familiar publications are documented.

Fears, J. Rufus. "Emperor's Cult." *Encyclopedia of Religion.* Ed. Mircea Eliade.16 vols.
    New York: Macmillan, 1987. Print.

For an anonymous article, references begin with the article's title.

Government Documents

The basic information for a federal, provincial, or foreign government publication that is documented using the MLA system includes the name of the author, the title of the publication, the name of the government and the agency issuing the publication, the place of publication, the name of the printing group, if known, the date, and the medium of publication. If no author is named, begin by identifying the government and then cite the government agency as the author.

Centre of Expertise in Marine Mammalogy. *Marine Mammal Research: An Overview.* Communications Branch, Fisheries and Oceans Canada. Ottawa, 2006. Print.

Helix, Jefferson. *Environmental Impact of Fish Farming in British Columbia.* British Columbia Ministry of Environment. Victoria: Queen's Printer for British Columbia, 1997. Print.

United States. Cong. Office of Technology Assessment. *The Biology of Mental Disorders.* 102nd Cong., 2nd sess. Washington: GPO, 1992. Print.

Other Sources

■ Book Reviews

Koenig, Rhoda. "Billy the Kid." Rev. of *Billy Bathgate,* by E. L. Doctorow. *New York* 20 Feb. 1989: 20–21. Print.

If the review is untitled, follow the above format but omit the missing element.

■ Published Interviews

Noriega, Manuel. "A Talk with Manuel Noriega." By Felipe Hernandez. *News Report* 20 Mar. 1997: 28–30. Print.

If the interview is untitled, then in place of a title, use the word "Interview," without quotation marks or italics.

■ Personal Interviews

If you conducted the interview yourself, start with the name of the person interviewed and follow it with the kind of interview and the date conducted.

Harper, Stephen. Personal interview. 19 Nov. 2008.

■ Audiovisual Media

Frankenstein. Dir. James Whale. Perf. Boris Karloff, John Boles, Colin Clive, and Mae Clarke. Universal, 1931. Film.

If you are interested in the contribution of a particular person, start with that person's name. Use the same model for videocassette and DVD recordings, and add release dates and distributors.

Whale, James, dir. *Frankenstein.* Perf. Boris Karloff, John Boles, Colin Clive, and Mae
    Clarke. Universal, 1931. Film.

Whale, James, dir. *Frankenstein.* Perf. Boris Karloff, John Boles, Colin Clive, and Mae
    Clarke. 1931. Universal, 1999. DVD.

■ Television and Radio Programs

The Independent Eye. Prod. M. Paris and J. Robertson. Knowledge Network. Know,
    Burnaby. 13 Feb. 1999. Television.

Use this format when additional information is pertinent:

Peril at End House. By Agatha Christie. Dir. Renny Rye. Prod. Brian Eastman.
    Perf. David Suchet and Hugh Fraser. *Mystery.* Introd. Diana Rigg. PBS. WKAR,
    East Lansing. 12 Aug. 1993. Television.

■ Music and Sound Recordings

Smith, Bessie. *The World's Greatest Blues Singer.* Columbia, 1948. LP.

Give the recording date, followed by the medium (CD, Audiocasette, Audiotape,
CD, or LP). If you mention the name of a particular item on the sound recording,
set it off with quotation marks, as shown below.

Smith, Bessie. "Down Hearted Blues." By Alberta Watson. *The World's Greatest Blues
    Singer.* Columbia, 1948. LP.

■ Computer Software

Data Desk. Vers. 6.0. Data Description, 1997. Computer software.

■ CD-ROMs and Other Databases

Norman, J. L. "Barcelona." *Software Toolworks Multimedia Encyclopedia.* Disc 1.
    Danbury: Grolier, 1996. CD-ROM.

Online Sources

Because data from the internet are often incomplete—perhaps lacking an author, a
title, or any recognizable page or paragraph number—ask your instructor what
format to follow and then use that format consistently. Include all the available information, including the online address only if your reader couldn't find it otherwise or
if your instructor requires you to do so.

■ Books on the Web

The basic information for a book on the Web includes the name(s) of the
author(s), if known; the title of the book; the place and date of original publication,

if applicable; the electronic site, if named; the date of electronic publication if the online version has never been published in print, or if it is part of a scholarly project; the title of the database or website (in italics); the medium of publication (*Web*); and the date the material was retrieved.

Locke, John. *An Essay Concerning Human Understanding.* London, 1690. *Institute of Learning Technologies.* 1995. Columbia U. Web. 24 June 2000.

When some of the basic information is not provided, use whatever is available.

Chaney, Walter J., William J. Diehm, and Frank Seeley. *The Second 50 Years: A Reference Manual for Senior Citizens.* Weed: London Circle, 1999. Web. 8 Aug. 2000.

To cite part of an electronic book, place the part's title after the name(s) of the author(s).

Dawson, Marie. Introduction. *Methods of Sociological Investigation.* New York: Harmon, 1997. Web. 6 Sept. 2000.

■ Periodicals on the Web

Periodicals online include specialized occupational and scholarly journals, popular magazines, newspapers, and newsletters. The basic information for a periodical is much the same as for a print publication: include the author's name, if known; the title of the article; the title of the periodical; the volume and issue numbers; the date the article was published; the page numbers (or if it's an online publication that doesn't include page numbers, "n.pag."); the medium of publication (*Web*); and the date the material was retrieved.

Cervetti, Nancy. "In the Breeches, Petticoats, and Pleasures of Orlando." *Journal of Modern Literature* 20.2 (1996): 165-75. Web. 8 Jan. 1998.

Navarro, Mireya. "Women in Sports Cultivating New Playing Fields." *New York Times.* New York Times, 13 Feb. 2001. Web. 22 Feb. 2001.

"No Link Found in Violence, Videos." *Boston Globe.* Boston Globe, 8 Aug. 2000. Web. 27 Aug. 2000.

Oakes, Jeannie. "Promotion or Retention: Which One Is Social?" *Harvard Education Letter* 15.1 (1999): n. pag. Web. 8 Aug. 2000.

■ Periodicals Accessed through an Online Library Service or Large Network Provider

Increasingly, full-text articles are available online at libraries or at home through services provided by private institutions such as LexisNexis and ProQuest Direct, or public institutions such as governments that maintain extensive databases. For a work in a periodical in an online database, cite the author's name, if known; the title of the article; the title of the periodical; the date the article was published; the page numbers for the article; the name of the database, in italics; the medium of publication (*Web*); and the date the material was accessed.

Clemetson, Lynette. "A Ticket to Private School." *Newsweek* 27 Mar. 2000.

LexisNexis. Web. 5 May 2000.

■ Encyclopedia Articles

The basic information for an encyclopedia article accessed online includes the author's name, if known; the title of the article; the name of the encyclopedia; the name of the overall Web site (in italics); version or edition used, the publisher; the date of the edition; the medium of publication (*Web*); and the date of access. For encyclopedia articles accessed through a CD-ROM, include the same information as for the printed version, putting the medium of publication as "CD-ROM."

"Western Music. "*Encyclopaedia Britannica Online.*" Encyclopaedia Britannica, 2009.

Web. 22 Apr. 2009.

■ Government Documents

The basic information for a government document includes the name of the author, if known; the title; the name of the government and agency issuing the document; the place of publication and printing group, if known; the date of publication; the medium of publication (*Web*); and the date the material was retrieved. If no author is given, begin by identifying the government and then give the government agency as the author.

Georgia State. Probation Division of the Georgia Department of Corrections.

Alternatives to Incarceration. 1 July 1997. Web. 3 Feb. 1998.

■ Personal Home Page

The basic information for a personal homepage documented according to the MLA style system includes the name of its originator, if known; the title of the site, if any (use *Home page* or other such description if no title is given); the medium of publication (*Web*); and the date the material was retrieved from the site.

Lanthrop, Olin. Home page. Web. 24 June 2000.

■ Online Postings and Email

For online posting such as newsgroups or mailing lists, use the label "Online posting" where the title would go. For an email message, give the name of the writer; the subject line of the message, if there is one, as the title in quotation marks; the words "Message to" and the name of the recipient; the date of the message, and the medium.

Corelli, Aldo. "Colleges and Diversity." Online posting. *Learninghouse,* 20 Apr. 1993.

Web. 24 June 2000.

Nicholson, Brad. "Casino Gambling." Message to author. 2 Feb. 2001. Email.

MLA

PREPARING APA BIBLIOGRAPHIC REFERENCES

Books

The basic bibliographic reference for a book includes the name of the author, the title of the book, the place of publication, the name of the publisher, and the date of publication. Other information is added as necessary. The APA system uses initials rather than first and middle names for authors, editors, and translators.

■ **A Book with One Author**

Ondaatje, M. (1993). *The English patient.* Toronto: Vintage Books.

■ **A Book with Two Authors**

Finnbogason, J., & Valleau, A. (1997). *A Canadian writer's guide.* Toronto: Nelson.

■ **A Book with More Than Three Authors**

Alder, R. W., Finn, T., Bradley, M. A., & Li, A. W. (1971). *Mechanisms in organic chemistry.* New York: Wiley.

The APA system gives up to and including six author or editor names in the reference list. Substitute "et al." for the seventh or more.

■ **A Book with a Title That Includes Another Title**

The APA offers no guidelines for this specific situation. However, the general guidelines for italics apply.

Tanner, J. (1992). *Anxiety in Eden: A Kierkegaardian reading of* Paradise Lost. Oxford: Oxford University Press.

■ **A Book with Corporate or Association Authorship**

United Nations, Public Administration Division. (1968). *Local government training.* New York: Author.

When the author of the work is also the publisher, the APA system uses the word "Author" following the place of publication. If the work is published by another organization, its name replaces "Author."

■ **An Edition Other Than the First**

Waldman, N., & Norton, S. (1996). *Canadian content* (3rd ed.). Toronto: Harcourt.

■ **A Book in Two or More Volumes**

Bartram, H. C. (1959). *The cavalcade of America* (Vols. 1–2). New York: Knopf.

■ **A Reprint of an Older Work**

Matthiessen, F. O. (1970). *American renaissance: Art and expression in the age of Emerson and Whitman.* New York: Oxford. (Original work published 1941)

APA

■ A Book with an Editor Rather Than an Author

Toye, W. (Ed.). (1983). *The Oxford companion to Canadian literature*. Toronto: Oxford.

■ A Book with Both an Author and an Editor

Conrad, J. (1995). *Heart of darkness* (R. Hampson, Ed.). London: Penguin. (Original
    work published 1902)

■ A Translation

Beauvoir, S. de. (1974). *All said and done* (P. O'Brian, Trans.). New York: Putnam.
    (Original work published 1972)

■ An Essay or Chapter in a Collection of Works by One Author

Woolf, V. (1925). The lives of the obscure. In V. Woolf, *The common reader*, first series
    (pp. 111–118). New York: Harcourt.

■ An Essay or Chapter in an Anthology

Blaise, C. (1993). A class of new Canadians. In E. C. Karpinski & I. Lea (Eds.),
    Pens of many colours: A Canadian reader (pp. 218–226). Toronto: Harcourt.

APA

Periodicals

The basic information for a periodical article includes the name of the article's
author, the date of publication, the title of the article, the name of the periodical, the page range of the entire article, and, for scholarly journals, the volume
number of the periodical.

■ An Article in a Scholarly Journal Consecutively Paged through the Entire Volume

Pfennig, D. (1997). Kinship and cannibalism. *Bioscience, 47*, 667–675.

■ An Article in a Scholarly Journal That Pages Each Issue Separately

Block, J. W. (1976). Sodom and Gomorrah: A volcanic disaster. *Journal of Geological
    Education, 23*(5), 74–77.

■ An Unsigned Article in a Scholarly Journal

Baby, it's cold inside. (1997). *Science, 276*, 537–538.

■ A Signed Article in an Occupational or a Popular Magazine

Gopnik, A. (1997, November 24). The good soldier. *The New Yorker, 73*, 106–114.

■ An Unsigned Article in an Occupational or a Popular Magazine

Robot productivity. (1982, May). *Production Engineering, 29*, 52–55.

■ A Signed Article in a Daily Newspaper

Aird, E. (1998, February 14). Take men as sexual victims, please. *Vancouver Sun,* p. A5.

■ An Unsigned Article in a Daily Newspaper

The arithmetic of terrorism. (1997, November 14). *Washington Post*, p. A26.

Encyclopedia Articles

The APA system requires complete information for all encyclopedia citations.

Fears, J. R. (1987). Emperor's cult. In *The encyclopedia of religion*
    (Vol. 5, pp. 101–102). New York: Macmillan.

For an anonymous article, references begin with the article's title. Position the publication date, within parentheses, after this title. The remaining format is identical to citations with an author.

Government Documents

The APA system includes the name of the author, the date of publication, and the place of publication and adds a cataloguing code where one exists.

Helix, J. (1997). *Environmental impact of fish farming in British Columbia.* British
    Columbia, Ministry of Environment. Victoria: Queen's Printer for British Columbia.

Canadian Department of Finance. (1993). *Annual report 1991–1992.* Ottawa: Queen's
    Printer.

U.S. Congress, Office of Technology Assessment. (1992). *The biology of mental
    disorders* (SUDOCS No. Y3.T22/2:2/B57/10). Washington, DC: U.S. Government
    Printing Office.

Other Sources

■ Book Reviews

Koenig, R. (1989, February 20). Billy the Kid [Review of the book *Billy Bathgate*]. *New
    York, 20–21.*

If the review is untitled, follow the above format but omit the missing element.

■ Published Interviews

The APA system does not include a documentation format for published interviews. If your paper includes material from a published interview, we suggest that you document as follows:

Hernandez, F. (1997, Mar. 20). A talk with Manuel Noriega. [Interview with Manuel
    Noriega]. *News Report, 15,* 28–30.

If the interview is untitled, follow the example above, omitting mention of a title.

■ Personal Interviews

For the APA system, a personal interview is considered personal correspondence and is not included in the References list. Use only an in-text parenthetical citation.

Include the name of the person interviewed, the notation "personal communication," and the date: (P. Newman, personal communication, May 18, 2005).

■ Film

The citation begins with an individual's name and his or her contribution to the *motion picture* (use this term, not *film*). The country of origin (where it was made and released) is required.

Whale, J. (Director). (1931). *Frankenstein* [Motion picture].United States: Universal.

■ Television and Radio Programs

Paris, M., & Robertson, J. (Producers). (1999, February 13). *The independent eye* [Television broadcast]. Burnaby, BC: Knowledge Network.

Use the following format when additional information is pertinent:

Exton, C. (Script Writer), & Rye, R. (Director). (1993). Peril at End House [Television series episode]. In B. Eastman (Producer), *Mystery*. Washington, DC: Public Broadcasting Service.

Note that the name of the scriptwriter appears first the author's position, followed by the director. Any in-text references begin with the first name in the bibliographical reference (for example, Exton, 1993).

■ Music and Sound Recordings

The APA format requires identification of all formats, including a CD.

Smith, B. (1948). *The essential Bessie Smith*. [CD]. New York: Columbia Records.

Hunter, A. (1921). Down hearted blues [Recorded by B. Smith]. On *The world's greatest blues singer* [CD]. New York: Columbia Records. (Original recording February 17, 1925.)

Recording dates, if different from the copyright year, follow the entry, enclosed in parentheses, with no final period.

■ Computer Software

Data Desk (Version 6.0) [Computer software]. (1997). Ithaca, NY: Data Description.

Only specialized software or computer programs are listed in the References. Standard commercial software and languages should be cited by their proper name and version in the text itself.

■ CD-ROMs and Other Databases

Norman, J. L. (1992). Barcelona. *Software Toolworks Multimedia Encyclopedia* [CD-ROM]. Boston: Grolier.

The APA *Manual* (5th ed.) takes the view that all aggregated databases are the same type of source, regardless of the format or manner of access (CD-ROM, library or university server, or online Web supplier). Follow the model above when you need to cite an entire CD-ROM (not a document from it). In a reference to information taken from a database (even a CD-ROM), give a "retrieval statement" containing the date you retrieved the document, article, or piece of data, as well as the full, correct name of the database. When you retrieve information from an online database, end the entry with a correct and complete URL for the specific document or version. In this case, the name of the database is omitted, unless this information will help in retrieval from a large or complex site. (See online samples in the next section.)

Online Sources

While the 2001 fifth edition of the *Publication Manual of the American Psychological Association* provides guidelines for documenting online sources, the most up-to-date information is in the *APA Style Guide to Electronic References,* published online in 2007. This 24-page PDF can be ordered from the association's website.

> http://www.apastyle.org/elecref.html

Be sure to ask your instructor which format to follow and then use that format consistently. If the data from the internet are incomplete, perhaps lacking an author, a title, or recognizable page or paragraph number, include all the available information. APA guidelines recommend that you include the same elements for an online reference as you would include for a print source, adding as much extra information as a reader would need to find the document.

■ Retrieval Date Only for Material Likely to Change

Include the date you retrieved material only if it is likely to be updated or altered, such as a blog or a wiki. A retrieval date is usually not needed for journal articles or books.

■ Include Name and Location of Source

Because much internet content changes frequently, many academic publishers now assign a Digital Object Identifier (DOI) to scholarly documents. A DOI is a unique string of numbers and letters assigned by a registration agency, is more stable than a URL and should be used instead of a URL when available. It can usually be found on the first page of the article. If there is no DOI, include the URL, such as the example below of the URL for the Social Science and Humanities Research Council of Canada:

> http://www.sshrc.ca/site/home-accueil-eng.aspx

For convenience and accuracy, you can copy and paste the DOI, if one is available, or the URL. Because your goal is to allow the reader to locate the source you have used, you should test URLs in a new browser session to ensure they actually work.

■ Books on the Web

Follow the general guidelines for a printed book and conclude with appropriate electronic source information, as modelled here.

Locke, J. (1995). *An essay concerning human understanding.* New York: Columbia University. (Original work published 1690). Retrieved from http://www.ilt.columbia.edu/projects/digitexts/locke/understanding/title.html

When some of the basic information is not provided, use whatever is available.

Chaney, W. J., Diehm, W. J., & Seeley, F. (1999). *The second 50 years: A reference manual for senior citizens.* Weed: London Circle. Retrieved from http://londoncircle.com/2d50.html

To cite part of an electronic document or book, place the part's title after the date of publication and cite a chapter or section identifier following the title of the complete document.

Canadian Food Inspection Agency. (2008). Nutrition labelling. In *Guide to food labelling and advertising* (chap. 5). Retrieved from http://www.inspection.gc.ca/english/fssa/labeti/guide/ch5e.shtml

APA

■ Periodicals on the Web

The APA recommends using the models for print periodicals when documenting online articles. When the article has a DOI assigned, no retrieval date, database name (if one is used), or URL is necessary. If the article does not have a DOI assigned, give the exact URL if access to the journal is open, and give the home page of the journal if the article is accessible only by subscription. A retrieval date is not necessary.

■ Journal Article with DOI Assigned

Raver, C., et al. (2009). Targeting children's behavior problems in preschool classrooms: A cluster-randomized controlled trial. *Journal of Consulting and Clinical Psychology, 77,* 302–316. doi: 10.1037/a0015302

■ Journal Article with No DOI Assigned

Sprott, J., & Doob, A. (2008). Youth crime rates and the youth justice system. *Canadian Journal of Criminology and Criminal Justice, 50,* 621–639. Retrieved from http://www.ccja-acjp.ca/en/cjc.html

■ Book Reviews and Peer Commentaries

Galbo, J. (2008). Anxious academics: Mission drift and sliding standards in the modern Canadian university [Review of the book *Ivory tower blues: A university system in crisis*]. *Canadian Journal of Sociology, 33,* 404–417. Retrieved from http://ejournals.library.ualberta.ca/index.php/CJS/article/viewFile/4548/3694

Beare, M. (2008). [Response to David Hicks's peer comment on *Money laundering in Canada: Chasing dirty and dangerous dollars*]. *Canadian Journal of Sociology, 33,* 1065–1067. Retrieved from http://ejournals.library.ualberta.ca/index.php/CJS/article/view/4546/3693

■ Newspaper or Newsletter Articles

Laucius, J. (2009, March 26). Students need real civics lessons: Educator. *Ottawa Citizen.* Retrieved from http://www.ottawacitizen.com/Life/Students+need+real+civics+lessons+educator/1428192/story.html

Oakes, J. (1999, January–February). Promotion or retention: Which one is social? *Harvard Education Letter.* Retrieved August 8, 2000, from http://www.edletter.org/ pst/issues/1999-jf-promotion.shtml

■ Encyclopedia Articles

The basic information for an encyclopedia article accessed through the Web includes the author's name, if known; the date of the edition; the title of the article; the name of the encyclopedia; the date the material was retrieved; and the URL of the home or index page.

Greene, G., & Spier, S. Banff Centre for the Arts. In *Encyclopedia of music in Canada.* Retrieved March 1, 2009, from http://www.thecanadianencyclopedia.com/ index.cfm?PgNm=EMCSubjects&Params=U2

■ Bibliography from Website

Library and Archives Canada. (2006). *Aboriginal stories: English annotated titles.* Retrieved from Read Up on It 2006-2007, Library Archives Canada website: http://www.collectionscanada.gc.ca/read-up-on-it/015020-062000-e.html#a

■ Government Documents

The basic information for a government document includes the name of the author, if known; the date of publication; the title; a cataloguing code if one is available; the date the material was retrieved; and the online address. If no author is given, begin by identifying the government agency as the author.

Statistics Canada. (2008). *Educational portrait of Canada, 2006 census.* Retrieved April 24, 2009, from http://www12.statcan.ca/english/census06/analysis/ education/pdf/97-560-XIE2006001.pdf

■ Annual Report

Petro-Canada. (2008). *Petro-Canada annual report: Strength to deliver.* Retrieved from http://www.petro-canada.ca/pdfs/investors/2008_annual_report-e.pdf

■ Personal Home Page

The APA *Manual* offers no specific guidelines for personal home pages. We suggest that you follow the following pattern, which conforms to general APA practice. Note that the APA system includes the date of the latest webpage revision, if known, in parentheses.

Lanthrop, O. (2000, May 28). Home page. Retrieved June 24, 2000, from http://www.cognivis.com/olin/photos.htm

■ Alternative Media Sources

Format a podcast as follows.

McDonald, B. (Producer). (2009, February 28). The evolution of moral disgust. *Quirks and Quarks.* Podcast retrieved from http://www.cbc.ca/quirks/

For a weblog (blog), use the words "Message posted to" before the address.

Raskin, R. (2009, March 4). Should learning be rewarded with "stuff"? Message posted to http://www.robinraskin.com/blog/category/your-digital-kids/

■ Newsgroups, Electronic Mailing Lists, and Email

APA format treats email as personal communications, which are cited in parentheses in the text only. Newsgroups, online forums, discussion groups, and electronic mailing lists that maintain archives can be cited in the References, but the APA advises that you do so with caution.

Trehub, A. (2002, January 28). The conscious access hypothesis [Msg. 18]. Message posted to University of Houston Psyche Discussion Forum: http://listserv.uh.edu/cgi-bin/wa?A2=ind0201&L=psyche-b& F=&S=&P=2334

APA

EXERCISE

1. **Using the MLA or APA system, write a proper reference for each of the unstyled sets of information that follow:**

    a. A book entitled Gas Conditioning Fact Book. The book was published in 1962 by Dow Chemical Company in Midland, Michigan. No author is named.

    b. An unsigned article entitled Booze Plays a Big Role in Car Crashes. The article was published in the November 28, 1997, state edition of the Detroit News. It appears on page 2 of section C.

    c. An essay written by C. Wright Mills and entitled The Competitive Personality. The essay appeared in a collection of Mills's writings entitled Power, Politics, and People. The collection was published in 1963 by Ballantine Books in New York. The book is edited and introduced by Irving Louis Horowitz. The essay appears on pages 263 through 273.

    d. An unsigned article entitled Global Warming Fears on Rise. The article was published in the October 25, 1997, issue of Newswatch magazine. It appears on pages 29 to 31.

    e. A book written by Guy Vanderhaeghe and entitled The Englishman's Boy. The book was published in 1996 by McClelland & Stewart Inc. in Toronto.

    f. A book written by Kate Chopin and entitled The Awakening. The book, edited by Margaret Culley, was published in 1976 by W. W. Norton and Company in New York.

    g. An article written by James E. Cooke and entitled Alexander Hamilton. The article appears on pages 31 and 32 of the World Book Encyclopedia, Volume 9, published in 1996.

    h. An article written by Sarah McBride and entitled Young Deadbeats Pose Problems for Credit-Card Issuers. The article was published in the November 28, 1997, Toronto edition of The Globe and Mail. It appears on pages 1 and 6 of section B.

    i. A book written by Magdalena Dabrowski and Rudolph Leopold and entitled Egon Schiele. The book was published in 1997 by the Yale University Press in New Haven, Connecticut.

j. A book written by Jean Descola and entitled A History of Spain. The book, translated by Elaine P. Halperin, was published in 1962 by Alfred A. Knopf in New York.

k. An article written by John T. Flanagan and Raymond L. Grimer and entitled Mexico in American Fiction to 1850. The article was published in 1940 in a journal called Hispania. It appears on pages 307 through 318. The volume number is 23.

l. A Canadian government document entitled Marine Fisheries Review. It was published by the Federal Department of Fisheries in 1993. No author is given.

m. A book written by David Kahn and entitled The Codebreakers. The second edition of the book was published in 1996 by Scribner's in New York.

n. A book written by Joseph Blotner and entitled Faulkner: A Biography. The book was published in two volumes in 1974 by Random House in New York.

o. An article written by Calvin Tompkins and entitled The Importance of Being Elitist. The article was published in the November 24, 1997, issue of The New Yorker. It appears on pages 58 through 69.

p. A book written by Thomas Beer and entitled Stephen Crane: A Study in American Letters. The book was published in 1923 and reprinted in 1972 by Octagon Books in New York.

q. A review of a book written by Jacques Barzun and entitled The Culture We Deserve. The review, by Beth Winona, appeared in the March 1989 issue of American Issues magazine and was titled Barzun and Culture. It appeared on pages 46 through 50.

r. An interview of playwright Neil Simon. The interview was entitled Neil Simon on the New York Theater and appeared in the September 3, 1997, issue of the Long Island News, on pages C4–5. The interviewer was Pearl Barnes.

s. A film entitled Casablanca. The film was directed by Michael Curtiz and starred Humphrey Bogart, Ingrid Bergman, Claude Rains, and Paul Henreid. It was released in 1942 by Warner Brothers.

t. A television program entitled Grizzly. It appeared on CBUT, Vancouver, on February 3, 1997. The station is part of the CBC.

2. **Prepare a proper MLA or APA reference for each of the works you plan to use in writing a paper.**

HANDLING IN-TEXT CITATIONS

Both the MLA and APA systems use notations that appear within the text and are set off by parentheses. The systems are illustrated by the following examples.

Basic Citation Form

For the MLA system, the citation consists of the last name of the author and the page number(s) of the material from the original source. The APA system identifies the last name of the author or authors and the year of publication. When the same work is referenced within a paragraph, the first in-text citation requires the date; subsequent references in the text of that paragraph only need the author's name. A page number is provided in APA with quotations and when the information is so specific that it is important to reference the specific page.

■ Bibliographic Reference*

Rothenberg, Randall. "Life in Cyburbia." *Esquire* Feb. 1996: 56–63. Print.

■ Passage and Citation

> A mania for the internet has invaded many important aspects of our culture. Newspapers run stories on it, businesses have rushed to set up websites, and the Speaker of the House of Representatives has stated that even our poorest children have a stake in the internet (Rothenberg 59). `MLA`

> Rothenberg states that a mania for the internet has invaded many important aspects of our culture. Newspapers run stories on it, businesses have rushed to set up websites, and the Speaker of the House of Representatives has stated that even our poorest children have a stake in the internet (59). `MLA`

> . . . our poorest children have a stake in the Internet (Rothenberg, 1996, p. 59). `APA`

> Rothenberg (1996) states . . . have a stake in the Internet (p. 59). `APA`

In-Text

■ Bibliographic Reference

Weider, Benjamin, and David Hapgood. *The Murder of Napoleon.* New York: Congdon, 1982. Print.

■ Passage and Citation

> Four different autopsy reports were filed. All the reports agreed that there was a cancerous ulcer in Napoleon's stomach, but none of them declared that the cancer was the cause of death. Nevertheless, cancer has become accepted as the cause (Weider and Hapgood 72). `MLA`

> . . . Nevertheless, cancer has become accepted as the cause (Weider & Hapgood, 1982, p. 72). `APA`

If a source has more than three authors (more than six for the APA), use "et al.," meaning "and others," for all but the first-named one.

■ Bibliographic Reference

Baugh, Albert C., et al. *A Literary History of England.* New York: Appleton, 1948. Print.

■ Passage and Citation

> Although no one knows for certain just when Francis Beaumont and John Fletcher started collaborating, by 1610 they were writing plays together (Baugh et al. 573). `MLA`

> . . . writing plays together (Baugh et al., 1948, p. 573). `APA`

* The bibliographic references in this section are in MLA style.

Authors with the Same Last Name

If your citations include authors with the same last name, use the initials of their first names to distinguish them.

■ Bibliographic References

Adler, Jerry. "Search for an Orange Thread." *Newsweek* 16 June 1980: 32–34. Print.

Adler, William L. "The Agent Orange Controversy." *Detroit Free Press* 18 Dec. 1979, state ed.: B2. Print.

■ Passage and Citation

In-Text

| MLA | As early as 1966, government studies showed that dioxin-contaminated 2,4,5-T caused birth defects in laboratory animals. Later studies also found that this herbicide was to blame for miscarriages, liver abscesses, and nerve damage (J. Adler 32). |

| APA | . . . miscarriages, liver abscesses, and nerve damage (J. Adler, 1980, p. 32). |

Separate Works by the Same Author

If your references include two or more works by the same author, add shortened forms of the titles to your in-text citation if you follow the MLA system. Underline shortened book titles and use quotation marks around article and essay titles. For the APA system, use the conventional name-date-page number entry. (Note: Page numbers are not always needed.)

■ Bibliographic References

Mullin, Dennis. "After U.S. Troops Pull Out of Grenada." *U.S. News & World Report* 14 Nov. 1983: 22–25. Print.

--- "Why the Surprise Move in Grenada—and What Next." *U.S. News & World Report* 7 Nov. 1983: 31–34. Print.

■ Passage and Citation

| MLA | As the rangers evacuated students, the marines launched another offensive at Grand Mal Bay, then moved south to seize the capital and free the governor (Mullin, "Why the Surprise" 33). |

| APA | . . . and free the governor (Mullin, 1983b, p. 33). |

As the APA example illustrates, if the two works by the same author appeared in the same year, put an "a" or a "b," without quotation marks, after the date to identify whether you are referring to the first or second entry for that author in the bibliography.

Two Sources for the Same Citation

If two sources provide essentially the same information and you wish to mention both in one parenthetical citation, alphabetize them according to their authors' last names, group them together with a semicolon between them, and position the citation as you would any other citation. (Citations using MLA do not need to be listed alphabetically.)

■ Bibliographic References

Bryce, Bonnie. "The Controversy over Funding Community Colleges." *Detroit Free Press* 13 Nov. 1988, state ed.: A4. Print.

Warshow, Harry. "Community College Funding Hits a Snag." *Grand Rapids Press* 15 Nov. 1988, city ed.: A2. Print.

■ Passage and Citation

In contending that a 3 percent reduction in state funding for community colleges would not significantly hamper their operations, the governor overlooked the fact that community college enrollment was expected to jump by 15 percent during the next year (Bryce A4; Warshow A2).

> MLA

. . . enrollment was expected to jump by 15 percent during the next year (Bryce, 1988, p. A4; Warshow, 1988, p. A2).

> APA

In-Text

Unsigned References

When you use a source for which no author is given, the in-text citation consists of all or part of the title, the appropriate page numbers, and, for the APA system, the date.

■ Bibliographic Reference

"Money and Classes." *Progressive* Oct. 1997: 10. Print.

■ Passage and Citation

According to the General Accounting Office, repairing the country's dilapidated school buildings would carry a price tag of over 110 billion dollars. Furthermore, constructing the 6000 buildings needed to end classroom overcrowding would cost many billions more ("Money and Classes" 10).

> MLA

. . . many billions more ("Money and Classes," 1997, p. 10).

> APA

Citing Quotations

When the quotation is run into the text, position the citation as shown below.

■ Bibliographic Reference

Schapiro, Mark. "Children of a Lesser God." *Harper's Bazaar* Apr. 1996: 205–6+. Print.

■ Passage and Citation

MLA

U.N. investigators who have studied the extent of child labour in Third World countries estimate that "as many as 200 million children go to work rather than to school . . . making everything from clothing and shoes to handbags and carpets" (Schapiro 205).

APA

" . . . handbags and carpets" (Schapiro, 1996, p. 205).

With longer, indented quotations, skip two horizontal spaces after the end punctuation and type the reference in parentheses.

In-Text

■ Bibliographic Reference

Kymlicka, Will. "Immigrants, Multiculturalism and Citizenship." *Strategies for Successful Writing.* 2nd Canadian ed. Ed. James A. Reinking et al. Toronto: Pearson, 2006: 46–63. Print.

■ Passage and Citation

MLA

One commentator offers this assessment of the focus of Canada's multiculturalism policy, which is often misunderstood by its critics:

> In reality, most of the focus of multiculturalism policy (and most of its funding) has been directed to promoting civic participation in the larger society and to increasing mutual understanding and co-operation between the members of different ethnic groups. More generally, the multiculturalism policy has never stated or implied that people are under any duty or obligation to retain their ethnic identity/practices "freeze-dried," or indeed to retain them at all. On the contrary, the principle that individuals should be free to choose whether to maintain their ethnic identity has been one of the cornerstones of the policy since 1971 and continues to guide existing multiculturalism programs. Multiculturalism is intended to make it possible for people to retain and express their identity with pride if they so choose, by reducing the legal, institutional, economic or societal obstacles to this expression. It does not penalize or disapprove of people who choose not to identify with their ethnic group, or describe them as poor citizens or as lesser Canadians. (Kymlicka 46)

APA

. . . describe them as poor citizens or as lesser Canadians. (Kymlicka, 2006, p. 46)

Indirect Citations

If you use a quotation from person A that you obtained from a book or article written by person B, or you paraphrase such a quotation, put "qtd. in" before the name of the publication's author in the parenthetical reference. For APA style, name the original work in the text, then give the secondary source in parentheses preceded by "as cited in" rather than "qtd.in."

■ Bibliographic Reference

Klein, Joe. "Ready for Rudy." *New York* 6 Mar. 1989: 30–37. Print.

■ Passage and Citation

Rudolph Giuliani favours the death penalty for "the murder of a law-enforcement officer, mass murder, a particularly heinous killing" but would impose it only "when there is certainty of guilt well beyond a reasonable doubt" (qtd. In Klein 37). `MLA`

Rudolph Giuliani favours " . . . certainty of guilt well beyond a reasonable doubt" (as cited in Klein, 1989, p. 37). `APA`

In-Text

Authors Identified in Text

Sometimes you need to introduce a paraphrase, summary, or quotation with the name of its author. In this case, the page number may be positioned immediately after the name or follow the material cited.

■ Bibliographic Reference

Jacoby, Susan. "Waiting for the End: On Nursing Homes." *New York Times Magazine* 31 Mar. 1974, city ed.: 80. Print.

■ Passage and Citation

Susan Jacoby (80+) sums up the grim outlook of patients in bad nursing homes by noting that they are merely waiting to die. `MLA`

Susan Jacoby sums up the grim outlook of patients in bad nursing homes by noting that they are merely waiting to die (80+).

Susan Jacoby (1974, p. 80) sums up . . . `APA`

Susan Jacoby (1974) sums up . . . waiting to die (p. 80).

EXERCISE *Using the MLA system, write a proper in-text citation for each of the bibliographic references you prepared for part 2 on page 484. Assume that you have not used the author's name to introduce the material you cite.*

HANDLING QUOTATIONS

Set off quotations fewer than five lines long (fewer than forty words long for the APA system) with quotation marks and run them into the text of the paper. For longer quotations, omit the quotation marks and indent the material 2.5 centimetres (1 inch) from the left-hand margin; (1 centimetre (1/2 inch) for the APA system). Double-space the text. If you quote part or all of one paragraph, don't further indent the first line. If you quote two or more consecutive paragraphs, indent each one's first line an additional 0.5 centimetre (1/4 inch); 1 centimetre (1/2 inch) for the APA system. Use single quotation marks for a quotation within a shorter quotation and double marks for a quotation within a longer, indented quotation. The following examples illustrate the handling of quotations. The documentation and indentation follow the MLA guidelines.

■ Short Quotation

Ellen Goodman offers this further observation about writers who peddle formulas for achieving success through selfishness: "They are all Doctor Feelgoods, offering placebo prescriptions instead of strong medicine. They give us a way to live with ourselves, perhaps, but not a way to live with each other" (16).

■ Quotation within Short Quotation

The report further stated, "All great writing styles have their wellsprings in the personality of the writer. As Buffon said, 'The style is the man'" (Duncan 49).

■ Quotation within Longer, Indented Quotation

Barbara Tuchman's *The Proud Tower* presents a somewhat different view of the new conservative leaders:

Besides riches, rank, broad acres, and ancient lineage, the new government also possessed, to the regret of the liberal opposition, and in the words of one of them, "an almost embarrassing wealth of talent and capacity." Secure in authority, resting comfortably on their electoral majority in the House of Commons and on a permanent majority in the House of Lords, of whom four-fifths were conservatives, they were in a position, admitted the same opponent, "of unassailable strength." (4)

Always provide some context for material that you quote. Various options exist. When you quote from a source for the first time, you might provide the author's full name and the source of the quotation, perhaps indicating the author's expertise as well. The passage just above omits the author's expertise; the passage below includes it.

Writing in *Newsweek* magazine, Riena Gross, chief psychiatric social worker at Illinois Medical Center in Chicago, said, "Kids have no real sense that they belong anywhere or to anyone as they did ten or fifteen years ago. Parents have loosened the reins, and kids are kind of floundering" (74).

Or you might note the event prompting the quotation and then the author's name.

> Addressing a seminar at the University of Toronto, Dr. Joseph Pomeranz speculated that "acupuncture may work by activating a neural pain suppression mechanism in the brain" (324).

On other occasions you might note only the author's full name and expertise.

> Economist Richard M. Cybert, president of Carnegie-Mellon University, offers the following sad prediction about the steel industry's future: "It will never be as large an industry as it has been. There are a lot of plants that will never come back and many laborers that will never be rehired" (43).

After first citing an author's full name, use only the last name for subsequent references.

> In answering the objections of government agencies to the U.S. Freedom of Information Act, Wellford commented, "Increased citizen access should help citizens learn of governmental activities that weaken our First Amendment freedoms. Some administrative inconvenience isn't too large a price to pay for that" (137).

When quoting from a source with no author given, introduce the quotation with the name of the source.

> Commenting upon the problems that law enforcement personnel have in coping with computer crime, *Credit and Financial Management* magazine pointed out, "A computer crime can be committed in three hundredths of a second, and the criminal can be thousands of miles from the 'scene,' using a telephone" ("Computer Crime" 43).

Page numbers are not helpful when you cite passages from plays and poems since these literary forms are available in many editions. When you quote from a play, identify the act, scene, and line numbers. Use Arabic numbers separated by periods. Here's how to cite Act 2, Scene 1, lines 295–300 of Shakespeare's *Othello:*

> That Cassio loves her, I do well believe it;
> That she loves him, 'tis apt, and of great credit:
> The Moor, how be it that I endure him not,
> Is of a constant, loving, noble nature;
> And I dare think he'll prove to Desdemona
> A most dear husband. (*Othello* 2.1. 295–300)

When quoting from a short poem, use "line" or "lines" and the line number(s).

> In "Dover Beach," Matthew Arnold offers this melancholy assessment of the state of religion:

> The Sea of Faith
> Was once, too, at the full, and round earth's shore

> Lay like the folds of a bright girdle furl'd.
>
> But now I only hear
>
> Its melancholy, long, withdrawing roar. (lines 21–25)

In quoting poetry that has been run into the text, use a slash (/) to indicate the shift from one line to the next in the original:

> In his ode "To Autumn," Keats says that autumn is the "Season of mists and mellow fruitfulness, / Close bosom-friend of the maturing sun" (lines 1–2).

AVOIDING PLAGIARISM

While documenting your sources properly strengthens the authority of your writing, failing to document properly weakens your personal and academic or professional credibility. This failure to document, whether intentional or not, may be regarded as plagiarism.

Plagiarism is a form of academic dishonesty. It occurs when a writer uses another person's material without properly acknowledging the debt. Almost all students know that the most obvious forms of plagiarism—such as buying a paper from a paper mill—are unethical. Often, however, plagiarism happens because students are careless in their note taking, or because they simply don't understand what must be acknowledged and documented. In our computerized world, where we have become used to downloading music and sharing software, it might be tempting to rationalize that material from the internet is free for the taking. Some students might imagine that they can escape the obligation to cite sources by changing a word here or there, or cutting and pasting information from different sources. However, unless the material is clearly common knowledge that will not ever be questioned or challenged, any material from external sources, including the internet, must be cited. Both intentional and unintentional plagiarism are unacceptable.

Plagiarism is a serious ethical breach. It degrades the quality of education for students and for institutions. It is unfair to the majority of students who are struggling to learn the challenging task of incorporating relevant research into their own writing in a responsible way. Students who plagiarize cheat themselves of genuine learning; they are also robbing the original writer of due recognition.

The consequences of plagiarism are often severe. Depending on the school policy, students caught plagiarizing risk getting a zero for that assignment, failing the course, or even being suspended or expelled. In 2002, 44 business and economics students at a major B.C. university were suspended for plagiarizing a tutor's work; the suspensions were noted on the students' transcripts. Large groups of students at other Canadian universities have been suspended for academic dishonesty. Instructors who are used to reading student essays can usually notice when the voice of the writer changes, or when the quality of the writing is inconsistent. In addition, many schools have plagiarism detection software that helps instructors track plagiarism, even if it is just a few sentences that have been raided from a source. It's easy for professors to use search engines to check whether particular phrases, sentences, or paragraphs have been copied from websites—and many do.

Any summary, paraphrase, quotation, statistics, or graphics you include in your paper must be documented. The only types of information escaping this requirement are those listed below:

1. *Common knowledge.* Common knowledge is information that most educated people would know. For instance, there's no need to document a statement that the Pacific National Exhibition attracts thousands of visitors each year. However, if you include precise daily, monthly, or yearly figures, then documentation is necessary.

2. *Your own conclusions.* As you write your paper, you incorporate your own conclusions at various points. Such comments require no documentation. The same holds true for your own research. If you polled students on a campus issue, simply present the findings as your own.

3. *Facts found in many sources.* Facts such as the year of Shakespeare's death, the size of the national debt, and the location of the Taj Mahal need not be documented. However, where there may be disputes about the facts in question or where there may be some need to enforce the credibility of your figures, provide the source for your facts. If you are not certain that something is common knowledge, indicate your source.

4. *Standard terms.* Terms widely used in a particular field require no documentation. Examples include such computer terms as *mouse, hard drive,* and *download.*

Any piece of information not set off with quotation marks must be in your own words. Otherwise, even though you name your source, you are plagiarizing by presenting the original phrasing as your own.

The following passages illustrate the improper and proper use of source material in conveying James L. Buckley's thoughts on the potential environmental impact of development in the United States.

Original Passage

One might contend, of course, that our country's biological diversity is so great and the land is so developed—so criss-crossed with the works of man—that it will soon be hard to build a dam anywhere without endangering some species. But as we develop a national inventory of endangered species, we certainly can plan our necessary development so as to exterminate the smallest number possible . . .

James L. Buckley, "Three Cheers for the Snail Darter,"
National Review, September 14, 1979: 1144–45. Print.

■ Plagiarism

Our country's biological diversity is so great and the land is so developed that it will soon be hard to build a dam anywhere without endangering some species. But as we develop a national inventory of endangered species, we certainly can plan our necessary development so as to exterminate the smallest number possible.

This writer has clearly plagiarized. The absence of Buckley's name and the failure to enclose his words in quotation marks create the impression that this passage is the student's own work.

■ Plagiarism

> Given the extensive diversity of species in America, development such as the construction of dams is likely to endanger some species, whether it is a rare plant, a species of frog, or a rare variety of fish. By creating a database of endangered species, however, we can facilitate a planning process that will place the minimum number of species at risk.

While this writer uses original language, the absence of documentation suggests that these ideas are the student's without any recognition of Buckley's contribution. Despite the paraphrase, this is still plagiarism.

■ Plagiarism

> Our country's biological diversity is so great and the land so developed that in the near future we may pose a threat to some creature whenever we construct a dam. By developing a national inventory of endangered species, however, we can plan necessary development so as to preserve as many species as possible (Buckley 1144).

This version credits the ideas to Buckley, but the student has plagiarized by failing to put quotation marks around the phrasing (underlined above) that was copied from the original. As a result, readers will think that the passage represents the student's own wording.

■ Proper Use of Original

> The United States has so many kinds of plants and animals, and it is so built up, that in the near future we may pose a threat to some living thing just by damming some waterway. If, however, Americans knew which of their nation's plants and animals were threatened, they could use this information to preserve as many species as they can (Buckley 1144).

This student has identified the author and used her own words. As a result, she has not plagiarized.

Students who are uncertain about what constitutes plagiarism are responsible to educate themselves. They may consult resources available through online sources such as various documents available at

http://www.plagiarism.org/learning_center/printable_docs.html

Whenever you are unsure whether material requires documentation, supply a reference. And always handle direct quotations by following the guidelines beginning on page 490.

READER

Daniel Francis

My Life with Riley

Daniel Francis originally published this article in the Fall 1996 issue of Geist *magazine. In the following essay, Francis narrates a lively, even humorous, account of the relationship he had with his blind dog. The essay, which shows the effects of the discovery of his dog's blindness on himself initially and then on other people, may allow for the discussion of ethical issues relating to disabilities.*

1   We were driving through Stanley Park, talking about what to call the new dog when my son piped up from the back seat, "Why not Stanley Bark?" It was his first joke (a pretty good one, too) and we all laughed appreciatively, but in the end, families being what they are and democracy being what it is, we settled on Riley.

2   Collectors of political trivia will recall that in 1990 Barbara Bush's dog Millie published her first book. Titled simply *Millie's Book*, it was a heartwarming dog's-eye view of life in the White House, illustrated with many colour photographs of Millie going about her daily activities as the most powerful dog in the free world.

3   Millie was a springer spaniel. So was Riley. A coincidence, but when I learned about it I took it as a sign that we had chosen the right breed. The Dog of Presidents. But this was as far as the similarity went. Millie was obviously a gifted dog. After all, she had written a book. Riley, on the other hand, did not write books. To be honest, he could not even read them. Riley was blind.

4   Until Riley came into my life, I was not what is commonly called a dog lover. Not like the President and Mrs. Bush. My only other canine encounter was with a yappy, anorexic Chihuahua purchased by my parents when I was a boy. They called him Rex. I suppose it was meant to be a joke. Rex had a serious problem with continence and soon moved on to alternative accommodation where white rugs were not an issue. This brief experience in no way prepared me for the implications of Riley's disability.

5   We did not realize that Riley was blind until some time after we purchased him. I remember looking into his eyes. They seemed completely blank, like Orphan Annie's dog in the comic strip, but it did not occur to me that there was nobody there looking back. Finally, when Riley began walking into walls and falling off the back porch, we began to suspect there was something wrong. Still, it came as a complete shock when the dog ophthalmologist diagnosed two detached retinas. They were floating in his eyeballs like small collapsed trumpets, the doctor said. Riley couldn't see a thing.

6   The world immediately divided into two camps. On one side were those who counselled us to replace Riley with a "healthy" dog. They argued that any dog,

but especially a natural-born retriever, could not be happy blind. For the sake of the animal, for the sake of our children, we should try again. Which, of course, meant having Riley euthanized. And we had better do it soon before we grew attached to him.

7   The other camp argued that there was nothing wrong with a blind dog, that it was a kind of insane consumerism that treated a dog like a faulty vacuum cleaner to be traded in for a better model. One friend said, "When the dog's time comes, it will come, but it's not now." Life seemed to be filled with conversations like that. In the end we decided, for better or worse, not to kill the dog.

8   I acquired one of those long retractable leashes which extend to a reasonable distance and began taking Riley for strolls through the neighbourhood. His walk was erratic; he tacked from side to side like a sailboat heading into the wind. Of course, his handicap remained invisible to people we met along the way, many of whom were reluctant to accept the fact when told. I did not want to be a mendicant begging for sympathy on Riley's behalf, but when an obvious dog lover stopped us to make conversation about Riley I usually let drop the fact that he was blind. As a matter of mutual interest. On more than one occasion these strangers tried to convince me that I was wrong. I recall an elderly gentleman who dropped to his knees on the sidewalk and began passing his finger back and forth in front of Riley's eyes, claiming that Riley was actually following the movement and therefore could not be blind. It is too absurd to think that he thought I was lying, that I was so desperate for sympathy that I spent my time cruising the neighbourhood with a cockamamie story about a blind dog. I guess he just thought I had made a horrible mistake.

9   (And then there was the neighbour who emerged from her house one day and, seeing Riley and me standing in the front yard, cheerily called out, "Is he still blind?" as she got into her car and drove off.)

10   When it wakes up, how does a blind dog remember where it went to sleep? This question occurred to me one evening when I arrived home and found Riley snoozing in the living room. At the sound of my voice he wakened, totally disoriented. First he stepped onto the hearth and stared into the fireplace for a few seconds. Then he spun around and trotted into the far corner of the room where he became entangled in the legs of a table. I called him and he came back across the room and stumbled into a chair. Finally it occurred to me that this would work better if I went to him.

11   We strove to treat Riley as a normal, sighted dog whenever possible. To this end, my wife enrolled him in obedience class. But he was overstimulated by the smells and sounds of movement around him and proved impossible to discipline. Eventually my wife began going to obedience class by herself, leaving Riley at home. I guess the idea was that we would convey all the information to him at some later time, but it never happened. He remained completely untrained, though my wife became very good at fetching the newspaper.

12   In the end, Riley developed intractable ear infections which we could not seem to eradicate. The operation was going to cost more money than we had, and might leave him deaf anyway. After another prolonged moral struggle, we concluded that we were not doing this dog a favour. The vet agreed that perhaps it was time to put him down.

13   It fell to me, of course, to deliver Riley to his own execution. He came happily; he had always trusted me completely, which just made it worse. The vet explained that I could remain with Riley and hold his head as he drifted out of consciousness but such stoicism was beyond my emotional range. As it was I dissolved in tears in the parking lot. It was a scene out of *Lassie*, except Lassie always recovered from her injuries to do another show.

14   For a long time afterward, I was burdened with a deep sense of guilt. I wondered if perhaps instead of giving Riley the final injection the vet might have passed him on to a more caring owner who would not put his own convenience ahead of the welfare of a loyal pet. I began eyeing other black and white spaniels in the street, wondering if perhaps one of them was actually Riley, his sight and hearing restored through the intervention of expensive surgery.

15   Eventually the irrationality subsided, the grieving process came to an end. I am not sure what I learned from this episode. I know only that I will never own another dog. The emotional and moral demands are too extreme.

16   And Riley, if you're out there reading this, forgive me.

DISCUSSION QUESTIONS

1. What is the effect of the references to dogs that are not the focus of the essay—Millie and Rex (paragraphs 1–4)?

2. Why does the author withhold the information that "Riley was blind" until the end of the third paragraph? How does the subject of Riley's blindness bring up ethical implications that extend beyond this particular family's dilemma (paragraphs 6–7)?

3. Why do you suppose "strangers tried to convince" the writer that he was wrong about Riley's blindness (paragraph 8)? What other responses do people have to information about Riley's blindness, and what is the larger significance of their reactions?

4. How does the narrator avoid sentimentality in the treatment of Riley's blindness (paragraphs 8–11) and Riley's death (paragraph 13)? What is the tone, or attitude, of the writer in the essay as a whole? Consider what the references to *Millie's Book* (paragraph 2), Orphan Annie's dog (paragraph 5), and the *Lassie* show (paragraph 13) contribute to the tone.

5. What does the writer mean when he says that he will "never own another dog" because "the emotional and moral demands are too extreme" (paragraph 15)?

TOWARD KEY INSIGHTS

After learning that Riley is blind, the narrator finds the world "divided into two camps"—those who believe that Riley should be euthanized, and those who argue that Riley should not, in effect, simply "be traded in for a better model." What do you imagine the arguments would be for or against keeping the dog? To what extent are similar arguments applied to humans?

SUGGESTIONS FOR WRITING

1. If you or someone you are close to has a visible or invisible disability, write about an experience that illustrates the effects of this disability on you, or on others.

2. If you have lost a pet for any reason, write a narrative about what you learned from this experience without falling into sentimentality.

3. Write a narrative about an instance in which people have challenged a personal decision that you felt ethically or emotionally committed to.

Evelyn Lau

An Insatiable Emptiness

Evelyn Lau, born in 1970 in Vancouver, British Columbia, is the author of Runaway: Diary of a Street Kid. *She has also written five volumes of poetry and prose. In Lau's essay, "An Insatiable Emptiness," which first appeared in* The Georgia Straight, *she uses vivid detail to describe the effects of an eating disorder that she eventually overcame.*

1   I no longer clearly remember the first time I forced myself to throw up. What I do remember is how inexpert I was and how long it took before I succeeded in actually vomiting instead of just gagging and retching. I began by sticking my finger down my throat and wiggling it around, but this produced few results; it wasn't until articles about bulimia appeared in women's magazines that I finally thought to use the handle of a toothbrush instead of my forefinger. It became easy after that.

2   In my mid-teens, I was too young to believe I was anything but immortal. It didn't occur to me that what I was doing was dangerous—instead, it seemed a smart and practical way of coping with things. I went through months of throwing up once or twice a day, then brief periods when I did not throw up at all, when I seemed to have broken the pattern. Surely this meant I was in control. But by the time I turned 18, the months of not throwing up had diminished to weeks, and when I *was* vomiting I was doing it four, five, six times a day. I had become addicted to the sensation. It was no longer a penance I had to perform after eating, but the reward at the end of a binge. I loved the feeling I had after purging, of being clean and shiny inside like a scrubbed machine, superhuman. I would rise from the bathroom floor, splash my face with cold water, vigorously brush the acid from my mouth. I would take a wet cloth, wipe off the vomit that had spattered my arms, and feel as energized as someone who had just woken from a nap or returned from an invigorating jog around the block. I felt as if everything disgusting inside me had been displaced so that it was now outside myself. Not only all the food I had eaten, but my entire past.

3   No one could tell me to stop, not even my friends who eventually knew what I was doing. They could not control this part of my life or any other. This was mine alone—the chemical flower smell of the blue water in the toilet, the vomit that shot out as a burning liquid, drenching the sides of the bowl. After a session

in the bathroom, a certain emptiness would sing inside me, a sensation of having become a cage of bones with air rushing through it. I craved this feeling so much I no longer cared what I had to eat in order to vomit—I would cram clusters of bananas into my mouth, or tubs of ice cream that lurched back up my throat in a thin and startlingly sweet projectile.

4   When I left the bathroom, I felt like someone who had achieved some great thing—climbed a mountain, written a book—and survived. I was overweight by only 10 pounds or so, but when I looked in the mirror all I saw was buttery flesh covering my body. My stomach had become swollen and globular from the gorging and purging; I had earned it the way other women earn washboard stomachs and lean waists from hours of sit-ups and crunches at the gym.

5   As a child, I had been thin and healthy, with a flat belly and limbs that turned brown in the summer. I had my first period when I was 11, and for the next several years the blood welled out of me in thick, rust-coloured gouts that no tampons or pads could contain. My body had somehow become a vessel filled with secret, terrible workings, and I longed to make it translucent, pared-down, clean as a whistle. But the blood spread in the shapes of clouds on my skirts and pants, for 10 or 12 days each month, and my hips and breasts pressed outwards. I hated what was happening to my body, once so straight and uninflected. I attracted the attention of one of my parents' friends, who stared at the fuzzy-dark crook at the top of my thighs when I sat cross-legged in front of him, who asked me to perform somersaults and splits while his thick lips hung open with desire. My own father grew awkward around me, refusing to touch me or meet my eyes, driven away by this growing body that forced him out like a giant balloon expanding in a small room. I was in despair. I wanted to trick my body back into childhood by starving it, but I was hungry all the time; I craved food during the week prior to my traumatic periods. Sometimes I would consume a whole bag of shortbread cookies or three chocolate bars; the sugar and fat would induce a heavy, mucousy lethargy.

6   My breasts continued to develop, horrifying my mother, who frequently made me undress in front of her so she could ridicule them. Her actions convinced me there was something wrong with my body. She decided to put the whole family on a diet, serving small portions of steamed fish and vegetables, chicken with the skin removed. During dinner, and in the hungry hours of the evening that followed, she would say over and over again, "It's because of you we didn't get enough to eat, that we're going to bed hungry. Look at the sacrifices we're making for you." I would sit at the dinner table, staring down at my plate with tears in my eyes, grief forming a hot, choking knot in my throat. I would watch my father slowly raise his fork to his mouth while my eagle-eyed mother watched me triumphantly, eating only half of what was on her plate in order to set an example.

7   My mother was so thin and white that whenever I glimpsed her undressing behind a half-closed door, her thighs looked like those of the Holocaust survivors I examined in photographs in history class at school. Meanwhile, I began to put on weight, growing chubby beneath sweatshirts and loose jeans. I stole chocolates from the drugstore, bought greasy bags of day-old cookies from the bakery, consumed candies in a blind rush on the mile-long walk from school to home. I crammed myself with food, yet I hated food: its veils of grease, its sauces

like paste. I hated its fragility beneath my hands, could not bear the delicacy of pastry. But once I started eating, I could not stop, and after I gave in I would again have to cope with the horrible feeling of satiation—a feeling so uncomfortable and guilt-ridden it threatened to annihilate me.

8   I hated the unaccustomed thickness of my body, yet I took a secret, perverse pride in the space I was filling up, the air I was pushing aside in the family home in order to make room for myself. I looked in scorn upon my mother, who wore tiny pink sweaters with pearl buttons, size XS. Her legs were like bleached sticks, the skin white and crepey; her hipbones jutted visibly beneath her skirts, and she reminded me of a starving cow, its ribs and hips holding up the tent of skin. At 13, I had grown to match my father's weight. But at 130 pounds, he was small for a man, his arms straight, the biceps undefined. He was weak, useless in the battle that had sprung up between my mother and myself. He would not protect me, he took no sides in the daily tug-of-war for power. He merely absented himself, took the coward's way out. For this, I knew, one day I would make him suffer.

9   I thought that if I were to physically fight my mother I could break her dry arms like twigs. I could twist her skeleton between my hands; I could sit on her and suffocate her. But it never came to that. Instead, with each pound I gained, my mother became more controlling. I felt that in my entire world there was only one thing my mother could not take away from me: my body. She was trying, of course, with her diets and carefully calibrated meals and calorie counters set up around the kitchen. She wanted to watch me day and night, but in this she inevitably encountered frustration and failure: she could not see the junk food I snuck between meals and hid between textbooks and in my locker at school.

10   And it was driving my mother crazy, I began to realize. She turned to the only thing she could control 24 hours a day: her own body. For every pound I gained, she lost one. In Grade 9, when I came home from school I found her doing jumping jacks and skipping rope in the living room, or following an aerobics show on television. She had virtually stopped eating, complaining that I was doing enough eating for us both. Her eyes grew large in her face, and her hair began to fall out in swirls that clogged up the drain in the sink and the shower. When I stood up from the table and looked down at my mother's skull, I could see the wide, white swathe of the part in her hair.

11   For a while, my father insisted that she eat, but he soon gave up and came home less and less, always too late for the dinner hour, fraught as it was with its agonizing tensions: my mother staring at me with fascination as I ate, her eyes transfixed with hunger. I thought I could no longer stand it; I was as guilty as a murderer with every bite. At night, I lay in my room contemplating suicide and listening to the footsteps of my father pacing his study, waiting for his wife to fall asleep before daring to enter their bedroom. When I trespassed there, I saw pink walls, pink curtains, a pink throw on the queen-sized bed. The bedroom faced south, and all day the sun shone relentlessly through the gauze curtains, revealing the motes of dust in the air. When I opened the dresser drawers, I found beautiful, tiny clothes, beaded and jewelled, carefully folded and wrapped in plastic, as if their owner had already died. I knew these clothes would never again be worn by my mother, and I would never be small enough to wear them.

I knew this was a source of bitterness in my mother's life—she could not pass her-self on to me; she could not live her life again through me. In order to survive, I would have to deny my mother this second life and claim my own.

12   In the en suite bathroom I found orange lipsticks dried to hard, wax nubs, cakes of powder that crumbled at a touch, an old tube of KY Jelly squeezed from the bot-tom like toothpaste. All of it seemed a shrine to my mother's glamorous past. She had been a beauty in her youth, with thick hair that hung down to her waist, so much hair it was almost impossible to bind into ponytails. She had pale skin and pink cheeks like apple blossoms, and she wore short skirts and high heels to work.

13   What my mother didn't know was that I was already beginning to incorporate her inside me. She didn't know that she was winning and that for the rest of my life I would contain aspects of her—both the young beauty turning men's heads and the wasted figure doing sit-ups on the living room floor. I would grow up to wear contact lenses and to put a wave in my hair; I would admire myself in mirrors and spend small fortunes on clothes and cosmetics. Beneath this evidence of self-esteem, though, I would learn to cultivate a parallel self-hatred: my thoughts would repeat themselves obsessively; I would become compulsive in my behav-iour, desperate for control; I would avoid other women because I was afraid they would be like my mother; and I would live at the mercy of my emotions, the end-less stream of hatred that poured out of my mouth when I bent over the toilet.

14   "You will never succeed at anything," my mother told me day after day. "You're like your father—spineless, weak, good for nothing."

15   The last time I saw them, when I was 17 and they were in their 50s, he seemed bewildered by what had happened to our family. She had become a confused, agitated woman who plucked ceaselessly at the strap of her purse with an anguished tic. She had become powerless to control me, this piece of herself that had separated from her. She had lost me in her attempt to keep me forever.

16   I was 20 years old when I began to lose the feeling of immortality. I thought my body would regenerate itself in time, that once again everything would be new and resilient. But it only got worse. My body began showing sings of wear—my throat constantly ached from throwing up, and when I opened my mouth I saw in the mirror a red, inflamed pendulum dangling behind rows of teeth soft-ened and eroded by acid. My own teeth, once so enamel white—the sort of teeth parents thank God for; the sort of teeth a man meeting me for the first time would go away remembering—had, overnight it seemed, turned pitted and yellow, the back ones worn down to shrunken saddles. When I looked in the mirror, they were translucent as X-rays, made, it seemed, of water and putty. I began to brush more vigorously after each purge, not knowing then that I was accelerating the process, scrubbing my teeth with my own stomach acid.

17   I waited for the day when I would throw up blood. Already I could taste it at the back of my throat, inching farther upward with each heartbeat. Now after vomiting, I would rise shakily from my knees, gripping the edge of the counter for balance, my heart knocking wildly in my chest. A column of flame speared me from my stomach to my throat—my esophagus a two-edged blade in my chest, a tunnel set on fire, a steel pole thrust through me.

18   Now when I threw up, I reeled from the pain. I was not throwing up half-digested food, as I had for years, but what felt like complete objects—plastic

balls, pieces of Lego, nuts and bolts that tore at me as they came out of my body. Afterwards, my stomach would hurt so much that for the rest of the evening any sustenance I sought would have to be the sort given to a convalescent or a starvation victim: thin porridge, vegetable soup, herbal tea.

19   I no longer thought of myself as a girl or a woman. I no longer felt sexual desire. I was an "it," a conduit for a constant stream of ugliness that had to pass through it in order for me to stay pure.

20   In some dim part of me, I knew that when I left my apartment to go out into the street, other people did not see me as I saw myself. They did not recoil from me in horror, as I expected. I knew I was a reasonably attractive young woman, like so many young women in the city, neither fat nor thin. But I felt somehow grotesque and abnormal. Strangers knew nothing of my secret; friends were helpless; my dentist would only shake his head over my open mouth and tap his pencil along my teeth to track the path of corrosion the vomit had left in its wake.

21   Once, in a determined moment, I called the Eating Disorder Clinic at St. Paul's Hospital, but the waiting list meant I would not get in for a year. At that time, a year seemed forever, so I did not add my name to the list. Surely in a year's time everything would change, resolve itself. Twelve months later I called again, but by this time the list was even longer, and again I did not add my name.

22   I finally stopped being bulimic nearly two years ago, when I was 22. It ended not because of willpower or therapy or something so banal as an increased sense of self-esteem. It ended because the pain from throwing up rendered the pleasure slight by comparison. It ended when my softened teeth cringed at every mouthful and when I woke several times each night with cramps wracking my stomach from one side of my waist to the other. It ended when I arrived at the point where I could no longer feel my feet. Months later, when I went to the doctor, he would diagnose it as an electrolyte imbalance caused by the vomiting up of so many vitamins and minerals. But for a long time, I didn't know what it was, and it frightened me—sometimes when I stood up, I nearly fell over. My feet were like dead fish, cold and clammy, disconnected from the rest of my body. Once in a while they flared suddenly to life, a constellation of pins and needles, so that I could not bear to press my soles to the floor. When I tried to go to the bathroom in the middle of the night, I felt in the underwater light of that hour as if I had transformed into the fairy-tale mermaid who had chosen her lover over the sea: with each step, I landed on knife points.

23   By then I had also developed a hiatus hernia—a portion of my stomach protruded through my esophagus—and my teeth became so compromised that one day one of them simply disintegrated under pressure.

24   "Your tooth isn't going to grow back," the dentist said flatly, and it was then I understood for the first time that my body did not possess some secret store of replacement parts, that physical damage, like its psychological counterpart, left marks that could remain a lifetime.

25   The last time I forced myself to throw up, it felt like internal surgery. Grief, love, rage, pain—it all came pouring out, yet afterwards it was still there inside me. I had been bulimic off and on for eight years, and in all that vomiting I had not purged myself of any of the things that were making me sick.

DISCUSSION QUESTIONS

1. Examine the ways that Evelyn Lau describes the sensations associated with her former compulsion in paragraphs 1–3. What is the effect of the different sensory details and images? How does she use comparisons, or metaphors, to make her experiences vivid to the reader?

2. What impression does Lau convey about crossing into puberty? What associations does she suggest between her eating disorder and sexuality?

3. What connection is implied between the daughter's hunger and the mother's hunger (paragraphs 5–11)? How do you interpret the reference to "the daily tug-of-war for power" (paragraph 8)?

4. What does the writer mean when she says that she "began to lose the feeling of immortality" at a certain age (paragraph 16)?

5. After referring to paragraph 22, explain in your own words why Lau stops being bulimic. Why do you suppose her compulsion continued as long as it did?

6. What is your emotional reaction to this essay? Do you feel sympathy or empathy for the writer? Explain your answer.

TOWARD KEY INSIGHTS

Do you or does someone you know have a compulsion or addiction? What are the reactions of others to this compulsion? What is the effect of these reactions?

What rewards or compensations did Lau receive from the addiction at first? Does her essay suggest that cultural pressures caused her eating disorder, or does it imply that there were other contributing factors?

SUGGESTIONS FOR WRITING

1. Write an essay that describes the overcoming of a compulsion—even a minor one.

2. Write an essay describing how you lost your feeling of immortality.

John Gimlette

Down Labrador

John Gimlette practises law in London, England. He regularly contributes articles on travel to the Condé Nast Traveller. *This selection is from the author's second book,* Theatre of Fish: Travels through Newfoundland and Labrador.

1   Jim Jones steered a thoughtful path through the last of the season's ice.

2   "This is all frozen over in the winter," he said, distractedly. "When I was a child they used to drop the mail over Mary's Harbour, and then a dog-slide would bring it out to Battle."

3   It was a twelve-mile journey. After the open water, we shrank into the flanks of Great Caribou Island, the *Iceberg Hunter* creaking and groaning with the surge. Jim said she was launched in the sixties, but with her funnels and copper pipes she seemed so much more Vintage Steam than Space Age. I thought of Curwen belting up here on the *Albert*, a record four days out of St. John's. Two days behind him was Grenfell, lurching along in his steam-launch, not unlike our own.

4   Great Caribou rolled and sprawled, and cracked and frothed, and then ended in a full stop. This was Battle Harbour, a third of a mile long and an eighth wide. Between the islands was a channel, big enough for a hundred schooners, too shallow for the icebergs to get among them.

5   *Batal*, the Portuguese called it, the Boat. Then came the horse-faced Basques and the scraggy livyers, landless Scots and bony Norwegians, merging their fortunes with the Esquimaux girls. By 1862, Battle was the capital of fish, and "the most lawless and disorderly place on the whole coast." By the time Curwen appeared, there were three hundred permanent residents—"the Wintermen"—and ten times that in summer. There was no law, no police, no representation, and the place was terrorized by dogs. But the killing and "making" of cod was industrial; over two-and-a-quarter million pounds of "Labrador Cure" were being shipped out every year, along with 5,000 barrels of herring for New York. The stink of fish pip and gurry carried way out to sea, and the rocks were rotten with slime.

6   But—despite itself—Battle had never ceased to please. Grenfell was so delighted that he chose it as the centre for his Labrador, even though it was solid half the year. Curwen was more circumspect in his praise: "An odd-looking place," he wrote, "but picturesquely situated on the rock."

7   But what was merely surprising for Curwen left me gaping with disbelief. Of course, I'd lived with his photographs all my life, and now here it was, almost exactly as he'd left it. I had a feeling not unlike homecoming, even though the place I'd known was fogged with sepia and age. Now here was Battle transfused with colour; seal-oil scarlet, carvenous white fish-sheds, wharves, salt warehouses, a tiny church, and the hillside writhing with sundew and vetch. It was like memory in reverse, faint recollections bursting into life.

8   "They nearly burnt it all down," he told me, "in 1992."

9   With the cod gone, pretty Battle was almost lost. Even the Spearings had stopped visiting their old home, and Victorian woodwork had begun to flap apart. But then, unable to watch it perish, the Labradorians had restored it. A handful of them had even stayed on—cooks, boatmen, joiners and clerks—to feed the curious and sustain the myth. It was an uncanny resurrection; Battle much as Curwen had described it but without the fish, of course, and the tuberculosis. Someone had hung copies of his photographs in the net shed, a reminder that life hadn't always been so quaint.

10   I climbed upwards, through a mercantile complex known as "The Room."

11   "It was all made in England," said the carpenter, "two hundred years ago." Every knee and joint was shipped over, he said, and slotted together without a nail.

12   Most of the stores still smelt of industry, of seals and pine, salmon, flour and herrings. "No spitting," said the signs, although the salt had gone; drifts of seven hundred tons once loomed out of the darkness like alps. Curwen had often held services in here, among the stench and grind. It was a bleak ordeal, he noted, the men "sleepy and unresponsive." The floorboards still bore the mark of their exhaustion, furrows sculpted by seaboots and heavy feet.

13   "Most think of nothing," wrote Curwen, "but fish, fish, fish."

14   Only a fraction of the fish flake had survived, a platform of latticed spruce. In 1893, it had sprawled up the hill like a basketwork rash. To the armies and workers of Europe, it truly was a bread basket, crusts of fish warming in the sun. Three-quarters of each fillet would evaporate, leaving a husk of concentrated protein (it took 75 lbs. of salt and 225 lbs. of fish to produce 112 lbs. of Labrador Cure). The Spearings explained the metamorphosis. First, they said, the fish was pitch-forked from the boats, split and lightly salted for twenty-one days. Then, the "beach women" spread it on the flake, flipping it skin-up if it rained. There it dried for up to four days, until an aromatic amber.

15   "Too much salt, she burns," said Levi. "Too little she had redshanks."

16   Finally, the fish was sorted for export: Choice and Prime for Europe, and the broken cullage for the Caribbean. Battle carried on like this until the age of fridges. "We stopped makin' fish in about the fifties," said Alfred. "After that, people wanted it frozen, see."

      . . .

17   Elsewhere, there'd been a few refinements since Curwen's day.

18   The Doctors' House, I noticed, was new. As the Mission had grown, Grenfell had had it shipped out from England, complete with gingerbread gables and leather-buttoned chairs. The "Big House" too was enjoying a little splendour; there was William Morris wallpaper, and linen for the guests, and polish and caribou cutlets. Even the Battle Store was in the throes of renaissance. There was still the old counter, of course, and the brass scales and bags of split peas and hard tack, but there were apples too, and tins of meat. Curwen would remember just the caplin and "porpoise chops," all emphatically fishy.

19   "Anything by way of fresh meat," reported Grenfell, "is a treat in this country."

20   Only Curwen's tiny hospital was missing. In his photographs, it's all new; walls of rough-hewn planks caulked, or *chinsed* with straw and felt, eight iron beds, biblical tracts and a shelf of unguents. It will be the first hospital outside St. John's, but already things aren't right; they realise—too late—that it'll have to close for winter, and the *Albert* has brought the bacon instead of the drugs. It's an inauspicious start, but the hospital will do brave work—until it's carbonised by a careless cigarette in 1930. The Spearings had watched it burn.

21   "It was a bit o' fun," said Albert, "'til we heard about the gun-powder . . . "

22   "Then we was running," said Levi, "like pigs before thunder . . . "

23   But the Rooms didn't blow. The fire moved off harmlessly, into Battle's miniature barrens. The only other casualty was the Marconi station. "Battle Harbour Burning . . . " it squeaked as it melted into the rock. Now, there was nothing left but four blobs of metal in the moss.

24   I often took the same path as the fire, out into the muskeg. Battle's barrens made up for their size with their ferocity. There were always signs of struggle; kittiwakes bombing the sea, fierce golden rod and snarly dogwood, pieces of an aircrash, and the icebergs booming like artillery. It was easy to see how Grenfell had been ignited by such beauty. Curwen was different; his curiosity endlessly stimulated, but deep affection never aroused. I decided that nowadays it was possible to feel all these things; Battle had ironed out its cruelty, but was still as savage as ever.

25   That night, I slept out on the headland, above the battle of the hulks. They fought through until dawn, roaring and imploding, and collapsing in clouds of diamond dust. Then there was a lull, and a new cathedral floated into the bay.

DISCUSSION QUESTIONS

1. What overall impression does the selection seem to create?
2. What impact does the reference to the history of Battle and the island have on the description.
3. What specific senses does the writer evoke in this piece?
4. What verbs do you find that are effectively vivid and help the description?
5. What dominant technique does the author use to convey a sense of the island?
6. How did the author organize the description?

TOWARD KEY INSIGHTS

This author places his description of Battle in a historical context, indicating how it was viewed in the past, and the changes it experienced. In what ways can the appearance of things be related to their history?

In paragraph 7, the author contrasts his experience of Battle through a photograph and its appearance when he visits it in person. How do the actual environments when they are visited in person differ from their pictures?

SUGGESTION FOR WRITING *Read about the history of a place near you that you can visit. Visit the location and then write a description of your visit, providing historical background where appropriate.*

Douglas Todd

Beware the Boredom Boom

Douglas Todd is the religion and ethics writer for The Vancouver Sun. *He began his journalism career as a political reporter at* The Columbian *daily newspaper in New Westminster prior to moving to* The Vancouver Sun *in 1983, where he initially covered higher education and wrote award-winning features. Todd has received numerous regional, national, and international journalism awards. He is also the author of two books:* Brave Souls: Writers and Artists Wrestle with God, Love, Death and the Things That Matter *and* The Soul-Searcher's Guide to the Galaxy.

1   In the shopping mall—despite its sparkling light, Muzak and invitations to buy everything from jewelry to sportswear—there are many kinds of boredom.

2   There is the boredom of seniors like Zen Gregory, who is 76 and has a cold. The retired millwright has walked over to the Oakridge mall food court for a cup of tea and muffin because he's weary of being trapped alone in his apartment.

3   "To tell you the truth," Gregory says, "I'm bored with Vancouver. There's nothing to do here." He's tired not only of his jigsaw puzzles and TV shows, but with feeling he has to pay money to do anything in Vancouver. He's thinking of moving back to Ontario; at least he'll be near his daughters.

4   In the mall, there's also the boredom of teenagers, the cohort most people think about when they reflect on this contemporary disease—which, paradoxically, is growing more severe as the level of stimulation escalates.

5   Five Grade 11 friends from Eric Hamber Secondary sit at a table next to Gregory. Elliot Lo says his group doesn't find the mall "that special." But at least it's a place to hang out. In school, it becomes clear, the teenagers suffer from the kind of boredom that prisoners experience—the kind you can't escape.

6   The famous Danish existential philosopher Soren Kierkegaard once called boredom "the root of all evil." The English poet, Wordsworth, referred to it as "savage torpor." A thousand years ago, Christian monks called it "acedia," a form of inner sloth judged a sin.

7   But in our increasingly plugged-in, hyped-up, 24–7 society, chronic boredom is becoming a crisis. We feel we have a right not to be bored. We fear boredom as much as we fear death (and more than a few scholars say there's a connection.)

8   Boredom is not a subject to be treated tongue-in-cheek. Boredom matters. The rise of boredom raises many complex questions about the human condition.

ILLUSTRATION   **509**

9   Boredom is the all-encompassing name we now give our discontent. As Patricia Spacks says in the groundbreaking book, *Boredom: A Literary History of a State of Mind*, it is a modern-day "menace," the ghost that haunts our every moment.

10   Boredom is also something we deny. How can we admit to being bored when others seem so busy and, especially on TV, fabulously excited? Confessing to being bored is like admitting to being a loser.

11   Drinking Starbucks coffee or juice from Orange Julius, the teens in the Oakridge mall say math and physics are the most enervating subjects.

12   "'What is the square root of 14?' It's like time is moving in slow motion when the teacher asks stuff like that. I watch the clock all the time," says JoJo Smith.

13   Most of the group also admit to having watched a lot of TV and having played a few too many thousand video games. Decent students, they're beginning to find electronic media repetitive.

14   Yet what are you going to do, Smith asks, when you're so bored in school you can't wait to get out, but you're also bored during summer vacation?

15   Smith feels bad about her boredom; because one of her favourite actors, Viggo Mortensen, the hunk swordsman in *The Lord of the Rings*, recently declared there's no excuse for it.

16   That's the kind of moralizing that's long pushed boredom underground, making it hard to discuss or research. Yet the scholars and psychologists who are now probing boredom believe it's one of the major diseases of our era.

17   We're in a "Boredom Boom," says the U.S.–based Yankelovich Monitor, a consumer survey.

18   Almost three out of four North Americans say they crave more novelty in their lives, says the Monitor. Sixty-nine per cent agree with the statement: "Even though I have so much to do, I'm always looking for something new and exciting to do." More than four out of five said they were bored with TV and the Internet.

19   California psycho-psychologist Augustin de la Pena, who has studied boredom for 30 years, says the subject intimidates most researchers because it's hard to measure, funding agencies aren't interested and most people think humans are motivated by more noble purposes than sheer boredom.

20   However, de la Pena maintains boredom is key to understanding humans. Survey results like those from the Yankelovich Monitor reveal the human mind is always upping the ante for stimulation, just as a drug addict needs larger doses to get high.

21   It's not only seniors and high-school students who are bored. Clock-watching employees and managers are causing executives to fret because uninterested staff cost companies billions of dollars.

22   The father of modern capitalism, Adam Smith, worried in the 1700s that mind-numbing industrial jobs would make humans dull and ignoble. Now, some economists worry the fastest-growing category of new jobs is in the low-paying service sector, where hundreds of thousands of cashiers, clerks, security guards, fast-food staff and others endure deadly dull repetition.

23   Business is so afraid of boredom that high-tech shopping carts are now being designed with DVD players so kids don't get bored while their parents strive to buy things.

24   As well, the entertainment industry is becoming boring to many—witness declining ratings for everything from the Grammys to professional sports.

25   Meanwhile, in our relationships, divorce rates are rising because spouses are bored with each other. Many people are over-eating because they're bored. And surveys show many are bored with sex. TV's *Desperate Housewives* are, by definition, desperately bored; so they're on the sexual warpath.

26   Here's what various health specialists say are signs of boredom:

27   ■ Lack of interest.
       ■ Vague discontent.
       ■ Frequent drowsiness.
       ■ Listlessness and fatigue.
       ■ The slow passage of time.
       ■ Wishful thinking.
       ■ Preoccupation with romantic or heroic fantasies.
       ■ Vanity and self-absorption.
       ■ Moderate to severe depression.

28   What causes boredom?

29   Humans and other animals seem to have an innate curiosity.

30   "The eyes want to see and the ears want to hear," said early American psychologist Robert Woodworth. When our curiosity is stifled, when our inner energy cannot be expressed, we grow frustrated.

31   Human beings have a need for stimulation. In a room without windows, decorations, telephones or other outlets, we grow unbearably bored. Even rats will actively explore parts of a maze that have stripes, and avoid walled areas without patterns.

32   Some may be glad to hear that boredom could be more prevalent among intelligent people. Psychologist Eric Fromm was among the first to propose the theory when he noted higher-functioning animals, such as apes and bears, often get bored in zoos. But snakes and crocodiles don't appear to have the same problem.

33   The evils of boredom enter our lives in two distinct ways.

34   The first is called situational boredom.

35   It's what teenagers experience in a math class or patients feel waiting in a doctor's office. More seriously, it's what prisoners endure in jail, and what millions of seniors experience in badly run residences. It's involuntary boredom; it arises out of monotonous situations we can't control.

36   The more troubling type of boredom is chronic.

37   It's the kind that Madame Bovary experienced in the 1856 literary classic by Gustave Flaubert. Madame Bovary, restricted by social convention, was bored with her husband, bored with her community, and bored with her life.

38   In her endless tedium, she created idealistic fantasies and entered into two love affairs, both of which turned disastrous. She took her life through arsenic.

39   Like Madame Bovary, it's common to blame something else for our boredom.

40   We complain we're bored with our spouses, our teachers, with meetings, with surfing the Web, with our "no-fun" city.

41   Given all the finger-pointing, theologian Paul Tillich said, "Boredom is rage spread thin."

ILLUSTRATION   511

42   It is deadened anger, or resentment.

43   Yet while it's often expressed as irritation with others, it's really anger at ourselves.

44   Vancouver's Bonnelle Strickling sees them every morning: The bored college students. At home they're plugged into exploding electronic media, but in the classroom they can't seem to concentrate.

45   Later in the day, in her private counselling office, Strickling sees the bored adults, who feel empty. They're stressed because they feel glued to the work treadmill; they've lost their zest because they're too damn busy.

46   Since Strickling wears dual hats—as a Langara College philosophy instructor and a psychotherapist in private practice—she finds herself fighting on two fronts to counteract the deadening effects of hyperactivity.

47   She's not the only one concerned about today's paradoxical problem: That our over-stimulated society is breeding widespread, insidious boredom.

48   Although a good portion of Strickling's second-year students continue to be engrossed in her philosophy classes, after three decades at Langara College, she notes a sudden decline in many first-year students' ability to comprehend the basics.

49   "A lot of my students seem to have the attention span of a gnat," she says. "They act in class like they're watching TV. They talk to each other while I'm teaching. There seems to be this kind of constant need for stimulation."

50   Plugged in at home and on the street to TV, the Internet, laptops, DVDs, cell-phones and MP3s, many young people are becoming merely reactive, Strickling says.

51   Prof. Michael Raposa, a specialist in boredom based at Lehigh University in the U.S., says we live in a attention-deficit-disorder culture, and the effects are becoming crippling.

52   "Students today are very good at retrieving information," Raposa says. "They can scan the Web quickly and find what they need. But to get them to read just a paragraph in a text, to really mull it over and make sense of it, is increasingly difficult. As a result, some of their cognitive skills atrophy."

53   As a therapist, Strickling sees a related kind of inattention, or flatness, in adults. She often listens to the pain-filled stories of baby boomers who feel so pressured and over-scheduled that "all the colour seems to have gone out of everything."

54   They might ingest the North American drug of choice, caffeine, and they might race from meeting to meeting, but they don't display much energy, much *elan vital.*

55   "They seem cut off," Strickling says—uninterested in work, relationships or spending time with their families. "They don't care about the things they used to care about. It's very disconcerting. I think boredom is the neutral name we give to our lack of meaning."

56   The Archbishop of Canterbury is among those worried that today's fast-paced world is creating chronic boredom; by making people impatient with questions that don't offer immediate answers.

57   "Why do we want to escape from the glories and difficulties of everyday life?" the Welsh theologian asks. "Why do we want to escape into gambling or drugs or any other kind of fantasy?"

58   Picking up on how boredom can lead to addiction, Simon Fraser University philosopher Mark Wexler says that when things that were once satisfying become unsatisfying, we often end up wanting to do more of them. Compulsively. He defines addiction as "the tendency to try to relieve anxiety by repeating things."

59   Bored with your job? Take an extra job on the side. Bored with your spouse? Have an affair. Bored with your daily routine? Jack yourself up on more coffee. Bored with having a beer with friends? Drink to excess.

60   It's one of the many ways that our fear of being bored can become destructive.

61   It's not hard to see how, in this endless pursuit of stimulation to escape feeling empty, boredom can become a special curse on the affluent.

62   It was impossible to be bored in hard-scrabble primitive days because the fight for survival kept you forever on your toes.

63   But boredom can be a critical issue for spoiled children; little princesses and princes who have been given everything and not had to struggle for any of it.

64   Although we generally associate boredom with being underchallenged, Wexler says there's no doubt boredom also comes from being overchallenged.

65   We just don't get the math class. We find it too nerve-racking to face another tense business meeting. We know we should be realizing more out of the situation. To protect ourselves from feeling inadequate in the face of such frustration and threat, Wexler says we often become jaded. Cynical.

66   What's going on in the minds of sullen 14-year-old boys or girls who come home from school in a daze, then settle into endless TV-watching or video games until bed? Wexler believes the sad young teens are often reacting to the often-overwhelming academic and social demands of high school, which they find threatening and which make them feel like losers.

67   Such teens are retreating into a safer, private world of TV and electronic games—filled with guns, cars, gladiators and wizards; at least it's a world they feel they can control.

68   They enter an artificial cyberspace that may symbolize the paradox of our time—because, as Wexler suggests, it's a place where teens are both stimulated and bored at the same time.

DISCUSSION QUESTIONS

1. Why does the writer begin his essay with a reference to a shopping mall and Muzak? What examples does he use in the first five paragraphs to illustrate that there are "many kinds of boredom" in our society?

2. In paragraph 6, Todd mentions how a philosopher, a poet, and a monk characterize boredom. Explain in your own words what these descriptions of boredom mean, and how they might fit the writer's overall purpose. Do you consider boredom to be a moral problem (paragraph 16)? Explain.

3. To what extent do you agree with the claim that "we fear boredom as much as we fear death" (paragraph 7)? What possible connection could exist between the fear of boredom and the fear of death?

ILLUSTRATION **513**

4. Todd refers to teens who say they are bored by math and physics, by school in general, and even by summer vacation (paragraphs 11–14). Do you think that boredom is especially epidemic among teens? If so, what reasons for this boredom do you imagine?

5. What does Todd mean by his distinction between situational boredom and chronic boredom (paragraphs 34–40)? What examples does he use to bring out the distinction?

6. What does Todd seem to be implying about the link between boredom and overexposure to the electronic media (paragraphs 13, 18, 24, 44, 50, 66–68)? Do you agree that it is possible to be stimulated and bored at the same time (paragraphs 47, 68)?

TOWARD KEY INSIGHTS

Do you agree with the writer that increased stimulation leads to increased boredom (paragraph 4)? Why or why not? What level of stimulation seems optimal to you? What kinds of stimulation do your find energizing, and what kind do you find possibly draining? Give examples.

How do you respond to Todd's analysis of the "crippling effects" (paragraphs 51–60) of boredom? What do you think of the possibility that boredom could contribute to addiction (paragraphs 58–59)?

Do you agree that boredom is a "special curse on the affluent" (paragraph 61)? Why or why not?

In your experience, what is the effect of boredom at school, at work, or in human relationships?

What cures for boredom would you propose?

SUGGESTIONS FOR WRITING

1. Todd suggests different possible ways to define boredom, such as the "name we now give our discontent" (paragraph 9), "one of the major diseases of our era" (paragraph 16), the frustration of not being able to express our curiosity or "inner energy" (paragraph 30), or "deadened anger" that is really anger at ourselves (paragraphs 42–43). Take one of these ways to conceptualize boredom, or another of Todd's claims about boredom, and develop it in depth, using examples of your own.

2. Write an essay arguing that we should accept and perhaps even embrace boredom as part of the human condition because it can lead to creativity or other positive results. Use examples.

Tim Folger

Waves of Destruction

Tim Folger has served as contributing editor and reporter for Discover *and* Science Digest. *He is the series editor for the annual anthology* The Best American Science and Nature Writing.

1   Like most people in Nicaragua, Chris Terry didn't feel the mild earthquake that shook the country at about 8 PM on September 1, 1992. He didn't notice anything out of the ordinary until some minutes later. Terry and his friend Scott Willson, both expatriate Americans, run a charter fishing business in San Juan del Sur, a sleepy village on Nicaragua's Pacific coast. On the evening of the earthquake they were aboard their boat in San Juan del Sur's harbor. "We were down below," says Terry. "We heard a slam." The sound came from the keel of their boat, which had just scraped bottom in a harbor normally more than 20 feet deep. Somehow the harbor had drained as abruptly as if someone had pulled a giant plug.

2   Terry and Willson didn't have much time to contemplate the novelty of a waterless harbor. Within seconds they were lifted back up by a powerful wave. "Suddenly the boat whipped around very, very fast," says Terry. "It was dark. We had no idea what had happened."

3   The confusion was just beginning. As Willson and Terry struggled to their feet, the boat began dropping once again, this time into the trough of a large wave. Willson was the first to get out to the deck. There he found himself staring into the back side of a hill of water rushing towards the shore. "He was seeing the lights of the city through the water," says Terry. "And then the swell hit, and the lights went out, and we could hear people screaming."

4   One of those on the shore was Inez Ortega, the owner of a small beachfront restaurant. She hadn't noticed the earthquake either. While preparing dinner she glanced out at the harbor and noticed that the water seemed unusually low. "I didn't pay much attention at the time," she says. But when she looked up again, a swell of water at least five feet high was racing up the beach toward her restaurant.

5   "I started running, but I didn't even get out of the restaurant when the wave hit," she says. Ortega and several of her customers spent about half an hour swimming in a debris-filled stew before they managed to drag themselves out of the water.

6   Ortega and everyone else in San Juan del Sur looked about themselves in stunned silence. The waves had swept away restaurants and bars lining the beach, as well as homes and cars—and people—hundreds of yards inland. Terry and Willson managed to ride out the disaster on their boat. Still reeling, they witnessed the receding wake of the last wave.

7   "When the wave came back out, it was like being in a blender," says Terry. Collapsed homes bobbed in the water around their boat.

8   Terry, Willson, and Ortega had survived a tsunami, a devastating wave triggered by an undersea earthquake. Although the waves that hit San Juan del Sur were extremely powerful, they rose only 5 to 6 feet high. Other parts of Nicaragua weren't so lucky. All told, the offshore earthquake sent tsunamis crashing along a 200-mile stretch of the coast, and newspapers reported 65-foot waves in some places (though seismologists consider that figure unlikely; a more realistic wave height might be about 30 feet). The waves killed about 170 people, mostly children who were sleeping when the waves came. More than 13,000 Nicaraguans were left homeless.

9   Destructive tsunamis strike somewhere in the world an average of once a year. But the period from September 1992, the time of the Nicaraguan tsunami, through last July was unusually grim, with three major tsunamis. In December 1992 an earthquake off Flores Island in Indonesia hurled deadly waves against the shore, killing more than 1,000 people. Entire villages washed out to sea. And in July 1993 an earthquake in the Sea of Japan generated one of the largest tsunamis ever to hit Japan, with waves washing over areas 97 feet above sea level; 120 people drowned or were crushed to death.

10   In Japanese *tsunami* literally means "harbor wave." In English the phenomenon is often called a tidal wave, but in truth tsunamis have nothing to do with the tame cycle of tides. While volcanic eruptions and undersea landslides can launch tsunamis, earthquakes are responsible for most of them. And most tsunami-spawning earthquakes occur around the Pacific rim in areas geologists call subduction zones, where the dense crust of the ocean floor dives beneath the edge of the lighter continental crust and sinks down into Earth's mantle. The west coasts of North and South America and the coasts of Japan, East Asia, and many Pacific island chains border subduction zones in the Caribbean, and tsunamis have occurred there, but the Atlantic is seismically quiet compared with the restless Pacific.

11   More often than not, the ocean crust does not go gentle into that good mantle. As it descends, typically at a rate of a few inches a year, an oceanic plate can snag like a Velcro strip against the overlying continent. Strain builds, sometimes for centuries, until finally the plates spasmodically jerk free in an earthquake. As the two crustal plates lumber past each other into a new locked embrace, they sometimes permanently raise or lower parts of the seafloor above. A 1960 earthquake off Chile, for example, took only minutes to elevate a California-size chunk of real estate by about 30 feet. In some earthquakes, one stretch of the sea bottom may rise while an adjoining piece drops. Generally, only earthquakes that directly raise or lower the seafloor cause tsunamis. Along other types of faults—for example, the San Andreas, which rims under California and into the ocean—crustal plates don't move up and down but instead scrape horizontally past each other, usually without ruffling the ocean.

12   Seismologists believe the sudden change in the seafloor terrain is what triggers a tsunami. When the seafloor rapidly sinks—or jumps—during an earthquake, it lowers (or raises) an enormous mountain of water, stretching from the

seafloor all the way to the surface. "Whatever happens on the seafloor is reflected on the surface," says Eddie Bernard, an oceanographer with the National Oceanic and Atmospheric Administration (NOAA). "So if you imagine the kind of deformation where a portion of the ocean floor is uplifted and a portion subsides, then you'd have—on the ocean surface—a hump and a valley of water simultaneously, because the water follows the seafloor changes."

13   One major difference between the seafloor and the ocean surface, however, is that when the seafloor shifts, it stays put, at least until the next earthquake. But the mound of water thrust above normal sea level quickly succumbs to the downward pull of gravity. The vast swell, which may cover up to 10,000 square miles depending on the area uplifted on the ocean floor, collapses. Then the water all around the sinking mound gets pushed up, just as a balloon bulges out around a point where it's pressed. This alternating swell and collapse spreads out in concentric rings, like the ripples in a pond disturbed by a tossed stone.

14   Although you might think a tsunami spreading across the ocean would be about as inconspicuous as a tarantula walking on your pillow, the wave is, in fact, essentially invisible in deep ocean water. On the open sea, a tsunami might be only ten feet high, while its wavelength—the distance from one tsunami crest to another—can be up to 600 miles. The tsunami slopes very gently, becoming steeper only by an inch or so every mile. The waves so feared on land are at sea much flatter than the most innocuous bunny-run ski slope; they wouldn't disturb a cruise ship's shuffleboard game. Normal surface waves hide tsunamis. But that placid surface belies the power surging through the water. Unlike wind-driven waves, which wrinkle only the upper few feet of the ocean, a tsunami extends for thousands of fathoms, all the way to the ocean bottom.

15   Tsunamis and surface waves differ in another crucial respect: tsunamis can cross oceans, traveling for thousands of miles without dissipating, whereas normal waves run out of steam after a few miles at most. Tsunamis are so persistent that they can reverberate through an ocean for days, bouncing back and forth between continents. The 1960 Chilean earthquake created tsunamis that registered on tide gauges around the Pacific for more than a week.

16   "You've got to remember how much energy is involved here," says Bernard. "Look at the size of these earthquakes. The generating mechanism is like a huge number of atomic bombs going off simultaneously, and a good portion of that energy is transferred into the water column."

17   The reason for tsunamis' remarkable endurance lies in their unusually long wavelengths—a reflection of the vast quantity of water set in motion. Normal surface waves typically crest every few feet and move up and down every few seconds. Spanning an ocean thus involves millions of wavelengths. In a tsunami, on the other hand, each watery surge and collapse occurs over perhaps 100 miles in a matter of minutes. For a large subduction-zone earthquake magnitude 8 or more—the earthquake's impulse can be powerful enough to send tsunamis traveling across the Pacific—from the Chilean coast to Japan, Australia, Alaska and all the islands en route as well.

18   For much the same reason, tsunamis can race through the ocean at jetliner speeds—typically 500 miles an hour. To span a sea, they need to travel a distance equal to just a few dozen of their own wavelengths, a few swells and collapses.

That means the wave only has to rise and fall a handful of times before the surge reaches its destination. The outsize scale of a tsunami makes an ocean seem like a pond.

19   As a tsunami speeds on its covert way, undersea mountains and valleys may alter its course. During the 1992 Indonesian earthquake, villages on the south side of Babi Island were the hardest hit, even though the source of the tsunami was to the north of the island. Seismologists believe that the underwater terrain sluiced the tsunami around and back toward the island's south coast.

20   Only when a tsunami nears land does it reveal its true, terrible nature. When the wave reaches the shallow water above a continental shelf, friction with the shelf slows the front of the wave. As the tsunami approaches shore, the roiling waves in the train pile onto the waves in front of them, like a rug crumpled against a wall. The resulting wave may rear up to 30 feet before hitting the shore. Although greatly slowed, a tsunami still bursts onto land at freeway speeds, with enough momentum to flatten buildings and trees and to carry ships miles inland. For every five-foot stretch of coastline, a large tsunami can deliver more than 100,000 tons of water. Chances are if you are close enough to see a tsunami, you won't be able to outrun it.

21   As Inez Ortega and Chris Terry witnessed in San Juan del Sur, the first sign of a tsunami's approach is often not an immense wave but the sudden emptying of the harbor. This strange phenomenon results from tremendous magnification of normal wave motion. In most waves, the water within the crest is actually moving in a circular path; a wave is like a wheel rolling towards the shore, with only the top half of the wheel visible. When that wave is 100 miles long, the water in the crest moves in long, squashed ellipses rather than in circle. Near the front and bottom of the wave, water is actually on the part of the elliptical "wheel" moving backward—towards the wave and out to sea. If you've ever floated in front of a wave, you've probably felt the pull of the wave as water sloshes back towards the crest. With a tsunami, that seaward pull reaches out over tens of miles, sometimes with tragic result: when an earthquake and tsunami struck Lisbon in 1755, exposing the bottom of the city's harbor, the bizarre sight drew curious crowds who drowned when the tsunami rushed in a few minutes later. Many people died in the same way when a tsunami hit Hawaii in 1946.

22   Although seismologists and oceanographers understand in broad terms how tsunamis form and speed across oceans, they are still grappling with some nagging fundamental questions. One of the major mysteries is why sometimes relatively small earthquakes generate outlandishly large waves. Such deceptive earthquakes can be particularly devastating because they may be ignored by civil agencies that are charged with issuing tsunami warnings.

23   The Nicaraguan earthquake is a case in point. By conventional measures, it shouldn't have produced a tsunami at all. The earthquake registered magnitude 7.0 on the Richter scale, not puny by any means, but not large enough, seismologists believed, to pose much of a tsunami risk. The quake's epicenter was 60 miles offshore, distant enough to dampen the tremors on land. Yet people who had not even felt the quake found themselves swept out to sea minutes later.

DISCUSSION QUESTIONS

1. What is the advantage of starting this essay with the detailed experience of two individuals?

2. The actual presentation of the process of a tsunami starts in paragraph 11. The author does not use typical transitions to indicate steps in a process. Why might the author have made that decision? Did it help or hurt the essay and why?

3. This essay uses a number of metaphors and similes to make a massive, complex process vivid. What are some of the metaphors and similes and how effective are they?

4. Re-read paragraph 11. What are some of the concrete verbs that the author uses and how do they make the description of the process more vivid?

5. Find examples in paragraphs 14, 15, 16, 17, 18, and 20 where the writer uses comparison or contrast to help the reader understand the nature of tsunamis.

6. How does the writer shift the focus from the tsunami in Nicaragua to more general information about tsunamis? Where and why does the writer return to the story of the Nicaraguan earthquake?

TOWARD KEY INSIGHTS

Often the description of processes and an account of causes overlap. Many causes take place as a series of steps and many steps in a process can be explained as a relationship of cause and effect. To what extent is this account of tsunamis a description of a process and to what extent is this an analysis of a cause-and-effect relationship?

All accounts of processes could go into more or less detail. What additional steps could the writer of this essay have addressed in more detail?

SUGGESTION FOR WRITING *Closely observe a tame or wild creature (cat or dog or squirrel or bird, for example) that is doing something such as eating or playing. Notice how the creature moves and reacts to things or people in the environment. Help your reader to notice more closely by describing the processes you see in subtle detail, using any metaphors or similes that seem helpful.*

Allen Abel

Sweet Nothings

Allen Abel is the author of three books and has been an on-air host for the CBC. He has also received the National Newspaper Award. Abel's article "Sweet Nothings," which first appeared in Saturday Night *magazine, shows how damaging patronizing language, referred to as "elderspeak," may be to senior citizens. Students may be surprised to learn that social stereotyping may be quite subtle and may even stem from good intentions. The essay could easily be paired with another essay that brings up issues related to stages of life: "The Sweet Bird of Youth Is Showing Signs of Age (page 522)."*

1   Somewhere between ambition and extinction, between Whitman's "exquisite realization of health" and Browning's "last of life, for which the first was made," stretches a shifting, invisible frontier—the boundary of old age.

2   On one side of this customs house, we stockpile growth and advancement; on the other, we store retreat and decline. We assume that those who cross the border can never reverse their journey, and that, once beyond it, they have entered the realm of darkness. A look, a shrug, a word is enough to hold them there, for they are old and helpless, and we are young and strong. Both sides are complicit in the game—a conspiracy of shunning and surrender.

3   "There is a global time when old age happens," a much younger woman tells me. "It may happen when you move into a nursing home. It may be when you are already in the nursing home and they move you onto the full-time-care floor. It may be when you are retiring, or after a heart attack or a stroke, or when your spouse dies.

4   "When this happens, you ask yourself, 'How is it going to be now?' You look in the social mirror and the social mirror says, 'You are old.' The negative stereotype is so ingrained that, if there's any decline at all, we assume that this is the new you."

5   "Why are we so afraid of old people?" I ask.

6   "It is our cultural fear of death," Dr. Ellen Bouchard Ryan replies. "In the nursing home, and within the family, there is a fear of ageing and the aged that creates a distance between the old and the young. Our behaviour and our language perpetuate this distance. But the irony is, most of the diminishment of old people's competence is done with a nurturing intent."

7   Dr. Ryan's life's work is the study of how the way we talk to the old helps make them old. (Within her academic discipline, the condescending, exaggerated baby talk often used with older adults is known as "elderspeak.") She is a professor of psychology at McMaster University in Hamilton, Ontario, and one of Canada's foremost gerontologists. Her ancestry on the Bouchard side can be traced back to eighth-century France. One of her Québécois progenitors sailed with Champlain. She has an uncle named Lucien. (But not *that* Lucien.)

8   "There are things we do to be nice to dear old people that aren't good for them," she says, summarizing nearly twenty years of work in one sentence. Then she immediately retracts the word "dear."

9   Ryan's research papers are unequivocal: terms such as *dearie* and *sweetie;* patronizing directives (*Shall we get our pants on?; Let's get you into bed*); commands (*Move it, lady*); and even praise (*Good girl!*) can ravage an older person's self-esteem as surely as a fractured hip. Non-verbal communication can be just as damaging—family members rolling their eyes as Grandmother begins to tell yet another story about the Dirty Thirties; a restaurant server asking the youngest person at the table what the oldest will have to eat.

10   The academic investigators of elderspeak pepper their papers with microscopic dissections of intergenerational conversations that count "left-branching

clauses" and "repetitions per utterance" and "percentage of Long Words." Researchers pair student and senior volunteers, record the interactions, and count the *honeys* and *sweeties* and *dearies*.

11   The scholars' conclusions are hardly surprising. In one journal article, Dr. Ryan announces that "stereotyped expectations about elderly adults' cognitive decline" can create "a self-fulfilling prophecy." Passivity continues the downward spiral, she writes.

12   "Just when you need extra encouragement to stay active, society encourages you to lie down and rest," Dr. Ryan says. "If we are young, and we're having a really good day and somebody puts us down, we react by saying 'That person has a problem.' But when we're vulnerable, those comments go deep down.

13   "Older people *know* that old age is going to hit. They know the face of the person in the mirror is ageing, but they don't feel like that person. They use expressions such as 'Those old people in the nursing homes.' But then, on a bad day, they forget where their car is parked in the lot at the mall. Or they want to introduce someone and they forget that person's first name and then they suddenly feel old.

14   "It's like hearing yourself in a tape recorder for the first time—it's a different voice. Suddenly, it's not you. You're hurt, and then you start to get this negative feedback from society. The older person thinks, 'I know I need a hearing aid but I don't want to wear one. I *know* I need a cane but [then] when I go in a shop, the clerk will call me Dearie.'

15   "The problem in the nursing home," Dr. Ryan says, "is that the staff tend to give off so many clues that the older person is not competent—'I'm in control and you're not'—and for people who may have few other adult contacts, that has a tremendously debilitating effect.

16   "But when I talk to service providers about this, they line up to defend themselves. They say, 'I'm communicating to them that I love them.' Then it sort of dawns on them that they wouldn't like it either."

17   "What should service providers do?" I inquire.

18   "*Listen!*" the professor replies.

19   "I have heard it many times in the hospital," a seventy-eight-year-old fireball named Katie Allen tells me. "*'Put this leg in your pants, darling.' 'Come on, dear, we'd better go to bed now.'* Well, I think you get what you deserve. I never let it slide, not even *once*."

20   Katie Allen is the founder of a group of older memoirists who meet every other Tuesday at the police station in Dundas, Ontario, and call themselves Writer's Cramp. When I meet her at her home in a wide spot in the road called, aptly, Copetown, she has just finished firing off an e-mail message to the president of the United States. She and her associates, some of whom take part in Dr. Ryan's studies of young-old speech patterns, do not intend to go gently.

21   "You're *letting* them patronize you," she asserts. "Older people should make it plain that they are *not* children. They're *adults* and capable of doing it themselves—and even if they're *not* capable, they shouldn't be talked down to. I'm aggressive enough *not* to be put down. I *don't* accept it. I tell them, 'I am *not* your sweetie, sir.'"

22   Unprompted, she begins to quote Browning: "Grow old along with me, the best is yet to be . . . "

23   "What should older people do?" I ask.

24   "Get *out* of the damn rocking chair and *quit* watching TV."

25   On August 13, 1995, the automobile carrying Ellen Bouchard Ryan, her husband Patrick (a mathematician and computer scientist at McMaster), and two of their three children was halted at a stop sign not far from their home when it was rear-ended by another vehicle travelling eighty kilometres an hour. Three of the Ryans were unhurt. Ellen suffered a neck injury so severe that, two years later, she still needs the support of a walking stick.

26   Some days, the overachieving scholar—chair of the Department of Psychology at the University of Notre Dame in Indiana before she was thirty—is "close to what I was." More often, a horrible pain above her right eye, vertigo, and nausea are crippling. An attempt at yoga left her hardly able to move her head. Aquatic exercise made it even worse. Only acupuncture seems to help, and then only for a few hours.

27   Halfway to one hundred, her "exquisite realization of health" suddenly gone, perhaps forever, Dr. Ryan has had no shortage of time to ponder the metaphysics of her own predicament. She speaks of spiritual and emotional development, inspirational books: *Chicken Soup for the Soul.*

28   "Do you feel like the universe has provided you with a taste of old age?" I ask her, thinking myself insightful, as she sinks into her recliner in her sunken living room.

29   "It is unfortunate that, in our society, when people feel *ill,* we say they feel *old,*" she replies. "There are many, many, many, many ways to be old. Just as in childhood—you can have a good old age or a bad old age. And, just as in childhood, what makes the difference is a sense of meaning and purpose in life.

30   "I am trying to teach the diversity of old age. The message is, there is pain and suffering—and glory—in the human condition, no matter how old you are."

DISCUSSION QUESTIONS

1. Analyze paragraph 2. Paraphrase what the writer is saying in your own words. What does Abel mean when he says "Both sides are complicit in the game"?

2. What reasons does the writer suggest for negative stereotypes of old age (paragraphs 5–6)? Why is it ironic that we may have a "nurturing intent" when we diminish "old people's competence" (paragraph 6)?

3. What are the verbal and nonverbal ways that Dr. Ryan claims we patronize old people (paragraphs 7–10)? What is meant by the term "elderspeak" (paragraph 7)?

4. According to Dr. Ryan, what are the effects on older people of realizing the inevitable fact of their old age? (paragraphs 13–14)?

5. Why do you suppose the writer includes the story about the effects of a severe automobile accident on Dr. Ryan (paragraphs 25–29)?

6. What is the significance of paragraphs 19–24? How do you respond to the allusions to poetry (paragraphs 20, 22) here?

7. What does Dr. Ryan mean by "the diversity of old age" in the last paragraph? How effective is the conclusion?

TOWARD KEY INSIGHTS

Have you seen examples of "elderspeak"—or any other kinds of condescending, simplified language to certain kinds of people? What might be the reasons that people speak this way? What might be the effects of this kind of language on others?

Drawing on your own experiences in school, with family, or in other relationships, comment on whether you think people tend to meet others' expectations, falling into a downward or an upward spiral depending on what is expected of them.

How is it possible that a person's apparently good intentions may have damaging effects?

SUGGESTION FOR WRITING *Write an essay tracing the effects of a subtle form of negative stereotyping at school or in another social grouping you are familiar with.*

Andrew Beyak

The Sweet Bird of Youth Is Showing Signs of Age

Andrew Beyak was born in Toronto in 1971. After studying zoology at the University of Western Ontario, Beyak moved to Montreal for graduate work at Concordia University. While his educational background was in the sciences, he also has had a lifelong interest in literature, journalism, and music. Beyak's article "The Sweet Bird of Youth" has appeared previously in both The Hour, *the Montreal arts weekly, and* The Georgia Straight, *the Vancouver arts and entertainment weekly. "The Sweet Bird of Youth Is Showing Signs of Age" argues that the definition of "youth" is too elastic when it includes people from 18 to 30. Beyak suggests that there may be a political or economic agenda for those who would extend the period of "youth," enabling us collectively to dismiss the problem of unemployment as "youth unemployment."*

1   According to my 1956 edition of *Webster's New World Dictionary*, youth is: "1. the state or quality of being young. 2. the period of life coming between childhood and maturity; adolescence. 3. an early stage of growth or existence."

2   More recently, according to corporate, political, and media interests, youth is: "1. not employed; without work. 2. not being used; idle."

3   In case you haven't noticed, the term *youth* is increasingly becoming a euphemism for *unemployed and underemployed adults.* It no longer has anything to do with age or maturity. Rather, the term *youth* has been co-opted by corporate and government interests as a means of evading responsibility for both their actions and their inactions—actions and inactions that are having an impact on a generation of young, and not-so-young, adults.

4   Virtually all of the programs in the federal government's current Youth Employment Strategy are available to "youths" under the age of 30. All of these programs are aimed at attacking the relatively recent problem of "youth unemployment," a problem that used to go by the name of "unemployment." Meanwhile, the Youth Employment Services Centre in Montreal offers services to "youths" between the ages of 16 and 35. Yes, that's right. Thirty-five. These days, you are considered a "youth" until you have lived almost one-half of the average male life, which is currently around 75 years long. Or, to give this some historical perspective, today you are a youth for what was the entire duration of the average life just over a century ago. With the ever-expanding usage of the term *youth*, I am sure you would not have to look very far to find some youths out there with youths of their own.

5   On CBC Television's *Youth Town Hall* program during the last federal election campaign, 18- to 25-year-olds had a go at the politicians. Prior to this, I had taken it for granted that the idea behind the age of majority was to officially recognize an age at which citizens are considered mature enough to decide the fate of our country. In other words, they are no longer youths, but adults. Unfortunately, none of the leaders of our official political parties seem to share this view, as was evidenced by their absence from the *Youth Town Hall* forum. Were these leaders absent due to conceit, or did they simply fear the wrath of an increasingly ostracized group? Whatever the reason, today 18- to 25-year-olds are routinely separated from the rest of the clear-thinking, mature adults and are labelled "youths," not because of their state of maturity or development, but because of their economic circumstances.

6   Many people in their 20s and early 30s may enjoy the term *youth* and be somewhat reluctant to give it up. Thus, many of us in this age bracket are accomplices in the escalating abuse and misuse of this word, for it suggests that we are still hip, beautiful, vibrant, and intimately in touch with the nuances of popular culture. However, there is something far more sinister than mere flattery going on here.

7   By referring to a segment of the most-educated generation of adults to date as "youth," older generations, corporations, and governments have succeeded in leaving the impression that these people are not getting ahead in life because, "well, it's just not quite time yet." They would have you believe that it has nothing to do with employee-taxation laws. It has nothing to do with the fact that many salaried employees are logging more than 60 hours a week. It is not that CEOs' salaries have skyrocketed since the 1960s. It is not a lack of jobsharing. It is not that many corporate leaders are given bonuses based on short-term, rather than long-term, performance. It is not greed. Not the unrealistic expectations of relatively unskilled university graduates. Not demographics. Not resource scarcity. Not automation. Not NAFTA. Not globalization. No, that's not it. It's just that the "youths" in our society, those in the 18-to-35 bracket, have a little more growing up to do. In other words, it is just a matter of time.

8   Unfortunately, there is something of a self-fulfilling prophecy here, in that many young adults only aspire to live up to their recently attenuated expectations. The consequences of this go beyond economics; they are also social in

scope. Furthermore, these consequences will likely carry over to the next generation. Moving away from home, marriage, and parenthood, as well as many other rites of passage in adults' lives, are increasingly being put off until people are well into their 30s. These events are now postponed until careers are firmly established and new cars and houses are bought. And why not, in a society that equates money with maturity, and full employment with adulthood?

9   By replacing the term *adult* with *youth*, governments, corporations, and the media can offer the majority of the electorate and the majority of society (baby boomers, if you will) an easy explanation for why those aged 18 to 35 are not receiving what they as adults need—namely employment, a living wage, and a minimal level of independence. At the same time, those with a vested interest in the status quo are creating a diversion from a multitude of other issues that will inevitably have to be addressed. All of this with one word.

DISCUSSION QUESTIONS

1. How does Beyak rewrite the traditional definition of "youth"? Why does he begin with a dictionary definition?

2. In paragraph 7, Beyak uses a number of negative statements beginning with "It is not," "Not," or "No." What is the effect of the many negatives?

3. According to the author, how does our society define maturity or adulthood (paragraphs 8–9)?

4. What are the negative social and economic consequences of calling people aged 18–35 "youth"?

5. Find the thesis statement, and paraphrase it. Why is it located where it is?

6. What is the tone of this article? Explain.

TOWARD KEY INSIGHTS

What does Beyak mean when he says that "the term *youth* has been co-opted by corporate and government interests"? Can you think of another term or concept that has been redefined or co-opted by certain interests?

What do you consider to be the dividing line between youth and adulthood? Do you consider people between 18 and 35 adults? Explain.

What rites of passage do you associate with maturity?

What is your response to Beyak's suggestion that one cause of unemployment or underemployment is "unrealistic expectations of relatively unskilled university graduates" (paragraph 7)?

SUGGESTION FOR WRITING *Write an essay exploring how a word or term that once seemed relatively simple has taken on "ever-expanding usage" or changed its meaning according to a changing political, social, or economic climate.*

Bob Harvey

Loyalty: A Last Virtue; Me-First Attitude Is Stripping Away Our Sense of Community

Bob Harvey is a journalist for the Ottawa Citizen, *in which this article first appeared. This essay provides an extended definition of loyalty, partly by saying what it is not. True loyalty, the allegiance to something larger than the self, has faded in the West, eroded by our emphasis on subjectivity and individualism. This 1996 essay could be fruitfully paired with Laurence Shames's essay "The Sweet Smell of Success Isn't All That Sweet" (page 243).*

> Loyal: 1. Steadfast in support and devotion to and never betraying the interests of one's homeland, government, or sovereign. 2. Faithful to a person, ideal or custom; constantly supporting or following. (French, from Old French *loyal, loial, leial, fait*)
>
> —*Reader's Digest Illustrated Encyclopedic Dictionary*

1   The Roman senator, Seneca, called it "the holiest virtue in the human head." For most of the 2,000 years since, few would have disagreed with his call for loyalty to the gods, to the state, to family and to duty.

2   But loyalty, that once-essential virtue, is fading fast, and our sense of community and identity is disappearing with it.

3   Recent headlines tell some of the story. Last month, actor Elizabeth Taylor filed for divorce from husband No. 8, and all it merited was a news brief. We've become used to the breakdown in marital loyalty. The Canadian divorce rate has shot up by 400 percent since 1970.

Everyone's Not Doing It

4   This month, it was Wayne Gretzky who quit on a relationship. He pushed the Los Angeles Kings to trade him to the St. Louis Blues because he wants to be on a winning team. But it's not only athletes who'd rather switch than commit. In the last year, the owners of the Quebec Nordiques, the Winnipeg Jets and the Cleveland Browns have all chosen cash over their loyal fans.

5   Loyalty's gone in almost every sphere. Canadian voters have deserted the Tories and the New Democrats. Many Quebecois want to quit Canada. Consumers are dumping brand names. Believers are switching denominations and even bigger numbers are quitting organized religion altogether.

6   Today's new version of loyalty, according to people who've thought about this issue, is loyalty to self, as summed up by what was originally meant to be ironic advice to Hamlet: "To thine own self be true."

7   Philosopher Donald De Marco says what's happened is that "we've lost the sense of a common good. We've made an invalid of loyalty."

8   He says that without an accepted common good, or allegiance to something beyond the self, loyalty crumbles.

9   "If you're saying the highest loyalty is to self, you can't get beyond self. Therefore you're missing an essential element of loyalty. It's not a virtue to be

loyal to oneself. It's a vice to be selfish," says De Marco, who teaches in St. Jerome's College at the University of Waterloo.

10   Graeme Hunter, who teaches philosophy at the University of Ottawa, says that in the West, Christianity kept me-first individualism in check for hundreds of years.

11   "Religious commitments weren't just restricted to the sphere of the church. They affected one's whole life. You had a responsibility to your community, to your employer and to the State."

12   In fact, the sacred scriptures of all the major faiths not only teach that God is loyal and faithful, but also urge we follow that divine example: "Those who faithfully observe their trust and their covenants will inherit Paradise," says the Koran.

13   Loyalty has been valued in all cultures, as witness this 16th-century advice to the Japanese samurai warrior: "The business of the samurai consists in discharging loyal service to his master, in devoting himself to duty above all."

14   But secularism and individualism are making inroads in all cultures, and taking away not only the religious backing for loyalty to others, but also some of the cultural emphasis on it. "If there is no God, there is no absolute foundation to anything," says Hunter.

First Fading Hints

15 The notion of loyalty began to fade first in the West, in the late 19th century, as exemplified by this 1889 musing by diarist Alice James: "When will women begin to have the first glimmer that above all other loyalties is the loyalty to Truth, i.e. to yourself, that husband, children, friends and country are as nothing to that."

16   Will Sweet, who teaches philosophy at St. Francis Xavier University in Antigonish, N.S., says, however, that this tendency to value self above community or duty began at least 400 years ago. René Descartes, the father of modern philosophy, wrote *cogito ergo sum* (I think therefore I am) and began the shift from an emphasis on absolute values and absolute truths to an emphasis on subjectivity and the value of the individual.

But Which Good?

17 A hundred years later, Adam Smith and other economists speeded up the shift to me-first individualism by teaching that if we just pursued our own economic self-interest, all would benefit. Suddenly the common good was equated with the individual good. Only now are we beginning to see some of the problems with this notion, including the spread of poverty in spite of continuing increases in the production of goods.

18   Pollster Andrew Grenville says many aspects of modern life also contribute to the decline in loyalty. Greater prosperity makes divorce more possible when relationships break down, and *technology* makes it possible to market not only thousands of different products, but also thousands of different ideas.

19   Grenville, vice-president of the Angus Reid polling firm, says that along with these new choices comes a fragmentation in identities.

20   Instead of identifying with our neighbors, or our nation, we're developing new micro-identities as Internet surfers or evangelical Christians that transcend old boundaries, says Grenville.

21   Greg Walters teaches ethics at Ottawa's Saint Paul University and says loyalty got a bad name during the Second World War, when it became clear that not all loyalties are good loyalties.

22   The Nazis and other totalitarian regimes made us suspicious of authority and less willing to give uncritical loyalty to a State, or an institution.

23   However, he says the yearning for loyalty hasn't gone away. In spite of the current high divorce rate, surveys by Alberta sociologist Reg Bibby show that 97 percent of Canadian teens still confidently expect to marry only once.

24   *Technology* and the breakdown of tradition have made it necessary to redefine ourselves and our loyalties, says Walters. And although we're still groping for new structures and new ways of thinking to help us to do it, he says history teaches us that it's probably just a matter of time until we do.

Terrible Tribalism

25 Sweet says the resurgence of nationalism and tribalism is more evidence of this yearning for enduring connections.

26   In some nations, like Rwanda and the former Yugoslavia, this new assertion of tribal or national identity community has turned psychopathic. In places like Quebec, the process is more peaceful. Like other thinkers, Sweet is philosophical about the new stain on our loyalties,

27   "It's the effect of a process that's been going on for 400 years. We can't expect any sudden changes in a lifetime."

DISCUSSION QUESTIONS

1. What is accomplished by introducing a dictionary definition of loyalty, followed by an ancient Roman senator's definition of loyalty, at the beginning of this essay?

2. How does the author define loyalty partly through negation?

3. How does the author make the subject of loyalty seem of universal and contemporary significance?

4. Find places where methods of development such as cause-and-effect analysis, contrast, or illustration are used. What larger purpose does the author have in using each of these strategies?

5. What connections does the author make between loyalty and religious faith? loyalty and economic philosophy? loyalty and technology?

6. In your own words, explain why Nazi and other totalitarian regimes might have contributed to the decline of loyalty (paragraphs 25–26).

TOWARD KEY INSIGHTS

The author quotes a philosopher who says that loyalty needs "allegiance to something beyond the self." Do you agree that "loyalty to self" is not true loyalty? Why or why not?

Compare and contrast the way that Bob Harvey defines "loyalty" and the way that Stephen Carter defines "integrity" in "The Insufficiency of Honesty" (page 241). How do both essays include an element of argument? Which essay do you find more effective?

SUGGESTION FOR WRITING *Write an essay in which you develop an expanded definition of a concept such as "commitment" or "faith" or "discipline." Draw from personal observation or experience in order to make a statement about this concept, showing, for instance, that the principle of commitment is alive and well, in decline, or simply changing.*

Marilyn Baker

Greed Works

Marilyn Baker was born in Carman, Manitoba. She graduated with a Bachelor of Science degree from the University of Manitoba in 1963; and for the next thirty-four years, she worked in the computer sector. Baker has also been writing professionally for ten years. Currently, she is working on a novel and is a freelance writer based in Richmond, British Columbia.

1   If I had to choose among the seven deadly sins, I would pick Greed. In a ranking from best to worst, Greed comes in first. Envy on the other hand, comes dead last, trailing a bunch of more or less innocuous sins, like Gluttony and Lust.

2   Greed has many mitigating virtues, such as honesty "What's in it for me?" is the enthusiastic cry of the greedy, who worship at the Holy Grail of The Market—honest by definition. The greedy don't have time to inflict shame on ordinary passers-by. They're too busy trying to get a piece of the action for themselves.

3   In contrast, envy uses every dishonest trick in the book to spoil the successes of the greedy. The envious lay about, railing against the rich, and accusing them of selfishness. Deceitful to the core, they couch their bad-tempered rants in a thinly disguised veil of moral superiority. Claiming humanitarian motives gives them permission to become self-righteous and denounce greed.

4   But the thing is—as Gordon Gekko succinctly put it in the movie *Wall Street*—greed works. Greed goes with the flow. Pragmatic to the core, greedy people recognize that greed is a basic human instinct. Ever optimistic, they decide to milk the situation. They know that there is a sucker born every minute and that hey, a buck can be made here.

5   Greed is energizing. Heads down and bums up, the greedy busily seek ways to make more money. Greed generates wealth, and in its wake, pulls everyone up to a new level, making for a richer, happier society. Greed celebrates success. Since wealth is measurable and therefore taxable, greed generates the money that societies need to move our civilization forward a notch.

6   Envy dissipates energy in negative and exhausting ways. Discouraged by successful greed, the envious seek to expunge greed through shame, punishment, legislation, and coercion. They want to seize the assets of the greedy and redistribute them to the "less fortunate." Ever pessimistic, the envious assume that greedy people gain their wealth through Luck. Envy belittles success and denigrates profit. In vilifying greed, envy succeeds in creating black markets—sans regulations and taxable profits. When envious people achieve their goal of driving greed out of their domain, those left are much poorer in material things.

7   Greed is expansive and global in scope. "The world is a market for my better mousetrap," the greedy exult, rubbing their hands in glee. The greedy snap to attention when someone complains about bad service because it might cause

them to lose a money-producing customer. The greedy landlord doesn't care who pays the rent, as long as the rent cheque doesn't bounce. Greed fosters tolerance for diversity.

8   Envy is parochial and mean-spirited. Always measuring their success in comparison to others, the envious fuss obsessively about the gap between the rich and the poor, constantly redefining poverty to prove their point. Envy kills hope and pits people against each other. Envy breeds societies that are negative and intolerant.

9   Excessive greed is self-regulating. Fear is a built-in governor that moderates intemperate greed. The greedy reluctantly accept fair regulations, because they know that they must breathe the same air, drink the same water, and fly in the same airplanes that give them the profits they seek. The end result is a pull away from the fringes of excess and back to a balance in the centre.

10   Envy has no natural predator to induce moderation. The envious devise arbitrary rules to regulate the amount of wealth and happiness allotted to each citizen. Envy breeds more envy, resulting in the unfettered growth of mediocrity.

11   Greed brings out the best in human beings. Compassion, springing spontaneously from the heart, benefits both the giver and the receiver. Civilization is enriched and takes a tiny step towards nobility. Never easy, nobility is made even more difficult for greedy people; when achieved, it becomes even more noble.

12   Envy brings out the worst in mankind. Coveting Other People's Money, the envious seek to legislate and moralize their way to nobility. Nobility becomes a cheap confection that anyone can have merely by joining a protest march or slinging accusations at a Big Bank. But it is no longer noble. Envy justifies theft. The *Tales of Robin Hood* is a great story but immoral in its fundamentals. Ever anxious to share other people's wealth, envy is silent on how to deal with their debts.

13   Greedy people are generous. Realistic to the core, they accept death. They know they can't take it with them, preferring to give away the fruits of their successes. The greedy know that the real fun lies in the journey, not the destination.

14   The envious, with their malnourished souls, miss the point of the circus called life. Always one step behind, they measure their success in comparison to others. Since there will always be someone richer than they are, they're never satisfied and never happy. Unable to deal with generosity, they conclude that charity is evil because it invites gratitude, which they equate with humiliation.

15   Greedy people are fun to be around. The envious lay a wet blanket on the party. The greedy, even those who encounter innumerable setbacks on their quest, have more fun in a single day than the envious do in a lifetime.

16   I'm glad I'm greedy. I would hate to be envious.

DISCUSSION QUESTIONS

1. Discuss the significance and meaning of the title. How does it relate to the essay, and how does it indicate that the writer will take an unusual slant on this topic? What tone, or point of view, does the title suggest?

2. Comparisons between two items or ideas must have some common ground between them. What is the basis for the comparison between greed and envy? What are seven distinctions between greed and envy that the author explores?

3. What pattern of comparison does Marilyn Baker use to structure her essay—the block method, the alternating method, or a blend of the two? Examine the first sentence in paragraphs 3 through 12, and explain how the writer moves from one paragraph to the next.

4. What is the point of the reference to the movie *Wall Street* in paragraph 4, and to *The Tales of Robin Hood* in paragraph 12? Does it matter whether you have seen the movie *Wall Street* or read about Robin Hood in order to grasp the significance of these allusions? Why or why not?

5. To develop her argument that greed is better than envy, the author often uses cause-and-effect reasoning, particularly causal chains, where one effect becomes a cause of something else. Trace the cause-and-effect development in paragraphs 5–12.

6. What does the writer mean by the last two sentences? What is the tone here? Does the essay have a serious point, or is it written simply to entertain? Explain.

TOWARD KEY INSIGHTS

Identify references to money or wealth that suggest this essay is more about economics than about sin. What comment does it make about economics? To what extent does it celebrate capitalism, and to what extent does it cause the reader to think about the "gap between the rich and the poor" (paragraph 8)?

What does the writer mean when she says that "greed is expansive and global in scope" (paragraph 7) or, more surprisingly, that "greedy people are generous" (paragraph 13)?

Do your experiences or observations confirm Baker's claims that "envy dissipates energy" (paragraph 6) or that it creates perpetual discontent and dissatisfaction (paragraph 14)? Use examples.

SUGGESTION FOR WRITING *Write a comparison essay between two other deadly sins, such as lust and gluttony, or pride and envy, emphasizing the merits of one over another. You may choose to adopt an ironic or a straightforward tone.*

Henry Jenkins

Art Form for the Digital Age

Video games shape our culture. It's time we took them seriously.

Henry Jenkins is the John E. Burchard Professor of Humanities and Director of the Comparative Media Studies graduate program at MIT. His column "The Digital Renaissance," from which this selection was taken, was featured in the journal Technology Review Monthly *in September 2000.*

1   Last year, Americans bought over 215 million computer and video games. That's more than two games per household. The video game industry made almost as much money from gross domestic income as Hollywood.

2   So are video games a massive drain on our income, time and energy? A new form of "cultural pollution," as one U.S. senator described them? The "nightmare before Christmas," in the words of another? Are games teaching our children to kill, as countless op-ed pieces have warned?

No. Computer games are art—a popular art, an emerging art, a largely unrecognized art, but art nevertheless.

3   Over the past 25 years, games have progressed from the primitive two-paddles-and-a-ball Pong to the sophistication of Final Fantasy, a participatory story with cinema-quality graphics that unfolds over nearly 100 hours of play. The computer game has been a killer app for the home PC, increasing consumer demand for vivid graphics, rapid processing, greater memory and better sound. The release this fall of the Sony Playstation 2, coupled with the announcement of next-generation consoles by Nintendo and Microsoft, signals a dramatic increase in the resources available to game designers.

4   Games increasingly influence contemporary cinema, helping to define the frenetic pace and model the multi-directional plotting of *Run Lola Run,* providing the role-playing metaphor for *Being John Malkovich* and encouraging a fascination with the slippery line between reality and digital illusion in *The Matrix.* At high schools and colleges across the country, students discuss games with the same passions with which earlier generations debated the merits of the New American Cinema. Media studies programs report a growing number of their students want to be game designers rather than filmmakers.

5   The time has come to take games seriously as an important new popular art shaping the aesthetic sensibility of the 21st century. I will admit that discussing the art of video games conjures up comic images: tuxedo-clad and jewel-bedecked patrons admiring the latest Streetfighter, middle-aged academics pontificating on the impact of Cubism on Tetris, bleeps and zaps disrupting our silent contemplation at the Guggenheim. Such images tell us more about our contemporary notion of art—as arid and stuffy, as the property of an educated and economic elite, as cut off from everyday experience—than they tell us about games.

6   New York's Whitney Museum found itself at the center of controversy about digital art when it recently included Web artists in its prestigious biannual show. Critics didn't believe the computer could adequately express the human spirit. But they're misguided. The computer is simply a tool, one that offers artists new resources and opportunities for reaching the public; it is human creativity that makes art. Still, one can only imagine how the critics would have responded to the idea that something as playful, unpretentious and widely popular as a computer game might be considered art.

7   In 1925, leading literary and arts critic Gilbert Seldes took a radical approach to the aesthetics of popular culture in a treatise titled *The Seven Lively Arts.* Adopting what was then a controversial position, Seldes argued that America's primary contributions to artistic expression had come through emerging forms of popular culture such as jazz, the Broadway musical, the Hollywood cinema and the comic strip. While these arts have gained cultural respectability over the past 75 years, each was disreputable when Seldes staked out his position.

8   Readers then were skeptical of Seldes' claims about cinema in particular for many of the same reasons that contemporary critics dismiss games—they were suspicious of cinema's commercial motivations and technological origins, concerned about Hollywood's appeals to violence and eroticism, and insistent that cinema had not yet produced works of lasting value. Seldes, on the other hand, argued that cinema's popularity demanded that we reassess its aesthetic qualities.

9   Cinema and other popular arts were to be celebrated, Seldes said, because they were so deeply imbedded in everyday life, because they were democratic arts embraced by average citizens. Through streamlined styling and syncopated rhythms, they captured the vitality of contemporary urban experience. They took the very machinery of the industrial age, which many felt dehumanizing, and found within it the resources for expressing individual visions, for reasserting basic human needs, desires and fantasies. And these new forms were still open to experimentation and discovery. They were, in Seldes' words, "lively arts."

10   Games represent a new lively art, one as appropriate for the digital age as those earlier media were for the machine age. They open up new aesthetic experiences and transform the computer screen into a realm of experimentation and innovation that is broadly accessible. And games have been embraced by a public that has otherwise been unimpressed by much of what passes for digital art. Much as the salon arts of the 1920s seemed sterile alongside the vitality and inventiveness of popular culture, contemporary efforts to create interactive narrative through modernist hypertext or avant-garde installation art seem lifeless and pretentious alongside the creativity that game designers bring to their craft.

11   Much of what Seldes told us about the silent cinema seems remarkably apt for thinking about games. Silent cinema, he argued, was an art of expressive movement. He valued the speed and dynamism of D.W. Griffith's last-minute races to the rescue, the physical grace of Chaplin's pratfalls and the ingenuity of Buster Keaton's engineering feats. Games also depend up on an art of expressive movement, with characters defined through their distinctive ways of propelling themselves through space, and successful products structured around a succession of spectacular stunts and predicaments. Will future generations look back on Lara Croft doing battle with a pack of snarling wolves as the 21st-century equivalent of Lillian Gish making her way across the ice floes in *Way Down East*? The art of silent cinema was also an art of atmospheric design. To watch a silent masterpiece like Fritz Lang's *Metropolis* is to be drawn into a world where meaning is carried by the placement of shadows, the movement of machinery and the organization of space. If anything, game designers have pushed beyond cinema in terms of developing expressive and fantastic environments that convey a powerful sense of mood, provoke our curiosity and amusement, and motivate us to explore.

12   Seldes wrote at a moment when cinema was maturing as an expressive medium and filmmakers were striving to enhance the emotional experience of going to the movies—making a move from mere spectacle towards character and consequence. It remains to be seen whether games can make a similar transition. Contemporary games can pump us full of adrenaline, they can make us laugh, but they have not yet provoked us to tears. And many have argued that, since games don't have characters of human complexity or stories that stress the

consequences of our actions, they cannot achieve the status of true art. Here, we must be careful not to confuse the current transitional state of an emerging medium with its full potential. As I visit game companies, I see some of the industry's best minds struggling with this question and see strong evidence that the games released over the next few years will bring us closer and closer to the quality of characterization we have come to expect from other forms of popular narrative.

13   In the March 6 [2000] issue of *Newsweek*, senior editor Jack Kroll argued that audiences will probably never be able to care as deeply about pixels on the computer screen as they care about characters in films: "Moviemakers don't have to simulate human beings; they are right there, to be recorded and orchestrated. . . . The top-heavy titillation of *Tomb Raider*'s Lara Croft falls flat next to the face of Sharon Stone. . . . Any player who's moved to tumescence by digibimbo Lara is in big trouble." Yet countless viewers cry when Bambi's mother dies, and World War II veterans can tell you they felt real lust for *Esquire*'s Vargas girls. We have learned to care as much about creatures of pigment as we care about images of real people. Why should pixels be different?

14   In the end, games may not take the same path as cinema. Game designers will almost certainly develop their own aesthetic principles as they confront the challenge of balancing our competing desires for storytelling and interactivity. It remains to be seen whether games can provide players the freedom they want and still provide an emotionally satisfying and thematically meaningful shape to the experience. Some of the best games—Tetris comes to mind—have nothing to do with storytelling. For all we know, the future art of games may look more like architecture or dance than cinema.

15   Such questions warrant close and passionate engagement not only within the game industry or academia, but also by the press and around the dinner table. Even Kroll's grumpy dismissal of games has sparked heated discussion and forced designers to refine their own grasp of the medium's distinctive features. Imagine what a more robust form of criticism could contribute. We need critics who know games the way Pauline Kael knew movies and who write about them with an equal degree of wit and wisdom.

16   When *The Seven Lively Arts* was published, silent cinema was still an experimental form, each work stretching the medium in new directions. Early film critics played vital functions in documenting innovations and speculating about their potential. Computer games are in a similar phase. We have not had time to codify what experienced game designers know, and we have certainly not yet established a canon of great works that might serve as exemplars. There have been real creative accomplishments in games, but we haven't really sorted out what they are and why they matter.

17   But games do matter, because they spark the imaginations of our children, taking them on epic quests to strange new worlds. Games matter because our children no longer have access to real-world play spaces at a time when we've paved over the vacant lots to make room for more condos and the streets make parents nervous. If children are going to have opportunities for exploratory play, play that encourages cognitive development and fosters problem-solving skills, they will do so in the virtual environments of games. Multi-player games create opportunities for leadership, competition, teamwork and collaboration—for

nerdy kids, not just for high school football players. Games matter because they form the digital equivalent of the Head Start program, getting kids excited about what computers can do.

18   The problem with most contemporary games isn't that they are violent but that they are banal, formulaic and predictable. Thoughtful criticism can marshal support for innovation and experimentation in the industry, much as good film criticism helps focus attention on neglected independent films. Thoughtful criticism could even contribute to our debates about game violence. So far, the censors and culture warriors have gotten more or less a free ride because we almost take for granted that games are culturally worthless. We should instead look at games as an emerging art form—one that does not simply simulate violence but increasingly offers new ways to understand violence—and talk about how to strike a balance between this form of expression and social responsibility. Moreover, game criticism may provide a means of holding the game industry more accountable for its choices. In the wake of the Columbine shootings, game designers are struggling with their ethical responsibilities as never before, searching for ways of appealing to empowerment fantasies that don't require exploding heads and gushing organs. A serious public discussion of this medium might constructively influence these debates, helping identify and evaluate alternatives as they emerge.

19   As the art of games matures, progress will be driven by the most creative and forward-thinking minds in the industry, those who know that games can be more than they have been, those who recognize the potential of reaching a broader public, of having a greater cultural impact, of generating more diverse and ethically responsible content and of creating richer and more emotionally engaging stories. But without the support of an informed public and the perspective of thoughtful critics, game developers may never realize that potential.

DISCUSSION QUESTIONS

1. What seems to be the author's main purpose in comparing video games with cinema?

2. What points of comparison does the essay make between video games and cinema? Do those points of comparison seem valid?

3. What was the rhetorical advantage of referring to Gilbert Seldes' 1925 essay in paragraph 7 and 8?

4. How is paragraph 11 organized and why is this paragraph important to the overall comparison?

5. What differences does the author point out between cinema and video games? Do these differences undercut or support his main purpose?

6. In paragraph 2, the author asks whether games teach our children to kill. Does his essay answer the question, and if it does not, does this weaken his comparison-based argument?

7. The author does not mention a lot of specific games. Why might he have made that rhetorical choice? Does it weaken his comparison?

TOWARD KEY INSIGHTS

Often comparisons can be used to see something familiar in a new way. In this case, the author is attempting to get us to see the ways video games might be an art form. How might our idea of everyday things change if we looked at advertisements as art, everyday objects as sculpture, or short messages as poetry? Are such startling comparisons appropriate or useful?

The author stresses a number of similarities between video games and cinema. A critical response to comparisons requires us to look for points of disagreement. In what ways may video games be significantly and forever different from cinema?

SUGGESTIONS FOR WRITING *1. Write about how some other popular culture events or objects might be like art. For example, basketball could be like dance; comic books could be like visual art; extreme sports could be like ballet.*

2. Video games such as Lara Croft have been made into movies and movies such as The Matrix *have been made into video games. Compare a specific video game with its movie counterpart.*

Scott Russell Sanders

The Men We Carry in Our Minds

Scott Russell Sanders was born (1945) in Memphis, Tennessee. After earning a B.A. degree from Brown University in 1967 and a Ph.D. from Cambridge University in 1971, he joined the English faculty at Indiana University, where he is a full professor. Sanders is the author of numerous books of fiction and nonfiction. These books span a wide range of genres, including science fiction, historical novels, children's stories, folk tales, biographies, and personal essays. He has contributed to several essay anthologies, and his articles have appeared in literary journals and popular magazines. He has won several awards for his writing. In this essay, Sanders, in light of what he knows about the lives of working men, examines the view that power is rooted in gender.

1   The first men, besides my father, I remember seeing were black convicts and white guards, in the cottonfield across the road from our farm on the outskirts of Memphis. I must have been three or four. The prisoners wore dingy gray-and-black zebra suits, heavy as canvas, sodden with sweat. Hatless, stooped, they chopped weeds in the fierce heat, row after row, breathing the acrid dust of boll-weevil poison. The overseers wore dazzling white shirts and broad shadowy hats. The oiled barrels of their shotguns flashed in the sunlight. Their faces in memory are utterly blank. Of course those men, white and black, have become for me an emblem of racial hatred. But they have also come to stand for the twin poles of my early vision of manhood—the brute toiling animal and the boss.

2   When I was a boy, the men I knew labored with their bodies. They were marginal farmers, just scraping by, or welders, steel workers, carpenters; they swept floors, dug ditches, mined coal, or drove trucks, their forearms ropy with muscle; they trained horses, stoked furnaces, built tires, stood on assembly lines wrestling parts

onto cars and refrigerators. They got up before light, worked all day long whatever the weather, and when they came home at night they looked as though somebody had been whipping them. In the evenings and on weekends they worked on their own places, tilling gardens that were lumpy with clay, fixing broken-down cars, hammering on houses that were always too drafty, too leaky, too small.

3   The bodies of the men I knew were twisted and maimed in ways visible and invisible. The nails of their hands were black and split, the hands tattooed with scars. Some had lost fingers. Heavy lifting had given many of them finicky backs and guts weak from hernias. Racing against conveyor belts had given them ulcers. Their ankles and knees ached from years of standing on concrete. Anyone who had worked for long around machines was hard of hearing. They squinted, and the skin of their faces was creased like the leather of old work gloves. There were times, studying them, when I dreaded growing up. Most of them coughed, from dust or cigarettes, and most of them drank cheap wine or whiskey, so their eyes looked bloodshot and bruised. The fathers of my friends always seemed older than the mothers. Men wore out sooner. Only women lived into old age.

4   As a boy I also knew another sort of men, who did not sweat and break down like mules. They were soldiers, and so far as I could tell they scarcely worked at all. During my early school years we lived on a military base, an arsenal in Ohio, and every day I saw GIs in the guardshacks, on the stoops of barracks, at the wheels of olive drab Chevrolets. The chief fact of their lives was boredom. Long after I left the Arsenal I came to recognize the sour smell the soldiers gave off as that of souls in limbo. They were all waiting—for wars, for transfers, for leaves, for promotions, for the end of their hitch—like so many braves waiting for the hunt to begin. Unlike the warriors of older tribes, however, they would have no say about when the battle would start or how it would be waged. Their waiting was broken only when they practiced for war. They fired guns at targets, drove tanks across the churned-up fields of the military reservation, set off bombs in the wrecks of old fighter planes. I knew this was all play. But I also felt certain that when the hour for killing arrived, they would kill. When the real shooting started, many of them would die. This was what soldiers were *for*, just as a hammer was for driving nails.

5   Warriors and toilers: those seemed, in my boyhood vision, to be the chief destinies for men. They weren't the only destinies, as I learned from having a few male teachers, from reading books, and from watching television. But the men on television—the politicians, the astronauts, the generals, the savvy lawyers, the philosophical doctors, the bosses who gave orders to both soldiers and laborers—seemed as remote and unreal to me as the figures in tapestries. I could no more imagine growing up to become one of these cool, potent creatures than I could imagine becoming a prince.

6   A nearer and more hopeful example was that of my father, who had escaped from a red-dirt farm to a tire factory, and from the assembly line to the front office. Eventually he dressed in a white shirt and tie. He carried himself as if he had been born to work with his mind. But his body, remembering the earlier years of slogging work, began to give out on him in his fifties, and it quit on him entirely before he turned sixty-five. Even such a partial escape from man's fate as he had accomplished did not seem possible for most of the boys I knew. They

joined the Army, stood in line for jobs in the smoky plants, helped build highways. They were bound to work as their fathers had worked, killing themselves or preparing to kill others.

7   A scholarship enabled me not only to attend college, a rare enough feat in my circle, but even to study in a university meant for the children of the rich. Here I met for the first time young men who had assumed from birth that they would lead lives of comfort and power. And for the first time I met women who told me that men were guilty of having kept all the joys and privileges of the earth for themselves. I was baffled. What privileges? What joys? I thought about the maimed, dismal lives of most of the men back home. What had they stolen from their wives and daughters? The right to go five days a week, twelve months a year, for thirty or forty years to a steel mill or a coal mine? The right to drop bombs and die in war? The right to feel every leak in the roof, every gap in the fence, every cough in the engine, as a wound they must mend? The right to feel, when the layoff comes or the plant shuts down, not only afraid but ashamed?

8   I was slow to understand the deep grievances of women. This was because, as a boy, I had envied them. Before college, the only people I had ever known who were interested in art or music or literature, the only ones who read books, the only ones who ever seemed to enjoy a sense of ease and grace were the mothers and daughters. Like the menfolk, they fretted about money, they scrimped and made-do. But, when the pay stopped coming in, they were not the ones who had failed. Nor did they have to go to war, and that seemed to me a blessed fact. By comparison with the narrow, ironclad days of fathers, there was an expansiveness, I thought, in the days of mothers. They went to see neighbors, to shop in town, to run errands at school, at the library, at church. No doubt, had I looked harder at their lives, I would have envied them less. It was not my fate to become a woman, so it was easier for me to see the graces. Few of them held jobs outside the home, and those who did filled thankless roles as clerks and waitresses. I didn't see, then, what a prison a house could be, since houses seemed to me brighter, handsomer places than any factory. I did not realize—because such things were never spoken of—how often women suffered from men's bullying. I did learn about the wretchedness of abandoned wives, single mothers, widows; but I also learned about the wretchedness of lone men. Even then I could see how exhausting it was for a mother to cater all day to the needs of young children. But if I had been asked, as a boy, to choose between tending a baby and tending a machine, I think I would have chosen the baby. (Having now tended both, I know I would choose the baby.)

9   So I was baffled when the women at college accused me and my sex of having cornered the world's pleasures. I think something like my bafflement has been felt by other boys (and by girls as well) who grew up in dirt-poor farm country, in mining country, in black ghettos, in Hispanic barrios, in the shadows of factories, in Third World nations—any place where the fate of men is as grim and bleak as the fate of women. Toilers and warriors. I realize now how ancient these identities are, how deep the tug they exert on men, the undertow of a thousand generations. The miseries I saw, as a boy, in the lives of nearly all men I continue to see in the lives of many—the body-breaking toil, the tedium, the call to be tough, the humiliating powerlessness, the battle for a living and for territory.

10   When the women I met at college thought about the joys and privileges of men, they did not carry in their minds the sort of men I had known in my child-hood. They thought of their fathers, who were bankers, physicians, architects, stockbrokers, the big wheels of the big cities. These fathers rode the train to work or drove cars that cost more than any of my childhood houses. They were attended from morning to night by female helpers, wives and nurses and secre-taries. They were never laid off, never short of cash at month's end, never lined up for welfare. These fathers made decisions that mattered. They ran the world.

11   The daughters of such men wanted to share in this power, this glory. So did I. They yearned for a say over their future, for jobs worthy of their abilities, for the right to live at peace, unmolested, whole. Yes, I thought, yes yes. The difference between me and these daughters was that they saw me, because of my sex, as destined from birth to become like their fathers, and therefore as an enemy to their desires. But I knew better. I wasn't an enemy, in fact or in feeling. I was an ally. If I had known, then, how to tell them so, would they have believed me? Would they now?

DISCUSSION QUESTIONS

1. Why is the essay titled "The Men *We* Carry in *Our Minds*" rather than "The Men *I* Carry in *My Mind*"?

2. Other than starting the essay, what does paragraph 1 accomplish?

3. What primary categories of men does Sanders discuss? What principle of classification does he use?

4. Sanders uses a number of comparisons, such as "zebra suits, heavy as canvas" in paragraph 1, to enhance his writing. Point out other comparisons and comment on their effectiveness.

5. The last sentence of paragraph 10 and the second, sixth, and eighth sentences of paragraph 11 are short statements. What do you think Sanders accomplishes with these statements?

6. Judging by what Sanders writes in the essay, how do you think he would answer the questions he poses in the final two sentences of paragraph 11?

TOWARD KEY INSIGHTS

To what extent do you believe that the views expressed in the essay by the college women and Sanders reflect the views of today's college women and men?

How do you account for any changes you might note?

SUGGESTION FOR WRITING *Write an essay classifying the different grade school or high school teachers that you carry in your mind. Develop your categories with specific, informative details.*

Rick Salutin

The Mystery of Teaching

Rick Salutin is a Canadian playwright, novelist, and critic and is known for his background as a social activist and union organizer. He is the award-winning writer of the plays 1837 *(1976) and* Les Canadiens *(1977), and has written several books of non-fiction, including* Kent Rowley: A Canadian Union Life *(1980). In 1989 he won the Books in Canada First Novel Award for his novel* A Man of Little Faith. *Salutin has taught Canadian media and culture at the University of Toronto since the late 1970s. His work has appeared in several North American publications such as* Harper's *and* This Magazine *and he writes a regular column for* The Globe and Mail.

1   I've always written about kids and education. People used to challenge my right: "You don't have kids," they'd say. I could only answer, "But I was a kid." Teaching is also a thing everyone has the right to opine about, not because everyone has been a teacher, but because everyone has been taught.

2   The education discussion tends to focus on big issues: human nature, relations between the biological unit of the family and social units like the nation, the values that ground personal and collective behaviour, the good society, the demands of citizenship. When I was a kid in the 1950s, writers like Paul Goodman (*Growing Up Absurd*) and Edgar Z. Friedenberg (*Coming of Age in America*) went into schools like classical anthropologists searching for the noble savage or like anarchists who travelled Europe in the late nineteenth century, stirring up revolution whenever their train stopped long enough. Starting in the 1960s, Jonathan Kozol wrote bestsellers about US ghetto classrooms, like a war correspondent at the front. For twenty years, I worked for an alternative journal now called *This Magazine,* which began life as a homespun publication called *This Magazine is About Schools.* That was when education still engendered grand, resonant debates.

3   One effect of the deficit hysteria and budget slashing of the late twentieth century was to throttle discussion about public education. People with a passion for it were reduced to fighting rear-guard actions to save what they could, holding bake sales so the kids would have textbooks or pencils. People who would have been happier attacking the system in order to humanize it were forced to fight for its mere existence. It has been everyone's loss. Education is always a mess; it's always damaging kids and others. It needs critics even more than it needs defenders.

4   I student-taught at my Toronto synagogue from age seventeen. We made lesson plans and used audiovisual aids like film strips. During university, I worked at summer camps. Inspired by A.S. Neill's book on his free school in England, *Summerhill,* I tried to abolish cabin cleanup. For twenty-nine years, I've taught a half-course in Canadian Studies at the University of Toronto. I run it as a discussion, though it has grown from 20 to 175 students. "That class was real '60s," said a former student. I prefer to think of it as Socratic. When I taught Plato's

The Republic to undergrads on Long Island in the vrai sixties, I told them the basis of political authority was "They got the guns, man!" My eight-year-old, Gideon, heard me say that while reminiscing with old friends. He cracked up. "I can't believe you said, 'They got the guns, man!'" I hope it's the 'man' that convulsed him, but I fear it's the pomposity.

5   Gideon is my only kid. He started attending private daycare at ten months. It seemed tragically early, but he thrived. There were kids of many ages and they looked after each other. Some, like Gideon, attended all day; others, after school or just for lunch. ("Graduates" dropped in sometimes because they still felt attached to the place.) For Gideon, daycare may have helped compensate for not having siblings or an accessible extended family. He formed intense friendships, many of which he's maintained. I deduce from this that you never know what value a kid will glean from a setting. In that way education is like dating: no one knows what they really want until they get it.

6   Gideon went to a Montessori school for kindergarten. There, each kid works separately, on skills such as math and geography or a physical task such as pouring. The teacher deals with one student, teaching a new skill until the kid grasps it; then the kid continues alone, or aided by an older kid, until he's mastered it; then the kid moves on to something new. For the teacher it looks exhausting. She keeps glancing around to check on others. Occasionally, a kid comes to her with a problem, and she deals with it. There is no lockstep learning, no time-limited and testing-based units of study. It is total decentralization. Kids work at their own pace, and eventually everyone covers the same skill sets. The teacher keeps track. It is collective and individual, and there are few discipline problems since there is no attempt to keep everyone on the same track. It only looks anarchic; it's actually highly structured and task-driven. The kids respond positively, and I see little reason why this approach couldn't be applied to public systems.

7   Maria Montessori designed her teaching style for slum kids in Italy a century ago, though at Gideon's school SUVs lined up at the end of a day to pick the kids. He loved his first year there but not the second; the difference was his reaction to two different teachers. Other kids had the reverse experience with the same teachers. From this, I deduce that regardless of method, the teacher is central. I mean this as more than the pablum it sounds. I'll return to it.

8   Gideon went to Clinton, our local public school, for grade one. Some of his old daycare friends were there, he wanted to join them, and there was a financial consideration, but the main point was educational. What you learn in the public system is what the world you live in is like and that you are a part of it. That's because the public system must let everyone in. Some kids might bully you, and the school should help you cope with that. In the yard after school, a wayward kid might kill a butterfly that your class carefully raised from pupa stage—enraging parents, but the kids understand because, after all, so-and-so did it, and he's sort of like that. Sending a kid into the public system, for those who can afford otherwise, isn't an altruistic choice to support public education, or it shouldn't be. I think Gideon sensed that Clinton was a "real school," in the sense of a public institution that was a part of the larger world in which we live, and that's why he wanted to go. He strutted through the halls in a way he hadn't at Montessori.

9   But the mystery that is teaching is most striking for me at Gideon's karate classes. I've sat through hundreds at Northern Karate Schools, twice a week, never bored, rapt each time trying to figure out why this teaching is so good. Gideon went briefly to another karate school that was quasi-military—lots of *Sir, yes sir*—but it didn't take. Northern Karate has none of that, though it's disciplined and highly structured. He can attend any of several classes each day of the week. Teachers vary along with the composition of each class, so his experience doesn't depend on one teacher. Classes are brief: usually thirty minutes, and drills shift often, so attention doesn't flag. But at the bottom, it's the teachers.

10   They have vastly different personalities. Dominic is stocky and ebullient, with a voice like Aaron Neville's. Ricky Bonaparte (great name) is intense and demanding. "Ricky makes you want to work hard," says Gideon. Vince is methodical. Claire is maternal. They were well trained in conveying specific karate techniques but, says Andrea, another teacher, they each had to work out an underlying approach for themselves. This is a kind of teaching where the teachers are taught to find their own way.

11   The teachers pay the same attention to three-year-olds as they do to black belts. When the students are taken through moves or stances or full routines (*katas*) that they've done thousands of times, there is always something to learn. Noam Chomsky was once asked on CBC-TV if he ever got tired repeating the same points about politics year after year. He chuckled, adjusted a pesky earpiece, and said, "No, after we finish this interview, I'm going into a linguistics seminar where we'll discuss issues I've been thinking about a lot longer. There's always something to learn."

12   Teaching is one of the most basic human activities, like breathing and seeing. There's no end to it, just deeper depths. The best part about watching Gideon's karate teachers is that I can't nail down why they are so effective. It's *fun,* I think, but there's more to it than that. Or: *they like kids*. But the nub keeps slipping away. That's why it's teaching, a kind of activity that exists in the doing and that constantly reshapes according to context. This doesn't mean that method doesn't matter. But there is always that other, independent variable: the relationship between teacher and student. It is like the mystery of therapy. Teaching and therapy are the two remaining institutional redoubts of the oral tradition in our society. Aside from them, the oral tradition survives mainly in gossip, chitchat, and folklore. Aside from teaching and therapy, the written rules. No one has yet succeeded in reducing teaching or therapy to written form, despite correspondence courses and self-help books. It doesn't even require speech; silence can be the best teacher. Some of the most famed cases involve the sage or therapist saying nothing at a crucial moment.

13   Pedagogy is unavoidable, as is a curriculum. But it is the nature of oral discourse that it cannot have definitive rules or a stable end point. You can offer these provisionally but there is no authoritative method or conclusion, any more than there is in friendship, a marriage, or therapy. The relationship can stray somewhere unexpected; it can stop or unfold further. Teaching is essentially open-ended, because it belongs among those normal human activities that are embedded in time, and can't be extracted from their unfolding process and formalized. It is in their nature that any human being can do them and in some form, everyone does.

14   In this light—that teaching is a normal human function—I'd like to make a modest proposal: why not extend teaching duty, in an assistant capacity, to members of the community in order to help solve the classroom crisis everyone talks about? To the extent that schools require extra help in the classroom, citizens would be called on to serve, as they are in jury duty, with similar allowances for being excused and/or omitted. These community members would help so that teachers themselves could spend more time with individual students, as in Montessori classrooms. This would address the problems of class size and also of discipline. Let me linger over discipline.

15   It is impossible to run a teaching institution, or any institution, without some element of order and mutual respect. Reports in the spring from C.W. Jefferys Collegiate Institute in Toronto, where a fatal shooting occurred, and from elsewhere, tell of students threatening teachers, ignoring them, verbally abusing and physically abusing them. This is not just an education issue, it is a sign of serious social breakdown.

16   In the past, order was generally maintained through a social fabric that was hierarchical and patriarchal. It included religion, a moral code, parental authority, and sanctions like the threat of hell, all of it internalized in a sense of guilt and shame over violations. It worked in the sense that it largely kept the lid on violent impulses or channelled them elsewhere, but the human and emotional costs were monstrous.

17   People were dulled to their own experiences and each other. I would not want to restore this set of constraints if we could, and we can't. Particular players—parents, schools, teachers, courts, governments—can try to impose controls and limits, but they will not be nearly as effective as they were within a total framework that no longer exists. The issue now is: can our society devise a set of social controls that permits learning but does not require severe repression and an impossible return to the undesirable framework of earlier eras?

18   Of what use would the conscription of classroom citizen assistants be in this respect? One of the serious causes of the breakdown is that many youth believe their surrounding society doesn't really give a damn, and does little to ease their way through school and beyond. Their job prospects are uncertain, and they are told to prepare for constant change. This amounts to saying, "You're on your own." The models they see for success in the adult world tend to be grandiose and egocentric, and lack social purpose or contribution. The presence of community members in classrooms would represent a social commitment, in personal form. (My Uncle Eddie, a cosmetic surgeon, used to go into British Columbia prisons to operate on inmates who felt a different look might help them change. The results were good, and the warden said that this was mostly because the convicts knew Eddie wanted to be there.) Today, adult society appears to have largely opted out of its responsibilities to coming generations. Youth get this and respond variously, from violence to sullenness. A way for adults to address this response would be to opt back in.

19   Besides, I don't think teaching should be a full-time activity. It is too demanding and too normal. Teaching a two-hour university class is exhausting. What can it mean to teach a room full of kids, all day, five days a week? Summers off don't solve the problem. The kids teem back in September. Teachers should teach only

part-time because teaching, like eating, is a part-time activity. Then they could teach at their best. Since this may have to await a more utopian future, the least the rest of us can do for now is to get in there and share the burden, as well as the vast reward.

DISCUSSION QUESTIONS

1. Why do you think Salutin begins his essay with a general contextualization of his personal experience and historical knowledge of teaching and being taught? What effect does this opening create?

2. Does this essay have a stated or an implied thesis? What is the thesis?

3. What does Salutin hope to accomplish through his argument?

4. How does Salutin organize his essay? How does this organization advance his purpose?

5. Explain what you think Salutin means by suggesting teaching is one of two "remaining institutional redoubts of the oral tradition in our society"?

6. What is Salutin's modest proposal? What opportunities and barriers do you imagine would accompany his proposal if enacted?

TOWARD KEY INSIGHTS

To what extent do you think we are all obligated to act as teachers to facilitate a stronger, healthier, more respectful society? Explain your answer.

SUGGESTION FOR WRITING *Write an essay proposing that university students should be required to do some kind of community service, whether in the public schools, non-profit agencies, prisons, or other public institutions.*

Martin Luther King, Jr.

I Have a Dream

Martin Luther King, Jr. (1929–1968) has earned lasting fame for his part in the civil rights struggles of the 1950s and 1960s. Born in Atlanta, Georgia, he was ordained a Baptist minister in his father's church in 1947. A year later, he graduated from Morehouse College, then went on to take a Bachelor of Divinity degree at Crozier Theological Seminary (1951) and a Ph.D. in Philosophy at Boston University (1954), after which he accepted a pastorate in Montgomery, Alabama. King's involvement with civil rights grew when he organized and led a boycott that succeeded in desegregating Montgomery's bus system. In 1957, he founded and became the first president of the Southern Christian Leadership Conference and assumed a leading role in the civil rights movement. King advocated a policy of nonviolent protest based on the beliefs of

Thoreau and Gandhi and never veered from it despite many acts of violence directed at him. The success of King's crusade helped bring about the passage of the Civil Rights Act of 1964 and the Voting Rights Act of 1965 and won him the Nobel Peace Prize in 1964. King was assassinated on April 4, 1968, in Memphis, Tennessee. The speech "I Have a Dream" was delivered August 28, 1963, at the Lincoln Memorial in Washington, D.C., before a crowd of 200 000 people who had gathered to commemorate the centennial of the Emancipation Proclamation and to demonstrate for pending civil rights legislation. It stands as one of the most eloquent pleas ever made for racial justice.

1   I am happy to join with you today in what will go down in history as the greatest demonstration for freedom in the history of our nation.

2   Five score years ago, a great American, in whose symbolic shadow we stand today, signed the Emancipation Proclamation. This momentous decree came as a great beacon light of hope to millions of Negro slaves who had been seared in the flames of withering injustice. It came as a joyous daybreak to end the long night of their captivity.

3   But one hundred years later, the Negro still is not free; one hundred years later, the life of the Negro is still sadly crippled by the manacles of segregation and the chains of discrimination; one hundred years later, the Negro lives on a lonely island of poverty in the midst of a vast ocean of material prosperity; one hundred years later, the Negro is still languishing in the corners of American society and finds himself in exile in his own land.

4   So we've come here today to dramatize a shameful condition. In a sense we've come to our nation's capital to cash a check. When the architects of our republic wrote the magnificent words of the Constitution and the Declaration of Independence, they were signing a promissory note to which every American was to fall heir. This note was the promise that all men, yes, black men as well as white men, would be guaranteed the unalienable rights of life, liberty, and the pursuit of happiness.

5   It is obvious today that America has defaulted on this promissory note in so far as her citizens of color are concerned. Instead of honoring this sacred obligation, America has given the Negro people a bad check; a check which has come back marked "insufficient funds." But we refuse to believe that the bank of justice is bankrupt. We refuse to believe that there are insufficient funds in the great vaults of opportunity of this nation. And so we've come to cash this check, a check that will give us upon demand the riches of freedom and the security of justice.

6   We have also come to this hallowed spot to remind America of the fierce urgency of now. This is no time to engage in the luxury of cooling off or to take the tranquilizing drug of gradualism. Now is the time to make real the promises of democracy; now is the time to rise from the dark and desolate valley of segregation to the sunlit path of racial justice; now is the time to lift our nation from the quicksands of racial injustice to the solid rock of brotherhood; now is the time to make justice a reality for all of God's children. It would be fatal for the nation to overlook the urgency of the moment. This sweltering summer of the Negro's legitimate discontent will not pass until there is an invigorating autumn of freedom and equality.

7   Nineteen sixty-three is not an end, but a beginning. And those who hope that the Negro needed to blow off steam and will now be content will have a rude awakening if the nation returns to business as usual. There will be neither rest nor tranquility in America until the Negro is granted his citizenship rights. The whirlwinds of revolt will continue to shake the foundations of our nation until the bright day of justice emerges.

8   But there is something that I must say to my people, who stand on the worn threshold which leads into the palace of justice. In the process of gaining our rightful place, we must not be guilty of wrongful deeds. Let us not seek to satisfy our thirst for freedom by drinking from the cup of bitterness and hatred. We must forever conduct our struggle on the high plain of dignity and discipline. We must not allow our creative protests to degenerate into physical violence. Again and again we must rise to the majestic heights of meeting physical force with soul force. The marvelous new militancy, which has engulfed the Negro community, must not lead us to a distrust of all white people. For many of our white brothers, as evidenced by their presence here today, have come to realize that their destiny is tied up with our destiny. And they have come to realize that their freedom is inextricably bound to our freedom. We cannot walk alone. And as we walk, we must make the pledge that we shall always march ahead. We cannot turn back.

9   There are those who are asking the devotees of Civil Rights, "When will you be satisfied?" We can never be satisfied as long as the Negro is the victim of the unspeakable horrors of police brutality; we can never be satisfied as long as our bodies, heavy with the fatigue of travel, cannot gain lodging in the motels of the highways and the hotels of the cities; we cannot be satisfied as long as the Negro's basic mobility is from a smaller ghetto to a larger one; we can never be satisfied as long as our children are stripped of their selfhood and robbed of their dignity by signs stating "For Whites Only"; we cannot be satisfied as long as the Negro in Mississippi cannot vote and a Negro in New York believes he has nothing for which to vote. No! No, we are not satisfied, and we will not be satisfied until "justice rolls down like waters and righteousness like a mighty stream."

10   I am not unmindful that some of you have come here out of great trials and tribulations. Some of you have come fresh from narrow jail cells. Some of you have come from areas where your quest for freedom left you battered by the storms of persecution and staggered by the winds of police brutality. You have been the veterans of creative suffering. Continue to work with the faith that unearned suffering is redemptive. Go back to Mississippi. Go back to Alabama. Go back to South Carolina. Go back to Georgia. Go back to Louisiana. Go back to the slums and ghettos of our Northern cities, knowing that somehow this situation can and will be changed. Let us not wallow in the valley of despair.

11   I say to you today, my friends, that even though we face the difficulties of today and tomorrow, I still have a dream. It is a dream deeply rooted in the American dream. I have a dream that one day this nation will rise up and live out the true meaning of its creed, "We hold these truths to be self-evident, that all men are created equal." I have a dream that one day on the red hills of Georgia, sons of former slaves and the sons of former slave owners will be able to sit down together at the table of brotherhood. I have a dream that one day even the state of Mississippi, a

state sweltering with the heat of injustice, sweltering with the heat of oppression, will be transformed into an oasis of freedom and justice. I have a dream that my four little children will one day live in a nation where they will not be judged by the color of their skin, but by the content of their character.

12   I have a dream today!

13   I have a dream that one day down in Alabama—with its vicious racists, with its Governor having his lips dripping with the words of interposition and nullification—one day right there in Alabama, little black boys and black girls will be able to join hands with little white boys and white girls as sisters and brothers.

14   I have a dream today!

15   I have a dream that one day every valley shall be exalted, every hill and mountain shall be made low. The rough places will be plain and the crooked places will be made straight, "and the glory of the Lord shall be revealed, and all flesh shall see it together."

16   This is our hope. This is the faith that I go back to the South with. With this faith we will be able to hew out of the mountain of despair, a stone of hope. With this faith we will be able to transform the jangling discords of our nation into a beautiful symphony of brotherhood. With this faith we will be able to work together, to pray together, to struggle together, to go to jail together, to stand up for freedom together, knowing that we will be free one day. And this will be the day. This will be the day when all of God's children will be able to sing with new meaning, "My country 'tis of thee, sweet land of liberty, of thee I sing. Land where my fathers died, land of the pilgrim's pride, from every mountain side, let freedom ring." And if America is to be a great nation, this must become true.

17   So let freedom ring from the prodigious hilltops of New Hampshire; let freedom ring from the mighty mountains of New York; let freedom ring from the heightening Alleghenies of Pennsylvania; let freedom ring from the snowcapped Rockies of Colorado; let freedom ring from the curvaceous slopes of California. But not only that. Let freedom ring from Stone Mountain of Georgia; let freedom ring from Lookout Mountain of Tennessee; let freedom ring from every hill and molehill of Mississippi. "From every mountainside, let freedom ring."

18   And when this happens, and when we allow freedom to ring, when we let it ring from every village and every hamlet, from every state and every city, we will be able to speed up that day when all of God's children, black men and white men, Jews and Gentiles, Protestants and Catholics, will be able to join hands and sing in the words of the old Negro spiritual: "Free at last. Free at last. Thank God Almighty, we are free at last."

DISCUSSION QUESTIONS

1. Why do you think King begins with a reference to Lincoln?

2. Does this speech have a stated or an implied proposition? What is the proposition?

3. What does King hope to accomplish by the speech? How does he go about achieving his aim(s)?

4. What is the audience for the speech?

5. How does King organize his speech? How does this organization advance his purpose?

6. Which type(s) of argumentative appeal does King use? Cite appropriate parts of the speech.

7. What kinds of stylistic devices does King use? Where do they occur? How do they increase the effectiveness of the speech?

TOWARD KEY INSIGHTS

To what extent do people of all races relate to King's message today? Explain your answer.

SUGGESTION FOR ORAL ARGUMENT *Research the following proposition, and come to class prepared to argue either side:*

In order to promote more social justice, the Canadian government should institute an affirmative action program for racial minorities.

SUGGESTION FOR WRITING *Look up Barack Obama's 2004 Democratic National Keynote Address "The Audacity of Hope" on the internet, and write an essay pointing out echoes and differences between Obama's speech and King's speech. How do both speeches reflect their respective historical periods?*

Deborah A. Sullivan

Social Bodies: Tightening the Bonds of Beauty

Deborah A. Sullivan teaches sociology at Arizona State University. She is the co-author of Labor Pains: Modern Midwives and Home Birth, *in addition to a number of articles. The selection here is taken from the first chapter of her book* Cosmetic Surgery: The Cutting Edge of Commercial Medicine in America. *In this section she examines the reasons for and changing meanings of tattooing.*

1   Every culture has some customs that prescribe deliberately changing a body's natural appearance (Brain 1979). The methods, however, are diverse and particular to a culture at a specific period of time. Paints, for example, are used to decorate bodies in many cultures, but the pigments, patterns, permanency, and purpose of each culture's body customs vary widely. Only a nineteenth-century Bedouin woman could appreciate the eroticism of painting the whites of a man's eyes blue. While she would have regarded her own culture's customs as highly "civilized," she

probably would have thought the full body designs of Aboriginal Australians, American Indians, and Africans savage. Like eighteenth-century European explorers, she might have considered the tattooing and tooth-blackening in the Pacific region bizarre, and found the deeply carved black spirals and curves on Maori faces frightening and repulsive. It is no more likely that she could have discerned the beauty intended by the African and South American tribes who create elaborate patterns of raised scars, insert large lip plates and ear and nose plugs, and file teeth to sharp points. Nor is it likely that she could have appreciated the charm of Chinese women's bound "lotus" feet, Padaung women's elongated necks, or Western women's constricted waists during the Victorian era and augmented breasts in recent decades. Instead, in the implausible circumstance that a nineteenth-century Bedouin woman was exposed to such body customs, she probably would have regarded them as barbaric mutilations, much as contemporary Americans' view of female circumcision, which she might have considered normal.

2   The diversity of body customs has led anthropologists (e.g., Douglas 1970; Strathern 1996) to conclude that a body is both a physical and a symbolic artifact, forged by nature and by culture at a particular moment in history. Social institutions, ideology, values, beliefs, and technology transform a physical body into a social body. The resulting social body bears the imprint of the more powerful elements of its cultural context. Bodies, therefore, provide important clues to the mechanics of society.

3   There are many well-documented examples of the cultural construction of a social body. Although some body customs may be merely decorative, many, if not most, have social significance. Cultures in which female circumcision is common are strongly patriarchal and pronatalist. Women in these traditional cultures are believed to be weak and incapable of controlling their sexual urges. They are allowed little contact with men outside their families and are expected to hide their bodies from public view. Their social roles are circumscribed to child care and domestic functions. They receive little education and are economically dependent on men and politically powerless. They are socialized by their mothers to believe that removal of external female genitalia is a religious obligation that promotes purity, cleanliness, and fertility and that unexcised women are unattractive and beastly. Their identities as desirable women depend on the submission of their physical bodies to the dictates of social norms. The custom embodies their inferior status.

4   As female circumcision illustrates, the body can be a site for the expression of power in a culture. It also is used to communicate group membership, individual status, and social identity, along with associated beliefs and values. The body is often ritually modified in connection with major life transitions. In the Australian Aboriginal culture, for example, one or two front teeth are removed at puberty. Some time later boys are painted white, secluded, and circumcised to symbolize their passage into the world of men. At the end of the ceremony, they are painted red to celebrate their reentry into society as young men with all the corresponding rights and expectations of their new status. In some tribes young men undergo a subincision ceremony in which their urethra is split open before they marry and assume full adult male rights. Rites of passage between life stages in many other cultures are marked by ritualized patterns of scarification,

piercing, and tattooing. These same techniques are used to proclaim more permanent kinds of social status, such as gender and social class, as are head molding and other body modifications.

5   Using the body to communicate power, group membership, individual status, and social identity is not limited to exotic non-Western societies. It is ubiquitous in modern societies as well. American sailors, prisoners, bikers, and other gang members have tattooed their bodies throughout most of the twentieth century. Clinton Sanders (1989) argues that they use this particular body custom, considered vulgar by most middle-class, middle-aged Americans, to proclaim their resistance to conventional social norms of appearance and behavior. Their preference for death symbols, predatory animals, insulting and salacious images further enhances their rebellious statement.

6   After the mid-1960s the shock value of tattoos made them popular among some younger artistic individuals looking for attention and innovative, creative modes of expression. By the 1980s they were de rigueur among heavy metal and rap performers seeking a following among adolescents and young adults based on flaunting the conventional values and beliefs of their parents and other authority figures. Punks, freaks, Goths, skinheads, stoners, tweakers, and other disaffected young adults who identified with the counterculture heroes of their generation went to shops with names like Hierarchy, Crawling Squid, and Pigments of Imagination to record their sense of alienation on their bodies.

7   The meaning of tattoos changed in the 1990s. They became a badge of youth. Professional athletes, middle-class college students, blue-collar workers, and even some suburban housewives marked their bodies with tribal patterns, Kanji lettering, and sexy butterflies and flowers. As the shock value of tattoos declined, the most alienated subgroups added other forms of body modifications to advertise their contempt for middle-class conventions. They pierced their ears, noses, eyebrows, lips, tongues, nipples, navels, and genitalia with safety pins, barbells, studs, and various rings. These cultural pioneers established Internet news groups to share information about techniques, complications, public reaction, and erotic effects. Pop singers and other media celebrities adopted less extreme versions of this new body custom to advertise their hip identity. High school girls turned nose studs and navel rings into a fashion statement, undermining their deviance value. Those seeking a body symbol of resistance capable of generating strong public revulsion experimented with more extreme forms of self-stigmatization, such as scalp implants and scarification, to proclaim their marginalized status.

8   Tattooing and piercing at the end of the twentieth century appear to have much in common with previous fashion fads that visually differentiated each young generation over the course of the twentieth century, although some cultural observers (e.g., Polhemus and Randall 1996) find deeper meaning in these trends. They suggest the practices express a yearning for continuity, community, and commitment in a fragmented postmodern culture where ritual is rare and anomie prevails. Tattooing and piercing offer more permanent ways of recording life transitions and one's place in society.

9   All body customs, whether temporary, like tweezing eyebrows and clipping nose hair, or more permanent, like tattoos and cosmetic surgery, are forms of

self-creation. They are an effort to achieve a desired identity and connection with a reference group—marginal, hip, or mainstream. The process of reincarnation is universal.

10   Kim Hewitt (1997) additionally argues that body customs, particularly painful ones, can be used as part of a self-chosen health ritual. She theorizes that the physiological effects of pain can stimulate at least a temporary reprieve from numbing feelings of alienation (118). The acute awareness of feeling alive induced by pain has the potential to replace psychological fragmentation with holistic integration and a euphoric feeling of self-mastery. She claims that young women who starve and cut their bodies, like the punks and other marginalized subgroups who customize their bodies in extreme ways, are not only rebelling against societal constrictions, they also are trying to reclaim control of their bodies and establish individuality and autonomy. Other body customs, including female bodybuilding (Heywood 1998) and cosmetic surgery (Davis 1995), have been similarly interpreted as methods of psychological healing and cultural empowerment.

11   Those with a more Foucauldian perspective, such as Susan Bordo (1993, 1997), argue that such "disciplinary" body customs are outward manifestations of internalized cultural oppression. The discipline comes from an awareness of prevailing values, beliefs, norms and voluntary self-surveillance. Consequently, the sense of power experienced by disciplining one's own body, whether to resist prevailing cultural dictates with tattoos and piercings or successfully conform to them with diets and cosmetic surgery, is merely a personal achievement that lacks political effect to change the culture. Instead, as Rosemary Gillespie (1996) points out, customs such as cosmetic surgery perpetuate wider social inequalities.

12   This debate raises perennial philosophical questions about the nature of social control and the extent of free will. It also raises contemporary concerns that interpreting personal behavior as victimization deprives individuals of agency and castes them as gullible cultural dupes. My own perspective is similar to that of Bordo. Respect for the right of competent adults to make decisions about their own bodies should not blind us to the impact of the larger cultural and social context in which personal choices occur. My aim is to bring the structural aspects of this context, aspects that construct cosmetic surgery, into sharper focus. This larger cultural and social context influences individual body choices, gives them social meaning, and makes some, like cosmetic surgery, common enough to be considered body customs.

Works Cited

Bordo, Susan. *Unbearable Weight: Feminism, Western Culture, and the Body.* Berkeley: U of California Press, 1993.

Bordo, Susan. "Braveheart, Babe, and the Body: Contemporary Images of the Body." In *Twilight Zone: The Hidden Life of Cultural Images from Plato to O.J.,* ed. Susan Bordo. Berkeley: U of California Press, 1997.

Brain, Robert. *The Decorated Body.* London: Hutchinson, 1979.

Davis, Kathy. *Reshaping the Female Body: The Dilemma of Cosmetic Surgery.* New York: Routledge, 1995.

Douglas, Mary. *Natural Symbols: Explorations in Cosmology.* New York: Pantheon, 1970.

Gillespie, Rosemary. 1996. "Women, the Body, and Brand Extension in Medicine: Cosmetic Surgery and the Paradox of Choice." *Women and Health* 24: 69–85.

Hewitt, Kim. *Mutilating the Body: Identity in Blood and Ink.* Bowling Green, Ohio: Bowling Green State U Popular Press, 1997.

Heywood, Leslie. 1998. *Bodymakers: A Cultural Anatomy of Women's Body Building.* New Brunswick, NJ: Rutgers U Press.

Polhemus, Ted, and Housk Randall. *The Customized Body.* New York: Serpent's Tale, 1996.

Sanders, Clinton. *Customizing the Body: The Art and Culture of Tattooing.* Philadelphia: Temple UP, 1989.

Strathern, Andrew. 1996. *Body Thoughts.* Ann Arbor: Michigan Press.

DISCUSSION QUESTIONS

1. Identify the author's thesis statement. Explain as fully as possible what the author means by the thesis statement.

2. What are the advantages of the author's using many examples of body modification? How does that help make her point?

3. In the introduction, the author starts by describing the possible reaction of a nineteenth-century Bedouin woman to a variety of body modifications. What are the effects of this approach?

4. Why does the author discuss the changing meaning of tattooing?

5. This selection not only illustrates the author's thesis but does so by specifying possible causes for body modification. Identify the causes the author discusses. Do those that apply to modern tattooing seem correct to you?

6. This selection from a chapter of a book draws on a variety of sources and is extensively documented. What effect does this have on the essay?

7. In the conclusion of this selection, the author raises a number of broader questions. What role do these questions play given that this selection is part of the first chapter of a book? Are they effective here where they are serving as a conclusion?

TOWARD KEY INSIGHTS

Tattooing, piercing, and scarification are increasingly common practices. What reasons do you see for these practices?

Are those who participate in such practices "cultural dupes" who blindly follow cultural expectations or free individuals who make personal choices?

SUGGESTION FOR WRITING *Write a paper that illustrates a cultural practice that you think is significant, such as the crucial role of music in the life of many university students and teens.*

HANDBOOK

Learning the parts of English sentences won't in itself improve your writing, but it will equip you to gain more control over your writing as you learn to identify and repair errors at the sentence level. For example, before you can identify and correct unwarranted shifts from past to present time, you need to know about verbs and their tenses. Similarly, to recognize and correct pronoun case errors, you need to know what pronouns are and how they are used. This section first covers subjects and predicates, then complements, appositives, and the parts of speech, and finally phrases and clauses.

SUBJECTS AND PREDICATES

The subject of a sentence tells who or what the sentence is about. A *simple subject* consists of a noun (that is, a naming word) or a noun substitute. A *complete subject* consists of a simple subject plus any words that limit or describe it.

The predicate tells something about the subject and completes the thought of the sentence. A *simple predicate* consists of one or more verbs (words that show action or existence). A *complete predicate* includes any associated words. In the following examples, the simple subjects are underlined <u>once</u> and the simple predicates <u>twice</u>. The subjects and predicates are separated with slash marks.

<u>William</u>/<u>laughed</u>.

<u>Mary</u>/<u>has moved</u>.

<u>Sarah</u>/<u>painted</u> the kitchen.

The <u>student</u> over there in the corner/<u>is majoring</u> in art.

Complex subjects can be very long; it is helpful to be able to pick the simple subject out of a complex subject.

The <u>storms</u> in March, which dropped a record rainfall in one week, <u>resulted</u> in fierce floods.

A sentence can have a compound subject (two or more separate subjects), a compound predicate (two or more separate predicates), or both.

The <u>elephants</u> and their <u>trainer</u>/<u>bowed</u> to the audience and <u>left</u> the ring.

Sentences that ask questions don't follow the usual simple subject–simple predicate order. Instead, the word order may be changed slightly.

When questions use forms of the verb *be* (*is, am, are*), the verb appears before the subject while the rest of the predicate still follows the subject.

<u>Is</u>/<u>Angela</u>/ an experienced mountain climber?

When the sentences include auxiliary, or helping, verbs, the auxiliary is moved in front of the subject while the rest of the predicate remains in the same place.

<u>Has</u>/<u>a package</u>/ <u>arrived</u> yet for me?

Sometimes a question word such as *when, why, who,* or *where* appears in front of the sentence with the helping verb.

When <u>will</u>/<u>we</u>/<u>be allowed</u> to park on campus?

Sometimes certain types of phrases and clauses can fall between the subject and the predicate. These should not be confused with the subject. They are usually easy to detect since they can be moved elsewhere in the sentence. The subject is underlined.

sent

<u>My dog</u>, *since he has gotten old*, simply lies around the house.

<u>My dog</u> simply lies around the house *since he has gotten old*.

Sometimes a phrase that is not part of the subject can introduce the sentence. This phrase can also usually be moved.

After we have repaired the rock wall, <u>we</u> will begin to plant the new flowers.

<u>We</u> will begin to plant the new flowers *after we have repaired the rock wall*.

Usage Considerations   Because subjects are such important sentence elements, make sure that your subjects are clearly spelled out, not vague or misleading. Read the example below:

Our government has failed to repeal the Goods and Services Tax.

This statement can be expressed more precisely:

The *House of Commons* has failed to repeal the Goods and Services Tax.

The *prime minister* has rejected proposals to repeal the GST.

Paying close attention to subjects lets you present your ideas more accurately and clearly.

EXERCISE *Place a slash mark between the complete subject and the complete predicate; then underline the simple subject once and the verb(s) twice. If a subject comes between two verbs, set it off with two slash marks.*

1. The full moon rose majestically over the mountain peak.
2. John was ill on the day of the big test.
3. The boys and girls laughed and splashed happily in the pool.
4. That man by the door is my uncle.
5. The judge revoked Rudy's parole and ordered him to jail.
6. The tall oak shaded almost the entire backyard.
7. My favourite subject is English.
8. Mr. Eames has bought a wicker chair for his living room.

COMPLEMENTS

A complement is a word or word group that forms part of the predicate and helps complete the meaning of the sentence. Anything that comes after the verb is usually a complement. There are many kinds of complement, including phrases and clauses, which will be reviewed later in this chapter.

sent

- I think *that Glenn Gould was the quintessential Canadian musician.*
- Robert hesitated *to trap the groundhog behind his house.*
- We were late *because our car would not start.*

The four common complements of traditional grammar are direct objects, indirect objects, subject complements, and object complements.

A *direct object* names whatever receives, or results from, the action of a verb.

The millwright repaired the *lathe.* (Direct object receives action of verb *repaired.*)

Hilary painted a *picture.* (Direct object results from action of verb *painted.*)

They took *coffee* and *sandwiches* to the picnic. (Direct objects receive action of verb *took.*)

An *indirect object* identifies someone or something that receives whatever is named by the direct object.

Doris lent *me* her calculator. (Indirect object *me* receives *calculator,* the direct object.)

Will and Al bought their *boat* new sails. (Indirect object *boat* receives *sails,* the direct object.)

An indirect object can be converted to a prepositional phrase that begins with *to* or *for* and follows the direct object.

Doris lent her calculator *to me.*

Will and Al bought new sails *for their boat.*

A *subject complement* follows a linking verb—one that indicates existence rather than action. It renames or describes the subject.

Desmond is a *carpenter.* (Complement *carpenter* renames subject *Desmond.*)

The lights are too *bright* for Percy. (Complement *bright* describes subject *lights.*)

An *object complement* follows a direct object and renames or describes it.

The council named Donna *treasurer.* (Object complement *treasurer* renames direct object *Donna.*)

The audience thought the play *silly.* (Object complement *silly* describes direct object *play.*)

If a word is an object complement, you can form a short test sentence using *is*.

Donna is *treasurer*.

The play is *silly*.

Usage Considerations   Like subjects, direct objects can be revised for greater precision, as these examples show:

John sent *a gift*.

John sent *a giant colouring book as a birthday gift*.

Often, you can carry the revision one step further by adding an indirect object, subject complement, or other complement to the sentence.

John sent his *niece* a giant colouring book as a birthday gift. (Indirect object added.)

APPOSITIVES

An appositive is a noun, or word group serving as a noun, that follows another noun or noun substitute and expands its meaning. Appositives may be restrictive or nonrestrictive. Restrictive appositives distinguish whatever they modify from other items in the same class. They are written without commas.

My sister *Heidi* is a professional golfer. (Appositive *Heidi* distinguishes her from other sisters.)

I have just read a book by the novelist *Henry James*. (Appositive *Henry James* distinguishes him from other novelists.)

Nonrestrictive appositives provide more information about whatever they modify. This sort of appositive is set off by a pair of commas, except at the end of a sentence; then it is preceded by a single comma.

Anatoly Karpov, *the Russian chess player,* was interviewed on TV. (Appositive names *Karpov's* occupation.)

Todd plans to major in paleontology, *the study of fossils*. (Appositive defines the term *paleontology*.)

Usage Considerations   When a brief definition is necessary, appositives can help you improve your sentences.

John Cage wrote hundreds of pieces for prepared piano.

John Cage, *a twentieth-century avant-garde composer,* wrote hundreds of pieces for prepared pianos, *instruments with odds and ends stuck between their strings to provide unusual effects*.

However, avoid cluttering your writing with appositives that provide unneeded information; the overload will impede and irritate your reader.

EXERCISE *Identify each italicized item as a direct object (DO), an indirect object (IO), a subject complement (SC), an object complement (OC), or an appositive (AP).*

1. Harry is a *student* in business administration.
2. Mr. Ames gave his *son* money for the movies.
3. The study group found Kant's philosophy *difficult.*
4. Dan lost his *umbrella* in the subway.
5. Speed Spedowski, *our best pitcher,* won twenty-three games last season.
6. Bill borrowed several *CDs* for the party.
7. The newspaper named Melissa *editor.*
8. Nelson was *overjoyed* at winning the essay contest.

PARTS OF SPEECH

Traditional English grammar classifies words into eight parts of speech: *nouns, pronouns, verbs, adjectives, adverbs, prepositions, conjunctions,* and *interjections.* This section discusses these categories as well as verbals, phrases, and clauses, which also serve as parts of speech.

It is important to recognize that words that may look like one part of speech can function as another part of speech. For example, the verb *swim* can function as a noun:

Swimming is good for your health.

To identify a word as a part of speech is to identify how it functions in a sentence.

Traditional grammar defines nouns as words that name persons, places, things, conditions, ideas, or qualities. Most nouns can take a plural (*book, books*), possessive (*Andy, Andy's*), or article (*bench, the bench*).

Proper Nouns   Some nouns, called *proper nouns,* identify one-of-a-kind items like the following and are commonly capitalized.

France	Thanksgiving
Pacific Ocean	Saskatchewan
Man Booker Prize	Stanley Cup
Canadarm	Fantasy Corporation
Charter of Rights and Freedoms	Capilano College

Common Nouns   Common nouns name general classes or categories of items. Some common nouns are *abstract* and name a condition, idea, or quality that we can't experience with our five senses. *Abstract nouns* often cannot accept the plural; we cannot usually say we have *envies*. *Concrete nouns* identify something that we can experience with one or more of our senses and usually have plural forms.

Abstract Nouns	Concrete Nouns
arrogance	man
fear	bicycle
liberalism	desk
sickness	cartoon
understanding	lemon

noun

Count and Non-Count Nouns   Most nouns identify things we can count, and such nouns usually can take the plural form: *three bananas, a book, two children.* Some nouns, including many abstract nouns, cannot accept a plural: *underwear, patriotism, honesty.*

Usage Considerations   Good writing demands precise, potent nouns that have been carefully chosen. Ill-chosen nouns suggest poor thinking. Note how the vague word *freedom* robs the following sentence of any specific meaning:

Our *freedom* needs to be protected.

What did the writer have in mind? Here are a few possibilities:

Our *right to free speech* needs to be protected.

Our *private behaviour* needs to be protected.

Our *national sovereignty* needs to be protected.

Even when meaning does not present problems, sentences can be sharpened by careful attention to nouns. Note the greater precision of the second sentence below:

Our *dog* has a savage bite.

Our *pit bull* has a savage bite.

EXERCISE *Identify the nouns in the following sentences:*

1. Jeremy has undertaken the task of learning conversational German this summer.
2. Scrabble is a pleasant game to play on a cold, wet evening.
3. The chairperson will tell you about the decision of the committee.
4. The tree was covered with blossoms around which many bees buzzed.
5. My new apartment is in St. John's, Newfoundland.
6. Marcy Johnson jumped in her car, revved its engine, and roared off down the road.

Pronouns

Pronouns are a special class of words that can sometimes take the place of a noun in a sentence. Pronouns can help you avoid the awkward repetition of nouns.

Personal Pronouns   Personal pronouns refer to identifiable persons or things. Personal pronouns have different cases. The subjective case is used when the pronoun serves as the subject of the sentence or clause. **I** *helped Steve.* The objective case is used when the pronoun is the object of a verb or preposition. *Steve helped* **me.** *We spoke about* **him.** The possessive case shows possession or ownership. *That is* **my** *briefcase. My, your, our,* and *their* always precede nouns, as in *their car. Mine, hers, ours, yours,* and *theirs* do not precede nouns, as in *That book is mine. His* and *its* may or may not precede nouns.

	Subjective	Objective	Possessive
Singular			
First person	I	me	my, mine
Second person	you	you	your, yours
Third person	he, she, it	him, her, it	his, her, hers, its
Plural			
First person	we	us	our, ours
Second person	you	you	your, yours
Third person	they	them	their, theirs

Relative Pronouns   A relative pronoun relates a subordinate clause—a word group that has a subject and a predicate but does not express a complete idea—to a noun or pronoun, called an antecedent, in the main part of the sentence. The relative pronouns include the following:

who	whose	what	whoever	whichever
whom	which	that	whomever	whatever

Who in its various forms refers to people, *which* to things, and *that* to either things or groups of people.

Mary Beth Cartwright, *who* was arrested last week for fraud, was Evansville's "Model Citizen" two years ago. (The antecedent of *who* is *Mary Beth Cartwright.*)

He took the electric razor, *which* needed a new cutting head, to the repair shop. (The antecedent of *which* is *electric razor.*)

David Bullock is someone *whom* we should definitely hire. (The antecedent of *whom* is *someone.*)

Montreal is a city *that* I've always wanted to visit. (The antecedent of *that* is *city.*)

Which typically introduces nonrestrictive clauses, that is, clauses that provide more information about whatever they modify (see page 582).

The palace, *which* was in bad condition a century ago, is finally going to be restored. (Clause adds information about palace.)

That is typically used in other situations, especially to introduce restrictive clauses: those that distinguish the things they modify from others in the same class (see page 582).

The used car *that* I bought last week at Honest Bill's has already broken down twice. (Clause distinguishes writer's used car from others.)

Pages 601 and 664 explain the use of *who*, used in the subjective case, and *whom*, used only for the objective case.

pro

Interrogative Pronouns   Interrogative pronouns introduce questions. All of the relative pronouns except *that* also function as interrogative pronouns.

who	which	whoever	whichever
whom	what	whomever	whatever
whose			

What is the matter?

Who asked you?

Whatever do you mean?

When *what, which,* and *whose* are followed by nouns, they act as adjectives, not pronouns.

Which movie should we see?

Demonstrative Pronouns   As their name suggests, demonstrative pronouns point things out. There are four such pronouns:

this	these
that	those

This and its plural *these* identify recent or nearby things.

This is the play to see.

These are difficult times.

That and its plural *those* identify less recent or more distant things.

That is Mary's house across the road.

Those were very good peaches you had for sale last week.

Reflexive and Intensive Pronouns   A reflexive pronoun is used when the pronoun refers back to the noun in the same clause. An intensive pronoun lends emphasis to a noun or pronoun. The two sets of pronouns are identical.

myself	herself	ourselves
yourself	itself	yourselves
himself	oneself	themselves

My father cut *himself* while shaving. (reflexive pronoun)

The premier *himself* has asked me to undertake this mission. (intensive pronoun)

Don't substitute a reflexive pronoun for a personal pronoun.

Faulty	Jill and *myself* are going to a movie.
Revision	Jill and *I* are going to a movie.

Indefinite Pronouns These pronouns refer to unidentified persons, places, or things. One group of indefinite pronouns consistently acts as pronouns:

anybody	everything	one
anyone	nobody	somebody
anything	no one	someone
everybody	nothing	something
everyone		

A second group functions as either pronouns or adjectives.

all	any	most	few	much
another	each	either	many	neither

Here are some examples:

Everyone is welcome. (indefinite pronoun)

Many are called, but *few* are chosen. (indefinite pronouns)

Many men but only a *few* women attend the Air Force Academy. (adjectives)

Pages 560–561 discuss indefinite pronouns as antecedents.

Usage Considerations Many students use vague or ambiguous pronouns that damage the clarity of their writing. Problems include letting the same pronoun stand for different nouns or using a pronoun where detailed, vivid language would be more effective. The following passage illustrates poor pronoun usage:

My brother loves fly-fishing. He thinks *it* is the only way to spend a summer weekend. In fact, whenever he's off work, he'll do *it*.

Rewritten as follows, the passage has been notably improved:

My brother loves fly-fishing. He thinks that *wading a stream and casting leisurely for trout* is the only way to spend a summer weekend. In fact, whenever he's off work, he *can be found up to his hips in water, offering his hand-tied flies to the waiting rainbow trout.*

EXERCISE *Identify each pronoun in the following sentences and indicate its type (personal, relative, interrogative, demonstrative, reflexive, intensive, and indefinite). If it is a personal pronoun, indicate if it is in the subjective (S), objective (O), or possessive (P) case.*

1. This is the kind of movie that I like.
2. Everyone in the class came to the party she gave at term's end.
3. If you feel thirsty, pour yourself a glass of lemonade.
4. That is a terrible-looking chair. Who would buy it anyhow?
5. What do you think Sally and Bill bought each other for their wedding?
6. I myself will take the blame for anything that goes wrong with the experiment.

vbs

Verbs

A verb indicates action or existence. Main verbs fall into two classes: *action verbs* and *linking verbs*. A very different type of verb is the *auxiliary* (or *helping*) verb, which adds specific kinds of meaning to the main verb.

Action Verbs   As their name suggests, action verbs express action. Some action verbs are transitive, others intransitive. A transitive verb has a direct object that receives or results from the action and rounds out the meaning of the sentence.

The photographer *took* the picture.

Without the direct object, this sentence would not express a complete thought. In contrast, an *intransitive* verb requires no direct object to complete the meaning of the sentence.

Lee Ann *gasped.*

Little Tommy Tucker *sings* for his supper.

Many action verbs can play both transitive or intransitive roles, depending on the sentences they are used in.

Kari *rode* her bicycle into town. (transitive verb)

Karl *rode* in the front seat of the car. (intransitive verb)

Linking Verbs   A linking verb shows existence—what something is, was, or will be—rather than action. Linking verbs are intransitive and tie their subjects to subject complements. Some subject complements are nouns or noun substitutes that rename their subjects. Others are adjectives that describe their subjects.

Ms. Davis *is* our new director. (Complement *director* renames subject *Ms. Davis.*)

The soup *was* lukewarm. (Complement *lukewarm* describes subject *soup.*)

The most common linking verbs are forms of the verb *to be* (*is, are, am, was, were, be, being, been*). Likewise, verbs such as *seem, become, appear, remain, feel, look, smell, sound,* and *taste* function as linking verbs when they do not indicate actual physical action. In such cases, they are followed by adjectives (see pages 569–571). Here is an example:

Harry looked *angry.*

When such verbs do indicate physical action, they function as action verbs and are followed by adverbs (see pages 572–573).

Harry looked *angrily* at the referee.

vbs

Linking verbs can also be followed by adverbial phrases of place or time.

Your dinner is *on the table* (adverb phrase of place).

The meeting will be *at 8:00 A.M.* (adverb phrase of time).

Auxiliary Verbs　These helping verbs accompany action or linking verbs, and provide information about time, possibility, or obligation. They also establish the passive voice. *Have, be,* and *do* can function as both auxiliary and main verbs.

The auxiliary verbs *have (has, had)* and *be (is, are, was, were)* can provide information about time.

Carol *has* repaired your computer.

Carol *is* reformatting your hard drive.

The auxiliary verb *do* is inserted to form the negative or interrogative (question form) when there is no other auxiliary.

Ellen *did* not resign.

Did Ellen resign?

Auxiliary verbs called modals show time, obligation, possibility, or ability: *shall, should, will, would, can, could, may, might.*

With questions, the auxiliary verb is often moved to the front.

Will Ellen *resign?*

Auxiliary verbs called modals show time, obligation, possibility, or ability: *shall, should, will, would, can, could, may, might.*

Usage Considerations　Energetic writing requires precise verbs. Don't take verbs for granted; revise them as necessary in order to strengthen a sentence. Note the improved precision of the second example sentence:

I *gave* the maître d' a twenty-dollar bill.

I *slipped* the maître d' a twenty-dollar bill.

EXERCISE *Identify each verb in the following sentences and indicate its type:*

1. If Paul and Jim need transportation, my car will be available.
2. Please write your name on your quiz before you give it to me.

3. Marvin has been sitting in front of the TV all morning.

4. I will be watching the Toronto Raptors play tonight.

5. The movie offered lots of action, but the plot was poor.

6. Christine's assistance on this project has been invaluable.

Tense   Verbs change in form to show distinctions in time. Every main verb has two basic tenses: present and past.

The *present tense* shows present condition and general or habitual action, indicates permanent truths, tells about past events in the historical present, and sometimes denotes action at some definite future time.

Verbs in the present tense must agree with their subjects. If the subject of a verb is a singular noun or pronoun (*he, she, it*), add *s* or *es* (if the word ends with an *s, z,* or *ch* sound: *talks, teaches*). If the subject is plural or a second-person pronoun (*you*), the verb takes no ending (*talk, teach*).

Helen *looks* beautiful in her new gown. (present condition)

John *works* on the eighteenth floor. (general action)

I *brush* my teeth each morning. (habitual action)

The earth *rotates* on its axis. (permanent truth)

On November 11, 1918, the guns *fall* silent, and World War I *comes* to an end. (historical present)

On Monday, I *begin* my new job. (future action)

The past tense shows that a condition existed or an action was completed in the past. This verb tense leaves the time indefinite, but surrounding words may specify it. Most verbs are regular and form the past tense by adding *-ed: talk, talked.* Some verbs are irregular and form the past by changing the vowel: *run, ran.* A very few verbs do not change forms at all in creating the past: *set, set.*

Paul *was* angry with his noisy neighbours. (past condition, time indefinite)

Sandy *received* a long letter yesterday. (past action, time specified by *yesterday*)

Past Participle   In addition to the basic tenses, there is a *past participle* form of main verbs that is used to form the perfect form of the verb phrase (*He* **has talked** *to her*), as well as the passive voice (*the table* **was set**). For most verbs, the past participle form is identical to the past tense in form.

Present	Past	Past Participle
talk	talk**ed**	talk**ed**
stand	st**oo**d	st**oo**d
set	set	set

vbs

Some verbs have different past forms and past participles. This can often lead to errors, as less experienced writers may use the regular past (*He has* **swam** *this river before*) when the past participle form is required (*He has* **swum** *this river before*). Below is a table of many but not all of the irregular verbs for your reference.

Present Infinitive	Past	Past Participle
arise	arose	arisen
be	was, were	been
become	became	become
bite	bit	bitten
blow	blew	blown
break	broke	broken
choose	chose	chosen
come	came	come
do	did	done
draw	drew	drawn
drink	drank	drunk
drive	drove	driven
eat	ate	eaten
fall	fell	fallen
fly	flew	flown
freeze	froze	frozen
get	got	get *or* gotten
give	gave	given
grow	grew	grown
hide	hid	hidden
know	knew	known
ride	rode	ridden
see	saw	seen
shake	shook	shaken
slay	slew	slain
speak	spoke	spoken
spring	sprang	sprung
write	wrote	written

Time and Verb Forms   In addition to the tenses in English, many other forms of a verb are used to express time.

Future Time   *Future time* is frequently indicated by the auxiliary modals *shall* or *will* with the present tense form of the verb.

You *will feel* better after a good night's sleep. (future condition)

I *shall attend* the concert next week. (future action)

Perfect Verb Forms   The perfect form of a verb describes a past action or condition that continued. It is formed using the auxiliary verb *have* and the past participle of the verb.

The *present perfect* tense is formed with *has* or *have* and the past participle of the main verb. It shows that a past condition or action, or its effect, continues until the present time.

The players *have been* irritable since they lost the homecoming game. (Condition continues until present.)

Juanita *has driven* a truck for five years. (Action continues until present.)

William *has repaired* the snow blower. (Effect of action continues until present although the action itself was completed in the past.)

The *past perfect* tense combines *had* and the past participle of the main verb. It refers to a past condition or action that was completed before another past condition or action.

He *had been* in the army two years when the war ended. (Past perfect condition occurred first.)

Vivian moved into the house that she *had built* the summer before. (Past perfect action occurred first.)

The *future perfect* tense is formed from the verbs *shall have* or *will have* plus the past participle of the main verb. It shows that a condition or an action will have been completed at some time in the future. Surrounding words specify time.

Our sales manager *will have been* with the company ten years next July. (Condition will end.)

By the end of this year, I *shall have written* the great Canadian novel. (Action will be completed.)

Progressive Verb Forms   Each verb form, including the basic tenses, has a *progressive form* that indicates action in progress. The progressive is always indicated by some form of the verb *to be* followed by a present participle (or progressive), a verb that ends in *-ing*.

Present progressive	I am running.
Past progressive	I was running.
Future progressive	I will be running.
Present perfect progressive	I have been running.
Past perfect progressive	I had been running.
Future perfect progressive	I will have been running.

An easy way to identify the form of the verb phrase is to use the following formula (see page 564 for modal verbs):

(modal) + (have + en/ed) + (be + ing) + main verb

Simply read the first tense in the sentence. If the modal is *will* then that designates future time. Then if *have, has, or had* is present, the verb phrase is

vbs

perfect. If a form of *be* is present and the main verb ends with *ing*, then the verb phrase is progressive.

will	*have*	*been living*
future	perfect	progressive

Usage Considerations   While most students use regular tenses and the progressive accurately, many less experienced writers do not always use the perfect verb form where appropriate. This is acceptable in informal writing; it is not acceptable in most formal writing.

> *Not acceptable*   Jim *studied* accounting for the last three years.
> (This suggests that the action is over and done with.)
>
> *Acceptable*   Jim *has studied* accounting for the last three years. (The present perfect verb form shows that the action comes right up to the present and may not be finished yet.)

Pages 603–604 discuss unwarranted shifts in tense and their correction.

Voice   Transitive verbs have two voices: active and passive. A verb is in the *active voice* when the subject carries out the action named by the verb.

> Barry *planned* a picnic. (Subject *Barry* performs action.)

A verb is in the *passive voice* when the subject receives the action. The performer may be identified in an accompanying phrase or go unmentioned.

> A picnic *was planned* by Barry. (The phrase *by Barry* identifies the performer.)

> The picnic *was cancelled.* (The performer goes unmentioned.)

A passive construction always uses a form of *to be* and the past participle of an action verb. Like other constructions, the passive may show past, present, or future time.

> Amy *is paid* handsomely for her investment advice. (present tense)

> I *was warned* by a sound truck that a tornado was nearby. (past tense)

> I *will be sent* to Ghana soon by the Canada Corps. (future tense)

> I *have been awarded* a sizeable research grant. (present perfect tense)

> The city *had been shelled* heavily before the infantry moved in. (past perfect tense)

> By the end of this month, the site for our second factory *will have been chosen.* (future perfect tense)

To convert a sentence from the passive to the active voice, make the performer the subject, the original subject the direct object, and drop the form of *to be.*

> The treaty *was signed* by the general. (passive)

> The general *signed* the treaty. (active)

Technical and scientific writing commonly uses the passive voice to explain processes since its flat, impersonal tone adds an air of scientific objectivity and authority. However, other kinds of writing avoid the passive voice except when it is desirable to conceal the one performing the action or when the action is more significant than the actor. See pages 112–113 and 580 for more information on usage.

EXERCISE *Identify each verb in the following sentences, indicate its tense, and note any use of the passive voice:*

1. They will have arrived in Tokyo by this evening.
2. This TV program is relayed to Europe by satellite.
3. The Krause Corporation's new headquarters building will be dedicated June 30.
4. The school psychologist was asked whether she had any explanation for Tim's odd behaviour.
5. We have been told we face yet another 15 percent staff cutback.
6. Nancy bought an Arcade Fire CD.
7. The Northrups will start their vacation tomorrow.
8. Leslie works in the sales department of Canadian Time.

Adjectives

An adjective *modifies* a noun or pronoun by describing it, limiting it, or otherwise making its meaning more precise.

> The *brass* candlestick stood next to the *fragile* vase. (*Brass* modifies *candlestick*, and *fragile* modifies *vase*.)

> The cat is *long-haired* and *sleek*. (*Long-haired* and *sleek* modify *cat*.)

There are three general categories of adjectives: limiting, descriptive, and proper.

Limiting Adjectives   A limiting adjective identifies or points out the noun or pronoun it modifies. It may indicate number or quantity. Several categories of pronouns can serve as limiting adjectives, as can numbers and nouns.

> *Whose* briefcase is on the table? (interrogative adjective)

> The couple *whose* car was stolen called the police. (relative adjective)

> *This* restaurant has the best reputation for gourmet food. (demonstrative adjective)

> *Some* people have no social tact at all. (indefinite adjective)

> Sally swerved *her* car suddenly to avoid an oncoming truck. (possessive adjective)

> *Three* people entered the lecture hall late. (number as adjective)

> The *schoolgirl* look is fashionable this year. (noun as adjective)

adj

Descriptive Adjectives   A descriptive adjective names a quality, characteristic, or condition of a noun or pronoun. Two or more of these adjectives, members of the largest category of adjectives, may modify the same noun or pronoun.

The *yellow* submarine belongs to the Beatles.

He applied *clear* lacquer to the tabletop.

The *slim, sophisticated* model glided onto the runway.

The child was *active, happy,* and *polite.*

Proper Adjectives   A proper adjective is derived from a proper noun and is always capitalized.

Harwell is a *Shakespearean* actor.

Articles as Adjectives   Articles appear immediately before nouns and can therefore be considered adjectives. There are three articles in English: *a, an,* and *the. The* points to a specific item; *a* and *an* do not. *A* precedes words beginning with consonant sounds; *an* precedes words with vowel sounds, making pronunciation easier.

The right word at *the* right moment can save a friendship. (Definite articles suggest there is one right word and one right moment.)

A right word can save a friendship. (Indefinite article suggests there are several right words.)

I think I'd like *an* apple with my lunch. (No particular apple is specified.)

Sometimes the definite article refers to a class of items.

The tiger is fast becoming an endangered species.

Context shows whether such a sentence refers to particular items or entire classes.

Comparison with Adjectives   Adjectives may be used to show comparison. When two things are compared, shorter adjectives usually add *-er* and longer adjectives add *more.* When three or more things are compared, shorter adjectives usually add *-est* and longer ones add *most.*

John is *taller* than Pete. (short adjective comparing two people)

Sandra seems *more cheerful* than Jill today. (long adjective comparing two people)

John is the *tallest* of the three brothers. (short adjective comparing three people)

Sandra is the *most cheerful* girl in the class. (longer adjective comparing more than three people)

Some adjectives, like the examples below, have irregular forms for comparisons.

good—better—best

bad—worse—worst

Don't use the *-est* form of the shorter adjective for comparing just two things.

> *Faulty*   This is the *smallest* of the two castles.

Instead, use the *-er* form. (See pages 605–606 for revision of faulty comparisons.)

> *Revision*   This is the *smaller* of the two castles.

Position of Adjectives   Most adjectives come immediately before the words they modify. In a few set expressions (for example, heir *apparent*), the adjective immediately follows the word it modifies. Similarly, adjective pairs sometimes appear in a follow-up position for added emphasis (The rapids, *swift* and *dangerous,* soon capsized the raft). Adjectives can also serve as subject complements, where they follow their subjects (The puppy was *friendly*).

Usage Considerations   Some students overuse adjectives, especially in descriptions, but most underuse them. Review your sentences carefully to see where adding or cutting adjectives can increase the impact of your writing.

> My Cadillac is the talk of my friends.

> My *old, dilapidated, rusty, fenderless 1985* Cadillac is the talk of my friends.

> My *rusty, fenderless 1985* Cadillac is the talk of my friends.

The first sentence lacks adjectives that show why the car is discussed. The second sentence overcorrects this fault by including two adjectives that repeat the information provided by the others. The final sentence strikes the proper balance.

Determiners   Some words, called *determiners,* limit the noun or pronoun but do not name a quality or characteristic of the noun or pronoun. These words are sometimes classified with adjectives.

> *Three* sailboats raced around the island.

While we know how many sailboats are involved, there is no descriptive content added to the concept of sailboats.

There are many different kinds of determiners.

Determiners	Name
a, an	Indefinite article
the	Definite article
this, that, these, those	Demonstrative
one, two, three, four, five	Cardinal number
first, second, third, fourth	Ordinal number
my, our, your, his, her, hers, its, their	Possessive pronoun
some, any, no, every, another, enough	Indefinite pronoun
either, neither, all, both, each, less,	
other, many, more, most, few, several	
Tom's, Mary's	Possessive noun

adj

EXERCISE *Identify the adjectives in the following sentences:*

1. Tom is a very unhappy person.
2. Paul has an aunt who writes long, chatty letters to him regularly.
3. Sean ate an English muffin and drank a cup of black coffee.
4. Barton has an unusual sideboard in his dining room.
5. The tired carpenter tossed his tools into the red truck and drove home.
6. After buying a few gifts, Linda and Audrey took a slow stroll around the resort town.
7. Harvey ate three hamburgers and four helpings of salad at the picnic.
8. From the hilltop, the view was beautiful.

Adverbs

An adverb modifies a verb, an adjective, another adverb, or a whole sentence. Adverbs generally answer questions such as "How?" "When?" "Where?" "How often?" and "To what extent?"

The floodwaters receded *very* slowly. (Adverb modifies adverb and answers the question "How?")

My sister will visit me *tomorrow.* (Adverb modifies verb and answers the question "When?")

The coach walked *away from the bench.* (Adverb modifies verb and answers the question "Where?")

The tire is *too* worn to be safe. (Adverb modifies adjective and answers the question "To what extent?")

The teller is *frequently* late for work. (Adverb modifies adjective and answers the question "How often?")

Unfortunately, the game was cancelled because of rain. (The adverb modifies the whole sentence but does not answer any question.)

Formation of Adverbs Most adverbs are formed by adding *-ly* to adjectives.

The wind is *restless.* (*Restless* is an adjective modifying *wind.*)

He walked *restlessly* around the room. (*Restlessly* is an adverb modifying *walked.*)

However, many common adverbs (*almost, never, quite, soon, then, there,* and *too*) lack *-ly* endings.

> I *soon* realized that pleasing my boss was impossible.

> This movie is *too* gruesome for my taste.

Furthermore, some words such as *better, early, late, hard, little, near, only, straight,* and *wrong* do double duty as either adjectives or adverbs.

> We must have taken a *wrong* turn. (*Wrong* is an adjective modifying the noun *turn.*)

> Where did I go *wrong*? (*Wrong* is an adverb modifying the verb *go.*)

Comparison with Adverbs   Like adjectives, adverbs can show comparison. When two things are compared, adverbs add *more*. When three or more things are compared, *most* is used.

> Harold works *more* efficiently than Don. (adverb comparing two people)

> Of all the people in the shop, Harold works the *most* efficiently. (adverb comparing more than two people)

Some adverbs, like some adjectives, use irregular forms for comparisons.

> well—better—best

> much—more—most

Position of Adverbs   Adverbs are more movable than any other part of speech. Usually, adverbs that modify adjectives and other adverbs appear next to them to avoid confusion.

> Her *especially* fine tact makes her a welcome guest at any party. (Adverb *especially* modifies adjective *fine.*)

> The novel was *very* badly written. (Adverb *very* modifies adverb *badly.*)

Adverbs that modify verbs, however, can often be shifted around in their sentences without causing changes in meaning.

> *Quickly,* she slipped through the doorway.

> She slipped *quickly* through the doorway.

> She slipped through the doorway *quickly.*

adv

EXERCISE *Identify the adverbs in the following sentences:*

1. Harold is late more frequently than any other member of the crew.
2. After dinner, the children went outdoors and played noisily.
3. Lucy stepped quickly to the door and listened intently to the howling wind.
4. The pirate ship glided swiftly and silently toward the sleeping town.
5. The tired, perspiring runner staggered wearily across the finish line.
6. You'll have to work very fast to keep up with Jody.

Prepositions

A preposition links its object—a noun or noun substitute—to some other word in the sentence and shows a relationship between them. The relationship is often one of location, time, means, or reason or purpose. The word group containing the preposition and its object makes up a prepositional phrase.

The new insulation *in* the attic keeps my house much warmer now. (Preposition *in* links object *attic* to *insulation* and shows location.)

We have postponed the meeting *until* tomorrow. (Preposition *until* links object *tomorrow* to *postponed* and shows time.)

The tourists travelled *by* train. (Preposition *by* links object *train* to *travelled* and shows means.)

Warren swims *for* exercise. (Preposition *for* links object *exercise* to *swims* and shows reason or purpose.)

The following list includes the most common prepositions, some of which consist of two or more words:

above	beside	in	out of
after	between	instead of	over
against	by	into	since
along with	by reason of	like	through
among	contrary to	near	to
at	during	next to	toward
because of	except	of	under
before	for	on	with
below	from	onto	without

Many of these combine to form additional prepositions: *except for, in front of, by way of, on top of,* and the like.

Some prepositions such as *up, on,* and *in* can also function as a different part of speech called a *verb particle.* Here are two examples.

The instructor let Jeff make *up* the test.

The officer turned *in* his best friend.

The verb particle is closely associated with the verb and is a part of its meaning. If a word is used as a verb particle (rather than a preposition), it can usually be moved after the noun.

The instructor let Jeff make the test *up*.

The officer turned his best friend *in*.

Usage Considerations It is easy to use a small group of prepositions over and over in your writing. This habit often results in imprecise or misleading sentences. To avoid this problem, think carefully about your choice of prepositions as you revise. Read the following example:

He walked *by* the railway tracks on his way home.

Note that two interpretations are possible.

He walked *along* the railway tracks on his way home.

He walked *past* the railway tracks on his way home.

Clearly you want to use the preposition that conveys your intended meaning.

EXERCISE *Identify the prepositions and their objects in the following sentences:*

1. I finally finished waxing the car just before the rainstorm.
2. Aloe lotion will give you instant relief from sunburn.
3. For reasons of security, this gate must be kept locked at all times.
4. Shortly after dark, the group arrived at the camp.
5. Across the street, Gillian was working on her roof.
6. At the end of the concert, everyone in the hall stood and applauded.

Conjunctions

Conjunctions serve as connectors, linking parts of sentences or whole sentences. These connectors fall into three groups: coordinating conjunctions, subordinating conjunctions, and conjunctive adverbs.

Coordinating Conjunctions Coordinating conjunctions connect terms of equal grammatical importance: words, word groups, and simple sentences. These conjunctions can occur singly *(and, but, or, nor, for, yet, so)* or in pairs called correlative conjunctions *(either—or, neither—nor, both—and,* and *not only—but also).* The elements that follow correlative conjunctions must be parallel, that is, have the same grammatical form.

Tom *and* his cousin are opening a video arcade. (Coordinating conjunction connects nouns.)

conj

Shall I serve the tea in the living room *or* on the front porch? (Coordinating conjunction connects phrases.)

I am going to Europe this summer, *but* Marjorie is staying home. (Coordinating conjunction connects simple sentences.)

Amy *not only* teaches English *but also* writes novels. (Correlative conjunctions connect parallel predicates.)

You can study nursing *either* at the University of B.C. *or* at Kwantlen Polytechnic University. (Correlative conjunctions connect parallel phrases.)

Friendship is *both* pleasure *and* pain. (Correlative conjunctions connect parallel nouns.)

Subordinating Conjunctions   Like relative pronouns, subordinating conjunctions introduce subordinate clauses, relating them to independent clauses, which can stand alone as complete sentences. Examples of subordinating conjunctions include *because, as if, even though, since, so that, whereas,* and *whenever* (see pages 582–583 for more).

I enjoyed the TV program *because* it was so well acted. (Conjunction connects *it was so well acted* to rest of sentence.)

Whenever you're ready, we can begin dinner. (Conjunction connects *you're ready* to rest of sentence.)

Conjunctive Adverbs   Some connectors are adverbs that function as conjunctions. They serve as linking devices between elements of equal rank and as modifiers, showing such things as similarity, contrast, result or effect, addition, emphasis, time, and example.

The job will require you to travel a great deal; *however,* the salary is excellent.

Sean cares nothing for clothes; *in fact,* all of his socks have holes in their toes.

The following list groups the most common conjunctive adverbs according to function:

Similarity: likewise, similarly
Contrast: however, nevertheless, on the contrary, on the other hand, otherwise
Result or effect: accordingly, as a result, consequently, hence, therefore, thus
Addition: also, furthermore, in addition, in the first place, moreover
Emphasis or clarity: in fact, in other words, indeed, that is
Time: afterward, later, meanwhile, subsequently
Example: for example, for instance, to illustrate

Conjunctive adverbs should not be confused with coordinating conjunctions. Unlike other conjunctions and other adverbs, conjunctive adverbs can move, often to create a specific emphasis.

The job will require you to travel a great deal; the salary, *however,* is excellent.

The job will require you to travel a great deal; *however,* the salary is excellent.

Sean cares nothing for clothes; all of his socks, *in fact,* have holes in their toes.

Sean cares nothing for clothes; *in fact,* all of his socks have holes in their toes.

conj

Because conjunctive adverbs can move, the second independent clause must be treated as a complete sentence and either be joined to the previous independent clause with a semicolon or be separated by a period.

Usage Considerations   You can add variety to your writing by varying the conjunctions you use. For example, if you consistently rely on the conjunction *because,* try substituting *as* or *since.* When you have choppy sentences, try combining them by using a conjunction.

You can buy smoked salmon at Sally's Seafoods. You can buy it at Daane's Thriftland as well.

You can buy smoked salmon *either* at Sally's Seafoods *or* at Daane's Thriftland.

The revision is much smoother than the original sentence pair.

Interjections

An interjection is an exclamatory word used to gain attention or to express strong feeling. It has no grammatical connection to the rest of the sentence. An interjection is followed by an exclamation point or a comma.

Hey! Watch how you're driving! (strong interjection)

Oh, is the party over already? (mild interjection)

EXERCISE *Identify the coordinating conjunctions (CC), subordinating conjunctions (SC), conjunctive adverbs (CA), and interjections (I) in the following sentences:*

1. The car was not only dented but also dirty.
2. While Roger was at the movies, his brother bought a model airplane.
3. Rats! My computer ate my essay.
4. Although they felt under the weather, Marie and Sally attended the dance.
5. The candidate's views matched those of his audience; consequently, he received warm applause.
6. Sandra is no academic slouch; indeed, she was valedictorian of her high school class.

PHRASES AND CLAUSES

Phrases

A phrase is a group of words that lacks a subject and a predicate and serves as a single part of speech. This section discusses four basic kinds of phrases: *prepositional phrases, participial phrases, gerund phrases,* and *infinitive phrases.* The last three are based on participles, gerunds, and infinitives, verb forms known as verbals. A fifth type of phrase, the verb phrase, consists of sets of two or more verbs (*has fixed, had been sick, will have been selected,* and the like).

Prepositional Phrases   A prepositional phrase consists of a preposition, one or more objects, and any associated words. These phrases serve as adjectives or adverbs.

> The picture *over the mantel* was my mother's. (prepositional phrase as adjective)

> He bought ice skates *for himself.* (prepositional phrase as adverb modifying verb)

> The toddler was afraid *of the dog.* (prepositional phrase as adverb modifying adjective)

> Our visitors arrived late *in the day.* (prepositional phrase as adverb modifying another adverb)

Frequently, prepositional phrases occur in series. Sometimes they form chains in which each phrase modifies the object of the preceding phrase. At other times some or all of the phrases may modify the verb or verb phrase.

> John works *in a clothing store / on Main Street / during the summer.*

Here the first and third phrases serve as adverbs modifying the verb *works* and answering the questions "Where?" and "When?" while the second phrase serves as an adjective modifying *store* and answering the question "Where?"

Participial Phrases   A participial phrase consists of a participle plus associated words. Participles are verb forms that function as adjectives or adverbs when used in participial phrases. A present participle ends in *-ing* and indicates an action currently being carried out. A past participle ends in *-ed, -en, -e, -n, -d,* or *-t* and indicates some past action.

> The chef *preparing dinner* trained in France. (present participial phrase as adjective)

> The background, *sketched in lightly,* accented the features of the woman in the painting. (past participial phrase as adjective)

> She left *whistling a jolly melody.* (present participial phrase as adverb)

A perfect participial phrase consists of *having* or *having been* plus a past participle and any associated words. Like a past participial phrase, it indicates a past action.

> *Having alerted the townspeople about the tornado,* the sound truck returned to the city garage. (perfect participial phrase)

> *Having been alerted to the tornado,* the townspeople sought shelter in their basements. (perfect participial phrase)

phr

Some participial phrases that modify persons or things distinguish them from others in the same class. These phrases are written without commas. Other phrases provide more information about the persons or things they modify and are set off with commas.

> The man *fixing my car* is a master mechanic. (Phrase distinguishes man fixing car from other men.)

> Mr. Welsh, *fatigued by the tennis game,* rested in the shade. (Phrase provides more information about Mr. Welsh.)

Gerund Phrases   A gerund phrase consists of a gerund and the words associated with it. Like present participles, gerunds are verb forms that end in *-ing*. However, unlike participles, they function as nouns rather than as adjectives or adverbs.

> Kathryn's hobby is *collecting stamps.* (gerund phrase as subject complement)

> Kathryn's hobby, *collecting stamps,* has made her many friends. (gerund phrase as appositive)

> He devoted every spare moment to *overhauling the car.* (gerund phrase as object of preposition)

Infinitive Phrases   An infinitive phrase consists of the present principal part of a verb preceded by *to (to fix, to eat),* together with any accompanying words. These phrases serve as adjectives, adverbs, and nouns.

> This looks like a good place *to plant the shrub.* (infinitive phrase as adjective)

> Lenore worked *to earn money for tuition.* (infinitive phrase as adverb)

> My goal is *to have my own business some day.* (infinitive phrase as noun)

Gerunds can often be substituted for infinitives and vice versa.

> *To repair this fender* will cost two hundred dollars. (infinitive phrase as subject)

> *Repairing this fender* will cost two hundred dollars. (gerund phrase as subject)

At times the *to* in an infinitive may be omitted following verbs such as *make, dare, let,* and *help.*

Kristin didn't dare *(to) move* a muscle.

The psychiatrist helped me *(to) overcome* my fear of flying.

Verbals Not in Phrases　Participles, gerunds, and infinitives can function as nouns, adjectives, or adverbs, even when they are not parts of phrases.

That *sunbathing* woman is a well-known model. (participle as adjective)

Dancing is fine exercise. (gerund)

The children want *to play*. (infinitive as noun)

If you're looking for a job, Sally is the person *to see*. (infinitive as adjective)

I'm prepared *to resign*. (infinitive as adverb)

Usage Considerations　Phrases can often help clarify or develop the information in a sentence.

Original	My brother is fishing.
Revision	My brother is fishing *for trout just below Barnes Dam on Sidewinder Creek*. (prepositional phrases added)
Original	The boat barely made shore.
Revision	The boat, *listing heavily and leaking badly*, barely made shore. (participial phrases added)

Testing a Phrase's Function　To determine whether a phrase is functioning as noun, adjective, or adverb, try this substitution test. Try replacing the phrase in question with a common noun (*something, someone,* or *it*), with an adjective or adjective phrase, or with an adverb. Whichever choice works will demonstrate the function of the phrase.

Walking at a brisk pace is excellent exercise. (participial phrase)

Something is excellent exercise. (therefore, a **noun** phrase)

I am prepared *to finish the job*. (infinitive phrase)

I am prepared *completely*. (therefore, an **adverb** phrase)

He was a man *of unusual craftiness*. (prepositional phrase)

He was a *crafty* man. (therefore, an **adjective** phrase)

EXERCISE *Identify the italicized phrases as prepositional, participial, gerund, or infinitive and tell whether each is used as a noun, an adjective, or an adverb.*

1. *Walking the dog in the rain* made me grouchy for the rest of the day.
2. *To ride the Orient Express* was Marian's fondest ambition.

3. *Opening the door a tiny crack,* Michelle stared with horror at the scene before her.

4. Sue Ellen works *in a grocery store* during the summer.

5. Tom couldn't decide which refrigerator *to buy for his mother.*

6. Old-fashioned in every way, Chester shaves *with a straight razor.*

cl

Clauses

A clause is a word group that includes a subject and a predicate. An *independent clause,* sometimes called a main clause, expresses a complete thought and can function as a simple sentence. A *dependent clause,* or subordinate clause, cannot stand by itself. Subordinate clauses may serve as nouns, adjectives, or adverbs.

Noun Clauses   A noun clause can serve in any of the ways that ordinary nouns can.

What the neighbour told John proved to be incorrect. (noun clause as subject)

The woman asked *when the bus left for Sherbrooke.* (noun clause as direct object)

I'll give a reward to *whoever returns my billfold.* (noun clause as object of preposition *to*)

Noun clauses normally begin with one of the following words:

Relative Pronouns		**Interrogative Pronoun**
who	whoever	when
whom	whomever	why
whose	that	where
what	whatever	how
which	whichever	whether

The relative pronoun *that* is sometimes omitted from the beginning of a clause that acts as a direct object.

Dr. Kant thinks *(that) he knows everything.*

If a clause is serving as a noun, you can replace it with the word *something* or *someone,* and the sentence will still make sense.

Dr. Kant thinks *something.*

If the clause is serving as an adjective or an adverb, making the substitution turns the sentence into nonsense.

The person *who wins the lottery* will receive two million dollars.

The person *someone* will receive two million dollars.

cl

Adjective Clauses   Like ordinary adjectives, adjective clauses modify nouns and noun substitutes.

> Give me one reason *which could sway my opinion.* (Adjective clause modifies noun.)

> I'll hire anyone *that Dr. Stone recommends.* (Adjective clause modifies pronoun.)

> Generally, adjective clauses begin with one of the following words:

Relative Pronouns
who
whom
whose
what
which
that

Sometimes the word that introduces the clause can be omitted.

> The chair *(that) we ordered last month* has just arrived. (pronoun *that* omitted but understood)

> The man *(whom) we were talking to* is a movie producer. (pronoun *whom* omitted but understood)

An adjective clause may be restrictive and distinguish whatever it modifies from others in the same class, or it may be nonrestrictive and provide more information about whatever it modifies.

> Flora wiped up the cereal *that the baby had spilled.* (restrictive clause)

> Harriet Thomas, *who was born in Saskatchewan,* now lives in Alberta. (nonrestrictive clause)

As these examples show, restrictive clauses are not set off with commas, but nonrestrictive clauses are.

Adverb Clauses   These clauses modify verbs, adjectives, adverbs, and sentences, answering the same questions that ordinary adverbs do.

> You may go *whenever you wish.* (Adverb clause modifies verb.)

> Sandra looked paler *than I had ever seen her look before.* (Adverb clause modifies adjective.)

> Darryl shouted loudly *so that the rescue party could hear him.* (Adverb clause modifies adverb.)

> *Unless everyone cooperates,* this plan will never succeed. (Adverb clause modifies whole sentence.)

The word or word group that introduces an adverb clause is always a subordinating conjunction. Here are the most common of these conjunctions, grouped according to the questions they answer.

> *When?* after, as, as soon as, before, since, until, when, whenever, while

> *Where?* where, wherever

How? as if, as though

Why? as, because, now that, since, so that

Under what conditions? although, if, once, provided that, though, unless

To what extent? than

Usage Considerations   Like phrases, clauses can help develop sentences as well as smooth out choppiness.

Original	The old grandfather clock ticked loudly through the night.
Revision	The old grandfather clock *that my great-aunt gave me before she died* ticked loudly through the night. (Clause adds information.)
Original	The chemistry professor insisted on lab safety. He had been hurt in a lab explosion the previous year.
Revision	The chemistry professor, *who had been hurt in a lab explosion the previous year,* insisted on lab safety. (Clause adds smoothness.)

To avoid clumsiness, avoid overloaded sentences like the one below:

The old grandfather clock that my great-aunt gave me before she died *and that I took with me to England when my company transferred me there for two years* ticked loudly through the night.

EXERCISE *Identify the italicized clauses as noun, adjective, or adverb.*

1. Why do Bill's parents always give him *whatever he wants?*
2. Steve skated *as if an NHL scout were watching him.*
3. Gary is the only golfer *who putted well today.*
4. The dog barked loudly *because he was hungry.*
5. *Why anyone would want to skydive* is beyond me.
6. The secretary *Julie hired last month* has already received a raise.

Coordination and Subordination

Coordination and subordination are ways to rank ideas in sentences. Coordination makes ideas equal; subordination makes them unequal. To understand coordination and subordination, you need to know about four kinds of sentences: simple, compound, complex, and compound–complex.

Simple Sentences   A simple sentence has one subject and one predicate. Some simple sentences consist merely of a single noun and a single verb.

Millicent shouted.

Others can include elements such as compound subjects, compound verbs, direct objects, indirect objects, and subject complements.

crd

Jim and Sue have bought a car. *(compound subject, direct object)*

Lucretia Borgia smiled and mixed her guests a cocktail. *(compound verb, indirect object, direct object)*

Autumn is a sad season. *(subject complement)*

Most simple sentences are rather short and easy to understand. This trimness can add punch to your writing, but it can also make your writing sound childish and may waste words.

The audience was young and friendly. It was responsive. It cheered for each speaker.

Combined into a single simple sentence, the information is easier to follow and more interesting to read:

The young, friendly, responsive audience cheered for each speaker.

Compound Sentences   A compound sentence contains two or more independent clauses, each holding the same (coordinate) rank. As a result, the idea in the first clause receives the same emphasis as the idea in the second. In some cases, a comma and a coordinating conjunction *(and, but, or, nor, for, yet, so)* link successive clauses.

She named the baby William, and her mother approved.

The audience was young, friendly, and responsive, *so* it cheered for each speaker.

In others, a semicolon and a conjunctive adverb *(for example, however, in fact, likewise, meanwhile, instead,* and the like) furnish the connection.

Tod wants to see the play; *in fact,* he's talked about it for weeks.

Today, many young women do not rush into marriage and motherhood; *instead,* they spend several years establishing careers.

Finally, a writer may omit any connecting word and separate the clauses with a semicolon.

The sky grew pitch black; the wind died; an ominous quiet hung over the whole city.

Be sure to read this Robertson Davies novel; it shows the ramifications of a single small event.

As the preceding sentences show, compound sentences allow writers to express simple relationships among simple ideas. However, such sentences have one important limitation: They make it impossible to highlight one particular idea. To do this, we need to use complex sentences.

Complex Sentences   A complex sentence has one independent clause and one or more dependent clauses. Relegating an idea to a dependent clause shows that the writer wishes it to receive less emphasis than the idea in the main clause.

Because the young, friendly audience was responsive, it cheered for each speaker.

After the ball was over, Arthur collapsed on the sofa.

Once they had reached the lakeshore, the campers found a level spot *where they could pitch their tent.*

crd

Unlike compound sentences, complex ones allow writers to vary the emphasis of ideas.

While I watered the grass, I discussed stock options with Liz.

I watered the grass while I discussed stock options with Liz.

The first sentence emphasizes the talk with Liz, the second watering the lawn. By shifting emphasis a writer can change the meaning of a sentence.

While his bicycle was damaged, Pat walked to work.

While Pat walked to work, his bicycle was damaged.

Furthermore, complex sentences signal *how* ideas relate. Note the various relationships in the following sentences:

Because she was swimming well, Millicent did 200 laps today. *(reason)*

The CN Tower is taller *than the Empire State Building. (extent)*

Ms. Yoshira is the executive *for whom I am working. (relationship between persons)*

Compound–Complex Sentences   This type of sentence features two or more independent clauses and one or more dependent clauses. Here are two examples with the dependent clauses italicized:

Ms. Harris works as an investment manager, and Mr. Williams, *who lives next door to her,* owns a jewellery store.

If you are to communicate properly, your thoughts must be clear and correct; thoughts are wasted *when language is muddled.*

With compound–complex sentences writers can present more intricate relationships than with other sentences. In the following example, three sentences—one compound and two simple—have been rewritten as a compound–complex sentence. Notice how subordination improves the compactness and smoothness of the final version.

Mary hated to be seen in ugly clothing, but she wore an ugly dress with red polka dots. She had received the dress as a Christmas present. Her Aunt Ida had given it to her.

Mary hated to be seen in ugly clothing; nevertheless, she wore an ugly red-polka-dot dress that her Aunt Ida had given her for Christmas.

The second version condenses thirty-five words to twenty-six.

crd

EXERCISE

1. **Label the independent and dependent clauses in the sentences below. Then identify each sentence as simple, compound, complex, or compound–complex.**

    a. A career in broadcasting requires good verbal skills, an extensive wardrobe, and a pleasant smile.

    b. Because its bag was too full, the vacuum cleaner backfired, leaving the room dirtier than it had been before.

    c. When Tom arrived home, his roommate asked him where he had really gone; six hours seemed too long a time to spend in the library.

    d. My apple tree blossomed last week; however, the peach trees have withered, probably because of the freeze last month.

    e. It's risky to confide in a co-worker because one can never be sure that the confidence will be kept.

2. **Using coordination and subordination, rewrite the following passages to reduce words and/or improve smoothness.**

    a. He played the piano. He played the organ. He played the French horn. He did not play the viola.

    b. Life on Venus may be possible. It will not be the kind of life we know on Earth. Life on Mars may be possible. It will not be the kind of life we know on Earth.

    c. Albert lay in bed. He stared at the ceiling. Albert thought about the previous afternoon. He had asked Kathy to go to dinner with him. She is a pretty, blonde-haired woman. She sits at the desk next to his. They work at Hemphill's. She had refused.

    d. I went to the store to buy a box of detergent. I saw Bill there, and we talked about last night's game.

    e. Tim went to the newsstand. He bought a magazine there. While he was on the way home, he lost it. He had nothing to read.

Accepted usage improves the smoothness of your prose, makes your writing easier to understand, and demonstrates that you are a careful communicator. These assets, in turn, increase the likelihood that the reader will accept your ideas.

When you've finished revising the first draft of a piece of writing, edit it with a critic's eye to ensure that you eliminate all errors. Circle sentences or parts of them that are faulty or suspect. Then check your circled items against this section of the Handbook, which deals with the most common errors in writing.

frag

REVISING SENTENCE FRAGMENTS

A sentence fragment is a group of words that fails to qualify as a sentence but is capitalized and punctuated as if it were a sentence. To be a sentence, a word group must (1) have a subject and a verb and (2) make sense by itself. The first of the following examples has a subject and a verb; the second does not. Neither makes sense by itself.

> If you want to remain.

> His answer to the question.

Methods of Revision   Eliminating a sentence fragment is not hard. Careful reading often shows that the fragment goes with the sentence that comes just before or just after it. And sometimes two successive fragments can be joined. Note how we've corrected the fragments (italicized) in the following pairs:

Faulty	*Having been warned about the storm.* We decided to stay home.
Revision	Having been warned about the storm, we decided to stay home.
Faulty	*After eating.* The dog took a nap.
Revision	After eating, the dog took a nap.
Faulty	Sally went to work. *Although she felt sick.*
Revision	Sally went to work although she felt sick.
Faulty	Dave bought a new suit. *Over at Bentley's.*
Revision	Dave bought a new suit over at Bentley's.
Faulty	*That bronze clock on the mantel. Once belonged to my grandmother.*
Revision	That bronze clock on the mantel once belonged to my grandmother.

Joining a fragment to a sentence or to another fragment works only if the problem is simply one of mispunctuation. If the fragment stems from an improperly developed thought, revise the thought into correct sentence form.

Punctuating Your Corrections When you join a fragment to the following sentence, you need not place a comma between the two unless the fragment has six or more words or if omitting a comma might cause a misreading. When joining a fragment to the preceding sentence, omit a comma unless there is a distinct pause between the two items. The preceding examples illustrate these points.

Intentional Fragments Fragments are commonly used in conversation and the writing that reproduces it. Professional writers also use fragments to gain special emphasis or create special effects. (See pages 103–105.)

frag

CONNECTED DISCOURSE EXERCISE *Identify and correct the sentence fragments in the following letter:*

Dear Phone Company:

Recently I received a phone bill for over $500. While I do use the phone fairly extensively. Most of the calls I make are local ones. In this case, many of the calls on my bill were to other countries. Including a phone call to New Delhi, India. I can hardly be held responsible for these calls. Especially since I don't know anyone who lives overseas. Since the only long-distance call I made was to Sudbury, Ontario. I have deducted the charges for all the other long-distance calls from my bill and am sending you the balance. In order to prevent this type of error from happening again. Would you please have a representative determine why these charges appeared on my bill?

Sincerely,

Desperate

EXERCISE *Twelve main clauses paired with fragments are shown below. In each case identify the sentence (S) and the fragment (F) and then eliminate the fragment.*

1. The clerk handed the package to the customer. And walked swiftly away from the counter.
2. Exhausted by his efforts to push the car out of the snowbank. Paul slumped wearily into the easy chair.
3. The dinner honoured three retirees. One of them my father.
4. After tidying up the kitchen. My parents left for the movies.
5. If Dr. Frankenstein's experiment is a success. He'll throw a monster party to celebrate.
6. Even though Ned studied very hard. He had trouble with the test.
7. The dog barked at the stranger. And chased him from the property.
8. By leaving the ballpark before the last out was made. We avoided the after-game crowd.

REVISING RUN-ON SENTENCES AND COMMA SPLICES

A fused, or run-on, sentence occurs when one sentence runs into another without anything to mark their junction. A comma splice occurs when only a comma marks the junction. A comma is not strong enough punctuation to join independent clauses, or sentences. Here are several examples:

Fused sentence	Laura failed to set her alarm she was late for work.
Comma splice	Violets are blooming now, my lawn is covered with them.
Fused sentence	Rick refused to attend the movie he said he hated horror shows.
Comma splice	Perry watched the road carefully, he still missed his turn.
Fused Sentence	Janet worked on her term paper her friend studied for a calculus test.
Comma splice	Janet worked on her term paper, her friend studied for a calculus test.

fs cs

Testing for Errors   To check out a possible comma splice or fused sentence, read what precedes and follows the comma or suspected junction and see whether the two parts can stand alone as sentences. If *both parts* can stand alone, there is an error. Otherwise, there is not.

Darryl is a real troublemaker, someday he'll find himself in serious difficulty.

Examination of the parts preceding and following the comma shows that each is a complete sentence:

Darryl is a real troublemaker.

Someday he'll find himself in serious difficulty.

The writer has therefore committed a comma splice that needs correction.

Methods of Revision   You can correct fused sentences and comma splices in several ways.

1. Create two separate sentences.

Revision	Violets are blooming now. My lawn is covered with them.
Revision	Rick refused to attend the movie. He said he hated horror shows.

2. Join the sentences with a semicolon.

Revision	Violets are blooming now; my yard is covered with them.
Revision	Rick refused to attend the movie; he said he hated horror shows.

3. Join the sentences with a comma and a coordinating conjunction *(and, but, or, nor, for, yet, so)*.

Revision   Laura failed to set her alarm, *so* she was late for work.

Revision   Perry watched the road carefully, *but* he still missed his turn.

4. Join the sentences with a semicolon and a conjunctive adverb (see pages 576–577).

Revision   Laura failed to set her alarm; *consequently*, she was late for work.

Revision   Violets are blooming now; *in fact*, my yard is covered with them.

5. Introduce one of the sentences with a subordinating conjunction (see page 575).

Revision   *Because* Laura failed to set her alarm, she was late for work.

Revision   Janet worked on her term paper *while* her friend studied for a calculus test.

As our examples show, you can often correct an error in several ways.

fs cs

CONNECTED DISCOURSE EXERCISE *Identify and correct the comma splices and run-on sentences in the following letter:*

Dear Desperate:

We are sorry to hear that you are having difficulty paying your bill, it is, however, your responsibility. Unfortunately we have no way to prevent you from making overseas calls, you have to curb your own tendency to reach out and touch your friends. Following your instructions, we are sending a technician to remove your phone. Please be home this Friday morning he will arrive then. Even though we will remove your phone, you are still responsible for the unpaid portion of your bill, it is your financial obligation. We would dislike referring this matter to a collection agency, it could ruin your credit rating.

Sincerely,

Your friendly phone representative

EXERCISE *Indicate whether each item is correct (C), is a fused sentence (FS), or contains a comma splice (CS) and then correct the faulty items.*

1. Lee is a difficult person he becomes angry whenever he doesn't get his own way.
2. The student appeared puzzled by the instructor's answer to his question, but he said nothing more.
3. The doctor warned Allan about his high cholesterol level, he went on a high-fibre diet.
4. Sally researched her topic thoroughly and wrote her report carefully as a result she received an *A*.

5. It's nice to see you again; we should get together more often.

6. The horse stumbled and nearly fell in the backstretch, nevertheless it managed to finish second.

7. Janice thought the exercises would be easy, after finishing them she found that her whole body ached.

8. I've just started to take up chess, you can hardly expect me to play well.

CREATING SUBJECT–VERB AGREEMENT

sv agr

A verb should agree in number with its subject. Singular subjects should have singular verbs, and plural subjects should have plural verbs.

Correct	My *boss* is a grouch. (singular subject and verb)
Correct	The *apartments have* two bedrooms. (plural subject and verb)

Ordinarily, matching subjects and verbs causes no problems. However, the following special situations can create difficulties.

Subject and Verb Separated by a Word Group   Sometimes a word group that includes one or more nouns comes between the subject and the verb. When this happens, match the verb with its subject, not a noun in the word group.

Correct	Our *basket* of sandwiches *is* missing.
Correct	Several *books* required for my paper *are* not in the library.
Correct	*Mr. Schmidt*, along with his daughters, *runs* a furniture store.
Correct	The old *bus*, crammed with passengers, *was* unable to reach the top of the hill.

Two Singular Subjects   Most singular subjects joined by *and* take a plural verb.

Correct	The *couch* and *chair were* upholstered in blue velvet.

Sentences like the one above almost never cause problems. However, in sentences with subjects like *restoring cars* and *racing motorcycles,* singular verbs are often mistakenly used.

Faulty	*Restoring cars* and *racing motorcycles consumes* most of Frank's time.
Revision	*Restoring cars* and *racing motorcycles consume* most of Frank's time.

When *each* or *every* precedes the subjects, use a *singular* verb in place of a plural.

Correct	Every *book* and *magazine was* badly water-stained.

Singular subjects joined by *or, either/or,* or *neither/nor* also take singular verbs.

Correct	A *pear* or an *apple is* a good afternoon snack.
Correct	Neither *rain* nor *snow slows* our letter carrier.

Finally, use a singular verb when two singular subjects joined by *and* name the same person, place, or thing.

> *Correct*   My cousin and business partner is retiring next month.
> (Cousin and partner refer to the same person.)

One Singular and One Plural Subject   When one singular subject and one plural subject are joined by *or, either/or,* or *neither/nor,* match the verb with the closer of the two.

> *Correct*   Neither *John* nor his *parents were* at home.

> *Correct*   Neither his *parents* nor *John was* at home.

sv agr

As these examples show, the sentences are usually smoother when the plural subject follows the singular.

Collective Nouns as Subjects   Collective nouns (*assembly, class, committee, family, herd, majority, tribe,* and the like) are singular in form but stand for groups or collections of people or things. Ordinarily, collective nouns are considered singular and therefore take singular verbs.

> *Correct*   The *class is* writing a test.

> *Correct*   The *herd was* clustered around the water hole.

Sometimes, though, a collective noun refers to the separate individuals making up the grouping, and then it requires a plural verb.

> *Correct*   The *jury are* in dispute about the verdict.

Sentences in Which the Verb Comes Ahead of the Subject   The verb comes before the subject in sentences that begin with words such as *here, there, how, what,* and *where.* In such sentences, the verb must agree with the subject that follows it.

> *Correct*   Here *is* my *house.*

> *Correct*   Where *are* my *shoes?*

> *Correct*   There *is* just one *way* to solve this problem.

> *Correct*   There *go* my *chances* for a promotion.

CONNECTED DISCOURSE EXERCISE *Identify and correct the subject–verb agreement errors in the following letter:*

Regional Accounts Manager:

One of your area phone representatives have seriously misread a letter I submitted with my bill. I refused to pay for long-distance overseas calls since neither I nor my roommate know anyone who lives overseas. Instead of deducting the calls from my bill, she sent someone to remove my phone. Now my phone, along with many of my valuable possessions, have been removed. Unfortunately the technician, whom I allowed into my apartment only after carefully checking his credentials, were a thief. He locked me in a closet and cleared out the apartment. I have called the police, but I also expect the phone company to reimburse me for my losses. There is only two choices. Either the stolen items or a cheque covering the loss need to be sent to me immediately. Otherwise I am afraid I will be forced to sue. A jury are sure to rule in my favour. In addition, I expect to find that those overseas calls has been deducted from my bill.

Sincerely,

Desperately Desperate

pa agr

EXERCISE *Choose the correct verb form from the pair in parentheses.*

1. The pictures in the drawing room of the mansion (has, have) been insured for twelve million dollars.
2. Every dish and piece of stainless that I own (is, are) dirty.
3. Look! There (is, are) Kathy and her friend Marge.
4. Reading novels and watching TV (takes, take) up most of Stanley's time.
5. Each of these proposals (represents, represent) a great amount of work.
6. Two hamburgers or a hot beef sandwich (makes, make) an ample lunch.
7. (Has, Have) either of the orchids blossomed yet?
8. The automobile with the broken headlights and dented sides (was, were) stopped by the police.

ACHIEVING PRONOUN–ANTECEDENT AGREEMENT

The antecedent of a pronoun is the noun or pronoun to which it refers. Just as verbs should agree with their subjects, pronouns should agree with their antecedents: Singular antecedents require singular pronouns, and plural antecedents require plural pronouns. Ordinarily, you will have no trouble matching antecedents and pronouns. The situations below, however, can cause problems.

Indefinite Pronouns as Antecedents   Indefinite pronouns include words such as *each, either, neither, any, everybody, somebody,* and *nobody*. Whenever an indefinite pronoun is used as an antecedent, the pronoun that refers to it should be singular.

> *Faulty*   *Neither* of the actors had learned *their* lines.

> *Revision*   *Neither* of the actors had learned *his* lines.

As the revised example shows, this rule applies even when the pronoun is followed by a plural noun.

When the gender of the antecedent is unknown, you may follow it with *his or her;* if this results in awkwardness, rewrite the sentence in the plural.

> *Correct*   *Anyone* who has studied *his or her* assignments properly should do well on the test.

> *Correct*   *Those* who have studied *their* assignments properly should do well on the test.

Occasionally, a ridiculous result occurs when a singular pronoun refers to an indefinite pronoun that is obviously plural in meaning. When this happens, rewrite the sentence to eliminate the problem.

> *Faulty*   *Everybody* complained that the graduation ceremony had lasted too long, but I didn't believe *him.*

> *Revision*   *Everybody* complained that the graduation ceremony had lasted too long, but I didn't agree.

Two Singular Antecedents   Two or more antecedents joined by *and* ordinarily call for a plural pronoun.

> *Correct*   Her briefcase and umbrella were missing from *their* usual place on the hall table.

When *each* or *every* precedes the antecedent, use a singular pronoun.

> *Correct*   Every college and university must do *its* best to provide adequate student counselling.

Singular antecedents joined by *or, either/or,* or *neither/nor* call for singular pronouns.

> *Correct*   Neither Carol nor Irene had paid *her* rent for the month.

Applying this rule can sometimes yield an awkward or foolish sentence. When this happens, rewrite the sentence to avoid the problem.

> *Faulty*   Neither James nor Sally has finished *his or her* term project.

> *Revision*   James and Sally have not finished *their* term projects.

Singular antecedents joined by *and* that refer to the same person, place, or thing use a singular pronoun.

> *Correct*   My *cousin* and business *partner* is retiring to *his* condo in Florida next month.

Singular and Plural Antecedents   If one singular and one plural antecedent are joined by *or, either/or,* or *neither/nor,* the pronoun agrees with the closer one.

> *Correct*   Either Terrence James or the Parkinsons will let us use *their* lawn mower.

> *Correct*   Either the Parkinsons or Terrence James will let us use *his* lawn mower.

Sentences of this sort are generally smoother when the plural subject follows the singular.

pa agr

Collective Nouns as Antecedents   When a collective noun is considered a single unit, the pronoun that refers to it should be singular.

> *Correct*   The *troop* of scouts made *its* way slowly through the woods.

When the collective noun refers to the separate individuals in the group, use a plural pronoun.

> *Correct*   The *staff* lost *their* jobs when the factory closed.

CONNECTED DISCOURSE EXERCISE *Identify and correct the pronoun–antecedent agreement errors in the following letter:*

pa agr

Dear Desperately Desperate:

We were sorry to hear about the theft from your apartment. Apparently a gang of con artists recently had their base of operations in your city. It posed as repair technicians and presented false credentials to anyone expecting their phone to be repaired. Someone also must have intercepted your mail and written their own response since we have no record of any previous letter from you. Clearly neither the representative you mentioned nor the phony phone technician could have held their position with our company. Every one of our technicians must provide us with their fingerprints and take periodic lie detector tests. Further, none of our representatives will answer correspondence since it is not a part of their job description. For these reasons, we do not believe we are responsible for your losses. However, a review of our records shows that you owe $500; we have included a copy of the bill in case you have misplaced the original.

> Sincerely,
> Accounts Manager

EXERCISE *Choose the right pronoun from the pair in parentheses.*

1. If everybody does *(his or her, their)* part, the pageant should go smoothly.
2. Neither Greg nor the Snows had remembered to make *(his, their)* reservations at the ski lodge.
3. The graduating class filed by the principal and received *(its, their)* diplomas.
4. Each of the performers nervously waited *(his or her, their)* turn to audition.
5. Every boot and shoe I own needs to have *(its, their)* laces replaced.
6. Either Laurie or Alicia will show *(her, their)* slides at the party.
7. Dave and Bill loudly voiced *(his, their)* complaints about the restaurant's service.
8. Pleased with the performance, the audience showed *(its, their)* pleasure by applauding loudly.

USING EFFECTIVE PRONOUN REFERENCE

Any pronoun except an indefinite pronoun should refer to just one noun or noun substitute—its antecedent. Reference problems result when the pronoun has two or more antecedents, a hidden antecedent, or no antecedent. These errors can cause mixups in meaning as well as ridiculous sentences.

More Than One Antecedent   The following sentences lack clarity because their pronouns have two possible antecedents rather than just one:

Faulty   Take the screens off the windows and wash *them*.

Faulty   Harry told Will that *he* was putting on weight.

The reader can't tell whether the screens or the windows should be washed or who is putting on weight.

Sometimes we see a sentence like this one:

Faulty   If the boys don't eat all the Popsicles, put *them* in the freezer.

In this case, we know it's the Popsicles that should be stored, but the use of *them* creates an amusing sentence.

Correct these faults by replacing the pronoun with a noun or by rephrasing the sentence.

Revision   Wash the windows after you have taken off the screens.

Revision   Take off the screens so that you can wash the windows.

Revision   Harry told Will, "I am (you are) putting on weight."

Revision   Put any uneaten Popsicles in the freezer.

Hidden Antecedent   An antecedent is hidden if it takes the form of an adjective rather than a noun.

Faulty   The movie theatre is closed today, so we can't see *one*.

Faulty   As I passed the tiger's cage, *it* lunged at me.

To correct this fault, replace the pronoun with the noun used as an adjective or switch the positions of the pronoun and the noun and make any needed changes in their forms.

Revision   The theatre is closed today, so we can't see a movie.

Revision   As I passed its cage, the tiger lunged at me.

No Antecedent   A no-antecedent sentence lacks any noun to which the pronoun can refer. Sentences of this sort occur frequently in everyday conversation but should be avoided in formal writing. The examples below illustrate this error:

Faulty   The lecture was boring, but *they* took notes anyway.

Faulty   On the news program, *it* told about another flood in Quebec.

To set matters right, substitute a suitable noun for the pronoun or reword the sentence.

> *Revision*   The lecture was boring, but the students took notes anyway.

> *Revision*   The news program told about another flood in Quebec.

Sometimes *this, that, it,* or *which* will refer to a whole idea rather than a single noun. This usage is acceptable provided the writer's meaning is obvious, as in this example:

> *Correct*   The instructor spoke very softly, *which* meant we had difficulty hearing him.

However, problems occur when the reader can't figure out which of two or more ideas the pronoun refers to.

> *Faulty*   Ginny called Sally two hours after the agreed-upon time and postponed their shopping trip one day. *This* irritated Sally very much.

What caused Sally to be irritated—the late call, the postponement of the trip, or both? Again, rewording or adding a clarifying word will correct the problem.

> *Revision*   Ginny called Sally two hours after the agreed-upon time and postponed their shopping trip one day. This *tardiness* irritated Sally very much.

> *Revision*   Ginny called Sally two hours after the agreed-upon time and postponed their shopping trip one day. Ginny's *change of plans* irritated Sally very much.

The first of these examples illustrates the addition of a clarifying word; the second illustrates rewriting.

pr ref

CONNECTED DISCOURSE EXERCISE *Identify and correct any faulty pronoun references in the following memorandum:*

TO: Director of Food Services, Groan University

FROM: Vice-President of Services

DATE: February 19, 2008

SUBJECT: Student Complaints about Cafeteria

Complaints about food quality and cafeteria hours are common but easily resolved. They can be extended by simply installing vending machines. It might not make for a nutritious meal, but it certainly will undercut some of the dissatisfaction. Of course, no matter how good the food, they will complain. Still, you can partially defuse those complaints by having students list their major concerns and then meeting them. Of course, you can always increase student satisfaction by purchasing a soft ice cream machine and offering it for dessert.

EXERCISE *Indicate whether each sentence is correct (C) or contains a faulty pronoun reference (F) and then correct any faulty sentences.*

1. Ann told Jennifer that the boss wanted to see her.
2. Because the ring hurt her finger, Ruth took it off.
3. At the farmer's market they sell many kinds of produce.
4. I like the food in Thai restaurants because it is very spicy.
5. They tell me that the company's profits have risen 5 percent this quarter.
6. Knowing that my friends like hot dogs, I grilled them at the picnic.
7. When Jeffrey rose to make his speech, they all started laughing.
8. In the paper, it told about the province's budget surplus.

MANAGING SHIFTS IN PERSON

Pronouns can be in the first person, second person, or third person. *First-person* pronouns identify people who are talking or writing about themselves, *second-person* pronouns identify people being addressed directly, and *third-person* pronouns identify persons or things that are being written or spoken about. The following table sorts pronouns according to person:

First Person	Second Person	Third Person
I	you	he
me	your	she
my	yours	it
mine	yourself	him
we	yourselves	his
us		her
our		hers
ours		its
ourselves		one
		they
		them
		their
		theirs
		indefinite pronouns

All nouns are in the third person. As you revise, be alert for unwarranted shifts from one person to another.

Faulty I liked *my* British vacation better than *my* vacation in France and Italy because *you* didn't have language problems.

Revision I liked *my* British vacation better than *my* vacation in France and Italy because *I* didn't have language problems.

Faulty Holidays are important to *everyone*. They boost *your* spirits and provide a break from *our* daily routine.

Revision	Holidays are important to *everyone*. They boost *one's* spirits and provide a break from *one's* daily routine.
Faulty	The taller the *golfer,* the more club speed *you* will have with a normally paced swing.
Revision	The taller the *golfer,* the more club speed *he* or *she* will have with a normally paced swing.

As these examples show, the shift can occur within a single sentence or when the writer moves from one sentence to another.

Some shifts in person, however, are warranted. Read the following correct sentence:

Correct	*I* want *you* to deliver these flowers to Ms. Willoughby by three o'clock. *She* needs them for a party.

Here the speaker identifies himself or herself (*I*) while speaking directly to a listener *(you)* about someone else *(she).* In this case, shifts are needed to get the message across.

shft

CONNECTED DISCOURSE EXERCISE *Identify and correct the unwarranted shifts in person in the following paragraph:*

Good health is clearly important to you. But it is one's responsibility to ensure our own good health. You can start with simple exercises. We would like to provide you with a low-impact aerobics DVD for only $9. We guarantee that the more out of shape the customer, the quicker you will notice the benefits. The way our bodies feel affects the quality of one's lives. Let our tape help you to a better life.

EXERCISE *Indicate whether the sentence is correct (C) or contains an unwarranted shift in person (S). Correct faulty sentences.*

1. Because many of our tour guides spoke very poor English, the tourists soon became quite frustrated.

2. We like the location of our new house very much; you are close to a couple of large shopping centres.

3. If you want me to invite Gary to the party, I'll call him right now.

4. Be sure you tell the bakery clerk that we will need the cake by tomorrow noon.

5. If you complete a degree in vocational education, anyone can expect a rewarding career.

6. Once we learn to ride a bicycle, a person never forgets how.

7. Anyone wishing to make the trip to Kelowna should make your own hotel reservations.

8. After we had finished the test, the instructor told the students she would return it on Thursday.

USING THE RIGHT PRONOUN CASE

Case means the changes in form that a personal pronoun (see page 560) undergoes to show its function in a sentence. English has three cases: the *subjective,* the *objective* (nonsubjective), and the *possessive.* The following chart shows the different forms:

Subjective Form	Objective Form	Possessive Form
I	me	my, mine
he	him	his
she	her	her, hers
we	us	our, ours
you	you	your, yours
they	them	their, theirs
who	whom	whose

The subjective case is used for subjects and subject complements, and the objective is used for direct objects, indirect objects, and objects of prepositions. The possessive case shows ownership and is also used with gerunds.

The following pointers will help you select the proper pronoun as you revise.

We and Us Preceding Nouns   Nouns that serve as subjects take the pronoun *we.* Other nouns take the pronoun *us.*

Correct	*We* tourists will fly home tomorrow. (*We* accompanies the subject.)
Correct	The guide showed *us* tourists through the cathedral. (*Us* accompanies an object.)

If you can't decide which pronoun is right, mentally omit the noun and read the sentence to yourself, first with one pronoun and then with the other. Your ear will identify the correct form.

My mother made *(we, us)* children vanilla pudding for dessert.

Omitting *children* shows immediately that *us* is the right choice.

Correct	My mother made *us* children vanilla pudding for dessert.

Pronouns Paired with Nouns   When such a combination serves as the subject of a sentence or accompanies the subject, use the subject form of the pronoun. When the combination plays an object role, use the object form of the pronoun.

Correct	Arlene and *I* plan to join Katimavik. (*I* is part of the compound subject.)
Correct	Two people, Mary and *I,* will represent our school at the meeting. (*I* is part of a compound element accompanying the subject.)
Correct	The superintendent told Kevin and *him* that they would be promoted soon. (*Him* is part of a compound object.)
Correct	The project was difficult for Jeffrey and *him* to complete. (*Him* is part of a compound object.)

Again, mentally omitting the noun from the combination will tell you which pronoun is correct.

Who and Whom in Dependent Clauses   Use *who* for the subjects of dependent clauses; otherwise use *whom*.

> *Correct*   The Mallarys prefer friends *who are interested in the theatre.* (*Who* is the subject of the clause.)

> *Correct*   Barton is a man *whom very few people like.* (*Whom* is not the subject of the clause but the object of the verb *like.*)

A simple test will help you decide between *who* and *whom*. First, mentally isolate the dependent clause. Next, block out the pronoun in question and insert *he* (or *she*), and then *him* (or *her*) at the appropriate spot in the remaining part of the clause. If *he* (or *she*) sounds better, *who* is right. If *him* (or *her*) sounds better, *whom* is right. Let's use this test on the sentence below:

> The woman who(m) Scott is dating works as a mechanical engineer. Scott is dating (she, her.)

Clearly *her* is correct; therefore, *whom* is the proper form.

> *Correct*   The woman *whom Scott is dating* works as a mechanical engineer.

Pronouns as Subject Complements   In formal writing, pronouns that serve as subject complements (see page 556) always take the subject form.

> *Correct*   It is *I.*

> *Correct*   It was *she* who bought the old Parker mansion.

This rule, however, is often ignored in informal writing or casual speech.

> It's *her.*

> That's *him* standing over by the door.

Comparisons Using *than* or *as . . . as*   Comparisons of this kind often make no direct statement about the second item of comparison. When the second naming word is a pronoun, you may have trouble choosing the right one.

> Harriet is less outgoing than (*they, them*).

> My parents' divorce saddened my sister as much as *(I, me)*.

Not to worry. Expand the sentence by mentally supplying the missing material. Then try the sentence with each pronoun and see which sounds right.

> Harriet is less outgoing than (*they, them*) are.

> My parents' divorce saddened my sister as much as it did *(I, me)*.

Obviously *they* is the right choice for the first sentence, and *me* is the right choice for the second one.

case

Correct   Harriet is less outgoing than *they* are.

Correct   My parents' divorce saddened my sister as much as it did *me*.

Pronouns Preceding Gerunds   Use the possessive form of a pronoun that precedes a gerund (see page 579).

I dislike *their* leaving without saying goodbye.

Ted can't understand *her* quitting such a good job.

This usage emphasizes the action named by the gerund instead of the person or persons performing it. Thus, in the above sentences, the possessive form of the pronoun signals that it's the *leaving* the writer dislikes and the *quitting* that Ted can't understand. The people involved are secondary.

When the pronoun precedes a participle (see pages 578–579), it should be in the objective case. The emphasis is then on the actor rather than the action.

Jennifer caught *them* listening to CDs instead of studying.

In this example, Jennifer caught the listeners, not the listening.

If you have trouble deciding between the objective and possessive forms of a pronoun, ask yourself whether you want to emphasize the action or the actor; then proceed accordingly.

case

CONNECTED DISCOURSE EXERCISE *Identify and correct the pronoun case errors in the following paragraph:*

Between my brother and I, we are always able to pull at least five good-sized trout a day from the creek behind our house. Us rural trout fishermen just seem to have the knack. Of course, those city fishermen whom insist on employing artificial flies won't appreciate our methods even if they can't do as well as us. We just let our bait, usually a juicy worm, float downstream to the waiting trout. Of course, my brother won't let the fishing interfere with him sleeping. In fact, it was him that developed the idea of looping the line around his toe so that he would wake up when a trout took the bait. Others have told my brother and I that this method is dangerous, but neither of us has lost a toe yet. Of course, the people who we invite to dinner don't complain about our methods, and they seem to enjoy the fish.

EXERCISE *Choose the right form of the pronoun for each of the following sentences:*

1. Cherie is the one student *(who, whom)* I believe has the potential to become a professional acrobat.
2. Two students, Carrie and *(I, me)*, scored 100 on the calculus test.
3. *(We, Us)* Greens pride ourselves on our beautiful lawns.
4. Ken Conwell is the only candidate *(who, whom)* I like in this election.

5. Brandon has richer friends than *(I, me)*.

6. The friendly student told *(we, us)* visitors that we were in the wrong building.

7. As children Bill and *(I, me)* used to play tag.

8. My uncle has given Sandra and *(I, me)* tickets for tonight's Bach concert.

CREATING CONSISTENCY IN SHOWING TIME

Inconsistencies occur when a writer shifts from the past tense to the present or vice versa without a corresponding shift in the time of the events being described. The following paragraph contains an uncalled-for shift from the present tense to the past:

> As *The Most Dangerous Game* opens, Sanger Rainsford, a famous hunter and author, and his old friend Whitney are standing on the deck of a yacht and discussing a mysterious island as the ship passes near it. Then, after everyone else has gone to bed, Rainsford manages to fall overboard. He swims to the island and ends up at a chateau owned by General Zaroff, a refugee from the Communist takeover in Russia. Zaroff, bored with hunting animals, has turned to hunting humans on his desert island. Inevitably, Rainsford is turned out into the jungle to be hunted down. There were [shift to past tense] actually four hunts over a three-day period, and at the end of the last one, Rainsford jumped into the sea, swam across a cove to the chateau, and killed Zaroff in the general's own bedroom. Afterward he sleeps [shift back to present tense] and decides "he had never slept in a better bed."

The sentence with the unwarranted shift in tense should read as follows:

> There are actually four hunts over a three-day period, and at the end of the last one, Rainsford jumps into the sea, swims across a cove to the chateau, and kills Zaroff in the general's own bedroom.

The time shift in the quotation part of the final sentence is justified because the sleeping has occurred before Rainsford's thoughts about it.

A second kind of inconsistency results when a writer fails to distinguish the immediate past from the less immediate past. The following sentence illustrates this error:

Faulty   Mary *answered* all thirty test questions when the class ended.

This sentence states that Mary completed all thirty test questions during the final instant of the class. This is impossible. When you detect this type of error in your writing, determine which action occurred first and then correct the error by adding *had* to the verb. In this case, the first verb needs correcting:

Revision   Mary *had answered* all thirty test questions when the class ended.

time

Besides adding *had*, you may sometimes need to alter the verb form.

> *Faulty*   Before he turned twenty, John *wrote* two novels.
>
> *Revision*   Before he turned twenty, John *had written* two novels.

CONNECTED DISCOURSE EXERCISE *Identify and correct any inconsistencies in showing time in the following passage:*

> There is no better time to go swimming than at night. The summer after I had graduated from high school, I worked for a landscaping company. After a sweaty day mowing lawns and digging up gardens, all of us who worked there would jump into the back of Dick's old pickup and rattle out to Woods Lake. It is just dark as we arrive. The moon is beautiful, reflected in that black mirror set in a frame of hills. We stumble down a small, sandy hill to the beach, where we strip off our dusty jeans and sweaty shirts before plunging into the cool reflection of stars.

EXERCISE *Indicate whether each sentence is correct (C) or contains an unwarranted shift (S) in tense. Then correct the faulty sentences.*

1. Although the alarm rang, Bob continues to lie in bed.
2. When autumn arrives, we often go for long walks in the woods.
3. John is writing his dissertation but found the job tough going.
4. When the trapeze artist fell into the net, the audience gasps loudly.
5. When I baked the cake, I ate a slice.
6. Edward walks for half an hour before he ate dinner.
7. Sarah had many friends but sees them infrequently.
8. As Elaine walked toward the garden, a rabbit scampers quickly away.

USING ADJECTIVES AND ADVERBS EFFECTIVELY

Beginning writers often use adjectives when they should use adverbs, and they also often confuse the comparative and superlative forms of these parts of speech when making comparisons.

Misusing Adjectives as Adverbs   Although most adjectives can be misused as adverbs, the following five, listed with the corresponding adverbs, cause the most difficulty.

Adjectives	**Adverbs**
bad	badly
good	well

most	almost
real	really
sure	surely

The following sentences show typical errors:

Faulty Bryan did *good* in his first golf lesson. (*good* mistakenly used to modify verb *did*)

Faulty *Most* every graduate from our auto service program receives several job offers. (*Most* mistakenly used to modify adjective *every*)

Faulty The speech was delivered *real* well. (*real* mistakenly used to modify adverb *well*)

mis/
adj/*adv*

Because adverbs modify verbs, adjectives, and other adverbs (see pages 572–573), and adjectives modify nouns and noun substitutes (see pages 569–571), the above sentences clearly require adverbs.

Revision Bryan did *well* in his first golf lesson.

Revision *Almost* every graduate from our auto service program receives several job offers.

Revision The speech was delivered *really* well.

If you can't decide whether a sentence requires an adjective or an adverb, determine the part of speech of the word being modified and proceed accordingly.

Confusing the Comparative and Superlative Forms in Comparisons   The comparative form of adjectives and adverbs is used to compare two things, the superlative form to compare three or more things. Adjectives with fewer than three syllables generally add *-er* to make the comparative form and *-est* to make the superlative form (tall, tall*er*, tall*est*). Adjectives with three or more syllables generally add *more* to make the comparative and *most* to make the superlative (enchanting, *more* enchanting, *most* enchanting), as do most adverbs of two or more syllables (loudly, *more* loudly, *most* loudly).

When making comparisons, beginning writers sometimes mistakenly use double comparatives or double superlatives.

Faulty Harry is *more taller* than James. (double comparative)

Faulty The Hotel Vancouver has the *most splendidest* lobby I've ever seen. (double superlative)

The correct versions read as follows:

Revision Harry is *taller* than James.

Revision The Hotel Vancouver has the *most splendid* lobby I've ever seen.

In addition, writers may erroneously use the superlative form, rather than the comparative form, to compare two things.

Faulty   Barry is the *richest* of the two brothers.

Faulty   Jeremy is the *most talented* of those two singers.

Here are the sentences correctly written:

Revision   Barry is the *richer* of the two brothers.

Revision   Jeremy is the *more talented* of those two singers.

Reserve the superlative form for comparing three or more items.

Correct   Barry is the *richest* of the three brothers.

Correct   Jeremy is the *most talented* of those four singers.

mis / adj/adv

CONNECTED DISCOURSE EXERCISE *Identify and correct the adjective–adverb errors in the following paragraph:*

This year our football team is outstanding. Spike Jones, our quarterback, has been playing real good this past season. Stan Blunder, the most talented of our two ends, hasn't dropped a pass all season. The team can most always count on Stan to catch the crucial first-down pass. Of course, the team wouldn't be where it is today without John Schoolyard's good coaching. He has made this team much more better than it was a year ago. Only the kicking team has done bad this season. Of course, with this most wonderfulest offence, the defensive players haven't got much practice. The good news is, then, that we can sure expect to watch some terrific university football for years to come.

EXERCISE *For each of the following sentences, choose the proper word from the pair in parentheses:*

1. A person can become (*stronger, more stronger*) by lifting weights.
2. Canvasback Dunn is clearly the (*less, least*) formidable of the two main challengers for Killer McGurk's boxing crown.
3. Diane did (*good, well*) on her chemistry test.
4. (*Most, Almost*) all our salaried employees have degrees in business administration or engineering.
5. Carol wore the (*silliest, most silliest*) hat I've ever seen to the masquerade party.
6. Don was hurt (*bad, badly*) in the auto accident.
7. Brad was the (*funniest, most funniest*) of all the performers at the comedy club.
8. Clear Lake is the (*deeper, deepest*) of the three lakes in our county.

PLACING MODIFIERS CORRECTLY

A misplaced modifier is a word or word group that is improperly separated from the word it modifies. When separation of this type occurs, the sentence often sounds awkward, ridiculous, or confusing.

Usually, you can correct this error by moving the modifier next to the word it is intended to modify. Occasionally, you'll also need to alter some of the phrasing.

Faulty	There is a bicycle in the basement *with chrome fenders.* (The basement appears to have chrome fenders.)
Faulty	David received a phone call from his uncle *that infuriated him.* (The uncle appears to have infuriated David.)
Revision	There is a bicycle *with chrome fenders* in the basement.
Revision	David received an *infuriating* phone call from his uncle. (Note the change in wording.)

When shifting the modifier, don't inadvertently create another faulty sentence.

Faulty	Fritz bought a magazine with an article about Michael Jackson *at the corner newsstand.* (The article appears to tell about Jackson's visit to the corner newsstand.)
Faulty	Fritz bought a magazine *at the corner newsstand* with an article about Michael Jackson. (The corner newsstand appears to have an article about Jackson.)
Revision	*At the corner newsstand,* Fritz bought a magazine with an article about Michael Jackson.

As you revise, watch also for *squinting modifiers*—that is, modifiers positioned so that the reader doesn't know whether they are supposed to modify what comes ahead of them or what follows them.

Faulty	The man who was rowing the boat *frantically* waved toward the onlookers on the beach.

Is the man rowing frantically or waving frantically? Correct this kind of error by repositioning the modifier so that the ambiguity disappears.

Revision	The man who was *frantically* rowing the boat waved toward the onlookers on the beach.
Revision	The man who was rowing the boat waved *frantically* toward the onlookers on the beach.

EXERCISE *Indicate whether each sentence is correct (C) or contains a misplaced modifier (MM). Correct faulty sentences.*

1. The boss asked me after lunch to type a special report.
2. Brenda returned the cottage cheese to the store that had spoiled.

mm

3. The hikers tramped through the woods wearing heavy boots.

4. The movie was heavily advertised by the studio before sneak previews were shown.

5. Mark mailed a package to his friend sealed with masking tape.

6. The woman packing her suitcase hastily glanced out the window at the commotion in the yard.

7. We bought a dictionary that was bound in leather at the local bookstore.

8. Jerry bought an Inuit carving for his bedroom in Regina.

REVISING DANGLING MODIFIERS

dm

A dangling modifier is a phrase or clause that lacks clear connection to the word or words it is intended to modify. As a result, sentences are inaccurate, often comical. Typically, the modifier leads off the sentence, although it can also come at the end.

Sometimes the error occurs because the sentence fails to specify who or what is modified. At other times, the separation is too great between the modifier and what it modifies.

Faulty	*Walking in the meadow,* wildflowers surrounded us. (The wildflowers appear to be walking in the meadow.)
Faulty	Dinner was served *after saying grace.* (The dinner appears to have said grace.)
Faulty	*Fatigued by the violent exercise,* the cool shower was very relaxing. (The cool shower appears to have been fatigued.)

These sentences are faulty because they do not identify who walked, said grace, or found the shower relaxing.

You can correct dangling modifiers in two basic ways. First, leave the modifier unchanged and rewrite the main part of the sentence so that it begins with the term actually modified. Second, rewrite the modifier so that it has its own subject and verb, thereby eliminating the inaccuracy.

Revision	*Walking in the meadow,* we were surrounded by wildflowers. (The main part of the sentence has been rewritten.)
Revision	*As we walked in the meadow,* wildflowers surrounded us. (The modifier has been rewritten.)
Revision	Dinner was served *after we had said grace.* (The modifier has been rewritten.)
Revision	*Fatigued by the violent exercise,* Ted found the cool shower very relaxing. (The main part of the sentence has been rewritten.)
Revision	*Because Ted was fatigued by the violent exercise,* the cool shower was very relaxing. (The modifier has been rewritten.)

Ordinarily, either part of the sentence can be rewritten, but sometimes only one part can.

EXERCISE *Indicate whether each sentence is correct (C) or contains a dangling modifier (DM). Correct faulty sentences.*

1. Dancing at the wedding reception, my feet hurt.
2. Working in the yard, Pete was drenched by the sudden cloudburst.
3. Looking out the window, a velvety lawn ran down to the river's edge.
4. Having mangy fur, our parents wouldn't let us keep the stray cat.
5. Because of memorizing all the definitions, Pam scored 100 on the vocabulary test.
6. Reminiscing about my school days, a run-in with my principal came to mind.
7. Unaware of what had happened, the confusion puzzled Nan.
8. At the age of eight, my father wrote a best-selling novel.

//

MAINTAINING PARALLELISM

Nonparallelism results when equivalent ideas follow different grammatical forms. One common kind of nonparallelism occurs with words or word groups in pairs or in a series.

Faulty	Althea enjoys *jogging, to bike,* and *to swim.*
Faulty	The superintendent praised the workers *for their productivity* and *because they had an excellent safety record.*
Faulty	The banner was *old, faded,* and *it had a rip.*

Note how rewriting the sentences in parallel form improves their smoothness.

Revision	Althea enjoys *jogging, biking,* and *swimming.*
Revision	The superintendent praised the workers for *their productivity* and *their excellent safety record.*
Revision	The banner was *old, faded,* and *ripped.*

Nonparallelism also occurs when correlative conjunctions *(either/or, neither/nor, both/and,* and *not only/but also)* are followed by unlike elements.

Faulty	That sound *either* <u>was a thunderclap</u> *or* <u>an explosion.</u>
Faulty	The basement was *not only* <u>poorly lit</u> *but also* <u>it had a foul smell.</u>

Ordinarily, repositioning one of the correlative conjunctions will solve the problem. Sometimes, however, one of the grammatical elements must be rewritten.

Revision	That sound was *either* <u>a thunderclap</u> *or* <u>an explosion.</u> (*Either* has been repositioned.)
Revision	The basement was *not only* <u>poorly lit</u> *but also* <u>foul smelling.</u> (The element following *but also* has been rewritten.)

comp

EXERCISE *Indicate whether each sentence is correct (C) or nonparallel (NP). Correct faulty sentences.*

1. The lemonade was cold, tangy, and refreshing.
2. Although he had practised for several days, the scout could neither tie a square knot nor a bowline.
3. This job will involve waiting on customers, and you will need to maintain our inventory.
4. My summer job at a provincial park gave me experience in repairing buildings, the operation of heavy equipment, and assisting park visitors.
5. To maintain his rose bushes properly, Sam fertilizes, sprays, prunes, and waters them according to a strict schedule.
6. Once out of high school, Barry plans either to join the navy or the air force.
7. My favourite sports are swimming, golfing, and to bowl.
8. Janice's leisure activities include collecting coins, reading, and she also watches TV.

REVISING FAULTY COMPARISONS

A faulty comparison results if you (1) mention one of the items being compared but not the other, (2) omit words needed to clarify the relationship, or (3) compare different sorts of items. Advertisers often offend in the first way.

> *Faulty*   Irish tape has better adhesion.

With what other tape is Irish tape being compared? Scotch tape? All other transparent tape? Mentioning the second term of a comparison eliminates reader guesswork.

> *Revision*   Irish tape has better adhesion than any other transparent tape.

Two clarifying words, *other* and *else*, are frequently omitted from comparisons, creating illogical sentences.

> *Faulty*   Sergeant McNabb is more conscientious than any officer in his precinct.

> *Faulty*   Stretch French is taller than anyone on his basketball team.

The first sentence is illogical because McNabb is one of the officers in his precinct and therefore cannot be more conscientious than himself. Similarly, because French is a member of his basketball team, he can't be taller than anyone on his team. Adding *other* to the first sentence and *else* to the second corrects matters.

Revision	Sergeant McNabb is more conscientious than any *other* officer in his precinct.
Revision	Stretch French is taller than anyone *else* on his basketball team.

Comparing unlike items is perhaps the most common kind of comparison error. Here are two examples:

Faulty	The cities in Ontario are larger than Nova Scotia.
Faulty	The cover of this book is much more durable than the other book.

The first sentence compares the cities of Ontario with a province, while the second compares the cover of a book with a whole book. Correction consists of rewriting each sentence so that it compares like items.

Revision	The cities in Ontario are larger than *those in* Nova Scotia.
Revision	The cover of this book is much more durable than *that of* the other book.

comp

CONNECTED DISCOURSE EXERCISE *Identify and correct the misplaced modifiers, dangling modifiers, nonparallelism, and faulty comparisons in the following memorandum:*

TO: All Residency Hall Advisors in Knuckles Hall

FROM: John Knells, Residence Hall Director

DATE: March 13, 2008

SUBJECT: Noise in Residence Hall

Recently I received a report from a student that deeply disturbed me. Apparently, after quiet hours students still have visitors in their rooms, are playing their stereos loudly, and are even staging boxing matches in the halls. The student who wrote me desperately tries to study. However, he is often forced to leave his room disturbed by the noise. He was not the only one to complain. You should know that we have had more complaints about Knuckles Hall than any residence on campus. Since discussing this problem with you at the last staff meeting, things haven't seemed to get any better. The rules are not only poorly enforced but also they are completely ignored. Your job performance is worse than the students. If you don't improve immediately, I will be forced to dismiss you.

EXERCISE *Indicate whether each sentence is correct (C) or contains a faulty comparison (FC). Correct any faulty comparison.*

1. The houses on Parkdale Street are more modest than Windsor Terrace.
2. Maxine has more seniority than any other member of her department.
3. The finish on the dresser is not as smooth as the end table.
4. In contrast to your yard, I have an underground sprinkling system.
5. My mother's homemade jam has more flavour than any jam I've eaten.
6. The dresses sold at The Bay are much less expensive than the Tres Chic Shoppe.
7. The paint on the front of the house is much lighter than the back.

comp

Punctuation marks indicate relationships among different sentence elements. These marks help clarify the meaning of written material. Similarly, a knowledge of mechanics—capitalization, abbreviations, numbers, and italics—helps you avoid distracting inconsistencies.

This part of the Handbook covers the fundamentals of punctuation and mechanics. Review it carefully when you edit your final draft.

APOSTROPHES

Apostrophes (') show possession, mark contractions, and occasionally indicate plurals singled out for special attention.

Possession   Possessive apostrophes usually show ownership *(Mary's cat)*. Sometimes they identify the works of creative people *(Hemingway's novels)* or indicate an extent of time or distance *(one hour's time, one metre's distance)*.

The possessive form is easily recognized because it can be converted to a prepositional phrase beginning with *of*.

The collar of the dog

The whistle of the wind

The intention of the corporation

The birthday of Scott

Possessive apostrophes are used with nouns and with pronouns such as *someone, no one, everybody, each other,* and *one another*. To show possession with these pronouns, with singular nouns, and with plural nouns that do not end in an *s*, add an apostrophe followed by an *s*.

Someone's car is blocking our driveway. (possessive of pronoun *someone*)

The *manager's* reorganization plan will take effect next week. (possessive of singular noun *manager*)

The *women's* lounge is being redecorated. (possessive of plural noun *women*)

Sentences that make comparisons sometimes include two possessives, the second coming at the very end. In such cases, be sure to use an apostrophe with the second possessive as well.

York's football team is much better than *Toronto's*.

With singular nouns that end in *s*, some people form the possessive merely by adding an apostrophe *(James' helmet)*. However, the preferred usage is *'s* *(James's helmet)* unless the additional *s* would make pronunciation awkward.

Charles's dog was afraid of the water. (awkward pronunciation of *Charles's*)

Charles' dog was afraid of the water. (nonawkward pronunciation of *Charles'*)

Plural nouns ending in *s* form the possessive by adding only an apostrophe at the end.

All the *ladies'* coats are on sale today. (possessive of plural noun *ladies*)

The *workers'* lockers were moved. (possessive of plural noun *workers*)

To show joint ownership by two or more persons, use the possessive form for the last-named person only. To show individual ownership, use the possessive form for each person's name.

Ronald and *Joan's* boat badly needed overhauling. (joint ownership)

Laura's and *Alice's* term projects are almost completed. (individual ownership)

Hyphenated nouns form the possessive by adding *'s* to the last word.

My *mother-in-law's* house is next to mine.

Never use an apostrophe with the possessive pronouns *his, hers, whose, its, ours, yours,* or *theirs.*

This desk is *his;* the other one is *hers.* (no apostrophes needed)

Contractions   Contractions of words or numbers omit one or more letters or numerals. An apostrophe shows exactly where the omission occurs.

Wasn't that a disappointing concert? (contraction of *was not*)

Around here, people still talk about the ice storm of '98. (contraction of *1998*)

Don't confuse the contraction *it's,* meaning *it is* or *it has,* with the possessive pronoun *its,* which should never have an apostrophe. If you're puzzled by an *its* that you've written, try this test. Expand the *its* to *it is* or *it has* and see whether the sentence still makes sense. If it does, the *its* is a contraction and needs the apostrophe. If the result is nonsense, the *its* is a possessive pronoun and does not get an apostrophe. Here are some examples:

Its awfully muggy today.

Its been an exciting trip.

Every dog has *its* day.

The first example makes sense when the *its* is expanded to *it is.*

It is awfully muggy today.

The second makes sense when the *its* is expanded to *it has.*

It has been an exciting trip.

Both of these sentences therefore require apostrophes.

It's awfully muggy today.

It's been an exciting trip.

The last sentence, however, turns into nonsense when the *its* is expanded.

Every dog has *it is* day.

Every dog has *it has* day.

In this case, the *its* is a possessive pronoun and requires no apostrophe.

Every dog has *its* day.

Plurals   To improve clarity, the plurals of letters, numbers, symbols, and words being singled out for special attention are written with apostrophes.

Mind your *p's* and *q's.* (plurals of letters)

Your *5's* and *6's* are hard to tell apart. (plurals of numbers)

The formula was sprinkled with *¶'s* and *β's.* (plurals of symbols)

Don't use so many *however's* and *therefore's* in your writing. (plurals of words)

Apostrophes are sometimes used to form the plurals of abbreviations.

How many *CD's* (or *CDs*) do you own? (plurals of abbreviation for *compact discs*)

When no danger of confusion exists, an *s* alone will suffice.

During the late *1960s,* many university students demanded changes in academic life.

CONNECTED DISCOURSE EXERCISE *Supply, delete, or relocate apostrophes as necessary in the following memorandum:*

TO: The Records Office Staff

FROM: The Assistant Registrar

DATE: January 27, 2008

SUBJECT: Faulty Student Transcripts

Recently, we have had too many student complaints' about handwritten transcripts. Apparently its hard to tell the Bs and Ds apart. One staff members' handwriting is totally illegible. This staffs carelessness is unacceptable. Someones even gone so far as to write grade change's in pencil, which allows students to make changes. This cant continue. In a short time, John and Marys student assistants will be typing the past transcripts into our new computer system. Once grades are entered, the computers ability to generate grade reports will solve this problem. Until that time, lets make an effort to produce clear and professional-looking transcripts.

EXERCISE *Supply apostrophes where necessary to correct the following sentences:*

1. The bosss speech reviewed the companys safety record.
2. Lets find out whats wrong with Melanys bicycle.
3. Daves and Marvins fiancées are identical twins.
4. Its highly unlikely that this movie will ever earn back its production costs when its released.
5. Sues test score was higher than all her friends test scores.
6. There are two *l*s and two *es* in the name *Colleen*.
7. When everyones ready, well start the slide show.
8. Alice overloads her sentences with *consequently*s and *accordingly*s.

COMMAS

Since commas (,) occur more frequently than any other mark of punctuation, it's vital that you learn to use them correctly. When you do, your sentence structure becomes clearer, and your reader grasps your meaning without having to reread.

Commas separate or set off independent clauses, items in a series, coordinate adjectives, introductory elements, places and dates, nonrestrictive expressions, and parenthetical expressions.

Independent Clauses   When you link two independent clauses with a coordinating conjunction (*and, but, or, nor, for, yet,* or *so*), put a comma in front of the conjunction.

Arthur is majoring in engineering, *but* he has decided to work for a clothing store following graduation.

The water looked inviting, *so* Darlene decided to go for a swim.

Don't confuse a sentence that has a compound predicate (see pages 554 and 584) with a sentence that consists of two independent clauses.

Tom watered the garden and mowed the lawn. (simple sentence with compound predicate)

Tom watered the garden, *and* Betty mowed the lawn. (sentence with two independent clauses)

Items in a Series   A series consists of three or more words, phrases, or clauses following on one another's heels. Whenever you write a series, separate its items with commas.

> *Sarah, Paul,* and *Mary* are earning *A's* in advanced algebra. (words in a series)

> Nancy strode *across the parking lot, through the revolving door,* and *into the elevator.* (phrases in a series)

> The stockholders' report said *that the company had enjoyed record profits during the last year, that it had expanded its work force by 20 percent,* and *that it would soon start marketing several new products.* (clauses in a series)

Coordinate Adjectives   Use commas to separate coordinate adjectives—those that modify the same noun or noun substitute and can be reversed without altering the meaning of the sentence.

> Andrea proved to be an *efficient, co-operative* employee.

> Andrea proved to be a *co-operative, efficient* employee.

When reversing the word order wrecks the meaning of the sentence, the adjectives are not coordinate and should be written without a comma.

> Many new models of hybrid cars have come on the market lately.

Reversing the adjectives *many* and *new* would turn this sentence into nonsense. Therefore, no comma should be used.

Introductory Elements   Use commas to separate introductory elements—words, phrases, and clauses—from the rest of the sentence. When an introductory element is short and the sentence will not be misread, you can omit the comma.

> *Correct*   After bathing, Jack felt refreshed.

> *Correct*   Soon I will be changing jobs.

> *Correct*   Soon, I will be changing jobs.

> *Correct*   When Sarah smiles her ears wiggle.

> *Correct*   When Sarah smiles, her ears wiggle.

The first example needs a comma; otherwise, the reader might become temporarily confused.

> After bathing Jack . . .

Always use commas after introductory elements of six or more words.

> *Correct*   Whenever I hear the opening measure of Beethoven's *Fifth Symphony,* I get goose bumps.

Places and Dates   Places include mailing addresses and geographical locations. The following sentences show where commas are used:

Sherry Delaney lives at 651 Daniel Street, Westmount, Quebec H4Z 6W5.

I will go to Calais, France, next week.

Chicoutimi, Quebec, is my birthplace.

Note that commas appear after the street designation and the names of cities, countries, and provinces, except when the name of the province is followed by a postal code.

Dates are punctuated as shown in the following example:

On Sunday, June 8, 2008, Elaine received a degree in environmental science.

Here, commas follow the day of the week, the day of the month, and the year. With dates that include only the month and the year, commas are optional.

Correct	In July 2004 James played chess for the first time.
Correct	In July, 2004, James played chess for the first time.

Nonrestrictive Expressions   A nonrestrictive expression supplies added information about whatever it modifies. This information, however, is *nonessential* and does not affect the basic meaning of the sentence. The two sentences below include nonrestrictive expressions:

Premier Campbell, *the leader of the British Columbia Liberal Party,* faced a tough campaign for re-election.

My dog, *frightened by the thunder,* hid under my bed while the storm raged.

If we delete the phrase *the leader of the British Columbia Liberal Party* from the first sentence, we still know that Premier Campbell faced a tough re-election battle. Likewise, if we delete *frightened by the thunder* from the second sentence, we still know that the dog hid during the storm.

Restrictive expressions, which are written *without commas,* distinguish whatever they modify from other persons, places, or things in the same category. Unlike nonrestrictive expressions, they are almost always *essential* sentence elements. Omitting a restrictive expression alters the meaning of the sentence, and the result is often nonsense.

Any person *caught stealing from this store* will be prosecuted.

Dropping the italicized part of this sentence leaves us with the absurd statement that any person, not just those caught stealing, faces prosecution.

Parenthetical Expressions   A parenthetical expression is a word or a word group that links one sentence to another or adds information or emphasis to the sentence in which it appears. Parenthetical expressions include the following:

Clarifying phrases
Names and titles of people being addressed directly

Abbreviations of degree titles

Echo questions

"Not" phrases

Adjectives that come after, rather than before, the words they modify

The examples that follow show the uses of commas:

All of Joe's spare time seems to centre around reading. Kevin, *on the other hand,* enjoys a variety of activities. (phrase linking two sentences together)

Myra Hobbes, *our representative in Calgary,* is being transferred to Kamloops next month. (clarifying phrase)

I think, *Jill,* that you'd make a wonderful teacher. (name of person addressed directly)

Tell me, *Captain,* when the cruise ship is scheduled to sail. (title of person addressed directly)

Harley Kendall, *Ph.D.,* will be this year's commencement speaker. (degree title following name)

Alvin realizes, *doesn't he,* that he stands almost no chance of being accepted at McGill? (echo question)

Mathematics, *not drama,* was Tammy's favourite high school subject. ("not" phrase)

The road, *muddy and rutted,* proved impassable. (adjectives following word they modify)

Punctuating Conjunctive Adverbs   Writers often mistakenly punctuate conjunctive adverbs with commas and create, as a result, a comma splice.

Vancouverites do not experience the snowfall of their Northern neighbours, however, they do experience a lot of rainfall.

Conjunctive adverbs do not join sentences and can be moved, revealing the underlying comma splice.

Vancouverites do not experience the snowfall of their Northern neighbours, they do, however, experience a lot of rainfall.

To fix such comma splices, join the sentences with a semi-colon or punctuate with a period and start a new sentence.

Vancouverites do not experience the snowfall of their Northern neighbours; however, they do experience a lot of rainfall.

Vancouverites do not experience the snowfall of their Northern neighbours. However, they do experience a lot of rainfall.

CONNECTED DISCOURSE EXERCISE *Add or delete commas as necessary in the following letter:*

Dear Loy Norrix Knight:

While we know you will be busy this summer we hope you will take time to join us for the twenty-five-year reunion of the graduating class of 1991. The reunion will include a cocktail hour a buffet dinner and a dance. For your entertainment we are going to bring in a professional band and a band starring some of your good, old high school chums. John Mcleary who is now a well-known professional nightclub performer will serve as the emcee. Do you remember him hosting our Grade 12 assemblies?

Yes many of your former, hardworking teachers will be at the reunion. You can thank them for the difference they made in your life or you can tell them what you've thought of them all these years. This reunion will also be your opportunity to catch up on the lives of your former friends find out what that old flame now looks like and brag a little about your own successes. And if you are really lucky you might even be able to sneak a dance with your high school prom partner.

We hope you will make plans, to join us here at the Penticton Hilton on July 28 2011 at 7 P.M. Wear your best 1990s-style clothes. Remember revisiting the past, can be fun.

Sincerely,

The Reunion Committee

EXERCISE *Supply commas as necessary to correct the following sentences:*

1. Before leaving Jim stopped to say goodbye to Lisa.
2. Although our prices continue to go up people will probably keep buying our computer games.
3. This store's burglar alarm system which is very outdated should be replaced immediately.
4. Stepping into the cool pleasant bake shop Annette bought a large cinnamon doughnut for a snack.
5. Mr. Kowalski was born in Warsaw Poland and became a Canadian citizen on February 15 1994.
6. The brakes on our car aren't working so we'll have to take the bus.
7. The movie-going couple bought popcorn candy bars and large Cokes at the lobby concession stand.
8. For more information about the Scotland tour write Doreen Campbell 218 Riverdale Street Windsor Ontario M6T 3Y7.

SEMICOLONS

The main use of the semicolon (;) is to separate independent clauses, which may or may not be connected with a conjunctive adverb (see pages 576–577). Other uses include separating

two or more of a series of items,

items containing commas in a single series, and

independent clauses that contain commas and are connected with a coordinating conjunction.

Independent Clauses   The examples that follow show the use of semicolons to separate independent clauses.

The fabric in this dress is terrible; its designer must have been asleep at the swatch. (no conjunctive adverb)

Steve refused to write a term paper; *therefore,* he failed the course. (conjunctive adverb *therefore* joining independent clauses)

Conjunctive adverbs can occur within, rather than between, independent clauses. When they do, set them off with commas.

Marsha felt very confident. Jane, *on the other hand,* was nervous and uncertain. (conjunctive adverb within independent clause)

To determine whether a pair of commas or a semicolon and comma are required, read what comes before and after the conjunctive adverb. Unless both sets of words can stand alone as sentences, use commas.

Two or More Series of Items   With sentences that have two or more series of items, writers often separate the series with semicolons in order to reduce the chances of misreading.

My duties as secretary include typing letters, memos, and purchase orders; sorting, opening, and delivering mail; and making plane and hotel reservations for travelling executives.

The semicolons provide greater clarity than commas would.

Comma-Containing Items within a Series   When commas accompany one or more of the items in a series, it's often better to separate the items with semicolons instead of commas.

The meal included salmon, which was cooked to perfection; asparagus, my favourite vegetable; and brown rice, prepared with a touch of curry.

Once again, semicolons provide greater clarity than additional commas.

Independent Clauses with Commas and a Coordinating Conjunction
Ordinarily, a comma is used to separate independent clauses joined by a coordinating conjunction. However, when one or more of the clauses have commas, a semicolon provides clearer separation.

The long black limousine pulled up to the curb; and Jerry, shaking with excitement, watched the prime minister alight from it.

The semicolon makes it easier to see the two main clauses.

CONNECTED DISCOURSE EXERCISE *Add and delete semicolons as appropriate in the following letter. You may have to substitute semicolons for commas.*

Dear Student:

Our university, as you are well aware, has been going through a number of changes, and these developments, both in the registration system and the curriculum, will continue next year. In the end these improvements will only benefit you; but we know that many of you have been anxious about the exact nature of the changes. To answer your questions, we have arranged an open forum with Linda Peters, president of the university, Drake Stevens, the registrar, and Jerry Mash, vice-president of academic affairs. The meeting will be held in Johnston Hall; 2 P.M.; March 23. Please come with your questions, this is your opportunity to put your fears to rest.

Sincerely,

Jessica X. Pelle

Dean of Students

EXERCISE *Supply semicolons wherever they are necessary or desirable in the following sentences. You may have to substitute semicolons for commas. If a sentence is correct, write C.*

1. The garage sale included women's coats, hats, and purses, men's shoes, shirts, and ties, and children's scarves, mittens, and boots.
2. James couldn't stand his sarcastic boss, therefore, he quit his job.
3. Our house is far too small, we should start looking for a larger one.
4. Morris wanted to work for a company that was small, environmentally responsible, and located in a midsize city, and finally, after a dozen job interviews, he went to work for Greenland, Inc.
5. This has been a good year for raspberries, I've got more than thirty litres from my small patch of bushes.
6. The road ahead has been washed out by a flood; you'll have to make a detour.
7. After touring the company's facilities, we had lunch with Giles Seymour, its president, Cheryl James, its sales manager, and Daryl Brewer, its research director.
8. Penny is a real cat lover; in fact, she has six cats.

PERIODS, QUESTION MARKS, AND EXCLAMATION POINTS

Since periods, question marks, and exclamation points signal the ends of sentences, they are sometimes called *end marks*. In addition, periods and question marks function in several other ways.

Periods   Periods (.) end sentences that state facts or opinions, give instructions, make requests that are not in the form of questions, and ask indirect questions—those that have been rephrased in the form of a statement.

> Linda works as a hotel manager. (Sentence states fact.)
>
> Dean Harris is a competent administrator. (Sentence states opinion.)
>
> Clean off your lab bench before you leave. (Sentence gives instruction.)
>
> Please move away from the door. (Sentence makes request.)
>
> I wonder whether Ruthie will be at the theatre tonight. (Sentence asks indirect question.)

Periods also follow common abbreviations, as well as a person's initials.

Capt.	P.M.
B.C.E	a.s.a.p.
etc.	St.
A.M.	Corp.

> Mark J. Valentini, Ph.D., has consented to head the new commission on traffic safety.

Periods are usually omitted after abbreviations for the names of organizations or government agencies, as the following examples show:

CBC	GST	RCAF	TD
PST	IBM	UPS	WTO

An up-to-date dictionary will indicate whether a certain abbreviation should be written without periods.

Periods also precede decimal fractions and separate numerals standing for dollars and cents.

0.81 percent	$5.29
3.79 percent	$0.88

Question Marks   A question mark (?) ends a whole or a partial sentence that asks a direct question (one that repeats the exact words of the person who asked it).

> Do you know how to operate this movie projector? (whole sentence asking a direct question)
>
> Has Cinderella scrubbed the floor? swept the hearth? washed the dishes? (sentence and sentence parts asking direct questions)

Dr. Baker—wasn't she your boss once?—has just received a promotion to sales manager. (interrupting element asking a direct question)

The minister inquired, "Don't you take this woman to be your lawful wedded wife?" (quotation asking a direct question)

A question mark may be used to indicate uncertainty.

Jane Seymour (1509?–1537), third wife of Henry VIII, was a lady in waiting to his first two wives.

Exclamation Points   Exclamation points (!) are used to express strong emotion or especially forceful commands.

Darcy! I never expected to see you again!

Sam! Turn that radio down immediately!

Help! Save me!

Use exclamation points sparingly; otherwise, they quickly lose their force.

. ? !

CONNECTED DISCOURSE EXERCISE *Add, change, or remove end marks as necessary. You may want to do some slight rewording.*

It was horrifying, the mob of screaming fans grabbed Jack Slitherhips as he left the concert hall. Soon all I could see were his arms reaching for help. But it never came. Why do fans act this way. I am left wondering whether they love or hate their idols? They tore the clothes off Slitherhips, they tore out patches of his hair, someone even snatched his false teeth. Is this any way to treat a fading rock star. Jack is now in the hospital in a complete body cast; when I finally got to see him, he mumbled that he was giving up show business, he plans to settle down on a small farm. Who can blame him?

EXERCISE *Supply periods, question marks, or exclamation points wherever they are necessary. You may have to change existing punctuation marks. If a sentence is correct, write C.*

1. The instructor asked Margie why she hadn't finished her process paper.
2. The videotape of the movie *Casablanca* retails for $2995.
3. Good lord, quit popping that gum before you drive me nuts.
4. Lock the front door before you go to bed.
5. Where do you plan to spend your vacation this year.
6. While you were in Vancouver, did you go to GM Place and see a Canucks game.
7. Would you be interested in having dinner with me tonight.
8. When it's 5 PM in British Columbia, it's 8 PM in Ontario.

COLONS, DASHES, PARENTHESES, AND BRACKETS

Colons, dashes, parentheses, and brackets separate and enclose, thereby clarifying relationships among the various parts of a sentence.

Colon   Colons (:) introduce explanations and anticipated lists following words that could stand alone as a complete sentence.

> His aim in life is grandiose: to corner the market in wheat. (explanation)

> Three students have been selected to attend the conference: Lucille Perkins, Dan Blakely, and Frank Napolis. (list)

> Three factors can cause financial problems for farmers: (1) high interest rates; (2) falling land values; and (3) a strong dollar, which makes global sales of crops difficult. (numbered list)

The first of the following sentences is incorrect because the words preceding the colon can't stand alone as a sentence:

> *Faulty*   The tools needed for this job include: a hacksaw, a file, and a drill.

> *Revision*   The tools needed for this job include a hacksaw, a file, and a drill.

Colons also frequently introduce formal quotations that extend beyond a single sentence.

> The speaker stepped to the lectern and spoke forcefully: "I am here to ask for your assistance. Today several African nations face a food crisis because drought has ruined their harvests. Unless we provide help quickly, thousands of people will die of starvation."

Colons also separate hours from minutes (8:20 A.M.), titles of publications from subtitles (*The Careful Writer: A Guide to English Usage*), numbers indicating ratios (a 3:2:2 ratio), and chapter from verse in scriptural references (Luke 6:20–49).

Dashes   Like colons, dashes (—) set off appositives, lists, and explanations but are used in less formal writing. A dash emphasizes the material it sets off.

> Only one candidate showed up at the political rally—Jerry Manders. (appositive)

> The closet held only three garments—an out-at-the-elbows sports coat, a pair of blue jeans, and a tattered shirt. (list)

> I know what little Billy's problem is—a soiled diaper. (explanation)

Dashes set off material that interrupts the flow of thought within a sentence.

Her new car—didn't she get it just three months ago?—has broken down twice.

Similarly, dashes are used to mark an interrupted segment of dialogue.

"I'd like to live in England when I retire."

"In England? But what will your wife—?"

"My wife likes the idea and can hardly wait for us to make the move."

Dashes set off parenthetical elements containing commas, and a dash can set off comments that follow a list.

The comedian—short, fat, and squeaky-voiced—soon had everyone roaring with laughter. (parenthetical element with commas)

A brag, a blow, a tank of air—that's what the director is. (comment following a list)

Parentheses   Parentheses () are used to enclose numbers or letters that designate the items in a formal list and to set off incidental material within sentences. Except in the kind of list shown in the first example below, a comma does not usually precede a parenthesis.

Each paper should contain (1) an introduction, (2) several paragraphs developing the thesis statement, and (3) a conclusion.

Some occupations (computer programming, for example) may be overcrowded in ten years.

If the material in parentheses appears within a sentence, don't use a capital letter or period, even if the material is itself a complete sentence.

The use of industrial robots (one cannot foresee their consequences) worries some people today.

If the material in parentheses is written as a separate sentence, however, then punctuate it as you would a separate sentence.

Paula's angry outburst surprised everyone. (She had seemed such a placid person.)

If the material in parentheses comes at the end of a sentence, put the final punctuation after the closing parenthesis.

This company was founded by Willard Manley (1876–1951).

In contrast to dashes, parentheses de-emphasize the material they enclose.

Brackets   In quoted material, brackets [ ] enclose words or phrases that have been added to make the message clearer. They are also used with the word *sic* (Latin for "thus") to point out errors in quoted material.

"This particular company [Zorn Enterprises, Inc.] pioneered in the safe disposal of toxic wastes," the report noted. (The bracketed name is added to the original.)

"[John Chafin's] expertise in science has made him a popular figure on the lecture circuit," his friend stated. (The bracketed name replaces *his* in the original.)

"The principle [*sic*] cause of lung cancer is cigarette smoking," the article declared. (the word *principal* is misspelled "principle" in the original.)

To call attention to an error, follow it immediately with the bracketed *sic*. The reader will then know that the blame rests with the original writer, not with you.

CONNECTED DISCOURSE EXERCISE *Supply any necessary or appropriate colons, dashes, parentheses, and brackets in the following letter:*

[]

Wayout Auto Company

We at Oldfield Sales a subsidiary of Jip, Inc., have had a serious problem with the cars we ordered from your company for leasing to our customers who will probably never return to us again. Two major parts fell off while the cars were sitting in the customers' driveways the exhaust system and the transmission. If this had happened while they were driving thank goodness it didn't, our customers could have been killed. Just imagine what that especially once it got into the newspapers would have done to our business. We must hold you to your claim that "while our cars are the cheepest *sic* on the market, we garnishee *sic* every car we sell." We expect immediate reimbursement for all the cars we purchased from you plus one million dollars to cover the damage to our reputation. A menace, a rip-off, a bad business deal, that's what your cars are. If you don't issue a formal recall for all your vehicles by 530 P.M., Friday, July 23, we will be forced to forward this matter to the federal government.

       Sincerely,

       Ken Swindelle

       Service Manager

EXERCISE *Supply colons, dashes, parentheses, and brackets wherever they are necessary.*

1. Worthington's new house mansion would be a better term has twenty-eight rooms.
2. This resort offers unsurpassed facilities for three winter sports ice skating, skiing, and tobogganing.
3. Two long meetings, a shopping trip, a dinner engagement I've had a busy day!
4. The main parts of the pressure tester include 1 an indicator dial, 2 a hose connection, 3 a damper valve, and 4 a sensing unit.
5. At the tone, the time will be 330 P.M. exactly.
6. The headline stated, "Students Voice They're sic Disapproval of Tuition Hike."
7. "His Charles Darwin's book *On the Origin of Species* touched off a controversy that still continues," the lecturer declared.
8. One major social problem will remain with us for years the need for more affordable housing.

QUOTATION MARKS

Quotation marks (" ") set off direct quotations, titles of short written or broadcast works, subdivisions of books, and expressions singled out for special attention.

Direct Quotations   A direct quotation repeats a speaker's or writer's exact words.

"Tell me about the movie," said Debbie. "If you liked it, I may go myself."

The placement director said, "The recruiter for Procter and Gamble will be on campus next Thursday to interview students for marketing jobs." (spoken comment)

"The trade deficit is expected to reach record levels this year," the *Financial Times* noted. (written comment)

Jackie said the party was "a total flop."

As these sentences show, a comma or period that follows a direct quotation goes inside the quotation marks. When a quotation is a sentence fragment, the comma preceding it is omitted.

When an expression like "he said" interrupts a quoted sentence, use commas to set off the expression. When the expression comes between two complete quoted sentences, use a period after the expression and capitalize the first word of the second sentence.

"Hop in," said Jim. "Let me give you a ride to school."

"Thank you," replied Kelly, opening the car door and sliding into the front seat.

"I can't remember," said Jim, "when we've had a worse winter."

Titles of Short Works and Subdivisions of Books   These short works include magazine articles, essays, short stories, chapters of books, one-act plays, short poems, songs, and television and radio episodes.

> The article was entitled "The Real Conservatism." (article)

> Last night I read John Cheever's "The Enormous Radio," "Torch Song," and "The Swimmer." (short stories)

> Many Stompin' Tom Connors fans consider "Sudbury Saturday Night" to be his greatest piece of music. (song)

> The unsuccessful TV show *Pursued* ended its brief run with a segment titled "Checkmate." (TV episode)

Here, as with direct quotations, a comma or period that follows a title goes inside the quotation marks.

Expressions Singled Out for Special Attention   Writers who wish to call the reader's attention to a word or symbol sometimes put it inside quotation marks.

> The algebraic formula included a "p," a "Q," and a "D."

> "Bonnets" and "lifts" are British terms for car hoods and elevators.

More frequently, however, these expressions are printed in italics (page 639).

Again, any commas and periods that follow expressions set off by quotation marks go inside the marks.

Quotation Marks within Quotation Marks   When a direct quotation or the title of a shorter work appears within a direct quotation, use single quotation marks (' ').

> "I heard the boss telling the foreman, 'Everyone will receive a bonus,'" John said.

> The instructor told the class, "For tomorrow, read Jack Hodgin's 'Separating.'"

Note that the period goes inside both the single and double quotation marks.

Positioning of Semicolons, Colons, and Question Marks   Position semi-colons and colons that come at the end of quoted material *after*, not before, the quotation marks.

> Marcia calls Francine "that greasy grind"; however, I think Marcia is simply jealous of Francine's abilities.

> There are two reasons that I like "Babylon Revisited": the characters are interesting and the writing is excellent.

When a question mark accompanies a quotation, put it outside the quotation marks if the whole sentence rather than the quotation asks the question.

Why did Cedric suddenly shout, "This party is a big bore"?

Put the question mark inside the quotation marks if the quotation, but not the whole sentence, asks a question or if the quotation asks one question and the whole sentence asks another.

Marie asked, "What school is your brother planning to attend?" (The quoted material, not the whole sentence, asks the question.)

Whatever possessed him to ask, "What is the most shameful thing you ever did?" (The whole sentence and the quoted material ask separate questions.)

CONNECTED DISCOURSE EXERCISE *Use quotation marks correctly in the following paragraph.*

Mr. Silver recently lectured our class on Stephen Crane's The Bride Comes to Yellow Sky. One thing we shouldn't forget, Mr. Silver insisted, is that the town is deliberately named Yellow Sky. What is the significance of Crane's choice of the words Yellow Sky? Mr. Silver pointed out a number of possible associations, including cowardice, the setting sun, the open expanse of the West, freedom, and the sand in the concluding passage. The story, Mr. Silver stated, is drenched in colour words. For example, he pointed out, in the first three paragraphs alone Crane mentions vast flats of green grass, brick-coloured hands, new black clothes, and a dress of blue cashmere.

EXERCISE *Supply properly positioned quotation marks wherever they are necessary.*

1. Jeffrey called the novel's plot a hopeless mishmash.
2. I think, said Tom, that I'll go to Niagara Falls for the weekend.
3. What poem has the lines Home is the sailor, home from the sea, / And the hunter home from the hills?
4. Denise tells everyone, I prefer classical music; however, her CD collection includes only hard rock and country music.
5. In his closing argument, the attorney challenged the jury. How would any of us act if accused of a crime we didn't commit?
6. At last my paper is finished, John said happily. Now I can start typing it.
7. Does anyone here know the difference between affect and effect?
8. Why did Neil's wife ask him, How would you like me to dispose of your remains?

HYPHENS

Hyphens (-) are used to join compound adjectives and nouns, compound numbers and word-number combinations, and certain prefixes and suffixes to the words with which they appear. In addition, hyphens help prevent misreadings and awkward combinations of letters or syllables and are used to split words between two lines.

Compound Adjectives   Hyphens are often used to join separate words that function as single adjectives and come before nouns. Typical examples follow:

> Howard is a very *self-contained* person.

> The *greenish-yellow* cloud of chlorine gas drifted toward the village.

> Betty's *devil-may-care* attitude will land her in trouble someday.

When the first word of the compound is an adverb ending in *ly* or when the compound adjective follows the noun it modifies, no hyphen is used.

> The *badly* burned crash victim was rushed to the hospital.

> The colour of the chlorine gas was *greenish yellow.*

When two or more compound adjectives modify the same last term, the sentence flows more smoothly if that term appears just once, after the last item in the series. However, keep the hyphens accompanying the earlier terms in the series.

> Many seventeenth-, eighteenth-, and nineteenth-century costumes are on display in this museum.

Compound Nouns   Hyphenated nouns include such expressions as the following:

> secretary-treasurer   good-for-nothing   sister-in-law   man-about-town

Here is a sentence with a hyphenated noun:

> Denton is *editor-in-chief* of the largest newspaper in this province.

Compound Numbers and Word–Number Combinations   Hyphens are used to separate two-word numbers from twenty-one to ninety-nine and fractions that have been written out.

> Marcy has worked *twenty-five* years for this company.

> *One-quarter* of my income goes for rent.

Similarly, hyphens are used to separate numerals from units of measurement that follow them.

> This chemical is shipped in *200-litre* drums.

Prefixes and Suffixes   A prefix is a word or set of letters that precedes a word and alters its meaning. A suffix is similar but comes at the end of the word. Although most prefixes are not hyphenated, the prefixes *self-* and *all-* do get hyphens, as does the suffix *-elect*. Also the prefix *ex-* is hyphenated when it accompanies a noun.

> This stove has a *self-cleaning* oven.

> Let Claire Voyant, the *all-knowing* soothsayer, read your future in her crystal ball.

> Ethel is the *chairperson-elect* of the club.

> Several *ex-teachers* work in this department.

A prefix used before a capitalized term is always hyphenated.

> The *ex-RCMP* officer gave an interesting talk on the operations of that organization.

Preventing Misreadings and Awkward Combinations of Letters and Syllables   Hyphens help prevent misreadings of certain words and also break up awkward combinations of letters and syllables between certain prefixes and suffixes and their core words.

> The doctor *re-treated* the wound with a new antibiotic. (The hyphen prevents the misreading *retreated*.)

> The company plans to *de-emphasize* sales of agricultural chemicals. (The hyphen prevents the awkward repetition of the letter *e* in *deemphasize*.)

EXERCISE *Supply hyphens wherever they are necessary. If the sentence is correct, write C.*

1. The task of residing the house will take three days.
2. Margaret is the most selfsufficient person that I've ever met.
3. Judge Grimm gave the convicted arsonist a ten to twenty year prison sentence.
4. Nearly three quarters of our chemistry majors go on to graduate school.
5. When I was thirty five years old, I quit my boring job and opened my own small business.
6. Most of my exsoldier friends belong to veterans' organizations.
7. Jeremiah's antigovernment tirades have caused most of his friends to avoid him.
8. The orange red flowers growing next to the house contrasted strongly with the dark grey of its walls.

Capitalization

Capitalize the first word in any sentence, the pronoun *I*, proper nouns and adjectives, titles used with—or in place of—names, and the significant words in literary and artistic titles.

Proper Nouns   A proper noun names one particular person, group of persons, place, or thing. Such nouns include the following:

Persons

Organizations

Racial, political, and religious groups

Countries, provinces and states, cities, and streets

Companies and buildings

Geographical locations and features

Days, months, and holidays

Trademarks

Languages

Ships and aircraft

Abbreviations for academic degrees

Titles used in place of names

The sentences below show the capitalization of proper nouns (in italics):

> *Sigmund* works for the *National Psychoanalytical Institute,* an organization that has done much to advance the science of psychiatry.

> How much does this roll of *Saran Wrap* cost?

> *Gwen Greene* moved to *Paris, France,* when her father became the consul there.

> On *Friday, December* 8, 2006, *Celine Dion* visited our city.

> *Larry* has a master of arts degree, and his sister has a *Ph.D.*

> My father works for the *Ford Motor Company,* but I work for *Chrysler.*

Do not capitalize words such as *institute, college, company,* or *avenue* unless they form part of a proper name. Likewise, do not capitalize the names of educational courses unless they start a sentence, are accompanied by a course number, or designate a language.

> I have a 95 average in *Economics* 112 but only a 73 average in sociology.

> Harry plans to take intermediate *German* in his junior year.

> Do you plan to attend *Queen's University* or some other university?

cap

Proper Adjectives   Adjectives created from proper nouns are called proper adjectives. Like the nouns themselves, they should be capitalized.

Lolita Martinez, our class valedictorian, is of *Spanish* ancestry. (*Spanish* is derived from the proper noun *Spain*.)

Abbreviations   As a general rule, capitalize abbreviations only if the words they stand for are capitalized.

Milton DeWitt works for the *NDP*. (*NDP* is capitalized because *New Democratic Party* would be.)

The flask holds 1500 *ml* of liquid. (The abbreviation *ml* is not capitalized because *millilitres* would not be.)

A few abbreviations are capitalized even though all or some of the words they stand for aren't. Examples include TV (television) and CD (compact disc). Others are shown on the next page.

Personal Titles   Capitalize a personal title if it precedes a name or is used in place of a name. Otherwise, do not capitalize.

cap

The division is under the command of *General* Arnold Schafer.

Tell me, *Doctor,* do I need an operation?

The *dean* of our engineering division is Dr. Alma Haskins.

Many writers capitalize titles of high rank when they are used in place of names.

The *Prime Minister* will sign this bill tomorrow.

The *prime minister* will sign this bill tomorrow.

Either usage is acceptable.

Titles of Literary and Artistic Works   When citing the titles of publications, pieces of writing, movies, television programs, paintings, sculptures, and the like, capitalize the first and last words and all other words except *a, an, the,* coordinating conjunctions, and prepositions.

Last week I played *Gone with the Wind* on my DVD player and read Patricia Cornwell's *Book of the Dead.* (the preposition *with,* the article *the,* and the preposition *of* are not capitalized.)

John is reading a book called *The Movies of Abbott and Costello.* (The preposition *of* and the coordinating conjunction *and* are not capitalized.)

Although I'm no TV addict, I watched every episode of *The Red Green Show.* (All of the words in the title are capitalized.)

Note that the titles of literary and artistic works are italicized. If you don't have access to italic print on your computer, underline the titles.

EXERCISE *Identify any word or abbreviation that should be capitalized in the following sentences:*

1. The recipe for this stew comes from *the canadian family cookbook.*
2. My cousin has accepted a job with the federal national mortgage association and will move to ottawa, ont., in july.
3. The announcement said that sergeant brockway had received a second lieutenant's commission.
4. The newest municipal judge in boyle city is judge martha berkowicz.
5. Unless sales increase markedly in the next quarter, the delta corporation will be forced into bankruptcy.
6. We need to buy some shreddies, mum.
7. What are your postretirement plans, professor?

ABBREVIATIONS

ab

Items that are abbreviated include certain personal titles, names of organizations and agencies, Latin terms, and specific and technical terms.

Personal Titles   Abbreviate *Mister, Doctor,* and similar titles when they come just ahead of a name, and *Junior, Senior,* and degree titles when they follow names.

> Will *Mr.* Harry Babbitt please come to the front desk?

> Arthur Compton, *Sr.,* is a well-known historian; his son, Arthur Compton, *Jr.,* is a television producer.

> This article on marital discord was written by Irma Quarles, Ph.D.

Names of Organizations and Agencies   Many organizations and agencies are known primarily by their initials rather than their full names, for example

CAA	CTV	NATO	WHO
CARE	IMF	SPCA	WTO
CMA	IRA	UNESCO	CRTC

Latin Terms   Certain Latin terms are always abbreviated; others are abbreviated when used with dates or times.

e.g. (*exempli gratia:* for example)
i.e. (*id est:* that is)
etc. (*et cetera:* and [the] others)
vs. or v. (*versus:* against)
a.m. or A.M. (*ante meridiem:* before noon)
p.m. or P.M. (*post meridiem:* after noon)

The play starts at 8 P.M.

Many writers (*e.g.,* Dylan Thomas and Malcolm Lowry) have had serious problems with alcohol.

Scientific and Technical Terms   For brevity's sake, scientists and technicians abbreviate terms of measurement that repeatedly occur. Terms that the reader would not know are written out the first time they are used, and they are accompanied by their abbreviation in parentheses. Unfamiliar organizations and agencies that are mentioned repeatedly are handled in like manner.

The viscosity of the fluid measured 15 centistokes (cs) at room temperature.

Common practice calls for writing such abbreviations without periods unless they duplicate the spelling of some word.

Standard dictionaries list common abbreviations. When you don't recognize one, look it up. Use abbreviations sparingly in essays. If you're unsure about what is appropriate, don't abbreviate.

num

EXERCISE *Supply abbreviations wherever they are necessary or are customarily used.*

1. The conference on poverty in the twenty-first century will be chaired by Donald Frump, Doctor of Philosophy.
2. When writing, don't use Latin terms such as *id est* and *exempli gratia* except as comments in parentheses and footnotes.
3. The United Nations Educational, Scientific, and Cultural Organization sponsors programs in primary education throughout developing countries.
4. My physics instructor, Doctor Seth Greenfield, Junior, has just completed a textbook on optics.
5. The thermometer on my front porch says that the temperature is 19° Celsius.
6. At 10:20 *ante meridiem,* the local TV station announced that a tornado had been sighted near Leesville.
7. This fall, the Columbia Broadcasting System will air nine new sitcoms.
8. Which would you prefer, Mister Bartleby, tea or coffee?

NUMBERS

Some instructors ask their students to express numbers larger than ninety-nine as figures and to spell out smaller numbers.

Banff is *100* kilometres from here.

Banff is *ninety-nine* kilometres from here.

Other instructors prefer that students switch to figures beginning with the number ten.

My son will be *nine* years old on his next birthday.

My son will be *10* years old on his next birthday.

With either practice, the following exceptions apply.

Numbers in a Series   Write all numbers in a series the same way regardless of their size.

Gatsby has *64* suits, *110* shirts, and *214* ties.

In just one hour the emergency room personnel handled *two* stabbings, *five* shootings, and *sixteen* fractures.

We have *150* salespeople, *51* engineers, and *7* laboratory technicians.

Dates   Use figures for dates that include the year.

February *14, 2005* (not February 14th, 2005)

When the date includes the day but not the year, you may use figures or spell out the number.

June 9

June ninth

the ninth of June

Page Numbers and Addresses   Use figures for page numbers and street numbers in addresses.

Check the graph on page *415.*

I live at *111* Cornelia Street, and my office is at *620* Victoria Avenue.

Numbers Beginning Sentences   Spell out any number that begins a sentence. If this requires three or more words, rephrase the sentence so that the number comes after the opening and numerals can be used.

The year *2004* was a good year for this wine.

Sixty thousand fans jammed the stadium.

An army of *265 000* troops assaulted the city. (If this number began the sentence, five words—an excessive number—would be needed to write it out.)

Decimals, Percentages, Times   Use figures for decimals and percentages as well as for expressions of time that are accompanied by A.M. or P.M.

The shaft has a *0.37*-millimetre diameter.

Last year the value of my house jumped *25* percent.

The plane leaves here at *9:50* A.M. and reaches Winnipeg at *2:30* P.M.

num

One Number Following Another   When two numbers directly follow each other (such as a quantity number followed by a measurement number), spell out the first number if it is smaller than 100, and use numerals for the second one. If the first number is larger than 100, use numerals for it and spell out the second one.

We ordered *six 100-*litre drums of solvent for the project.

The supplier shipped us *600 hundred-*litre drums by mistake.

EXERCISE *Identify any miswriting of numbers in the following sentences and rewrite these numbers correctly:*

1. 50 000 people ride this city's buses each day.
2. The article on page fifty-nine of this week's issue of *Maclean's* discusses Alanis Morissette's latest CD.
3. Next Saturday at one-thirty P.M., the city will test its emergency warning sirens.
4. My grandparents' golden wedding anniversary was July seventeen, two thousand nine.
5. Mildred has 500 books, two hundred CDs, and fifty-five DVDs.
6. It is not uncommon for credit-card holders to pay interest rates of eighteen percent or more.
7. Laura's plane will leave for Halifax at two-thirty P.M. on May the sixteenth.
8. The thickness of this piece needs to be increased by fifteen hundredths of a centimetre.

Italics

Italics are used for the titles of longer publications, the names of vehicles and vessels, foreign words and phrases, and expressions singled out for special attention. Sometimes underlining is used as an alternative to italics.

Titles of Longer Publications and Artistic Works   These items may include the following:

books	record albums	long musical works and poems
magazines	paintings	plays
newspapers	movies	sculptures

As noted on page 629, quotation marks are used for the titles of *short* pieces—articles, short stories, short poems, and one-act plays. Longer, full-length works always take italics.

Last night I finished Michael Ondaatje's *The English Patient* and read two articles in *Geist.* (book, magazine)

Michelangelo's *David* is surely one of the world's greatest sculptures. (sculpture)

The Globe and Mail had praise for the revival of Tomson Highway's *The Rez Sisters*. (newspaper, play)

Stephen Vincent Benét's poem *John Brown's Body* won a Pulitzer Prize in 1929. (book-length poem)

Do not use italics when naming the Bible, Koran, Torah, other scriptural books, or any of their chapters.

Joanna's favourite book of the Bible is the Book of Ecclesiastes, part of the Old Testament.

Names of Vehicles and Vessels   Names of particular airplanes, ships, trains, and spacecraft are italicized.

The plane in which Charles Lindbergh flew over the Atlantic Ocean was named *The Spirit of St. Louis*.

Foreign Expressions   Use italics to identify foreign words and phrases that have not yet made their way into the English language.

The writer has a terribly pessimistic *weltanschauung*. (philosophy of life)

This season, long skirts are the *dernier cri*. (the latest thing)

When such expressions become completely assimilated, the italics are dropped. Most dictionaries use an asterisk (*), a dagger (†), or other symbol to identify expressions that need italicizing.

Expressions Singled Out for Special Attention   These expressions include words, letters, numerals, and symbols.

The Greek letter *pi* is written π.

I can't tell whether this letter is meant to be an *a* or an *o* or this number a *7* or a *9*.

In England, the word *lorry* means truck.

As noted on page 629, quotation marks can replace italics for this purpose.

ital

CONNECTED DISCOURSE EXERCISE *Use hyphens, capitalization, abbreviations, numbers, and italics properly in the following passage.*

Because I can speak Russian fluently, I was recruited by the central intelligence agency while still at Boston college. I suspected that it was professor Hogsbottom, a Political Science teacher, who had suggested that they consider me. After all, he had been a General during World War II and still had connections with the intelligence community. It turned out that my brother in law was responsible; he was an ex FBI agent. Soon I was an american spy located, of all places, in England. Who would suspect that we had to spy on the english? For 3 years I posed as a british aristocrat who was a general bon vivant and man about town. I went by the alias of Mister Henry Higgins, Junior. Everyone, of course, wanted to know if I had seen My Fair Lady. Personally I thought the whole thing was a monty python type of joke until I found a position in the british secret service. Who could have believed the british kept so many secrets from their american allies? For twenty one years I spied on the british without anyone suspecting that I was an all american boy. I did find out recently, however, that because of my fluent russian they had suspected me of being a russian spy and had been feeding me false information all along.

EXERCISE *Supply italics wherever they are necessary.*

1. To keep abreast of the business news, I read both Investor's Daily and Forbes.
2. Next week, Boris is taking the Siberian Express to Irkutsk, Siberia.
3. Of all my art prints, I like Erte's Fishbowl best.
4. There are few artistic statements against war as powerful as Picasso's Guernica.
5. My uncle served on the cruiser Indianapolis during World War II.
6. Because Pam lost her brother's copy of Moby Dick, she bought him a new one.
7. Sometimes when I try to print a b I make a d instead.
8. In Scotland, the term lum refers to a chimney.

"Why the big deal about accurate spelling?"

"Does it really make that much difference if I have an *i* and an *e* turned around or if I omit a letter when spelling a word?"

Students frequently question the importance of proper spelling. Perhaps the answer is suggested by the following sentence, taken from a student essay:

Children's video games are far too violet.

The omission of an *n* in *violet* makes this writer's criticism of video games sound absurd. Not only does inaccurate spelling suggest carelessness, but also it sometimes drastically alters meaning.

While there is no sure way of becoming a good speller, you can minimize difficulties by learning basic spelling rules, applying helpful spelling tips, and memorizing the proper spelling of troublesome words.

SPELLING RULES

The following four rules should ease many spelling pains.

Rule 1   If a word has the double vowels *ie* or *ei* and the combination has a long *e* sound (as in *me*), use *ie* except after *c*. If the combination has an *a* sound, use *ei*.

ie (as long *e*)	*ei* after *c*	*ei* (as *a*)
relieve	deceive	freight
belief	receive	neighbour
grieve	receipt	reign
piece	perceive	weigh

The main exceptions to this rule include *either, financier, leisure, neither, seize, species,* and *weird*.

Rule 2   If a one-syllable word (example: *sin*) ends in a single consonant preceded by a single vowel, double the consonant before adding a suffix that starts with a vowel. Apply the same rule to a word of two or more syllables: If the final syllable is accented (example: *admit, prefer*) and ends with a single consonant preceded by a vowel, or if the final consonant is *l, p, s,* or *t* (example: *travel*), double the final consonant.

Words with Single Syllables	Words with Two or More Syllables
rig—rigged	admit—admittance
sin—sinned	control—controller
stop—stopping	equip—equipped
counsel—counsellor	

sp

If the accent does not fall on the last syllable, do not double the final -consonant.

audit—audited   chatter—chattered   simmer—simmering

Rule 3   If a word ends in *y* preceded by a single consonant, change the *y* to an *i* unless you are adding the suffix *-ing*.

y changed to *i*	*y* retained
beauty—beautiful	copy—copying
fury—furious	defy—defying
easy—easily	dry—drying
vary—various	vary—varying

Rule 4   If a word ends in a silent *e*, the *e* is usually dropped when a suffix starting with a vowel is added.

blue—bluish   fame—famous
dense—density   grieve—grievous

In a few cases, the *e* is retained to avoid pronunciation difficulties or confusion with other words.

dye—dyeing (not dying)   singe—singeing (not singing)
shoe—shoeing (not shoing)

The *e* is also retained when it is preceded by a soft *c* sound (pronounced like the letter *s*) or a soft *g* sound (pronounced like the letter *j*) and the suffix being added starts with an *a* or an *o*.

peace—peaceable   courage—courageous
change—changeable   manage—manageable

HELPFUL SPELLING TIPS

Here are some tips that can further improve your spelling:

1. Examine each problem word carefully, especially prefixes (*im*probable, *intra*venous), suffixes (superintend*ent*, descend*ant*), and double consonants (sate*ll*ite, roo*mm*ate, and co*ll*apsible).
2. Sound out each syllable carefully, noting its pronunciation. Words such as *height, governor,* and *candidate* are often misspelled because of improper pronunciation.
3. Make a list of your problem words and review them periodically. Concentrate on each syllable and any unusual features (ar*c*tic, ambig*uous*).
4. Use any crutches that will help: There is *gain* in *bargain;* to *breakfast* is to *break a fast;* a disease causes *dis-ease.*
5. When you copy anything from a blackboard or textbook, copy it carefully. Writing a word correctly helps you to spell it correctly the next time.
6. Buy a good dictionary and look up the words you don't know how to spell (See page 117 for more information on dictionaries.)

7. Use the spell checker of your word processor, but double-check the suggested corrections. Spell checkers often use non-Canadian spellings, confuse parts of speech, and can't differentiate among homophones (e.g., *there, their, they're*).

LIST OF TROUBLESOME WORDS

Students frequently misspell the words in the following list. Study these words carefully until the correct spelling becomes automatic. Then ask a friend to read them to you while you write them down. Tag the ones you misspell, and whenever you revise a paper, check for these words.

abandoned	alley(s)	bachelor	chauffeur
abbreviate	allot	balance	chief
absence	allotted	balloon	colloquial
absorb	allowed	barbarous	colonel
absorption	all right	barbiturate	column
absurd	already	beautiful	commission
academy	although	beggar	commit
accelerate	altogether	believe	commitment
accept	always	beneficial	committed
access	amateur	benefit	committee
accessible	ambiguous	benefited	committing
accident	among	biscuit	comparatively
accidentally	analysis analyses	boundary	competent
accommodate	analyze	bourgeois	competition
accomplish	anonymous	breathe (v.)	concede
accumulate	anxiety	Britain	conceive
accustom	apartment	bulletin	condemn
achieve	apparent	bureau	condescend
achievement	appearance	bureaucracy	confident
acknowledge	appreciate	business	congratulations
acknowledgment	appropriate	cafeteria	connoisseur
acquaintance	architecture	calendar	conqueror
acquire	arctic	camouflage	conscience
acquit	argue	campaign	conscientious
acquitted	arguing	candidate	conscious
address	argument	carburetor	consistency
advice (n.)	arithmetic	carriage	consistent
advise (v.)	ascent	carrying	conspicuous
aerial	assassin	casual	contemptible
aggravate	assent	category	continuous
aggravated	assistance	causal	controversy
aggression	assistant	ceiling	convenience
aggressive	athlete	cellar	convenient
aging	athletics	cemetery	coolly
alcohol	attempt	changeable	cooperate
allege	attendance	changing	corollary
alleviate	average	characteristic	corps

sp

corpse	emphasis	hygiene	medieval
correlate	employee	hypocrisy	mediocre
counterfeit	engineer	hysterical	melancholy
courteous	enthusiastic	illiterate	miniature
criticism	environment	illogical	minute
criticize	equal	illusion	miscellaneous
cruelty	equip	immediate	mischievous
curiosity	equipment	implement	misspell
curriculum	equipped	impromptu	modifies
dealt	equivalent	inadequate	modify
deceit	especially	incident	modifying
deceive	exaggerate	incidentally	moral
decent	exceed	independent	morale
decision	excellent	indict	mortgage
defence	except	indispensable	mosquitoes
defendant	excerpt	individual	muscle
definite	excess	inevitable	mysterious
definitely	excitement	infinitely	necessary
dependent	exercise	ingenious	neither
descendant	existence	ingenuous	nevertheless
descent	experience	innocent	niece
describe	extraordinary	intelligent	noticeable
description	extremely	interest	obedience
desert	fallacy	interfere	occasion
desirable	familiar	irresistible	occasionally
despair	fascinate	irresponsible	occur
desperate	fascist	jeopardy	occurred
dessert	February	judgment	occurrence
develop	fiery	judicial	occurring
development	finally	knowledge	official
difference	financier	knowledgeable	omission
dilemma	foreign	laboratory	omit
disappear	foreword	legitimate	omitted
disastrous	forfeit	leisure	omitting
discernible	forward	library	opinion
disciple	friend	licence (n.)	opponent
discipline	fulfill	license (v.)	opportunity
discussion	gaiety	lightning	optimistic
disease	gases	loneliness	original
dissatisfied	gauge	loose	outrageous
dissipate	genius	lose	pamphlet
dominant	genuine	magnificent	parallel
drunkenness	government	maintain	paralysis
echoes	grammar	maintenance	parliament
ecstasy	guarantee	manoeuvre	particularly
efficiency	guard	manual	pastime
efficient	handkerchief	marriage	patent
eighth	harass	mathematics	peaceable
eligible	height	mattress	perceive
eliminate	heroes	meant	perfectible
embarrass	hindrance	medicine	perform

permanent
permissible
perseverance
persuade
physical
physician
picnic
picnicked
playwright
pleasant
pleasurable
politician
possess
possession
possible
potatoes
practice (n.)
practise (v.)
precede
precedent
precious
predominant
preference
preferred
prejudice
preparation
privilege
probably
procedure
proceed
professor
prominent
pronounce
pronunciation
propaganda
propagate
propeller
prophecy (n.)
prophesy (v.)
prostate
prostrate
protein
psychiatry
psychology
pursue
pursuit
quantity
questionnaire
quiet
quite
quiz

quizzes
realize
receipt
receive
recipe
recognizable
recommend
refer
reference
referring
reign
relevant
relieve
religious
remembrance
reminisce
reminiscence
reminiscent
rendezvous
repellent
repentance
repetition
representative
resemblance
resistance
restaurant
rhetoric
rhyme
rhythm
roommate
sacrifice
sacrilege
sacrilegious
safety
salary
sandwich
scarcely
scene
scenic
schedule
science
secretary
seize
sensible
separate
sergeant
severely
siege
similar
simultaneous
sincerely

skeptical
skiing
skilful (skillful)
skis
society
sophomore
source
specifically
specimen
sponsor
spontaneous
statistics
steely
strategy
studying
subtle
subtlety
subtly
succeed
success
successful
succinct
suffrage
superintendent
supersede
suppose
suppress
surprise
syllable
symmetry
sympathize
synonym
synonymous
tangible
tariff
technical
technique
temperament
temperature
temporary
tenant
tendency
thorough
thought
through
traffic
trafficking
tragedy
tranquillity
transcendent
transcendental

transfer
transferred
transferring
translate
tries
truly
twelfth
tyrannical
tyranny
unanimous
unconscious
undoubtedly
unmistakable
unnecessary
until
unwieldy
urban
urbane
usage
useful
using
usual
usually
vacancy
vacillate
vacuum
valuable
vegetable
vengeance
victorious
village
villain
waive
warrant
warring
weather
Wednesday
weird
whether
whole
wholly
wield
wintry
wiry
worshipped
wreak
wreck
writing
written
yield

sp

The English language has many words and expressions that confuse writers and thereby lessen the precision and effectiveness of their writing. These troublesome items include the following:

Word pairs that sound alike or almost alike but are spelled differently and have different meanings

Word pairs that do not sound alike but still are often confused

Words or phrases that are unacceptable in formal writing

The following glossary identifies the most common of these troublemakers. Familiarize yourself with its contents. Then consult it as you revise your writing if you have even the slightest doubt about the proper use of a word, phrase, or expression.

a, an   Use *a* with words beginning with a consonant sound (even if the first written letter is a vowel); use *an* with words beginning with a vowel sound.

a brush, *a* student, *a* wheel, *a* risky situation, *a* once-in-a-lifetime opportunity

an architect, *an* apple, *an* unworthy participant, *an* interesting proposal, *an* honest politician

accept, except   *Accept* is a verb meaning "to receive" or "to approve." *Except* is used as a verb or a preposition. As a verb, *except* means "to take out, exclude, or omit." As a preposition, it means "excluding," "other than," or "but not."

She *accepted* the bouquet of flowers.

Linda *excepted* Sally from the list of guests. (verb)

All of Linda's friends *except* Sally came to the party. (preposition)

access, excess   *Access* is a noun meaning "means or right to enter, approach, or use." In the computer field, it is a verb meaning "gain entrance to." *Excess* is an adjective meaning "too much; more than needed; lack of moderation."

I have *access* to a summer cottage this weekend.

The code permits users to *access* the computer.

The airline booked an *excess* number of passengers on that flight.

adapt, adopt   To *adapt* is "to adjust," often by modification. To *adopt* is "to take as one's own."

He *adapted* to the higher elevations of the Rocky Mountains.

She *adopted* the new doctrine expounded by the prophet.

advice, advise   *Advice* is a noun meaning "a recommendation about how to deal with a situation or problem." *Advise* is a verb meaning "to recommend or warn."

The young man followed his sister's *advice*.

Mr. Smith *advised* John to buy 10 000 shares of the stock.

affect, effect   Although both words may function as nouns and verbs, usually *affect* is a verb and *effect* is a noun. The verb *affect* means "to influence, cause a change in, or arouse the emotions of." The noun *affect* is a technical term in psychology and refers to feeling. The noun *effect* means "result or outcome." The verb *effect* means "to bring about or achieve."

His speech *affected* me greatly. (verb)

The *effect* of the announcement was felt immediately. (noun)

The doctor was soon able to *effect* a cure. (verb)

aggravate   *Aggravate* is a verb meaning "to intensify or make worse" an existing situation. The use of *aggravate* to mean "annoy" or "anger" is colloquial.

Colloquial	Susan's behaviour at the dance really *aggravated* me.
Standard	Marcy's interference only *aggravated* the conflict between Bill and Nadine.

all ready, already   *All ready* means "completely prepared" or "everyone is ready." *Already* means "previously, even now, even then."

The scouts are *all ready* for the camp out.

When we arrived we found he had *already* gone.

The report is *already* a week overdue.

all right, alright   *Alright* is a nonstandard spelling of *all right* and is not acceptable in formal writing.

all together, altogether   *All together* means "all in one place" or "in unison." *Altogether* is an adverb meaning "completely, entirely."

The family was *all together* at the wedding.

All together, push!

Mr. Doe is *altogether* at fault for writing the letter.

allusion, delusion, illusion   An *allusion* is an indirect reference. A *delusion* is a mistaken belief, often part of a psychological condition. An *illusion* is a deceptive appearance presented to the sight or created by the imagination.

In his lecture, the professor made many *allusions* to *The Odyssey*.

He suffers from the *delusion* that he is a millionaire.

They wore makeup to give the *illusion* of beauty.

a lot, alot   *Alot* is an erroneous spelling of the two words *a lot*. The phrase *a lot* is usually colloquial; in formal writing replace it with *many*.

usage

already　See *all ready, already.*

alright　See *all right, alright.*

alternately, alternatively　*Alternately* means "occurring by turns, one after the other." *Alternatively* means "providing a choice between two items."

> The American flag has seven red and six white stripes, arranged *alternately.*

> Highway 44 offers the most direct route to Junction City. *Alternatively,* Highway 88 is much more scenic.

altogether　See *all together, altogether.*

among, between　Use *between* when referring to two things and *among* when referring to more than two.

> He divided the candy *between* Allan and Stephanie.

> He divided the candy *among* the five children.

amoral, immoral　*Amoral* means "neither moral nor immoral; morally neutral." *Immoral* means "contrary to the moral code."

> The movie, which takes no clear position on the behaviour it depicts, seems curiously *amoral.*

> Murder is an *immoral* act.

amount, number　*Amount* refers to total quantities, things in bulk, or weight. *Number* refers to countable things. Never use *amount* when referring to people.

> Cassandra inherited a large *amount* of money.

> Cassandra now has a large *number* of friends.

an, a　See *a, an.*

and/or　Although often used in commercial and legal documents, this combination should be avoided in other writing.

angry, mad　*Mad* means "insane," although it is often used colloquially to mean "annoyed" or "angry." To be precise, use *mad* only to mean insane.

> *Colloquial*　I was *mad* at Serena.

> *Standard*　I was *angry* with Serena.

around　*Around* is colloquial use for "approximately" or "about."

> *Colloquial*　She arrived *around* 10:00 P.M.

> 　　　　　　The blouse cost *around* $35.

> *Standard*　She arrived at *approximately* 10:00 P.M.

> 　　　　　　The blouse cost *about* $35.

as   *As* is frequently used as a weak substitute for *because, since, when,* and *while.*

Weak	She ran out of the house *as* it was on fire.
Better	She ran out of the house *because* it was on fire.

as, like   *As* may be used as a conjunction that introduces an adverb clause, but *like* should not be used this way.

Unacceptable	*Like* my father always said, "You can fool some of the people all of the time."
Standard	*As* my father always said, "You can fool some of the people all of the time."

However, *like* may be used as a preposition.

In times *like* this, it's hard not to despair.

Any woman *like* Jennifer can expect a successful career in business.

assure, ensure, insure   To *assure* is "to make safe from risk, to guarantee" or "to convince." *Ensure* and *insure* can be variant spellings meaning "to make certain." *Insure,* however, is now generally associated with the business of insurance.

The counsellor tried to *assure* the students that they had made a wise choice.

The captain *assured* them that they would be rescued.

The father, wanting to *ensure* his son's higher education, applied for a federally *insured* loan.

awhile, a while   *A while,* consisting of the noun *while* and the article *a,* means "a period of time." *Awhile* is an adverb meaning "for a short time."

Dinner will be served in *a while.*

Sit *awhile* and tell me the latest gossip.

bad, badly   *Bad* is an adjective. *Badly* is an adverb. *Badly* is colloquial when used to mean "very much."

Unacceptable	She feels *badly* about her mistake.
	Tom behaved *bad* at the circus.
Colloquial	I want a new car *badly.*
Standard	She feels *bad* about her mistake. (adjective as subject complement)
	Tom behaved *badly* at the circus. (adverb)
	I want a new car *very much.*

beside, besides   Both words are prepositions, but they have different meanings. *Beside* means "at the side of," and *besides* means "in addition to."

Sheila and Bill sat *beside* the trailer to eat their lunch.

Besides Harvey, Seymour is coming to dinner.

between   See *among, between.*

breath, breathe   *Breath* is a noun and *breathe* is its verb counterpart.

Nicole stepped outside the stuffy cabin for a *breath* of fresh air.

The cabin was so stuffy that Nicole could hardly *breathe.*

broke   *Broke,* when used to mean "without money," is colloquial.

Colloquial   Because Shelley was *broke,* she had to miss the movie.

Standard   Because Shelley *had no money,* she had to miss the movie.

can, may   *Can* refers both to permission and to the ability to do something, while *may* refers to permission only.

I think I *can* pass the exam on Friday. (ability)

My mother says I *can* go to the movies. (permission)

When used to denote permission, *can* lends a less formal air to writing than does *may.*

cannot, can not   The use of *cannot* is preferred unless the writer wishes to italicize the *not* for emphasis.

You *cannot* expect a raise this year.

No, you can *not* expect a raise this year.

can't help but   In formal writing, this colloquial phrase should be revised to the simpler I *can't help* or *I cannot help.*

Colloquial   I *can't help but* wish that I were going to the concert.

Standard   I *can't help* wishing that I were going to the concert.

capital, capitol   *Capital* means "a city that serves as a seat of government." *Capitol* means "a building in which a legislature meets" in the U.S. or "the building in which Congress meets."

Winnipeg is the *capital* of Manitoba.

The *capitol* in Washington is popular with visitors.

Capital can also refer to wealth or assets, to an offence punishable by death, or to something excellent or first-rate.

My *capital* consists entirely of stocks and bonds.

Canada does not have *capital* punishment

That's a *capital* suggestion!

childish, childlike   Both of these terms mean "like a child." *Childish,* however, has a negative connotation.

He is fifty-two years old, but he behaves in a *childish* manner.

Jon's face has a *childlike* quality that everyone likes immediately.

cite, sight, site   *Cite* means "to mention or quote as an example," *sight* means "to see" or "a view," and *site* means "a location."

Cheryl *cited* E. J. Pratt's *Towards the Last Spike* in her talk.

He was able to *sight* the enemy destroyers through the periscope.

The building *site* is a woody area south of town.

complement, compliment   Both words can act as nouns or verbs. As a noun, c*omplement* means "something that completes or makes up the whole." As a verb, it means "to complete or perfect." As a noun, *compliment* means "a flattering or praising remark." As a verb, it means "to flatter or praise."

A *complement* of navy personnel boarded the foreign freighter. (noun)

This fruit will *complement* the meal nicely. (verb)

Scott paid Sara Jane a lovely *compliment* at the time of her graduation. (noun)

My mother *complimented* me for cleaning my room. (verb)

conscience, conscious   *Conscience* refers to the sense of moral right or wrong. *Conscious* refers to the awareness of one's feelings or thoughts.

Edgar's *conscience* forced him to return the money.

Basil was not *conscious* of his angry feelings.

Do not confuse *conscious* with *aware;* although these words are similar in meaning, one is *conscious* of feelings or actions but *aware* of events.

contemptible, contemptuous   *Contemptible* means "deserving of contempt." *Contemptuous* means "displaying contempt."

Peter's drunkenness is *contemptible*.

Mary is *contemptuous* of Peter's drunkenness.

could have, could of   *Could of* is an unacceptable substitute for *could have* because a preposition cannot substitute for a verb.

> *Unacceptable*   I *could of* gone with my parents to Portugal.

> *Standard*   I *could have* gone with my parents to Portugal.

council, counsel   A *council* is a group of people that governs or advises. *Counsel* can be used as both a noun and a verb. The noun means "advice," and the verb means "to advise."

The city *council* meets on the second Tuesday of every month.

The lawyer's *counsel* was sound. (noun)

The psychologist *counsels* many abused children. (verb)

couple   *Couple* denotes two things and should not be used to refer to more than that number.

criteria, criterion   *Criterion* is always singular, *criteria* always plural.

>   The primary *criterion* for performing this job is manual dexterity.

>   Manual dexterity is but one of many *criteria* on which you will be judged.

data   *Data* is the plural of *datum*. Although *data* is sometimes used with a singular verb, this use is considered incorrect.

>   *Standard*   These *data* are incorrect.

>   *Unacceptable*   This *data* is incorrect.

delusion   See *allusion, delusion, illusion.*

desert, deserts, dessert   *Desert* is land that is arid. With the accent on the last syllable, it is a verb meaning "to abandon." *Deserts* means "that which is deserved." *Dessert* is food served after dinner.

>   The Sonoran *desert* is full of plant life.

>   You'll get your just *deserts* if you *desert* me now.

>   They had cheesecake for *dessert* every Thursday night.

different from, different than   *Different from* is preferred to *different than.*

>   His ideas on marriage were *different from* those of his wife.

Different than is accepted, however, when a clause follows and the *from* construction would be wordy.

>   *Acceptable*   Fiona looks *different than* she did last summer.

>   *Wordy*   Fiona looks *different from* the way she looked last summer.

discreet, discrete   To be *discreet* means to be "prudent, tactful, or careful of one's actions." *Discrete* means "distinct or separate."

>   Jack was always *discreet* when he talked to his grandparents.

>   When two atoms of hydrogen combine with one atom of oxygen, they are no longer *discrete* entities.

disinterested, uninterested   A person who is *disinterested* is impartial or unbiased. A person who is *uninterested* is indifferent or not interested.

>   We need a *disinterested* judge to settle the dispute.

>   Joe is completely *uninterested* in sports.

due to   *Due to* has always been acceptable following a linking verb.

>   Her success was *due to* hard work.

Purists, however, object to *due to* when it is used in other situations, especially in introductory phrases.

Due to the many requests we have had, not everyone who wishes tickets will receive them.

In such cases, you may wish to recast the sentence.

Because we have had so many requests, not everyone who wishes tickets will receive them.

effect   See *affect, effect.*

e.g.   This abbreviation, from the Latin *exempli gratia,* means "for example." Avoid using it except in comments in parentheses and in footnotes.

elicit, illicit   *Elicit* is a verb that means "to draw forth." *Illicit* is an adjective meaning "not permitted."

A good professor can always *elicit* responses from students.

He was engaged in many types of *illicit* activities.

emigrate, immigrate   When people *emigrate,* they move out of a country. When people *immigrate,* they move into a country.

The family *emigrated* from Poland.

Many Russians *immigrated* to Canada.

ensure   See *assure, ensure, insure.*

enthused, enthusiastic   *Enthused* is a colloquial word and should not be used in place of *enthusiastic.*

Colloquial	John was *enthused* about the prospects for jobs in his hometown.
Standard	John was *enthusiastic* about the prospects for jobs in his hometown.

especially, specially   The term *especially* means "particularly, notably." *Specially* means "for a specific purpose."

He is an *especially* talented pianist.

He was *specially* chosen to represent his group.

et al.   This expression, from the Latin *et alia,* means "and others," referring to people. Ordinarily, the abbreviation should be used only in footnotes and bibliographic entries.

etc.   This abbreviation, from the Latin *et cetera,* means "and other things" and is used in reference to objects rather than people. It should be avoided except in comments in parentheses or in footnotes. It should never be preceded by *and.*

everyone, every one   *Everyone* means "every person." *Every one* means "every particular person or thing."

usage

Everyone who wants to go to the ball game should let me know today.

If you carefully check *every one* of your paragraphs, you can improve your writing.

except   See *accept, except.*

excess   See *access, excess.*

explicit, implicit   *Explicit* means "clearly expressed" or "straightforward." *Implicit* means "implied" or "understood without direct statement."

You must state your needs *explicitly* if you want them fulfilled.

When I took on the project, I made an *implicit* commitment to see it through.

farther, further   The traditional distinction is that *farther* refers to physical distance and *further* to distance in time. Only *further* should be used to mean "additional" or "additionally."

In the race for the Muscular Dystrophy Association, Janet ran *farther* than Cindy.

If you think *further* on the matter, I am certain we can reach an agreement.

Let me make one *further* point.

fewer, less   *Fewer* refers to countable items. *Less* refers to quantity or degree.

Mrs. Smith has *fewer* dogs than cats.

There is *less* money in Joan's chequing account than in Stanley's.

Jack was *less* ambitious in his later years.

Never use *less* to refer to people.

Unacceptable   *Less* people were there than I expected.

Standard   *Fewer* people were there than I expected.

formally, formerly   *Formally* means "according to established forms, conventions, and rules; ceremoniously." *Formerly* means "in the past."

The ambassador *formally* greeted his dinner guests.

Formerly, smallpox was one of our most serious diseases.

funny   *Funny* refers to something that is amusing. In formal writing it should not be used to mean "odd" or "unusual."

Colloquial   I felt *funny* visiting my old Grade 4 classroom.

Standard   I felt *odd* visiting my old Grade 4 classroom.

further   See *farther, further.*

get   *Get*, in any of its many colloquial senses, should not be used in writing.

Colloquial	Her way of looking at a man really *gets* me.
	I'll *get* him if it's the last thing I do.
Standard	Beth will *get* at least a *B* in this course.

good, well Do not mistakenly use *good* as an adverb when an adjective is required.

Unacceptable	John did *good* on his first test.
Standard	John is making *good* progress on his report.
	John is a *good* student.

Well can be used as an adjective meaning "in good health." Otherwise it should always be used as an adverb.

Last week I had a bad cold, but now I am *well*. (adjective)

John did *well* on his first test. (adverb)

got, gotten Both are acceptable past-participle forms of the verb *to get*.

hanged, hung People may be *hanged*. Objects may be *hung*.

The prisoner was *hanged* at noon.

Mavis *hung* the picture in the dining room.

hopefully *Hopefully* means "in a hopeful manner." In informal speaking, it is used to mean "it is hoped" or "I hope," but this usage is not correct in formal writing. (Compare this with *carefully*, which means "in a careful manner"; no one uses *carefully* to mean "it is cared.")

Colloquial	*Hopefully*, it will not rain during the class picnic.
Standard	Sally walked *hopefully* into the boss's office to ask for a raise.

usage

hung See *hanged, hung*.

i.e. This abbreviation, meaning "that is," comes from the Latin *id est*. Avoid using it except in comments in parentheses or footnotes.

if, whether *If* is used to introduce adverb clauses, where it means "assuming that."

If I finish my report on time, I'll attend the concert with you.

If and *whether* are often used interchangeably to introduce noun clauses that follow verbs such as *ask, say, doubt, know,* and *wonder.* In formal writing, however, *whether* is preferred.

Less Desirable	I don't know *if* we'll be able to see the North Star tonight.
More Desirable	I don't know *whether* we'll be able to see the North Star tonight.

illicit See *elicit, illicit*.

illusion   See *allusion, delusion, illusion.*

immigrate   See *emigrate, immigrate.*

immoral   See *amoral, immoral.*

impact   Although *impact* is sometimes used in colloquial speech as a verb meaning "affect," this use is unacceptable in formal writing.

> *Colloquial*   This new law will greatly *impact* political campaigning.
>
> *Standard*   This new law will greatly *affect* political campaigning.

implicit   See *explicit, implicit.*

imply, infer   To *imply* is "to indicate indirectly or give implication." To *infer* is "to conclude from facts, evidence, or indirect suggestions."

> Jack *implied* that he wanted a divorce.
>
> Doris *inferred* that Jack wanted a divorce.

As these examples indicate, speakers and writers *imply;* listeners and readers *infer.*

incidence, incidents   *Incidents* are separate, countable experiences. *Incidence* refers to the rate at which something occurs.

> Two *incidents* during childhood led to her reclusiveness.
>
> The *incidence* of cancer in Japan is less than that in Canada.

incredible, incredulous   *Incredible* means "fantastic, unbelievable." *Incredulous* means "skeptical, disbelieving."

> That she could run so fast seemed *incredible.*
>
> Why is Bill wearing that *incredulous* look?

infer   See *imply, infer.*

in regards to   This is an incorrect use of *in regard to.*

insure   See *assure, ensure, insure.*

inter-, intra-   *Inter-* means "between or among." *Intra-* means "within."

> From Calgary to Saskatoon is an *interprovince* drive of approximately 700 kilometres.
>
> From Osoyoos to Vancouver is an *intraprovince* drive of about 500 kilometres.

in terms of   Avoid this vague, overused expression.

> *Vague*   *In terms of* the price he is asking, I would not recommend purchasing Tom's car.
>
> *Preferred*   *Because* of the price he is asking, I would not recommend purchasing Tom's car.

usage

irregardless   This nonstandard form of *regardless* includes the repetitive elements of *ir* and *less,* both of which mean "without."

is when, is where   *Is when* properly refers only to time.

> April *is when* our lilac bush blooms.

Is where properly refers only to place.

> Athens *is where* I met him.

The following sentences are *faulty* because of poorly phrased predicates which indicate that muckraking is a place and an abscess is a time:

> Muckraking *is where* someone investigates corporate or governmental abuses of power.

> An abscess *is when* some spot in body tissue fills with pus.

These sentences should be rephrased to eliminate the faulty assertion.

> Muckraking is the investigation of corporate or governmental abuses of power.

> An abscess is a spot in body tissue that fills with pus.

its, it's, its'   *Its* is a possessive pronoun. *It's* is a contraction of *it is* or *it has.*

> The gold chair was ruined, for someone had torn *its* seat.

> *It's* all I have to offer. (It is all I have to offer.)

> *It's* been a difficult day. (It has been a difficult day.)

There is no correct use for *its'.*

kind of, sort of   In formal writing, these are unacceptable substitutes for *somewhat, rather,* or *slightly.*

> *Colloquial*   She is *sort of* angry.
>
> I am *kind of* glad she went away.
>
> *Standard*   She is *somewhat* angry.
>
> I am *rather* glad she went away.

When *kind* and *sort* refer to a type, use them with singular nouns and verbs. With their plural forms, *kinds* and *sorts,* use plural nouns and verbs.

> *Unacceptable*   These *kind* of exams are difficult.
>
> *Standard*   This *kind* of exam is difficult.
>
> These *kinds* of exams are difficult.

In such constructions, be certain that *kind of* or *sort of* is essential to your meaning.

later, latter, last   *Later* refers to time; *latter* points out the second of two items. If more than two items are listed, use last to refer to the final one.

usage

He arrived at the party *later* than he was expected.

Although professors Stein and Patterson both lectured during the course, only the *latter* graded the final exam.

Of my cats, Sheba, Tiger, and Spot, only the *last* needs the vaccination.

lay, lie   *Lie* means "to recline" or "to remain in a particular position." It never takes a direct object. *Lay* means "to place" and always takes a direct object. These verbs are often confused, in part because the past tense of *lie* is *lay*. (The past tense of *lay* is *laid*.)

If I *lie* here a minute, I shall feel better.

As I *lay* asleep, a robber entered by apartment and stole my stereo.

Lay the book on the table, please.

He *laid* a hand on her shoulder.

leave, let   *Leave* means "to depart," and *let* means "to allow." Never use *leave* when *let* is meant.

Unacceptable	*Leave* him figure it out alone.
Standard	*Let* him figure it out alone.

lend, loan   Traditionally, *loan* has been classed as a noun and *lend* as a verb. Today, the use of *loan* as a verb is so commonplace that it is accepted as colloquial English.

Standard	I have applied for a *loan* so that I can buy a car. (noun)
	Please *lend* me your class notes. (verb)
Colloquial	Please *loan* me your class notes. (verb)

less   See *fewer, less*.

like   See *as, like*.

literally   The word *literally* means "restricted to the exact, stated meaning." In formal writing, use *literally* only to designate factual statements.

Colloquial	It was 15 degrees outside, but I was *literally* freezing.
Standard	Our dog was *literally* foaming at the mouth.
	It was 15 degrees outside, but I felt *very* cold.

loan   See *lend, loan*.

loose, loosen, lose   *Loose* is used primarily as an adjective, meaning "unattached, unrestrained, not confined." *Loosen* is a verb meaning "undo or ease." *Lose* can be used only as a verb meaning "mislay, fail to win, fail to maintain."

One should wear *loose* clothing when bowling. (adjective)

When will Mrs. Brady *loosen* her control over young Tom?

You would *lose* your nose if it were not attached to your face.

lots, lots of   *Lots* and *lots of* colloquially mean "many, much, a large amount, or a great amount." Avoid these expressions in formal writing.

> *Colloquial*   I've spent *lots of* money in my life.
>
> *Standard*   I have spent *much* money in my life.

mad   See *angry, mad*.

many, much   *Many* is used when referring to countable items; *much* is used when referring to an indefinite amount or to abstract concepts.

> There are *many* students in the biology class.
>
> How did Betty learn so *much* in so little time?

may   See *can, may*.

may be, maybe   *May be* is always used as a verb phrase. *Maybe* is an adverb meaning "perhaps."

> I *may be* chairman of the board by next June.
>
> *Maybe* we will see Jim at home.

medium, media   *Medium* is the singular form of this word; *media* is the plural.

> The internet is the *medium* I use most to get the news.
>
> The *media* have given extensive coverage to the brain transplant story.

much   See *many, much*.

myself   *Myself* is an intensive and a reflexive pronoun; it cannot substitute for a personal pronoun such as *I* or *me*.

> *Unacceptable*   Four other students and *myself* founded the club.
>
> *Standard*   Four other students and *I* founded the club.

number   See *amount, number*.

on account of   When used to begin an adverb clause (see pages 582–583), this is a nonstandard substitute for *because*.

> *Unacceptable*   The team was unable to practise *on account of* everyone was still upset over Tuesday's loss.
>
> *Standard*   The team was unable to practise *because* everyone was still upset over Tuesday's loss.

When *on account of* precedes a single word or a phrase, it is considered to be colloquial.

> *Colloquial*   The game was called *on account of* rain.

passed, past   *Passed* is a verb designating activity that has taken place. *Past* is a noun or an adjective designating a former time.

The parade *passed* the reviewing stand at 10:30 A.M.

In the *past,* few people were concerned about the environmental effects of pesticides.

This *past* summer, I visited France.

personal, personnel   *Personal* is an adjective meaning "private, individual." *Personnel* are the people working in an organization.

Age is a *personal* matter that you do not have to reveal during a job interview.

The *personnel* of the sanitation department will not be involved in the city workers' strike.

precede, proceed   *Precede* means "to go before or ahead of." *Proceed* means "to go on" or "to go forward."

The ritual of sharpening his pencils always *preceded* doing his homework.

The guide then said, "If you will *proceed,* I will show you the paintings by da Vinci."

predominant, predominate   *Predominant* is an adjective meaning "chief, main, most frequent." *Predominate* is a verb meaning "to have authority over others."

The *predominant* European influence on South American culture was Spanish.

In Canada, the will of the people should *predominate.*

principal, principle   *Principal,* which means "chief," "most important," (including as a noun referring to the chief administrator in a school) or "the amount of money on which interest is computed," is used as both an adjective and a noun. *Principle* is used only as a noun and means "truths, beliefs, or rules generally dealing with moral conduct."

The *principal* suspect in the case was arrested last Friday by the police.

The *principal* of Lewiston High School is Alison Cooperstein.

At this interest rate, your *principal* will double in ten years.

His *principles* are unconventional.

proceed   See *precede, proceed.*

raise, rise   *Raise* is a transitive verb and therefore requires a direct object. *Rise,* its intransitive counterpart, takes no direct object.

We plan to *raise* horses on our new farm.

The temperature is expected to *rise* to 30°C tomorrow.

Raise can also be a noun meaning "an increase in pay."

Tammy received a 25 percent *raise* last week.

real, really *Real* is an adjective; *really* is an adverb.

> He had *real* plants decorating the bedroom.

When used as an adverb, *real* is a colloquialism and should be replaced with *really*.

> *Colloquial* We had a *real* good time at the party.
>
> *Standard* We had a *really* good time at the party.

reason is because, reason is that The *reason is because* is colloquial and unacceptable in formal writing; the *reason is that* is the correct usage.

> *Colloquial* The *reason is because* I love her.
>
> *Standard* The *reason is that* I love her.

respectfully, respectively *Respectfully* means "with respect." *Respectively* indicates that the items in one series are related to those in a second series in the order given.

> Joseph should treat his parents *respectfully*.
>
> Tom, Anna, and Susan were assigned *Bleak House, Great Expectations,* and *Dombey and Son, respectively,* for their reports.

rise See *raise, rise.*

sensual, sensuous *Sensual* refers to bodily or sexual sensations. *Sensuous* refers to impressions experienced through the five senses.

> Singles bars offered *sensual* pleasures without emotional commitments.
>
> The Tivoli Garden provides many *sensuous* delights for visitors.

set, sit Generally, *set* means "to place" and takes a direct object. *Sit* means "to be seated" and does not take a direct object.

> Alice *set* her glass on the mantel.
>
> May I *sit* in this chair?

When it refers to the sun, however, *set* is used without a direct object.

> As the sun *set,* we turned homeward.

shall, will *Shall* is used in first-person (see page 560) questions and in specialized forms of writing such as military orders and laws. Otherwise, *will* is generally used.

> *Shall* we go to the movies tonight?
>
> The company *shall* fall into formation at precisely twelve noon.
>
> No family home *shall* be assessed at more than 50 percent of its actual value.

should have, should of *Should of* is an unacceptable substitute for *should have* because a preposition cannot substitute for a verb.

usage

> *Unacceptable*   I *should of* gone to the lake.
>
> *Standard*   I *should have* gone to the lake.

[*sic*]   This Latin word, always enclosed in brackets, follows quoted errors in grammar, spelling, or information. Inclusion of [*sic*] indicates that the error appeared in the original, which is being quoted exactly.

sight   See *cite, sight, site.*

sit   See *set, sit.*

site   See *cite, sight, site.*

so   *So* is an acceptable coordinating conjunction but tends to add an informal effect to writing and should therefore be used sparingly. For example, "Tom said he was divorcing me, *so* I began to cry" would be more effective if restated as follows: "When Tom said he was divorcing me, I began to cry." Do not use *so* as a substitute for *extremely* or *very* except with adverb clauses beginning with *that.*

> *Colloquial*   You are *so* careless in what you say.
>
> The discussion was *so* informative that I took many notes.
>
> *Standard*   You are *very* careless in what you say.
>
> The discussion was *extremely* informative.

sometime, some time, sometimes   *Sometime* means "at a future unspecified time," *some time* means "a span of time," and *sometimes* means "occasionally."

> We should get together *sometime* and play bridge.
>
> The weather has been hot for *some time.*
>
> *Sometimes* I go to dinner with Ethel.

sort of   See *kind of, sort of.*

specially   See *especially, specially.*

such, such . . . that   The use of *such* when it means "very" or "extremely" is unacceptable unless it is followed by a *that* clause completing the thought.

> *Colloquial*   They were *such* good cookies.
>
> *Standard*   They were *such* good cookies *that* I asked Steve for his recipe.

suppose to, supposed to   *Suppose to* is the nonstandard form of *supposed to.* In speech, it is difficult to hear the final *d* on *supposed,* and one may say *suppose to* without being detected; however, the correct written form is always *supposed to.*

than, then   *Than* is used to make comparisons; *then* means "at that time, in that case," or "after that."

> Jill is taller *than* her brother.
>
> First we will eat, and *then* we will discuss business.

usage

that, which   These two words have the same meaning. *That* may refer both to things and groups of people; *which,* only to things. When referring to things, *that* is generally used with clauses that distinguish the things they modify from others in the same class (restrictive clauses). *Which* is generally used with clauses that add information about the things they modify (nonrestrictive clauses).

> Any book *that* she likes is certain to be trashy. (restrictive clause)

> The Winthrop Building, *which* cost two million dollars to construct, could not now be duplicated for ten times that much. (nonrestrictive clause)

See pages 581–582 of the Handbook for a more complete explanation of restrictive and nonrestrictive expressions.

their, there, they're   These three separate words are often confused because they sound alike. *Their* is the possessive form of *they. There* is an expletive that appears at the beginning of a sentence and introduces the real subject, or it is an adverb meaning "in or at that place, at that point." *They're* is a contraction of *they are.*

> It is *their* basketball.

> *There* are many reasons why I cannot come.

> Put the sofa down *there.*

> *They're* going to be here soon.

then   See *than, then.*

there   See *their, there, they're.*

thorough, through   *Thorough* means "careful, complete, exact, painstaking." *Through* means "in one side and out the other, from end to end, from start to finish, over the whole extent of, finished."

> Brenda has done a *thorough* job.

> Let's run *through* the plan again.

thusly   *Thusly* is a nonstandard form of *thus.*

to, too, two   *To* is a preposition meaning "as far as, toward, until, onto." *Too* is an adverb meaning "excessively" or "also." *Two* is a number.

> I'm going *to* the store.

> Are you going *too?*

> This car is *too* expensive for me.

> There are *two* characters in the play.

toward, towards   Both forms are correct. *Toward* generally is used in North America and *towards* in England.

two   See *to, too, two.*

usage

uninterested   See *disinterested, uninterested.*

unique   *Unique* means "without an equal" or "extremely unusual" and thus should not be modified by an adverb such as *very.*

use to, used to   *Use* to is the nonstandard form of *used to.* In speech it is difficult to hear the *d* on *used,* and one may say use to without being detected; however, the correct written form is always *used to.*

way, ways   *Ways* may be used to refer to two or more means or methods but not to time or distance.

Unacceptable	Puerto Vallarta is a long *ways* from Canada.
Standard	There are two *ways* of thinking about that issue.
	Puerto Vallarta is a long *way* from Canada.

well   See *good, well.*

were, where   *Were* is the past form of the verb *to be. Where* is an adverb or a pronoun meaning "in, at, to, from a particular place or situation" or "which or what place."

I'm sorry that you *were* ill yesterday.

Mr. Morris will show you *where* to register.

where . . . at, to   *At* and *to* are unnecessary after *where.*

Wordy	*Where* are you taking the car *to?*
	Where does she live *at?*
Standard	*Where* are you taking the car?
	Where does she live?

whether   See *if, whether.*

which   See *that, which.*

who, whom   In formal writing, *who* should be used only as a subject in clauses and sentences and *whom* only as an object.

Unacceptable	*Who* are you taking to dinner on Friday?
	I know *who* the boss will promote.
	John is the candidate *whom* I think will be elected.
Standard	*Whom* are you taking to dinner on Friday?
	I know *whom* the boss will promote.
	John is the candidate *who* I think will be elected.

See page 601 of the Handbook for a more detailed discussion of *who* and *whom.*

who's, whose   *Who's* is a contraction of *who is* or *who has,* and *whose* is the possessive form of *who.*

> *Who's* coming to see us tonight?

> I would like to know *who's* been dumping trash in my yard.

> *Whose* book is that?

will   See *shall, will.*

wise   Do not randomly add *wise* to the ends of nouns. Such word coinings are ineffective.

> *Ineffective*   Personality*wise,* Sheila is ideal for the job.

> *Standard*   Sheila has an *ideal personality* for the job.

would have, would of   *Would of* is an unacceptable substitute for *would have.* A preposition cannot substitute for a verb.

> *Unacceptable*   I *would of* enjoyed seeing the Picasso exhibit.

> *Standard*   I *would have* enjoyed seeing the Picasso exhibit.

would have been, had been   When *would* occurs in the main part of a sentence, use *had been* (not *would have been*) in an "if" clause.

> *Unacceptable*   If the engine *would have been* lubricated, the bearing *would not have* burned out.

> *Standard*   If the engine *had been* lubricated, the bearing *would not have* burned out.

your, you're   *Your* is a possessive form of *you; you're* is a contraction of *you are.*

> Where is *your* history book?

> Tell me when *you're* ready to leave.

usage

Allen Abel, "Sweet Nothings," *Saturday Night*, Oct. 1997: 13–14.

R.T. Allen, "The Porcupine," from *Children, Wives and Other Wildlife* by Robert Thomas Allen. Copyright © 1970 by Robert Thomas Allen (New York: Doubleday, 1970).

"Antigen," *Encyclopaedia Britannica*, 1974, I, 417.

Margaret Atwood, *Alias Grace*. Copyright © 1996 by O.W. Toad Ltd. (Toronto: McClelland & Stewart, Inc. *The Canadian Publishers*, 1996.)

Patricia A. Baird, "Should Human Cloning Be Permitted?" Reprinted by the permission of Dr. Patricia Baird, University Distinguished Professor Emeritas.

Marilyn Baker, "Greed Works," *Vancouver Sun*, 15 Sept. 2004. Reprinted by permission of the author.

Kerry Banks, "As a Dad, Will I Do Right by My Daughter?" *Chatelaine*, June 1993.

Brian Bergman, "When Children Are Vicious," *Maclean's*, Aug. 12, 1996: 12.

Bruno Bettelheim, "Joey: A 'Mechanical Boy,'" *Scientific American*, March 1959, p. 122.

Andrew Beyak, "The Sweet Bird of Youth Is Showing Signs of Age," *Georgia Straight*, Jan. 1–8, 1998: 11.

Neil Bissoondath, "No Place Like Home," *New Internationalist*, Sept. 1998, Issue 305, p. 20+.

Dionne Brand, "Blossom: Priestess of Oya, Goddess of Winds, Storms and Waterfalls" from *Other Solitudes: Canadian Multicultural Fictions* (Don Mills, Ont: Oxford University Press, 1990).

Claude Brown, *Manchild in the Promised Land* (New York: Macmillan, 1965), p. 304.

Canadian Government, *Canadian Multiculturalism: An Inclusive Citizenship*. 10 Jul 2002, p. 8, http://www.pch.gc/progs/multi/inclusive_e.cfm.

Emily Carr, "D'Sonoqua" from *Klee Wyck*. Copyright © Gage Educational Publishing Limited, 1941.

Gladys Hasty Carroll, *Sing Out the Glory* (Boston: Little Brown, and Co., 1958).

Rachel Carson, *Silent Spring* (Boston: Houghton Mifflin, 1962).

Wayson Choy, "I'm a Banana and Proud of It." Copyright © 1997 by Wayson Choy. First published in Canada by *The Globe and Mail*. Reprinted by permission of the author.

Cecil Clutton and John Stanford, *The Vintage Motor-Car* (New York: Charles Scribner's Sons, 1955), p. 135.

Joseph Conrad, *Lord Jim* (New York: Holt, Rinehart and Winston, 1957), p. 13.

"Controlling Phobias through Behavior Modification." *USA Today*, August 1978.

Robertson Davies, "Living in a Country Without a Mythology," *The Merry Heart: Reflections on Reading, Writing, and the World of Books*, Toronto: Viking Penguin, 1997, p. 50.

Lester del Ray, *The Mysterious Sky* (New York: Chilton Book Company, 1964).

Magda Denes, *In Necessity and Sorrow: Life and Death in an Abortion Hospital* (New York: Basic Books, 1976), p. xiv.

Joan Didion, "On Self-Respect," in *Slouching Toward Bethlehem* (New York: Farrar, Strauss and Giroux, 1968), pp. 143–44.

Leo Durocher, *Nice Guys Finish Last* (New York: Simon & Schuster, 1975), p. 54.

Wayne Dyer, *What Do You Really Want for Your Children?* (New York: Simon & Schuster, 1975), p. 54.

Loren Eiseley, "The Judgment of the Birds," in *The Immense Journey* (New York: Random House, 1956), pp. 174–5.

Howard Ensign Evans, *Life on a Little-Known Planet* (New York: E.P. Dutton, 1968), pp. 107–8.

Harry Fairlie, "A Victim Fights Back," *The Washington Post*, April 30, 1978.

Candace Fertile, "The Oldest Profession: Shopping," from *POP CAN: Popular Culture in Canada*, Toronto: Prentice Hall, 1999: 77–81. Reprinted with permission by Pearson Education Canada Inc.

David Finkelstein, "When the Snow Thaws," *The New Yorker*, Sept. 10, 1979, p. 127.

Tim Folger, "Waves of Destruction," *Discover*, v. 15, May 1994, pp. 66–73. Copyright held by the magazine publisher.

Daniel Francis, "My Life with Riley," *Geist 23*, Fall 1996.

Adam Frank, excerpts from "Winds of Change," in *Discover*, June 1994, pp. 100–4.

Chief Dan George, "I Am a Native of North America," *My Heart Soars*. Clarke Irwin, 1974.

John Gimlette, "Down Labrador," from *Theatre of Fish: Travels through Newfoundland and Labrador* (New York: Alfred A. Knopf, 2005), pp. 194–197. Copyright held by the author.

Charles Gordon, "A Guided Tour of the Bottom Line," from *Reader's Choice: Essays for Thinking, Reading, and Writing*, Second Canadian Ed., Michael Flachmann, et al., Scarborough: Prentice Hall, 1997, pp. 439–440.

Dan Greenburg, "Sound and Fury." Reprinted by permission of the author. All rights reserved.

Amy Gross, "The Appeal of the Androgynous Man," *Mademoiselle*. Copyright © 1976 by The Condé Nast Publications, Inc. Reprinted by permission of Amy Gross.

L.D. Hamilton, "Antibodies and Antigens," *The New Book of Knowledge*, 1967, I, 317.

Bob Harvey, "Loyalty: A Last Virtue; Me-First Attitude Is Stripping Away Our Sense of Community," *Ottawa Citizen*, Mar. 2, 1996: C5.

Lesley Hazleton, "Assembly Line Adventure," Reprinted with the permission of The Free Press, a division of Simon & Schuster, Inc., from *Driving to Detroit: An Automotive Odyssey* by Lesley Hazleton, Copyright © 1998 by Lesley Hazleton.

Trevor Herriot, "Generation unto Regeneration," *The Globe and Mail*, May 25, 2002: A15. Reprinted with permission.

John Hersey, *Hiroshima* (New York: Modern Library, 1946), p. 4.

Nancy K. Hill, "Scaling the Heights: The Teacher as Mountaineer," *The Chronicle of Higher Education*, June 16, 1980, p. 48.

Jack Hodgins, "Separating," from *Spit Delaney's Island*. Copyright © Jack Hodgins 1976. (Toronto: The Macmillan Company of Canada Limited, 1976).

Dina Ingber, "Computer Addicts," *Science Digest*, July 1981.

Bruce Jackson, "Who Goes to Prison: Caste and Careerism in Crime," *Atlantic Monthly*, Jan. 1966, p. 52.

Robert Jastrow, *Until the Sun Dies* (New York: Norton, 1977).

Henry Jenkins, "Art Form for the Digital Age," from *Technological Review Monthly*, v. 103 no. 5, September and October 2000, pp. 117–120. Copyright held by magazine publisher.

Perry T. Jensen, "Lament for the Short and Stubby," *The Globe and Mail*, May 29, 1998: A22.

Marina Jiménez, "Domestic Crisis," *Chatelaine*, May 2005, pp. 76–83.

Martin Luther King, Jr., "I Have a Dream." Reprinted by arrangement with the heirs to the Estate of Martin Luther King, Jr., c/o Joan Daves Agency as agent for the proprietor. Copyright © 1963 by Martin Luther King, Jr., copyright renewed 1991 by Coretta Scott King.

Mark Kingwell, "Ten Steps to Creating a Modern Media Icon." *Marginalia: A Cultural Reader*. Copyright © Mark Kingwell. Reprinted by permission of Penguin Group (Canada), a division of Pearson Penguin Canada Inc.

Charles Krauthammer, "Crossing Lines," from *The New Republic*, v. 226, no. 16 (April 29, 2002), p. 20. Reprinted by permission.

Will Kymlicka, "Immigrants, Multiculturalism and Canadian Citizenship." The material in this paper is drawn from the book *Finding Our Way: Rethinking Ethnocultural Relations in Canada*, by Will Kymlicka (Oxford University Press, 1998), which contains more detailed discussion and citations of the statistics. Reprinted by permission of the author.

Evelyn Lau, "An Insatiable Emptiness," *The Georgia Straight*, 1995.

John Lovesey, "A Myth Is as Good as a Mile," *Sports Illustrated*, Nov. 9, 1964.

Robert M. MacGregor, "I Am Canadian: National Identity in Beer Commercials," *Journal of Popular Culture*, Vol. 37, No. 2, 2003, pp. 276–85. Reprinted by permission of Blackwell Publishing (UK) and of Prof. Robert M. Macgregor, Williams School of Business, Bishop's University.

James MacKinnon and Jeremy Nelson, "The True Cost of Groceries," *Adbusters*, Nov/Dec 2002, 24 Oct 2002, http://www.adbusters.org/magazine/44/articles/true_cost_groceries/ch.

Chris MacDonald, "Yes, Human Cloning Should Be Permitted," *Annals of The Royal College of Physicians and Surgeons of Canada*, Volume 33, Number 7, October 2000, pp. 437–438. © The Royal College of Physicians and Surgeons of Canada.

Marilyn Machlowitz, "Workaholism: What's Wrong with Being Married to Your Work?" *Working Woman*, May 1978, p. 51.

Marshall Mandell, "Are You Allergic to Your House?" *Prevention*, Sept. 1979, p. 101.

Marya Mannes, "Wasteland," in *More in Anger* (Philadelphia: J.B. Lippincott, 1958), p. 40.

Susan McClelland, "Distorted Images," *Maclean's*, August 14, 2000.

Bernice McCarthy, "A Tale of Four Learners" from *Educational Leadership*, v. 54, March 1997, pp. 46–51.

Peter McKnight, "The Specious Arguments against Cloning," *Vancouver Sun*, 24, November, 2007: C5. Material reprinted with the express permission of "Pacific Newspaper Group Inc.," a CanWest Partnership.

Rod McQueen, "Millionnaire Questionnaire," *Financial Post*, February 26, 1998: 25.

Thomas H. Middleton, "The Magic Power of Words," *Saturday Review*, Dec. 11, 1976, p. 90.

Don Ethan Miller, "A State of Grace: Understanding the Martial Arts," *Atlantic Monthly*, Sept. 1980. Copyright © 1980 by Don Ethan Miller.

Celia Milne, "Pressures to Conform," *Maclean's*, January 12, 1998: 60.

Moses Milstein, "Memories of Montreal—and Richness," *The Globe and Mail*, April 28, 1998: A16.

Susanna Moodie, *Roughing It in the Bush*. London: Richard Bentley, 1852.

Christine Nyhout, "Send in the Clowns," *Chatelaine*, April 1998: 165–166.

Michael Ondaatje, *In the Skin of a Lion*, Copyright © Michael Ondaatje, 1987 (Toronto: Penguin Books Canada Ltd., 1988).

George Orwell, excerpt from "Shooting an Elephant," in *Shooting an Elephant and Other Essays*. Copyright © 1950 by Sonia Brownell Orwell; renewed 1978 by Sonia Pitl-Rivers. Reprinted by permission of Harcourt, Inc.

Jo Goodwin Parker, "What Is Poverty?" in George Henderson, *America's Other Children: Public Schools Outside Suburbia* (University of Oklahoma Press. 1971).

Lord Ritchie-Calder, "The Doctor's Dilemma," *The Center Magazine*, Sept–Oct. 1971.

Rick Salutin, "The Mystery of Teaching." Reproduced with permission of Rick Salutin.

Scott Russell Sanders, "The Men We Carry in Our Minds," copyright © 1984 by Scott Russell Sanders; first appeared in *Milkweed Chronicle*; reprinted by permission of the author and Virginia Kidd Agency, Inc.

Laurence Shames, "The Sweet Smell of Success Isn't All That Sweet." Copyright © 1986 by The New York Times Company. Reprinted by permission.

Carol Shields, *Larry's Party*, Random House of Canada, 1997, pp. 242–243.

Elliott L. Smith and Andrew W. Hart, *The Short Story: A Contemporary Looking Glass* (New York: Random House, 1981).

Russell Smith, "Battered by Blandness," *The Globe and Mail*, 24 Oct 2002: R7.

Mariflo Stephens, "Barbie Doesn't Live Here Anymore." Reprinted with permission of Simon & Schuster Adult Publishing Group, from *The Barbie Chronicles*, edited by Yona Zeldis McDonough. Copyright © 1999 by Mariflo Stephens. Copyright © 1999 by Yona Zeldis McDonough. Barbie is a registered trademark of Mattel, Inc.

Andrew Struthers, "How Spell-Check Is Destroying English: With No Governing Body, Our Language Lies Prone to Market Forces," *Vancouver Sun*, 17 Aug. 2002: H8. Reprinted with permission by *The Vancouver Sun.*

Deborah A. Sullivan, "Social Bodies: Tightening the Bonds of Beauty," from *Cosmetic Surgery: The Cutting Edge of Commercial Medicine in America*, copyright © 2001 by Deborah A. Sullivan.

Joyce Susskind, "Surprises in a Woman's Life," *Vogue*, Feb. 1979, p. 252.

Deems Taylor, "The Monster" in *Of Mice and Music* (New York: Simon & Schuster, 1965).

Lewis Thomas, excerpt from "Societies as Organisms," in *The Lives of a Cell* by Lewis Thomas. Copyright © 1971 by The Massachusetts Medical Society.

Douglas Todd, "Beware the Boredom Boom," Douglass Todd/*Vancouver Sun* (May 6, 2005, p. A4).

Douglas Todd, "In a Girl's World It Can Be Tough Being a Boy," *Vancouver Sun*, Feb. 10, 1998: G3. Reprinted with permission by *The Vancouver Sun.*

Richard Tomkins, "Old Father Time Becomes a Terror." *Financial Times*, March 20, 1999.

Julie Traves, "The Church of Please and Thank You," *This Magazine*, March/April 2005, pp. 22–25.

Steve Whysall, "Don't Let Emotion Guide Your E-Mail." Steve Whysall/*Vancouver Sun*, October 19, 2004, pp. C1–C4.

Marion Winik, "What Are Friends For?" from *Telling* by Marion Winik, Copyright © 1994 by Marion Winik. Used by permission of Villard Books, a division of Random House, Inc.

Tom Wolfe, *The Pump House Gang* (New York: World Journal Tribune, 1966), p. 293.

Orville Wyss and Curtis Eklund, *Microorganisms and Man* (New York: John Wiley and Sons, 1971), pp. 232–33.

David Zimmerman, "Are Test-Tube Babies the Answer for the Childless?" *Woman's Day*, May 1979, p. 26.

INDEX

Note: Entries for figures are followed by *"f"*.

EDITING SYMBOLS

Symbol	Problem	Page	Symbol	Problem	Page
ab	improper abbreviation	635–36	nsu	nonstandard usage	
agr pa	faulty agreement of pronoun and antecedent	593–95	¶	new paragraph needed	
agr sv	faulty agreement of subject and verb	591–93	no ¶	new paragraph not needed	
ⱽ or apos	missing or misused apostrophe	613–16	⊙	period needed	623–24
awk	awkward phrasing		|| or para	nonparallelism	609–10
bib	faulty bibliographic form	467–84	? or ques	missing or misused question mark	623–24
cap	capital letter needed	633–35	" /" or quot	missing or misused quotation marks	628–30
case	wrong case	600–602	ref	unclear reference of pronoun to antecedent	596–98
cl	cliché	126	ro	run-on sentence	589–90
⋏ or com	missing or misused comma	616–20	; or sem	missing or misused semicolon	621–22
cs	comma splice	589–90	sp	spelling error	641–45
comp	faulty comparison	610–12	shift p	shift in person	598–99
dm	dangling modifier	608–09	shift t	shift in tense	603–04
⊙ or ellip	missing or misused ellipsis	416	sq	squinting modifier	607–08
frag	sentence fragment	587–88	t or tense	wrong tense	565–69
ital	missing or misused italics	638–39	trans	poor transition	
lc	lowercase (small) letter needed	633–35	vb	wrong verb form	
ll or lev	wrong level of usage	9–13	wdy	wordiness	101–102
log	faulty logic		ww	wrong word	
mm	misplaced modifier	608–09	ℒ	delete (omit)	
num	use numerals	636–38	⋀	material omitted	
			(?)	meaning unclear or word illegible	